KU-167-368

PATRICIA ROBERTS COLLECTION

PATRICIA ROBERTS COLLECTION

W.H. ALLEN · LONDON

Printed and bound in Italy
for the publishers,
W.H. Allen & Co. PLC,
44 Hill Street, London W1X 8LB

ISBN 0 491 03930 1

Reprinted 1985, 1986

Photographs on pages 126,127,130,131,133,146,147,156,174,175,182,183, 222,223 by Rolph Gobits

Photographs on pages 142,143,156,166,167,178,179,190,191,194,195,210, 211,214,215 by Cameron Mcvey

Photograph on page 123 by Chris Simpson, reproduced by permission of *Harpers & Queen*

Photograph on page 134 by Neil Kirk, reproduced by permission of *Company Magazine*

Photograph on page 151 by Tony McGee, reproduced by permission of *The Observer*

Photograph on page 199 by Chris Grant Smith, reproduced by permission of *Ms London*

Photograph on page 203 by Chris Duffy, reproduced by permission of *19 Magazine* (IPC Magazines Ltd)

All other photographs by

James Wedge

Stylist pages 1-119: Caroline Baker

Hair:

Pages: 11,18,19,38,39,46,47,62,63,67,98,99,102 and 103 by Harry Cole at Trevor Sorbet
Pages: 14,15,22,23,34,35,50,51,54,55,58,59,66,70,71,86,87,94,95,110 and 111 by Vicki at Molton Brown
Pages: 30,31,42,43,74,75,78,79,82,83,90,91,106,107,114 and 119 by Kathy at Smile

Acknowledgements:

Brown's, 27 South Molton Street, London W1; Memphis, 55 South Molton Street, London W1; Joseph, 6 Sloane Street, London SW1; Rider Shoes, 8 South Molton Street, London W1; Lunn Antiques, 86 New Kings Road, London SW6; Margaret Howell, 25/26 St Christophers Place, London W1; Butler and Wilson, 189 Fulham Road, London SW7

CONTENTS

1

How to Knit

to Cast On

Illustrations by Connie Jude

There are several methods of casting on stitches. The 'thumb' method is used at the start of work, as it has more elasticity. The 'through stitch' method is used for casting on once a piece of knitting has been started, for instance when working a buttonhole.

the thumb method

Leaving a length of yarn sufficient to make the required number of stitches, make a loop and place it on the needle held in the right hand. With the yarn from the ball in the right hand, take a loose end of yarn in the left hand and form a loop on the left thumb. Insert the point of the right hand needle into the loop on the thumb. Wrap the yarn round the point of the needle. Draw the yarn through the loop on the thumb, while slipping the loop off the thumb and tightening the left hand thread. Continue in the same way.

the through stitch method

Insert the right hand needle into the front of the first st. on the left hand needle. Wrap the yarn round the right hand needle. With this needle draw the yarn through the stitch on the left hand needle, then place this loop onto the left hand needle, and tighten thread. Continue working into last stitch made.

With the needle containing the cast on stitches in the left hand, insert the right hand needle into the front of the first stitch on the left hand needle, so that the point of the right hand needle passes towards the back of the work beneath the left hand needle. Wrap the yarn round the right hand needle. With this needle draw the yarn through the stitch on the left hand needle, while slipping the stitch off the left hand needle. Continue in this way with the yarn to the back of the work.

With the yarn to the front of the work, insert the right hand needle into the front of the first stitch on the left hand needle, so that the point of the right hand needle passes towards the front of the work beneath the left hand needle. Wrap the yarn round the right hand needle. With this needle draw the loop through the stitch on the left hand needle, while slipping the stitch off the left hand needle.

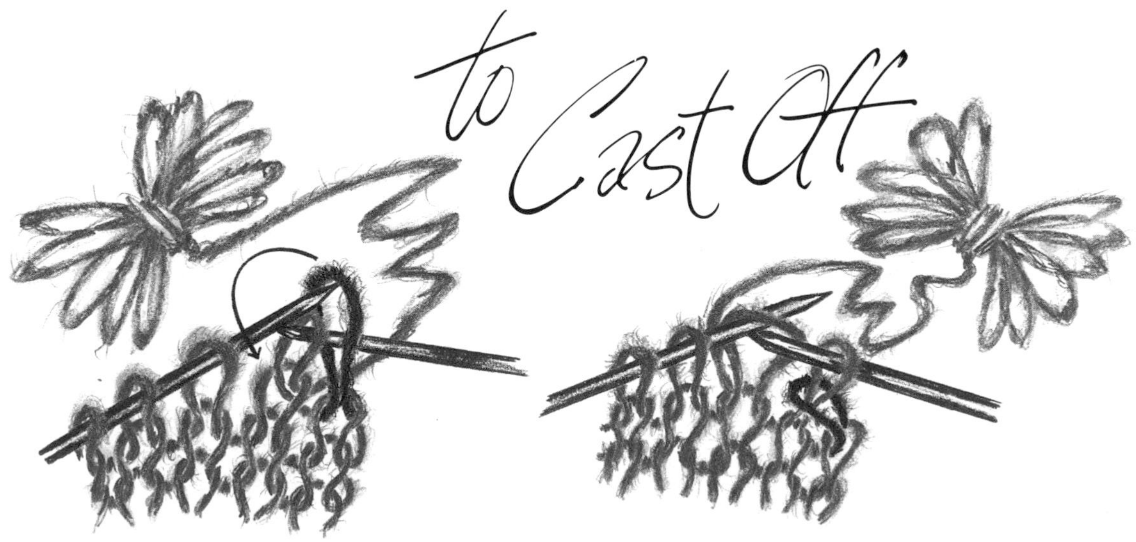

Knit or purl as appropriate 2 stitches. Pass the first of these stitches over the second stitch. *Work 1 more stitch, then pass the previous stitch over this one; repeat from * as required. When casting off all the stitches on left hand needle, one stitch will remain on right hand needle; break off yarn leaving a long end and thread it through the remaining st. Pull yarn firmly and fasten off. Care should be taken not to cast off too tightly; to avoid this a larger sized needle may be used.

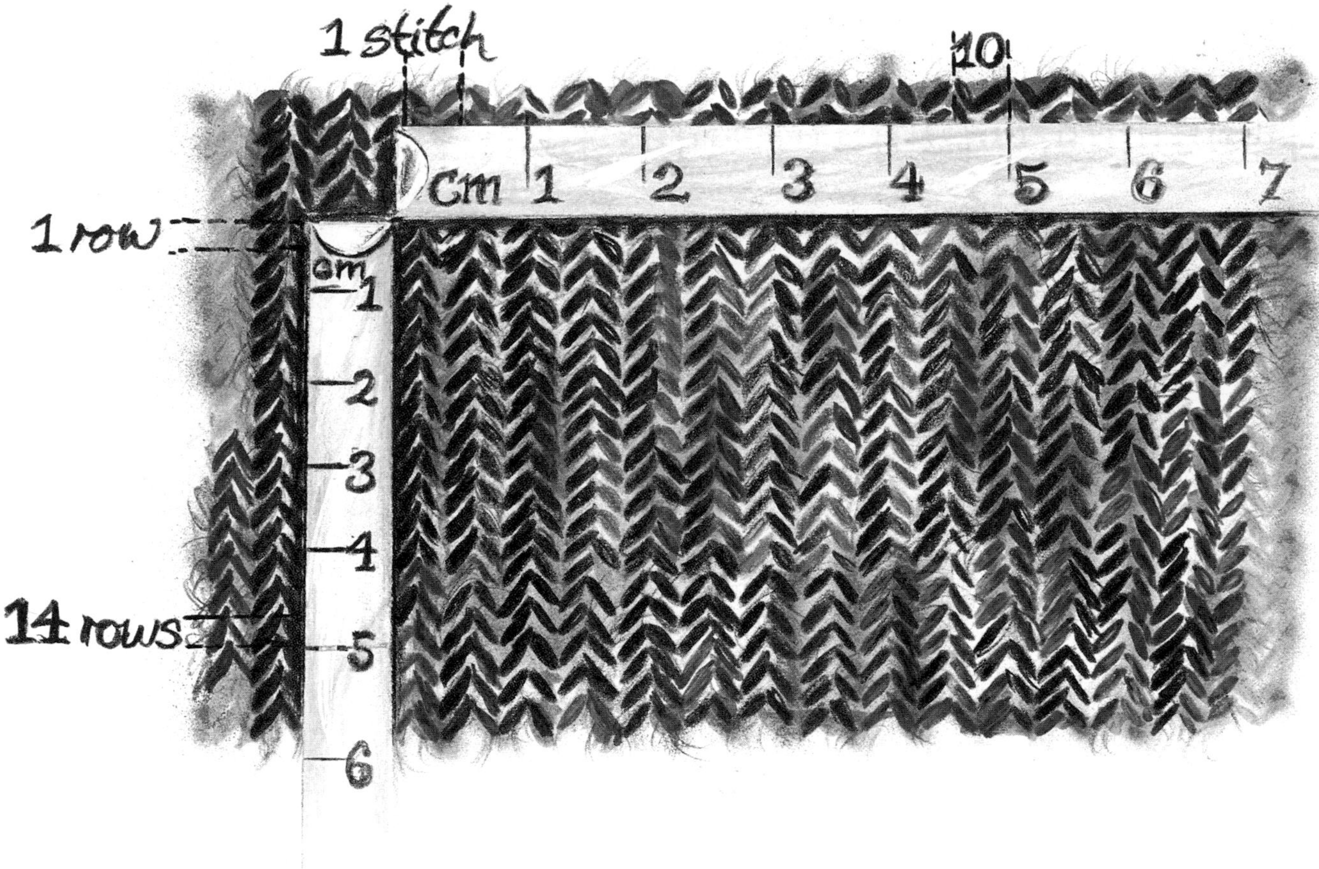

Illustrations by Connie Jude

The essential rule for successful knitting is to work at the correct tension. This is given at the beginning of each knitting pattern. Every knitter's tension varies slightly; which is the reason it is so important to check your tension before commencing work. To do this, knit a small test piece in the pattern, over which the tension is given and using the size needles recommended. Measure the number of stitches and rows to the number of centimetres (inches) stated in the pattern. If your tension is too tight – too many stitches and rows to the measure – test it again using a size larger needles. If it is still too tight, test it yet again using even larger needles and so on until your tension is correct. If your tension is too loose – too few stitches and rows to the measure – test your tension again with smaller needles until it is correct. Only a garment knitted at the correct tension will have the measurements given in the knitting pattern.

Yarns

Always use the yarn recommended in the knitting pattern. Different brands of yarn vary in thickness. This makes it difficult to obtain the correct tension and affects the amount of yarn required. Inferior yarns will produce inferior garments, regardless of the merits of the design. Natural fibre yarns are the most suitable for hand knitting.

Abbreviations

At the beginning of each set of instructions there is a list of abbreviations for that particular pattern. Never assume that you understand how to work an abbreviation without first reading its explanation. There are many different ways to work certain stitches and therefore the explanations of how to work them will vary from pattern to pattern.

Pressing

After completing the knitting, pin out all pieces, except the ribbed parts, with the wrong side of the work upwards, to the measurements given in the pattern. Using an iron heated in accordance with the making-up paragraph in each pattern, carefully press the knitting over a cloth which may be dry, damp or wet according to the pattern. Pressing should be done with an upwards and downwards movement and not from side to side.

Making Up

Use either the same yarn as the knitting itself, or a finer matching yarn to make up the garment. There are various methods for making up hand knitting; invisible seaming is a particularly successful method of making up, although a fine back stitch seam is also acceptable. The needle used for making up knitted garments is called a bodkin.

Invisable seaming

Place the first finger of the left hand between the two pieces of knitting to be joined, holding them edge to edge, with the right side of the work facing you. Secure the yarn at one edge, making sure that the bodkin is on the right side of the work. Taking the needle to the second edge, insert it under the thread that lies between the first and second stitches and draw the yarn through. Take the needle back to the first edge, and insert it under the thread between the first and second stitches and draw the yarn through. Take the yarn back to the second edge inserting the bodkin under the thread above the one worked previously and draw the yarn through. Return to the first edge and work in the same way. Continue until the seam is complete. Working seams in this way, it is not necessary to use pins, for the number of rows to be joined should match exactly.

Cleaning

Hand knits may be dry cleaned or washed by hand. Hand washing is often preferable although certain yarns are only suitable for dry cleaning.

hand washing

Carefully hand wash knitted items with the water at the temperature indicated on the yarn label. Using a spin dryer, spin briefly without any heat to remove excess water. Lay the garment flat on a towel and dry away from direct heat or sunlight. Never dry sweaters on a washing line, or they will become misshapen.

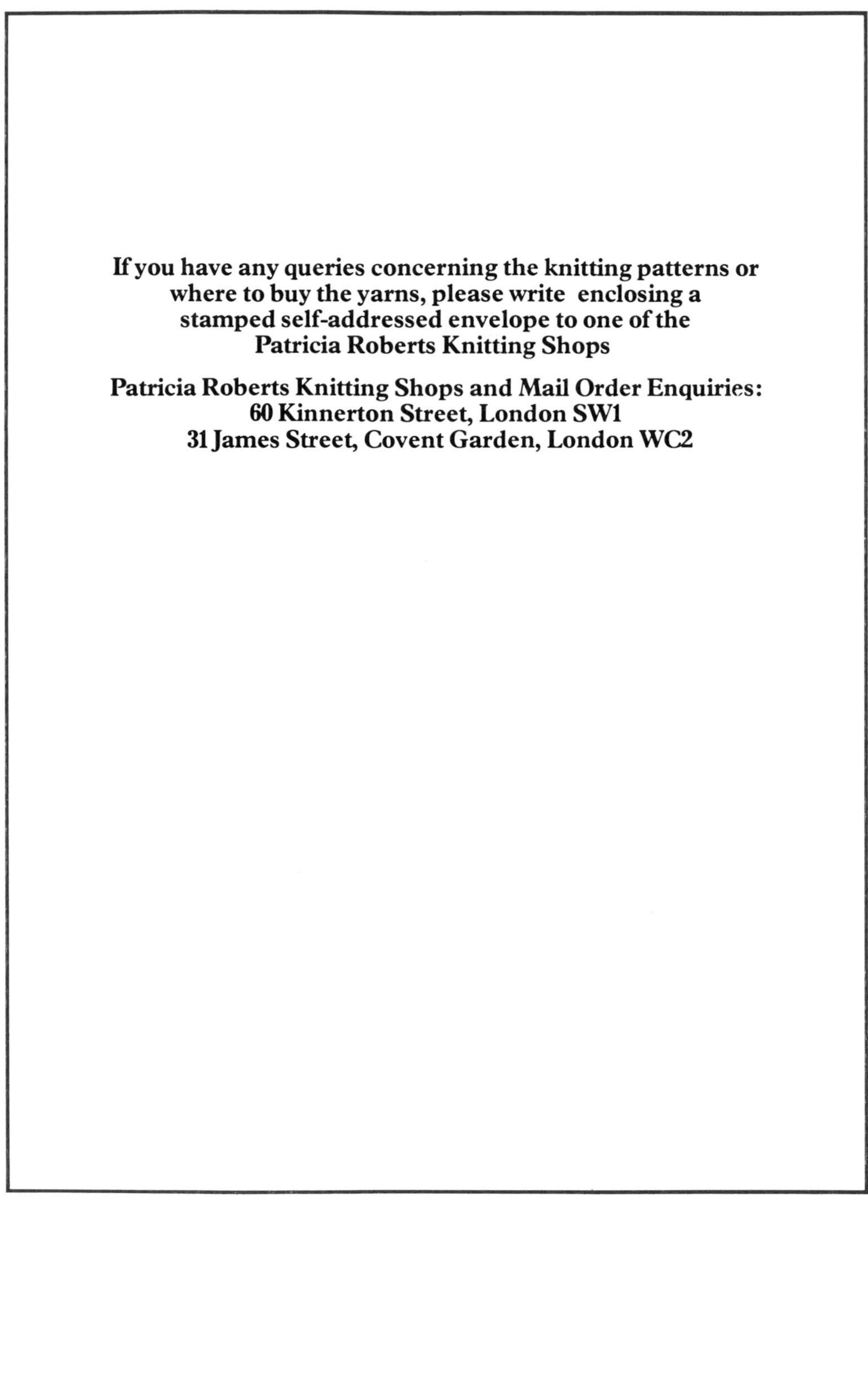

If you have any queries concerning the knitting patterns or where to buy the yarns, please write enclosing a stamped self-addressed envelope to one of the Patricia Roberts Knitting Shops

Patricia Roberts Knitting Shops and Mail Order Enquiries:
60 Kinnerton Street, London SW1
31 James Street, Covent Garden, London WC2

pot-pourri

pot-pourri

ARGYLL SCARF

MATERIALS
Either 5 20 gram balls of "Woollybear Angora" in main colour, 2 balls in first contrast and 1 ball in each of the 5 other contrast colours, or 5 ounce (28 gram) hanks of "Woollybear Real Shetland" in main colour, 2 hanks in first contrast and 1 hank in each of the 5 other contrast colours; a pair of size 2¾mm. (No. 12) Aero knitting needles.

TENSION
16 stitches and 20 rows to 5 centimetres (2 inches) over the pattern using size 2¾mm. (No. 12) needles. If you cannot obtain the correct tension using the size needles suggested, use larger or smaller ones accordingly.

ABBREVIATIONS
As given for "Pierrot" on page 50.

MEASUREMENTS
The measurements are given in centimetres followed by inches in brackets.

29 centimetres (11½ inches) in width before making up and 127.5 centimetres (51 inches) in length excluding fringe.

TO WORK
With size 2¾mm. (No. 12) needles and m. cast on 92 sts. and k.4 rows.

Now work in pattern as follows. Use separate balls of m. and a. for each section of the pattern, so that colours not in use are not taken across the back of the work.

1st foundation row: With m. k.1, with a. k.2, * with m. (p.1, k.1) 13 times. with a. k.4; repeat from * ending last repeat with a. k.2, with m. k.1.

2nd foundation row: With m. k.1, with a. p.2, *with m. (k.1, p.1) 6 times, with d. p.2, with m. (k.1, p.1) 6 times, with a. p.4; repeat from * using c. instead of d. on the first repeat, then b. instead of d. on the next repeat.

The last row sets the position of the contrast colours. Now work the 1st to 55th pattern rows as given for "Pierrot" on page 50 in the colours as set.

56th row: With m. k.1, with a. p.2, *with m. (k.1, p.1) 6 times, with b. - note colour change - p.2, with m. (k.1, p.1) 6 times, with a. p.4; repeat from * using f. instead of b., then e. instead of b. and ending last repeat with a. p.2, with m. k.1.

The last row sets the position of the colours for the next repeat of the pattern, work the 1st to 55th rows as set.

Continuing in pattern as set, but in the colours given in the chart, repeat the 56 pattern rows 7 times, ending with a 55th pattern row.

With m. only k.5 rows, then cast off.

Pin out to size and press all parts lightly on the wrong side with a warm iron over a damp cloth. Fold in half lengthways and join outer edges.

THE FRINGING
To make a tassel: Cut 6 lengths of m. each 24 centimetres (6 inches) long, fold these in half, then using a large crochet hook, insert hook into one corner of cast on edge of scarf and draw the 6 looped ends through, then pass cut ends through the loops and pull firmly to form a tassel.

In the same way, make 7 more tassels along cast on edge. Then make 8 tassels in the same way along cast off edge.

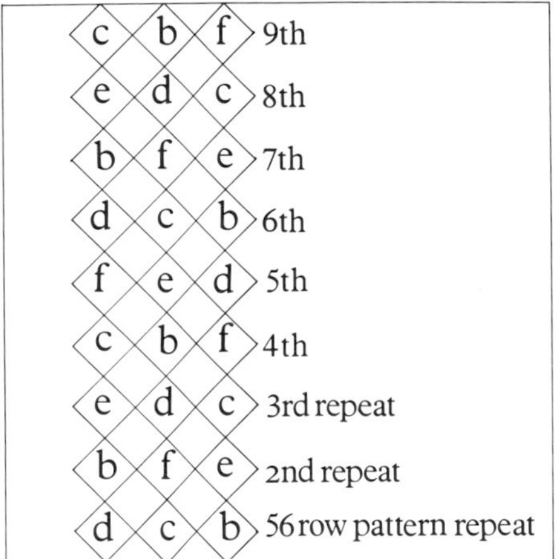

PATCHWORK SCARF AND MITTENS

MATERIALS
For mittens: either 2 20 gram balls of "Woollybear Angora" by Patricia Roberts or 3 25 gram balls of "Woollybear Lambswool" in main colour and oddments of the same yarn in each of the 4 contrast colours; a pair each of size 2¼mm. (No. 13) and size 2¾mm (No. 12) Aero knitting needles.

For the scarf: either 3 20 gram balls of "Woollybear Angora" by Patricia Roberts in main colour and 2 balls in each of the 4 contrast colours, or 3 25 gram balls of "Woollybear Lambswool" by Patricia Roberts in main colour and 2 balls in each of the 4 contrast colours; a pair of size 2¾mm. (No. 12) Aero knitting needles.

TENSION
16 stitches and 20 rows to 5 centimetres (2 inches) using size 2¾mm. (No. 12) needles. If you cannot obtain the correct tension using the size needles suggested, use larger or smaller ones accordingly.

ABBREVIATIONS
K., knit; p., purl; st., stitch; tog., together; inc., increase (by working twice into same st.); sl., slip; p.s.s.o., pass sl. st. over; up 1, pick up the loop which lies between the needles, slip it onto left hand needle, then k. into back of it; 5 from 1, k.1, y.r.n., k.1, y.r.n., k.1 all into 1 st.; y.r.n., yarn round needle; single rib is k.1 and p.1 alternately; s.s. stocking stitch is k. on ther right side and p. on the wrong side; m. ch., make chain thus, with m. k.1, *slip this st. back onto left hand needle and still with m. k. into it; repeat from * once; cr. 3rt., cross 3 right thus, with b. k. into front of 4th - long st. and 1st st. on left hand needle tog., then k. 2nd and 3rd sts. separately through back of loops; cr. 3lt., slip next long st. onto cable needle at front of work, k. 2, then k. st. from cable needle tog. with next st.; 3 from 1, k.1, y.r.n., k.1 all into 1 st.; w.s., wrong side; p.1 long, p.1 wrapping yarn round needle twice; sl. 1e., slip 1 dropping extra loop; 4 over 1, pass 2nd, 3rd, 4th and 5th sts. on left hand needle over 1st st. then with b. on mittens or m. on scarf k. this st.; m.b., make bobble thus, with a k.1, y.r.n., k.1 all into next st., turn, p.3, turn, sl. 1,k.2 tog., p.s.s.o.; m., main colour; a., first contrast; b., second contrast; c., third contrast; d., fourth contrast.

MEASUREMENTS
The measurements are given in centimetres followed by inches in brackets.

	Mittens	Scarf
Length	23.5(9½)	115(46)
Width before making up	22.5(9)	25(10)

THE MITTENS

THE LEFT MITTEN
With size 2¼mm. (No. 13) needles and m. cast on 64 sts. and work 19 rows in single rib.

Change to size 2¾mm. (No. 12) needles.

Increase row: Rib 4, *up 1, rib 8; repeat from * ending last repeat rib 4. - 72 sts.

Beginning with a k. row s.s. 4 rows.

Now work in pattern as follows. This is worked in s.s. except where indicated, so only the colour details are given.

1st row: 4m., 2a., 2b., 2a., 2b., 2a., 58m.

The last row sets the position of the pattern given in the chart. Work the 2nd to 24th rows as set.

Now divide the sts. for the thumb: Next row: Pattern 24, slip next 9 sts. onto a safety pin until required for thumb, turn, cast on 9, turn, work to end.

**On 72 sts. work 35 rows in pattern as set.

1st Decrease row: K.2, sl.1, k.2 tog., p.s.s.o., k.26, sl.1, k.2 tog., p.s.s.o., k.4, sl.1, k.2 tog., p.s.s.o., k.26, sl.1, k.2 tog., p.s.s.o., k.2. - 64 sts.

S.s. 3 rows.

2nd Decrease row: K.2, sl.1, k.2 tog., p.s.s.o., k.22, sl.1, k.2 tog., p.s.s.o., k.4, sl.1, k.2 tog., p.s.s.o., k.22, sl.1, k.2 tog., p.s.s.o., k.2. - 56 sts.

S.s. 3 rows.

3rd Decrease row: K.2, sl.1, k.2 tog., p.s.s.o., k.18, sl.1, k.2 tog., p.s.s.o., k.4, sl.1, k.2 tog., p.s.s.o., k.18, sl.1, k.2 tog., p.s.s.o., k.2. - 48 sts.

P.1 row.

Repeat the last 2 rows twice, working 4 sts. less between the decreases on each successive repeat. - 32 sts.

Next row: K.2 tog., *sl.1, k.2 tog., p.s.s.o.; repeat from * to end. - 12 sts.

Break off yarn leaving a long end. Thread through remaining sts., draw up and fasten off.

The thumb: With right side of work facing rejoin m. to the 9sts. left on safety pin for thumb, cast on 10 sts., then on 19 sts. beginning with a k. row s.s. 22 rows.

Next row: K.1, *k.2 tog.; repeat from * to end.

Break off yarn leaving a long end, thread through remaining sts. and draw up firmly. Using the long end neatly join row ends of thumb, then join cast on edges.

THE RIGHT MITTEN
Work as given for left mitten until the 24th pattern row has been worked.

Now divide the sts. for the thumb: Next row: K.39, slip next 9 sts. onto a safety pin until required for thumb, turn, cast on 9 sts. over those cast off, turn, k. to end.

Work as given for left mitten from ** to end.

TO COMPLETE
Fold in half lengthways and join row end edges. Press lightly.

THE SCARF

TO WORK
With size 2¾mm. (No. 12) needles and m. cast on 54 sts. and beginning with a k. row s.s. 2 rows. Break off m. Join in a.

***For the stripe section: Increase row: With a. *k.1, inc. in next st.; repeat from * to end. - 81 sts.

1st row: With a. all p.

2nd and 3rd rows: With b. all k.

4th row: With a. all k.

5th row: With a. all p.

6th row: With a. all k.

Repeat the last 6 rows 5 times, then work the first 5 rows again. Break off a. and b.

**Decrease row: Join in m., with m. *k.1, k.2 tog.; repeat from * to end. - 54 sts.

With m. p.1 row, k.1 row, then p.1 row.**

For the spotted patch: With m. work the increase row given for stripe section, and on 81 sts. p.1 row, then work as follows:

1st row: With m. k.4, *with c. 5 from 1, with m. k.7; repeat from * ending last repeat k.4.

2nd row: With m. p.4, *with c. p.5 long, with m. p.7; repeat from * ending last repeat p.4.

3rd row: With m. k.4, *sl. 5e., with m. k.7; repeat from * ending last repeat k.4.

4th row: With m. p.4, *sl.5, p.7; repeat from * ending last repeat p.4.

5th row: With m. k.4, *4 over 1, with m. k.7; repeat from * ending last repeat k.4.

6th, 7th and 8th rows: With m. in s.s.

9th row: With m. k.8, *with c. 5 from 1, with m. k.7; repeat from * ending last repeat k.8.

10th row: With m. p.8*, with c. p.5 long, with m. p.7; repeat from * ending last repeat with m. p.8.

11th row: With m. k.8, *sl. 5e., k.7.; repeat from* ending last repeat k.8.

12th row: With m. p.8, *sl.5, with m.p.7 repeat from *ending last repeat with m. p.8.

13th row: With m.k.8. *4 over 1, with m.k. this st., with m. k.7; repeat from *ending last repeat k.8.

14th, 15th and 16th rows: With m. in s.s.

Repeat the last 16 rows once more, then work the first 8 rows again.

Work from ** to ** as before.

For the check section: With d., work the increase row given for stripe section, and on 81 sts. p.1 row, then work as follows:

1st row: *With d. k.2, with c. k.2; repeat from * ending last repeat with d. k.1.

2nd row: With d. p.1, *with c. p.2, with d. p.2; repeat from * to end.

3rd row: *With c. k.2, with d. k.2; repeat from * ending last repeat with c. k.1.

4th row: With c. p.1, *with d. p.2, with c. p.2; repeat from * to end.

Repeat the last 4 rows 8 times more, then work the first 2 rows again.

With d. s.s. 2 rows.

Repeat from ** to ** as before.

For the zig-zag section: With b. work the increase

row given for stripe section and on 81 sts. p.1 row, then work as follows:

1st row: With b. k.2 tog., *k.3, 3 from 1, k.3, sl.1, k.2 tog. p.s.s.o.; repeat from * ending last repeat k.2 tog.

2nd row: With b. all p.

3rd row: With b. all k.

4th row: With b. all p.

5th row: With m. as 1st row.

6th row: With m. all k.

Repeat these last 6 rows 5 times, then work the first 4 rows again.

Repeat from ** to ** as before.

For the dot section: With d. work the increase row as for stripe section and on 81 sts. p.1 row, then work as follows:

1st row: With d. k.4, *with a. m.b., with d. k.3; repeat from * ending last repeat k.4.

2nd, 3rd and 4th rows: With d. in s.s.

5th row: With d. k.2, *with a. m.b., with d. k.3; repeat from * ending last repeat k.2.

6th, 7th and 8th rows: With d. in s.s.

Repeat the last 8 rows 4 times more.***

Work from ** to ** as before.

Repeat from *** to ***.

With m. work the decrease row, then p.1 row and k.1 row, then cast off.

TO COMPLETE

Fold in half lengthways and join outer edges. With m. make tassels as follows. Cut 6 lengths of m. each 10 inches long. Fold in half. Insert a crochet hook into one corner of cast on edge of scarf and draw the 6 folded ends through together. Pass the cut ends through the loop of the folded ends and draw up firmly. Make 5 more tassels in the same way equally spaced along this edge. Similarly work tassels along cast off edge.

ROSEBUD HAT & GLOVES

MATERIALS

Either 4 20 gram balls of "Woollybear Angora" in main colour and 2 balls in each of first and second contrast colours, or 4 50 gram balls of "Woollybear Cotton Crepe" in main colour and 2 balls in each of first and second contrast colours; a pair each of size 2¾mm. (No. 12), size 3mm (No. 11), 3¼mm. (No. 10) and 3¾mm. (No. 9) Aero knitting needles.

TENSION

20 sts. – 2 repeats of the rosebud pattern to 9 centimetres (3½ inches) in width and 18 rows to 5 centimetres (2 inches) in length over the pattern using size 3¾mm. (No. 9) needles. If you cannot obtain the correct tension using the size needles suggested use larger or smaller ones accordingly.

ABBREVIATIONS

K., knit; p., purl; st, stitch; tog., together; sl., slip; p.s.s.o., pass sl. st. over; up 1, pick up the loop which lies between the needles, slip it onto left hand needle, then k. into back of it; single rib is k.1 and p.1 alternately; m., main colour; a., first contrast; b., second contrast; m. b., make bobble thus, with a. k.1, p.1, k.1, p.1 all into next st., turn, k.4, turn, p.4, turn, k.4, turn, pass 2nd, 3rd and 4th sts. on left hand needle over first st., then with m.k. this st., knot ends in a. leaving sufficiently long ends to darn in at completion of work; ch.5, chain st. 5 thus, *with b. k. next st., slip the st. just made onto left hand needle pulling b. firmly; repeat from *4 times, with m. k.1.

THE HAT

TO WORK

With size 2¾mm. (No. 12) needles and a. cast on 141 sts. and work 6 rows in single rib. Break off a., join in m. and change to size 3mm. (No. 11) needles.

Increase row: K. 1, *up 1, k.2; repeat from * to end. – 211 sts.

Moss st. row: P.1, *k.1, p.1; repeat from * to end.

Now work in rosebud pattern as follows: Use separate short lengths of a. for each bobble and separate small balls of b. for each diagonal stripe.

1st row: With m. p.1, *with a. m.b. – see abbreviations, with m. p.1, k.1, p.1, k.1, p.1, k.1, p.1, k.1, p.1; repeat from * to end.

2nd row and every wrong side row: With m. p.1, *k.1, p.1; repeat from * to end.

3rd row: With m. p.1, *k.1, with b. ch. 5, with m. k.1, p.1, k.1, p.1, k.1, p.1, k.1, with b. ch. 5; repeat from * to end.

5th row: *With m. p.1, k.1, p.1, with b. ch. 5, with m. p.1, k.1, p.1, k.1, p.1, with b. ch. 5; repeat from * until 1 remains, with m. p.1.

7th row: With m. p.1, * k.1, p.1, k.1, with b. ch. 5, with m. k.1, p.1, k.1, with b. ch.5, with m. k.1, p.1; repeat from * to end.

9th row: With m. p.1, *k.1, p.1, k.1, p.1, with b. ch.5, with m. p.1, with b. ch. 5, with m. p.1, k.1, p.1; repeat from * to end.

10th row: As 2nd row.

Change to 3¼mm. (No. 10) needles.

11th row: With m. p.1, *k.1, p.1, k.1, p.1, k.1, with a. m.b., with m. k.1, p.1, k.1, p.1; repeat from * to end.

12th to 20th rows: Work 10th row back to 2nd row.

Continued on page 21.

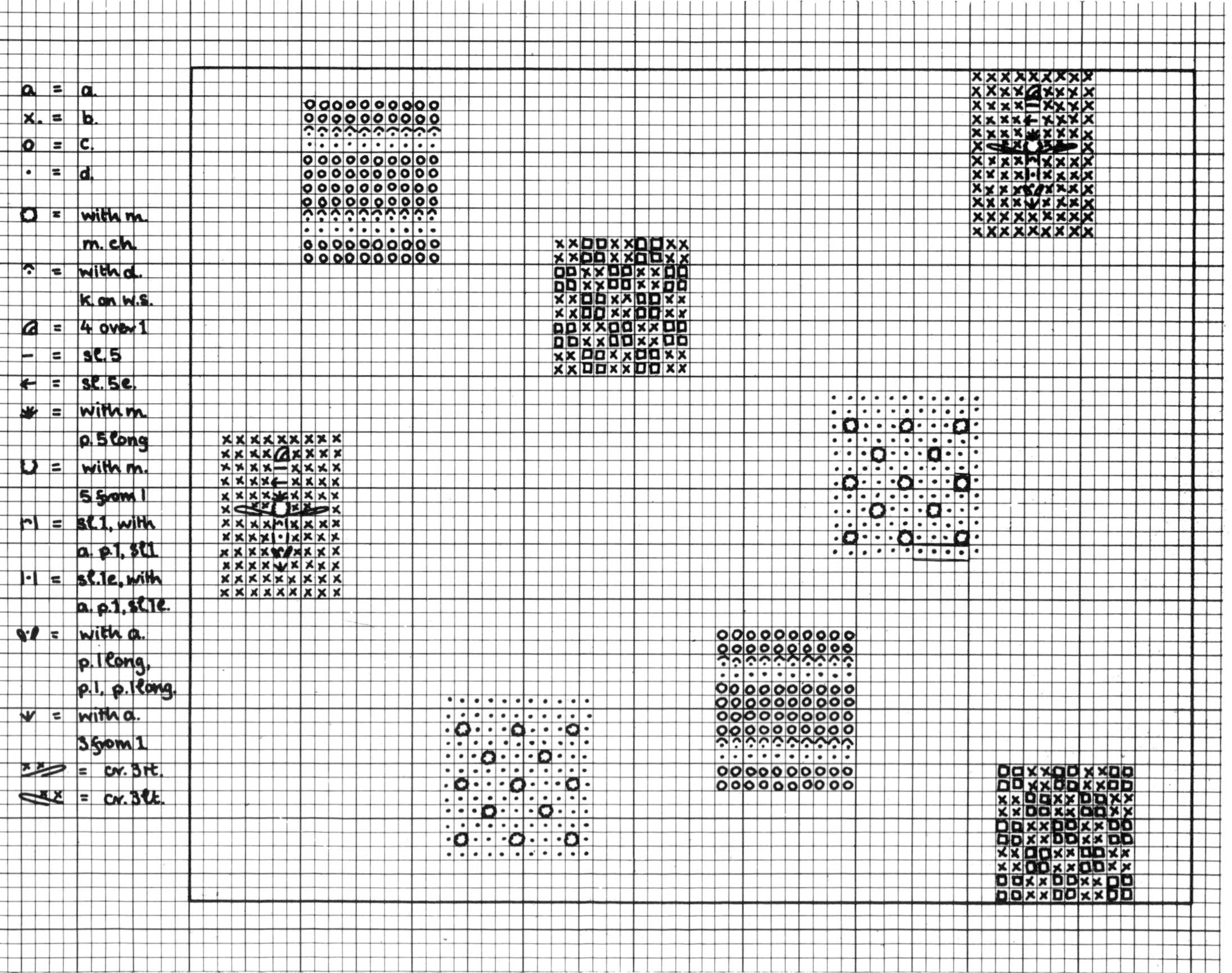

Trousers, shorts and hats by Kamikaze from Patricia Roberts, Covent Garden. T shirts from Memphis. Jewelry from Butler and Wilson.

romany

MATERIALS

Any of the following "Woollybear Yarns" by Patricia Roberts may be used for this design and "Woollybear Angora" may be substituted for any of the contrast colours, when using the other "Woollybear Yarns". For simplification, the yarn amounts are given for the cardigan, followed by those for the sweater in the first brackets and those for the waistcoat in the second brackets.

"Woollybear Lambswool" in 25 gram balls: 11 (9) (8) balls in main colour, 5 (5) (3) balls in first contrast, 5 (4) (3) balls in second contrast, 7 (6) (3) balls in third contrast and 5 (4) (3) balls in fourth contrast.

"Woollybear Pure Silk" in 25 gram balls: 8 (8) (7) balls in main colour, 4 (4) (2) balls in first contrast, 3 (3) (2) balls in second contrast, 6 (4) (2) in third contrast and 3 (3) (2) balls in fourth contrast.

"Woollybear Angora" in 20 gram balls 10 (7) (7) balls in main colour, 4 (4) (3) balls in first contrast, 4 (4) (2) balls in second contrast, 6 (5) (3) balls in third contrast and 4 (4) (3) balls in fourth contrast.

"Woollybear Fine Cotton" in 25 gram balls: 12 (10) (9) balls in main colour, 5 (5) (3) balls in first contrast, 5 (4) (3) balls in second contrast, 7 (6) (3) balls in third contrast and 5 (4) (2) balls in fourth contrast.

For any of the garments: a pair each of size $2\frac{1}{4}$ mm. (No. 13) and size $2\frac{3}{4}$ mm. (No. 12) Aero knitting needles. For the sweater, 1 button, for the cardigan or waistcoat. 4 buttons.

TENSION

The pattern is based on a stocking stitch tension of 16 stitches and 20 rows to 5 centimetres (2 inches) using size $2\frac{3}{4}$ mm. (No. 12) needles. If you cannot obtain this tension using the size needles suggested, use larger or smaller needles accordingly.

ABBREVIATIONS

K., knit; p., purl; st., stitch; tog., together; dec., decrease (by working 2 sts. tog.); inc., increase (by working twice into same st.); single rib is k. 1 and p. 1 alternately; s.s., stocking stitch is k. on the right side and p. on the wrong side; up 1, pick up the loop, which lies between the needles, slip it onto left hand needle, then k. into back of it; sl., slip; p.s.s.o, pass sl. st. over; y.r.n., yarn round needle; s.s.k., sl. 1, k. 1, p.s.s.o.; m., main colour; a., first contrast colour; b., second contrast colour; c., third contrast colour; d., fourth contrast colour; 3 from 1, k. 1, y.r.n., k. 1 all into next st.; 24 from 16 is (k. 1, inc. in next st.) 8 times; m.b., make bobble thus, k. 1, y.r.n., k. 1 all into next st., turn, p. 3, turn, sl. 1, k.2tog., p.s.s.o.; m.b. p.wise, make bobble purlwise as m.b. but reading p. for k. and k. for p.; 5 from 1, k. 1, y.r.n., k. 1, y.r.n., k. 1 all into one st.; 4 over 1, pass 2nd, 3rd, 4th and 5th sts. on left hand needle over first st., then with m. k. this st.

MEASUREMENTS

The measurements are given in centimetres followed by inches in brackets,

Underarms – cardigan & waistcoat	92.5 (37)
Underarms – sweater	90 (36)
Side seam	37.5 (15)
Length	57.5 (23)
Sleeve seam – sweater & cardigan	42.5 (17)

NOTE

Instructions in brackets are worked the number of times stated after the brackets.

THE CARDIGAN

THE BACK

With size $2\frac{1}{4}$ mm. (No. 13) needles and m. cast on 116 sts. and work 35 rows in single rib.

Now divide the sts. for easier working: Next row: Rib 58, and leave these sts. on a spare needle until required for left half back, work to end and continue on these 58 sts. for the right half back.

The right half back: Change to size $2\frac{3}{4}$ mm. (No. 12) needles and beginning with a k. row s.s. 2 rows. Now work in pattern as follows; using separate short lengths of m. for each vertical stripe and separate balls of contrast colours for each square. On wrong side rows take care to wrap m. firmly round contrast colours at the edges of the squares.

1st row: With m. k. 2, with a. 24 from 16, turn, with a. p.24, turn, with a. k.24, with m. k.3, with b. 24 from 16, turn, with b. p.24, turn, with b. k.3, (with a. k.2, with b. k.2) 5 times, with b. k.1 more, with m. k.3, with c. 24 from 16, turn, with c. p.24, turn, with c. k.24, with m. k.2.

2nd row: With m. p.2, with c. p.24, with m. p.3, with b. p.3, (with a. p.2, with b. p.2) 5 times, with b. p.1 more, with m. p.3, with a. p.24, with m. p.2.

3rd row: With m. k.2, wih a. k.24, turn, with a. p.24, turn, with a. k.24, *with m. k.3, with b. k.1, (with a. k.2, with b. k.2) 5 times, with a. k.2, with b. k.1, turn, with b. p.1, (with a. p.2, with b. p.2) 5 times, with a. p.2, with b. p.1, * *turn, with b. k.3, (with a. k.2, with b. k.2) 5 times, with b. k.1 more*, with m. k.3, with c. k.24, turn, with c. p.24, turn, with c. k.24, with m. k.2.

4th to 9th rows: Repeat 2nd and 3rd rows 3 times.

10th row: As 2nd row.

11th row: Work as given for 3rd row until * * is reached, turn, with b. k.24, with m. k.3, with c. k.24, turn, with c. p.24, turn, with c. k.24, with m. k.2.

12th row: With m. p.2, with c. p.24, with m. p.3, with b. p.24, with m. p.3, with a. p.24, with m. p.2.

13th row: With m. k.2, *(k.2tog., k.1) 8 times, k.3; repeat from * ending last repeat k.2.

14th, 15th and 16th rows: With m. in s.s.

17th row: With m. k.2, with d. 24 from 16, turn, with d. p.24, turn, with m. k.2tog., k.1, 3 from 1, k.2, (sl. 1, k.2tog., p.s.s.o., k.2, 3 from 1, k.2) twice, s.s.k., k.3, still with m. 24 from 16, turn, with m. p.24, turn, with m. k.24, then k.3, with a. 24 from 16, turn, with a. p.24, turn, with a. k.2, (with c. m.b., with a. k.3) 5 times, with c. m.b., with a. k.1, with m. k.2.

18th row: With m. p.2, with a. p.24, with m. p.30, still with m. k.24, p.2.

19th row: With m. k.2, with d. k.2tog., k.1, 3 from 1, k.2, (sl. 1, k.2tog., p.s.s.o., k.2, 3 from 1, k.2) twice, s.s.k., turn, with d. p.24, turn, with d. k.24, with m. k.3, then k.24, turn, with m. p.24, turn, with m. k.24, then k.3, with a. k.24, *turn, with a. p.24, turn, with a. k.24, with m. k.2.

20th row: With m. p.2, (with a. p.3, with c. m.b. p.wise) 5 times, with a. p.4, with m. p.30, with d. p.24, with m. p.2.

21st row: With m. k.2, still with m. *k.2tog., k.1, 3 from 1, k.2, (sl. 1, k.2tog., p.s.s.o., k.2, 3 from 1, k.2) twice, s.s.k. *, turn, with m. k.24, turn, with d. repeat from * to * with m. k.3, then k.24, turn, p.24, turn, k.24, then k.3, with a. k.24, turn, p.24, * *turn, k.24, with m. k.2.

22nd row: With m. p.2, with a. p.24, with m. p.30, with d. p.24, with m. p.2.

23rd row: With m. k.2, with d. k.24, turn, p.24, turn, with m. work from * to * on 21st row, then with m. k.3, then k.24, turn, p.24, turn, k.24, then k.3, with a. k.2, (with c. m.b., with a. k.3) 5 times, with c. m.b, with a. k.1, turn, with a. p.24, turn, with a. k.24, with m. k.2.

24th row: As 18th row.

25th row: Work as for 19th row until * is reached, turn, (with a. p.3, with c. m.b p.wise) 5 times, with a. p.4, turn, with a. k.24, with m. k.2.

26th row: As 22nd row.

27th row: Work as for 21st row until * * is reached, turn, with a. k.2, (with c. m.b., with a. k.3) 5 times, with c. m.b., with a. k.1, with m. k.2.

28th row: As 22nd row.

29th to 32nd rows: As 13th to 16th rows.

33rd row: With m. k.2, with b. 24 from 16, turn, p.24, turn, k.24, with m. k.3, with c. 24 from 16, turn, with c. p.24, turn, with d. k.24, with m. k.3, with d. 24 from 16, turn, with d. p.24, turn, with d. k.24, with m. k.2.

34th row: With m. p.2, with d. p.24, with m. p.3, with d. k.24, with m. p.3, with b. p.24, with m. p.2.

35th row: With m. k.2, with b. k.24, turn, p.24, turn, k.24, with m. k.3, with c. k.24, turn, p.24, turn, k.24, with m. k.3, with d. k.24, turn, p.24, turn, k.24, with m. k.2.

36th row: With m. p.2, with d. p.24, with m. p.3, with c. p.24, with m. p.3, with b. p.24, with m. p.2.

37th row: With m. k.2, with b. k.24, turn, p.24, turn, k.24, with m. k.3, with d. k.24, turn, with d. k.24, turn, with c. k.24, with m. k.3, with d. k.24, turn, p.24, turn, k.24, with m. k.2.

38th row: As 36th row.

39th row: With m. k.2, with b. k.24, turn, p.24, turn, k.24, with m. k.3, with c. k.24, turn, p.24, turn, with d. k.24, with m. k.3, with d. k.24, turn, p.24, turn, k.24, with m. k.2.

40th to 44th rows: As 34th to 38th rows.

45th to 48th rows: As 13th to 16th rows.

49th row: With m. k.2, with m. 24 from 16, turn, with m. p.24, turn, with m. k.3, (with b. 5 from 1, with m. k.7) twice, with b. 5 from 1, with m. k.4, then k.3 more, with a. 24 from 16, turn, with a. p.24, turn, with a. k.24, with m. k.3, with b. 24 from 16, turn, with b. p.24, turn, with b. k.3, (with a. k.2, with b. k.2) 5 times, with b. k.1 more, with m. k.2.

50th row: With m. p.2, with b. p.3, (with a. p.2, with b. p.2) 5 times, with b. p.1 more, with m. p.3, with a. p.24*, (with m. p.7, with b. p.5 winding yarn round needle twice for each st.) 3 times, with m. p.5.

51st row: With m. k.5, (slip 5 dropping extra loops, with m. k.7) twice, slip 5 dropping extra loops, with m. k.4, turn, with m. p.4, (sl.5, p.7) twice, sl.5, p.3, turn, with m. k.3, (4 over 1, k.7) 3 times, with a. k.24, turn, p.24, turn, k.24 * *, work as given for 3rd row from * to *, with m. k.2.

52nd row: Work as given for 50th row until * is reached, with m. p. to end.

53rd row: With m. k.2, then still with m. k.24, turn. p.24, turn, (with m. k.7, with b. 5 from 1) twice, with m. k.11, with a. k.24, turn, p.24, turn, k.24, work as given for 3rd row from * to *, with m. k.2.

54th row: Work as given for 50th row until * is reached, with m. p.11, (with b. p.5 winding yarn round needle twice for each st., with m. p.7) twice, with m. p.2.

55th row: With m. k.2, then (with m. k.7, sl.5 dropping extra loops) twice, with m. k.8, turn, with m. p.8, (sl.5, p.7) twice, turn, (with m. k.7, 4 over 1) twice, with m. k.11, with a. k.24, turn, p.24, turn, k.24, work as given for 3rd row from * to *, with m. k.2.

56th row: As 52nd row.

57th row: With m. k.26, turn, p.24, turn, with m. k.3, (with b. 5 from 1, with m. k.7) 3 times, with a. k.24, turn, p.24, turn, k.24, work as given for 3rd row from * to *, with m. k.2.

58th row: As 50th row.

59th row: Work as for 51st row until * * is reached, then as given for 3rd row from * to * *, turn and with b. k.24, with m. k.2.

60th row: With m. p.2, with b. p.24, with m. p.3, with a. p.24, with m. p.29.

61st to 64th rows. As 13th to 16th rows.

65th row: With m. k.2, with c. 24 from 16, turn, with c. p.24, turn, with c. k.24, with m. k.3, with d. 24 from 16, turn, p.24, turn, with m. k.2tog., k.1, 3 from 1, k.2, (sl. 1, k.2tog., p.s.s.o., k.2, 3 from 1, k.2) twice, s.s.k., still with m. k.3, then 24 from 16, turn, with m. p.24, turn, with m. k. to end.

66th row: With m. p.29, still with m. k.24, then p.3, with c. p.24, with m. p.2.

67th row: With m. k.2, with c. k.24, turn, p.24, turn, k.24, with m. k.3, with d. k.2tog., k.1, 3 from 1, k.2, (sl. 1, k.2tog., p.s.s.o, k.2, 3 from 1, k.2) twice, s.s.k., turn, with d. p.24, turn, k.24, with m. k.27, turn, p.24, turn, k.26.

68th row: With m. p.29, with d. p.24, with m. p.3, with c. p.24, with m. p.2.

69th row: With m. k.2, with c. k.24, turn, p.24, turn, k.24, with m. k.3, then still with m. *k.2tog., k.1, 3 from 1, k.2, (sl. 1, k.2tog., p.s.s.o., k.2, 3 from 1, k.2) twice, s.s.k. *, turn, with m. k.24, turn, with d. repeat from * to *, with m. k.27, turn, p.24, turn, k.26.

70th row: As 68th row.

71st row: With m. k.2, with c. k.24, turn, p.24, turn, k.24, with m. k.3, with d. k.24, turn, with d. p.24, turn, with m. work from * to * on 69th row, still with m. k.27, turn, p.24, turn, k.26.

72nd to 76th rows: As 66th to 70th rows.

77th to 80th rows: As 13th to 16th rows.

81st row: With m. k.2, with a. 24 from 16, turn, with a. p.24, turn, with a. k.2, (with c. m.b., with a. k.3) 5 times, with c. m.b, with a. k.1, with m. k.3, with b. 24 from 16, turn, with b. p.24, turn, with b. k.24, with m. k.3, with c. 24 from 16, turn, with c. p.24, turn, with d. k.24, with m. k.2.

82nd row: With m. p.2, with d. k.24, with m. p.3, with b. p.24, with m. p.3, with a. p.24, with m. p.2.

83rd to 94th rows: The last 2 rows set the position of the pattern squares, thus work one square in a. with bobbles in c. as on rows 17 to 30, one in b. alone and the other in c. with garter st. stripes as on rows 33 to 46.

To shape the armhole: 95th row: With m. cast off 8, k. to end. – 50 sts.

96th row: With m. all p.

97th row: With m. k.2, with d. (k.1, inc. in next st.) 4 times, turn, with d. p.12, turn, k.12, with m. k.3, then still with m. 24 from 16, turn, p.24, turn, with m. k.3, (with b. 5 from 1, with m. k.7) 3 times, * *with a. 24 from 16, turn, with a. p.24, turn, k.24, then with m. k.2.

98th row: With m. p.2, with a. p.24, (with m. p.7, with b. p.5 winding yarn round needle twice for each st.) 3 times, with m. p.6, with d. p.12 with m. p.2.

99th to 108th rows: The last 2 rows set the colours and pattern of the squares, thus work one in d. alone one in m. with dots in b. as on rows 51 to 60 and one in a. alone.

109th row: With m. k.2, (k.2tog., k.1) 4 times, k.3, (k.2tog., k.1) 8 times, k.3, (k.2tog., k.1) 8 times, k.2.

110th to 112th rows: With m. in s.s.

113th row: With m. k.2, with b. (k.1, inc. in next st.) 4 times, turn, with b. p.12, turn, with b. k.3, with a. k.2, with b. k.2, with a. k.2, with b. k.3, with m. k.3, with c. 24 from 16, turn, with c. p.24, turn, with c. k.24, with m. k.3, * *with d. 24 from 16, turn, with d. p.24, turn, with m. k.2tog., k.1, 3 from 1, k.2 (sl.1, k.2tog., p.s.s.o., k.2, 3 from 1, k.2) twice, s.s.k., with m. k.2.

114th to 124th rows: The last row sets the position of the patterns and colours, thus work one square in b. with checks in a. as on 2nd to 12th rows, one in c. alone and one in d. with zig-zags as on 18th to 28th rows.

125th to 128th rows: As 109 to 112th rows.

129th row: With m. k.2, still with m. (k.1, inc. in next st.) 4 times, turn, with m. p.12, turn, k.12, then k.3, with a. 24 from 16, turn, p.24, turn, with a. k.2, (with c. m.b., with a. k.3) 5 times, with c. m.b., with a. k.1, with m. k.3 * *, with b. 24 from 16, turn, with b. p.24, turn, k.24, with m. k.2.

130th to 140th rows: Work in pattern as set, one square in m., one in a. with bobbles in c. and one in b. alone.

141st to 144th rows: As 109th to 112th rows.

145th row: With m. k.2, with c. (k.1, inc. in next st.) 4 times, turn, p.12, turn, with d. k.12. with m. k.3, with d. 24 from 16, turn, p.24, turn, k.24, with m. k.3, then still with m. 24 from 16, turn, p.24, turn, wih m. k.3, (with b. 5 from 1, with m. k.7) twice, with b. 5 from 1, with m. k.6

146th to 156th rows: Work in pattern as set, one square in c. with garter st. stripes in d., one in d. alone and one in m. with dots in b.

157th and 158th rows: As 109th and 110th rows.

To slope the shoulder: With m. cast off 29 sts. loosely, using a size larger needle.

On 21 sts. work 1 row, then cast off very loosely, using a size larger needle.

The left half back: With right side of work facing rejoin m. to inner edge of the 58 sts. left on spare needle.

With size 2¾ mm. (No. 12) needles and m. beginning with a k. row s.s. 2 rows.

Now using separate short lengths of m. for the vertical stripes and taking care to wrap m. firmly round contrast colours at the edges of the squares, work in pattern as follows.

Work the 17th to 94th pattern rows given for right half back.

79th and 80th rows: With m. in s.s.

81st row: With m. k.2, with d. 24 from 16, turn, with d. p.24, turn, k.24, with m. k.3, then still with m. 24 from 16, turn, with m. p.24, turn, with m. k.3, (with b. 5 from 1, with m. k.7) 3 times, with a. 24 from 16, turn, p.24, turn, k.24, with m. k.2.

82nd to 95th rows: Work in pattern as set working one square in d. only, one in m. with dots in b. as before and one in a. only.

To shape the armhole: 96th row: With m. cast off 8 sts., p. to end. – 50 sts.

97th row: With m. k.2, with b. 24 from 16, turn, with b. p.24, turn, with b. k.3 (with a. k.2, with b. k.2) 5 times, with b. k.1 more, * *with m. k.3, with c. 24 from 16, turn, with c. p.24, turn, with c. k.24, with m. k.3, with d. (k.1, inc. in next st.) 4 times, turn, with d. p.12, turn, with m. k.2tog., k.1, 3 from 1, k.2, sl.1, k.2tog., p.s.s.o., k.2, inc. in next

						Rows
c.	b. checks in a.	a.	m. dots in c.	d.	c. stripes in d.	160 ↕ 145
m. dots in b.	d.	c. stripes in d.	b.	a. bobbles in c.	m.	144 ↕ 129
b.	a. bobbles in c.	m.	d. zig-zags in m.	c.	b. checks in a.	128 ↕ 113
d zig-zags in m.	c.	b. checks in a.	a.	m. dots in b.	d.	112 ↕ 97
a.	m. dots in b.	d.	c. stripes in d.	b.	a. bobbles in c.	96 ↕ 81
c. stripes in d.	b.	a. bobbles in c.	m.	d. zig-zags in m.	c.	80 ↕ 65
m.	d. zig-zags in m.	c.	b. checks in a.	a.	m. dots in b.	64 ↕ 49
b. checks in a.	a.	m. dots in b.	d.	c. stripes in d.	b.	48 ↕ 33
d.	c. stripes in d.	b.	a. bobbles in c.	m.	d zig-zags in m.	32 ↕ 17
a. bobbles in c.	m.	d. zig-zags in m.	c.	b. checks in a.	a.	16 ↕ 1

st., with m. k.2.

98th to 108th rows: In pattern as set, working one square in b. with checks in a., one in c. and one in d. with zig-zags in m.

109th row: With m. k.2, (k.2tog., k.1) 8 times, k.3, (k.2tog., k.1) 8 times, k.3, (k.2tog., k.1) 4 times, k.2 more.

110th to 112th rows: With m. in s.s.

113th row: With m. k.2, still with m. 24 from 16, turn, p.24, turn, k.27, with a. 24 from 16, turn, with a. p.24, turn, with a. k.2, (with c. m.b., with a. k.3) 5 times, with c. m.b., with a. k.1, with m. k.3, with b. (k.1, inc. in next st.) 4 times, turn, p.12, turn, k.12, with m. k.2.

114th to 128th rows: In pattern as set, working one square in m., one in a. with bobbles in c. and one in b. as set.

129th row: With m. k.2, with c. 24 from 16, turn, with c. p.24, turn, with d. k.24, with m. k.3, with d. 24 from 16, turn, with d. p.24, turn, k.24, with m. k.3, then still with m. (k.1, inc. in next st.) 4 times, turn, p.12, turn, k.3, with b. 5 from 1, with m. k.7, with b. 5 from 1, with m. k.2.

130th to 144th rows: In pattern as set, working one square in c. with stripes in d., one in d. alone and one in m. with dots in b. as set.

145th row: With m. k.2, with a. 24 from 16, turn, p.24, turn, k.24, with m. k.3, with b. k.24, turn, p.24, turn, with b. k.3, (with a. k.2, with b. k.2) 5 times, with b. k.1 more, with m. k.3, with c. (k.1, inc. in next st.) 4 times, turn, p.12, turn, k.12, with m. k.2.

146th to 157th rows: In pattern as set, working one square in a., one in b. with checks in a. and one in c.

To slope the shoulder: With m. cast off 29 sts. loosely using a large needle.

On 21 sts. work 1 row, then cast off very loosely, using a larger needle.

THE SLEEVES (both alike)

With size 2¼ mm. (No. 13) needles and m. cast on 64 sts. and work 35 rows in single rib.

Increase row: Rib 2, *up 1, rib 5; repeat from * ending rib 2 – 77 sts.

Change to size 2¾ mm. (No. 12) needles and beginning with a k. row s.s. 2 rows.

Now work in pattern as follows using separate lengths of m. for the vertical stripes and taking great care to wrap m. firmly round contrast colours at the edges of squares on wrong side rows.

1st row: With m. k.2, with b. 24 from 16, turn, p.24, turn, with b. k.3, (with a. k.2, with b. k.2) 5 times, with b. k.1 more, with m. k.3, with c. 24 from 16, turn, with c. p.24, turn, k.24, with m. k.3, with d. 24 from 16, turn, with d. p.24, turn, with m. k.2tog., k.1, 3 from 1, k.2, (sl.1, k.2 tog., p.s.s.o., k.2, 3 from 1, k.2) twice, s.s.k., then with m. k.3, still with m. 24 from 16, turn, p.24, turn, k.26.

The last row sets the position of the pattern, this is the same as the centre of the back.

Now work the 2nd to 112th rows as set, increasing 1 st. at the end of the last row – 78 sts. Break off m., join in b. and a. and work in check pattern as follows; taking great care, not to pull colours tightly across the back of the work.

1st row: With b. k.2, *with a. k.2, with b. k.2; repeat from * to end.

2nd row: With b. p.2, *with a. p.2, with b. p.2; repeat from * to end.

3rd row: With a. k.2, *with b. k.2, with a. k.2; repeat from * to end.

4th row: With a. p.2, * with b. p.2, with a. p.2; repeat from * to end.

Continuing in pattern as set, work 8 rows straight, marking each end of the last row with coloured threads.

Dec. 1st at each end of the next row and the 18 following alternate rows.

On 40 sts. work 1 row.

Cast off 3 sts. at the beginning of the next 6 rows, then 4 sts. on the 4 following rows.

Cast off the remaining 6 sts.

THE LEFT FRONT

With size 2¼ mm. (No. 13) needles and m. cast on 58 sts. and work 36 rows in single rib.

Change to size 2¾ mm. (No. 12) needles and beginning with a k. row s.s. 2 rows.

Work the 1st to 81st pattern rows given for right half back.

To slope the front edge: Decrease row: With m. p.2, with appropriate colour p.2tog., work to end as set.

Pattern 1 row as set.

Repeat the last 2 rows 4 times, then work the dec. row again, thus ending with the 92nd pattern row.

93rd row: With m., k.2, (k.2tog., k.1) 8 times, k.3, (k.2tog., k.1) 8 times, k.3, (k.2 tog., k.1) 6 times, k.2. – 54 sts.

94th row: With m. all p.

To shape the armhole: 95th row: With m. cast off 8, k. to end. – 46 sts.

96th row: With m. all p.

97th row: As given for 97th row on right half back until * * is reached, with a. (k.1, inc. in next st.) 6 times, turn, with a. p.18, turn, k.18, then with m. k.2.

Dec. 1 st. as before on the next row and the 5 following alternate rows.

109th row: With m. k.2, (k.2tog., k.1) 4 times, k.3, (k.2tog., k.1) 8 times, k.3, (k.2tog., k.1) 4 times, k.2.

110th to 112th rows: With m. in s.s.

Continued on page 20

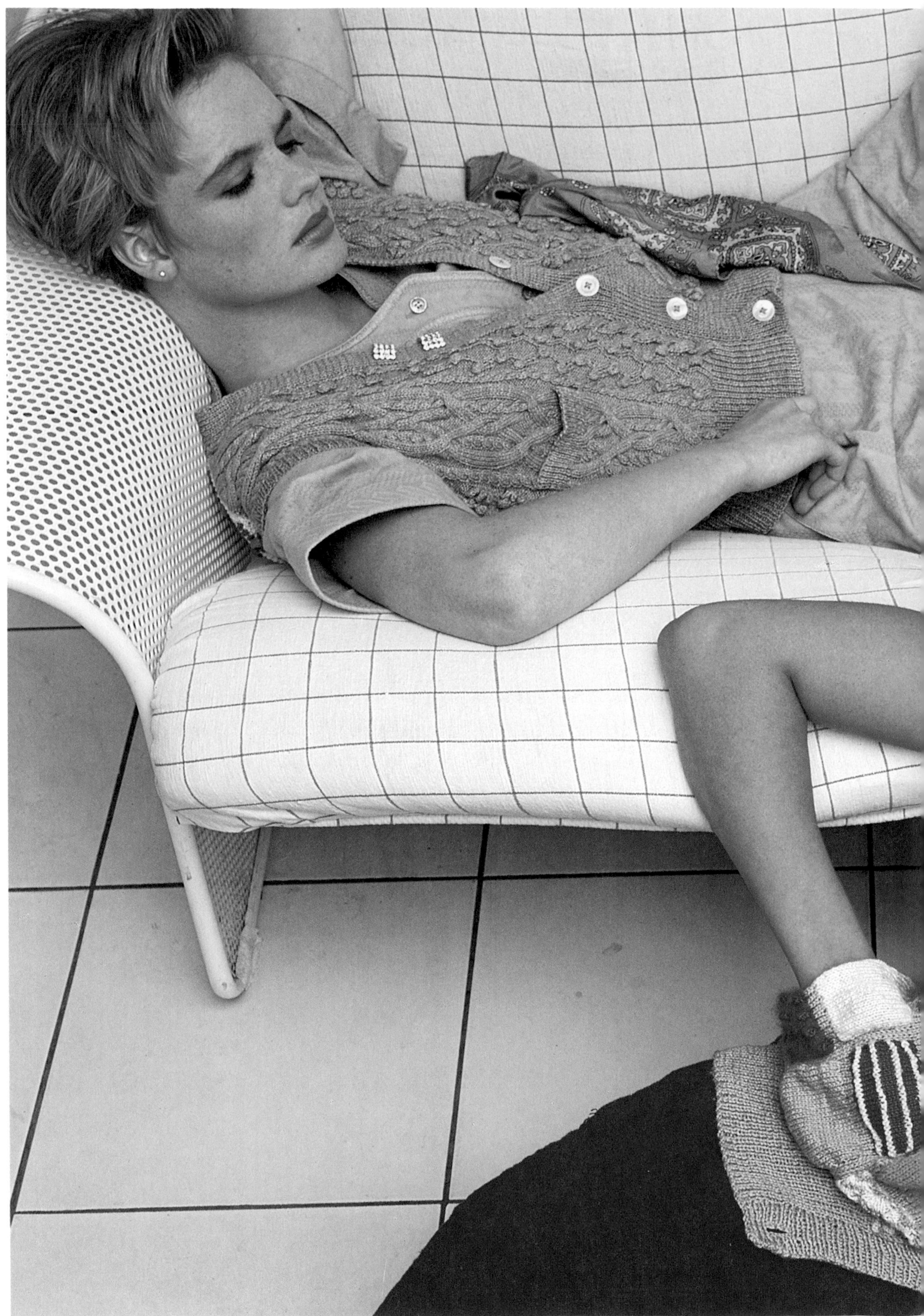

urchin

Trousers, shirt and dungarees

romany

icia Roberts, Covent Garden

Continued from page 17.

113th row: As given for 113th row on right back until ** is reached, with d. (k.1, inc. in next st.) 4 times, turn, with d. p.12, turn, with m. k.2tog., k.1, 3 from 1, k.2, sl.1, k.2tog., p.s.s.o., k.2, inc. in next st., with m. k.2.

114th to 124th rows: In pattern as set, but decreasing 1 st. as before for front edge on each wrong side row.

125th row: With m. k.2, (k.2tog., k.1) 4 times, k.3, (k.2tog., k.1) 8 times, k.3, (k.2tog., k.1) twice, k.2.

126th to 128th rows: With m. in s.s.

129th row: Work as for 129th row on right half back until ** is reached, with b. (k.1, inc. in next st.) twice, turn, with b. p.6, turn, k.6, with m. k.2.

130th to 140th rows: In pattern as set, but decreasing as before for front edge on each wrong side row.

141st row: With m. k.2, (k.2tog., k.1) 4 times, k.3, (k.2tog., k.1) 8 times, k.1, k.2tog., k.2.

142nd to 158th rows: In pattern as set, but decreasing by working the 3rd and 4th sts. from front edge tog. as before on 143rd and 145th rows.

To slope the shoulder: Cast off the remaining 31 sts. loosely using a size larger needle.

THE RIGHT FRONT

With size 2¼ mm. (No. 13) needles and m. cast on 58 sts. and work 36 rows in single rib.

Change to size 2¾ mm. (No. 12) needles and beginning with a k. row s.s. 2 rows.

Work the 1st to 81st pattern rows given for left half back.

To slope the front edge: Decrease row: Pattern as set until 4 remain, with appropriate colour p.2tog., with m. p.2.

Pattern 1 row as set.

Repeat the last 2 rows 4 times more, then work the decrease row again, ending with the 92nd pattern row.

93rd row: With m. k.2, (k.2tog., k.1) 6 times, k.3, (k.2tog., k.1) 8 times, k.3, (k.2tog., k.1) 8 times, k.2.

94th and 95th rows: With m. in s.s.

To shape the armhole: 96th row: With m. cast off 8 sts., p. to end. – 46 sts.

97th row: With m. k.2, with b. (k.1, inc. in next st.) 6 times, turn, p.18, turn, with b. k.1, (with a. k.2, with b. k.2) 4 times, with b. k.1 more, work as for 97th row on left half back from ** to end.

Work the 98th to 159th rows as set, but decreasing at front edge, by working the 3rd and 4th sts. from front edge tog. on the 98th row and the 5 following alternate rows, then on the 114th row and the 5 following alternate rows, then on the 130th row and 5 following alternate rows and finally on the 141st row and 2 following alternate rows.

To slope the shoulder: Cast off the remaining 31 sts. loosely with a size larger needle.

THE BUTTONBAND

With right side of work facing rejoin m. to left front edge at the 80th pattern row and using size 2¾ mm. (No. 12) needles pick up and k. 104 sts. from row end edge up to cast on edge.

Work 11 rows in single rib, then cast off loosely in rib, using a size larger needle.

THE BUTTONHOLE BAND

With right side of work facing rejoin m. at cast on edge of right front and using size 2¾ mm. (No. 12) needles pick up and k. 104 sts. from row end edge, up to the 80th pattern row.

Work 5 rows in single rib.

1st Buttonhole row: Rib 6, *cast off 6, rib next 23 sts; repeat from * ending last repeat rib 1.

2nd Buttonhole row: Rib 2, *turn, cast on 6, turn, rib 24; repeat from * ending last repeat rib 6.

Rib 4 rows, then cast off in rib very loosely.

THE HALF COLLAR (2 pieces alike)

With size 2¾ mm. (No. 12) needles and c. cast on 64 sts. and work in pattern as follows:

1st row: With c. all k.
2nd row: With c. all p.
3rd & 4th rows: With d. all k.
5th & 6th rows: As 1st and 2nd rows.

The last 6 rows form the pattern; repeat them 11 times more. then work the first 2 rows again.

Continuing in pattern as set. dec. 1 st. at each end of the next row and the 23 following alternate rows.

On 16 sts. work 1 row, then cast off.

THE POCKET BACKS (2 alike)

With size 2¾ mm. (No. 12) needles and m. cast on 48 sts. and work 60 rows in s.s., then cast off.

TO MAKE UP THE CARDIGAN

Do not press. Neatly join centre back seams; do not do this too firmly. Join shoulder seams. Set in sleeves, so that the 12 check pattern rows below the marking threads on sleeve top are sewn to the cast off groups at underarms. Neatly sew one row end edge of each pocket back to the row ends of the first 3 squares on each side of back. Join sleeve seams. Join side seams, neatly slip-stitching pockets in place at back of fronts. Join cast on edges of half collar pieces. Fold in half lengthways. Neatly sew row end edges of collar in place at neck edge, neatly sewing cast off edges of collar to row ends of button and buttonhole bands.

THE SWEATER

THE BACK

Work as given for the back of the cardigan until the 112th pattern row and the armhole shaping has been worked on both the left and right half backs. Leave the 50 sts. of each half back on a spare needle until required for yoke.

THE FRONT

Work as given for back.

THE BACK YOKE

With right side of work facing rejoin c. to the 50 sts. of right half back and using size 2¾ mm. (No. 12) needles work as follows: Increase row: K.5, *up 1, k.8; repeat from * ending last repeat k.5, then onto the same needle, work this increase row across the 50 sts. of left half back. – 112 sts.

P.1 row.

Now work in pattern as follows: 1st and 2nd rows: With d. all k.

3rd to 6th rows: With c. beginning with a. k. row in s.s.

The last 6 rows form the pattern; repeat them 8 times more, then work the first 4 rows again.

To slope the shoulders: Cast off 10 sts. at the beginning of the next 6 rows.

Leave the remaining 52 sts. on a spare needle until required for collar.

THE LEFT FRONT YOKE

With right side of work facing rejoin c. to the 50 sts. of left half front and using size 2¾ mm. (No. 12) needles and with c. work as follows:

Increase row: K.5, *up 1, k.8; repeat from * ending last repeat k.5, turn, cast on 3 sts. – 59 sts.

Next row: K.3, p. to end.

Now work in pattern, with garter st. edging as follows:

1st row: With d. k. until 3 remain, with c. k.3.
2nd row: With c. k.3, with d. k. to end.
3rd row: With c. all k.
4th row: With c. k.3, p. to end.
5th & 6th rows: As 3rd and 4th rows.

Repeat the last 6 rows 3 times more, then work the first row again.

To shape the neck: Continuing in pattern as set, cast off 5 sts. at the beginning of the next row, then dec. 1 st. at the neck edge on each of the next 24 rows.

On 30 sts. work 8 rows.

To slope the shoulder: Cast off 10 sts. at the beginning of the next row and the following alternate row. On 10 sts. work 1 row, then cast off.

THE RIGHT FRONT YOKE

With right side of work facing rejoin c. to the 50 sts. of right front yoke and using size 2¾ mm. (No. 12) needles and work as follows:

Increase row: Cast on 3 sts., k. these 3 sts., then k. next 5 sts., *up 1, k.8; repeat from * ending last repeat k.5. – 59 sts.

Next row: P. until 3 remain, k.3.

Now work in pattern with garter st. edging.

1st row: With c. k.3, with d. k. to end.
2nd row: With d. k. until 3 remain, with c. k.3.
3rd row: With c. all k.
4th row: With c. p. until 3 remain, k.3.
5th & 6th rows: As 3rd and 4th rows.

Work the first 4 pattern rows again.

1st Buttonhole row: With c. k.3, cast off 5, k. to end.

2nd Buttonhole row: With c., p. until 3 remain, turn, cast on 5, turn, k. to end.

Pattern 14 rows as set.

To shape the neck: Work as given for left front yoke neck shaping to end.

THE COLLAR

First join shoulder seams. With right side of work facing rejoin c. at right front neck edge, then using size 2¾ mm. (No. 12) needles pick up and k. 48 sts. from right front neck edge, k. across the 52 sts. at centre back edge, then pick up and k. 48 sts. from left front neck edge. – 148 sts.

Work 9 rows in single rib.

Increase row: Rib 4, 3 from 1, rib until 5 remain, 3 from 1, rib 4.

Repeat the last 10 rows 3 times more.

On 164 sts. rib 5 rows, then cast off loosely in rib.

THE SLEEVES

Work as given for sleeves of cardigan until 112 pattern rows have been worked.

Break off m., join in a. and work as follows:

Increase row: K.2, *up 1, k.4; repeat from * ending last repeat k.3. – 96 sts.

P.1 row.

Now join in c. and work in bobble pattern as follows.

1st row: With a. k.2, *with c. m.b, with m. k.3; repeat from * ending with a. k.1.

2nd, 3rd 4th & 5th rows: With a. in s.s.

6th row: *With a. p.3, with c. m.b. p.wise; repeat from * until 4 remain, with a. p.4.

7th to 10th rows: With a. in s.s.

The last 10 rows form the pattern; mark each end of the last row with coloured threads.

Continuing in pattern as set, dec. 1 st. at each end of the next row and the 9 following alternate rows.

On 76 sts. work 1 row.

Dec. 1 st. at each end of the next 20 rows.

Cast off 3 sts. at the beginning of the next 4 rows, then 4 sts. on the 4 following rows.

Cast off the remaining 8 sts.

TO MAKE UP THE SWEATER

Do not press. Set in sleeves, so that the 12 row ends in a. below the marking threads are sewn to the cast off groups at underarms. Join sleeve and side seams. Join centre back and centre front seams up to yoke very neatly, taking care not to pull yarn too firmly. Neatly sew 3 st. cast on groups of button and buttonhole edges of yoke in place at centre front. Sew on button.

THE WAISTCOAT

THE BACK

Work exactly as given for cardigan.

THE LEFT AND RIGHT FRONTS

Work as given for cardigan.

THE BUTTONBAND

First join shoulder seams. With right side of work facing rejoin m. to back neck edge of left half back, and using size 2¾ mm. (No. 12) needles, pick up and k. 24 sts. from left back neck edge, then 70 sts. from shaped row ends of left front down to the 81st pattern row, then pick up and k. 104 sts. from the 80th row down to cast on edge.

On 198 sts. work 11 rows in single rib.

Cast off loosely, using a size larger needle.

THE BUTTONHOLE BAND

With right side of work facing rejoin m. at cast on edge of right front and using size 2¾ mm. (No. 12) needles pick up and k. 104 sts. up to the 80th pattern row, then 70 sts. from shaped row end edge up to shoulder, then 24 sts. from right back neck.

On 198 sts. work 5 rows in single rib.

1st Buttonhole row: Rib 6, *cast off 6, rib next 23 sts.; repeat from * twice more, cast off 6, rib to end.

2nd Buttonhole row: Rib 96, *turn, cast on 6, turn, rib 24; repeat from * ending rib 6.

Rib 4 rows, then cast off in rib very loosely.

THE POCKET BACKS (2 alike)

As given for cardigan.

THE ARMBANDS (both alike)

With right side of work facing rejoin m. and using size 2¾ mm. (No. 12) needles pick up and k. 144 sts. from all round armhole edge. Work 7 rows in single rib, then cast off in rib.

TO MAKE UP THE WAISTCOAT

Do not press. Join centre back seam. Sew one row end edge of each pocket back to row ends of first 3 squares on each side of back. Join side seams, neatly slip stitching pockets in place at back of fronts. Sew on buttons.

urchin

MATERIALS
Either 18 25 gram balls of "Woollybear Fine Cotton" or 12 28 gram (ounce) hanks of "Woollybear Real Shetland" or 12 25 gram balls of "Woollybear Pure Cashmere" all by Patricia Roberts; a pair each of size 2¼mm. (No. 13) and size 2¾mm. (No. 12) Aero knitting needles, 2 fine cable needles; 4 buttons.

TENSION
As for "Brownie" on page 108.

ABBREVIATIONS
As for "Brownie" on page 108.

MEASUREMENTS
The measurements are given in centimetres followed by inches in brackets.

Underarms	95(38)
Side seam	30(12)
Length	51(20½)

THE BACK
With size 2¼mm. (No. 13) needles cast on 128 sts. and work 33 rows in single rib.

Increase row: Rib 3, *up 1, rib 2, up 1, rib 3; repeat from * to end. - 178 sts.

Change to size 2¾mm. (No. 12) needles and work the 28 pattern rows given for back of "Brownie" cardigan twice, then work the pocket and pattern 9 rows more.

To shape the armholes: Work as given for armhole shaping on back of "Brownie" cardigan on page 109 to end.

THE POCKET BACKS (2 alike)
With size 2¼mm. (No. 12) needles cast on 42 sts. and work 50 rows in single rib, then leave these sts. on a stitch-holder until required.

THE LEFT FRONT
With size 2¼mm. (No. 13) needles cast on 65 sts. and work 33 rows in single rib.

Increase row: Rib 2, up 1, rib 3, *up 1, rib 2, up 1, rib 3; repeat from * to end. - 90 sts.

Change to size 2¾mm. (No. 12) needles and work the 28 pattern rows as given for left front of "Brownie" cardigan twice, then work the pocket row and pattern 9 rows more.

Now work as given for left front of "Brownie" cardigan from ** to end.

THE RIGHT FRONT
Work as given for left front until the increase row has been worked.

Change to size 2¾mm. (No. 12) needles and work the 28 pattern rows given for the right front of the cardigan twice, then work the pocket row and pattern 10 rows more.

Now work as given for left front of "Brownie" cardigan from ** to end.

THE POCKET TOPS (2 alike)
With right side of work facing rejoin yarn to the 42 sts. left on stitch-holder and using size 2¼mm. (No. 13) needles work 8 rows in single rib, then cast off in rib.

THE FRONT BANDS
First join shoulder seams. With size 2¼mm. (No. 13) needles cast on 15 sts. and work 6 rows in single rib.

1st Buttonhole row: Rib 6, cast off 3, rib to end.

2nd Buttonhole row: Rib 6, turn, cast on 3 over those cast off, rib to end.

Rib 28 rows.

Repeat the last 30 rows twice, then work the 2 buttonhole rows again.

Continue in rib until the band is long enough to fit up right front edge, with last buttonhole in line with first front edge decrease, until the band is long enough fo fit round neck edge and down left front. Sew in place, casting off when correct length is assured.

THE ARMBANDS (both alike)
With right side of work facing rejoin yarn and using size 2¼mm. (No. 13) needles, pick up and k. 136 sts. from all round armhole edge, work 7 rows in single rib, then cast off in rib.

TO MAKE UP THE WAISTCOAT
Pin out to size and press all parts except the ribbing very lightly on the wrong side with a warm iron over a dry cloth. Neatly sew pocket backs and row ends of pocket tops in place. Join side seams. Sew on buttons.

"**Pot-pourri**" continued from page 13.

The last 20 rows form the rosebud pattern: Change to size 3¾mm. (No. 9) needles and work the 20 pattern rows again but without changing needles after 10th row, then work the 1st and 2nd rows again.

Now work in stripe pattern and decrease as follows.

1st Decrease row: With b. k.1, *sl.1, k.2 tog., p.s.s.o., k.11; repeat from * to end. - 181 sts.

With b. k.1 row.

With m. k.1 row, then moss st. - as before - 3 rows.

2nd Decrease row: With a. k.1, *sl.1, k.2 tog., p.s.s.o., k.9; repeat from * to end. - 151 sts.

With a. k.1 row.

With m. k.1 row, then moss st. 3 rows.

3rd Decrease row: With b. k.1, *sl.1, k.2 tog., p.s.s.o., k.7; repeat from * to end. - 121 sts.

With b. k.1 row.

With m. k.1 row, then moss st. 3 rows.

4th Decrease row: With a. k.1, *sl.1, k.2 tog., p.s.s.o., k.5; repeat from * to end. - 91 sts.

With a k.1 row.

With m. k.1 row, then moss st. 3 rows.

5th Decrease row: With b. k.1, *sl.1, k.2tog., p.s.s.o., k.3; repeat from * to end. - 61 sts.

With b. k.1 row.

With m. k.1 row, then moss st. 3 rows.

6th Decrease row: With a. k.1, *sl.1, k.2 tog., p.s.s.o., k.1; repeat from * to end. - 31 sts.

With a. k.1 row.

With m. k.1 row, then moss st. 1 row.

7th Decrease row: With m. k.1, *sl.1, k.2 tog., p.s.s.o.; repeat from * to end. - 11 sts.

Break off m. leaving a long end, thread this through the remaining sts. and draw up firmly, then with this end join row end edges neatly.

THE FINGERLESS GLOVES

THE LEFT GLOVE
With size 3¼mm. (No. 10) needles and m. cast on 51 sts. and work 6 rows in single rib.

Change to size 3¾mm. (No. 9) needles and using the same size needles throughout, work the 20 pattern rows given for the hat twice.

Change to size 3¼mm. (No. 10) needles and work the 20 pattern rows twice more. Work 1 extra row here, when working right glove.

Now divide the sts. for the thumb: Next row: Pattern 22, then slip the next 8 sts. onto a safety pin until required, in their place, turn and cast on 8 sts., turn, pattern to end.

Pattern 19 rows as set.

Now divide the sts. for the fingers: Next row: Pattern 5 and leave these sts. on a safety pin until required for little finger, cast off 1, pattern next 5 sts., then slip these 6 sts. onto a safety pin for third finger, cast off 1, pattern next 5 sts. and leave these 6 sts. on a safety pin for second finger, cast off 1, pattern next 10 sts., then leave these 11 sts. on a safety pin until required for first finger, cast off 1, pattern next 5 sts. and slip these 6 sts. onto the safety pin already holding 6 sts., for second finger, cast off 1, pattern next 5 sts. and slip these 6 sts. onto the safety pin holding sts. for third finger, cast off 1, pattern to end and slip these 5 sts. onto the safety pin holding sts. for little finger.

The finger edgings (all alike): With right side of work facing rejoin a. to the sts. left on one safety pin, and using size 3¼mm. (No. 10) needles k.4 rows, then cast off.

The thumb edging: With right side of work facing rejoin a. to the 8 sts. left on safety pin and using size 3¼mm. (No. 10) needles k. across these sts., turn, cast on 9 sts.

On 17 sts. k.3 rows, then cast off.

THE RIGHT GLOVE
Work as given for left glove, noting the variation in the rows, before dividing the sts. for the thumb.

TO COMPLETE
Neatly join seams between fingers. Join row end edges. Sew cast on edge of thumb to the sts. cast on for edging and join row ends of edging. Press lightly with a warm iron over a damp cloth.

Trousers, dress and white hat by Kamikaze from Patricia Roberts, Covent Garden.

henly

MATERIALS
For the sweater: Either 24 25 gram balls of "Woollybear Fine Cotton" or 24 25 gram balls of "Woollybear Lambswool" by Patricia Roberts. A pair each of size 2¼mm. (No. 13) and size 2¾mm. (No. 12) Aero knitting needles, a fine cable needle, 3 buttons.
For the cardigan: Add one extra ball to any of the yarns given for the sweater and 7 buttons.

TENSION
15 stitches and 24 rows to 5 centimetres (2 inches) over garter stitch using size 2¾mm. (No. 12) needles. If you cannot obtain the correct tension using the size needles suggested use larger or smaller ones accordingly.

NOTE
The instructions given in the brackets are worked the number of times stated after the brackets.

ABBREVIATIONS
K., knit; p., purl; st., stitch; tog., together; dec., decrease (by working 2 sts. tog.); inc., increase (by working twice into same st.); garter st. is k. plain on every row; single rib is k. 1 and p. 1 alternately; sl., slip; p.s.s.o., pass sl. st. over; y.r.n., yarn round needle; s.s.k., sl. 1, k. 1, p.s.s.o.; 9 from 1, k. 1, y.r.n., k. 1, y.r.n., k. 1, y.r.n., k. 1, y.r.n., k. 1 all into next st.; 8 over 1, pass 2nd, 3rd, 4th, 5th, 6th, 7th, 8th and 9th sts. on left hand needle over first st., then k. this st.; up 1, pick up the loop, which lies between the needles, slip it onto left hand needle, then k. into back of it; up 2, as up 1, but knitting into front and back of loop; cable 6, slip next 3 sts. onto cable needle and leave at front of work, k. 3, then k. 3 from cable needle; m.a., make apple thus, 9 from 1, turn, *k. 1, (p. 1, k. 1) 4 times, turn, k. 1, (p. 1, k. 1) 4 times, turn, k. 1, (p. 1, k. 1) 4 times, turn, k. 1, (p. 1., k. 1) 4 times *, turn, k. 1, p. 1, k. 1, sl. 1, k. 2 tog., p.s.s.o., y.r.n., k. 1, p. 1, k. 1, turn, k. 1, p. 1, k. 1, inc. in next st., (p. 1, k. 1) twice, turn; repeat from * to *, 8 over 1; 5 from 1 is k. 1, y.r.n., k. 1, y.r.n., k. 1 all into 1 st.; m.b., make bobble thus, 5 from 1., turn, p. 5, turn, k. 5, turn, p. 5, turn, k. 5, turn, p. 5, 4 over 1; 4 over 1 is pass 2nd, 3rd, 4th and 5th sts, on left hand needle over first st.; m.h., make head thus, 9 from 1, turn, p. 9, turn, k. 9, turn, p. 9, turn, k. 9, turn, p. 9, turn, k. 5, k. the next st., then (sl. the st. just knitted back onto left hand needle and k. into it) 4 times, k. 3, turn, p. 9, turn, 8 over 1; k. 1 down, insert right hand needle into st. 6 rows below next st. on left hand needle, wrap yarn round needle and draw loop through, then k. this loop together with next st. on left hand needle; m.h.b., make half bobble, thus, k. 9, turn, p. 9, turn, k. 9, turn, p. 9, turn, k. 4, k. next st., then (sl. the st. just knitted back onto left hand needle and k. into it) 6 times, k. 4, turn, p. 9, turn, 8 over 1; 3 from 1, k. 1, y.r.n., k. 1 all into next st.; tw.3lt., twist 3 left, thus, k. into back of 3rd st. on left hand needle, then k. into front of 1st and 2nd sts.; cr.3rt., cross 3 right, k. into front of 3rd st. on left hand needle, then k. first and 2nd sts; cr.3lt., cross 3 left, slip next st. onto cable needle and leave at front of work, k. 2, then k. 1 from cable needle; s.b., start bee, thus, k. 1, y.r.n., k. 1, y.r.n., k. 1, y.r.n., k. 1 all into next st., turn, k. 7, turn, p. 7; f.b., finish bee, thus, k. 7, turn, p. 7, turn, p. 7, turn, k. 7, turn, pass 2nd, 3rd, 4th, 5th, 6th and 7th sts. on left hand needle over first st., k. this st.; s.w.rt., small wing right, working into next st., cast on 4 sts., k. 4, turn, k. 4, turn, k. 3, turn, k. 2, turn, k. 1, turn, k. 2, turn, cast off 4; s.wlt., small wing left, sl. 1, turn and work as given for s.wrt., then turn and k. 1 remaining st.; l.w.rt., large wing right, working into next st., cast on 7 sts., k. 7, turn, k. 7, turn, k. 6, turn, k. 5, turn, k. 4, turn, k. 3, turn, k. 2, turn, k. 1, turn, cast off 7; l.w.lt., large wing left, sl. 1, turn and work as for l.w.rt., then turn and k. 1 remaining st.; b.w.rt., butterfly wing right, working into next st., cast on 9 sts., then working across these sts., (s.s.k., y.r.n.) 5 times, turn, p. 10, turn, k. 9, turn, k. 8, turn, k. 7, turn, k. 6, turn, k. 5, turn, k. 4, turn, k. 3, turn, k. 2, turn, k. 1, turn, k. 5, turn, cast off 9; b.w.lt., butterfly wing left, sl. 1, turn and work as given for b.w.rt., then turn and k. 1 remaining st.; cl., cloud, 5 from 1, turn, k. 5, turn, cast off 4; m.d.b., make double bobble, 3 from 1, 3 from 1, (turn, p. 6, turn, k. 6) twice, turn, p. 6, turn, (sl. 1, k. 2 tog., p.s.s.o.) twice; tw.3rt., twist 3 right, thus, k. into front of 2nd and 3rd sts. on left hand needle, then k. into back of 1st st.; m.k., make knot thus, k. 1, y.r.n., k. 1 all into one st., turn, p. 3, turn, k. 3, turn, p. 3, turn, sl. 1, k. 2 tog., p.s.s.o.; cable 9, slip next 3 sts. onto cable needle and leave at back of work, k. 6, then k. 3 from cable needle, w.s., wrong side; r.s., right side; 4 slant 6, is inc. in each of 4 sts., turn, k. these 8 sts., turn, p. 8, turn, k. 6, turn, p. 6; k. 1 long, k. 1, winding yarn round needle twice.

MEASUREMENTS
The measurements are given in centimetres followed by inches in brackets.

Underarms – sweater	95	(38)
Underarms – cardigan	99	(39½)
Side seam	42.5	(17)
Length	62.5	(25)
Sleeve seam	46	(18½)

THE SWEATER

THE SLEEVES (both alike)
With size 2¼mm. (No. 13) needles cast on 64 sts. and work 29 rows in single rib.
Increase row: Rib 1, *up 1, rib 2; repeat from * ending last repeat rib 1. – 96 sts.
Change to size 2¾mm. (No. 12) needles and work in cable pattern as follows:
1st row: All k.
2nd row: K. 3, p. 6, *k. 18, p. 12; repeat from * ending last repeat p. 6, k. 3.
3rd and 4th rows: As 1st and 2nd rows.
5th row: K. 3, *cable 6, k. 18, cable 6; repeat from * until 3 remain, k. 3.
6th row: As 2nd row.
7th and 8th rows: As 1st and 2nd rows.
9th row: K. 3, up 1, k. 6, *k. 2 tog., k. 14, s.s.k., k. 6, up 2 – see abbreviations, k. 6; repeat from * ending last repeat up 1, k. 3 instead of up 2, k. 6.
10th row: K. 4, *p. 6, k. 16, p. 6, k. 2; repeat from * ending last repeat k. 4.
11th row: K. 4, *up 1, k. 6, k. 2 tog., k. 12, s.s.k., k. 6, up 1, k. 2; repeat from * ending last repeat k. 4.
12th row: K. 5, *p. 6, k. 14, p. 6, k. 4; repeat from * ending last repeat k. 5.
13th row: K. 5, *up 1, cable 6, k. 2 tog., k. 10, s.s.k., cable 6, up 1, k. 4; repeat from * ending last repeat k. 5.
14th row: K. 6, *p. 6, k. 12, p. 6, k. 6; repeat from * to end.
15th row: K. 6, *up 1, k. 6, k. 2 tog., k. 8, s.s.k., k. 6, up 1, k. 6; repeat from * to end.
16th row: K. 7, *p. 6, k. 10, p. 6, k. 8; repeat from * ending last repeat k. 7.
17th row: K. 7, *up 1, k. 6, k. 2 tog., k. 6, s.s.k., k. 6, up 1, k. 8; repeat from * ending last repeat k. 7.
18th row: K. 8, *p. 6, k. 8, p. 6, k. 10; repeat from * ending last repeat k. 8.
19th row: K. 8, *up 1, k. 6, k. 2 tog., k. 4, s.s.k., k. 6, up 1, k. 10; repeat from * ending last repeat k. 8.
20th row: K. 9, *p. 6, k. 6, p. 6, k. 12; repeat from * ending last repeat k. 9.
21st row: K. 9, *up 1, cable 6, k. 2 tog., k. 2, s.s.k., cable 6, up 1, k. 12; repeat from * ending last repeat k. 9.
22nd row: K. 10, *p. 6, k. 4, p. 6, k. 14; repeat from * ending last repeat k. 10.
23rd row: K. 10, *up 1, k. 6, k. 2 tog., s.s.k., k. 6, up 1, k. 14; repeat from * ending last repeat k. 10.
24th row: K. 11, *p. 6, k. 2, p. 6, k. 16; repeat from * ending last repeat k. 11.
25th row: K. 11, *up 1, k. 5, k. 2 tog., s.s.k., k. 5, up 1, k. 16; repeat from * ending last repeat k. 11.
26th row: K. 12, *p. 12, k. 18; repeat from * ending last repeat k. 12.
27th row: All k.
28th row: As 26th row.
29th row: K. 12, *cable 6, cable 6, k. 18; repeat from * ending last repeat k. 12.
30th to 35th rows: repeat 26th and 27th rows 3 times.
36th and 37th rows: As 28th and 29th rows.
38th, 39th and 40th rows: As 26th to 28th rows.
41st row: K. 10, *s.s.k., k. 6, up 2, k. 6, k. 2 tog., k. 14; repeat from * ending last repeat k. 10.
42nd row: K. 11, *p. 6, k. 2, p. 6, k. 16; repeat from * ending last repeat k. 11.
43rd row: K. 9, *s.s.k., k. 6, up 1, k. 2, up 1, k. 6, k. 2 tog., k. 12 repeat from * ending last repeat k. 9.
44th row: As 22nd row.
45th row: K. 8, *s.s.k., cable 6, up 1, k. 4, up 1, cable 6, k. 2 tog., k. 10; repeat from * ending last repeat k. 8.
46th to 56th wrong side rows: Work as given for wrong side rows from 20th row back to 10th row.
47th row: K. 7, *s.s.k., k. 6, up 1, k. 6, up 1, k. 6, k. 2 tog., k. 8; repeat from * ending last repeat k. 7.
49th row: K. 6, *s.s.k., k. 6, up 1, k. 8, up 1, k. 6, k. 2 tog., k. 6; repeat from * to end.
51st row: K. 5, *s.s.k., k. 6, up 1, k. 10, up 1, k. 6, k. 2 tog., k. 4; repeat from * ending last repeat k. 5.
53rd row: K. 4, *s.s.k., cable 6, up 1, k. 12, up 1, cable 6, k. 2 tog., k. 2; repeat from * ending last repeat k. 4.
55th row: K. 3, *s.s.k., k. 6, up 1, k. 14, up 1, k. 6, k. 2 tog; repeat from * until 3 remain, k. 3.
57th row: K. 3, *s.s.k., k. 5, up 1, k. 16, up 1, k. 5, k. 2 tog.; repeat from * until 3 remain, k. 3.
58th to 64th rows: As 2nd to 8th rows (right and wrong side row).
The last 64 rows form the pattern.
Continuing in cable pattern as set and working the extra sts. in garter st. as they occur, inc. 1 st. at each end of the next row and the 5 following 16th rows.
On 108 sts. pattern 47 rows as set.
This completes the cable pattern. * * *
To shape the sleevetop: Continuing in garter stitch only, cast off 6 sts. at the beginning of the next 2 rows, then dec. 1 st. at each end of the next row and the 5 following 4th rows, then on the 16 following alternate rows.
On 52 sts. k. 1 row.
Dec. 1 st. at each end of the next 12 rows, then cast off 4 sts. at the beginning of the next 6 rows. Cast off the remaining 4 sts.

THE BACK
With size 2¼mm. (No. 13) needles cast on 132 sts. and work 35 rows in single rib.
Increase row: Rib 11, *up 1, rib 10; repeat from * ending last repeat rib 11. – 144 sts.
Change to size 2¾mm. (No. 12) needles and work in pattern from chart as follows:
1st to 4th rows: All k. (Note the background is in garter st. throughout.)
5th row: K. 20, m.a., k. 86, 9 from 1, k. 36.
6th row: K. 36, then (k. 1, p. 1) 4 times, k. 1, then k. 86, up 1, p. 1, k. 2 tog., k. 18.
The last 6 rows set the position of the pattern given in the charts. Work the 7th to 164th rows as set.
To shape the armholes: Continuing in pattern as set and given in the chart, cast off 6 sts. at the beginning of the next 2 rows, then dec. 1 st. at each end of the next row and the 4 following alternate rows.
On 122 sts. pattern 5 rows ending with the 180th row.
Now work in cable pattern as follows:
1st row: All k.
2nd row: K. 1, p. 6, *k. 18, p. 12; repeat from * ending last repeat p. 6, k. 1.
3rd and 4th rows: As 1st and 2nd rows.
Thus working in cable pattern as given for sleeves, but omitting 2 sts. at each end of each row, work the 5th to 64th pattern rows, then work the first 10 rows again.
To slope the shoulders: Cast off 10 sts. at the beginning of the next 6 rows. – 62 sts. * *
Cast off.

THE FRONT
Work as given for the back until the 159th pattern row has been worked.
Now divide the sts. for the neck opening: Next row: Pattern 68 and leave these sts. on a spare needle until required for right half front, cast off 8, pattern to end and continue on these 68 sts. for the left half front.
The left half front: Work the 161st to 164th pattern rows as set.
To shape the armhole: Continuing in pattern from chart as set, cast off 6 sts. at the beginning of the next row, work 1 row back to armhole edge, then dec. 1 st. at the beginning of the next row and the 4 following alternate rows.
On 57 sts. work 5 rows, thus completing the pattern given in the chart.
Now work in cable pattern as follows: 1st row: All k.
2nd row: K. 20, p. 12, k. 18, p. 6, k. 1.
3rd and 4th rows: As 1st and 2nd rows.
5th row: K. 1, cable 6, k. 18, cable 6, cable 6, k. 20.
6th, 7th and 8th rows: As 2nd, 3rd and 4th rows.

9th row: K.1, up 1, k.6, k.2 tog., k.14, s.s.k., k.6, up 2, k.6, k.2 tog., k.14, s.s.k., k.1, up 1, k.1.

10th row: K.2, p.1, k.16, p.6, k.2, p.6, k.16, p.6, k.2.

11th row: K.2, up 1, k.6, k.2 tog., k.12, s.s.k., k.6, up 1, k.2, up 1, k.6, k.2 tog., k.12, s.s.k., k.2, up 1, k.1.

12th row: K.2, p.2, k.14, p.6, k.4, p.6, k.14, p.6, k.3.

13th row: K.3, up 1, cable 6, k.2 tog., k.10, s.s.k., cable 6, up 1, k.4, up 1, cable 6, k.2 tog., k.10, s.s.k., tw.3lt., up 1, k.1.

14th row: K.2, p.3, k.12, p.6, k.6, p.6, k.12, p.6, k.4.

15th row: K.4, up 1, k.6, k.2 tog., k.8, s.s.k., k.6, up 1, k.6, up 1, k.6, k.2 tog., k.8, s.s.k., k.4, up 1, k.1.

16th row: K.2, p.4, k.10, p.6, k.8, p.6, k.10, p.6, k.5.

17th row: K.5, up 1, k.6, k.2 tog., k.6, s.s.k., k.6, up 1, k.8, up 1, k.6, k.2 tog., k.6, s.s.k., k.5, up 1, k.1.

18th row: K.2, p.5, k.8, p.6, k.10, p.6, k.8, p.6, k.6.

19th row: K.6, up 1, k.6, k.2 tog., k.4, s.s.k., k.6, up 1, k.10, up 1, k.6, k.2 tog., k.4, s.s.k., k.6, up 1, k.1.

20th row: K.2, p.6, k.6, p.6, k.12, p.6, k.6, p.6, k.7.

21st row: K.7, *up 1, cable 6, k.2 tog., k.2, s.s.k., cable 6, up 1, k.12; repeat from * ending last repeat k.2.

The last 21 rows set the position of the pattern given for the sleeves, now work the 22nd to 41st rows as set.

***To shape the neck: Continuing in pattern as set, cast off 9 sts. at the beginning of the next row, then dec. 1 st. at the neck edge on each of the next 18 rows.

On 30 sts. pattern 14 rows as set.

To slope the shoulder: Cast off 10 sts. at the beginning of the next row and following alternate row. On 10 sts. work 1 row, then cast off.

The right half front: With right side of work facing rejoin yarn to inner edge sts. left on spare needle and work 165th to 169th pattern rows as set.

To shape the armhole: Cast off 6 sts. at the beginning of the next row, then dec. 1 st. at the end - armhole edge on the next row and the 4 following alternate rows. On 57 sts. work 5 rows, completing the pattern in the chart.

Now work in cable pattern as follows:

1st row: All k.

2nd row: K.1, p.6, k.18, p.12, k.20.

3rd and 4th rows: As 1st and 2nd rows.

5th row: K.20, cable 6, cable 6, k.18, cable 6, k.1.

6th, 7th and 8th rows: As 2nd, 3rd and 4th rows.

9th row: K.1, up 1, k.1, k.2 tog., k.14, s.s.k., k.6, up 2, k.6, k.2 tog., k.14, s.s.k., k.6, up 1, k.1.

10th row: K.2, p.6, k.16, p.6, k.2, p.6, k.16, p.1, k.2.

The last 10 rows set the position of the pattern given for the sleeves, thus continuing to introduce sts. into cable panel at neck edge as on left front, work the 11th to 42nd rows as set.

Now work as given for left half front from *** to end.

THE FRONTBANDS AND NECKBAND

With size 2 ¼mm. (No. 13) needles cast on 12 sts. and work 12 rows in single rib, marking each end of the last row with a coloured thread.

Work 4 rows in single rib.

1st Buttonhole row: Rib 4, cast off 4, rib to end.

2nd Buttonhole row: Rib 4, turn, cast on 4, turn, rib to end.

Rib 24 rows, then work the 2 buttonhole rows again. Rib 22 rows.

**Now work turning rows as follows: 1st and 2nd rows: Rib 11, turn, rib to end.

3rd and 4th rows (Buttonhole rows): Rib 4, cast off 4, turn, k.1, turn, cast on 4 over those cast off, turn, rib to end.

5th and 6th rows: Rib 7, turn, rib to end.

7th and 8th rows: Rib 5, turn, rib to end.

9th and 10th rows: Rib 3, turn, rib to end.

11th and 12th rows: Rib 4, turn, rib to end.

13th and 14th rows: Rib 6, turn, rib to end.

15th and 16th rows: Rib 8, turn, rib to end.

17th and 18th rows: Rib 10, turn, rib to end.**

Now on all 12 sts. rib 188 rows.

Now work turning rows as follows:

1st and 2nd turning rows: Rib 11, turn, rib to end.

3rd and 4th turning rows: Rib 9, turn, rib to end.

5th to 18th turning rows: Work as for 5th to 18th turning rows before.

On 12 sts. rib 54 rows, then cast off in rib.

TO MAKE UP THE SWEATER

Do not press. Join shoulder seams. Set in sleeves. Join sleeve and side seams. Neatly sew cast off edge of buttonband to sts. cast off at centre front neck, sew row end edges of buttonband, neckband and buttonhole band in place, so that the 12 rows of buttonhole band below the marking thread hang free below sts. cast off at centre front neck, neatly catch buttonhole band in place across this line. Sew on buttons.

THE CARDIGAN

THE SLEEVES

As given for the sweater.

THE BACK

Work as given for back of sweater until ** is reached. Cast off 6 sts. at the beginning of the next 2 rows. Cast off the remaining 50 sts.

THE LEFT FRONT

With size 2 ¼mm. (No, 13) needles cast on 66 sts. and work 35 rows in single rib.

Increase row: Rib 6, *up 1, rib 9; repeat from * ending last repeat rib 6. – 73 sts.

Change to size 2¾mm. (No. 12) needles and work in pattern from chart as follows:

1st to 4th rows: All k.

5th row: K.20, m.a., k.52.

6th row: K.52, up 1, p.1, k.2 tog., k.18.

The last 6 rows set the position of the pattern given in the charts, work the 7th to 164th rows as set.

To shape the armhole: Cast off 6 sts. at the beginning of the next row, work 1 row back to armhole edge, then dec. 1 st. at the beginning – armhole edge on the next row and the 4 following alternate rows.

* * *On 62 sts. pattern 5 rows.

Now work in cable pattern as follows:

1st row: All k.

2nd row: K.1, p.6, k.18, p.12, k.18, p.6, k.1.

The last 2 rows set the position of the cable pattern given for the sleeves; work the 3rd to 33rd rows as set; work 1 extra row here when working right front.

To shape the neck: Cast off 8 sts. at the beginning of the next row, then dec. 1 st. at the neck edge on each of the next 18 rows.

On 36 sts. pattern 22 rows.

To slope the shoulder: Cast off 10 sts. at the beginning of the next row and the 2 following alternate rows. On 6 sts. work 1 row, then cast off.

THE RIGHT FRONT

Work as given for left front until the increase row has been worked.

Change to size 2¾mm. (No. 12) needles and work in pattern as follows:

1st to 4th rows: All k.

5th row: K.36, 9 from 1, k.36.

6th row: K.36, then (k.1, p.1) 4 times, k.1, then k. to end.

The last 6 rows set the position of the pattern given in the charts. Work the 7th to 165th rows.

To shape the armhole: Cast off 6 sts. at the beginning of the next row, then dec. 1 st. at the end-armhole edge on the next row and the 4 following alternate rows. – 62 sts.

Work as given for left front from * * * to end.

THE BUTTONHOLE BAND AND HALF NECKBAND

With size 2 ¼mm. (No. 13) needles cast on 12 sts. and work 8 rows in single rib.

1st Buttonhole row: Rib 4, cast off 4, rib to end.

2nd Buttonhole row: Rib 4, turn, cast on 4, rib to end.

Rib 28 rows.

Repeat the last 30 rows 5 times, then work the 2 buttonhole rows again. Rib 26 rows.

Work as given for neckband on sweater from ** to **.

Mark the end of last row with a coloured thread.

On 12 sts. rib 80 rows, then cast off.

THE BUTTONBAND AND HALF NECKBAND

With size 2 ¼mm. (No. 13) needles cast on 12 sts. and work 216 rows in single rib. 1st and 2nd turning rows: Rib 11, turn, rib to end.

3rd and 4th turning rows: Rib 9, turn, rib to end.

Now work as given for Buttonhole band and neckband from 5th and 6th turning rows to end.

THE RIGHT HALF COLLAR

First sew button and buttonhole bands in place up front edges, but do not sew neckband in place. With right side of work facing rejoin yarn to neckband at the marking thread and using size 2 ¼mm. (No. 13) needles pick up and k. 54 sts. from the row end edge of right neckband, then work 7 rows in single rib.

** 1st and 2nd turning rows: Rib 24, turn, rib to end.

3rd and 4th turning rows: Rib 20, turn, rib to end.

5th and 6th turning rows: Rib 16, turn, rib to end.

7th and 8th turning rows: Rib 12, turn, rib to end.

9th and 10th turning rows: Rib 8, turn, rib to end.

11th and 12th turning rows: Rib 4, turn, rib to end.

On all 54 sts. rib 4 rows, then cast off in rib.

THE LEFT HALF COLLAR

With right side of work facing rejoin yarn to left neckband and using size 2 ¼mm. (No. 13) needles pick up and k. 54 sts. from neckband ending at marking thread. Work 8 rows in single rib, then work as given for right half collar from ** to end.

TO MAKE UP THE CARDIGAN

Do not press. Join shoulder seams. Set in sleeves. Join sleeve and side seams. Join row ends of half collar and cast off edges of neckband, then sew neckband in place.

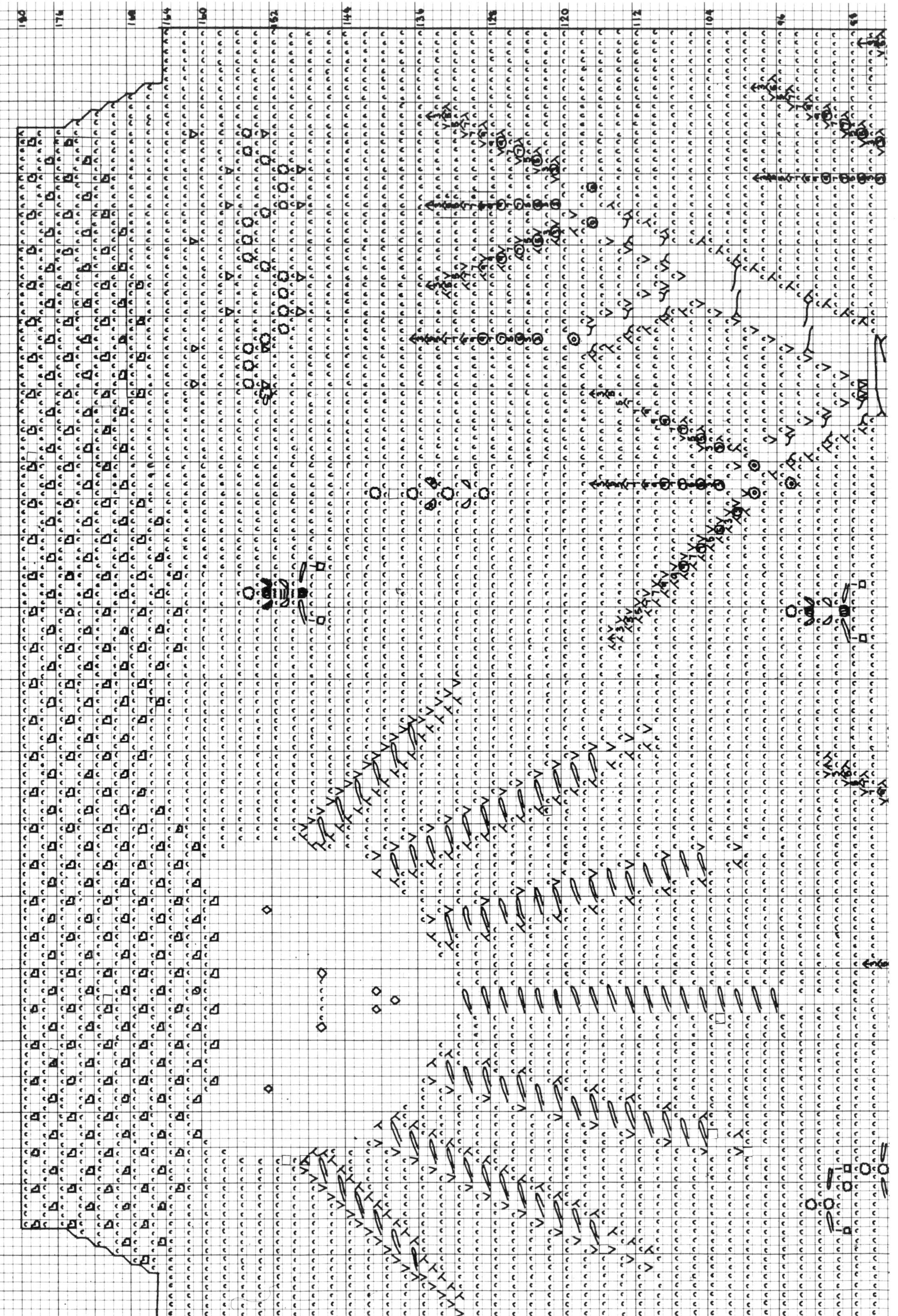

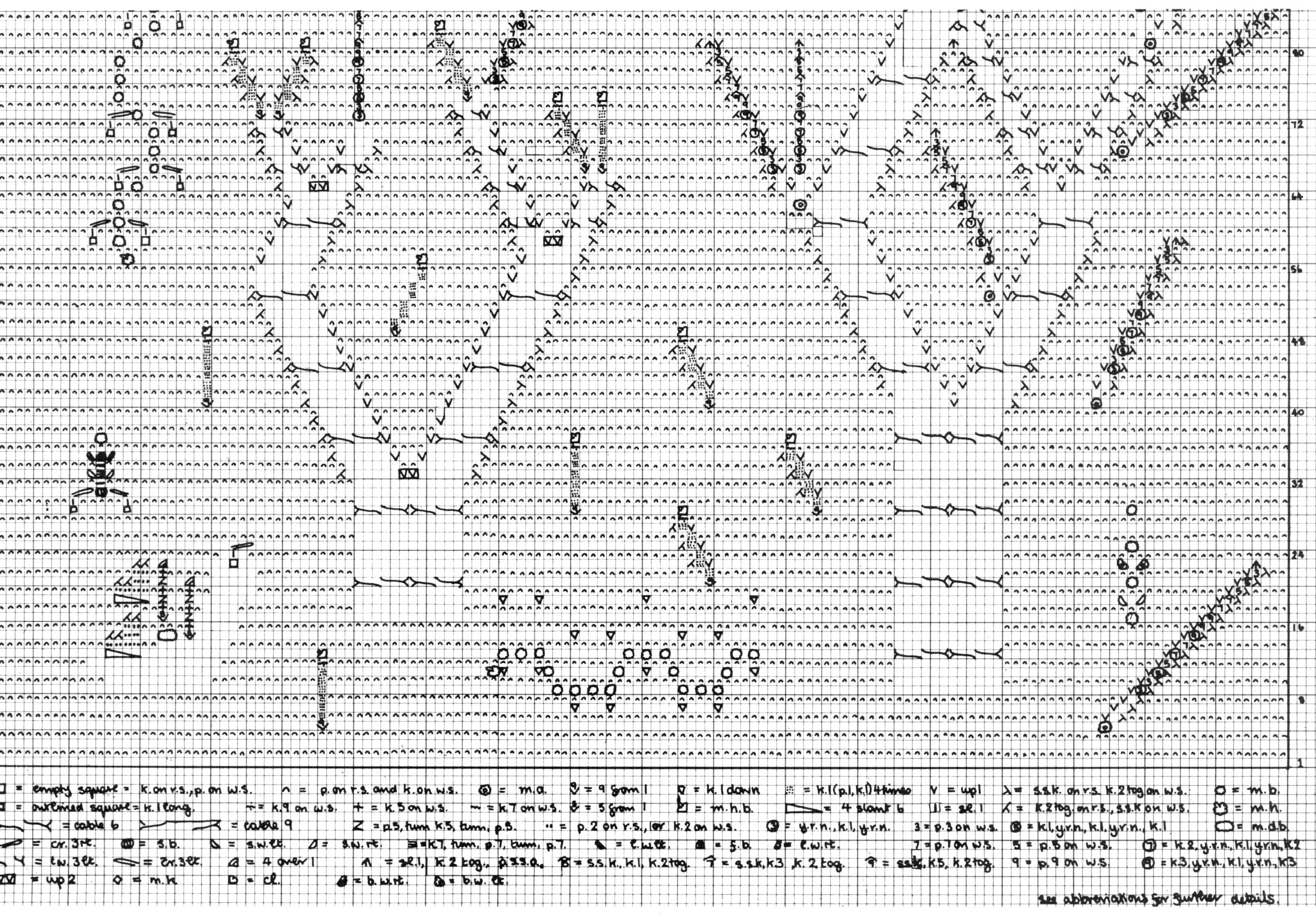
1
8
16
24
32
40
48
56
64
72
80
= empty square = k. on r.s., p. on w.s.
= p. on r.s. and k. on w.s.
= m.a.
= 9 from 1
= k.1 down
= k.1 (p.1, k.1) 4 times
V = up1
λ = s.s.k. on r.s. k.2 tog on w.s.
= m.b.
= outlined square = k.1 long.
= k.9 on w.s.
+ = k.5 on w.s.
~ = k.7 on w.s.
= 5 from 1
= m.h.b.
= 4 slant 6
= sl.1
= k.2 tog. on r.s., s.s.k on w.s.
= m.h.
= cable 6
= cable 9
Z = p.5, turn k.5, turn, p.5.
·· = p.2 on r.s., or k.2 on w.s.
= y.r.n., k.1, y.r.n.
3 = p.3 on w.s.
= k.1, y.r.n., k.1, y.r.n., k.1
= m.d.b.
= cr.3 rt.
= s.b.
= s.w. lt.
= s.w. rt.
= k.7, turn, p.7, turn, p.7.
= l.w. lt.
= s.b.
= l.w. rt.
7 = p.7 on w.s.
5 = p.5 on w.s.
= k.2, y.r.n., k.1, y.r.n., k.2
= tw.3 lt.
= cr.3 lt.
= 4 over 1
= sl.1, k.2 tog., p.s.s.o.
= s.s.k., k.1, k.2 tog.
= s.s.k, k.3, k.2 tog.
= s.s.k, k.5, k.2 tog.
9 = p.9 on w.s.
= k.3, y.r.n., k.1, y.r.n., k.3
= up 2
= m.k.
= cl.
= b.w. rt.
= b.w. lt.
see abbreviations for further details.

scrabble

MATERIALS
For the sweater: Either 18 25 gram balls of "Woollybear Fine Cotton", or 15 25 gram balls of "Woollybear Pure Silk", or 12 ounce (28 gram) hanks of "Woollybear Real Shetland" all by Patricia Roberts; a pair each of size 2 mm. (No. 14) and size 2¾ mm. (No. 12) Aero knitting needles; a fine cable needle.
For the cardigan: Add 2 balls or hanks of any of the yarns recommended, and 7 buttons.
For the shawl: 23 25 gram balls of "Woollybear Fine Cotton" or 14 ounce (28 gram hanks of "Woollybear Real Shetland" or 13 25 gram balls of "Woollybear Pure Cashmere" all by Patricia Roberts; a pair of size 2¾ mm. (No. 12) Aero knitting needles.

TENSION
The pattern is based on a stocking stitch tension of 16 stitches and 20 rows to 5 centimetres (2 inches) using size 2¾ mm. (No. 12) needles. If you cannot obtain the correct tension using the size needles suggested, use larger or smaller ones accordingly.

ABBREVIATIONS
K., knit; p., purl; st., stitch; tog., together; dec., decrease (by working 2 sts. tog.); inc., increase (by working twice into same st.); single rib is k. 1 and p. 1 alternately; up 1, pick up the loop which lies between the needles, slip it onto left hand needle, then k. into back of it; cable 8 thus, slip next 4 sts. onto cable needle and leave at front of work, k.4, then k.4 from cable needle; y.r.n., yarn round needle; sl., slip; p.s.s.o., pass sl. st. over; s.s.k., sl.1, k.1, p.s.s.o.; m.b., make bobble thus, k.1, y.r.n., k.1, y.r.n., k.1 all into next st., turn, k.5, turn, p.5, turn, k.5, turn, pass 2nd, 3rd, 4th and 5th sts. on left hand needle over first st., then k. this st.; 3 from 3, p. next 3 sts. tog., y.r.n., then p. these 3 sts. tog. again allowing loops to fall from left hand needle; s.s., stocking stitch is k. on right side and p. on the wrong side; r.s.s. reversed stocking stitch is p. on the right side and k. on the wrong side; 3 from 1, k.1 winding yarn round needle twice, p.1, then k.1 winding yarn round needle twice all into next st.; cr.3rt., cross 3 right thus, working into the front of the sts. knit the fourth st. on left hand needle together with the first st., then knit the 2nd and 3rd sts. in the usual way; cr.3lt., cross 3 left thus, slip next long st. off left hand needle to front of work, k.2, then k. the long st. at front of work together with the next st.; cable 4 thus, slip next 2 sts. onto cable needle and leave at front of work, k.2, then k.2 from cable needle.

NOTE
The instructions are given in one size only. Instructions in brackets are worked the number of times stated after the last bracket.

MEASUREMENTS
The measurements are given in centimetres followed by inches in brackets.

THE SWEATER AND THE CARDIGAN

Underarms	91 (36½)
Side seam	40 (16)
Length	60 (24)
Sleeve seam	41 (16½)

THE SWEATER

THE BACK
With size 2 mm. (No. 14) needles cast on 132 sts. and work 38 rows in single rib.
Increase row: K.6, *up 1, k.8; repeat from * ending last repeat k.6. – 148 sts.
Change to size 2¾ mm. (No. 12) needles and k.1 row, then work in pattern given in chart as follows: 1st row (right side): (s.s.k., y.r.n.) 16 times, k.1, y.r.n., sl.1, k.2 tog., p.s.s.o., y.r.n., k.1, (y.r.n., k.2 tog.) 15 times, y.r.n., sl.1, k.2 tog., p.s.s.o., y.r.n. k.8, y.r.n., sl.1, k.2 tog., p.s.s.o., y.r.n., (s.s.k., y.r.n.) 15 times, k.1, y.r.n., sl.1, k.2 tog., p.s.s.o., y.r.n., k.1, (y.r.n., k.2 tog.) 16 times.
2nd row: (wrong side): K.70, p.8, k.70.
3rd and 4th rows: As 1st and 2nd rows.
5th row: S.s.k., y.r.n., k.31, y.r.n., sl.1, k.2 tog., p.s.s.o., y.r.n., k.31, y.r.n., sl.1, k.2 tog., p.s.s.o., y.r.n., k.8, (y.r.n., sl.1, k.2 tog., p.s.s.o., y.r.n., k.31) twice, y.r.n., k.2 tog.
6th row: K.2, p.31, k.3, p.2, (k.1, p.1) 13 times, k.1, p.2, k.3, p.8, (k.3, p.31) twice, k.2.
7th row: S.s.k., y.r.n., k.3, (y.r.n., s.s.k., k.5) 4 times, y.r.n., sl.1, k.2 tog., p.s.s.o., y.r.n., k.31, y.r.n., sl.1, k.2 tog., p.s.s.o., y.r.n., k.8, y.r.n., sl.1, k.2 tog., p.s.s.o., y.r.n., (k.1, p.1) 5 times, 3 from 1, (p.1, k.1) 4 times, p.1, 3 from 1, (p.1, k.1) 5 times, y.r.n., sl.1, k.2 tog., p.s.s.o., y.r.n., k.31, y.r.n., k.2 tog.
8th row: K.2, p.31, k.3, p.2, (k.1, p.1) 4 times, sl.3 p.wise, (p.1, k.1) 4 times, p.1, sl.3 p.wise, (p.1, k.1) 4 times, p.2, k.3, p.8, (k.3, p.31) twice, k.2.
The last 8 rows set the position of the pattern given in the chart, now work the 9th to 124th rows from the chart as set.
To shape the armholes: Continuing in pattern from chart as set, cast off 10 sts. at the beginning of the next 2 rows, then dec. 1 st. at each end of the 4 rows. – 120 sts.
Now work the yoke pattern as follows: 1st row: K.9, *y.r.n., sl.1, k.2 tog., p.s.s.o., y.r.n., k.8; repeat * ending last repeat k.9.
2nd row: K.12, *p.8, k.14; repeat from * ending last repeat k.12.
3rd and 4th rows: As 1st and 2nd rows.
5th row: K.9, *y.r.n., sl.1, k.2 tog., p.s.s.o., y.r.n., cable 8, y.r.n., sl.1, k.2 tog., p.s.s.o., y.r.n., k.8; repeat from * ending last repeat k.9.
6th row: As 2nd row.
7th and 8th rows: As 1st and 2nd rows.
The last 8 rows form the cable lace pattern; repeat them 7 times more, then work the first 2 rows again.
To slope the shoulders: Cast off 9 sts. at the beginning of the next 8 rows. – 48 sts. * *
Change to size 2 mm. (No. 14) needles and work 8 rows in single rib.
Cast off in rib.

THE FRONT
Work as given for the back until the 8 cable lace pattern rows have been worked 4 times, then work the first row again.
Now divide the sts. for the neck: Next row: Pattern 50 and leave these sts. on a spare needle until required for right front shoulder, cast off 20, pattern to end and continue on these 50 sts. for the left front shoulder.
The left front shoulder: Continuing in pattern as set, dec. 1 st. at the neck edge on each of the next 14 rows. – 36 sts.
Pattern 18 rows.
To slope the shoulder: Cast off 9 sts. at the beginning of the next row and the 2 following alternate rows. On 9 sts. work 1 row, then cast off.
The right front shoulder: With right side of work facing rejoin yarn to inner edge of sts. left on spare needle and work to end of row, then work as given for left front shoulder to end.

THE FRONT NECKBAND
With right side of work facing rejoin yarn at left front neck edge and using size 2 mm. (No. 14) needles pick up and k. 34 sts. from left front neck edge, 20 sts. from centre front neck and 34 sts. from right front neck edge.
On 88 sts. work 7 rows in single rib, then cast off in rib.

THE SLEEVES (both alike)
With size 2 mm. (No. 14) needles cast on 66 sts. and work 44 rows in single rib.
Increase row: K.1, *up 1, k.3; repeat from * ending last repeat k.2. – 88 sts.
Change to size 2¾ mm. (No. 12) needles and k.1 row, then work in pattern as follows: 1st row (right side): K.3, y.r.n., sl.1, k.2 tog., p.s.s.o., y.r.n., k.1, (y.r.n., k.2 tog.) 15 times, y.r.n., sl.1, k.2 tog., p.s.s.o., y.r.n., k.8, y.r.n., sl.1, k.2 tog., p.s.s.o., y.r.n., (s.s.k., y.r.n.) 15 times, k.1, y.r.n., sl.1, k.2 tog., p.s.s.o., y.r.n., k.3.
2nd row: K.40, p.8, k.40.
3rd and 4th rows: As 1st and 2nd rows.
5th row: K.3, *y.r.n., sl.1, k.2 tog., p.s.s.o., y.r.n., k.31, y.r.n., sl.1, k.2 tog., p.s.s.o., y.r.n., k.8; repeat from * ending k.3.
6th row: K.6, p.2, (k.1, p.1) 13 times, k.1, p.2, k.3, p.8, k.3, p.31, k.6.
7th row: K.3, y.r.n., sl.1, k.2 tog., p.s.s.o., y.r.n., k.3, (y.r.n., s.s.k., k.5) 4 times, y.r.n., sl.1, k.2 tog., p.s.s.o., y.r.n., k.8, y.r.n., sl.1, k.2 tog., p.s.s.o., y.r.n., (k.1, p.1) 5 times, 3 from 1, p.1, (k.1, p.1) 4 times, 3 from 1 (p.1, k.1) 5 times, y.r.n., sl.1, k.2 tog., p.s.s.o., y.r.n., k.3.
8th row: K.6, p.2, (k.1, p.1) 4 times, sl.3, p.1, (k.1, p.1) 4 times, sl.3, (p.1, k.1) 4 times, p.2, k.3, p.8, k.3, p.31, k.6.
9th row: K.3, y.r.n. sl.1, k.2 tog., p.s.s.o., y.r.n., k.3, (y.r.n., s.s.k., m.b., k.4) 4 times, y.r.n., sl.1, k.2 tog., p.s.s.o., y.r.n., cable 8, y.r.n., sl.1, k.2 tog., p.s.s.o., y.r.n., k.1, (p.1, k.1) 3 times, cr.3rt., sl.1, cr.3lt., k.1, p.1, k.1, cr.3rt., sl.1, cr3lt., (k.1, p.1) 3 times, k.1, y.r.n., sl.1, k.2 tog., p.s.s.o., y.r.n., k.3.
10th row: As 6th row.
The last 10 rows set the position of the pattern, given at the centre of the chart, but working the house picture instead of the letter H on the 5th to 41st rows, the ship instead of the letter S on the 47th to 83rd rows, and the tree instead of the letter T on the 89th to 124th rows. Now work the 11th to 24th rows as set, with 3 sts. in garter st. at each end of rows. Continuing in pattern as set, and working the extra sts. in garter st. as they occur, inc. 1 st. at each end of the next row and the 3 following 24th rows. On 96 sts. pattern 27 rows, ending at the 124th pattern row.
To shape the sleevetop: Continuing in pattern from chart, cast off 10 sts. at the beginning of the next 2 rows, then dec. 1 st. at each end of the next row and the following alternate row. – 72 sts.
Next row: K.32, p.8, k.32.
Now work in garter st. with centre lace and cable pattern as follows:
1st row: K.2 tog., k.27, y.r.n., sl.1, k.2 tog., p.s.s.o., y.r.n., k.8, y.r.n., sl.1, k.2 tog., p.s.s.o., y.r.n., k.27, k.2 tog.
2nd row: K.31, p.8, k.31.
3rd row: K.2 tog., k.26, y.r.n., sl.1, k.2 tog., p.s.s.o., y.r.n., k.8, y.r.n., sl.1, k.2 tog., p.s.s.o., y.r.n., k.26, k. 2 tog.
4th row: K.30, p.8, k.30.
5th row: K.2 tog., k.25, y.r.n., sl.1, k.2 tog., p.s.s.o., y.r.n., cable 8, y.r.n., sl.1, k.2 tog., p.s.s.o., y.r.n., k.25, k.2 tog.
6th row: K.29, p.8, k.29.
7th and 8th rows: As 3rd and 4th rows but working 2 sts. less in garter st. at each end of rows. – 64 sts.
The last 8 rows form the cable pattern. Continuing in pattern as set, dec. 1 st. at each end of the next row and the 12 following alternate rows.
Cast off 3 sts. at the beginning of the next 10 rows, then cast off the remaining 8 sts.

TO MAKE UP THE SWEATER
If working in "Pure Silk" do not press. If working in any of the other recommended yarns, pin out to size and press all parts except the ribbing with a warm iron over a damp cloth. Join shoulder seams. Set in sleeves. Join sleeve and side seams. Press seams except when using silk.

THE CARDIGAN

THE BACK
Work as given for the back of the sweater until * * is reached, then cast off.

THE SLEEVES
Work as given for the sleeves on sweater.

THE LEFT FRONT
With size 2 mm. (No. 14) needles cast on 62 sts. and work 38 rows in single rib.
Increase row: K.7, *up 1, k.8; repeat from * ending last repeat k.7. – 69 sts.
Change to size 2¾ mm. (No. 12) needles and k.1 row, then work in pattern as follows: 1st row: (S.s.k., y.r.n.) 16 times, k.1, y.r.n., sl.1, k.2 tog., p.s.s.o., y.r.n., k.1, (y.r.n., k.2 tog.) 16 times:
2nd row: All k.
3rd and 4th rows: As 1st and 2nd rows.
5th row: S.s.k., y.r.n., k.31, y.r.n., sl.1, k.2 tog., p.s.s.o., y.r.n., k.31, y.r.n., k.2 tog.
6th row: K.2, p.31, k.3, p.31, k.2.
7th row: S.s.k., y.r.n., k.3, (y.r.n., s.s.k., k.5) 4 times, y.r.n., sl.1, k.2 tog., p.s.s.o., y.r.n., k.31, y.r.n., k.2 tog.
8th row: As 6th row.
The last 8 rows set the position of the pattern given on the right hand side of the chart, now work the 9th to 124th rows from the chart as set.
To shape the armhole: Continuing in pattern from chart as set, cast off 10 sts. at the beginning of the next row, work 1 row back to armhole edge. Dec. 1 st. at the armhole edge on each of the next 4 rows. – 55 sts.
Now work the yoke pattern as follows: 1st row: K.9, *y.r.n., sl.1, k.2 tog., p.s.s.o., y.r.n., k.8;

repeat from * until 2 sts. remain, y.r.n., k.2 tog.
2nd row: K.13, p.8, k.14, p.8, k.12.
The last 2 rows set the position of the cable lace pattern given for the back. Work the 3rd to 8th rows as set. Repeat these 8 rows 3 times more, then work the first row again.
**To shape the neck: Continuing in pattern as set, cast off 5 sts. at the beginning of the next row. – 50 sts.
Now work as given for left front shoulder on front of sweater to end.

THE RIGHT FRONT
Work as given for left front until the first 5 pattern rows have been worked.
6th row: K.2, p.31, k.3, p.2, (k.1, p.1) 13 times, k.1, p.2, k.2.
7th row: S.s.k., y.r.n., (k.1, p.1) 5 times, 3 from 1, (p.1, k.1) 4 times, p.1, 3 from 1, (p.1, k.1) 5 times, y.r.n., sl.1, k.2 tog., p.s.s.o., y.r.n., k.31, y.r.n., k.2 tog.
The last 7 rows set the position of the pattern given on the left hand side of the chart, now work the 8th to 125th rows from the chart as set.
To shape the armhole: Cast off 10 sts. at the beginning of the next row, then dec. 1 st. at the armhole edge on each of the next 4 rows.
Now work the yoke pattern as follows: 1st row: S.s.k., y.r.n., *k.8, y.r.n., sl.1, k.2 tog., p.s.s.o., y.r.n.; repeat from * until 9 remain, k.9.
2nd row: K.12, p.8, k.14, p.8, k.13.
The last 2 rows set the position of the cable lace pattern given for back, work the 3rd to 8th rows as set; repeat these 8 rows 3 times more, then work the first 2 rows again.
To shape the neck: Work as given for left front from ** to end.

THE BUTTONBAND
With size 2 mm. (No. 14) needles cast on 10 sts. and work 204 rows in single rib, then cast off.

THE BUTTONHOLE BAND
With size 2 mm. (No. 14) needles cast on 10 sts. and work 6 rows in single rib.
1st Buttonhole row: Rib 3, cast off 4, rib to end.
2nd Buttonhole row: Rib 3, turn, cast on 4, turn, rib to end.
Rib 30 rows.
Repeat the last 32 rows 5 times more, then work the 2 buttonhole rows again.
Rib 4 rows, then cast off in rib.

THE BACK COLLAR
With size 2¾ mm. (No. 12) needles cast on 97 sts. and work in edging pattern as follows: 1st row: K.2 tog., *k.4, up 1, k.1, up 1, k.4, sl.1, k.2 tog., p.s.s.o.; repeat from * ending last repeat sl.1, k.1, p.s.s.o.
2nd row: All k.
Repeat the last 2 rows 3 times more.
Now work in lace pattern as follows: 1st row: K.7, *y.r.n., k.2 tog.; repeat from * until 6 remain, k.6.
2nd row: All k.
Repeat the last 2 rows 20 times more.
To slope the shoulders: Cast off 8 sts. at the beginning of the next 4 rows and 9 sts. on the 2 following rows.
Cast off the remaining 47 sts.

THE LEFT FRONT COLLAR
With size 2¾ mm. (No. 12) needles cast on 49 sts. and work as given for back collar until 9 rows have been worked in lace pattern – work 1 extra row here when working right front collar.
To shape the neck: Continuing in lace pattern as set, cast off 10 sts. at the beginning of the next row, then dec. 1 st. at the neck edge on each of the next 14 rows. – 25 sts.
Pattern 18 rows – with garter st. edging at shoulder edge only.
To slope the shoulder: Cast off 8 sts. at the beginning of the next row and the following alternate row.
On 9 sts. work 1 row, then cast off.

THE RIGHT FRONT COLLAR
Work as given for left front collar, noting the variation in the number of rows, before shaping the neck.

TO MAKE UP THE CARDIGAN
Work as given for sweater, then join shoulder seams of collar pieces. Sew collar in place all round neck edge. Sew front bands in place. Sew on buttons. Press seams – except when using silk.

THE SHAWL

THE PANELS (4 alike)
With size 2¾ mm. (No. 12) needles cast on 141 sts. and work edging pattern as follows:
1st row: K.1, *up 1, k.8, sl.1, k.2 tog, p.s.s.o., k.8, up 1, k.1; repeat from * to end.
2nd row: All k.
Repeat the last 2 rows 14 times more, then work the first of these rows again**.
Decrease row: K.29, *k.2 tog, k.26; repeat from * to end. – 137 sts.
Now work in lace pattern as follows:
1st row: (s.s.k., y.r.n.) 16 times, k.1, y.r.n., sl.1, k.2 tog., p.s.s.o., y.r.n., k.1, (y.r.n., k.2 tog.) 15 times, y.r.n., sl.1, k.2 tog., p.s.s.o., y.r.n., (s.s.k., y.r.n.) 15 times, k.1, y.r.n., sl.1, k.2 tog., p.s.s.o., y.r.n., k.1, (y.r.n., k.2 tog.) 16 times.
2nd row: All k.
3rd and 4th rows: As 1st and 2nd rows.
5th row: S.s.k., *y.r.n., k.31, y.r.n., sl.1, k.2 tog., p.s.s.o.; repeat from * ending last repeat k.2 tog. instead of sl.1, k.2 tog., p.s.s.o.
6th row: K.2, p.31, k.3, p.2, (k.1, p.1) 13 times, k.1, p.2, k.3, p.31, k.3, p.31, k.2.
7th row: S.s.k., y.r.n., k.3, (y.r.n., s.s.k., k.5) 4 times, y.r.n., sl.1, k.2 tog., p.s.s.o., y.r.n., k.31, y.r.n., sl.1, k.2 tog., p.s.s.o., y.r.n., (k.1, p.1) 5 times, 3 from 1, p.1, (k.1, p.1) 4 times, 3 from 1, (p.1 k.1) 5 times, y.r.n., sl.1, k.2 tog., p.s.s.o., y.r.n., k.31, y.r.n., k.2 tog.
The last 7 rows set the position of the pattern given in the chart but omitting the centre 8 st. cable and 3 st. lace panel; now work the 8th to 170 rows as set and given in the chart. Cast off.

THE EXTRA EDGINGS (4 alike)
Work as given for the panels until ** is reached. Cast off.

TO MAKE UP THE SHAWL
Pin out to size and press very lightly on the wrong side with a warm iron over a damp cloth. Join panels. Sew cast off edges of extra edgings in place.

scrabble

Antique lace from a selection at Lumm Antiques.

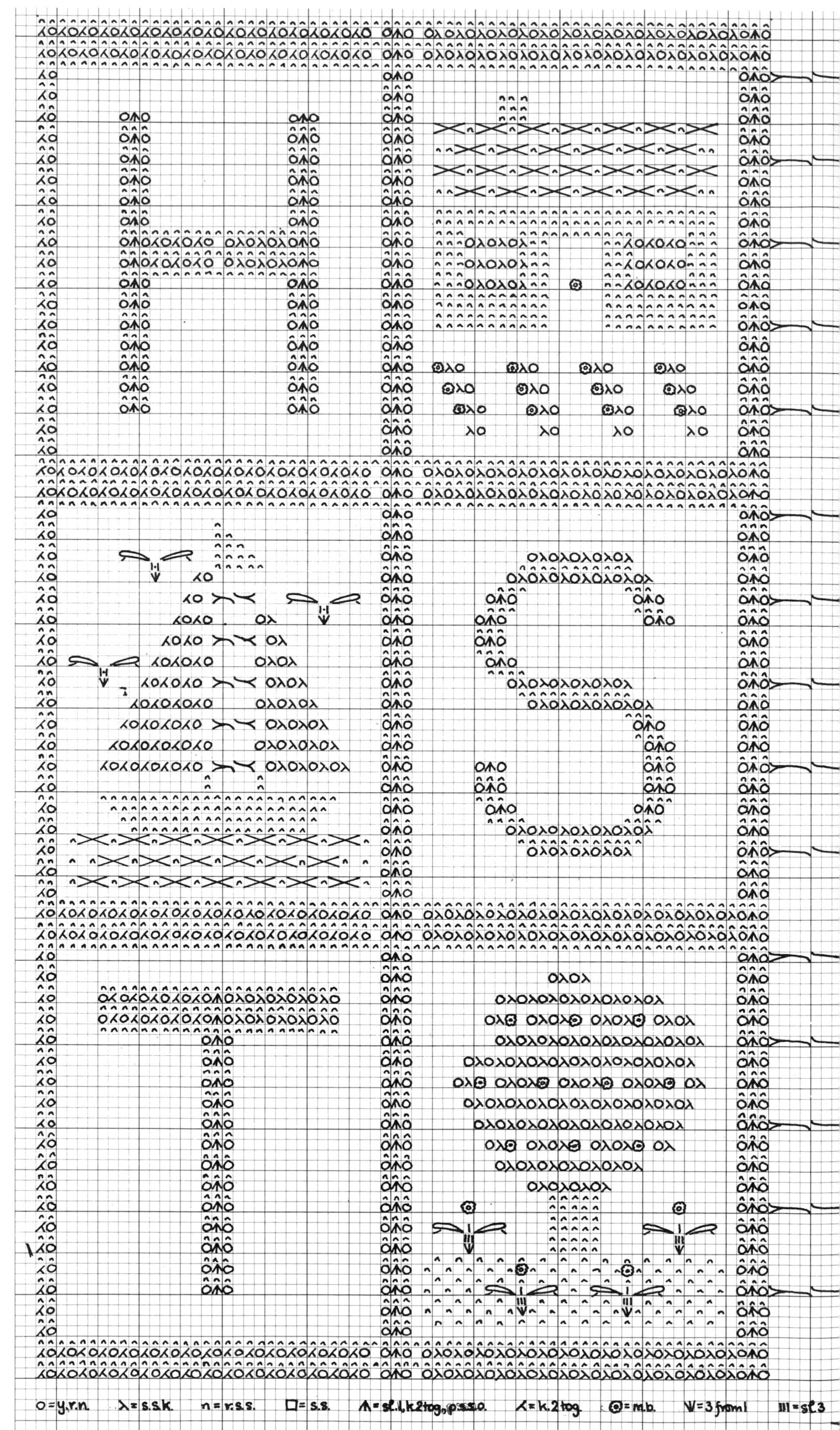
O = y.r.n.
λ = s.s.k.
n = r.s.s.
□ = s.s.
Λ = sl.1, k.2 tog, p.s.s.o.
⋌ = k.2 tog.
⊙ = m.b.
Ѱ = 3 from 1
III = sl.3

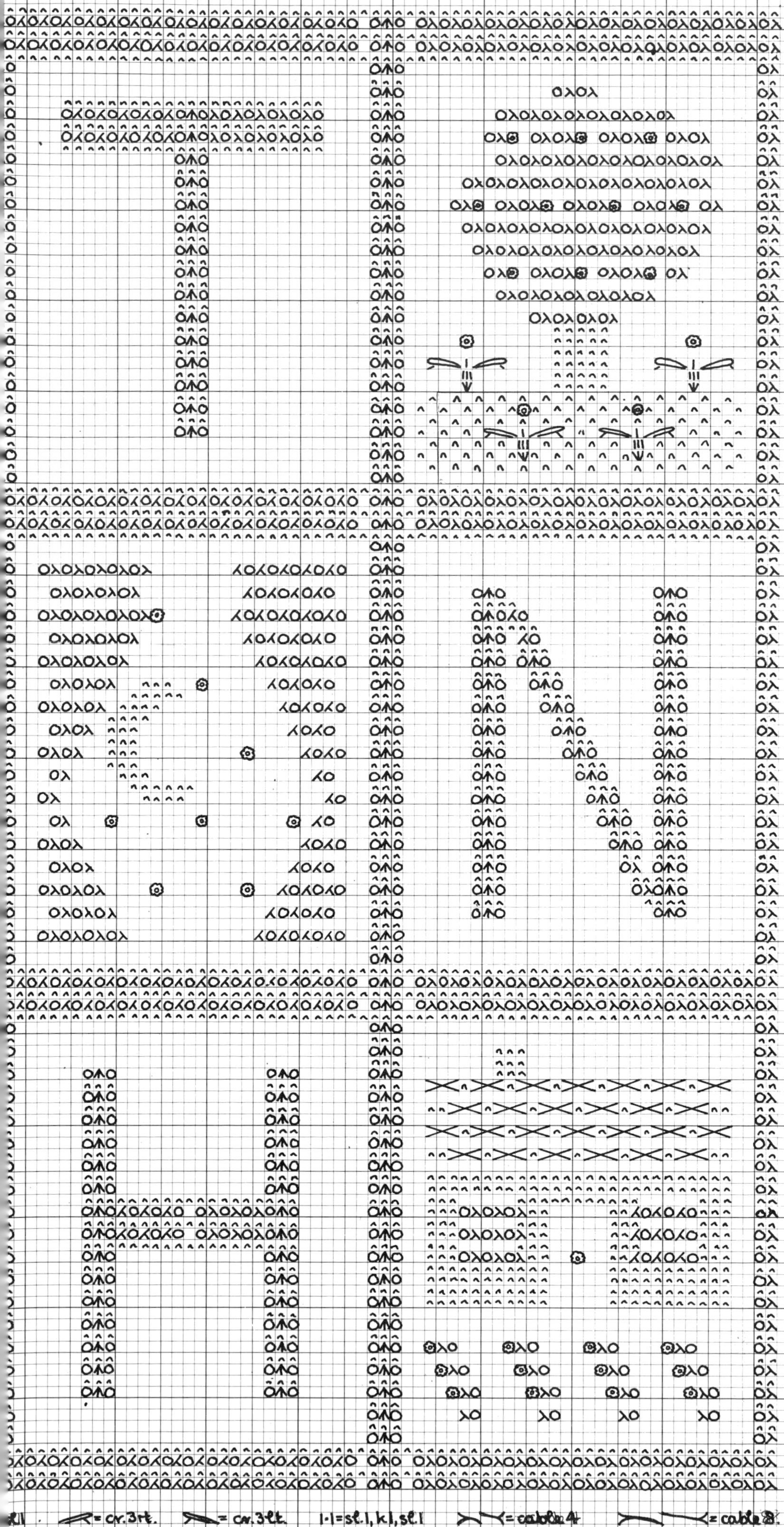

scrabble

Trousers by Katherine Hamnett, Jewelry from Butler & Wilson.

crackers

MATERIALS
Any of the following "Woollybear Yarns" by Patricia Roberts may be used for this pattern. For simplification the yarn amounts are given for the cardigan followed by those for the sweater in brackets.

"Woollybear Pure Silk" in 25 gram balls: 11 (7) balls in main colour; 11 (6) balls in first contrast and 2 (1) ball(s) in each of the 4 other contrast colours.

"Woollybear Fine Cotton" in 25 gram balls: 16 (10) balls in main colour; 16 (9) balls in first contrast and 2 (2) balls in each of the 4 other contrast colours.

"Woollybear Real Shetland" in 28 gram (1 ounce) hanks: 9 (6) hanks in main colour; 9 (6) hanks in first contrast and 2 (1) hank(s) in each of the 4 other contrast colours.

For the cardigan only: 7 buttons.

For either garment: a pair each of size 2¼mm. (No. 13) and size 2¾mm. (No. 12) Aero knitting needles; a fine cable needle.

TENSION
18 stitches and 34 rows to 5 centimetres (2 inches) over the chequer board pattern using size 2¾mm. (No. 12) needles. If you cannot obtain the correct tension using the size needles suggested use larger or smaller ones accordingly.

ABBREVIATIONS
K., knit; p., purl; st., stitch; tog., together; dec., decrease (by working 2 sts. tog.); inc., increase (by working twice into same st.); single rib is k. 1 and p. 1 alternately; sl., slip; y.f., yarn forward; y.b., yarn back; c.b., chequer board pattern; m.lp., make loop thus, with appropriate contrast colour given in instructions, working into next st., cast on 10 sts., k. 1, then cast off next 8 sts., with a. cast off the last of these sts., note the one k. stitch in contrast colour will remain on right hand needle; cr. 3rt., cross 3 right, insert right hand needle into front of 4th contrast colour st., then into first st. on left hand needle and with either a. or appropriate contrast colour as indicated in pattern, k. these 2 sts. tog., then slip 1 st. in m. and k. next st. in a., allowing loop of 4th st. to fall from left hand needle; beg.cr., begin cracker thus, working into next st., with appropriate contrast colour, cast on 6 sts., work in single rib across these sts., turn, rib these 6 sts., turn, k.6; make cluster, thus, slip next 6 sts. onto cable needle at front of work, wrap appropriate contrast firmly around these sts. 3 times, then k. these 6 sts. from cable needle; m.s.lp., make small loop, as m.lp. but casting on 6 sts. instead of 10 and casting off 4 instead of 8 in contrast colour; cr. 4lt., slip next st. – contrast colour one – onto cable needle at front of work, with a. k. 1, sl. 1, k. 1, then with either a. or appropriate contrast as indicated, k. the next st. tog. with st. from cable needle; m.d.b., make double bobble thus, with e. k. 1, y.r.n., k. 1 into each of next 2 sts., turn, p.6, turn, k.6, turn, p.6, turn, k.6, turn, (slip 1, p. 2 tog., p.s.s.o.) twice, turn, with e. k. these 2 sts.; ch. 12, chain 12 thus, with d. k. into next st. on left hand needle, then * slip the st. just made onto left hand needle and k. this st.; repeat from * 10 times more; ch. 6, as ch. 10, but repeating from * 4 times instead of 6; m., main colour; a., first contrast; b., second contrast; c., third contrast; d., fourth contrast; e., fifth contrast; p.s.s.o., pass slip stitch over; y.r.n., yarn round needle; 3 from 1, k. 1, y.r.n., k. 1 all into next st.; upl, pick up the loop, which lies between the needles, slip it onto left hand needle, then k. into back of it.

MEASUREMENTS
The measurements are given in centimetres followed by inches in brackets.

	Cardigan		Sweater	
Underarms	99	(39½)	95	(38)
Side seam	44	(17½)	25	(10)
Length	64	(25½)	47.5	(19)
Sleeve seam	41	(16½)		

THE CARDIGAN

THE BACK
With size 2¼mm. (No. 13) needles and m. cast on 142 sts. and work 33 rows in single rib.

Increase row: Rib 4, *up 1, rib 5; repeat from * ending last repeat rib 3. – 170 sts.

Change to size 2¾mm. (No. 12) needles and work in chequer board pattern as follows:

1st and 2nd rows: With m. all k.

3rd row: With a. k.2, *sl. 1, k.2; repeat from * to end.

4th row: With a. k.2, *y.f., sl. 1, y.b., k.2; repeat from * to end.

5th and 6th rows: As 3rd and 4th rows.

The last 6 rows in m. and a. form the chequer board pattern. This is a background to the motifs and for simplification is referred to as c.b. in the following pattern rows. When working the colour motifs use separate small balls of contrast colours, so as not to take colours not in use across the back of the work. The ball motifs are knitted separately and sewn into the holes at completion of work. When working the holes use separate balls of m. and a. on each side of them.

7th and 8th rows: With m. in c.b. – as 1st and 2nd rows.

9th row: With a. c.b. 19 – as in 3rd row, *with b. m.lp. – see abbreviations, with a. c.b. 20, with c. m.lp., with a. c.b. 20; repeat from * ending last repeat with a. c.b. 3.

10th to 14th rows: In c.b. as set, but slipping the contrast colour lp. sts., with yarn to wrong side of work.

15th row: With a. c.b. 16, *with appropriate contrast cr. 3rt. – see abbreviations, with a. c.b. 18; repeat from * ending last repeat c.b. 4.

16th row: With a. c.b. 6, *y.f., slip the contrast colour st., y.b., c.b. 20; repeat from * ending last repeat c.b. 16.

17th row: With a. c.b. 16, *with b. m.s.lp. – see abbreviations, with a. c.b. 20; with c. m.s.lp., with a. c.b. 20; repeat from * ending last repeat c.b. 6.

18th to 20th rows: As 10th row.

21st row: With a. c.b. 13, *with a. cr. 3rt., c.b. 18, with a. cr. 3rt., c.b. 18, with a. cr. 3rt., c.b. 7, cast off 7 for hole, c.b. next 3 sts., with a. cr. 3rt., c.b. 18; repeat from * ending last repeat c.b. 7.

22nd row: In c.b. as set, but using separate balls of yarn at each side of holes.

23rd to 32nd rows: In c.b., but decreasing 1 st. at each side of holes on right side rows.

33rd row: With a. c.b. 4, *with d. m.lp., with a. c.b. 20, with e. beg.cr. – see abbreviations, take m. and a. firmly across back of cracker motifs, with a. c.b. 21, with d. m.lp., c.b. 11, k.2tog. at each side of hole, with a. c.b. 9; repeat from * ending c.b. 7.

34th row: With a. in c.b., slipping contrast colours loops and with e. purling across the 6 cracker sts.

35th row: *With a. c.b. up to cracker, slipping contrast colour lp. sts., with d. k. the 6 cracker sts., turn, p.6, turn, with e. k.6, with a. c.b. up to hole dec. 1 st. at each side, completing the decreases; repeat from *, then c.b. to end.

36th row: As 34th row.

37th row: *With m. work as set up to cracker, with e. make cluster – see abbreviations; repeat from *, work to end as set.

38th row: With m. as set, but with d. purling across 6 cracker sts.

39th row: With a. c.b. 4, *with d. cr. 4lt., with a. c.b. 17, slip 6 cracker sts. onto cable needle and leave at front of work, with a. c.b. 3, then work across the sts. from cable needle thus, with d. k.2, with a. k.2, with d. k.2, then with a. c.b. 18, with d. cr. 4lt., with a. c.b. 8, hole, c.b. 9; repeat form * ending last repeat c.b. 7.

40th row: *With a. work as set up to cracker, with d. p.2, with a. p.2, with d. p.2; repeat from *, work to end as set.

41st row: With a. c.b. 7, *with d. m.s.lp., with a. c.b. 20, with d. k.6 cracker sts., turn, with e. p.6, turn, k.6, with a. c.b. 21, with d. m.s.lp., with a. c.b. 8, –hole–, with a. c.b. 12; repeat from * ending c.b. 7.

42nd row: As 34th row.

43rd and 44th rows: As 37th and 38th rows.

45th row: With a. c.b. 7, *with a. cr. 4lt., with a. c.b. 17, with d. k.6, turn, with e. p.6, turn, single rib 6, with a. c.b. 21, with a. cr. 4lt., c.b. 5, hole, c.b. 12; repeat from * ending c.b. 7.

46th row: With a. in c.b., working in single rib, with e. across the cracker sts.

47th row: With a. c.b. 28, *with e. cast off 6 cracker sts., with a. c.b. 28, inc. 1 st. at each side of hole, with a. c.b. 32; repeat from * ending c.b. 6.

48th to 56th rows: With m. and a. in c.b., increasing 1 st. at each side of holes on each right side row.

57th row: With a. c.b. 19, *with c. m.lp., with a. c.b. 20, with b. m.lp., with a. c.b. 20, with c. m.lp., with a. inc. in next st., hole, inc., c.b. 7, with b. m.lp., with a. c.b. 20; repeat from * ending last repeat c.b. 3.

58th to 60th rows: With a. work as set, slipping contrast colour loops and increasing 1 st. at each side of hole on 59th row.

61st row: With m. k. 19, *sl. 1, k. 21, sl. 1, k. 21, sl. 1, k. 4, turn, cast on 7, turn, k. 10, sl. 1, k. 21; repeat from * ending last repeat k. 4.

62nd to 68th rows: As 14th to 20th rows, but using b. instead of c. and c. instead of b.

69th row: With a. c.b. 13, *with a. cr. 3rt., c.b. 18; repeat from * ending last repeat c.b. 7.

70th to 80th rows: With m. and a. in c.b.

81st row: With a. c.b. 4, *with e. m.lp., with a. c.b. 20, with d. m.lp. with a. c.b. 20; repeat from * ending last repeat with a. c.b. 18.

82nd to 86th rows: In c.b. as set, slipping contrast colour sts.

87th row: With a. c.b. 4, *with appropriate contrast cr. 4lt., with a. c.b. 17; repeat from * ending last repeat c.b. 15.

88th row: In c.b., slipping contrast colour sts.

89th row: With a. c.b. 7, *with e. m.s.lp., with a. c.b. 20, with d. m.s.lp., with a. c.b. 20; repeat from * ending last repeat c.b. 15.

90th to 92nd rows: In c.b., slipping contrast colour sts.

93rd row: With a. c.b. 7, *with a. cr. 4lt., with a. c.b. 17; repeat from * ending last repeat c.b. 12.

94th to 98th rows: In c.b.

99th row: With a. c.b. 23, *with e. m.d.b. – see abbreviations, with a. c.b. 12, with e. m.d.b., c.b. 68; repeat from * ending c.b. 47.

100th row: With a. c.b. 47, *with c. p.2, with a. c.b. 11, with e. p.2, with c. p.1, with a. c.b. 68; repeat from *ending c.b. 23.

The last 2 rows set the position of the horse 23 row motif given in the chart, the background is in c.b. as set and the horse motif in s.s. except where indicated.

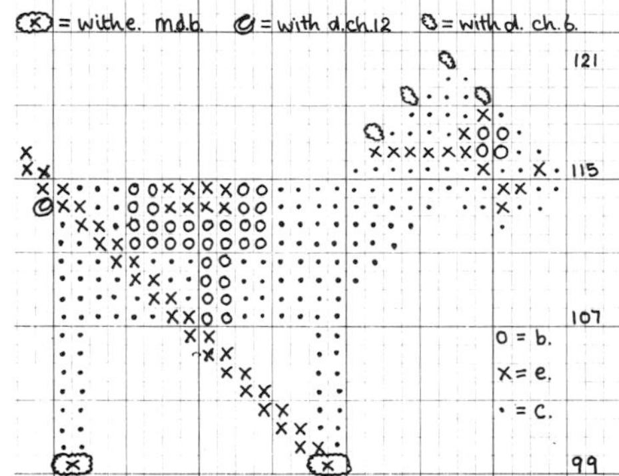

101st to 104th rows: In c.b. with horse motif.

105th row: Work in c.b., with horse motif as set, across 61 sts., *with b. beg.cr. – see abbreviations, with a. c.b. 21, with c. m.lp. *, *work in c.b. and horse motif across 62 sts.; repeat from * to *, with a. c.b. 3.

106th to 110th rows: Working in c.b. with horse motif as set work the crackers as given in the 34th to 38th rows, using b. instead of e. and c. instead of d.

111th row: Work in c.b. with horse motif across 58 sts., *slip next 3 sts. onto cable needle at back of work, then with c. k.2, with a. k.2, with c. k.2, across the cracker sts., with a. k. 1, sl. 1, k. 1 across the sts. from the cable needle, with a. c.b. 18, with c. cr. 3rt. *, work as set across next 60 sts.; repeat from * to *, with a. c.b. 4.

112th row: As 40th row using c. instead of d.

113th row: Work as set across 58 sts., *for cracker with c. k.6, turn, with b. p.6, turn, k.6, with a. c.b. 21, with c. m.s.lp. *, work as set across 62 sts.; repeat from * to *, with a. c.b. 6.

114th to 116th rows: As 42nd to 44th rows, using b. instead of e. and c. instead of d.

117th row: Work as set across 58 sts., *then for the cracker with c. k.6, turn, with b. p.6, turn, rib 6, with a. c.b. 18, with a. cr. 3rt. *, work as set across 63 sts.; repeat from * to *, with a. c.b. 7.

118th row: As set, but working in rib with b. across cracker sts.

119th row: As set, but with b. casting off the 6 cracker sts.

120th and 121st rows: In c.b. completing horse motif as set.

122nd to 128th rows: In c.b.

129th to 144th rows: As 81st to 96th rows.

The last 144 rows form the pattern; now using c. instead of b. and b. instead of c. and e. instead of d. and d. instead of e. when working the loops and the crackers, work the first 102 pattern rows again. Work should now measure 44 cms. (17½ inches) from beginning.

To shape the armholes: Continuing in pattern as set, cast off 4 sts. at the beginning of the next 2 rows, then dec. 1 st. at each end of the next row and the 12 following alternate rows.

On 136 sts. pattern 93 rows, noting that the hole nearest the armhole will be a half hole.

To slope the shoulders: Cast off 5 sts. at the beginning of the next 14 rows and 6 sts. on the 2 following rows. – 54 sts.

Change to size 2¼mm. (No. 13) needles and with m. and a. together work 12 rows in single rib, then cast off in rib.

THE POCKET BACKS (2 alike)

With size 2¾mm. (No. 12) needles and m. cast on 44 sts. and work the 6 rows chequer board pattern given for back 14 times, then leave these sts. on a stitch-holder until required.

THE LEFT FRONT

With size 2¼mm. (No. 13) needles and m. cast on 76 sts. and work 33 rows in single rib.

Increase row: Rib 6, *up 1, rib 7; repeat from * to end. – 86 sts.

Change to size 2¾mm. (No. 12) needles and work 96 rows in pattern as given for back.

Pocket row: Pattern 21, slip next 44 sts. onto stitch-holder and leave at front of work, then in their place work across the 44 sts. of one pocket back, pattern to end.

Work the 98th to 144th pattern rows, then the 1st to 102nd rows again; work 1 extra row here when working right front.

To shape the armhole: Continuing in pattern as set, cast off 4 sts. at the beginning of the next row. Work 1 row straight.

Dec. 1 st. at the beginning of the next row and the 12 following alternate rows.

On 69 sts. pattern 23 rows.

To slope the neck edge: Dec. 1 st. at the end of the next row and the 27 following alternate rows.

On 41 sts. pattern 15 rows.

To slope the shoulder: Cast off 5 sts. at the beginning of the next row and the 6 following alternate rows. On 6 sts. work 1 row, then cast off.

THE RIGHT FRONT

Work as given for left front, noting the variation in the number of rows before shaping the armhole and noting that the hole above the armhole will be a half hole.

THE POCKET TOPS (both alike)

With right side of work facing rejoin m. and using size 2¼mm. (No. 13) needles k. 4 rows, then cast off.

THE BUTTONBAND

With right side of work facing rejoin m. and a. together at left front neck edge, and using size 2¾mm. (No. 12) needles pick up and k. 41 sts. up to first front edge dec., then pick up andk k. 164 sts. down to cast on edge. – 205 sts.

With m. and a. together work 3 rows in single rib.

Next row: Rib 40, 3 from 1, rib to end.

Rib 3 rows.

Next row: Rib 41, 3 from 1, rib to end.

Rib 3 rows, then cast off loosely in rib.

THE BUTTONHOLE BAND

With right side of work facing rejoin m. and a. and using size 2¾mm. (No. 12) needles pick up and k. 164 sts. from cast on edge up to first front edge dec., then 41sts. up to shoulder. – 205 sts.

With m. and a. together work 3 rows in single rib.

Next row: Rib 164, 3 from 1, rib to end.

Rib 1 row.

1st Buttonhole row: Rib 6, *cast off 4, rib next 21 sts.: repeat from * 5 times more, cast off 4, rib to end.

2nd Buttonhole row: Rib 41, * turn, cast on 4, turn, rib 22, repeat from * ending last repeat rib 6.

Next row: Rib 165, *3 from 1, rib to end.

Rib 3 rows, then cast off loosely in rib.

THE SLEEVES (both alike)

With size 2¼mm. (No. 13) needles and m. cast on 86 sts. and work 23 rows in single rib.

Increase row: Rib 2, *up 1, rib 2; repeat from * to end. – 128 sts.

Change to size 2¾mm. (No. 12) needles and work the first 20 pattern rows given for back.

21st row: With a. c.b.13, *with a. cr.3rt., c.b. 18, with a. cr.3rt., c.b.18, with a. cr.3rt. *, c.b.7, cast off 7 for hole, c.b. next 3 sts.; repeat from * to *, c.b.7.

The last row sets the position of the pattern given for back, work the 22nd to 98th rows.

99th row: With a. c.b.23, *with e. m.d.b. – see abbreviations, with a. c.b.12, with e. m.d.b., c.b.68; repeat from * ending c.b.5.

The last row sets the position of the horse motifs. Work the 100th to 144th pattern rows, then work the first 96 rows again, using c. instead of b., b. instead of c., e. instead of d. and d. instead of e. when working the loops and crackers.

Decrease row: With m. k.8, *pass 2nd, 3rd and 4th sts. on left hand needle over first st., with m. k. this st., k. 14; repeat from * ending last repeat k.8. – 107 sts.

K. 1 row.

Now work in striped rib pattern as follows. Break off m., join in b.

1st row: All k.

2nd row: K.2, *y.f., sl. 1, y.b., k.2; repeat from * to end.

The last 2 rows form the stripe pattern. Working in stripe sequence of 2 rows c., 2 rows d., 2 rows e. and 2 rows b., work 2 rows straight.

To shape the armhole: Working in stripe sequence as set, cast off 4 sts. at the beginning of the next 2 rows, then dec. 1 st. at each end of the next row and the 9 following 4th rows, then on the 15 following alternate rows. On 49 sts. work 1 row.

Cast off 3 sts. at the beginning of the next 4 rows, 4 sts. on the 4 following rows, 5 sts. on the 2 following rows. Cast off the remaining 11 sts.

THE BALL MOTIFS (14 alike)

(5 for the back; 5 for the front and 2 for each sleeve.)

With size 2¾mm. (No. 12) needles and b. cast on 8 sts. and work as follows:

*1st and 2nd rows: All k.

3rd and 4th turning rows: K.7, turn, k. to end.

5th and 6th turning rows: K.6, turn, k. to end.

7th and 8th turning rows: K.5, turn, k. to end.

9th and 10th turning rows: K.4, turn, k. to end.

11th and 12th turning rows: K.3, turn, k. to end.

13th and 14th turning rows: K.2, turn, k. to end.

Break off b., join in c., work the last 14 rows, break of c., join in d., work these 14 rows again, break off d., join in e., work these 14 rows again **. Break off e., join in b.

Repeat from * to **, then cast off. Neatly join cast on and cast off edges, and darn in ends.

THE HALF BALL MOTIF (2 alike)

Work as given for ball motif until ** is reached. Darn in ends.

TO MAKE UP THE CARDIGAN

Do not press silk garments. For other "Woollybear Yarns" pin out to size and press all parts except the ribbing with a warm iron over a damp cloth. Neatly sew ball motifs and half motifs in position in the holes in the knitting. Join shoulder seams. Set in sleeves. Join sleeve and side seams. Neatly sew pocket backs and row ends of pocket tops in place. Sew on buttons.

THE SWEATER

THE BACK AND FRONT (alike)

With size 2¼mm. (No. 13) needles and m. cast on 170 sts. and work 10 rows in single rib.

Change to size 2¾mm. (No. 12) needles and work in pattern as given for back of long sweater until 154 rows have been worked in pattern.

To shape the armholes: Continuing in pattern as set, cast off 2 sts. at the beginning of the next 2 rows, then dec. 1 st. at each end of the next row and the 2 following 4th rows.

On 160 sts. pattern 106 rows.

Now divide the sts. for the neck: Next row: Pattern 66 and leave these sts. on a spare needle until required for second shoulder, cast off 28, pattern to end and continue on these 66 sts. for the first shoulder.

The first shoulder: Continuing in pattern as set dec. 1 st. at the neck edge on each of the next 26 rows. – 40 sts.

To slope the shoulder: Cast off 10 sts. at the beginning of the next row and the 2 following alternate rows. On 10 sts., work 1 row, then cast off.

The second shoulder: With right side of work facing rejoin yarn to inner edge of sts. left on spare needle and work to end of row, then work as given for first shoulder to end.

THE BACK AND FRONT NECKBANDS (alike)

With right side of work facing rejoin m. and using size 2¼mm. (No. 13) needles pick up and k. 85 sts. from neck edge.

Work 11 rows in single rib.

1st Increase row: Rib 6, *3 from 1, rib 11; repeat from * ending last repeat rib 6. – 99 sts.

Rib 9 rows.

2nd Increase row: Rib 7, *3 from 1, rib 13; repeat from * ending last repeat rib 7. – 113 sts.

Rib 9 rows, then cast off in rib.

THE ARMBANDS (both alike)

First join shoulder seams, continuing seams across neckbands. With right side of work facing rejoin m. and pick up and k. 145 sts. and work 11 rows in single rib.

Increase row: Rib 6, *3 from 1, rib 11; repeat from * ending last repeat rib 6. – 169 sts.

Work 9 rows in single rib, then cast off in rib.

TO MAKE UP THE SWEATER

Press as for cardigan – not silk. Join side seams.

Trousers from Patricia Roberts, Convent Garden

r sy

more crackers

MATERIALS
Either 13 25 gram balls of "Woollybear Fine Cotton" in main colour, 13 balls in first contrast and 3 balls in each of the 4 other contrast colours, or 9 25 gram balls of "Woollybear Pure Silk" in main colour, 10 balls in first contrast and 2 balls in each of the 4 other contrast colours, or 12 20 gram balls of "Woollybear Angora" in both main and first contrast colours, plus 2 balls in each of the 4 other contrast colours; a pair each of size 2¼mm (No. 13) and size 2¾mm (No. 12) Aero knitting needles; a fine cable needle.

TENSION
As for "Crackers"

ABBREVIATIONS
M.k., make knot thus, with a. k.1, y.r.n., k.1 all into 1 st., turn, k.3, turn, with e. sl.1, k.2 tog., p.s.s.o., all other abbreviations are as given for "Crackers".

MEASUREMENTS
The measurements are given in centimetres followed by inches in brackets.

Underarms	95(38)
Side seam	44(17½)
Length	64(25½)
Sleeve seam	41(16½)

THE BACK
Work as given for back of "Crackers" cardigan until the shoulders have been shaped.

Change to size 2¼mm. (No. 13) needles and m. only work 8 rows in single rib, then cast off in rib.

THE FRONT
Work as given for the back until the armhole shaping rows have been worked.

On 136 sts. pattern 30 rows.

Now divide the sts. for the neck: Next row: Pattern 55, and leave these sts. on a spare needle until required for right front shoulder, cast off 26, pattern to end and continue on these 55 sts. for the left front shoulder.

The left front shoulder: To shape the neck: Dec. 1 st. at the neck edge on the next row and the 13 following alternate rows.

On 41sts. pattern 13 rows.

To slope the shoulder: Cast off 5 sts. at the beginning of the next row and the 6 following alternate rows.

On 6 sts. work 1 row, then cast off.

The right front shoulder: With right side of work facing rejoin yarn to inner edge of sts. left on spare needle and work to end of row, then work as given for left front shoulder to end.

THE SHOULDER PIECES (2 alike)
With size 2¾mm. (No. 12) needles and e. cast on 41 sts. and k.4 rows, then work in pattern as follows:

1st row: With e. k.2, *with a. m.k. – see abbreviations, with e. k.5; repeat from * ending last repeat k.2.

2nd, 3rd and 4th rows: With e. all k.

5th row: With e. k.5, *with a. m.k., with e. k.5; repeat from * to end.

6th, 7th and 8th rows: With e. all k.

9th to 12th rows: As 1st to 4th rows.

Cast off.

THE SLEEVES (both alike)
As given for "Crackers" cardigan.

THE BALL MOTIFS (14 alike)
As given for "Crackers" cardigan.

THE HALF BALL MOTIFS (2 alike)
As given for "Crackers" cardigan.

THE FRONT NECKBAND
First sew shoulder pieces in place – to front shoulders. Then with right side of work facing rejoin m. at left front shoulder, and using size 2¼mm. (No. 13) needles pick up and k. 12 sts. from row ends of shoulder piece; 14 sts. from left front neck edge, 24 sts. from centre front neck, 14 sts. from right front neck edge, then 12 sts. from row ends of shoulder piece.

On 76 sts. work 7 rows in single rib, then cast off.

TO MAKE UP THE SWEATER
Do not press silk. For other "Woollybear Yarns" pin out to size and press all parts except the ribbing with a warm iron over a damp cloth. Neatly sew ball motifs and half motifs in position in the holes. Join shoulder seams. Set in sleeves. Join sleeve and side seams.

"**Rosy**" continued from opposite page.

Now work the 60 pattern rows given for back twice, then work the first 26 rows again.

To shape the sleevetop: Continuing in pattern as set, cast off 4 sts. at the beginning of the next 2 rows, then dec. 1 st. at each end of the next row and the 19 following alternate rows.

On 50 sts. work 1 row.

Cast off 3 sts. at the beginning of the next 4 rows, then 4 sts. on the 6 following rows. Cast off the 14 remaining sts.

THE SHORT SLEEVES (both alike)
With size 2¼ mm. (No. 13) needles cast on 80 sts. and work 17 rows in single rib.

Increase row: Rib 6, *up1, rib 4, repeat from * ending last repeat rib 6. – 98 sts.

Change to size 2¾ mm. (No. 12) needles and beginning with a k. row s.s. 4 rows.

Now work the 31st. to 60th pattern rows given for back, then work the 1st to 26th rows.

To shape the sleevetop: Work as given for sleevetop on long sleeves.

THE COLLAR
With size 2¾ mm. (No. 12) needles and m. cast on 15 sts. and k. 2 rows.

Now work in lace pattern, working the instructions in brackets the number of times stated after the brackets.

Foundation row: K.2, (y.r.n.) 4 times, k. 2 tog., (y.r.n., k.2 tog.) 5 times, k.1.

1st row: K.12, then k.1, p.1, k.1, p.1 all into the 4 y.r.n. loops of previous row, k.2.

2nd and 3rd turning rows: K. until 3 remain, turn, k. to end.

4th row: K.2, (y.r.n.) 5 times, k.2 tog., k.1, (y.r.n., k.2 tog.) 6 times, k.1.

5th row: K.15, then k.1, p.1, k.1, p.1, k.1 all into the 5 y.r.n. loops of the previous row, k.2.

6th and 7th turning rows: K. until 3 remain, turn, k. to end.

8th row: Cast off 7, then k.1, (y.r.n.) 4 times, k. 2 tog., (y.r.n., k.2 tog.) 5 times, k.1.

The last 8 rows form the pattern; repeat them 26 times more, then work the first 7 of these rows again.

Cast off.

TO MAKE UP THE SWEATER
Do not press silk. For cotton pin out to size and press all parts except the ribbing very lightly with a warm iron over a damp cloth. Join shoulder seams. Set in sleeves. Jóin sleeve and side seams. Neatly sew collar in place.

THE CARDIGAN

THE BACK
Work as given for the sweater.

THE LEFT FRONT
With size 2¼ mm. (No. 13) needles and m. cast on 64 sts. and work 35 rows in single rib.

Increase row: Rib 5, *up 1, rib 6; repeat from * ending last repeat rib 5 – 74 sts.

Change to size 2¾ mm. (No. 12) needles and beginning with a k. row s.s. 4 rows.

Now work in pattern as follows; noting the information given for the back **.

1st row: K.9, p.15, k.33, p.15, k.2.

2nd row: P.2, k.15, p.33, k.15, p.9.

The last 2 rows set the position of the pattern given for the back. Now work the 3rd to 60th rows as set and given for back, then work the first 56 rows again.

To shape the armholes: Continuing in pattern as set, cast off 4 sts. at the beginning if the next row. Work 1 row back to armhole edge. Dec. 1 st. at the beginning of the next row and the 3 following alternate rows.

On 66 sts. pattern 40 rows.

To shape the neck: Cast off 8 sts. at the beginning of the next row, then dec. 1st at the neck edge on each of the next 17 rows.

On 41 sts. pattern 13 rows.

To slope the shoulder: Cast off 8 sts. at the beginning of the next row and the 3 following alternate rows. On 9 sts. work 1 row, then cast off.

THE RIGHT FRONT
Work as given for left front until **is reached.

1st row: K.33, p.15, k.26.

2nd row: P.26, k.15, p.33.

The last 2 rows set the position of the pattern given for the back. Work the 3rd to 60th rows as set, then work the first 57 rows again.

To shape the armholes: Work as given for left front armhole shaping to end.

THE SLEEVES (both alike)
As given for the sweater.

THE BUTTONHOLE BAND
With size 2¼ mm. (No. 13) needles and m. cast on 10 sts. and work 4 rows in single rib.

1st Buttonhole row: Rib 3, cast off 4, rib to end.

2nd Buttonhole row: Rib 3, turn, cast on 4, turn, rib to end.

Rib 30 rows.

Repeat the last 32 rows 5 times more, then work the 2 buttonhole rows again.

Rib 4 rows.

Cast off in rib.

THE BUTTONBAND
With size 2¼ mm. (No. 13) needles and m. cast on 10 sts. and work 202 rows in single rib, then cast off.

THE COLLAR
As given for the sweater.

TO MAKE UP THE CARDIGAN
Press as for sweater – not silk. Make up as for sweater. Then sew front bands in place. Sew on buttons.

rosy

MATERIALS

For the sweater or the cardigan with long sleeves: 16 25 gram balls of "Woollybear Pure Silk" by Patricia Roberts in main colour and one ball of the same yarn in each of the 3 contrast colours, or 21 25 gram balls of "Woollybear Fine Cotton" by Patricia Roberts in main colour, one ball in second contrast colour and 2 balls in first and third contrasts; for the short sleeved version allow 2 balls less in silk or 4 balls less in cotton in main colour; a pair of each of size 2¼ mm. (No. 13) and size 2¾ mm. (No. 12) Aero knitting needles. For the cardigan 7 buttons.

TENSION

Work at a tension of 16 stitches and 20 rows to 5 centimetres (2 inches) over stocking stitch using size 2¾ mm. (No. 12) needles. If you cannot obtain the correct tension using the size needles suggested, use larger or smaller needles accordingly.

ABBREVIATIONS

K., knit; p., purl; st., stitch; tog., together; dec., decrease (by working 2 sts. tog.); inc., increase (by working twice into same st.); single rib is k. 1 and p. 1 alternately; s.s., stocking stitch is k. on the right side and p. on the wrong side; y.r.n., yarn round needle; sl., slip; p.s.s.o., pass slip st. over; y.f., yarn forward; y.b., yarn back; m.b., make bobble thus, k. 1, y.r.n., k. 1, y.r.n., k. 1 all into next st., turn, k. 5, turn, p. 5, turn, k. 1, sl. 1, k. 2 tog., p.s.s.o., k. 1, turn, p. 3 tog.; m.s., make streamer thus, with a. working into next st., cast on 20 sts., then cast off these 20 sts., thus 1 st. has been worked from left hand needle, – for easier working use a spare size 2¾ mm. (No. 12) needle to cast on and off; 9 from 1, with c. k. 1, y.r.n., k. 1, y.r.n., k. 1, y.r.n., k. 1, y.r.n., k. 1 all into one st.; m., main colour; a., first contrast; b., second contrast; c., third contrast colour.

SPECIAL NOTE

Instructions in brackets should be worked the number of times stated after the last bracket.

MEASUREMENTS

The measurements are given in centimetres followed by inches in brackets.

All round at underarms	90	(36)
Side seam	37.5	(15)
Length	59	(23½)
Sleeve seam-long	42.5	(17)
Sleeve seam-short	19	(7½)

THE SWEATER

THE BACK

With size 2¼ mm. (No. 13) needles and m. cast on 128 sts. and work 35 rows in single rib.

Increase row: Rib 5, *up 1, rib 7; repeat from * ending last repeat rib 4. – 146 sts.

Change to size 2¾ mm. (No. 12) needles and beginning with a k. row s.s. 4 rows.

Now work in pattern as follows. This is worked entirely in m. except where indicated for the streamers and rosebuds – use separate small balls of contrast colours for these.

1st row: K. 9, *p. 15, k. 33; repeat from * ending last repeat k. 26.

2nd row: P. 26, *k. 15, p. 33; repeat from * ending last repeat p. 9.

3rd and 4th rows: As 1st and 2nd rows.

5th row: K. 10, *p. 1, k. 1, p. 1, k. 1, p. 1, k. 1, p. 1, k. 1, p. 1, k. 1, p. 1, k. 1, p. 1, k. 35; repeat from * ending last repeat k. 27.

6th row: P. 26, *k. 1, p. 1, k. 1, p. 1, k. 1, p. 1, k. 1, p. 1, k. 1, p. 1, k. 1, p. 1, k. 1, p. 1, k. 1, p. 33; repeat from * ending last repeat p. 9.

7th row: K. 10; *m.b., k. 1, p. 1, m.b., p. 1, k. 1, m.b., k. 1, p. 1, m.b., p. 1, k. 1, m.b., k. 35; repeat from * ending last repeat k. 27.

8th row: As 6th row.

9th row: As 5th row.

10th row: P. 32, *k. 1, p. 1, k. 1, p. 45; repeat from * ending last repeat p. 15.

11th row: K. 8, *k. 2 tog., y.r.n., k. 2 tog., y.r.n., k. 2 tog., y.r.n., k. 2, m.b., k. 2, y.r.n., sl. 1, k. 1, p.s.s.o., y.r.n., sl. 1, k. 1, p.s.s.o., y.r.n., sl. 1, k. 1, p.s.s.o., k. 14, with a. m.s. – see abbreviations, with m. k. 1, with a. m.s., with m. k. 14; repeat from * ending last repeat k. 8.

12th row: P. 24, *p. 2 tog.b., y.r.n., p. 2 tog.b., y.r.n., p. 4, k. 1, p. 1, k. 1, p. 4, y.r.n., p. 2 tog., y.r.n., p. 2 tog., p. 29; repeat from * ending last repeat p. 7.

13th row: K. 6, * * * k. 2 tog., y.r.n., k. 2 tog., y.r.n., k. 1, k. 2 tog., y.r.n., k. 2 tog., y.r.n., k. 1, p. 1, k. 1, y.r.n., sl. 1, k. 1, p.s.s.o., y.r.n., sl. 1, k. 1, p.s.s.o., k. 1, y.r.n., sl. 1, k. 1, p.s.s.o., y.r.n., sl. 1, k. 1, p.s.s.o., k. 13. * * Now work the leaf and bud as follows, noting that both are worked into the same st., thus with b., working into next st., cast on 5, k. these 5 sts., turn, k. them again, turn, cast off 4 sts., leaving 1 st. in b. on the right hand needle, now for the bud, working into the next st. again, with c. 9 from 1, *turn, (y.f., sl. 1 p.wise, y.b., k. 1) 5 times *, noting that the last st. worked was the 1st in b., repeat from * to * 7 times more, turn, so that the wrong side of the work is now facing, sl. 1, still with c. cast off 8, turn, sl. 1, with m. k. 1, then p.s.s.o., this completes the bud * *, continuing with m. k. 13; repeat from * * * ending last repeat k. 9.

14th row: P. 22, *p. 2 tog.b., y.r.n., p. 2 tog.b., y.r.n., p. 15, y.r.n., p. 2 tog., y.r.n., p. 2 tog., p. 25; repeat from * ending last repeat p. 5.

15th row: K. 4, *k. 2 tog., y.r.n., k. 2 tog., y.r.n., k. 2, k. 2 tog., y.r.n., k. 2 tog., y.r.n., k. 1, y.r.n., sl. 1, k. 2 tog., p.s.s.o., y.r.n., k. 1, y.r.n., sl. 1, k. 1, p.s.s.o., y.r.n., sl. 1, k. 1, p.s.s.o., k. 2, y.r.n., sl. 1, k. 1, p.s.s.o., y.r.n., sl. 1, k. 1, p.s.s.o., k. 12, work the leaf and bud as given for 13th row between * * and * *, then continuing with m. k. 10; repeat from * ending last repeat k. 8.

16th row: P. 20, *p. 2 tog.b., y.r.n., p. 2 tog.b., y.r.n., p. 19, y.r.n., p. 2 tog., y.r.n., p. 2 tog., p. 21; repeat from * ending last repeat p. 3.

17th row: K. 2, *k. 2 tog., y.r.n., k. 2 tog., y.r.n., k. 3, k. 2 tog., y.r.n., k. 2 tog., y.r.n., k. 2, y.r.n., sl. 1, k. 2 tog., p.s.s.o., y.r.n., k. 2, y.r.n., sl. 1, k. 1, p.s.s.o., y.r.n., sl. 1, k. 1, p.s.s.o., k. 3, y.r.n., sl. 1, k. 1, p.s.s.o., y.r.n., sl. 1, k. 1, p.s.s.o., k. 19; repeat from * to end.

18th row: All p.

19th row: K. 3, *y.r.n., sl. 1, k. 2 tog., p.s.s.o., y.r.n., k. 2, k. 2 tog., y.r.n., k. 2 tog., y.r.n., k. 3, y.r.n., sl. 1, k. 2 tog., p.s.s.o., y.r.n., k. 3, y.r.n., sl. 1, k. 1, p.s.s.o., y.r.n., sl. 1, k. 1, p.s.s.o., k. 2, y.r.n., sl. 1, k. 2 tog., p.s.s.o., y.r.n., k. 21; repeat from * ending last repeat k. 20.

20th row: All p.

21st row: K. 3, *y.r.n., sl. 1, k. 2 tog., p.s.s.o., y.r.n., k. 3 *; repeat from * to * 3 times more, y.r.n., sl. 1, k. 2 tog., p.s.s.o., y.r.n., k. 21; repeat from first * ending last repeat k. 20.

22nd row: All p.

23rd row: K. 4, *m.b., k. 4, y.r.n., sl. 1, k. 2 tog., p.s.s.o., y.r.n., k. 3, y.r.n., sl. 1, k. 2 tog., p.s.s.o., y.r.n., k. 3, y.r.n., sl. 1, k. 2 tog., p.s.s.o., y.r.n., k. 4, m.b., k. 23; repeat from * ending last repeat k. 21.

24th row: All p.

25th row: K. 10, *m.b., k. 4, y.r.n., sl. 1, k. 2 tog., p.s.s.o., y.r.n., k. 4, m.b., k. 35; repeat from * ending last repeat k. 27.

26th row: All p.

27th row: K. 16, *m.b., k. 47; repeat from * ending last repeat k. 33.

28th to 30th rows: In s.s.

31st row: *K. 33, p. 15; repeat from * until 2 remain, k. 2.

32nd row: P. 2, *k. 15, p. 33; repeat from * to end.

33rd and 34th rows: As 31st and 32nd rows.

35th row: K. 34, *(p. 1, k. 1) 6 times, p. 1, k. 35; repeat from * ending last repeat k. 3.

36th row: P. 2, (k. 1, p. 1) 7 times, k. 1, p. 33; repeat from * to end.

37th row: K. 34, *m.b., k. 1, p. 1, m.b., p. 1, k. 1, m.b., k. 1, p. 1, m.b., p. 1, k. 1, m.b., k. 35; repeat from * ending last repeat k. 3.

38th and 39th rows: As 36th and 35th rows.

40th row: P. 8, *k. 1, p. 1, k. 1, p. 45; repeat from * ending last repeat p. 39.

41st row: K. 15, *with a. m.s., with m. k. 1, with a. m.s., with m. k. 14, k. 2 tog., y.r.n., k. 2 tog., y.r.n., k. 2 tog., y.r.n., k. 2, m.b., k. 2 (y.r.n., sl. 1, k. 1, p.s.s.o.) 3 times, k. 14; repeat from * ending last repeat k. 1.

42nd row: *P. 2 tog.b., y.r.n., p. 2 tog.b., y.r.n., p. 11, y.r.n., p. 2 tog., y.r.n., p. 2 tog., p. 29; repeat from * ending last repeat p. 31.

43rd row: K. 1, *y.r.n., sl. 1, k. 1, p.s.s.o., k. 13, now work the stem and bud as given for 13th row between * * and * *, k. 13, k. 2 tog., y.r.n., k. 2 tog., y.r.n., k. 1, k. 2 tog., y.r.n., k. 2 tog., y.r.n., k. 1, p. 1, k. 1, y.r.n., sl. 1, k. 1, p.s.s.o., y.r.n., sl. 1, k. 1, p.s.s.o., k. 1, y.r.n., sl. 1, k. 1, p.s.s.o.; repeat from * until 1 remains, k. 1.

44th row: *P. 2 tog.b., y.r.n., p. 15, y.r.n., p. 2 tog., y.r.n., p. 2 tog., p. 25, p. 2 tog.b., y.r.n.; repeat from * until 2 remain, p. 2.

45th row: K. 1, *y.r.n., sl. 1, k. 1, p.s.s.o., y.r.n., sl. 1, k. 1, p.s.s.o., k. 12, work the stem and bud given for 13th row between * * and * *, k. 10, k. 2 tog., y.r.n., k. 2 tog., y.r.n., k. 2, k. 2 tog., y.r.n., k. 2 tog., y.r.n., k. 1, y.r.n., sl. 1, k. 2 tog., p.s.s.o., y.r.n., k. 1, y.r.n., sl. 1, k. 1, p.s.s.o., y.r.n., sl. 1, k. 1, p.s.s.o., k. 2; repeat from * ending last repeat k. 3.

46th row: *P. 19, y.r.n., p. 2 tog., y.r.n., p. 2 tog., p. 21, p. 2 tog.b., y.r.n., p. 2 tog.b., y.r.n.; repeat from * until 2 remain, p. 2.

47th row: K. 3, *y.r.n., sl. 1, k. 1, p.s.s.o., y.r.n., sl. 1, k. 1, p.s.s.o., k. 19, k. 2 tog., y.r.n., k. 2 tog., y.r.n., k. 3, k. 2 tog., y.r.n., k. 2 tog., y.r.n., k. 2, y.r.n., sl. 1, k. 2 tog., p.s.s.o., y.r.n., k. 2, y.r.n., sl. 1, k. 1, p.s.s.o., y.r.n., sl. 1, k. 1, p.s.s.o., k. 3; repeat from * ending last repeat k. 2.

48th row: All p.

49th row: K. 3, *y.r.n., sl. 1, k. 2 tog., p.s.s.o., y.r.n., k. 21, y.r.n., sl. 1, k. 2 tog., p.s.s.o., y.r.n., k. 2, k. 2 tog., y.r.n., k. 2 tog., y.r.n., k. 3, y.r.n., sl. 1, k. 2 tog., p.s.s.o., y.r.n., k. 3, y.r.n., sl. 1, k. 1, p.s.s.o., y.r.n., sl. 1, k. 1, p.s.s.o., k. 2; repeat from * ending last repeat k. 1.

50th row: All p.

51st row: K. 3, *y.r.n., sl. 1, k. 2 tog., p.s.s.o., y.r.n., k. 21 (y.r.n., sl. 1, k. 2 tog., p.s.s.o., y.r.n., k. 3) 4 times; repeat from * ending last repeat k. 2.

52nd row: All p.

53rd row: K. 4, *m.b., k. 23, m.b., k. 4, y.r.n., sl. 1, k. 2 tog., p.s.s.o., y.r.n., k. 3, y.r.n., sl. 1, k. 2 tog., p.s.s.o., y.r.n., k. 3, y.r.n., sl. 1, k. 2 tog., p.s.s.o., y.r.n., k. 4; repeat from * ending last repeat k. 2.

54th row: All p.

55th row: K. 34, *m.b., k. 4, y.r.n., sl. 1, k. 2 tog., p.s.s.o., y.r.n., k. 4, m.b., k. 35; repeat from * ending last repeat k. 3.

56th row: All p.

57th row: K. 40, *m.b., k. 47; repeat from * ending last repeat k. 9.

58th to 60th rows: In s.s.

The last 60 rows form the pattern, work the first 56 rows again.

To shape the armholes: Maintaining the continuity of the pattern as set cast off 4 sts. at the beginning of the next 2 rows, then dec. 1 st. at each end of the next row and the 3 following alternate rows.

On 130 sts. pattern 71 rows.

To slope the shoulders: Cast off 8 sts. at the beginning of the next 8 rows and 9 sts. on the 2 following rows.

Cast off the remaining 48 sts.

THE FRONT

Work as given for the back until the armhole shaping rows have been worked

On 130 sts. pattern 36 rows.

Now divide the sts. for the neck: Next row: Pattern 53 and leave these sts. on a spare needle until required for right front shoulder, cast off 24 sts. pattern to end and continue on these 53 sts. for the left front shoulder.

The left front shoulder: To shape the neck: Dec. 1 st. at the neck edge on each of the next 9 rows, then on the 3 following alternate rows.

On 41 sts. pattern 19 rows.

To slope the shoulder: Cast off 8 sts. at the beginning of the next row and the 3 following alternate rows. On 9 sts. work 1 row, then cast off.

The right front shoulder: With right side of work facing rejoin m. to inner edge of sts. left on spare needle and work to end of row, then work as given for left front shoulder to end.

THE LONG SLEEVES (both alike)

With size 2¼ mm. (No. 13) needles and m. cast on 66 sts. and work 23 rows in single rib.

Increase row: Rib 2, *up 1, rib 2; repeat from * to end. – 98 sts.

Change to size 2¾ mm. (No. 12) needles and beginning with a k. row s.s. 4 rows.

Continued opposite.

spectrum

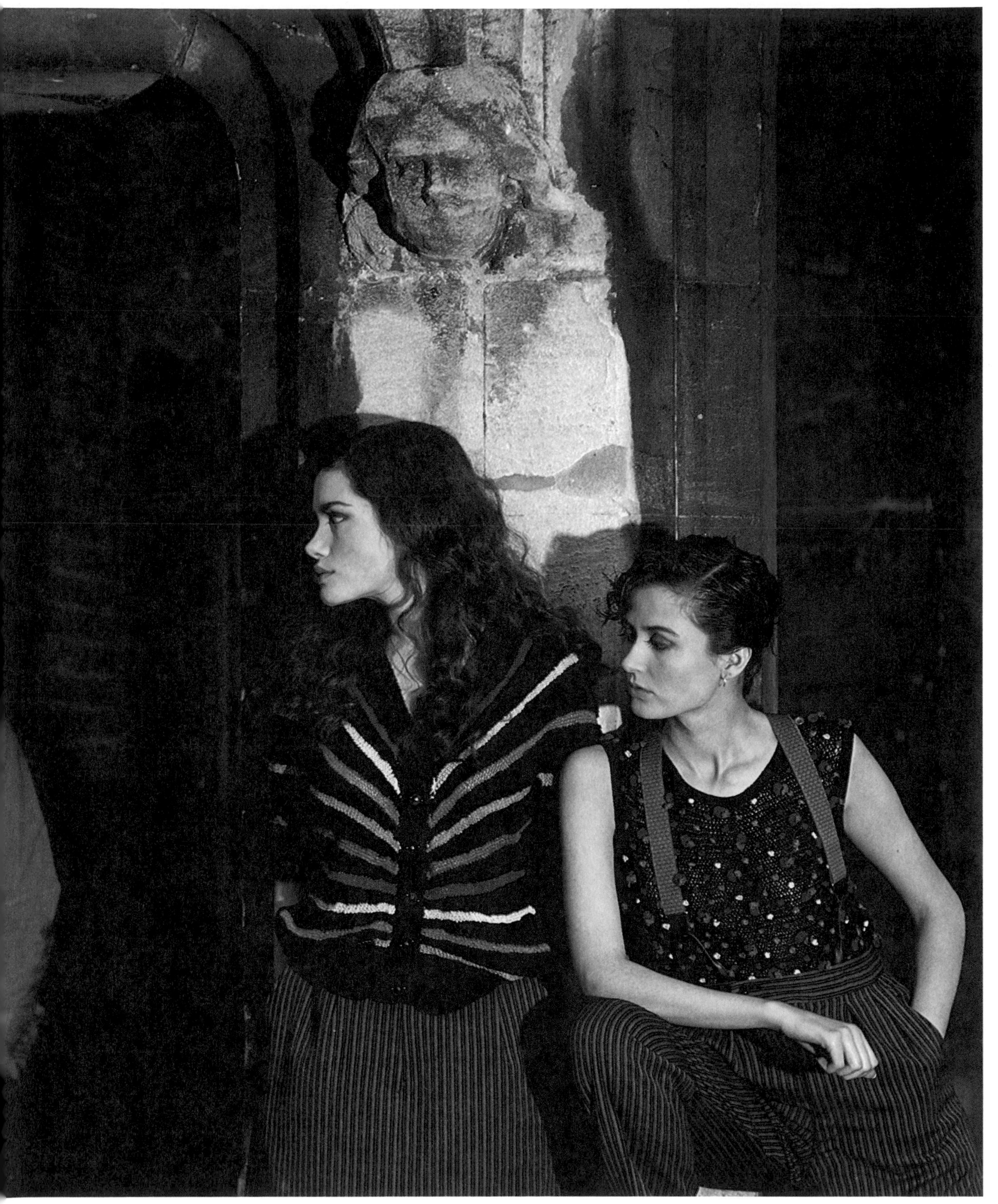

rosebud

Trousers and skirt from Margaret Howell.

spectrum

MATERIALS
For the cardigan or sweater with short sleeves: 9 50 gram balls of "Woollybear Cotton Bouclé" by Patricia Roberts in main colour and 1 ball of "Woollybear Fine Cotton" by Patricia Roberts in each of the 5 contrast colours; a pair each of size 3¼ mm. (No. 10) and size 3¾ mm. (No. 9) Aero knitting needles; for the cardigan only 6 buttons.

For the cardigan or sweater with long sleeves: Add 1 extra 50 gram ball of "Woollybear Cotton Bouclé" in main colour.

SPECIAL NOTE
These garments may also be knitted in "Woollybear 100% Mohair" by Patricia Roberts in main colour instead of the "Cotton Bouclé". The short sleeved cardigan or sweater will require 14 25 gram balls and the long sleeved cardigan or sweater will require 15 25 gram balls. To obtain the correct tension it is necessary to use size 4 mm. (No. 8) needles instead of size 3¾ mm. (No. 9) needles and size 3¾ mm. (No. 9) needles instead of size 3¼ mm. (No. 10) needles throughout.

TENSION
19 stitches and 36 rows to 10 centimetres (4 inches) over the garter stitch using size 3¾ mm. (No. 9) needles and "Woollybear Cotton Bouclé". Using "Woollybear 100% Mohair" the same tension should be obtained by using size 4 mm. (No. 8) needles. If you cannot obtain the correct tension using the size needles suggested, use larger or smaller ones accordingly.

ABBREVIATIONS
K., knit; p., purl; st., stitch; tog., together; dec., decrease (by working 2 sts. tog.); inc., increase (by working twice into same st.); single rib is k. 1 and p. 1 alternately; s.s., stocking stitch is k. on the right side and p. on the wrong side; garter st. is k. plain on every row; m., main colour; a., first contrast; b., second contrast; c., third contrast; d., fourth contrast; e., fifth contrast; up 1, pick up the loop which lies between the needles, slip it onto left hand needle, then k. into back of it; sl., slip; p.s.s.o., pass sl. st. over.

MEASUREMENTS
The measurements are given in centimetres followed by inches in brackets.

Sizes	small	medium
Underarms (sweater)	90 (36)	95 (38)
Underarms (cardigan)	92 (37½)	99 (39½)
Side seam	39 (15½)	39 (15½)
Length,	57.5 (23)	59 23½)
Sleeve seam (short)	11 (4½)	11 (4½)
Sleeve seam (long)	42.5 (17)	42.5 (17)

THE CARDIGAN

THE SHORT SLEEVES (both alike)
With size 3¼ mm. (No. 10) needles and m. cast on 48 (50) sts. and work 10 rows in single rib.

Change to size 3¾ mm. (No. 9) needles and work as follows: Increase row: K.2 (3), *up 1, k.4; repeat from * ending last repeat k.2 (3). – 60 (62) sts.

K. 13 rows.

***Break off m., join in e. and beginning with a k. row s.s. 4 rows. Break off e., join in m.

With m. k. 14 rows.

To shape the sleevetop: Cast off 4 sts. at the beginning of the next 2 rows, then dec. 1 st. at each end of the next row and the following alternate row. – 48 (50) sts.

Now divide the sts. for the back and front shoulders: Next row: K.24 (25) and leave these sts. on a stitch-holder until required, k. to end and leave these 24 (25) sts. on a stitch-holder until required.

THE LONG SLEEVES (both alike)
With size 3¼ mm. (No. 10) needles and m. cast on 40 (42) sts. and work 20 rows in single rib.

Change to size 3¾ mm. (No. 9) needles and work as follows: Increase row: K.2 (3), *up 1, k.4; repeat from * ending last repeat k.2 (3). – 50 (52) sts.

K.3 rows.

Break off m., join in e. and beginning with a k. row s.s. 4 rows. Break off e., join in m.

With m. k. 18 rows, increasing 1 st. at each end of the 9th of these rows.

Instead of e. for the s.s. stripes, using a. for the first repeat, b. for the second repeat; c., for the third repeat and d. for the fourth repeat; repeat the last 22 rows 4 times. – 60 (62) sts.

Now work as given for the short sleeves from *** to end.

THE RIGHT HALF BACK
With size 3¼ mm. (No. 10) needles and m. cast on 38 (40) sts. and work 19 rows in single rib.

Increase row: Rib 5 (6), *up 1, rib 7; repeat from * ending last repeat rib 5 (6). – 43 (45) sts.

Change to size 3¾ mm. (No. 9) needles and work the foundation panel as follows: K.2 rows.

Now work turning rows as follows: 1st and 2nd turning rows: K. until 8 remain, turn, k. to end.

3rd and 4th turning rows: K. until 16 remain, turn, k. to end.

5th and 6th turning rows: K. until 24 remain, turn, k. to end.

7th and 8th turning rows: K. until 32 remain, turn, k. to end.

Working across all the sts. k. 2 rows.

Now work the panels as follows:

1st panel: Break off m., join in a; with a. beginning with a k. row s.s. 4 rows, then break off a. and join in m.

With m. k. 2 rows.

1st and 2nd turning rows: K. until 6 remain, turn, k. to end.

3rd and 4th turning rows: K. until 12 remain, turn, k. to end.

5th and 6th turning rows: K. until 18 remain, turn, k. to end.

7th and 8th turning rows: K. until 24 remain, turn, k. to end.

9th and 10th turning rows: K. until 30 remain, turn, k. to end.

11th and 12th turning rows: K.4, up 1, k. until 36 remain, turn, k. to end.

Working across all sts. k.2 rows. – 44 (46) sts.

2nd panel: Break off m., join in b.; with b. beginning with a k. row, s.s. 4 rows, break off b., join in m.

K.1 row, decreasing 1 st. at end – centre back edge. K.1 row back to side seam edge.

1st and 2nd turning rows: K.4, up 1, k. until 6 remain, turn, k. to end.

Now work as given for 1st panel from 3rd and 4th turning rows to end. 45 (47) sts.

3rd panel: Using c. instead of b., work as given for 2nd panel until the 1st and 2nd turning rows have been worked.

3rd and 4th turning rows: K.4, up 1, k. until 12 remain, turn, k. to end.

5th and 6th turning rows: K.4, up 1, k. until 18 remain, turn, k. to end.

Work the 7th to 12th turning rows given for 1st panel.

13th and 14th turning rows: K.4, up 1, k. until 42 remain, turn, k. to end.

Next row: K. until 2 remain, dec.

K. 1 row. – 48 (50) sts.

4th panel: Using d. instead of b. work as given for 2nd panel until the 1st and 2nd turning rows have been worked.

Work the 3rd to 6th turning rows as given for 3rd panel.

7th and 8th turning rows: K.4, up 1, k. until 24 remain, turn, k. to end.

Work the 9th to 12th turning rows given for 1st panel.

13th and 14th turning rows: K.4, up 1, k. until 42 remain, turn, k. to end.

15th and 16th turning rows: K.4, up 1, k. until 48 remain, turn, k. to end.

Next row: K. until 2 remain, dec.

K.1 row. – 53 (55) sts.

5th panel: Using e. instead of d. work as given for 4th panel until the 8th turning row has been worked.

9th and 10th turning rows: K.4, up 1, k. until 30 remain, turn, k. to end.

11th and 12th turning rows: K.4, up 1, k. until 36 remain, turn, k. to end.

To shape the armhole: 13th and 14th turning rows: Cast off 4, k. until 42 remain, turn, k. to end.

15th and 16th turning rows: K. until 48 remain, turn, k. to end.

Next row: K. until 2 remain, dec.

Next row: Dec., k. to end. – 52 (54) sts.

6th panel: Break off m., with right side of work facing rejoin a. to the centre of right sleeve and k. across the 24 (25) sts. left on one stitch-holder then onto the same needle, k. across the 52 (54) sts. of right half back. – 76 (79) sts.

****With a. beginning with a p. row s.s. 3 rows, break off a., join in m.

**With m. k.2 rows, decreasing 1 st. at centre back edge on each row – work 1 row less here on left half back.

Work the first 10 turning rows given for 1st panel.

11th and 12th turning rows: K. until 36 remain, turn, k. to end.

13th and 14th turning rows: K. until 42 remain, turn, k. to end.

15th and 16th turning rows: K. until 48 remain, turn, k. to end.

17th and 18th turning rows: K. until 54 remain, turn, k. to end.

With m. k.2 rows more decreasing 1 st. at centre back edge on each row – work 1 row more here when working left half back. – 72 (75) sts. ***

7th panel: Break off m., join in b., with b. beginning with a k. row s.s. 4 rows, decreasing 1 st. at the centre back edge on the first and third of these rows. Break off b., join in m.

Work as given for 6th panel from ** to ***, but decreasing 1 st. at the beginning – shoulder edge – on the 3rd, 7th, 11th and 15th turning rows. – 62 (65) sts.

8th panel: Break off m., join in c., with c. beginning with a k. row s.s. 4 rows, decreasing 1 st. at centre back edge on each row.

Work as given for 6th panel from ** until the first 14 turning rows have been worked, but decreasing 1 st. at the beginning of the 1st, 5th, 9th and 13th turning rows.

With m. k.2 rows more, decreasing 1 st. at centre back edge on each row – work 1 row more here when working left half back. – 50 (53) sts.

9th panel: Break off m., join in d., with d. beginning with a k. row s.s. 4 rows, decreasing 1 st. at centre back edge on each row.

Work as given for 6th panel from ** until the first 6 turning rows have been worked, but decreasing 1 st. at the beginning – shoulder edge on the 1st and 5th turning rows. – 42 (45) sts. Mark the end of the last row with a coloured thread.

Work the 7th to 12th turning rows given for the 6th panel, decreasing 1 st. at the shoulder edge on the 1st and 5th of these rows.

With m. k.1 row, decreasing 1 st. at centre back edge.

Cast off 6 sts. at the beginning – centre back edge of the next row. – When working left half back, k.1 row more decreasing 1 st. at centre back edge. – 33 (36) sts.

10th panel: Break off m., join in e., with e. beginning with a k. row s.s. 4 rows, casting off 4 sts. at the beginning of the 2nd and 4th of these rows. – 25 (28) sts.

Work as given for 6th panel from ** until the first 6 turning rows have been worked, but decreasing 1 st. at the beginning of the 3rd and 5th of these rows. When working left half back, k.1 row, decreasing 1 st. at centre back edge.

Cast off the remaining 21 (24) sts.

THE LEFT HALF BACK
Work as given for right half back until the increase row has been worked.

Change to size 3¾ mm. (No. 9) needles and k. 1 row.

Work the 8 turning rows given for foundation panel on right half back, then with m. k.3 rows.

1st panel: Break off m., join in a. With a. beginning with a k. row s.s. 4 rows. Break off a., join in m.

With m. k.1 row.

Work the 12 turning rows given for 1st panel on right half back.

With m. k.3 rows. – 44 (46) sts.

2nd panel: Break off m., join in b. With b. beginning with a k. row s.s. 4 rows. Break off b., join in m.

With m. k.1 row decreasing 1 st. at the beginning – centre back edge.

Work the 12 turning rows given for 2nd panel on right half back.

K.3 rows. – 45 (47) sts.

3rd panel: Using c. instead of b., work as given for 2nd panel, until the 1st and 2nd turning rows have been worked, then work given for 3rd panel on

rosebud

right half back from the 3rd turning row to end, then k. 1 row more. – 48 (50) sts.

4th panel: Using d. instead of b., work as given for 2nd panel until the 1st and 2nd turning rows have been worked, then work given for 4th panel given for right half back from the 3rd turning row to end then k. 1 row more. – 53 (55) sts.

5th panel: Break off m., join in e. With e., beginning with a k. row s.s. 4 rows. Break off e., join in m.

With m. k. 1 row decreasing 1 st. at centre back edge.

Work as given for 5th panel on right half back from 1st turning row to end, then k. 1 row more.

6th panel: Break off m., join in a.

Next row: K. across these 52 (54) sts., then onto same needle k. across the 24 (25) sts. of sleeve left on stitch holder – ending a centre of sleeve. – 76 (79) sts.

Now work as given for right half back, from * * * * to end, noting the variation in the number of rows, where indicated.

THE LEFT HALF FRONT

Work as given for right half back, until the 6th turning row of the 9th panel has been worked, then cast off the remaining 42 (45) sts. loosely.

THE RIGHT HALF FRONT

Work as given for left half back, until the 6th turning row of the 9th panel has been worked, then k. 1 row, decreasing 1 st. at centre back edge, cast off the remaining 42 (45) sts. loosely.

THE POCKET BACKS (2 alike)

With size $3\frac{3}{4}$ mm. (No. 9) needles and m. cast on 24 sts. and beginning with a k. row s.s. 34 rows, then cast off.

THE FRONT BAND

With size $3\frac{1}{4}$ mm. (No. 10) needles and m. cast on 7 sts. and k. 6 rows.

1st Buttonhole row: K. 2, cast off 3, k. to end.

2nd Buttonhole row: K. 2, turn, cast on 3, turn, k. to end.

K. 20 rows.

Repeat the last 22 rows 4 times more, then work the 2 buttonhole rows again.

K. 334 (344) rows more, then cast off.

TO MAKE UP THE CARDIGAN

Do not press. Join shoulder seams, so that the cast off edge at front neck is in line with the marking threads on half backs. Join centre back seam. Join sleeve seams. Join side seams for 14 centimetres ($5\frac{1}{2}$ inches) down from armhole. Sew cast off edge of pocket back to side seam edges of back only, then join remainder of side seams. Neatly sew pocket backs in place. Sew front band in place, so that the last buttonhole is in line with the row end of the final front neck edge cast off row. Sew on buttons.

TO COMPLETE THE CARDIGAN

With right side of work facing rejoin m. to the free row end edges of front at one side seam edge and using size $3\frac{3}{4}$ mm. (No. 9) needles pick up and k. 25 sts. from this pocket edge, turn and cast off. Work along the other front pocket edge in the same way.

THE SWEATER

TO WORK

The sleeves, the right half back, the left half back, the left half front and the right half front are all worked as given for the cardigan.

THE NECKBAND

First join centre front seam, up to the final cast off edge, then join centre back seam, then the right shoulder seam, so that the marking thread on back is in line with cast off edge on front. With right side of work facing rejoin m. at left front shoulder and using size $3\frac{1}{4}$ mm. (No. 10) needles pick up and k. 42 (45) sts. from left front neck edge, 42 (45) sts. from right front neck edge, then 28 sts. from back neck edge.

On 112 (118) sts. work 1 row in single rib.

Next row: Rib to within 2 sts. of centre front neck, sl. 1, k. 1, p.s.s.o., k. 2 tog., rib to end.

Repeat the last 2 rows twice more, then cast off in rib.

TO MAKE UP THE SWEATER

Do not press. Join left shoulder seam, continuing seam across neckband. Join sleeve and side seams.

MATERIALS

8 25 gram balls of either "Woollybear Pure Silk" or "Woollybear Fine Cotton" by Patricia Roberts in main colour, 2 balls in first contrast colour and 1 ball in each of the 4 other contrast colours; a pair each of size $2\frac{1}{4}$ mm. (No. 13) and size $2\frac{3}{4}$ mm. (No. 12) Aero knitting needles; 3 buttons.

TENSION

10 stitches and 12 rows to 5 centimetres (2 inches) over the lace pattern, using size $2\frac{3}{4}$ mm. (No. 12) needles. If you cannot obtain the correct tension using the size needles suggested, use larger or smaller ones accordingly.

ABBREVIATIONS

K., knit; p., purl; st., stitch; tog., together; dec., decrease (by working 2 sts. tog.); inc., increase (by working twice into same st.); single rib is k. 1 and p. 1 alternately; y.r.n. yarn round needle; m.b., make bobble thus, with appropriate contrast colour k. 1, y.r.n., k. 1 all into next st., turn, p. 3, turn, k. 3, turn, p. 3, turn, sl. 1, with m. k. 2 tog., then pass slip stitch over; sl., slip; m., main colour; a., first contrast; b., second contrast; c., third contrast; d., fourth contrast; e., fifth contrast; p.s.s.o., pass sl. st. over; up 1, pick up loop which lies between the needles, slip it onto left hand needle, then k. into back of it; y.f., yarn forward; y.b., yarn back; 9 from 1, k. 1, y.r.n., k. 1, y.r.n., k. 1, y.r.n., k. 1, y.r.n., k. 1 all into next st.

NOTE

The instructions in the brackets are worked the number of times stated after the last bracket.

MEASUREMENTS

The measurements are given in centimetres followed by inches in brackets.

Sizes	Small
All round at underarms	90 (36)
Side seam	40 (16)
Length	60 (24)

THE BACK

With size $2\frac{1}{4}$ mm. (No. 13) needles and m. cast on 121 sts. and work 35 rows in single rib.

Decrease row: *K. 2, k. 2 tog.; repeat from * ending last repeat k. 1. – 91 sts.

Change to size $2\frac{3}{4}$ mm. (No. 12) needles and work in pattern as follows. This is worked entirely in a lace stitch, which is a special way of knitting, except for the bobbles and roses. When working the bobbles use separate short lengths – approximately 30 centimetres (12 inches) – of contrast colour for each bobble, and leaving sufficiently long ends to knot and darn in at completion of work.

To work the lace stitch, insert right hand needle into first st. on left hand needle as if to knit, bring the yarn from the back of the work between the needles to the front, take it round in front of left hand needle and then to the front between the needles, then take it behind the right hand needle and back again between the needles to the front of the work, draw this loop through onto right hand needle, allowing the original stitch and extra loops to fall from left hand needle in the usual way.

1st and 2nd rows: All knit lace as explained above.

3rd row: With m. work 5 sts. in knit lace, *with a. m.b., with m. knit lace 7 sts., with b. m.b., with m. knit lace 7 sts.; repeat from * ending last repeat with a. m.b., with m. knit lace 5. Knot the ends on each bobble firmly, leaving ends to darn in at completion of work.

4th, 5th and 6th rows: With m. in knit lace.

7th row: With m. knit lace 1 st., *with c. m.b., with m. knit lace 7 sts., with d. m.b., with m. knit lace 7 sts.; repeat from * ending last repeat with m. knit lace 1 st. instead of 7; knot ends on each bobble firmly.

8th, 9th and 10th rows: With m. in knit lace.

11th row: With m. work 5 sts. in knit lace, * * *with e. m.b., with m. knit lace 7, * * now work the flower, noting that the stem and the bud are both worked into the same st., thus with b. working into the next st. cast on 5 sts., then k. these 5 sts., turn, k. these 5 sts. again, turn, cast off 4 sts., leaving 1 st. in b. on right hand needle. Now for the bud, with a. 9 from 1, *turn, (y.f., sl. 1 p.wise, y.b., k. 1) 5 times*, note that the last st. worked was the 1st. in b.; repeat from * to * 7 times, turn, so that the wrong side of work is now facing, sl. 1, with a. cast off 8, turn, with m. sl. 1, k. 1 p.s.s.o., the remaining sts. in a. * *, with m. knit lace 7; repeat from * * * ending last repeat with e. m.b., with m. knit lace 5; knot the ends on bobbles and flowers firmly.

12th, 13th and 14th rows: With m. in knit lace.

15th row: As 7th row, but using b. instead of c. and c. instead of d. for the bobbles.

16th, 17th and 18th rows: With m. in knit lace.

19th row: As 3rd row, but using d. instead of a. and e. instead of b.

20th, 21st and 22nd rows: With m. in knit lace.

23rd row: With m. knit lace 1 st., *with a. m.b., with m. knit lace 7 sts., now work the flower as given for 11th row between * * and * *, with m. knit lace 7 sts.; repeat from * ending last repeat knit lace 1 st.

24th row: With m. in knit lace.

The last 24 rows form the pattern, work them again using c. instead of a., d. instead of b., e. instead of c., a. instead of d., and b. instead of e. for the bobbles – the flowers are always in a. and b.

Now work them again, using e. instead of a., a. instead of b., b. instead of c., c. instead of d., and d. instead of e. for the bobbles.

Using b. instead of a., c. instead of b., d. instead of c., e. instead of d. and a. instead of e. for the bobbles, on the next repeat of the pattern, work the first 6 pattern rows. Work should now measure 40 cms. (16 inches) from beginning.

To shape the armholes: Continuing in pattern as set, cast off 4 sts. at the beginning of the next 2 rows, then dec. 1 st. at each end of the next row and the 3 following alternate rows.

On 75 sts. pattern 9 rows, thus completing the last repeat of the pattern.

Work the 24 pattern rows once more, but using d. instead of a., e. instead of b., a. instead of c., b. instead of d. and c. instead of e. for the bobbles. * * * *

To slope the shoulders: Continuing in pattern as set in the colours as originally given, cast off very loosely 6 sts. at the beginning of the next 6 rows. – 39 sts.

Change to size $2\frac{1}{4}$ mm. (No. 13) needles and work as follows:

Increase row: K. 1, *up 1, k. 2; repeat from * to end. – 58 sts.

Work 5 rows in single rib, then cast off in rib.

THE FRONT

Work as given for back until the armhole shaping rows have been worked.

On 75 sts. pattern 9 rows, completing a repeat of the pattern.

Using d. instead of a., e. instead of b., a. instead of c., b. instead of d. and c. instead of e. for the bobbles on the next repeat of the pattern, work the first 11 rows.

Now divide the sts. for the neck: Next row: Pattern 28 and leave these sts. on a spare needle until required for right front shoulder; pattern 19 and leave these sts. on a stitch-holder until required for neckband, pattern to end and continue on these 28 sts. for the left front shoulder.

The left front shoulder: Continuing in pattern as set, dec. 1 st. at the neck edge, on each of the next 10 rows.

On 18 sts. work 2 rows.

To slope the shoulder: Cast off very loosely 6 sts. at the beginning of the next row and the following alternate row. On 6 sts. work 1 row, then cast off very loosely.

The right front shoulder: With right side of work facing rejoin yarn to inner edge of sts. left on spare needle and work to end of row, then work as given for left shoulder to end.

THE FRONT NECKBAND

With right side of work facing rejoin m. and using size $2\frac{1}{4}$ mm. (No. 13) needles pick up and k. 32 sts. from left front neck edge, then across the sts. at centre neck edge, k. 1, *up 1, k. 2; repeat from * to end, then pick up and k. 32 sts. from right front neck edge. – 92 sts.

Work 5 rows in single rib, then cast off in rib.

THE ARMBANDS

First join right shoulder seam, then join left shoulder seam for 2.5 centimetres (1 inch) at armhole edge. With right side of work facing rejoin m. and using size $2\frac{1}{4}$ mm. (No. 13) needles pick up

Continued on page 48.

matelot

Trousers

na Lino

marina

matelot

MATERIALS
Either 13 50 gram balls of "Woollybear Cotton Crêpe" by Patricia Roberts in main colour, 4 balls in first contrast, 1 ball in each of second and third contrasts and one ball in fourth contrast; a pair each of size 3mm (No.11) and size 3¾mm (No. 9) Aero knitting needles; a medium sized cable needle; shoulder pads (optional).

TENSION
15 stitches – 1 repeat of the pattern and 16 rows to 5 centimetres (2 inches) over the cable pattern using size 3¾mm. (No. 9) knitting needles. If you cannot obtain the correct tension using the size needles suggested, use larger or smaller ones accordingly.

ABBREVIATIONS
K., knit; p., purl; st. stitch; tog., together; dec., decrease (by working 2 sts. tog.); inc., increase (by working twice into same st.); single rib is k.1 and p.1 alternately; cable 6, thus, slip next 3 sts. onto cable needle and leave at front of work, k.3, then k.3 from cable needle; m., main colour; a., first contrast; b., second contrast; c., third contrast; d., fourth contrast; sl., slip; p.s.s.o., pass sl. st. over; up 1, pick up the loop which lies between the needles, slip it onto left hand needle, then k. into back of it.

MEASUREMENTS

The measurements are given in centimetres followed by inches in brackets.

Underarms	97.5(39)
Side seam	45(18)
Length	67.5(27)
Sleeve seam	40(16)

THE BACK AND THE FRONT (alike)
With size 3mm. (No. 11) needles and m. cast on 119 sts. and work 23 rows in single rib, beginning right side rows with p.1 and wrong side rows with k.1.

Increase row: Rib 4, *inc. p. wise in each of the next 3 sts., rib 9; repeat from * ending last repeat rib 4. 149 sts.

Change to size 3¾mm. (No.9) needles and work in pattern as follows. Use separate balls of contrast colours for each vertical stripe.

1st Foundation row: With m. k.3, p.1, k.6, p.1, k.2, *with a. k.3, with m. k.2, p.1, k.6, p.1, k.2; repeat from * using b. instead of a. for the first repeat, c. instead of a. for the second, d. instead of a. for the third, then a. again for the fourth repeat, followed by b., c., d. and a. again for the following repeats, with m. k. the remaining st.

2nd Foundation row: With m. k.1, p.1, k.1, p.8, k.1, p.1, *with a. k.1, p.1, k.1, with m. p.1, k.1, p.8, k.1, p.1; repeat from * using d., then c., then b., a. again, then d., c., b. and a. again for the contrast colour stripes, with m. k.1 remaining st.

Now work in pattern as follows:

1st row: With m. k.3, p.1, k.6, p.1, k.2, *with appropriate contrast colour, k.1, p.1, k.1, with m. k.2, p.1, k.6, p.1, k.2; repeat from * with contrast colours as set in foundation rows and ending last repeat with m. k.3 instead of 2.

2nd row: With m. k.1, p.1, k.1, p.8, k.1, p.1, *with appropriate contrast k.1, p.1, k.1, with m. p.1, k.1, p.8, k.1, p.1; repeat from * until 1 remains, k.1 more.

3rd and 4th rows: As 1st and 2nd rows.

5th row: With m. k.3, p.1, cable 6, p.1, k.2, * with appropriate contrast k.1, p.1, k.1, with m. k.2, p.1, cable 6, p.1, k.2; repeat from * ending last repeat k.3.

6th row: As 2nd row.

7th to 12th rows: As 1st to 6th rows.

13th and 14th rows: As 1st and 2nd rows.

The last 14 rows form the pattern; repeat them 7 times more, then work the first 6 rows again. Work should now measure 45 centimetres (18 inches) from beginning.

To shape the armholes: Cast off 6 sts. at the beginning of the next 2 rows, then dec. 1 st. at each end of the next row and the 9 following alternate rows. – 117 sts.

Pattern 14 rows.

Decrease row: With m. p.1, *k.1, p.3, p.2 tog., p.3, k.1, p.5; repeat from * ending last repeat p.1 instead of p.5. – 109 sts.

Leave these sts. on a spare needle until required for yoke.

THE SLEEVES (both alike)
With size 3mm. (No. 11) needles and m. cast on 60 sts. and work 17 rows in single rib.
Increase row: Rib 3, *up 1, rib 5; repeat from * ending last repeat rib 2. – 72 sts.

Now work in pattern as follows: Change to size 3¾mm. (No. 9) needles.

1st Foundation row: With m. k.2, p.1, k.6, p.1, k.2, * with b. k.3, with m. k.2, p.1, k.6, p.1, k.2; repeat from * using c. instead of b. for the first repeat, d. instead of b. for the second, then b. again for the third repeat.

2nd Foundation row: With m. p.1, k.1, p.8, k.1, p.1, *with b. k.1, p.1, k.1, with m. p.1, k.1, p.8, k.1, p.1; repeat from * using d. then c., and then b. for the contrast colour vertical stripes.

The last 2 rows set the position of the pattern given for the back. Work the 14 pattern rows as set.

Continuing in cable pattern as set, and working the extra sts. into the pattern as they occur – the colour stripes introduced at each end of the rows – will both be in a., – inc. 1 st. at each end of the next row and the 15 following 6th rows.

On 104 sts. pattern 5 rows.

To shape the sleevetop: Cast off 6 sts. at the beginning of the next 2 rows, then dec. 1 st. at each end of the next row and the 9 following alternate rows.

On 72 sts. pattern 14 rows.

Decrease row: With m. k.2 tog., *p.3, p.2tog., p.3, k.1, p.5, k.1; repeat from * once more, p.2, p.2 tog., and leave these 32 sts. on a stitch-holder until required for yoke, then across remaining sts, p.2 tog., p.2, *k.1, p.5, k.1, p.3, p.2 tog., p.3; repeat from * until 2 remain, k.2 tog. and leave these 32 sts. on a stitch-holder until required for yoke.

THE BACK YOKE
With right side of work facing rejoin m. at centre of right sleeve and using size 3mm. (No. 11) needles, beginning with k.1, work in single rib across the 32 sts. of one sleeve, then onto the same needle work in single rib across the 109 sts. of the back, then across the first 32 sts. of left sleeve. – 173 sts.

Work 3 rows in single rib.

Decrease row: Rib 10, sl.1, k.2 tog., p.s.s.o., rib until 13 remain, sl.1, k.2 tog., p.s.s.o., rib to end.

Repeat the last 4 rows twice more.

Work 1 row in single rib.

Next Decrease row: K.2 tog., rib 8, sl.1, k.2 tog., p.s.s.o., rib until 13 remain, sl.1, k.2 tog., p.s.s.o., rib until 2 remain, k.2 tog.**

Repeat the last 2 rows 7 times more, working 1 st. less between the first and last decreases on each successive repeat.

On 113 sts. rib 1 row.

To slope the shoulders: Cast off 14 sts. at the beginning of the next 4 rows.

On 57 sts. work 2 rows in single rib, then cast off in rib.

THE FRONT YOKE
Work as given for the back yoke until ** is reached.

Now divide the sts. for the neck: Next row: Rib 69 and leave these sts. on a stitch-holder until required for right front shoulder, rib 17 and leave these sts. on a spare double pointed needle until required, rib to end and continue on these 69 sts. for the left front shoulder.

Decrease row: K.2 tog., rib 7, sl.1, k.2 tog., p.s.s.o., rib until 3 remain, then slip these 3 sts. onto the needle holding the sts. at centre front neck.

Rib 1 row.

Repeat the last 2 rows once more, working 1 st. less between the decreases.

Next Decrease row: K.2 tog., rib 5, sl. 1, k.2 tog., p.s.s.o., rib until 2. remain, slip these 2 sts. onto needle at centre front.

Rib 1 row.

Repeat the last 2 rows 4 times more, working 1 st. less between the decreases on each successive repeat.

To slope the shoulder: Next row: Cast off 14 sts., then rib until 2 remain and slip these sts. onto needle at centre front.

Rib 1 row.

Next row: Cast off 14 sts., then leave the 2 remaining sts. on needle at centre front.

The right front shoulder: With right side of work facing rejoin yarn to inner edge of sts. left on stitch-holder and work as follows:

Decrease row: Rib until 12 remain, sl. 1, k.2 tog., p.s.s.o., rib 7, k.2 tog.

Next row: Rib until 3 remain, slip these 3 sts. onto spare needle at centre front.

Repeat the last 2 rows once more, then the decrease row again, but working 1 st. less between the decreases on each successive decrease row.

Next row: Rib until 2 remain, slip these 2 sts. onto needle at centre front.

Repeat the last 2 rows, working 1 st less between the decreases on each successive repeat, 4 times.

Rib 1 row straight.

To slope the shoulder: Work as given for left front shoulder.

To complete the front: Rejoin yarn to the 57 sts. now on needle at centre front. Work 2 rows in single rib, then cast off very loosely.

THE POCKET BACKS (2 alike)
With size 3¾mm. (No. 9) needles and m. cast on 40 sts. and work 40 rows in single rib, then cast off.

TO MAKE UP THE SWEATER
Pin out to size and press all parts very lightly on the wrong side with a warm iron over a damp cloth. Join shoulder seams. Neatly sew one row end edge of each pocket at each side of back 5 centimetres (2 inches) above ribbing. Join sleeve seams. Join side seams, neatly sewing pocket backs in place on wrong side of front. Join underarm seams. Catch shoulder pads in place if required.

"**Rosebud**" continued from page 45.
and k. 125 sts. from all round armhole edge. Work 5 rows in single rib, then cast off in rib.

THE LEFT SHOULDER EDGING
Rejoin m. at left back shoulder and using size 2¼ mm. (No. 13) needles pick up and k. 24sts. from left back shoulder, then 24sts. from left front shoulder. –48sts.

1st Buttonhole row: K.2, *cast off 3sts., k. next 4 sts.; repeat from * once, cast off 3 sts., k. to end.

2nd Buttonhole row: K.27, turn, cast on 3, turn, k.5; repeat from * ending last repeat k.2.

Cast off. Sew on buttons.

TO COMPLETE
DO NOT PRESS. Join side seams.

marina

MATERIALS
Either 12 25 gram balls of "Woollybear Fine Cotton" by Patricia Roberts in main colour and 3 balls of the same yarn in each of the 5 contrast colours; or 9 25 gram balls of "Woollybear Pure Silk" by Patricia Roberts in main colour and 2 balls of the same yarn in each of the 5 contrast colours: a pair each of size $2\frac{1}{4}$mm. (No. 13) and size $2\frac{3}{4}$mm. (No. 12) Aero knitting needles; a fine cable needle.

TENSION
Work at a tension of 24 sts. - 1 repeat of the pattern to 5 centimetres (2 inches) in width and 22 rows to 5 centimetres (2 inches) in depth over the cable pattern using size $2\frac{3}{4}$mm. (No. 12) needles. If you cannot obtain the correct tension using the size needles suggested use larger or smaller needles accordingly. Some knitters may find it necessary to use a size larger needle, when using "Woollybear Pure Silk".

ABBREVIATIONS
K., knit; p., purl; st., stitch; tog., together; dec., decrease (by working 2 sts. tog.); inc., increase (by working twice into same st.); single rib is k.1 and p.1 alternately; up 1, pick up the loop, which lies between the needles, slip it onto left hand needle, then k. into back of it; cable 6f., cable 6 front thus, slip next 3 sts. onto cable needle and leave at front of work, k.3, then k.3 from cable needle; cable 6b., cable 6 back, as cable 6f., but leaving sts. on cable needle at back of work; cr.6b., cross 6 back thus, slip next 3 sts. onto cable needle and leave at back of work, k.3, then p.3 from cable needle; cr.6f., cross 6 front thus, slip next 3 sts. onto cable needle at front of work, p.3, then k.3 from cable needle; cr.5f., cross 5 front thus, slip next 3 sts. onto cable needle and leave at front of work, p.2, then k.3 from cable needle; cr.5b., cross 5 back thus, slip next 2 sts. onto cable needle and leave at back of work, k.3, then p.2 from cable needle; m., main colour; a., first contrast colour; b., second contrast; c., third contrast; d., fourth contrast; e., fifth contrast.

MEASUREMENTS
The measurements are given in centimetres followed by inches in brackets.

Underarms - including side pieces	100(40)
Length of back and front	42.5(17)
Length of sleeves	35(14)

THE BACK AND FRONT (alike)
With size $2\frac{1}{4}$mm. (No. 13) needles and m. cast on 146 sts. and work 11 rows in single rib.

Increase row: Rib 2, *up 1, rib 2; repeat from * to end. - 218 sts.

Change to size $2\frac{3}{4}$mm. (No. 12) needles, break off m., join in a. and work in pattern as follows:

1st row: P.4, *k.6, p.6; repeat from * ending last repeat p.4.

2nd row: K.4, *p.6, k.6; repeat from * ending last repeat k.4.

3rd and 4th rows: As 1st and 2nd rows.

5th row: P.4, *cable 6f., p.6, cable 6b., p.6; repeat from * ending last repeat p.4.

6th row: As 2nd row.

7th and 8th rows: As 1st and 2nd rows.

Break off a., join in m.

9th to 16th rows: Repeat 1st to 8th rows.

Break off m., join in b.

17th to 24th rows: As 1st to 8th rows.

Break off b., join in m.

25th row: P.2, *cr.5b., cr.6f., cr.6b., cr.5f., p.2; repeat from * to end.

26th row: K.2, *p.3, k.5, p.6, k.5, p.3, k.2; repeat from * to end.

27th row: P.2, *k.3, p.5, k.6, p.5, k.3, p.2; repeat from * to end.

28th row: As 26th row.

29th row: P.2, *k.3, p.5, cable 6b., p.5, k.3, p.2; repeat from * to end.

30th to 32nd rows: As 26th to 28th rows.

Break off m., join in c.

33rd row: P.2, *cr.5f., cr.6b., cr.6f., cr.5b., p.2; repeat from * to end.

34th to 40th rows: As 2nd to 8th rows.

Break off c., join in m.

41st to 48th rows: As 1st to 8th rows.

Break off m., join in d.

49th to 56th rows: As 1st to 8th rows.

Break off d., join in m.

57th to 64th rows: As 1st to 8th rows.

Break off m., join in e.

65th row: P.1, *cr.6b., cr.5f., p.2, cr.5b., cr.6f.; repeat from * until 1 remains, p.1.

66th row: K.1, p.3, *k.5, p.3, k.2, p.3, k.5, p.6; repeat from * ending last repeat p.3, k.1 instead of p.6.

67th row: P.1, k.3, *p.5, k.3, p.2, k.3, p.5, k.6; repeat from * ending last repeat k.3, p.1.

68th row: As 66th row.

69th row: P.1, k.3, *p.5, k.3, p.2, k.3, p.5, cable 6f.; repeat from * ending last repeat k.3, p.1 instead of cable 6f.

70th to 72nd rows: As 66th to 68th rows.

Break off e., join in m.

73rd row: P.1, *cr.6f., cr.5b., p.2, cr.5f., cr.6b.; repeat from * until 1 remains, p.1.

74th to 80th rows: As 2nd to 8th rows.

The last 80 rows form the pattern. Work the first 36 rows again; mark each end of the last row with coloured threads to denote armholes.

Work the 37th to 80th pattern rows, then the first 12 rows again.

To slope the shoulders: Continuing in pattern as set, cast off 21 sts. at the beginning of the next 4 rows. - 134 sts.

Change to size $2\frac{1}{4}$mm (No. 13) needles and continue with m. as follows:

Decrease row: K.1, p.1, k.2 tog., p.1, k.1, *p.2 tog., k.1, p.1, k.2 tog., p.1, k.1; repeat from * to end. - 101 sts.

Work 3 rows in single rib, then cast off in rib.

THE SLEEVES (both alike)
With size $2\frac{1}{4}$mm (No. 13) needles and m. cast on 98 sts. and work 33 rows in single rib.

Increase row: Rib 1, *up 1, rib 2; repeat from * ending last repeat rib 3. - 146 sts.

Change to size $2\frac{3}{4}$mm (No. 12) needles, break off m., join in a. and work the first 72 pattern rows given for back. Mark each end of the last row with coloured threads.

Work the 73rd to 80th rows as set, then work the first 32 rows again.

Break off m., join in c., with c. k.12 rows, then cast off.

THE SIDE PIECES (2 alike)
With size $2\frac{1}{4}$mm (No. 13) needles and m. cast on 17 sts. and work 12 rows in single rib.

Change to size $2\frac{3}{4}$mm (No. 12) needles, join in c. and work as follows:

1st and 2nd rows: With c. all k.

3rd row: With m. all k.

4th row: With m. all p.

The last 4 rows form the pattern; repeat them 18 times more.

Continuing in stripe pattern, inc. 1 st. at each end of the next row and the 7 following 4th rows. - 33 sts.

Work 1 row, marking each end with coloured threads.

Work 2 rows, then dec. 1 st. at each end of the next row and the 14 following 3rd rows.

Work 2 rows, then take the 3 remaining sts. tog., and fasten off.

TO MAKE UP THE SWEATER
Do not press "Pure Silk". For "Fine Cotton" pin out to size and press all parts except the ribbing lightly on the wrong side with a warm iron over a damp cloth. Join shoulder seams. Sew cast off edges of sleeves to the row ends of the back and front between the marking threads. Join sleeve seams up to the marking threads. Sew side pieces in position, so that the marking threads match up with those on back and front and the shaped row ends are sewn to the free row ends of the sleeves.

pierrot

Trousers, skirts and shirts by Kamikaze from Patricia Roberts, Covent Garden.

pierrot

MATERIALS

For the vee-necked sweater: Either 11 (12) 25 gram balls of "Woollybear Fine Cotton" by Patricia Roberts or 9 (10) 25 gram balls of "Woollybear Pure Silk" or 9 (10) 28 gram (ounce) hanks of "Woollybear Real Shetland" in main colour and in the same yarn 3 balls or hanks in first contrast and 2 balls or hanks in each of the 5 other contrasts; angora may be substituted for 2 or 3 contrasts. For the short sweater: Either 9 25 gram balls of "Woollybear Fine Cotton" or 6 25 gram balls of "Woollybear Pure Silk" in main colour and in the same yarn 3 balls in first contrast, 1 ball in second and fourth contrasts and 2 balls in the 3 other contrasts; angora may be substituted for 2 or 3 contrasts. For the cardigan: Add 1 ball or hank of the appropriate yarn in main colour to the quantities given for the vee-necked sweater and 5 buttons.

For any of the garments: a pair each of size $2\frac{1}{4}$ mm. (No. 13) and either $2\frac{3}{4}$ mm. (No. 12) for the woman's garments or size 3 mm. (No. 11) Aero knitting needles for the man's; a fine cable needle.

TENSION

Either 16 stitches and 20 rows to 5 centimetres (2 inches) over the moss stitch pattern using size $2\frac{3}{4}$ mm. (No. 12) needles for the women's garments or for the man's 15 stitches and 19 rows to 5 centimetres (2 inches) over the moss stitch using size 3 mm. (No. 11) needles. If your cannot obtain the correct tension using the size needles suggested use larger or smaller ones accordingly.

ABBREVIATIONS

K., knit; p., purl; st., stitch; tog., together; dec., decrease (by working 2 sts. tog.); inc., increase (by working twice into same st.); single rib is k. 1 and p. 1 alternately; m., main colour; a., first contrast; b., second contrast; c., third contrast; d., fourth contrast; e., fifth contrast; f., sixth contrast; up 1, pick up the loop, which lies between the needles, slip it onto left hand needle, then k. into back of it; cable 4, slip next 2 sts. onto cable needle and leave at front of work, with a. k. 2, then k. 2 from cable needle; cr. 4f., slip next 2 sts. onto cable needle and leave at front or work, with m. or appropriate contrast colour k. 2, with a. k. 2 from cable needle; cr. 4b., slip next 2 sts. onto cable needle and leave at back of work, with a. k. 2, with m. or appropriate contrast colour k. 2 from cable needle; cr. 3 lt., cross 3 left, slip next 2 sts. onto cable needle and leave at front of work, with m. or appropriate contrast k. 1, then with a. k. 2 from cable needle; cr. 3rt., cross 3 right, slip next st. onto cable needle and leave at back of work, with a. k. 2, with m. or appropriate contrast k. 1 from cable needle; m.b., make bobble thus, with c. k. 1, y.r.n., k. 1, y.r.n., k. 1, all into next st., turn, k. 5, turn, p. 5, turn, k. 5, turn, pass 2nd, 3rd, 4th and 5th sts. on left hand needle over first st. on left hand needle, with m. k. this st., break off c. and knot ends firmly leaving sufficiently long ends to darn in at completion of work; ch. 1, work chain thus, with f. k. into next st., without alllowing original loop to fall from left hand needle, slip st. just made, back onto left hand needle, *k. into this st. in the usual way and slip it back onto left hand needle; repeat from * twice more, with m. k. together the last st. just made with the original st. through back of sts.; y.r.n., yarn round needle; sl., slip; p.s.s.o., pass sl. st. over.

MEASUREMENTS

The measurements are given in centimetres followed by inches in brackets.

THE VEE NECKED SWEATER AND CARDIGAN

	Woman's	Man's
Underarms-sweater	95 (38)	101 ($40\frac{1}{2}$)
Underarms-cardigan	97.5 (39)	104 ($41\frac{1}{2}$)
Side seam	40 (16)	41 ($16\frac{1}{2}$)
Length	64 ($25\frac{1}{2}$)	66 ($26\frac{1}{2}$)
Sleeve seam	40 (16)	49 ($19\frac{1}{2}$)

THE SHORT SWEATER

Underarms	105 (42)
Length	44 ($17\frac{1}{2}$)
Sleeve seam	34 ($13\frac{1}{2}$)

THE VEE NECKED SWEATER

THE BACK

With size $2\frac{1}{4}$ mm. (No. 13) needles and m. cast on 132 sts. and work 33 rows in single rib.

Increase row: Rib 9, *up 1, rib 6; repeat from * ending last repeat rib 9. – 152 sts.

**Change to size $2\frac{3}{4}$ mm. (No. 12) needles for the woman's sweater or size 3 mm. (No. 11) needles for the man's and work in pattern as follows: Use separate balls of m. and a. for each section of the pattern, so that colours not in use are not taken across the back of the work.

1st foundation row: With m. k. 1, with a k. 2, *with m. (p. 1, k. 1) 13 times, with a. k. 4; repeat from * ending last repeat with a. k. 2, with m. k. 1.

2nd foundation row: With m. k. 1, with a. p. 2, *with m. (k. 1, p. 1) 6 times, with b. p. 2, with m. (k. 1, p. 1) 6 times, with a. p. 4; repeat from * using c. instead of b. on the first repeat, d. instead of b. on the 2nd, e. instead of b. on the 3rd and f. instead of b. on the 4th repeat and ending this last repeat, with a. p. 2, with m. k. 1.

Now work in pattern as follows: 1st row: With m. k. 1, with a. k. 2, *with m. (p. 1, k. 1) 5 times, p. 1, with f. k. 2, p. 1, k. 1, with m. (k. 1, p. 1) 5 times, k. 1, with a. cable 4; repeat from * using e. instead of f., then d., c. and b. instead of f. on each successive repeat and ending last repeat, with a. k. 2, with m. k. 1.

2nd row: With m. k. 1, with a. p. 2, *with m. (k. 1, p. 1) 5 times, k. 1, with b. (p. 1, k. 1) twice, with m. p. 1 (k. 1, p. 1) 5 times with a. p. 4; repeat from *using c., then d., then e. and then f. instead of b. on each successive repeat and ending last repeat, with a. p. 2, with m. k. 1.

3rd row: With m. k. 1, *with a. and m. cr. 4f., with m. (p. 1, k. 1) 4 times, with f. (k. 1, p. 1) twice, then k. 2, with m. (p. 1, k. 1) 4 times, with a. and m. cr. 4b. *; repeat from * to * using e., then d., then c., and then b. instead of f. on each successive repeat, then with m. k. 1.

4th row: With m. k. 2, p. 1, *with a. p. 2, with m. (k. 1, p. 1) 4 times, with b. (k. 1, p. 1) 3 times, with m. (k. 1, p. 1) 4 times, with a. p. 2, with m. (k. 1, p. 1) twice; repeat from * using c., then d., then e., then f. instead of b. on each successive repeat, and ending last repeat with m. k. 1, p. 1, k. 1.

5th row: With m. k. 1, p. 1, k. 1, * with a. and m. cr. 3lt., with m. (k. 1, p. 1) 3 times, with f. k. 2, (p. 1, k. 1) 3 times, with m. (k. 1, p. 1) 3 times, with a. and m. cr. 3rt., with m. (p. 1, k. 1) twice; repeat from * using appropriate contrasts instead of f. on each successive repeat and ending last repeat with m. p. 1, k. 2.

6th row: With m. k. 2, p. 1, k. 1, * with a. p. 2, with m. (p. 1, k. 1) 3 times, with b. (p. 1, k. 1) 4 times, with m. (p. 1, k. 1) 3 times, with a. p. 2, with m. (p. 1, k. 1) 3 times; repeat from * using appropriate contrast colours instead of b. on each successive repeat and ending last repeat with m. (p. 1, k. 1) twice.

The last 6 rows set the position of the pattern given in the chart. Now work the 7th to 55th rows from the chart in colours as set.

56th row: With m. k. 1, with a. p. 2, *with m. (k. 1, p. 1) 6 times, with d. – note the colour change – p. 2, with m. (k. 1, p. 1) 6 times, with a. p. 4; repeat from * using e., then f., then b., and then c. instead of d. on the following repeats and ending last repeat with a. p. 2, with m. k. 1.

The last 56 rows form the pattern; work the first 55 rows again, but with the contrast colours in the order set in the 56th pattern row of the last pattern repeat.

Next row: With m. k. 1, with a. p. 2, *with m. (k. 1, p. 1) 6 times, with f. p. 2, with m. (k. 1, p. 1) 6 times, with a. p. 4; repeat from * using b., then c., then d., then e. instead of f. on each successive repeat, and ending last repeat with a. p. 2, with m. k. 1.**

The last row sets the order of the colours for the next repeat of the pattern. Work 16 rows.

To shape the armholes: Maintaining the continuity of the pattern, cast off 8 sts. at the beginning of the next 2 rows, then dec. 1 st. at each end of the next row and the 7 following alternate rows.

On 120 sts. work 22 rows, ending with a 55th pattern row.

Next row: With c. p. 1, *with m. (k. 1, p. 1) 6 times, with b. p. 4, with m. (k. 1, p. 1) 6 times, with d. p. 2; repeat from * using e., then f., then b. on each successive repeat and ending last repeat p. 1 instead of 2.

The last row sets the order of the colours for the next repeat of the pattern. Now pattern 48 rows.

To slope the shoulders: Cast off 10 sts. at the beginning of the next 4 rows, then 12 sts. on the 2 following rows. – 56 sts.

Change to size $2\frac{1}{4}$ mm. (No. 13) needles and using m. only, work 8 rows in single rib, work 12 rows when working cardigan, then cast off in rib.

THE FRONT

Work as given for back, until the first 3 armhole shaping rows have been worked. – 134 sts.

Next row: Pattern 67 sts. and leave these sts. on a

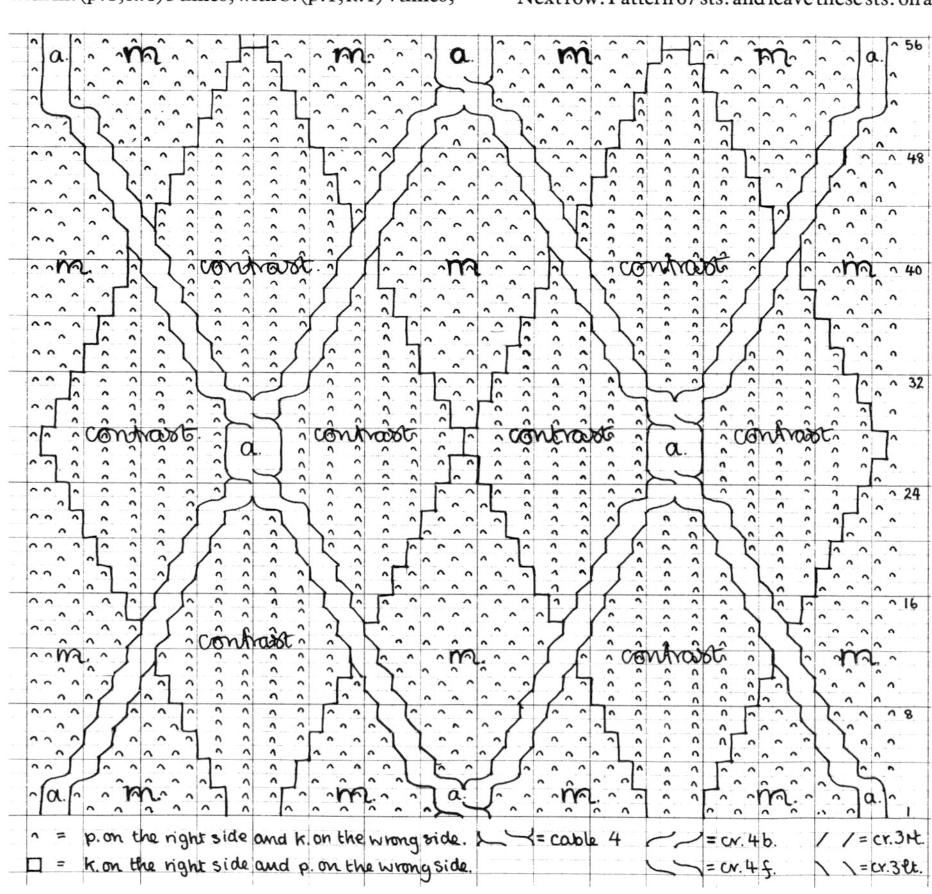

spare needle until required for right front shoulder, pattern to end and continue on these 67 sts. for the left front shoulder.

* * *The left front shoulder: To slope the neck and continue to shape the armhole: Continuing in pattern as set and given for back, dec. 1 st. at each end of the next row and the 6 following alternate rows.

On 53 sts. work 1 row.

Dec. 1 st. at the neck edge on the next row and the 20 following alternate rows.

On 32 sts. pattern 29 rows.

To slope the shoulder: Cast off 10 sts. at the beginning of the next row and following alternate row.

On 12 sts. work 1 row, then cast off.

The right front shoulder: With right side of work facing rejoin yarn to inner edge of sts. left on spare needle, and work to end of row, then work as given for left front shoulder to end.

THE FRONT NECKBAND

With right side of work facing rejoin m. to left front neck edge and using size 2¼ mm. (No. 13) needles pick up and k. 76 sts. from left front neck edge, then 76 sts. from right front neck edge. – 152 sts.

Work 1 row in single rib.

Next row: Rib to within 2 sts. of centre front neck, sl. 1, k. 1, p.s.s.o., k. 2 tog., rib to end.

Repeat the last 2 rows twice.

Rib 1 row, then cast off in rib.

THE SLEEVES (both alike)

With size 2¼ mm. (No. 13) needles and m. cast on 82 sts. and work 33 rows in single rib.

Increase row: Rib 5, *up 1, rib 8; repeat from * ending last repeat rib 5. – 92 sts.

* * *Change to size 2¾ mm. (No. 12) needles for the woman's garment or size 3 mm. (No. 11) needles for the man's and work in pattern as follows, noting the information given before commencing pattern on back.

For the man's sweater only: 27th pattern row: As given for 27th row on back, but using c. for the first diamond, b. for the second and f. for the third.

The last row sets the position of the pattern and the colours; now work the 28th to 55th rows as set.

For the woman's sweater: Work the 1st foundation row given for the back.

For both the man's and the woman's sweater:

Next row: With m. k. 1, with a. p. 2, *with m. (k. 1, p. 1) 6 times, with c. p. 2, with m. (k. 1, p. 1) 6 times, with a. k. 4, repeat from * using d. instead of c., then e. instead of c, ending last repeat with a. k. 2, with m. k. 1.

The last row sets the position of the pattern and the colours given for the centre 3 pattern repeats on the back. * * *

Pattern 28 rows as set.

* * * *Maintaining the continuity of the pattern and working the extra sts. into the pattern as they occur, inc. 1 st. at each end of the next row and the 9 following 10th rows.

On 112 sts. pattern 9 rows.

To shape the sleevetop: Continuing in pattern as set cast off 8 sts. at the beginning of the next 2 rows, then dec. 1 st. at each end of the next row and the 3 following alternate rows. Work 1 row straight.

Dec. 1 st. at each end of the next 20 rows.

Cast off 4 sts. at the beginning of the next 10 rows.

Cast off the remaining 8 sts.

TO MAKE UP THE SWEATER

Do not press silk garments. For other yarns, pin out to size noting the measurements given at beginning. Press with a warm iron over a damp cloth, all parts except the welts. Join shoulder seams. Set in sleeves. Join sleeve and side seams.

THE SHORT SWEATER

THE BACK AND FRONT (alike)

With size 2¼ mm. (No. 13) needles and m. cast on 152 sts. and work 12 rows in single rib.

Work as given for back of vee necked sweater from ** to ** marking each end of the 48th row of the second repeat of the pattern with coloured threads to denote armholes.

The last row sets the order of the colours for the next repeat of the pattern. * * * Work 50 rows.

To slope the shoulders: Cast off 16 sts. at the beginning of the next 4 rows.

Change to size 2¼ mm. (No. 13) needles and on 88 sts. with m. only, work 4 rows in single rib, then cast off in rib.

THE LEFT SLEEVE

With size 2¼ mm. (No. 13) needles and m. cast on 92 sts. and work 34 rows in single rib.

Change to size 2¾ mm. (No. 12) needles and work the 1st foundation row given for back of vee necked sweater.

2nd foundation row: With m. k. 1, with a. p. 2, *with m. (k. 1, p. 1) 6 times, with c. p. 2, with m. (k. 1, p. 1) 6 times, with a. p. 4; repeat from * using d. instead of c., then e. instead of c., ending last repeat with a. p. 2, with m. k. 1.

The last row sets the position of the pattern and the colours given for the centre 3 pattern repeats on back of vee necked sweater. Work the 1st to 55th pattern rows as set.

56th row: With m. k. 1, with a. p. 2, *with m. (k. 1, p. 1) 6 times, with e. p. 2, with m. (k. 1, p. 1) 6 times, with a. p. 4; repeat from * using f. and then b. instead of e. on the following repeats and ending last repeat with a. p. 2, with m. k. 1.

The last row sets the order of the contrast colours for the next repeat of the pattern.

Pattern 48 rows, marking each end of the 12th row with coloured threads.

With a. only, k. 12 rows, then cast off.

THE SIDE PIECES (2 alike)

With size 2¼ mm. (No. 13) needles and m. cast on 17 sts. and work 12 rows in single rib.

Change to size 2¾ mm. (No. 12) needles, join in a. and work as follows:

1st and 2nd rows: With a. all k.

3rd row: With m. all k.

4th row: With m. all p.

The last 4 rows form the pattern; repeat them 18 times more.

Continuing in stripe pattern inc. 1 st. at each end of the next row and the 7 following 4th rows. – 33 sts.

Work 1 row marking each end with coloured threads.

Work 2 rows.

Dec. 1 st. at each end of the next row and the 14 following 3rd rows.

Work 2 rows, then take the 3 remaining sts. tog. and fasten off.

THE RIGHT SLEEVE

With size 2¼ mm. (No. 13) needles and m. cast on 93 sts. and work 34 rows in single rib.

Change to size 2¾ mm. (No. 12) needles and work in pattern as follows. Use a separate ball of f. for each diagonal stripe.

1st row: With m. (k. 1, p. 1) 3 times, *with c. m.b. – see abbreviations, with m. p. 1, (k. 1, p. 1) 4 times; repeat from * ending last repeat with m. (p. 1, k. 1) 3 times.

2nd row and every wrong side row: With m. k. 1, *p. 1, k. 1; repeat from * to end.

3rd row: With m. (k. 1, p. 1) twice, k. 1, *with f. ch. 1 – see abbreviations –, with m. k. 1, with f. ch. 1, with m. k. 1, (p. 1, k. 1) 3 times; repeat from * ending last repeat with m. k. 1, (p. 1, k. 1) twice.

5th row: With m. (k. 1, p. 1) twice, *with f. ch. 1; with m. p. 1, k. 1, p. 1, with f. ch. 1, with m. p. 1, (k. 1, p. 1) twice; repeat from * ending last repeat with m. (p. 1, k. 1) twice.

7th row: With m. k. 1, p. 1, k. 1, *with f. ch. 1, with m. (k. 1, p. 1) twice, k. 1, with f. ch. 1, with m. k. 1, p. 1, k. 1; repeat from * to end.

9th row: With m. k. 1, p. 1, *with f. ch. 1, with m. p. 1, (k. 1, p. 1) 3 times, with f. ch. 1, with m. p. 1; repeat from * ending last repeat with m. p. 1, k. 1.

11th row: With m. k. 1, with c. m.b., *with m. (k. 1, p. 1) 4 times, k. 1, with c. m.b.; repeat from * ending last repeat with m. k. 1.

13th to 20th rows: Work 9th row back to 2nd row.

The last 20 rows form the pattern, repeat them twice more, then work the first 10 rows again. Mark each end of the last row with coloured threads.

Pattern 36 rows more.

With c. only, k. 12 rows, then cast off.

TO MAKE UP THE SWEATER

Do not press silk. For other yarns press as for vee necked sweater. Join shoulder seams. Sew cast off edges of sleeves to the row ends of back and front between the marking threads. Join sleeve seams up to marking threads. Sew side pieces in position so that the marking threads match up with those on back and front and the shaped row ends above the marking threads are sewn to the sleeves down to the marking threads.

THE CARDIGAN

THE BACK

As given for vee necked sweater.

THE SLEEVES

As given for vee necked sweater.

THE POCKET BACKS (two alike)

With size 2¼ mm. (No. 13) needles and m. cast on 41 sts. and work in moss st. as follows: Moss st. row: P. 1, *k. 1, p. 1; repeat from * to end.

Repeat the last row 49 times, then leave these sts. on a spare needle until required.

THE LEFT FRONT

With size 2¼ mm. (No. 13) needles and m. cast on 67 sts. and work 33 rows in single rib.

Increase row: Rib 7, *up 1, rib 6; repeat from * to end. – 77 sts.

Change to size 2¾ mm. (No. 12) needles for the woman's garment or size 3 mm. (No. 11) needles for the man's and work in pattern as follows:

1st foundation row: With m. k. 1, with a. k. 2, *with m. (p. 1, k. 1) 13 times, with a. k. 4, repeat from * once more, with m. (p. 1, k. 1) 7 times.

2nd foundation row: With d. p. 2, with m. (k. 1, p. 1) 6 times, with a. p. 4, with m. (k. 1, p. 1) 6 times, with e. p. 2, with m. (k. 1, p. 1) 6 times, with a. p. 4, with m. (k. 1, p. 1) 6 times, with f. p. 2, with m. (k. 1, p. 1) 6 times, with a. p. 2, wih m. k. 1.

* * * *The last 2 rows set the pattern and the colours given for the back; pattern 48 rows as set.

Pocket row: Pattern 18, slip next 41 sts. onto stitch-holder and leave at front of work; in their place, pattern across the 41 sts. of one pocket back, pattern to end.

Pattern 79 rows as given for appropriate side of back. Work 1 extra row here when working right front.

To shape the armhole: Cast off 8 sts. at the beginning of the next row. Work 1 row. Then dec. 1 st. at each end of the next row.

Work 1 row back to armhole edge, then work as given for left front shoulder of vee necked sweater from * * * to end.

THE RIGHT FRONT

Work as given for left front until the increase row has been worked.

Change to size 2¾ mm. (No. 12) needles for the woman's garment and size 3 mm. (No. 11) needles for the man's and work in pattern as follows:

1st foundation row: With m. (p. 1, k. 1) 7 times, *with a. k. 4, with m. (p. 1, k. 1) 13 times; repeat from * once, with a. k. 2 with m. k. 1.

2nd foundation row: With m. k. 1, with a. p. 2, *with m. (k. 1, p. 1) 6 times, with b. p. 2, with m. (k. 1, p. 1) 6 times, with a. p. 4; repeat from * using c. instead of b., with m. (k. 1, p. 1) 6 times, with d. p. 2.

Now work as given for left front from * * * * to end, noting the variation in the number of rows, before shaping the armhole.

THE POCKET TOPS (both alike)

With right side of work facing rejoin m. to the 41 sts. left on stitch-holder and using size 2¼ mm. (No. 13) needles k. 1 row, then work 5 rows in single rib, then cast off in rib.

THE LEFT FRONT BAND

With right side of work facing rejoin m. at left front shoulder and using size 2¼ mm. (No. 13) needles pick up and k, 80 sts. down to first front dec., then pick up and k. 148 sts. down to cast on edge.

On 228 sts. work 11 rows in single rib, then cast off in rib.

THE RIGHT FRONT BAND

With right side of work facing rejoin m. and using size 2¼ mm. (No. 13) needles pick up and k. 148 sts. up to first front edge dec., then 80 sts. up to shoulder.

On 228 sts. work 3 rows in single rib.

1st Buttonhole row: Rib 7, cast off 5, *rib next 28 sts., cast off 5; repeat from * 3 times, rib to end.

2nd Buttonhole row: Rib 80, *turn, cast on 5 over those cast off, rib 29; repeat from * ending last repeat rib 7.

Rib 6 rows, then cast off in rib loosely.

TO MAKE UP THE CARDIGAN

Do not press silk. For other yarns press as for sweater. Join shoulder seams. Set in sleeves. Join sleeve and side seams. Neatly sew pocket backs and row ends of pocket tops in place. Sew on buttons.

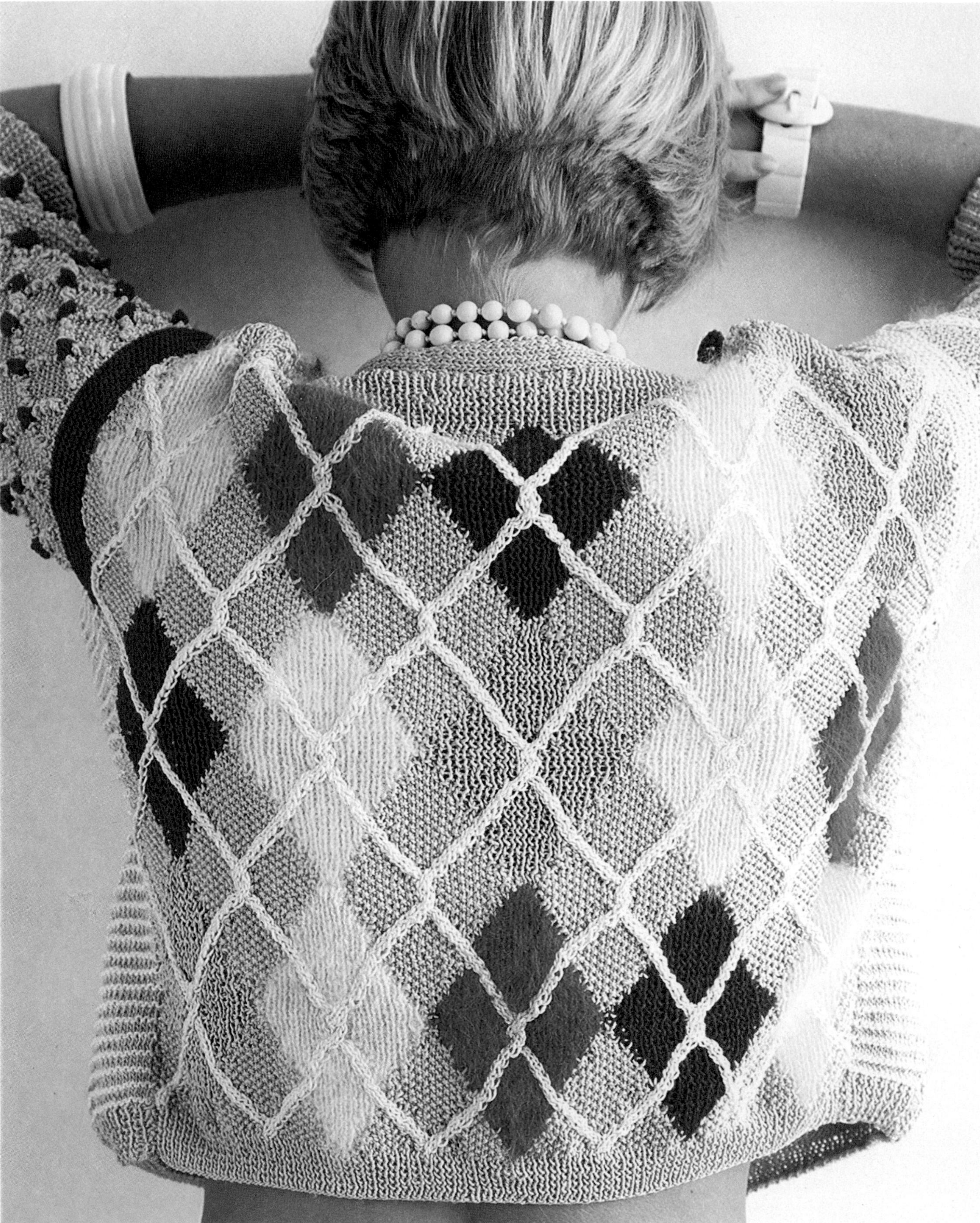

valentine

valentine

MATERIALS

Either 8 25 gram balls of "Woollybear Pure Silk" by Patricia Roberts in main colour, 4 balls in first contrast and 2 balls in each of the 5 other contrast colours, 1 ball of "Woollybear Angora" may be substituted for the second, fourth and fifth contrasts – as in the picture; or 11 25 gram balls of "Woollybear Fine Cotton" in main colour, 5 balls in first contrast and 2 balls in each of the 5 other contrasts; or 8 28 gram (ounce) hanks of "Woollybear Real Shetland" in main colour, 4 hanks in first contrast and 2 hanks in each of the 5 other contrasts, and pair each of size 2¼mm. (No. 13) and 2¾mm. (No. 12) Aero knitting needles, a fine cable needle; 4 buttons.

TENSION

It is especially important to work this pattern at the tensions stated. 16 stitches and 20 rows to 5 centimetres (2 inches) over the moss stitch using size 2¾mm. (No. 12) needles for the back and the sleeves. For the fronts work at a tension of 18 stitches and 34 rows to 5 centimetres (2 inches) over the chequer board pattern, using size 2¾mm. (No. 12) needles. If you cannot obtain the correct tensions using the size needles suggested, use larger or smaller ones accordingly.

ABBREVIATIONS

Refer to those given for the "Pierrot" and the "Happy Birthday" patterns as appropriate.

MEASUREMENTS

The measurements are given in centimetres followed by inches in brackets.

Underarms	105	(42)	Length	47.5	(19)
Side seam	29	(11½)	Sleeve seam	34	(13½)

THE BACK

Work as given for the back of the short "Pierrot" sweater – page 53 – until * * * is reached.

Work 55 rows in pattern as set.

With m. only, work 5 rows in single rib.

To slope the shoulders: Continuing in rib, cast off 12 sts. at the beginning of the next 4 rows, then 13 sts. on the 4 following rows.

Cast off the remaining 52 sts.

THE LEFT AND RIGHT SLEEVES

As given for the short "Pierrot" sweater.

THE SIDE PIECES (2 alike)

As given for the short "Pierrot" sweater.

THE POCKET BACKS (2 alike)

As given for "Happy Birthday" cardigan – page 61.

THE LEFT FRONT

With size 2¼mm. (No. 13) needles and m. cast on 87 sts. and work 12 rows in single rib.

Now work as given for left front of "Happy Birthday" cardigan – page 61 – from * * * until the 120 pattern rows have been worked. Work 1 extra row here when working right front.

To slope the front edge: Continuing in pattern as set, dec. 1 st. at the end of the next row and the 13 following 4th rows.

On 73 sts. work 1 row, marking the end of this row with a coloured thread.

Pattern 67 rows more, decreasing 1 st. at the front edge on every 4th row as before – 56 sts.

On 56 sts. pattern 47 rows.

To slope the shoulder: Cast off 9 sts. at the beginning of the next row and the 4 following alternate rows.

On 11 sts. work 1 row, then cast off.

THE RIGHT FRONT

Work as given for left front noting the variation in the rows before sloping the front edge.

THE POCKET TOPS (2 alike)

As given for "Happy Birthday" cardigan.

THE FRONT BAND

First join shoulder seams. With size 2¼mm. (No. 13) needles and m. cast on 12 sts. and work 6 rows. in single rib.

1st Buttonhole row: Rib 4, cast off 4, rib to end.

2nd Buttonhole row: Rib 4, turn, cast on 4, turn, rib to end.

Rib 24 rows.

Repeat the last 26 rows twice more, then work the 2 buttonhole rows again.

Continue in rib until the band is long enough to fit up right front with last buttonhole in line with first front edge dec., across back neck edge and down left front. Sew in place, casting off when correct length is assured.

TO COMPLETE

Do not press silk items, but for other "Woollybear" yarns pin out to size and press all parts except the ribbing with a warm iron over a damp cloth. Sew cast off edges of sleeves to the row ends of back and front between the marking threads. Join sleeve seams up to the marking threads. Sew side pieces in position so that the marking threads match up with those on back and front and the shaped row ends above the marking threads are sewn to the sleeves down to the marking threads. Sew pocket backs and row ends of pocket tops in place. Sew on buttons.

happy birthday

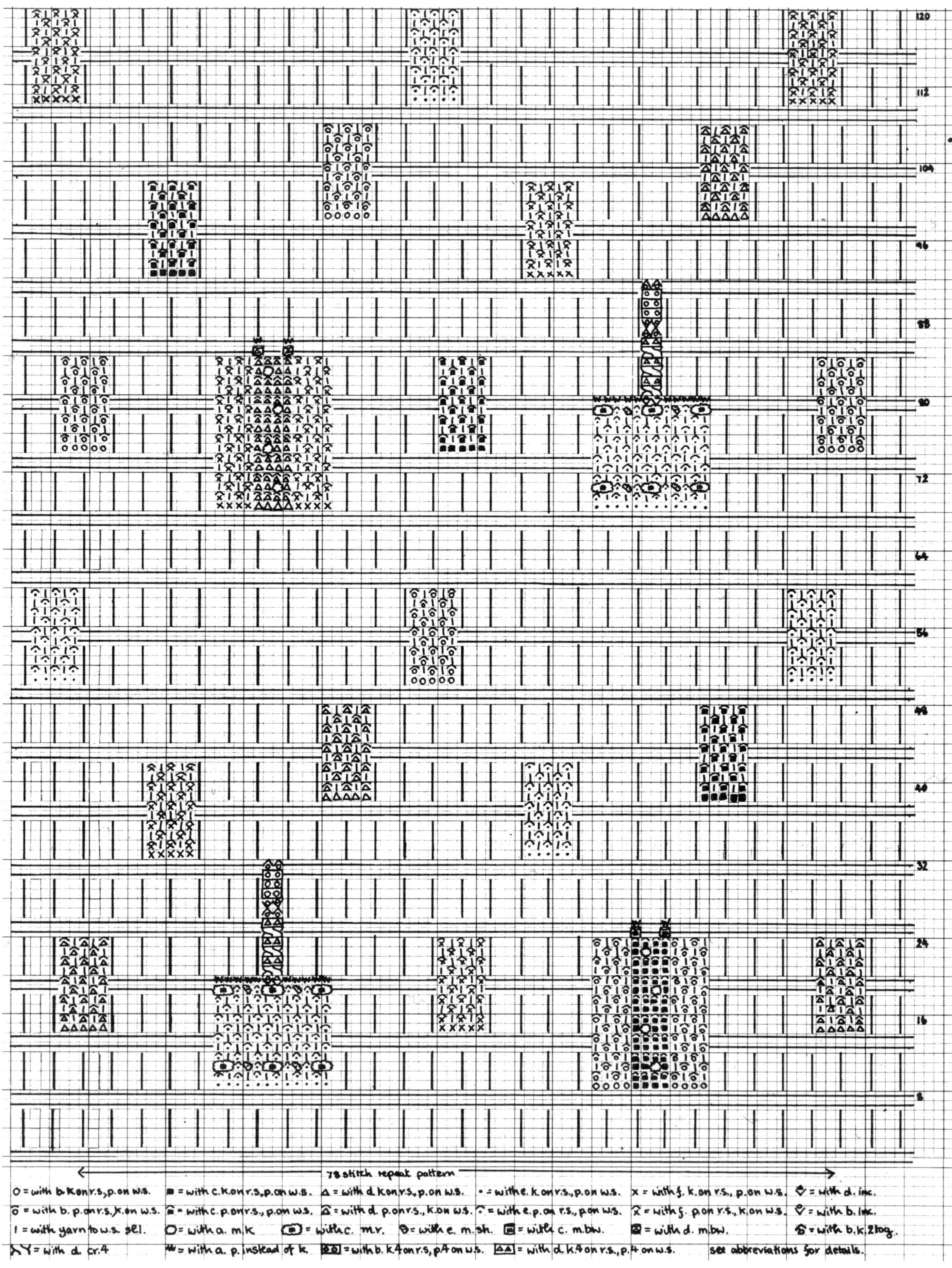

happy birthday

Grey suit by Kamikaze from Patricia Roberts, Covent Garden. Navy trousers and white shirt from Browns.

happy birthday

MATERIALS
Any of the following "Woollybear Yarns" by Patricia Roberts may be used for this design. For simplification the yarn amounts are given for the sweater, followed by those for the cardigan in the first brackets and those for the waistcoat in the second brackets.

"Woollybear Real Shetland" in 28 gram (ounce) hanks: 8 (8) (5) in main colour, 8 (8) (5) hanks in first contrast; 1 (1) (1) hank in second, fourth, fifth and sixth contrasts and 2 (2) (1) hank(s) in third contrast. "Woollybear 100% Mohair" may be used for the second, fifth and sixth contrasts, 2 (2) (1) 25 gram balls in each colour will be required.

"Woollybear Pure Silk" in 25 gram balls: 11 (11) (7) in main colour, 10 (10) (6) balls in first contrast; 2 (2) (1) balls in second, fourth, fifth and sixth contrasts and 3 (3) (2) balls in third contrast.

"Woollybear Fine Cotton" in 25 gram balls: 14 (14) (8) in main colour, 13 (13) (7) balls in first contrast; 2 (2) (1) balls in second, fourth, fifth and sixth contrasts and 3 (3) (2) balls in third contrast.

For any of the garments a pair each of size 2¼ mm. (No. 13) and size 2¾ mm. (No. 12) Aero knitting needles; a fine cable needle. For the cardigan 6 buttons, for the waistcoat 4 buttons.

TENSION
18 stitches and 34 rows to 5 centimetres (2 inches) over the chequer board pattern using size 2¾ mm. (No. 12) needles. If you cannot obtain the correct tension using the size needles suggested use larger or smaller ones accordingly.

ABBREVIATIONS
K., knit; p., purl; st., stitch; tog., together; dec., decrease (by working 2 sts. tog.); inc., increase (by working twice into same st.); single rib is k. 1 and p. 1 alternately; sl., slip; y.r.n., yarn round needle; m., main colour; a., first contrast; b., second contrast; c., third contrast; d., fourth contrast; e., fifth contrast; f., sixth contrast; y.f., yarn forward; y.b., yarn back; m.r., make rosette thus, with c. k. 1, y.r.n., k. 1 into each of next 2 sts., turn, k. 6, turn, k. 1, cast off 4, turn, k. 1, y.r.n., k. 1 into each of the remaining 2 sts., turn, with e. (sl. 1, k. 2 tog., p.s.s.o.) twice; p.s.s.o., pass sl. st. over; m.k., make knot thus, with a. k. 1 and p. 1, into same st., turn, k. 2, with either c. or d. as appropriate k. 2 tog.; m.sh., make shell thus, with e. k. 1, y.r.n., k. 1 all into same st., turn, k. 3, turn, cast off 2; cr. 4, cross 4 thus, sl. next 2 sts. onto cable needle and leave at front of work, with d. k. 2, then k. 2 from cable needle; m.bw., make bow thus, with with c. or d. as appropriate, k. 1, y.r.n., k. 1, y.r.n., k. 1 all into same st., turn, k. 5, turn, k. 1, with a. m.k., with c. or d. k. 3, (turn, k. 5) 3 times, turn, k. 3, with a. m.k., with c. or d. k. 1, (turn, k. 5) 3 times, turn, pass 2nd, 3rd, 4th and 5th sts. over 1st st. on left hand needle, with m., k. this st.; s.s., stocking stitch is k. on the right side and p. on the wrong side; ws., wrong side; r.s., right side.

MEASUREMENTS
The measurements are given in centimetres followed by inches in brackets.

	Sweater	Cardigan
Underarms	95 (38)	97.5 (39)
Side seam	40 (16)	30 (12)
Length	70 (28)	60 (24)
Sleeve seam	35 (14)	30 (12)
	Waistcoat	
Underarms	97.5 (39)	
Side seam	30 (12)	
Length	51 (20½)	

THE SWEATER

THE BACK
With size 2¼mm. (No. 13) needles and m. cast on 143 sts. and work 33 rows in single rib.

Increase row: Rib 4, *up 1, rib 5; repeat from * ending last repeat rib 4. – 171 sts.

Change to size 2¾ mm. (No. 12) needles and work in pattern as follows: Use separate small balls and lengths of contrast colours for each motif so that colours not in use are not taken across the back of the work.

1st and 2nd rows: With m. all k.

3rd row: With a. k. 1, *sl. 1, k. 2; repeat from * ending last repeat k. 1.

4th row: With a. k. 1, *y.f., sl. 1, y.b., k. 2; repeat from * ending last repeat k. 1.

5th and 6th rows: As 3rd and 4th rows.

The last 6 rows form the chequer board pattern, which forms a background to the motifs, continue as follows.

7th and 8th rows: As 1st and 2nd rows.

9th row: (With a. k. 1, sl. 1, k. 1) 7 times, *with b. k. 4, with c. k. 4, with b. k. 4, (with a. k. 1, sl. 1, k. 1) 9 times, with e. k. 12, (with a. k. 1, sl. 1, k. 1) 9 times; repeat from * but working instructions in last brackets 7 times instead of 9.

10th row: (With a. k. 1, y.f., sl. 1, y.b., k. 1) 7 times, *(with e. y.b., k. 1, y.f., sl. 1) 6 times, (with a. k. 1, y.f., sl. 1, y.b., k. 1) 9 times, with b. k. 1, y.f., sl. 1, y.b., k. 1, y.f., sl. 1, with c. k. 4, with b. k. 1, y.f., sl. 1, y.b., k. 1, y.f., sl. 1, (with a. k. 1, y.f., sl. 1, y.b., k. 1) 9 times; repeat from * ending by working instructions in last brackets 7 times.

11th row: (With a. k. 1, sl. 1, k. 1) 7 times, *with b. p. 1, y.b., sl. 1, y.f., p. 1, y.b., sl. 1, with c. k. 1, with a. m.k. – see abbreviations –, with c. k. 2, with b. p. 1, y.b., sl. 1, y.f., p. 1, y.b., sl. 1, (with a. k. 1, sl. 1, k. 1) 9 times, with c. m.r. – see abbreviations, (with e. p. 1, m.sh. – see abbreviations, p. 1, with c. m.r.) twice, (with a. k. 1, sl. 1, k. 1) 9 times; repeat from * ending by working instructions in last brackets 7 times.

12th row: As 10th row.

13th row: With m. k. 21, *with b. p. 1, y.b., sl. 1, y.f., p. 1, y.b., sl. 1, with c. k. 4, with b. p. 1, y.b., sl. 1, y.f., p. 1, y.b., sl. 1, with m. k. 27, (with e. y.f., p. 1, y.b., sl. 1) 6 times, with m. k. 27; repeat from * ending with m. k. 21 instead of 27.

14th row: With m. k. 21, (with e. y.b., k. 1, y.f., sl. 1) 6 times, with m. k. 27, with b. k. 1, y.f., sl. 1, y.b., k. 1, y.f., sl. 1, with c. k. 4, with b. k. 1, y.f., sl. 1, y.b., k. 1, y.f., sl. 1, with m. k. 27; repeat from * ending with m. k. 21.

15th row: With a. k. 1, sl. 1, k. 2, sl. 1, with d. k. 5, *sl. 1, (with a. k. 2, sl. 1) 3 times, with a. k. 1, with b. p. 1, y.b., sl. 1, y.f., p. 1, y.b., sl. 1, with c. k. 2, with a. m.k., with c. k. 1, with b. p. 1, y.b., sl. 1, y.f., p. 1, y.b., sl. 1, (with a. k. 1, sl. 1, k. 1) 3 times, with a. k. 1, sl. 1, with f. k. 5, sl. 1, (with a. k. 2, sl. 1) 3 times, with a. k. 1, (with e. y.f., p. 1, y.b., sl. 1) 6 times, with a. k. 1, (sl. 1, k. 2) 3 times, sl. 1, with d. k. 5; repeat from *, then sl. 1, with a. k. 2, sl. 1, k. 2.

To simplify the instructions, the 6 row chequer board pattern in m. and a. will be referred to as c.b. and the full instructions for the motifs only will be given in the following rows.

16th row: C.b. 5, with d. k. 1, (y.f., sl. 1, y.b., k. 1) twice, *c.b. 11, (with e. y.b., k. 1, y.f., sl. 1) 6 times, **c.b. 11, with f. k. 1, (y.f., sl. 1, y.b, k. 1) twice, c.b. 11, with b. k. 1, y.f., sl. 1, y.b., k. 1, y.f., sl. 1, with c. k. 4, with b. k. 1, y.f., sl. 1, y.b., k. 1, y.f., sl. 1, c.b. 11, with d. k. 1, (y.f., sl. 1, y.b., k. 1) twice**; repeat from *, then c.b. 5.

17th row: C.b. 5, with d. y.b., sl. 1, (y.f., p. 1, y.b., sl. 1) twice, *c.b. 11, with b. p. 1, y.b., sl. 1, y.f., p. 1, y.b., sl. 1, with c. k. 4, **with b. p. 1, y.b., sl. 1, y.f., p. 1, y.b., sl. 1, c.b. 11, with f. y.b., sl. 1, (y.f, p. 1, y.b., sl. 1) twice, c.b. 11**, (with e. y.f., p. 1, y.b., sl. 1) 6 times, c.b. 11, with d. y.b., sl. 1, (y.f., p. 1, y.b., sl. 1) twice; repeat from *, then c.b. 5.

18th row: As 16th row.

19th row: C.b. 5, with d. y.b., sl. 1, (y.f., p. 1, y.b., sl. 1) twice, *c.b. 11, with b. p. 1, y.b., sl. 1, y.f., p. 1, y.b., sl. 1, with c. k. 1, with a. m.k., with c. k. 2, work as for 17th row from ** to **, with c. m.r., (with e. p. 1, m.sh., p. 1, with c. m.r) twice, c.b. 11, with d. (y.b., sl. 1, y.f., p. 1, y.b., sl. 1) twice; repeat from *, then c.b. 5.

20th row: C.b. 5, with d. k. 1, (y.f., sl. 1, y.b., k. 1) twice, *c.b. 11, with m. p. 5, with d. inc. in each of next 2 sts., with m. p. 5; work as given for 16th row from ** to **; repeat from *, then c.b. 5.

The last 20 rows set the position of the pattern and method of working given in the chart, note that the chequer board pattern, given in full in the first 6 rows, is only indicated in the chart – by the straight lines. Work the 21st to 120th rows from the chart as set, then work the first 100 rows again.

To shape the raglan armholes: Continuing in pattern as set, cast off 3 sts. at the beginning of the next 2 rows, then dec. 1 st. at each end of the next row and the 18 following 6th rows.

Work 5 rows. ***

Dec. 1 st. at each end of the next row and the 11 following 4th rows, then on the 20 following alternate rows.

On 63 sts. work 1 row.

THE FRONT
Work as given for back until *** is reached.

Dec. 1 st. at each end of the next row and the 9 following alternate rows. – 107 sts.

Now divide the sts. for the neck: Next row: Pattern 40 and leave these sts. on a spare needle until required for right front shoulder, cast off 27, pattern to end and continue on these 40 sts. for the left front shoulder.

****The left front shoulder: To shape the neck and to slope the raglan: Continuing to slope the raglan on every alternate row, dec. 1 st. at the neck edge on each of the next 18 rows. – 13 sts.

Pattern 22 rows decreasing 1 st. at the shoulder edge on every alternate row as before.

Take the 2 remaining sts. tog. and fasten off.

The right front shoulder: With right side of work facing rejoin yarn to inner edge of sts. left on spare needle and work to end of row, then work as given for left front shoulder to end.

THE LEFT SLEEVE
With size 2¼ mm. (No. 13) needles and m. cast on 93 sts. and work 44 rows in single rib.

Change to size 2¾ mm. (No. 12) needles and noting the information given for back – in particular the 6 chequer board pattern rows – work the 49th to 70th pattern rows as given for back.

Continuing in pattern as set and working the extra sts. into the pattern as they occur, inc. 1 st. at each end of the next row and the 16 following 8th rows.

On 127 sts. work 19 rows.

Work 1 extra row here, when working right sleeve.

To shape the raglan sleevetop: Work as given for back until *** is reached.

**Dec. 1 st. at each end of the next row, then at the beginning only on the following alternate row. Work 1 row straight.

Repeat the last 4 rows 10 times more. – 50 sts.

Dec. 1 st. at each end of the next row and the 8 following alternate rows.

On 32 sts. work 1 row, marking the end of the last row with a coloured thread.

Dec. 1 st. at each end of the next row, then at the end only on the following row. Repeat the last 2 rows 9 times more. – 2 sts.

K. 2, then k. 2 tog. and fasten off.

THE RIGHT SLEEVE
Work as given for left sleeve, noting the variation in the number of rows before shaping the sleevetop.

THE NECKBAND
First join front raglan seams, so that the marking threads on the sleeves match with the top of the front points, then join right back raglan seam, noting that the row ends above the marking threads on front of sleeves form part of neck edge. With right side of work facing rejoin m. at top of left sleeve and using size 2¼ mm. (No. 13) needles pick up and k. 12 sts. from row ends of sleevetop up to marking thread, 20 sts. from left front neck edge, 20 sts. from centre front neck, 20 sts. from right front neck edge, 12 sts. from row ends of right sleevetop, then 56 sts. from back neck edge.

On 140 sts. work 9 rows in single rib, then cast off.

THE POCKET BACKS (2 alike)
With size 2¾ mm. (No. 12) needles and b. cast on 40 sts. and s.s. 50 rows, then cast off.

TO COMPLETE
Do not press silk garments. For other yarns pin out to size – see measurements – and press all parts lightly except the ribbing on the wrong side with a warm iron over a damp cloth. Join left back raglan seam. Neatly sew one row end edge of each pocket to each side of back 10 centimetres (4 inches) above cast on edge. Join sleeve and side seams, neatly sewing pocket backs in place on wrong side of front.

THE CARDIGAN

THE BACK
Work as given for back of sweater until the 120 pattern rows have been worked, then work the first 38 rows again.

To shape the raglan armholes: Work as given for back of sweater.

THE POCKET BACKS (2 alike)
With size 2¼ mm. (No. 13) needles and m. cast on 37 sts. and s.s. 34 rows, then leave these sts. on a stitch-holder until required.

THE LEFT FRONT
With size 2¼ mm. (No. 13) needles and m. cast on 72 sts. and work 33 rows in single rib.

Increase row: Rib 1, *up 1, rib 5; repeat from * ending last repeat rib 1. – 87 sts.

* * *Change to size 2¾ mm. (No. 12) needles and work the first 8 pattern rows as given for back of sweater.

9th row: (With a. k.1, sl.1, k.1) 7 times, with b. k.4, with c. k.4, with b. k.4, (with a. k.1, sl.1, k.1) 9 times, with e. k.12, (with a. k.1, sl.1, k.1) 5 times.

The last row sets the position of the pattern given for the back of the sweater, work the 10th to 60th pattern rows as set.

* *Pocket row: Pattern 25 as set, slip next 37 sts. onto a stitch-holder and leave at front of work, in their place pattern across the 37 sts. of one pocket back, pattern to end.

Now work the 62nd to 120th pattern rows as set, then work the first 38 rows again. Work 1 extra row here when working right front.

To slope the raglan armhole: Continuing in pattern as set, cast off 3 sts. at the beginning of the next row; work 1 row straight.

Dec. 1 st. at the beginning of the next row and the 18 following 6th rows.

On 65 sts. work 5 rows.

Dec. 1 st. at the beginning of the next row and the 9 following alternate rows. – 55 sts.

To shape the neck and continue to slope the raglan: Cast off 15 sts. at the beginning of the next row, then work as given for left front shoulder of sweater from * * * * to end.

THE RIGHT FRONT
Work as given for left front until the first 8 pattern rows have been worked.

9th row: (With a. k.1, sl.1, k.1) 5 times, with b. k.4, with c. k.4, with b. k.4, (with a. k.1, sl.1, k.1) 9 times, with e. k.12, (with a. k.1, sl.1, k.1) 7 times.

The last row sets the position of the pattern, given for the back of the sweater, work the 10th to 60th rows as set.

Now work as given for left front from * * to end, noting the variation in the rows, before sloping the raglan.

THE POCKET TOPS (both alike)
With right side of work facing rejoin m. to the 37 sts. left on stitch-holder and k.1 row, then work 5 rows in single rib, then cast off in rib.

THE BUTTONHOLE BAND
With size 2¼ mm. (No. 13) needles and m. cast on 12 sts. and work 8 rows in single rib.

1st Buttonhole row: Rib 4, cast off 4, rib to end.

2nd Buttonhole row: Rib 4, turn, cast on 4, turn, rib to end.

Rib 40 rows.

Repeat the last 42 rows 4 times more, then work the 2 buttonhole rows again.

Rib 8 rows, then cast off in rib.

THE BUTTONBAND
With size 2¼ mm. (No. 13) needles and m. cast on 12 sts. and work 228 rows in single rib, then cast off.

THE LEFT SLEEVE
With size 2¼ mm. (No. 13) needles and m. cast on 99 sts. and work 43 rows in single rib.

Increase row: Rib 1, *up 1, rib 3; repeat from * ending last repeat rib 2. – 132 sts.

Change to size 2¾ mm. (No. 12) needles and work the first 8 pattern rows given for back of sweater.

9th row: (With a. k.1, sl.1, k.1) 7 times, with b. k.4, with c. k.4, with b. k.4, (with a. k.1, sl.1, k.1) 9 times, with e. k.12, (with a. k.1, sl.1, k.1) 9 times, with b. k.4, with c. k.4, with b. k.4, (with a. k.1, sl.1, k.1) 7 times.

The last row sets the position of the pattern given in the chart, now work the 10th to 120th rows as set, then work the first 38 rows again.

To shape the raglan sleevetop: Cast off 3 sts. at the beginning of the next 2 rows, then dec. 1 st. at each end of the next row and the 15 following 6th rows, then on the 5 following 4th rows.

Work 1 row straight, dec. 1 st. at the beginning only on the next row, then work 1 row more. – 83 sts.

Now work as given for sleevetop on sweater from * * to end.

THE RIGHT SLEEVE
Work as given for left sleeve until the 120 pattern rows have been worked, then work the first 8 rows again.

Break off m., join in c.

Decrease row: K.2, *k.2tog., k.7; repeat from * ending last repeat k.2. – 117 sts.

K.3 rows.

Work in spot pattern as follows: 1st row: With c. k.4, *with a. m.k., with c. k.5; repeat from * ending last repeat k.4.

2nd, 3rd and 4th rows: With c. all k.

5th row: With c. k.1, *with a. m.k., with c. k.5; repeat from * ending last repeat k.1.

6th, 7th and 8th rows: With c. all k.

9th to 12th rows: As 1st to 4th rows.

Break off c., join in m.

Increase row: K.2, *up 1, k.8; repeat from * ending last repeat k.3. – 132 sts.

Next row: With m. all k.

Now work in pattern as follows: Next row: With a. k.1, sl.1, (k.2, sl.1) 11 times, with e. k.5, sl.1, (with a. k.2, sl.1) 11 times, with f. k.5, sl.1, (with a. k.2, sl.1) 11 times, with e. k.5, sl.1, (with a. k.2, sl.1) 4 times, k.1.

The last row sets the position of the pattern, now work the 34th to 39th rows as set.

To shape the raglan sleevetop: Work as given for left sleeve.

THE NECKBAND
First join raglan seams, matching the marking threads on sleeves with the top of the front points, so that the row ends above the marking threads form part of the neck edge. With right side of work facing rejoin m. and using size 2¼ mm. (No. 13) needles pick up and k.31 sts. from right front neck edge, 12 sts. from top of right sleeve, 56 sts. from back neck edge, 12 sts. from top of left sleeve and 31 sts. from left front neck edge.

On 142 sts. work 9 rows in single rib, then cast off.

THE BOW (2 pieces alike)
With size 2¼ mm. (No. 13) needles and c. cast on 81 sts. and k.3 rows.

Work the 12 spot pattern rows given for right sleeve, then cast off.

TO COMPLETE
Press as for sweater – not silk items. Join sleeve and side seams. Sew button and buttonhole bands in place. Neatly sew pocket backs and row ends of pocket tops in position. Sew on buttons. Sew one row end edge of each bow piece in place at centre of spotted part of right sleeve. Tie bow.

THE WAISTCOAT

THE BACK
Work as given for the back of the sweater until the 120 pattern rows have been worked, then work the first 34 rows again.

To shape the armholes: Continuing in pattern as set, cast off 7 sts. at the beginning of the next 2 rows, then dec. 1 st. at each end of the next row and the 13 following alternate rows.

On 129 sts. pattern 105 rows.

To slope the shoulders: Cast off 8 sts. at the beginning of the next 10 rows.

Cast off the remaining 49 sts.

THE POCKET BACKS (2 alike)
As given for cardigan.

THE LEFT FRONT
Work as given for left front of cardigan until the 120 pattern rows have been worked.

**To slope the front edge: Continuing in pattern as set, dec. 1 st. at the end of the next row and the 5 following 6th rows.

On 81 sts. work 3 rows back to side seam edge.

To shape the armhole and continue to slope the front edge: Still decreasing at front edge on every 6th row, cast off 7 sts. at the beginning of the next row, then dec. 1 st. at the beginning of the 14 following alternate rows. On 55 sts. work 3 rows.

Dec. 1 st. at the end – front edge – on the next row and the 14 following 6th rows.

On 40 sts. pattern 17 rows.

To slope the shoulder: Cast off 8 sts. at the beginning of the next row and the 3 following alternate rows. On 8 sts. work 1 row, then cast off.

THE RIGHT FRONT
Work as given for right front of cardigan until 121 pattern rows have been worked, then work as given for left front of waistcoat from ** to end.

THE POCKET TOPS (2 alike)
As given for cardigan.

THE FRONT BAND
First join shoulder seams.

With size 2¼ mm. (No. 13) needles and m. cast on 12 sts. and work 6 rows in single rib.

1st Buttonhole row: Rib 4, cast off 4, rib to end.

2nd Buttonhole row: Rib 4, turn, cast on 4, turn, rib to end.

Rib 32 rows.

Repeat the last 34 rows twice more, then work the 2 buttonhole rows again.

Continue in rib until the band is long enough to fit up right front, with last buttonhole in line with first front edge decrease, across back neck edge and down left front. Sew in place, casting off when correct length is assured.

THE ARMBANDS (both alike)
With right side of work facing rejoin m. and using size 2¼ mm. (No. 13) needles pick up and k. 128 sts. from all round armhole edge. K.5 rows, then cast off.

TO COMPLETE
Press as for sweater – not silk items. Join side seams. Neatly sew pocket backs and row ends of pocket tops in place. Sew on buttons.

sugar plum

fairy

Woman's skirt by Forma

sugar plum

MATERIALS
Either 6(7)(8) 20 gram balls of "Woollybear Angora" by Patricia Roberts in main colour and 2 balls in each of 5 contrast colours or 5(6)(7) 28 gram (ounce) hanks of "Woollybear Real Shetland" in main colour and 2 hanks in each of 5 contrast colours or for summer 6(7)(8) 25 gram balls of "Woollybear Fine Cotton" in main colour and 2 balls in each of 5 contrast colours; a pair each of size 2¼mm. (No. 13) and size 2¾mm. (No. 12) Aero knitting needles; 6 buttons.

STOCKISTS
Woollybear Yarns are available from Patricia Roberts Knitting Shops at 31 James Street, Covent Garden, London W.C.2., 60 Kinnerton Street, London S.W.1. and 1b Kensington Church Walk, London W.8. Mail order is available from the last 2 shops. Please write enclosing a stamped self-addressed envelope for price list.

TENSION
16 stitches and 20 rows to 5 centimetres (2 inches) over the stocking stitch using size 2¾mm. (No. 12) needles. If you cannot obtain the correct tension using the size needles suggested, use larger or smaller needles accordingly.

ABBREVIATIONS
K., knit; p., purl; st., stitch; tog., together; dec., decrease (by working 2 sts. tog.); inc., increase (by working twice into same st.); single rib is k.1 and p.1 alternately; y.r.n., yarn round needle; s.s., stocking stitch is k. on the right side and p. on the wrong side; sl., slip; p.s.s.o., pass sl. st. over; up1, pick up the loop, which lies between the needles, slip it onto left hand needle, then k. into back of it; 5 from 1, k.1, y.r.n., k.1, y.r.n., k.1 all into next st.; m.b., make bobble, thus, with appropriate contrast colour, k.1, y.r.n., k.1 all into next st., turn, p.3, turn, k.3, turn, p.3, turn, sl.1, k.2 tog., p.s.s.o.; m., main colour; a., first contrast; b., second contrast; c., third contrast; d., fourth contrast; e., fifth contrast.

NOTE
The instructions are given for the first size. Where they vary, work the instructions in the first brackets for the second size or the instructions in the second brackets for the third size.

MEASUREMENTS
The measurements are given in centimetres followed by inches in brackets.

Underarms	55(22)	60.5(24¼)	66(26½)
Side seam	22.5(9)	25(10)	27.5(11)
Length	35.5(14¼)	39(15¾)	43(17¼)
Sleeve seam	24(9½)	26(10½)	29(11½)

THE POCKET BACKS (2 alike)
With size 2¾mm. (No. 12) needles and m. cast on 20 sts. and beginning with a k. row s.s. 28 rows, then leave these sts. on a stitch-holder until required.

THE MAIN PART
With size 2¼mm. (No. 13) needles and m. cast on 154(170)(186) sts. and work 29 rows in single rib.

Increase row: Rib 5, *up 1, rib 8; repeat from * ending last repeat rib 5. – 173 (191)(209) sts.

Change to size 2¾mm. (No. 12) needles and work in pattern as follows: Use short lengths or small balls of contrast colour for each individual motif.

1st row: With m. all k.

2nd row: With m. all p.

3rd row: With m. k.3, *with a. 5 from 1, with m. k.17; repeat from * ending last repeat with m. k.7.

4th row: With m. p.7, *with a. p.5, with m. p.17; repeat from * ending last repeat with m. p.3.

5th row: With m. k.3, *with a. k.5, with m. k.17; repeat from * ending last repeat with m. k.7.

6th row: As 4th row.

7th row: With m. k.3, *with a. sl.1, k.1, p.s.s.o., k.1, k.2 tog., with m. k.3, with a. 5 from 1, with m. k.13; repeat from * ending last repeat with m. k.3.

8th row: With m. p.3, *with a. p.5, with m. p.3, with a. p.3. tog., with m. p.13; repeat from * ending last repeat with m. p.3.

9th row: With m. k.3, *with b. k.1, with m. k.3, with a. k.5, with m. k.13; repeat from * ending last repeat with m. k.3.

10th row: With m. p.3, *with a. p.5, with m. p.3, with b. p.1, with m. p.13; repeat from * ending last repeat with m. p.3.

11th row: With m. k.3, *with m. up1, with b. k.1, with m. k.2 tog., k.1, with a. sl.1, k.1, p.s.s.o., k.1, k.2 tog., with m. k.13; repeat from * ending last repeat with m. k.3.

12th row: With m. p.3, *with a. p.3 tog., with m. p.2, with b. p.1, with m. p.14; repeat from * ending last repeat with m. p.4.

13th row: With m. k.4, *with m. up1, with b. k.1, with m. k.2 tog., with b. k.1, with m. k.14; repeat from * ending last repeat with m. k.3.

14th row: With m. p.3, *with b. p.1, with m. p.1, with b. p.1, with m. p.15; repeat from * ending last repeat p.5.

15th row: With m. k.5, *with m. up1, with b. sl.1, k.1, p.s.s.o., k.1, with m. k.15; repeat from *ending last repeat with m. k.3.

-16th row: With m. p.3, *with b. p.2, with m. p.16; repeat from * ending last repeat with m. p.6.

17th row: With m. k.6, *with m. up1, with b. sl.1, k.1, p.s.s.o., with m. k.16; repeat from * ending last repeat with m. k.3.

18th row: With m. all p.

19th row: With m. all k.

20th row: With m. all p.

21st row: With m. k.16, *with c. m.b., with m. k.17; repeat from * ending last repeat with m. k.12.

22nd row: With m. p.11, *with c. p.3, with m. p.15; repeat from * ending last repeat p.15.

23rd row: With m. k. 15, * with c. m.b., k.1, m.b., with m. k.15; repeat from *ending last repeat with m. k.11.

24th row: With m. p.10, *with c. p.5, with m. p. 13; repeat from * ending last repeat with m. p.14.

25th row: With m. k.14, *with c. m.b., k.1, m.b., k.1, m.b., with m. k.13; repeat from * ending last repeat with m. k.10.

26th row: With m. p.9, *with c. p.7, with m. p.11; repeat from * ending last repeat with m. p.13.

27th row: With m. k.13, *with c. m.b., k.1, m.b., k.1, m.b., k.1, m.b., with m. k.11; repeat from * ending last repeat with m. k.9.

28th and 29th rows: As 24th and 25th rows.

30th row: With m. p.11, *with b. p.3, with m. p.15; repeat from * ending last repeat with m. p.15.

31st row: With m. k.14, *with b. k.5, with m. k.13; repeat from * ending last repeat with m. k.10.

32nd row: With m. p.12, *with b.p.1, with m. p.17; repeat from * ending last repeat with m. p. 16.

33rd row: With m. k.16, *with b. k.1, with m. k.17; repeat from * ending last repeat with m. k.12.

34th row: As 32nd row.

The last 34 rows form the pattern. Continuing in pattern as set, but using d. instead of a. and e. instead of c. on every alternate pattern repeat, work as follows.

Pocket row: With m. k.12, *sl. next 20 sts. onto a stitch-holder and leave at front of work, in their place k. across the 20 sts. of one pocket back*, k.109 (127)(145) sts.; then repeat from * to *, k.12.

Pattern 30(40)(50) rows.

Now divide the sts. for the armholes: Next row: Pattern 41(45)(49) and leave these sts. on a spare needle until required for left half front, cast off 4(5)(6), work across next 82(90)(98) sts. and leave these 83(91)(99) sts. on a spare needle, until required for back, cast off 4(5) (6) sts., pattern to end and continue on these 41(45)(49) sts. for the right half front.

The right half front: To shape the armhole: Maintaining the continuity of the pattern as set, dec. 1 st. at the armhole edge on each of the next 7(8)(9) rows.

On 34(37)(40) sts. pattern 21(24)(25) rows.

To shape the neck: Cast off 6(7)(7) sts. at the beginning of the next row, then dec. 1 st. at the neck edge on each of the next 8(8)(9) rows.

On 20(22)(24) sts. work 10(12)(13) rows.

To slope the shoulder: Cast off 10(11)(12) sts. at the beginning of the next row. On 10(11)(12) sts. work 1 row, then cast off.

The back: With right side of work facing rejoin yarn to the 83(91)(99) sts. left on spare needle and work as follows.

To shape the armholes: Continuing in pattern as set, dec. 1 st. at each end of the next 7(8)(9) rows.

On 69(75)(81) sts. pattern 41(46)(49)rows.

To slope the shoulders: Cast off 10(11)(12) sts. at the beginning of the next 4 rows, then leave the remaining 29(31)(33) sts. on a spare needle until required for neckband.

The left half front: With right side of work facing rejoin yarn to inner edge of sts. left on spare needle and work to end of row, then work as given for right half front to end.

THE SLEEVES (both alike)
With size 2¼mm. (No. 13) needles and m. cast on 47(51)(55) sts. and work 18 rows in single rib.

Change to size 2¾mm. (No. 12) needles and beginning with a k. row s.s. 2 rows.

Now work in pattern as follows:

21st row: With m. k.5 (7)(9), *with e. m.b., with m. k.17; repeat from * ending last repeat k.5(7)(9).

The last row sets the position of the pattern given for the back. Pattern 7 rows more.

Continuing in pattern as set and working the extra sts. into the pattern as they occur, inc. 1 st. at each end of the next row and the 8 following 8th (8th)(10th) rows.

On 65(69)(73) sts. pattern 7 (17)(11) rows.

To shape the sleevetop: Cast off 2(3)(3) sts. at the beginning of the next 2 rows, then dec. 1 st. at each end of the next row and the 5(6)(8) alternate rows.

On 49 sts. work 1 row.

Dec. 1 st. at each end of the next 16 rows.

Cast off 3 sts. at the beginning of the next 4 rows. Cast off the remaining 5 sts.

THE POCKET TOPS (2 alike)
With right side of work facing rejoin m. to the 20 sts. left on stitch-holder and using size 2¼mm. (No. 13) needles work 6 rows in single rib, then cast off in rib.

THE NECKBAND
First join shoulder seams. With right side of work facing rejoin m. at right front neck edge and using size 2¼mm. (No. 13) needles pick up and k. 28(30)(31) sts. from right front neck edge, k. across the 29(31)(33) sts. left on spare needle at back neck edge, then pick up and k. 28(30)(31) sts. from left front neck edge.

On 85(91)(95) sts. work 5 rows in single rib, then cast off in rib.

THE BUTTONBAND
With size 2¼mm (No. 13) needles and m. cast on 6 sts. and work 132(146)(158) rows in single rib, then cast off in rib.

THE BUTTONHOLE BAND
With size 2¼mm. (No. 13) needles and m. cast on 6 sts. and work 6 (8)(10) rows in single rib.

1st Buttonhole row: Rib 2, cast off 2, rib to end.

2nd Buttonhole row: Rib 2, turn, cast on 2, turn, rib to end.

Rib 22(24)(26) rows.

Repeat the last 24(26)(28) rows 4 times more, then work the 2 buttonhole rows again.

Rib 4(6)(6) rows, then cast off.

TO MAKE UP THE CARDIGAN
Pin out to size and press all parts except the ribbing lightly on the wrong side with a warm iron over a damp cloth. Join sleeve seams. Set in sleeves. Sew button and buttonhole bands in place. Sew pocket backs and row ends of pocket tops in position. Sew on buttons.

fairy

MATERIALS
Either 15(16)(17) 25 gram balls of "Woollybear Lambswool" by Patricia Roberts in main colour and one 20 gram ball of "Woollybear Angora" in second contrast colour and 2 balls in each of the 3 other contrasts; or for a summer sweater 13(14)(15) 25 gram balls of "Woollybear Fine Cotton" by Patricia Roberts in main colour, 2 balls of the same yarn in second contrast colour and 3 balls in each of the 3 other contrasts. A pair each of size 2¼mm (No. 13) and 2¾mm (No. 12) Aero knitting needles.

TENSION
16 stitches and 20 rows to 5 centimetres (2 inches) over stocking stitch using size 2¾mm (No. 12) needles. If you cannot obtain the correct tension using the size needles suggested, use larger or smaller ones accordingly.

ABBREVIATIONS
K., knit; p., purl; st., stitch; tog., together; dec., decrease (by working 2 sts. tog.); inc., increase (by working twice into same st.); single rib is k.1 and p.1 alternately; s.s., stocking stitch is k. on the right side and p. on the wrong side; up 1, pick up the loop, which lies between the needles, slip it onto left hand needle, then k. into back of it; y.r.n., yarn round needle; sl., slip; p.s.s.o., pass sl.st. over; 5 from 1, k.1, y.r.n., k.1, y.r.n, k.1 all into next st.; m.b., make bobble thus, k.1, y.r.n., k.1, all into next st., turn p.3, turn, k.3, turn, p.3, turn, sl.1, k.2 tog., p.s.s.o.; m., main colour; a., first contrast colour; b., second contrast; c., third contrast; d., fourth contrast.

NOTE
The instructions are given for the small size. Where they vary, work the instructions in the first brackets for the medium size or the figures in the second brackets for the large size.

MEASUREMENTS
The measurements are given in centimetres followed by inches in brackets.

Sizes	Small	Medium	Large
Underarms	87.5(35)	92.5(37)	99(39½)
Side seam	40(16)	40(16)	40(16)
Length	61(24½)	62(24¾)	62.5(25)
Sleeve seam	42.5(17)	42.5(17)	42.5(17)

THE BACK
With size 2¼mm (No. 13) needles and m. cast on 128(136)(144) sts. and work 33 rows in single rib.

Increase row: Rib 10(14)(9), *up 1, rib 9; repeat from * ending last repeat rib 10(14)(9). – 141(149)(159) sts.

Change to size 2¾mm (No. 12) needles and work in pattern as follows. Use separate lengths of contrast colours for each motif, but leave sufficiently long ends to darn in at completion of work.

1st row: With m. all k.

2nd row: With m. all p.

3rd row: With m. k.9(13)(9), *with a. 5 from 1, with m. k.17; repeat from * ending last repeat k.5(9)(5).

4th row: With m. p.5(9)(5), * with a. p.5, with m. p.17; repeat from * ending last repeat p.9 (13)(9).

5th row: With m. k.9(13)(9), *with a. k.5, with m. p.17; repeat from * ending last repeat k.5(9)(5).

6th row: As 4th row.

7th row: With m. k.9(13)(9), *with a. sl.1, k.1, p.s.s.o., k.1, k.2 tog., with m. k.3, with a. 5 from 1, with m. k.13; repeat from * ending last repeat k.1(5)(1).

8th row: With m. p.1(5)(1), *with a. p.5, with m. p.3, with a. p.3 tog., with m. p.13; repeat from * ending last repeat with m. p.9 (13)(9).

9th row: With m. k.9(13)(9), *with b. k.1, with m. k.3, with a. k.5, with m. k.13; repeat from * ending last repeat with m.k.1(5)(1).

10th row: With m. p.1(5)(1), *with a. p.5, with m. p.3, with b. p.1, with m. p.13; repeat from * ending last repeat with m. p.9(13)(9).

11th row: With m. k.9(13)(9), *with m. up 1, with b.k.1, with m.k.2 tog. k.1, with a. sl.1, k.1, p.s.s.o., k.1, k.2 tog., with m. k.13; repeat from * ending last repeat k.1(5)(1).

12th row: With m. p.1(5)(1), *with a. p.3 tog., with m. p.2, with b. p.1, with m. p.14; repeat from * ending last repeat with m. p.10(14)(10).

13th row: With m. k.10(14)(10), *with m. up 1, with b. k.1, with m. k.2 tog., with b. k.1, with m. k.14; repeat from * cnding last repeat with m. k.1(5)(1).

14th row: With m. p.1(5)(1), *with b. p.1, with m. p.1, with b. p.1, with m. p.15; repeat from * ending last repeat p.11(15)(11).

15th row: With m. k.11(15)(11), *with m. up 1, with b. sl.1, k.1, p.s.s.o., k.1, with m. k.15; repeat from * ending last repeat with m. k.1(5)(1).

16th row: with m. p.1(5)(1), *with b. p.2, with m. p.16; repeat from * ending last repeat with m. p.12(16)(12).

17th row: With m. k.12(16)(12), *with m. up 1, with b. sl.1, k.1, p.s.s.o., with m. k.16; repeat from* ending last repeat with m. k.1(5)(1).

18th row: With m. all p.

19th row: With m. all k.

20th row: With m. all p.

21st row: With m. k.4(8)(4), *with c. m.b., with m. k.17; repeat from * ending last repeat with m. k.10(14)(10).

22nd row: With m. p.9(13)(9), *with c. p.3, with m. p.15; repeat from * ending last repeat with m. p.3(7)(3).

23rd row: With m. k.3(7)(3), *with c. m.b., k.1, m.b., with m. k.15; repeat from * ending last repeat with m. k.9(13)(9).

24th row: With m. p.8(12)(8), *with c. p.5, with m.p.13; repeat from *ending last repeat with m. p.2(6)(2).

25th row: With m. k.2(6)(2), *with c. m.b., k.1, m.b., k.1, m.b., with m. k.13; repeat from * ending last repeat with m. k.8 (12)(8).

26th row: With m. p.7 (11)(7), *with c. p.7, with m. p.11; repeat from * ending last repeat with m. p.1(5)(1).

27th row: With m. k.1(5)(1), *with c. m.b., k.1, m.b., k.1, m.b., k.1, m.b., with m. k.11; repeat from * ending last repeat with m. k.7(11)(7).

28th and 29th rows: As 24th and 25th rows.

30th row: With m. p.9(13)(9), *with b. p.3, with m. p.15; repeat from * ending last repeat with m. p.3(7)(3).

31st row: With m. k.2(6)(2), *with b. k.5, with m. k.13; repeat from * ending last repeat with m. k.8(12)(8).

32nd row: With m. p.10(14)(10), *with b. p.1, with m. p.17; repeat from * ending last repeat with m. p.4(8)(4).

33rd row: With m. k.4(8)(4), *with b. k.1, with m. k.17; repeat from * ending last repeat with m. k.10(14)(10).

34th row: As 32nd row.

The last 34 rows form the pattern; using d. instead of a. and a. instead of c. repeat the 34 pattern rows again, then using c. instead of a. and d. instead of c. repeat them once more, noting that b. is used for the stems throughout. The last 3 repeats of the pattern form the colour sequence.

Continuing in pattern in colour sequence as set, pattern 28 rows more.

To shape the armholes: Continuing in pattern as set, cast off 6(7)(8) sts. at the beginning of the next 2 rows, then dec. 1 st. at each end of the next 10(11)(12) rows.

On 109(113)(119) sts. pattern 66(67)(68) rows.

To slope the shoulders: Cast off 7(8)(9) sts. at the beginning of the next 4 rows, then 8 sts. on the 4 following rows.

Leave the remaining 49(49)(51) sts. on a spare needle until required for neckband.

THE FRONT
Work as given for the back, until the armhole shaping has been worked.

On 109(113)(119) sts. pattern 33(32)(31) rows.

Now divide the sts., for the neck: Next row: Counting the 5 sts. of the cherries as 1 st., pattern across 46(48)(50) sts. and leave these sts. on a spare needle until required for right front shoulder, then cast off 17(17)(19) sts., but working the 5 cherry sts. tog. as they occur, then pattern to end as set and continue on these 46(48)(50) sts. for the left front shoulder.

The left front shoulder: To shape the neck: Dec. 1 st. at the neck edge on each of the next 16 rows.

On 30(32)(34) sts. pattern 16(18)(20) rows.

To slope the shoulder: Cast off 7(8)(9) sts. at the beginning of the next row and the following alternate row, then 8 sts. on the next alternate row.

On 8 sts. work 1 row, then cast off.

The right front shoulder: With right side of work facing rejoin yarn and work to end of row, then work as given for left front shoulder to end.

THE SLEEVES (both alike)
With size 2¼mm (No. 13) needles and m. cast on 64 sts. and work 27 rows in single rib.

Increase row: Rib 8, *up 1, rib 12; repeat from * ending last repeat rib 8. – 69 sts.

Change to size 2¾mm (No. 12) needles and beginning with the 19th pattern row, work 10 rows in pattern as given for first size on back.

Continuing in pattern as set and working the extra sts. into the pattern as they occur, inc. 1 st. at each end of the next row and the 13(15)(17) following 10th(8th)(6th) rows.

On 97(101)(105) sts. pattern 5(15)(33) rows.

To shape the sleeve top: Cast off 6(7)(8) sts. at the beginning of the next 2 rows, then dec. 1 st. at each end of the next row and the 19(20)(21) following alternate rows.

On 45 sts. work 1 row.

Cast off 3 sts. at the beginning of the next 4 rows, 4 sts. on the 4 following rows, then 5 sts. on the next 2 rows. Cast off the remaining 7 sts.

THE POCKET BACKS (2 alike)
With size 2¼mm (No. 12) needles and m. cast on 40 sts. and work 50 rows in s.s., then cast off.

THE NECKBAND
First join right shoulder seam. With right side of work facing pick up and k. 40(42)(44) sts. from left front neck edge, 17(17)(19) sts. from centre front neck, and 40(42)(44) sts. from right front neck edge, then k. across the 49(49)(51) sts. left on spare needle at back neck edge.

On 146(150)(158) sts. work 9 rows in single rib. Cast off in rib.

TO MAKE UP THE SWEATER
Pin out to size and press all parts except the ribbing lightly with a warm iron over a damp cloth. Join left shoulder seam. Set in sleeves. Neatly sew one row end edge of each pocket back to each side of back – 2.5 centimetres (1 inch) above ribbing. Join sleeve and side seams, neatly slip stitching around pocket back on wrong side of front.

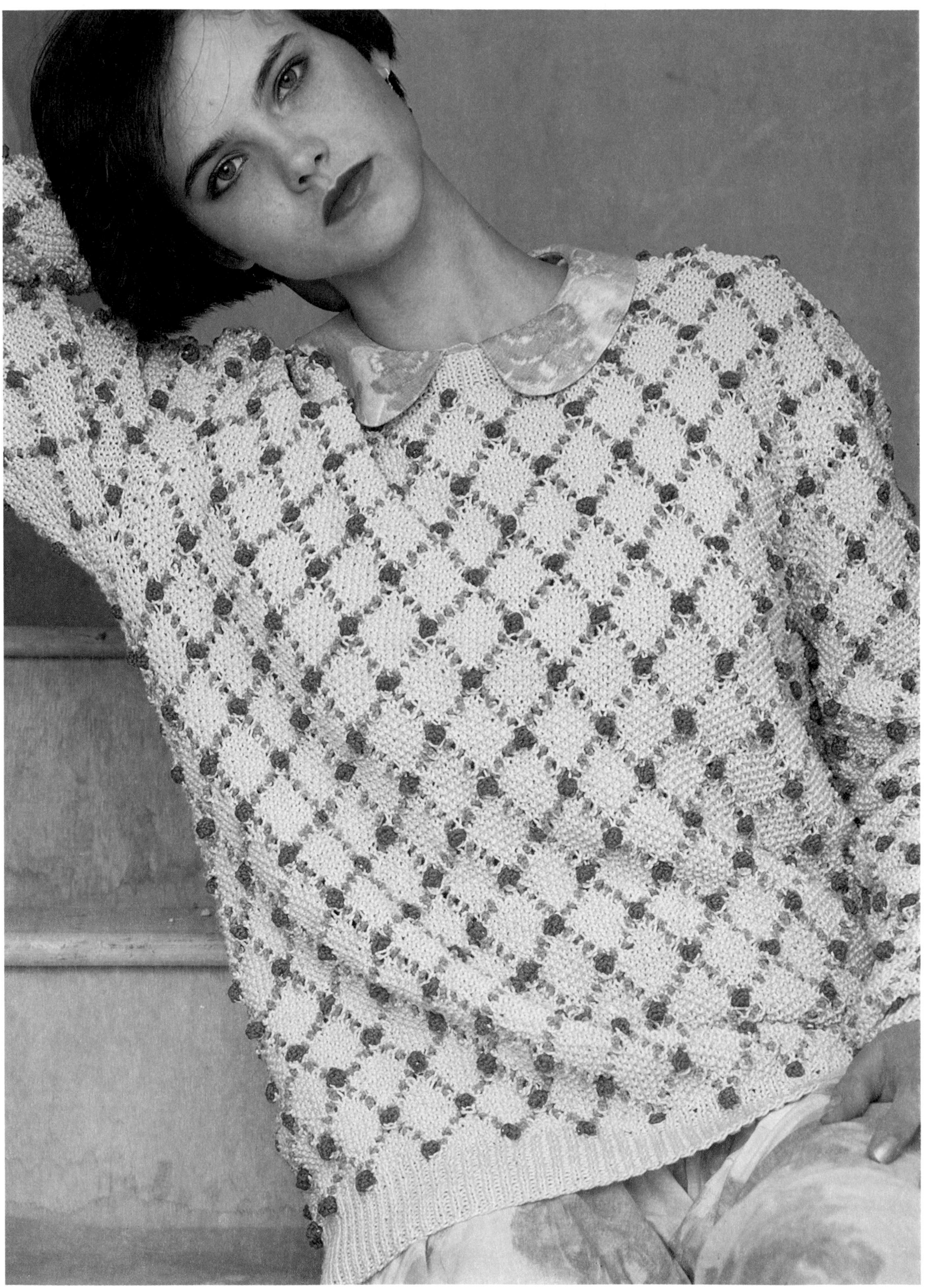

zelda

Shirt and culottes by Steven Lingard

zelda

zelda

MATERIALS

Either 14 50 gram balls of "Woollybear Cotton Crepe" by Patricia Roberts in main colour, 3 balls in first contrast and 5 balls in 2nd contrast or 17 20 gram balls of "Woollybear Angora" in main colour, 4 balls in first contrast and 6 balls in 2nd contrast; a pair each of size 3¼mm (No. 10) and size 3¾mm (No. 9) Aero knitting needles.

TENSION

Work at a tension of 20 sts. – 2 repeats of the pattern, to 9 centimetres (3½ inches) in width and 18 rows to 5 centimetres (2 inches) in length over the rosebud pattern using size 3¾mm. (No. 9) needles. If you cannot obtain the correct tension using the size needles suggested, use larger or smaller ones accordingly.

ABBREVIATIONS

K., knit; p., purl; st., stitch; tog., together; dec., decrease (by working 2 sts. tog.); inc., increase (by working twice into same st.); single rib is k. 1 and p. 1 alternately; m., main colour; a., first contrast; b., second contrast; m.b., make bobble thus, with a. k. 1, p. 1, k. 1, p. 1 all into next st., turn, k. 4, turn, p. 4, turn, k. 4, pass 2nd, 3rd and 4th sts. on left hand needle over first st., then with m. k. this st. Knot ends in a. leaving sufficiently long ends to darn in at completion of work; ch. 5, chain st. 5 thus, *with b. k. next st., then slip st. just made onto left hand needle, repeat from * 4 times, with m. k. 1, – when working chain sts. pull b. firmly throughout.

MEASUREMENTS

The measurements are given in centimetres followed by inches in brackets.

	Small		Medium	
Underarms	95	(39)	106	(42½)
Side seam	42.5	(17)	42.5	(17)
Length	65	(26)	65	(26)
Sleeve seam	40	(16)	40	(16)

THE BACK

With size 3¼mm. (No. 10) needles and m. cast on 101(111) sts. and work 19 rows in single rib.

Increase row: Rib 7(12), *up 1, rib 8; repeat from * ending last repeat rib 6(11). – 113(123) sts.

Change to size 3¾mm. (No. 9) needles and work in pattern as follows: Use separate balls of b. for each diagonal line of chain sts. so that contrast colours are not taken across the back of the work, when not in use. Note that a. is broken off after working each bobble and the ends firmly knotted.

1st row: With m. p. 1, *with a. m.b. – see abbreviations, with m. p. 1, k. 1, p. 1, k. 1, p. 1, k. 1, p. 1, k. 1, p. 1; repeat from * ending last repeat p. 1.

2nd row and every wrong side row: With m. p. 1, *k. 1, p. 1; repeat from * to end..

3rd row: with m. p. 1, k. 1, *with b. ch. 5, with m. k. 1, p. 1, k. 1, p. 1, k. 1, p. 1, k. 1, with b. ch. 5, with m. k. 1; repeat from * until 1 remains, p. 1.

5th row: * With m. p. 1, k. 1, p. 1, with b. ch. 5, with m. p. 1, k. 1, p. 1, k. 1, p. 1, with b. ch. 5; repeat from * until 3 remain, with m. p. 1, k. 1, p. 1.

7th row: With m. p. 1, k. 1, *p. 1, k. 1, with b. ch. 5, with m. k. 1, p. 1, k. 1, with b. ch. 5, with m. k. 1, p. 1, k. 1; repeat from * ending last repeat p. 1 more.

9th row: With m. p. 1, k. 1, *p. 1, k. 1, p. 1, with b. ch. 5, with m. p. 1, with b. ch. 5, with m. p. 1, k. 1, p. 1, k. 1; repeat from * ending last repeat p. 1 more.

11th row: With m. p. 1, k. 1, *p. 1, k. 1, p. 1, k. 1, with a. m.b., with m. k. 1, p. 1, k. 1, p. 1, k. 1; repeat from * ending last repeat p. 1 more

13th to 20th rows: work 9th row back to 2nd row.

The last 20 rows form the pattern; repeat them 5 times, then work the first 6 rows again.

To shape the armholes: Continuing in pattern as set, cast off 4(5) sts. at the beginning of the next 2 rows, then dec. 1 st. at each end of the next row and the 8(9) following alternate rows.

On 87(93) sts. pattern 25 rows.

Inc. 1 st. at each end of the next row and the following 8th rows.

On 91(97) sts. work 19 rows.

To slope the shoulders: Cast off 7 sts. at the beginning of the next 4 rows, then 7(8) sts. on the 4 following rows. – 35(37) sts.

Change to size 3¼mm. (No. 10) needles and with m. only, work 8 rows in single rib, then cast off.

THE FRONT

Work as given for the back until the armhole shaping rows have been worked.

On 87(93) sts. pattern 24 rows.

Now divide the sts. for the neck: Next row: Pattern 36(38) sts. and leave these sts. on a spare needle until required for right front shoulder, cast off 15(17), pattern to end and continue on these 36(38) sts. for the left front shoulder.

The left front shoulder: To shape the neck and the armhole: Work 10 rows, decreasing 1 st. at the neck edge on every row and at the same time increasing 1 st. at the armhole edge on the first and 9th of these rows.

On 28(30) sts. work 18 rows.

To slope the shoulder: Cast off 7 sts. at the beginning of the next row and the following alternate row, then 7(8) sts. on the next alternate row.

On 7(8) sts. work 1 row, then cast off.

The right front shoulder: With right side of work facing rejoin yarn to inner edge of sts. left on spare needle and work to end of row, then work as given for left front shoulder to end.

THE FRONT NECKBAND

With right side of work facing rejoin m. at left front neck edge and using size 3¼mm. (No. 10) needles pick up and k. 29 sts. from left front neck edge, 15(17) sts. from centre front neck, then 29 sts. from right front neck edge. – 73(75) sts.

Work 7 rows in single rib, then cast off in rib.

THE SLEEVES (both alike)

With size 3¼mm. (No. 10) needles and m. cast on 53 sts. and work 14 rows in single rib.

Change to size 3¾mm. (No. 9) needles and work 20 rows in pattern as given for back.

Continuing in pattern and working the extra sts. into the pattern as they occur, inc. 1 st. at each end of the next row and the 9(12) following 10th (8th) rows.

On 73(79) sts. pattern 15(9) rows.

To shape the sleevetop: Cast off 4(5) sts. at the beginning of the next 2 rows, then dec. 1 st. at each end of the next row and the 11 following 4th rows, then the 2(3) following alternate rows.

On 37(39) sts. work 1 row.

Dec. 1 st. at each end of the next 4 rows, then cast off 3 sts. at the beginning of the 4 following rows and 5 sts. on the next 2 rows.

Cast off the remaining 7(9) sts.

THE POCKET BACKS (2 alike)

With size 3¼mm. (No. 10) needles and a. cast on 31 sts. and work in moss st. as follows:

Moss st. row: P. 1, *k. 1, p. 1; repeat from * to end.

Repeat this row 45 times, then cast off.

TO MAKE UP THE SWEATER

Pin out to size and press very lightly on the wrong side with a warm iron over a damp cloth. Join shoulder seams. Set in sleeves. Sew one row end edge of each pocket to each side of back 5 centimetres (2 inches) above ribbing. Join sleeve and side seams, neatly sewing pocket backs in place on wrong side of front. Press seams.

french leave

MATERIALS

23 25 gram balls of "Woollybear 100% Mohair" in main colour, and one ball in each of the 5 contrast colours; a pair each of size 3¼mm. (No. 10), size 3¾mm. (No. 9) and size 4mm. (No. 8) Aero knitting needles; cable needle; 10 buttons; shoulder pads (optional).

TENSION

14 stitches and 13 rows to 5 centimetres (2 inches) over the cable rib pattern, using size 4mm. (No. 8) needles. If you cannot obtain the correct tension using the size needles suggested, use larger or smaller ones accordingly.

ABBREVIATIONS

K., knit; p., purl; st., stitch; tog., together; dec., decrease (by working 2 sts. tog.); inc., increase (by working twice into same st.); single rib is k. 1 and p. 1 alternately; cable 6, thus, slip next 3 sts. onto cable needle and leave at front of work, k. 3, then k. 3 from cable needle; sl., slip; p.s.s.o., pass sl.st. over; 3 from 1, k. 1, y.r.n., k. 1 all into same st.; m., main colour; a., first contrast; b., second contrast; c., third contrast; d., fourth contrast; e., fifth contrast; up 1, pick up the loop, which lies between the needles, slip it onto left hand needle, then k. into back of it; y.r.n. yarn round needle.

MEASUREMENTS

The measurements are given in centimetres followed by inches in brackets.

Underarms	110	(44)
Side seam	44	(17¾)
Length	74	(29½)
Sleeve seam	44	(17½)

NOTE

Instructions in brackets are worked the number of times stated after the brackets.

THE BACK

With size 3¾mm. (No. 9) needles and m. cast on 126 sts. and work 19 rows in single rib.

Increase row: Rib 3, *up 1, rib 5; repeat from * ending last repeat rib 3. – 151 sts.

Change to size 4mm. (No. 8) needles and work in pattern as follows:

1st row: P. 1, (k. 1, p. 1) twice, *k. 6, p. 1, (k. 1, p. 1) 4 times; repeat from * ending last repeat (k. 1, p. 1) twice instead of 4 times.

2nd row: K. 1, (p. 1, k. 1) twice, *p. 6, k. 1, (p. 1, k. 1) 4 times; repeat from * ending last repeat (p. 1, k. 1) twice.

3rd to 6th rows: Repeat 1st and 2nd rows twice.

7th row: P. 1, (k. 1, p. 1) twice, *cable 6, p. 1, (k. 1, p. 1) 4 times; repeat from * ending last repeat (k. 1, p. 1) twice.

8th row: As 2nd row.

9th and 10th rows: As 1st and 2nd rows.

The last 10 rows form the cable rib pattern.

Continuing in cable rib pattern as set work the spotted patch as follows; using separate balls of m. at each side of the patch.

1st row: With m. work in cable rib as set across 27sts., with a. k. 15, with m. pattern to end as set.

2nd row: With m. cable rib 109, with a. p. 15, with m. cable rib 27.

3rd row: With m. cable rib 27, with a. k. 1, with b. 3 from 1, (with a. k. 3, with b. 3 from 1) 3 times, with a. k. 1, with m. cable rib 109.

4th row: With m. cable rib 109, with a. p. 1, (with b. p. 3, with a. p. 3) 3 times, with b. p. 3, with a. p. 1, with m. cable rib 27.

5th row: With m. cable rib 27, with a. k. 1, sl. 1, k. 2tog., p.s.s.o., (k. 3, sl. 1, k. 2tog., p.s.s.o.) 3 times, k. 1, with m. cable rib 109.

6th row: As 2nd row.

7th row: With m. cable rib 27, (with a. k. 3, with b. 3 from 1) 3 times, with a. k. 3, with m. cable rib 109.

8th row: With m. cable rib 109, with a. p. 3, (with b. p. 3, with a. p. 3) 3 times, with m. cable rib 27.

9th row: With m. cable rib 27, (with a. k. 3, sl. 1, k. 2tog., p.s.s.o.) 3 times, with a. k. 3, with m. cable rib to end.

10th row: As 2nd row.

11th to 18th rows: As 3rd to 10th rows.

19th row: With m. cable rib 27, still with m. k. 15, then cable rib to end.

This completes the spotted patch.

Next row: All cable rib.

Now work the check patch as follows, again using separate balls of m. at each side of the patch.

1st row: With m. cable rib 91 sts., with c. k. 2, (with d. k. 2, with c. k. 2) 3 times, with m. cable rib 46.

2nd row: With m. cable rib 46, with c. p. 2, (with d. p. 2, with c. p. 2) 3 times, with m. cable rib 91 sts.

3rd row: With m. cable rib 91 sts., with d. k. 2, (with c. k. 2, with d. k. 2) 3 times, with m. cable rib 46.

4th row: With m. cable rib 46, with d. p. 2, (with c. p. 2, with d. p. 2) 3 times, with m. cable rib 91 sts.

5th to 16th rows: Repeat the 1st to 4th rows 3 times.

17th and 18th rows: As 1st and 2nd rows.

19th row: With m. cable rib 91, k. 14, cable rib to end.

This completes the check patch.

Cable rib 11 rows.

Now work the striped patch as follows:

1st row: With m. cable rib 50, with c. k. 14, with m. cable rib 87.

2nd row: With m. cable rib 87, with c. p. 14, with m. cable rib 50.

3rd and 4th rows: As 1st and 2nd rows.

5th to 8th rows: Using d. instead of c. repeat 1st to 4th rows.

9th to 12th rows: Using a. instead of c. as 1st to 4th rows.

13th to 16th rows: Using b. instead of c. as 1st to 4th rows.

17th to 20th rows: Using e. instead of c. as 1st to 4th rows.

21st row: With m. cable rib 50, k. 14, cable rib to end.

This completes the stripe patch.

Next row: All in cable rib.

Now work the spotted patch again in a different position as follows:

Next row: With m. cable rib 121, with a. k. 15, with m. cable rib 15.

The last row sets the position of the next spotted patch.

Continuing in cable rib with spotted patch as set and given before, pattern 13 rows more.

To shape the armholes: Still working the spotted patch as set, cast off 6 sts. in rib at the beginning of the next 2 rows, then dec. 1 st. at each end of the next 3 rows. The last row completes the spotted patch.

Continuing with m. in cable rib dec. 1 st. at each end of the next 6 rows. – 121 sts.

Cable rib 3 rows.

Now work the next check patch as follows:

Next row: With m. cable rib 15, with c. k. 2, (with d. k. 2, with c. k. 2) 3 times, with m. cable rib to end.

The last row sets the position of the check patch given before, now work the 2nd to 19th rows of the patch as set.

Work 1 row in cable rib.

Now work the stripe patch as follows: Next row: With m. cable rib 92, with c. k. 14, with m. cable rib 15.

The last row sets the position of the striped patch given before, work the 2nd to 21st rows as set.

Continuing with m. in cable rib only, work 3 rows, then inc. 1 st. at each end of the next row and the following 4th row.

On 125 sts. work 7 rows.

To slope the shoulders: Cast off 12 sts. at the beginning of the next 6 rows – 53 sts.

Change to size 3¼mm. (No. 10) needles and work 12 rows in single rib, then cast off in rib.

THE LEFT FRONT

With size 3¾mm. (No. 9) needles and m. cast on 64 sts. and work 19 rows in single rib.

Increase row: Rib 4, *up 1, rib 5; repeat from * to end. – 76 sts.

Change to size 4mm. (No 8) needles and work 10 rows in cable rib pattern as given for back.

Continuing in cable rib as set, work the patches as follows.

The spotted patch: 1st row: With m. cable rib 27, with a. k. 15, with m. pattern 34.

The last row sets the position of the spotted patch, now work the 2nd to 19th rows as set.

Cable rib 31 rows.

Now work the striped patch as follows: 1st row: With m. cable rib 50, with c. k. 14, with m. cable rib 12.

The last row sets the position of the striped patch, work the 2nd to 21st rows as set.

With m. cable rib 15 rows.

To shape the armhole: Continuing in cable rib, cast off 6 sts. at the beginning of the next row, work 1 row back to armhole edge. Dec. 1 st. at the armhole edge on each of the next 9 rows. On 61 sts. work 1 row.

To slope the front edge: Dec. 1 st. at the end – front edge on the next row. Work 1 row back to armhole edge.

Now work the check patch as follows: Next row: Cable rib 15, with c. k. 2, (with d. k. 2, with c. k. 2) 3 times, with m. cable rib 29, k. 2tog. for front slope.

The last row sets the position of the check patch; continuing in pattern with patch as set, and given for back, pattern 19 rows, decreasing 1 st. at the end – front edge on the 2nd of these rows and the 8 following alternate rows.

Continuing in cable rib only, dec. 1 st. at the end of the next row and the 11 following alternate rows.

**On 38 sts, work 1 row.

Still decreasing at front edge on every alternate row, inc. 1 st. at the armhole edge on the next row and the following 4th row.

On 37 sts. work 1 row.

Dec. 1 st. at the front edge on the next row.

On 36 sts. work 5 rows.

To slope the shoulder: Cast off 12 sts. at the beginning of the next row and following alternate row. On 12 sts. work 1 row, then cast off.

THE RIGHT FRONT

Work as given for left front until the 10 cable rib pattern rows have been worked.

Repeat these 10 rows twice more.

Now work the check patch as follows: 1st row: With m. cable rib 16, with c. k. 2, (with d. k. 2, with c. k. 2) 3 times, with m. cable rib 46.

The last row sets the position of the check patch given for back, work the 2nd to 19th rows as set.

Work 33 rows in cable rib.

Now work the spot patch as follows: Next row: With m. cable rib 46, with a. k. 15, with m. cable rib 15.

The last row sets the position of the spotted patch, given for back, work the 2nd to 15th rows as set.

To shape the armhole: Continuing in pattern as set, cast off 6 sts. at the beginning of the next row, then dec. 1 st. at the armhole edge on each of the next 9 rows, completing the patch on the 3rd of these rows.

On 61 sts. work 2 rows.

To slope the front edge: Dec. 1 st. at the end – front edge on the next row and the 10 following alternate rows. – 50 sts.

Now work the stripe patch as follows: Next row: With m. cable rib 21, with c. k. 14, with m. cable rib 15.

The last row sets the position of the striped patch given for back, work the 2nd to 21st rows as set, decreasing 1 st. at the front edge on every alternate row as before. – 40 sts.

Dec. 1 st. at the front edge on the next row and the following alternate row.

Work as given for left front from ** to end.

THE SLEEVES (both alike)

With size 3¾mm. (No. 9) needles and m. cast on 66 sts. and work 15 rows in single rib.

Increase row: Rib 6, *up 1, rib 6; repeat from * to end. – 76 sts.

Change to size 4mm. (No. 8) needles and work 10 rows in cable rib pattern given for back.

Continuing in cable rib and working the extra sts. into the pattern as they occur, inc. 1 st. at each end of the next row and the 2 following 4th rows.

On 82 sts. work 1 row.

Now work the striped patch as follows: Next row: With m. cable rib 15, with c. k. 14, with m. cable rib to end.

The last row sets the position of the striped patch given for back, work the 2nd to 21st rows as set, increasing 1 st. at each end of the 3rd row and the 4 following 4th rows.

Next row: Work in cable rib as set across all sts.

Continuing in cable rib, inc. 1 st. at each end of the next row and the 6 following 4th rows.

On 106 sts. work 3 rows.

Now work the check patch as follows: Next row: With m. pattern 64, with c. k. 2, (with d. k. 2, with c. k. 2) 3 times, with m. cable rib 28.

The last row sets the position of the patch given for the back. Continued on page 73

tea time

french leave

Trousers by Katherine Hamnett, shirts by Goldie.

ovaltinie

MATERIALS
For the pullover: either 5 ounce (28 gram) hanks of "Woollybear Real Shetland" by Patricia Roberts or 6 25 gram balls of "Woollybear Pure Silk" by Patricia Roberts in main colour and 1 ball or hank of the same yarn in each of the 8 contrast colours; a pair each of size 2¼ mm. (No. 13) and size 2¾ mm. (No. 12) Aero knitting needles. For the sweater: Add 2 hanks or balls in main colour and 1 in each contrast colour.

TENSION
19 stitches and 20 rows to 5 centimetres (2 inches) over the FairIsle pattern using size 2¾ mm. (No. 12) needles. If you cannot obtain the correct tension using the size needles suggested, use larger or smaller ones accordingly.

ABBREVIATIONS
K., knit; p., purl; st., stitch; tog., together; dec., decrease (by working 2 sts. tog.); inc., increase (by working twice into same st.); single rib is k. 1 and p. 1 alternately; s.s., stocking stitch is k. on the right side and p. on the wrong side; sl., slip; p.s.s.o., pass sl. st. over; m., main colour; a., first contrast; b., second contrast; c., third contrast; d., fourth contrast; e., fifth contrast; f., sixth contrast; g., seventh contrast; h., eighth contrast; up 1, pick up the loop, which lies between the needles, slip it onto left hand needle, then k. into back of it; garter st. is k. plain on every row.

MEASUREMENTS
The measurements are given in centimetres followed by inches in brackets.

Underarms	95 (38)
Side seam	40 (16)
Length	62.5 (25)
Sleeve seam (sweater only)	42.5 (17)

THE PULLOVER

THE BACK
With size 2¼ mm. (No. 13) needles and m. cast on 161 sts. and work 35 rows in single rib.

Increase row: Rib 5, *up 1, rib 8; repeat from * ending last repeat rib 4. – 181 sts.

Change to size 2¾ mm. (No. 12) needles and beginning with a k. row s.s. 2 rows. Now work in pattern as follows: This is worked entirely in s.s., so only the colour details are given. It is not necessary to weave in the wools, but care should be taken not to pull colours not in use, tightly across the back of the work or it will become puckered.

1st row: 2a., *3m., 3a.; repeat from * ending last repeat 2a.

2nd row: As 1st row.

3rd row: 2m., *3b., 3m.; repeat from * ending last repeat 2m.

4th row: As 3rd row.

5th and 6th rows: All m.

7th row: 1c., *5m., 1c.; repeat from * to end.

8th row: 2c., *4m., 2c., 3m., 2c., 4m., 3c.; repeat from * ending last repeat 2c.

The last 8 rows set the position of the pattern given in the chart. Now work the 9th to 128th rows from the chart as set.

To shape the armholes: Continuing in pattern from the chart as set, cast off 8 sts. at the beginning of the next 2 rows, then dec. 1 st. at each end of the next 12 rows.

On 141 sts. pattern 6 rows, ending with the 148th pattern row. **

Now work the 1st to 64th pattern rows again.

To slope the shoulders: Continuing in pattern from chart, cast off 14 sts. at the beginning of the next 6 rows.

Leave the remaining 57 sts. on a spare needle until required for neckband.

THE FRONT
Work as given for back until the 117th pattern row has been worked.

Now divide the sts. for the neck: Next row: P. 90 sts. as set and leave these sts. on a spare needle until required for right half front, p. 1 and leave this st. on a safety pin until required for neckband, p. to end and continue on these 90 sts. for the left half front.

The left half front: to slope the neck: Continuing in pattern as set, dec. 1 st. at the end – neck edge on the next row and at the same edge on the 3 following 3rd rows.

To shape the armhole and continue to slope the neck edge: Continuing to dec. at the neck edge on every 3rd row as set, cast off 8 sts. at the beginning of the next row, then dec. 1 st. at the armhole edge on each of the 12 following rows.

Pattern 59 rows decreasing 1 st. at the neck edge on every 3rd row as set.

On 42 sts. pattern 12 rows.

To slope the shoulder: Cast off 14 sts. at the beginning of the next row and the following alternate row.

On 14 sts. work 1 row, then cast off.

The right half front: With right side of work facing rejoin yarn to inner edge of sts. left on spare needle and work to end of row, then work as given for left half front to end.

THE NECKBAND
First join right shoulder seam. With right side of work facing rejoin m. at left front shoulder and using size 2¼ mm. (No. 13) needles pick up and k. 74 sts. from left front neck edge, k. 1 st. from safety pin at centre front, pick up and k. 74 sts. from right front neck edge, then k. across the 57 sts. at back neck edge – 206 sts.

Work 1 row in single rib.

Next row: Rib to within 2 sts. of st. at centre front, sl. 1, k. 1, p.s.s.o., k. centre st., then k. 2 tog., rib to end.

Repeat the last 2 rows 5 times more, then cast off in rib.

THE ARMBANDS (both alike)
First join left shoulder seam. With right side of work facing rejoin m. and using size 2¼ mm. (No. 13) needles pick up and k. 152 sts. from all round armhole edge. Work 9 rows in single rib, then cast off in rib.

TO MAKE UP THE PULLOVER
For Shetland garments, pin out to size and press all parts except the ribbing with a warm iron over a damp cloth. Do not press silk garments. Join side seams. Press seams.

THE SWEATER

THE BACK AND THE FRONT
Work as given for the pullover.

THE SLEEVES (both alike)
With size 2¼ mm. (No. 13) needles and m. cast on 67 sts. and work 47 rows in single rib.

Increase row: Rib 3, * up 1, rib 1, up 1, rib 2; repeat from * ending last repeat, rib 3. – 109 sts.

Change to size 2¾ mm. (No. 12) needles and work as given for back until the 32nd pattern row has been worked.

Continuing in pattern as set and working the extra sts. into the pattern as they occur inc. 1 st. at each end of the next row and the 2 following 32nd rows.

On 115 sts. pattern 31 rows ending with the 128th pattern row.

To shape the sleevetop: Continuing in pattern as set, cast off 8 sts. at the beginning of the next 2 rows, then dec. 1st. at each end of the next row and the 8 following alternate rows.

On 81 sts. work 1 row.

This completes the fairisle pattern.

Now working in garter st. in stripe sequence of 2 rows b., 2 rows e., 2 rows g., 2 rows f., 2 rows d., 2 rows a., 2 rows c., and 2 rows h., dec. 1 st. at each end of the first row and the 7 following 4th rows, then on the 7 alternate rows.

On 51 sts. work 1 row.

Cast off 3 sts. at the beginning of the next 4 rows, 4 sts. on the next 2 rows, 5 sts. on the 2 following rows and 6 sts. on the next 2 rows.

Cast off the remaining 9 sts.

THE 'V' NECK INSET
With right side of work facing rejoin m. to the st. left on safety pin at centre front neck edge and using size 2¼ mm. (No. 13) needles p. 1, k. 1, p. 1 all into this st., then work as follows.

Next row: Inc. in first st., p. 1, inc. in last st.

Next row: K. 1, p. 1, k. 1, p. 1, k. 1.

Next row: P. 1, k. 1, p. 1, k. 1, p. 1.

Continuing in rib as set, inc. 1 st. at each end of the next row and the 18 following 3rd rows. – 43 sts.

Now divide the sts. for the neck: Next row: Rib 12 and leave these sts. on a spare needle until

Continued on opposite page.

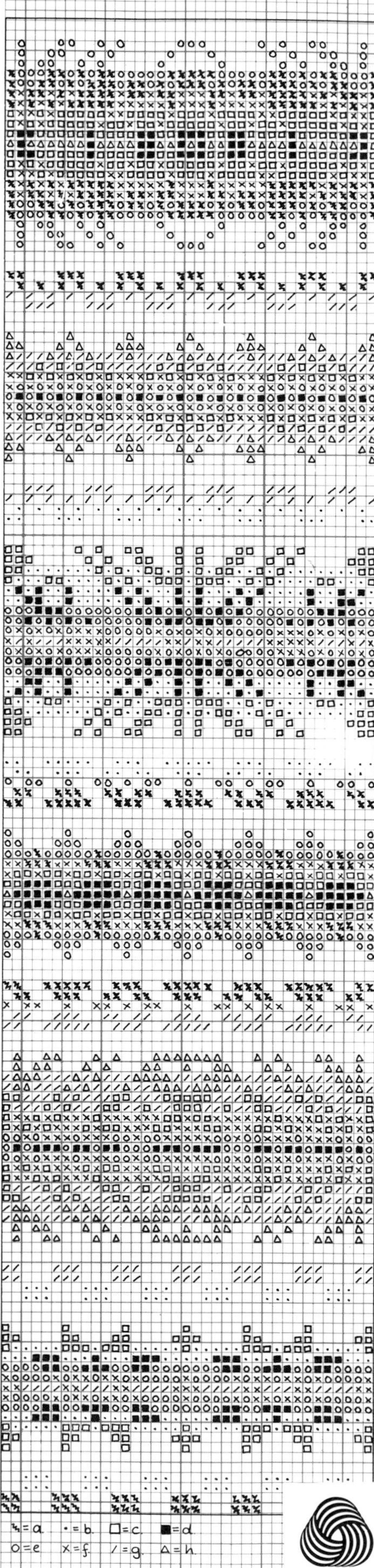

time for tea

MATERIALS
14 25 gram balls of "Woollybear Lambswool" by Patricia Roberts in main colour, 3 25 gram balls of "Woollybear 100% Mohair" in fourth contrast colour and 2 20 gram balls of "Woollybear Angora" in each of the 7 other contrast colours; a pair each of size 2¼mm (No. 13) and size 2¾mm (No. 12) Aero knitting needles; 5 buttons.

TENSION
As for Ovaltinie.

ABBREVIATIONS
As for Ovaltinie.

MEASUREMENTS
The measurements are given in centimetres followed by inches in brackets.

Underarms	102.5(41)
Side seam	42.5(17)
Length	65(26)
Sleeve seam	42.5(17)

THE BACK
With size 2¼mm (No. 13) needles and m. cast on 161 sts. and work 23 rows in single rib, then work as given for back of "Ovaltinie" pullover from the increase row until the armhole shaping has been worked, but working an extra 20 rows in Fair Isle pattern, before shaping the armholes.

On 141 sts. pattern 70 rows.

To slope the shoulders: Cast off 14 sts. at the beginning of the next 6 rows, then cast off the remaining 57 sts.

THE POCKET BACKS (2 alike)
With size 2¾mm (No. 12) needles and m. cast on 41 sts. and beginning with a k. row s.s. 48 rows, then leave these sts. on a stitch-holder until required.

THE LEFT FRONT
With size 2¼mm (No. 13) needles and m. cast on 81 sts. and work as given for back until 27 rows have been worked in pattern and noting that there are 91 sts. after the increase row.

28th row: 4h., 3m., 1h., 1m., 1h., 3m. 2h., 2m., 1h., 1m., *1h., 2m., 2h., 3m., 1h., 1m., 1h., 3m., 7h., 3m., 1h., 1m., 1h., 3m., 2h., 2m., 1h., 1m.; repeat from * once more.

29th row: 1m., *1h., 1m., 2h., 3m., 1h., 1m., 1h., 3m., 2h., 2m., 1h., 2m., 2h., 3m., 1h., lm., 1h., 3m., 2h., 1m., 1h., 1m.; repeat from * once more, then 1h., 1m., 2h., 3m., 1h., 1m., 1h., 3m., 2h., 2m., 1h.

The last 29 rows set the position of the pattern given in the chart, now work the 30th to 46th rows as set.

Pocket row: K.25, slip next 41 sts. onto a stitch-holder and leave at front of work, in their place k. across the 41 sts. of one pocket back, k. to end of row.

Continuing in pattern as set, work a further 88 rows ending with the 135th pattern row.

**To slope the front edge: Dec. 1 st. at the beginning of the next row. Pattern 2 rows.

Now work as given for left half front on front of pullover to end.

THE RIGHT FRONT
With size 2¼mm (No. 13) needles and m. cast on 81 sts. and work as given for the back until the 27th pattern row has been worked, noting that there are 91 sts. after the increase row.

28th row: 1m., *1h., 2m., 2h., 3m., 1h., 1m., 1h., 3m., 7h., 3m., 1h., 1m., 1h., 3m., 2h., 2m., 1h., 1m.; repeat from * once, then 1h., 2m., 2h., 3m., 1h., 1m., 1h., 3m., 4h.

The last row sets the position of the pattern given in the chart, work the 29th to 46th rows as set.

Work the pocket row given for left front, then work the 48th to 136th pattern rows as set.

Now work as given for left front from ** to end.

THE SLEEVES (both alike)
As given for "Ovaltinie" sweater.

THE POCKET TOPS (2 alike)
With right side of work facing rejoin m. to the 41 sts. left on stitch-holder and using size 2¼mm (No. 13) needles work 6 rows in single rib, then cast off in rib.

THE BUTTONBAND AND HALF COLLAR
With size 2¼mm (No. 13) needles and m. cast on 26 sts. and work 164 rows in single rib.

**Continuing in rib, inc. 1 st. at the beginning of the next row and the 29 following alternate rows.

On 56 sts. work 1 row.

Cast off in rib, marking the 11th of these sts. with a coloured thread.

THE BUTTONHOLE BAND AND HALF COLLAR
With size 2¼mm (No. 13) needles and m. cast on 26 sts. and work 10 rows in single rib.

1st Buttonhole row: Rib 10, cast off 6, rib to end.

2nd Buttonhole row: Rib 10, turn, cast on 6 over those cast off, turn, rib 10.

Rib 36 rows.

Repeat the last 38 rows 3 times then work the 2 buttonhole rows again.

Work 1 row in single rib, then work as given for buttonband and half collar from ** to end.

THE BACK COLLAR
With size 2¼mm (No. 13) needles and m. cast on 157 sts. and work 12 rows in single rib. Mark each end of the last row with coloured threads.

Dec. 1 st. at each end of the next row and the 9 following alternate rows.

On 137 sts. work 1 row, then cast off.

TO MAKE UP THE JACKET
Pin out to size and press all parts except the ribbing with a warm iron over a damp cloth. Join shoulder seams. Set in sleeves. Join sleeve and side seams. Neatly sew pocket backs and row ends of pocket tops in place. Sew shaped row end edge of button and buttonhole bands in place, so that the first decreases on front edges are in line with the first increases on collar pieces. Sew cast off and shaped row end edges of back collar in place, matching the marking threads. Sew on buttons. Press seams.

"**Ovaltine**" continued from opposite page.

required for the right front point, cast off 19 sts. for the neck, work to end and continue on these 12 sts. for the left front point.

The left front point: Pattern 14 rows, decreasing 1 st. at the neck edge on each row and at the same time increasing 1 st. at the outer edge on the 2nd, 5th, 8th and 11th of these rows.

Take the 2 remaining sts. tog. and fasten off.

The right front point: With right side of work facing rejoin m. to inner edge of sts. left on spare needle and work as given for the left front point to end.

Neatly sew neck inset in position, ending 26 rows from top of shoulder.

THE NECKBAND
First join right shoulder seam: With right side of work facing rejoin m. at left front shoulder and using size 2¼mm. (No. 13) needles pick up and k. 40 sts. from left front neck edge, 19 sts. from centre front neck edge and 40 sts. from right front neck edge, then k. across the 57 sts. at back neck edge.

On 156 sts. work 9 rows in single rib, then cast off in rib.

TO MAKE UP THE SWEATER
Press as for pullover. Join left shoulder seam, continuing seam across neckband. Set in sleeves. Join sleeve and side seams.

"**French Leave**" continued from page 69.

Work the 2nd to 19th rows of the patch as set.

Work 10 rows in cable rib.

Now work the spotted patch as follows: Next row: With m. cable rib 45, with a. k.15, with m. cable rib 46.

The last row sets the position of the spot patch, given for back. Work the 2nd row as set.

To shape the sleevetop: Continuing in cable rib with the 18 row spot patch as set, cast off 6 sts. at the beginning of the next 2 rows, then dec. 1 st. at each end of the next row and the 15 following alternate rows. On 62 sts. work 1 row.

Dec. 1 st. at each end of the next 8 rows. Cast off 4 sts. at the beginning of the next 2 rows, 6 sts. on the 2 following rows, and 8 sts. on the next 2 rows.

Cast off the remaining 10 sts.

THE BUTTONBAND
With right side of work facing rejoin m. at left front shoulder and using size 3¼mm. (No. 10) needles pick up and k. 60 sts. from left front neck edge, up to first front neck decrease, then pick up and k. 128 sts. from rest of front edge.

On 188 sts. work 7 rows in single rib.

Next row: Rib 60, 3 from 1, rib to end.

Next row: Rib as set.

Repeat the last 2 rows once more, then cast off loosely, using a size larger needle.

THE BUTTONHOLE BAND
With right side of work facing rejoin m. at right front edge and using size 3¼mm. (No. 10) needles, pick up and k. 128 sts. from right front edge, up to first front edge dec., then pick up and k. 60 sts. from front neck edge up to shoulder.

On 188 sts. rib 5 rows.

1st Buttonhole row: Rib 4, *cast off 3, rib next 14; repeat from * ending last repeat rib 18.

2nd Buttonhole row: Rib 19, *turn, cast on 3 over those cast off, turn, rib 15; repeat from * ending last repeat rib 4.

Next row: Rib 128, 3 from 1, rib to end.

Next row: Rib as set.

Repeat the last 2 rows once, then cast off loosely, using a size larger needle.

THE POCKET BACKS (2 alike)
With size 4mm. (No. 8) needles and m. cast on 26 sts. and work 30 rows in s.s., then cast off.

TO MAKE UP THE JACKET
Pin out to size and press all parts very lightly, with a warm iron over a damp cloth. Join shoulder seams. Set in sleeves. Join sleeve and side seams, inserting pocket backs in side seams 25 cms. (10 inches) below armholes, neatly sewing them in place on wrong side of fronts. Sew on buttons. Press seams. Catch (optional) shoulder pads in place.

ovaltinie

His shirt, tie and hat from Margaret Howell.

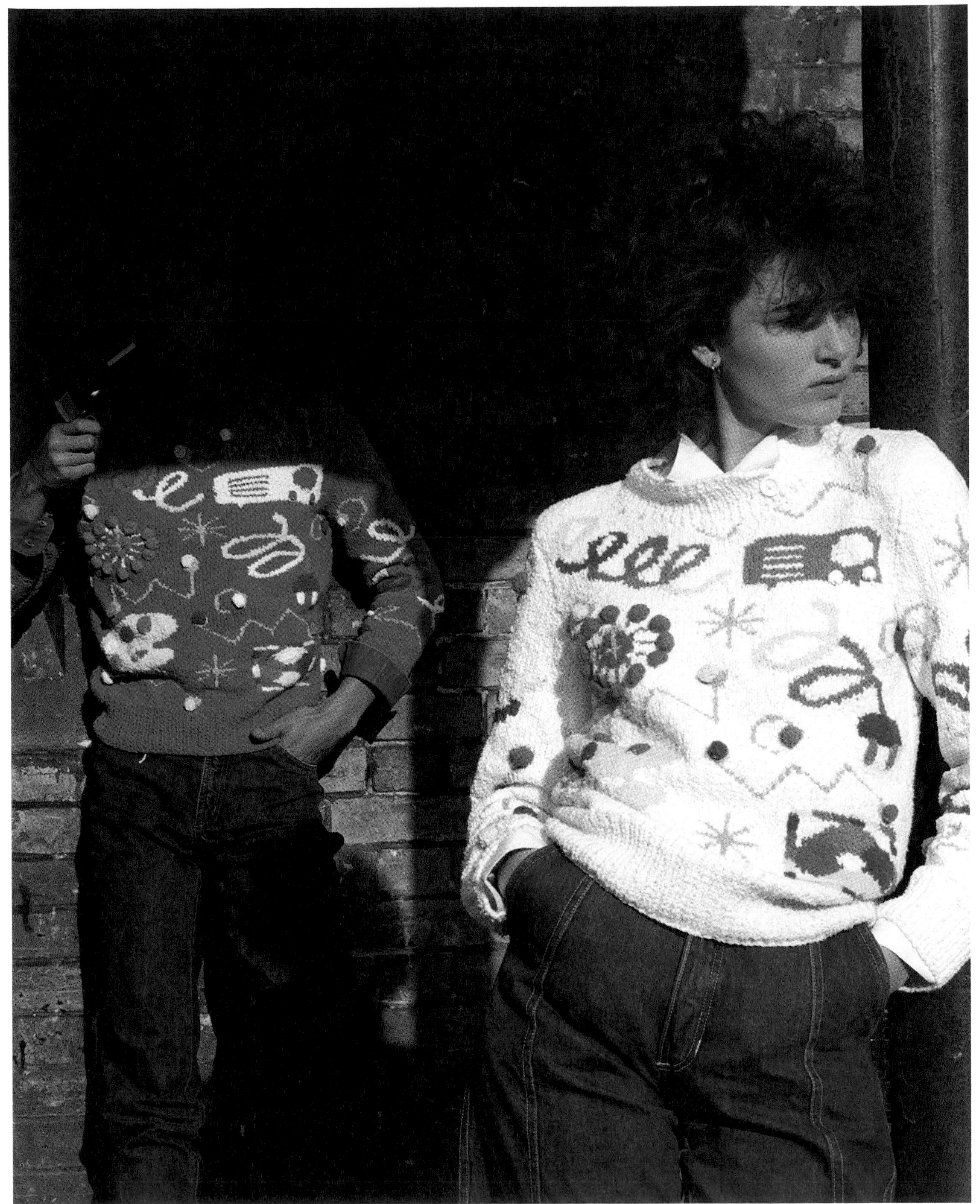

lucky strike

His shirt from Brown's, jeans from Pacific.

lucky strike

MATERIALS

For the woman's sweater: 9 50 gram balls of "Woollybear Cotton Bouclé" by Patricia Roberts in main colour; 2 balls in first contrast colour and 1 ball in each of the four other contrast colours; a pair each of size 3¼ mm. (No. 10) and size 3¾ mm. (No. 9) Aero knitting needles; 1 button.
For the man's sweater: Add an extra ball in main colour and size 4 mm. (No. 8) needles and omit the size 3¼ mm. (No. 10) needles and the button.

SPECIAL NOTE

The woman's sweater may also be knitted in "Woollybear 100% Mohair" by Patricia Roberts. It requires 12 25 gram balls in main colour, 3 balls in first contrast colour and 2 balls in each of the 4 other contrast colours. However, to obtain the correct tension it is necessary to use size 3¾ mm. (No. 9) needles, instead of size 3¼ mm. (No. 10) needles and size 4 mm. (No. 8) needles instead of size 3¾ mm. (No. 9) needles.

TENSION

For the woman's sweater, work at a tension of 10 stitches and 14 rows to 5 centimetres (2 inches) over stocking stitch using either 3¾ mm. (No. 9) needles and "Woollybear Cotton Bouclé" or size 4 mm. (No. 8) needles and "Woollybear 100% Mohair". For the man's sweater, work at a tension of 9 stitches and 13 rows to 5 centimetres (2 inches) over stocking stitch using size 4 mm. (No. 8) needles and "Cotton Bouclé". If you cannot obtain the correct tension using the size needles suggested, use larger or smaller ones accordingly.

ABBREVIATIONS

K., knit; p., purl; st., stitch; tog., together; dec., decrease (by working 2 sts. tog.); inc., increase (by working twice into same st.); single rib is k. 1 and p. 1 alternately; s.s., stocking stitch is k. on the right side and p. on the wrong side; 3 from 1, k. 1, p. 1, k. 1 all onto one st.; y.r.n., yarn round needle; m.b., make bobble thus, with appropriate contrast colour, k. 1, y.r.n., k. 1, y.r.n., k. 1 all into same st., turn, p. 5, turn, k. 5, turn, p. 5, turn, k. 5, turn, p. 5, turn, pass second, third, fourth and fifth sts. on left hand needle over first st., k. this st.; m.k., make knot thus, with m. k. 1, y.r.n., k. 1. all into next st., turn, p. 3, turn, k. 3, turn, p. 3, turn, pass second and third sts. over first st. on the left hand needle, with c. k. this st.; up 1, pick up the loop which lies between the needles, slip it onto left hand needle, then k. into back of it; m., main colour; a., first contrast colour; b., second contrast; c., third contrast; d., fourth contrast; e., fifth contrast;

MEASUREMENTS

The measurements are given in centimetres followed by inches in brackets.

	Woman's	Man's
Underarms	92.5 (37)	101 (40.5)
Side seam	37.5 (15)	40 (16)
Length	60 (24)	65 (26)
Sleeve Seam	42.5 (17)	45 (18)

WOMAN'S SWEATER

THE BACK

With size 3¼ mm. (No. 10) needles and m. cast on 80 sts. and work 25 rows in single rib.

Increase row: Rib 4, *up 1, rib 6; repeat from * ending last repeat rib 4. – 93 sts.

Change to size 3¾ mm. (No. 9) needles and k. 1 row. Now continuing in s.s. work in pattern from chart as follows. Use separate small balls of colour for each section of the pattern, so that colours not in use are not taken across the back of the work.

2nd row: (p. row): 40m., 3a., 50m.

3rd row: 49m., 5a., 39m.

4th row: 39m., 5a., 49m.

5th row: 49m., 2a., with b. m.b., 2 a., 39m.

6th row: As 2nd row.

The last 6 rows set the position of the pattern given in the chart, now work the 7th to 82nd rows from the chart as set.

To shape the armholes: Continuing in pattern from chart as set, cast off 5 sts. at the beginning of the next 2 rows, then dec. 1 st. at each end of the next row and the 5 following alternate rows.

On 71 sts. pattern 27 rows.

Inc. 1 st. at each end of the next row and the following 8th row. **

On 75 sts. pattern 8 rows.

Now divide the sts. for the back neck: Next row: Pattern 31 and leave these sts. on a spare needle until required for left back shoulder, cast off 13, pattern to end and continue on these 31 sts. for the right back shoulder.

The right back shoulder: Pattern 1 row back to neck edge. Cast off 7 sts. at the beginning of the next row, 8 sts. on the following row, then 7 sts. on the next row. Cast off the remaining 9 sts.

The left back shoulder: With right side of work facing rejoin yarn to inner edge of sts. left on spare needle and work to end of row, then work as given for right back shoulder to end.

THE BACK NECKBAND

With right side of work facing rejoin m. and using size 3¼ mm. (No. 10) needles pick up and k. 15 sts. from right back neck edge, 13 sts. from centre back neck edge, 15 sts. from left back neck edge.

On 43 sts. work 15 rows in single rib, then cast off.

THE FRONT

Work as given for the back until the armhole shaping has been worked.

On 71 sts. pattern 20 rows.

Now divide the sts. for the neck: Next row: Pattern 29 and leave these sts. on a spare needle until required for right front shoulder, cast off 13, pattern to end and continue on these 29 sts. for the left front shoulder.

The left front shoulder: to shape the neck: Continuing in pattern as set, dec. 1 st. at the neck edge on each of the next 6 rows, marking the neck edge on the last of these rows with a coloured thread.

Inc. 1 st. at the armhole edge at the beginning and dec. 1 st. at the neck edge on the next row. Dec. 1 st. at the neck edge on each of the next 7 rows.

Inc. 1 st. at the armhole edge on the next row.

On 17 sts. pattern 11 rows.

To slope the shoulder: Cast off 8 sts. at the beginning of the next row. On 9 sts. work 1 row, then cast off.

The right front shoulder: With right side of work facing rejoin yarn to inner edge of sts. left on spare needle and work to end of row, then work as given for left front shoulder to end, but omitting marked thread.

THE LEFT FRONT NECKBAND

With right side of work facing rejoin m. at left front neck edge, and using size 3¼ mm. (No. 10) needles pick up and k. 19 sts. up to marking thread, turn and cast on 5 sts.

On 24 sts. work 11 rows in single rib, then continuing in rib, dec. 1 st. at the marking thread end of row on each of the next 4 rows, then cast off in rib.

THE MAIN FRONT NECKBAND

With right side of work facing rejoin m. at marking thread on left front neck edge and using size 3¼ mm. (No. 10) needles pick up and k. 7 sts. from left front neck edge, 13 sts. from centre front neck edge, then 26 sts. from right front neck edge.

On 46 sts. work 5 rows in single rib.

1st Buttonhole row: Rib 2, cast off 3, rib to end.

2nd Buttonhole row: Rib until 2 remain, turn, cast on 3 over those cast off, turn, rib to end.

Rib 4 rows more.

Continuing in rib dec. 1 st. at the marking thread end of the row on each of the next 4 rows.

Cast off the remaining 42 sts.

THE SLEEVES (both alike)

With size 3¼ mm. (No. 10) needles and m. cast on 41 sts. and work 19 rows in single rib.

Increase row: Rib 3, * up 1, rib 4; repeat from * ending last repeat rib 2. – 51 sts.

Change to size 3¾ mm. (No. 9) needles and beginning with a k. row s.s. 3 rows.

Now work in pattern as follows noting the information given for back.

4th row: 40m., 3a., 8m.

5th row: 7m., 5a., 39m.

The last 2 rows set the position of the pattern given in the chart. Work the 6th to 20th rows as set.

Continuing in pattern from chart as set, inc. 1 st. at each end of the next row and the 4 following 16th rows.

On 61 sts. pattern 17 rows.

To shape the sleevetop: Cast off 5 sts. at the beginning of the next 2 rows, then dec. 1 st. at each end of the next row and the 12 following alternate rows. On 25 sts. work 1 row.

Dec. 1 st. at each end of the next 4 rows. Cast off 3 sts. at the beginning of the 4 following rows.

Cast off the 5 remaining sts.

TO MAKE UP THE SWEATER

Pin out to size and press all parts except the ribbing with a warm iron over a damp cloth. Join shoulder seams. Set in sleeves. Join sleeve and side

seams. * * * Neatly sew sts. cast on for left front neckband in place behind those picked up for main front neckband. Press seams. Sew button in place.

MAN'S SWEATER

THE BACK AND FRONT (alike)

Using size 3¾ mm. (No. 9) needles instead of size 3¼ mm. (No. 10) needles and size 4 mm. (No. 8) needles instead of size 3¾ mm. (No. 9) needles, work as given for the back of the woman's sweater until * * is reached.

On 75 sts. pattern 13 rows.

To slope the shoulders: Cast off 8 sts. at the beginning of the next 2 rows – 59 sts.

Change to size 3¾ mm. (No. 9) needles and decreasing 1 st. at each end of each row work 8 rows in single rib. Cast off the remaining 43 sts. in rib.

THE SLEEVES (both alike)

Using size 3¾ mm. (No 9) needles instead of size 3¼ mm. (No. 10) needles and size 4 mm. (No. 8) needles instead of size 3¾ mm. (No. 9) needles, work as given for the sleeves of the woman's sweater.

TO MAKE UP THE SWEATER

Work as for woman's sweater until * * * is reached.

beano

Tights from Brown's, shoulder bag from Elle.

beano

MATERIALS
For the cardigan: 11 (12) ounce (28 gram) hanks of "Woollybear Real Shetland" by Patricia Roberts in main colour, 2 hanks of the same yarn in each of the second, third and fourth contrast colours and 7 balls of "Woollybear 100% Mohair" in first contrast colour, 7 buttons.
For the sweater: 13 (14) 25 gram balls of "Woollybear Pure Silk" by Patricia Roberts in main colour, 4 balls of the same yarn in first contrast colour and 2 balls in each of the 3 other contrast colours; 3 buttons.
For either garment: A pair each of size 2¼ mm. (No. 13) and size 2¾ mm. (No. 12) Aero knitting needles.

TENSION
18 stitches and 20 rows to 5 centimetres (2 inches) over the cross stitch pattern using size 2¾ mm. (No. 12) needles. If you cannot obtain the correct tension using the size needles suggested, use larger or smaller ones accordingly.

ABBREVIATIONS
K., knit; p., purl; st., stitch; tog., together; dec., decrease (by working 2 sts. tog.); inc., increase (by working twice into same st.); single rib is k. 1 and p. 1 alternately; p. 2 from 2 thus, p. 2 sts. tog., then p. into the first of these sts. again allowing both loops to fall from left hand needle together; y.r.n., yarn round needle; 3 from 1, k. 1, y.r.n., k. 1 all into next st.; up 1, pick up the loop which lies between the needles, slip it onto left hand needle, then k. into back of it; inc. down thus, k. or p. as appropriate in the stitch below the next st. on left hand needle, then k. or p. the st. from left hand needle; 7 from 1, k. 1, y.r.n., k. 1, y.r.n., k. 1, y.r.n., k. 1 all into next st.; cable 6 thus, slip next 3 sts. onto cable needle and leave at front of work, k. 3, then k. 3 from cable needle; 2 over 1, pass 2nd and 3rd sts. on left hand needle over first st., with m. k. this st.; 6 over 1, pass 2nd, 3rd, 4th, 5th and 6th sts. on left hand needle over first st., then with m. k. this st.; m., main colour; a., first contrast; b., second contrast; c., third contrast; d., fourth contrast.

NOTE
The instructions are given for the small size. Where they vary work the figures in the brackets for the medium size.

MEASUREMENTS
The measurements are given in centimetres followed by inches in brackets.

Sizes	small	medium
Underarms (cardigan)	92.5 (37)	97.5 (39)
Underarms (sweater)	90 (36)	95 (38)
Side seam	40 (16)	40 (16)
Length	60 (24)	61 (24½)
Sleeve seam (short)	12.5 (5)	12.5 (5)
Sleeve seam (long)	42.5 (17)	42.5 (17)

THE CARDIGAN

THE BACK
With size 2¼ mm. (No. 13) needles and m. cast on 131 (139) sts. and work 35 rows in single rib.
Increase row: Rib 4 (8), *up 1, rib 4; repeat from * ending last repeat rib 3 (7). – 163 (171) sts.
**Change to size 2¾ mm. (No. 12) needles and work in pattern as follows. When working the motifs use separate small balls of contrast colours, for both neatness and ease of work. Use separate balls of m. and a. at each side of the jam tart motif, so as not to pucker work. When working the easter egg and marble motifs m. and a. should be taken firmly across back of work, as a raised effect is desired.
1st row: With m. k. 3, *p. 2 from 2 – see abbreviations, k. 2; repeat from * to end.
2nd row: With m. all p.
3rd row: With m. k. 1, p. 2 from 2, *k. 2, p. 2 from 2; repeat from * to end.
4th row: *With m. p. 2, with a. p. 2; repeat from * until 3 remain, with m. p. 3.
5th row: With m. k. 3, *with a. p. 2 from 2, with m. k. 2; repeat from * to end.
6th and 7th rows: As 2nd and 3rd rows.
8th row: As 2nd row.
9th row: As 1st row.
10th row: *With a. p. 2, with m. p. 2; repeat from * ending last repeat with m. p. 1.
11th row: With m. k. 1, with a. p. 2 from 2, *with m. k. 2, with a. p. 2 from 2; repeat from * to end.
12th row: With m. all p.
The last 12 rows form the all over pattern; continuing in this repeat pattern work the motifs as follows.
13th row: Pattern 10 (11) as set *for the jam tart motif with b. 3 from 1, k. 1, 3 from 1, with m. pattern 37 (39) as set; repeat from * ending last repeat pattern 30 (31).
14th row: Pattern 28 (29), *with m. p. 2 tog., with b. inc. down – see abbreviations, p. 5, inc. down, with m. p. 2 tog., pattern 33 (35) as set; repeat from * ending last repeat pattern 8 (9).
15th row: Pattern 9 (10) as set, with b. k. 9, with m. pattern 35 (37) as set; repeat from * ending last repeat pattern 29 (30).
16th row: With a. and m. pattern 27 (28) as set * with m. p. 2 tog., with b. inc. down, up 1, p. 7, up 1, inc. down, with m. p. 2 tog., with m. and a. pattern 31 (33); repeat from * ending last repeat pattern 7 (8).
*17th row: With m. and a. pattern 8 (9), *with b. cable 6, k. 1, cable 6, with m. and a. pattern 33 (35) as set; repeat from * ending last repeat pattern 28 (29).
18th row: With m. pattern 26 (27) as set, *with m. p. 2 tog., with b. inc. down, p. 4, with c. p. 1, 3 from 1, p. 1, with b. p. 4, inc. down, with m. p. 2 tog., then pattern 29 (31) as set; repeat from * ending last repeat pattern 6 (7).
19th row: With m. pattern 7 (8), *with b. k. 6, with c. k. 2, with a. k. 1, with c. k. 2, with b. k. 6, with m. pattern 31 (33); repeat from * ending last repeat pattern 27 (28).
20th row: Pattern 27 (28), *with b. p. 6, with c. inc. down, p. 3, inc. down, with b. p. 6, then with m. pattern 31 (33) as set; repeat from * ending last repeat pattern 7 (8).
21st row: Pattern 7 (8), *with b. cable 6, with c. k. 1, with a. k. 1, with c. k. 3, with a. k. 1, with c. k. 1, with b. cable 6, with m. pattern 31 (33) as set; repeat from * ending last repeat pattern 27 (28).
22nd row: With m. and a. pattern 27 (28), *with b. p. 6, with c. p. 7, with b. p. 6; with m. and a. pattern 31 (33); repeat from * ending last repeat pattern 7 (8).
23rd row: With m. and a. pattern 7 (8), with b. k. 6, with c. k. 3, with a. k. 1, with c. k. 3, with b. k. 6, with m. and a. pattern 31 (33) as set; repeat from * ending last repeat pattern 27 (28).
24th row: As 22nd row, but using m. only for all over pattern.
25th row: As 21st row.
26th row: Pattern 27 (28), *with b. p. 6, with c. p. 2 tog., p. 3, p. 2 tog., with b. p. 6, with m. pattern 31 (33); repeat from * ending last repeat pattern 7 (8).
27th row: As 19th row.
28th row: With m. and a. pattern 26 (27) as set, *with m. up 1, p. 1, with b. p. 2 tog., p. 4, with c. p. 1, p. 3 tog., p. 1, with b. p. 4, p. 2 tog., with m. p. 1, up 1, with m. and a. pattern 29 (31); repeat from * ending last repeat pattern 6 (7).
29th row: As 17th row.
30th row: With m. pattern 27 (28) as set, *with m. up 1, p. 1, with b. p. 2 tog., p. 2 tog., p. 5, p. 2 tog., p. 2 tog., with m. p. 1, up 1, pattern 31 (33); repeat from * ending last repeat pattern 7 (8)
31st row: As 15th row.
32nd row: Pattern 28 (29) as set, *with m. up 1, p. 1, with b. p. 2 tog., p. 5, p. 2 tog., with m. p. 1, up 1, then pattern 33 (35); repeat from * ending last repeat pattern 8 (9).
33rd row: Pattern 10 (11) as set, *with m. 2 over 1, k. 1, 2 over 1, then pattern 37 (39) as set; repeat from * ending last repeat pattern 30 (31). – 163 (171) sts.
34th to 48th rows: In all over pattern as set.
49th row: With m. pattern 30 (31) as set, *then for the marble motif, with d. 7 from 1, with c. 7 from 1, turn, with c. p. 7, with d. p. 7, turn, with a. k. 1, with d. k. 6, with b. k. 1, with c. k. 6, turn, with c. p. 6, with b. p. 1, with d. p. 6, with a. p. 1, turn, with a. inc. in this st., with d. k. 2 tog., k. 4, with b. inc., with c. k. 2 tog., k. 4, turn, with c. p. 5, with b. p. 2, with d. p. 5, with a. p. 2, turn, with a. k. 1, inc. down, with d. k. 2 tog., k. 3, with b. k. 1, inc. down, with c. k. 2 tog., k. 3, turn, with c. p. 4, with b. p. 3, with d. p. 4, with a. p. 3, turn, with a. k. 2, inc. down, with d. k. 2 tog., k. 2, with b. k. 2, inc. down, with c. k. 2 tog., k. 2, turn, with c. p. 3, with b. p. 4, with d. p. 3, with a. p. 4, turn, with a. k. 3, inc. down, with d. k. 2 tog., k. 1, with b. k. 3, inc. down, with c. k. 2 tog., k. 1, turn, with c. p. 2, with b. p. 5, with d. p. 2, with a. p. 5, turn, with a. k. 4, inc. down, with d. k. 2 tog., with b. k. 4, inc. down, with c. k. 2 tog., turn, with c. p. 1, with b. p. 6, with d. p. 1, with a. p. 6, turn, with m. 6 over 1, 6 over 1, with m. pattern 38 (40) as set; repeat from * ending last repeat pattern 11 (12).
50th to 62nd rows: In all over pattern as set.
63rd row: Pattern 11 (12) as set, *for the easter egg motif, using a spare needle and working into next st., with c. cast on 40 sts., cast off these 40 sts., then transfer the remaining st to right hand needle, with m. pattern 39 (41) as set; repeat from * ending last repeat pattern 31 (32).
64th row: With m. and a. pattern 30 (31), *with d. p. 3, with m. and a. pattern 37 (39); repeat from * ending last repeat pattern 10 (11).
65th row: With m. and a. pattern 9 (10), *with d. 3 from 1, 3 from 1, k. 1, 3 from 1, 3 from 1, with m. and a. pattern 35 (37); repeat from * ending last repeat pattern 29 (30).
66th row: With m. pattern 29 (30), *with d. p. 13, with m. pattern 35 (37); repeat from * ending last repeat pattern 9 (10).
67th row: With m. pattern 9 (10), *with d. 3 from 1, k. 1, with b. k. 1, with d. k. 3, with b. k. 1, with d. k. 3, with b. k. 1, with d. k. 1, 3 from 1, with m. pattern 35 (37); repeat from * ending last repeat pattern 29 (30).
68th row: With m. pattern 29 (30), *with d. p. 17, with m. pattern 35 (37); repeat from * ending last repeat pattern 9 (10).
69th row: With m. pattern 9 (10), *with d. 3 from 1, k. 15, 3 from 1, with m. pattern 35 (37); repeat from * ending last repeat pattern 29 (30).
70th row: With m. and a. pattern 29 (30), *with d. p. 4, with b. p. 1, with d. p. 3, with b. p. 1, with d. p. 3, with b. p. 1, with d. p. 3, with b. p. 1, with d. p. 4, with m. and a. pattern 35 (37); repeat from * ending last repeat pattern 9 (10).
71st row: With m. and a. pattern 9 (10), *with d. k. 21, with m. and a. pattern 35 (37); repeat from * ending last repeat pattern 29 (30).
72nd row: With m. pattern 29 (30), *with d. p. 21, with m. pattern 35 (37); repeat from * ending last repeat pattern 9 (10).
73rd row: With m. pattern 9 (10), *with d. k. 2, with b. k. 1, with d. k. 3, with b. k. 1, with d. k. 3, with b. k. 1, with d. k. 3, with b. k. 1, with d. k. 3, with b. k. 1, with d. k. 2, with m. pattern 35 (37); repeat from * ending last repeat pattern 29 (30).
74th row: As 72nd row.
75th row: As 71st row, but using m. only for all over pattern.
76th to 78th rows: As 70th to 72nd rows.
79th row: With m. pattern 9 (10), *with d. k. 3 tog. b., k. 3, with b. k. 1, with d. k. 3, with b. k. 1, with d. k. 3, with b. k. 1, with d. k. 3, k. 3 tog., with m. pattern 35 (37); repeat from * ending last repeat pattern 29 (30).
80th row: As 68th row.
81st row: With m. pattern 9 (10), *with d. k. 3 tog. b., k. 11, k. 3 tog., with m. pattern 35 (37); repeat from * ending last repeat pattern 29 (30).
82nd row: With m. and a. pattern 29 (30), *with d. p. 3 tog., p. 3 tog., p. 1, p. 3 tog., p. 3 tog., with m. pattern 35 (37); repeat from * ending last repeat pattern 9 (10).
83rd row: With m. and a. pattern 11 (12) as set, * using a spare needle with c. cast on 24 sts., then cast off these 24 sts., transfer the remaining st. to right hand needle, with m. and a. pattern 39 (41) as set; repeat from * ending last repeat pattern 31 (32) sts.
84th row: With m. in pattern as set.
The last 84 rows form the pattern. On the next repeat of the pattern the position of the motifs is reversed, so work the 1st to 12th rows as before, then work as follows:
13th row: Pattern 30 (31) as set, *for the jam tart motif with b. 3 from 1, k. 1, 3 from 1, with m. pattern 37 (39) as set, repeat from * ending last repeat pattern 10 (11).
The last row sets the position of the motifs for the next repeat of the pattern. Now work the 14th to 46th rows as set. Work should now measure 40 centimetres (16 inches) from beginning. **
To shape the armholes: Continuing in pattern as set, cast off 9 sts. at the beginning of the next 2 rows,

then dec. 1 st. at each end of the next row and the 8 (10) following alternate rows.

On 127 (131) sts. pattern 33 rows.

Inc. 1st. at each end of the next row and the following 8th row.

On 131 (135) sts. pattern 11 rows.

To slope the shoulders: Cast off 10 sts. at the beginning of the next 6 rows, then 8 (9) sts. on the 2 following rows.

Cast off the remaining 55 (57) sts.

THE LEFT FRONT

With size 2¼ mm. (No. 13) needles and m. cast on 67 (71) sts. and work 35 rows in single rib.

Increase row: Rib 4 (6), *up 1, rib 4; repeat from * ending last repeat rib 3 (5). – 83 (87) sts.

Now work as given for back from ** to **.

– Work 1 extra row here when working right front.

To shape the armhole: Continuing in pattern as set, cast off 9 sts. at the beginning of the next row, work 1 row back to armhole edge. Dec. 1 st. at the beginning of the next row and the 8 (10) following alternate rows.

On 65 (67) sts. pattern 20 rows.

To shape the neck: Cast off 10 (11) sts. at the beginning – neck edge – on the next row.

***Pattern 19 rows decreasing 1 st. at the neck edge on each row and at the same time increasing 1 st. at the armhole edge on the 13th of these rows.

On 37 (38) sts. pattern 1 row.

Inc. 1 st. at the beginning – armhole edge on the next row.

On 38 (39) sts. pattern 11 rows.

To slope the shoulders: Cast off 10 sts. at the beginning of the next row and the 2 following alternate rows.

On 8 (9) sts. work 1 row, then cast off.

THE RIGHT FRONT

Work as given for the left front, noting the variation in the number of rows before shaping the armhole.

THE LONG SLEEVES (both alike)

With size 2¼ mm. (No. 13) needles and m. cast on 72 (76) sts. and work 47 rows in single rib.

Increase row: Rib 6 (8), *up 1, rib 6; repeat from * ending last repeat rib 6 (8). – 83 (87) sts.

Change to size 2¾ mm. (No. 12) needles and work the first 24 pattern rows given for back.

Maintaining the continuity of the pattern as set, and working the extra sts. into the pattern as they occur, inc. 1 st. at each end of the next row and the 14 following 6th rows.

On 113 (117) sts. pattern 21 rows.

To shape the sleevetop: Continuing in pattern as set, cast off 9 sts. at the beginning of the next 2 rows.

Dec. 1 st. at each end of the next row and the 24 (26) following alternate rows.

On 45 sts. work 1 row.

Dec. 1 st. at each end of the next 4 rows. Then cast off 4 sts. at the beginning of the next 4 rows, then 6 sts. on the 2 following rows.

Cast off the 9 remaining sts.

THE NECKBAND

First join shoulder seams. With right side of work facing rejoin m. at right front neck edge and using size 2¼mm. (No. 13) needles pick up and k. 46 (47) sts. from right front neck edge, 51 (53) sts. from back neck edge, then 46 (47) sts. from left front neck edge.

On 143 (147) sts. work 9 rows in single rib, then cast off in rib.

THE BUTTONBAND

With size 2¼ mm. (No. 13) needles and m. cast on 10 sts. and work 216 (220) rows in single rib, then cast off in rib.

THE BUTTONHOLE BAND

With size 2¼ mm. (No. 13) needles and m. cast on 10 sts. and work 6 (8) rows in single rib.

1st Buttonhole row: Rib 3, cast off 4, rib to end.

2nd Buttonhole row: Rib 3, turn, cast on 4, turn, rib to end.

Rib 32 rows.

Repeat the last 34 rows 5 times more, then work the 2 buttonhole rows again.

Rib 4 (6) rows.

Cast off in rib.

TO MAKE UP THE CARDIGAN

For garments knitted in "Woollybear Real Shetland", pin out to size and press all parts except the ribbing with a warm iron over a damp cloth. For garments knitted in "Woollybear Pure Silk", DO NOT PRESS. Join shoulder seams, set in sleeves. Join sleeve and side seams. Sew front bands in place. Sew on buttons.

THE SWEATER

THE BACK

Work as given for the back of the cardigan.

THE FRONT

Work as given for the back until the armhole shaping has been worked.

On 127 (131) sts. pattern 20 rows.

Now divide the sts. for the neck: Next row: Pattern 55 (56) and leave these sts. on a spare needle until required for right front shoulder, cast off 17 (19) sts., pattern to end and continue on these 55 (56) sts. for the left front shoulder.

The left front shoulder: Work as given for left front of cardigan from *** to end.

The right front shoulder: With right side of work facing rejoin yarn at inner edge of sts. left on spare needle and work to end of row, then work as given for left front shoulder to end.

THE SHORT SLEEVES (both alike)

With size 2¼ mm. (No. 13) needles and m. cast on 113 (117) sts. and k. 10 rows.

Change to size 2¾ mm. (No. 12) needles and work the 5th to 12th pattern rows given for back of cardigan.

13th row: Pattern 5, *then for the jam tart motif, with b. 3 from 1, k. 1, 3 from 1, with m. pattern 37 (39) as set; repeat from * ending on last repeat pattern 25.

The last row sets the position of the pattern given for the back of the cardigan. Now work the 14th to 46th rows as set.

To shape the sleevetop: Continuing in pattern as set, work as given for sleevetop on long sleeves given for cardigan.

THE NECKBAND

First join the right shoulder seam, then join left shoulder seam for 2.5 centimetres (1 inch) at outer edge. With right side of work facing rejoin m. at left front neck edge and using size 2¼ mm. (No. 13) needles pick up and k. 36 sts. from left front neck edge, 17 (19) sts. from centre front neck, 36 sts. from right front neck edge, and 51 (53) sts. at back neck edge.

On 140 (144) sts. work 7 rows in single rib, then cast off loosely in rib.

THE SHOULDER EDGING

With right side of work facing rejoin m. to neck edge of left back shoulder, and using size 2¼ mm. (No. 13) needles pick up and k. 35 (36) sts. from left back shoulder and 35 (36) sts. from left front shoulder. – 70 (72) sts.

K. 1 row.

1st Buttonhole row: K. 39 (41), *cast off 3, k. next 9 sts.; repeat from * ending last repeat k. next st.

2nd Buttonhole row: K. 2, *turn, cast on 3 over those cast off, turn, k. 10; repeat from * ending last repeat k. 39 (41).

Cast off.

TO MAKE UP THE SWEATER

As given for cardigan, omitting front bands.

His Masters Voice continued from page 84.

1st Buttonhole row: Rib 2, cast off 2, rib to end.

2nd Buttonhole row: Rib 2, turn, cast on 2, rib to end.

Rib 22 rows.

Repeat the last 24 rows 5 times more, then work the 2 buttonhole rows again.

Rib 4 rows, then cast off.

POCKET EDGINGS (both alike)

With right side of front facing using size 3¾ mm. (No. 9) needles and m. pick up and k. 25 sts. between the 9th and 42nd rows at either side of front, then cast off.

TO MAKE UP THE CARDIGAN

Press as for sweater. Set in sleeves. Neatly sew one row end of each pocket back to each side of back between the 9th and 42nd rows. Join sleeve and side seams. Neatly catch pocket backs in place. Sew front bands in position. Press seams. Sew on buttons.

THE CORD

Cut 3 lengths of d. each 150 centimetres (60 inches) long. Knot together at one end. Twist firmly in one direction, fold in half, allowing the 2 halves to twist together in the opposite direction. Knot and neaten ends. Thread through eyelet holes at neck edge. With a. make 2 pom-poms 6 centimetres (2½ inches) in diameter. Sew one to each end of cord.

his masters voice

Plaid shirts, skirt and pantaloons from Brown's.

his masters voice

MATERIALS
14 25 gram balls of "Woollybear 100% Mohair" by Patricia Roberts in main colour, 5 balls in first contrast colour, 2 balls in second contrast and 1 ball in each of the three other contrast colours, plus an oddment in black; a pair of size 3¾ mm. (No. 9) and size 4 mm. (No. 8) Aero knitting needles. For the cardigan only, 7 buttons.

SPECIAL NOTE
These garments may also be knitted in "Woollybear Cotton Bouclé" by Patricia Roberts. They will require 10 50 gram balls in main colour, 4 balls in first contrast colour, 1 ball in each of four other contrast colours and an oddment in black. To obtain the correct tension it is necessary to use size 3¼ mm. (No. 10) needles instead of size 3¾ mm. (No. 9) needles and size 3¾ mm. (No. 9) needles instead of size 4 mm. (No. 8) needles throughout.

TENSION
10 stitches and 14 rows to 5 centimetres (2 inches) over stocking stitch using "Woollybear 100% Mohair" and size 4 mm. (No. 8) needles or "Woollybear Cotton Bouclé" and size 3¾ mm. (No. 9) needles. If you cannot obtain the correct tension using the size needles suggested, use larger or smaller ones accordingly.

ABBREVIATIONS
K., knit; p., purl; st., stitch; tog., together; dec., decrease (by working 2 sts. tog.); inc., increase (by working twice into same st.); single rib is k. 1 and p. 1 alternately; s.s., stocking stitch is k. on the right side and p. on the wrong side; m.b., make bobble thus, k. 1, y.r.n., k. 1 all into next st., turn, p. 3, turn, sl. 1, k. 2 tog., p.s.s.o.; sl., slip; p.s.s.o., pass slip st. over; y.r.n., yarn round needle; m., main colour; a., first contrast colour; b., second contrast; c., third contrast; d., fourth contrast; e., fifth contrast; f., sixth contrast – black; up 1, pick the loop, which lies between the needles, slip it onto left hand needle, then k. into back of it; 3 from 1, k. 1, y.r.n., k. 1 all into one st.; wrap 3, *slip next 3 sts. onto right hand needle, bring a. to front of work, slip these 3 sts. back to left hand needle, take a. to back of work; repeat from * twice more, then with a. k. 3; m.k., make knot thus, with e. p. 1, k. 1, p. 1 all into next st., turn, k. 3, turn, p. 3 tog.; m.b.w., make bow thus, working into the next st., with e. cast on 5 sts., then k. these 5 sts., *turn, p. 5, turn, k. 4, turn, p. 4, turn, k. 3, turn, p. 3, turn, k. 2, turn, p. 2, turn, k. 1, turn, p. 1, turn, k. 5, turn, p. 5, cast off 5 *, turn, cast on 5 sts. p. these 5 sts., reading p. for k. and k. for p. repeat from * to *, turn, and with m. knit this st.; m.r.b., make rosebud thus, noting that the leaf and rosebud are both worked into the same st. – thus, with b. working into next st., cast on 5 sts., then k. these 5 sts., turn and k. these 5 sts. again, turn, cast off 4 sts. leaving 1 st. in b. on right hand needle; for the bud, with a. k. 1, y.r.n., k. 1, y.r.n., k. 1, y.r.n., k. 1, y.r.n., k. 1 all into next st., * *turn, * yarn forward, slip 1, yarn back, k. 1, repeat from * 4 times more * *, noting that the last st. worked is the st. in b., then repeat from * * to * * 7 times more, turn, and with wrong side of work facing, sl. 1, cast off 8, turn, with m. sl. 1, k. 1, p.s.s.o., this complete the rosebud and leaf.

MEASUREMENTS
The measurements are given in centimetres followed by inches in brackets.

Underarms	92.5 (37)
Side seam	42.5 (17)
Length	62.5 (25)
Sleeve seam	42.5 (17)

THE SWEATER

THE BACK
With size 3¾ mm. (No. 9) needles and m. cast on 82 sts. and work 15 rows in single rib.

Increase row: Rib 6, *up 1, rib 7; repeat from * ending last repeat rib 6. – 93 sts.

Change to size 4 mm. (No. 8) needles and beginning with a k. row s.s. 4 rows.

Now work in pattern from the chart as follows. Where the pattern is worked in s.s., only the colour details are given. When working the motifs use separate balls of m. at each side of them and separate small balls of contrast colours for each section of a motif.

5th row: 4m., *with a. m.b., 5m.; repeat from * ending last repeat 4m.

6th to 10th rows: All m.

11th row: 1m., *with a. m.b., 5m., with a. m.b., 5m., m.r.b. – see abbreviations, 5m., with a. m.b., 5m.; repeat from * ending last repeat 1m.

12th to 16th rows: All m.

17th row: 4m., * with a. m.b., 5m.; repeat from * 7 times more, 4c., 3m., 3c., 2m., with a. m.b., 5m., with a. m.b., 3m., 3c., 3m., 4c., 4m., with a. m.b., 4m.

18th row: 9m., 4c., 3m., 4c., 11m., 4c., 2m., 4c., 52m.

The last 18 rows set the position of the pattern given in the chart. Now work the 19th to 106th rows as set.

To shape the armholes: Continuing in pattern as set, cast off 4 sts. at the beginning of the next 2 rows, then dec. 1 st. at each end of the next row and the 5 following alternate rows. * *

On 73 sts. pattern 21 rows.

Inc. 1 st. at each end of the next row and the following 8th row.

On 77 sts. work 7 rows.

To slope the shoulders: Cast off 8 sts. at the beginning of the next 4 rows, then 7 sts. on the 2 following rows.

Cast off the remaining 31 sts.

THE FRONT
Work as given for the back until * * is reached.

On 73 sts. pattern 14 rows.

Now divide the sts. for the neck: Next row: Pattern 31 and leave these sts. on a spare needle until required for right front shoulder, cast off 11, work to end and continue on these 31 sts. for the left front shoulder.

The left front shoulder: To shape the neck: Pattern 10 rows, decreasing 1 st. at the neck edge on each row and at the same time, increasing 1 st. at the armhole edge on the 7th of these rows.

On 22 sts. pattern 4 rows.

Inc. 1 st. at the armhole edge on the next row. Pattern 7 rows.

To slope the shoulder: Cast off 8 sts. at the beginning of the next row and the following alternate row. On 7 sts. work 1 row, then cast off.

The right front shoulder: With right side of work facing rejoin yarn to inner edge of sts. left on spare needle and work to end of row, then work as given for left front shoulder to end.

THE SLEEVES (both alike)
With size 3¾ mm. (No. 9) needles and m. cast on 42 sts. and work 15 rows in single rib.

Increase row: Rib 3, *up 1, rib 6; repeat from * ending last repeat rib 3. – 49 sts.

Change to size 4 mm. (No. 8) needles and work in pattern as follows. This is worked entirely in s.s., except where indicated.

1st to 4th rows: All m.

5th row: 3m., *with a. m.b., 5m.; repeat from * ending last repeat 3m.

6th to 10th rows: All m.

11th row: 6m., with a. m.b., *5m., with a. m.b., 5m., with a. m.b., 5m.*, m.r.b.; repeat from * to *, with a. m.b., 6m.

12th row: All m.

13th to 22nd rows: As 1st to 10th rows.

23rd row: 6m., *with a. m.b., 5m.; repeat from * ending last repeat 6m.

24th row: All m.

25th to 34th rows: As 1st to 10th rows.

35th row: 6m., with a. m.b., 5m., m.r.b., 5m., with a. m.b., 5m., with a. m.b., 5m., with a. m.b., 5m., m.r.b., 5m., with a. m.b., 6m.

36th row: All m.

37th to 48th rows: As 13th to 24th rows.

The last 48 rows form the pattern. Continuing in pattern as set, inc. 1 st. at each end of the next row and the 6 following 8th rows.

On 63 sts. pattern 7 rows.

To shape the sleevetop: Continuing in pattern as set, cast off 4 sts. at the beginning of the next 2 rows, then dec. 1 st. at each end of the next row and the 10 following alternate rows.

On 33 sts. work 1 row.

Dec. 1 st. at each end of the next 4 rows, then cast off 3 sts. at the beginning of the next 4 rows and 4 sts. on the 2 following rows.

Cast off the remaining 5 sts.

THE NECKBAND
First join right shoulder seam. With right side of work facing rejoin m. and using size 3¾ mm. (No. 9) needles pick up and k. 24 sts. from left front neck edge, 11 sts. from centre front neck edge, 24 sts. from right front neck edge and 31 sts. from back neck edge.

On 90 sts. work 7 rows in single rib, then cast off in rib.

TO MAKE UP THE SWEATER
Pin out to size and press very lightly on the wrong side all parts except the ribbing. Join left shoulder seam. Set in sleeves. Join sleeve and side seams. Press seams.

THE CARDIGAN

THE BACK
As given for back of sweater.

THE LEFT FRONT
With size 3¾ mm. (No. 9) needles and m. cast on 40 sts. and work 15 rows in single rib.

Increase row: Rib 5, *up 1, rib 6; repeat from * ending last repeat rib 5. – 46 sts.

Change to size 4 mm. (No. 8) needles and beginning with a k. row s.s. 4 rows. * *

Now work in pattern from the chart as follows, noting the information given for back.

5th row: 4m., *with a. m.b., 5m.; repeat from * to end.

6th to 10th rows: All m.

11th row: 1m., *with a. m.b., 5m., with a. m.b., 5m., m.r.b. – see abbreviations, 5m., m.b., 5m.; repeat from * ending with 2m. instead of 5m.

12th row: All m.

13th to 22nd rows: As 1st to 10th rows.

23rd row: 1m., *with a. m.b., 5m. *; repeat from * to * twice more, with a. m.b., 3m., 2d., with e. m.b.w., 3d., 2m.; repeat from * to * twice, with a. m.b., 2m.

The last 23 rows set the position of the pattern given on the right hand side of the chart. Now work the 24th to 106th pattern rows as set.

To shape the armhole: Continuing in pattern as set, cast off 4 sts. at the beginning of the next row, then work 1 row back to armhole edge. Dec. 1 st. at the beginning of the next row and the 5 following alternate rows.

On 36 sts. pattern 14 rows.

To shape the neck: Cast off 5 sts. at the beginning of the next row, then work as given for left front shoulder on front of sweater to end.

THE RIGHT FRONT
Work as given for left front until * * is reached.

Now work in pattern as follows: 5th row: 5m., *with a. m.b., 5m.; repeat from * ending last repeat 4m.

6th to 10th rows: All m.

11th row: 2m., *with a. m.b., 5m., with a. m.b., 5m., m.r.b., 5m., with a. m.b., 5m.; repeat from * ending 1m.

12th to 16th rows: All m.

17th row: 5m., 4c., 3m., 3c., 2m., with a. m.b., 5m., with a. m.b., 3m., 3c., 3m., 4c., 4m., with a. m.b., 4m.

The last 17 rows set the position of the pattern given on the left hand side of the chart. Now work the 18th to 107th rows from the chart as set.

To shape the armholes: Work as given for left front armhole shaping to end.

THE SLEEVES (both alike)
Work as given for sleeves on sweater.

THE NECKBAND
First join shoulder seams. With right side of work facing, using size 3¾ mm. (No. 9) needles and m., pick up and k. 29 sts. from right front neck edge, 30 sts. from back neck edge and 29 sts. from left front neck edge. – 88 sts.

Work 1 row in single rib.

Eyelet hole row: Rib 2, *y.r.n., k. 2 tog., sl. 1., k. 1, p.s.s.o., y.r.n., rib 6; repeat from * ending last repeat rib 2.

Rib 5 rows more, then cast off in rib.

THE POCKET BACKS (2 alike)
With size 4 mm. (No. 8) needles and m. cast on 25 sts. and work 34 rows in s.s., then cast off.

THE BUTTONBAND
With size 3¾ mm. (No. 9) needles and m. cast on 6 sts. and work 156 rows in single rib.

THE BUTTONHOLE BAND
With size 3¾ mm. (No. 9) needles and m. cast on 6 sts. and work 6 rows in single rib.

Continued on page 81.

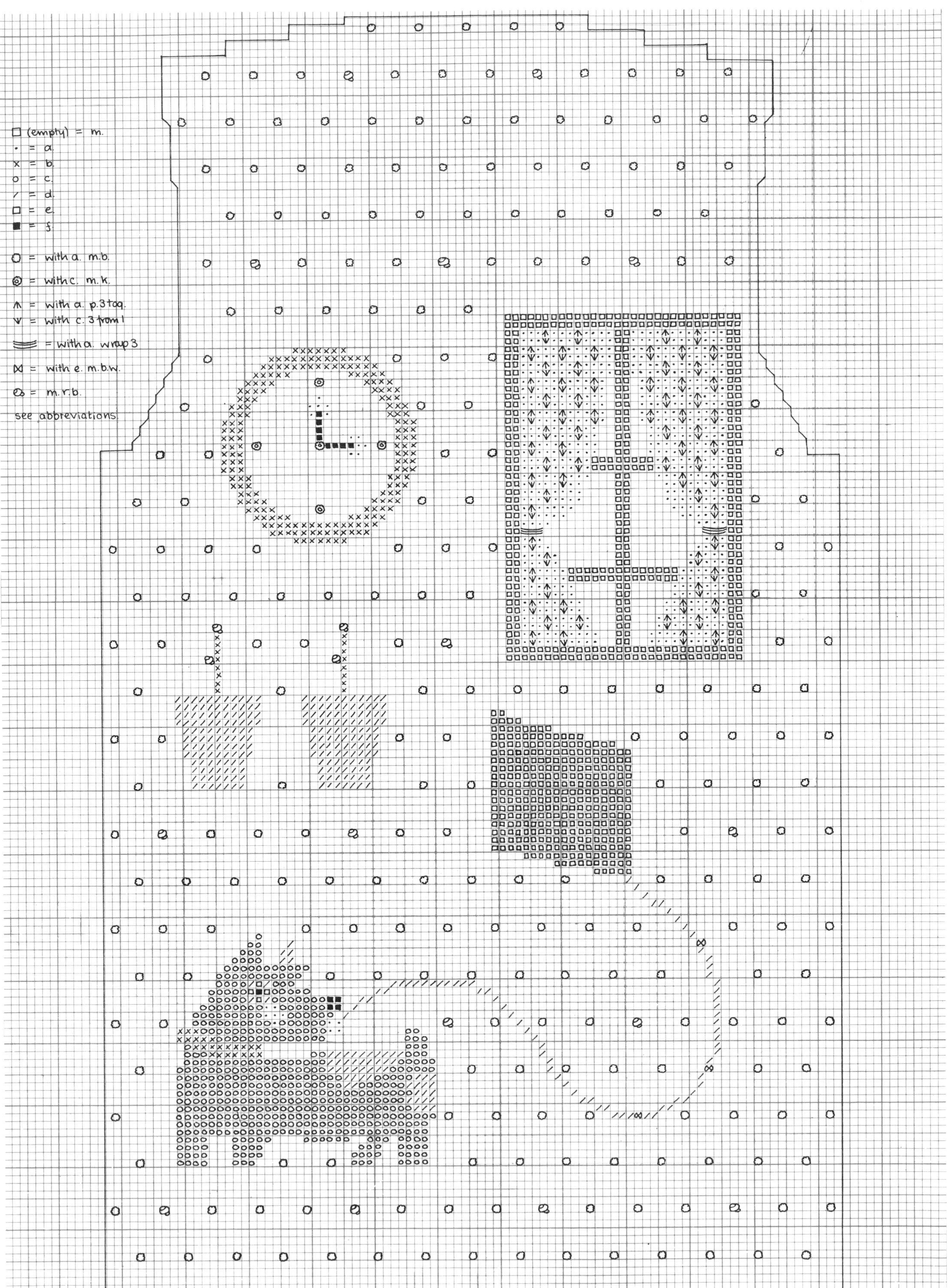
□ (empty) = m.
• = a.
x = b.
o = c.
/ = d.
□ = e.
■ = f.
O = with a. m.b.
◎ = with c. m.k.
∧ = with a. p.3 tog.
∨ = with c. 3 from 1
≡ = with a. wrap 3
⋈ = with e. m.b.w.
ʚ = m.r.b.
see abbreviations.

balmoral

Shorts and skirt by Kamikaze from Patricia Rober

collette

vent Garden. Man's trousers from Paul Smith.

balmoral

MATERIALS
2 (2) (3) (3) (3) (3) (3) (3) (4) (4) (4) (4) 28 gram (ounce) hanks of "Woollybear Real Shetland" by Patricia Roberts in main colour and 1 (1) (1) (1) (1) (1) (2) (2) (2) (2) (2) (2) hanks of the same yarn in each of the 9 contrast colours. "Woollybear 100% Mohair" may be substituted for up to 4 of the contrast colours, 1 (2) (2) (2) (2) (3) (3) (3) (3) (4) (4) (4) 25 gram balls in each colour will be required. A pair each of size 2¼mm. (No. 13) and 2¾mm. (No. 12) Aero knitting needles, 3 buttons for the first 3 sizes only.

TENSION
18 stitches and 20 rows to 5 centimetres (2 inches) over the FairIsle pattern using size 2¾mm. (No. 12) needles. If you cannot obtain the correct tension using the size needles suggested, use larger or smaller ones accordingly.

ABBREVIATIONS
K., knit; p., purl; st., stitch; tog., together; dec., decrease (by working 2 sts. tog.); inc., increase (by working twice into same st.); single rib is k. 1 and p. 1 alternately; s.s., stocking stitch is k. on the right side and p. on the wrong side; sl., slip; p.s.s.o., pass sl. st. over; m., main colour; a., first contrast; b., second contrast; c., third contrast; d., fourth contrast; e., fifth contrast; f., sixth contrast; g., seventh contrast; h., eighth contrast; i., ninth contrast; up 1, pick up the loop, which lies between the needles, slip it onto left hand needle, then k. into back of it.

MEASUREMENTS
The measurements are given in centimetres followed by inches in brackets.

Children's sizes			
Size	1	2	3
Underarms	55 (22)	60 (24)	65 (26)
Side seam	15 (6)	19 (7½)	22.5 (9)
Length	27.5 (11)	32.5 (13)	37.5 (15)
Sleeve seam	15 (6)	20 (8)	25 (10)

Children's sizes			
Size	4	5	6
Underarms	70 (28)	75 (30)	80 (32)
Side seam	26 (10½)	30 (12)	34 (13½)
Length	42.5 (17)	47.5 (19)	52.5 (21)
Sleeve seam	30 (12)	35 (14)	42 (16¾)

Women's sizes			
Size	7	8	9
Underarms	85 (34)	90 (36)	95 (38)
Side seam	37.5 (15)	37.5 (15)	37.5 (15)
Length	57.5 (23)	58 (23¼)	59 (23½)
Sleeve seam	42.5 (17)	42.5 (17)	42.5 (17)

Men's sizes			
Size	10	11	12
Underarms	95 (38)	100 (40)	105 (42)
Side seam	40 (16)	40 (16)	40 (16)
Length	62 (24½)	62.5 (25)	63 (25¼)
Sleeve seam	47.5 (19)	47.5 (19)	47.5 (19)

NOTE
The instructions are given for the first size. Where they vary, work the figures in the first brackets for the second size, the figures in the second brackets for the third size and so on. For easier working read through the pattern before commencing work and underline the figures to be worked.

THE BACK
With size 2¼mm. (No. 13) needles and m. cast on 86 (94) (102) (109) (117) (125) (133) (140) (148) (148) (156) (163) sts. and work 17 (19) (23) (25) (29) (31) (35) (35) (35) (35) (35) (35) rows in single rib.

Increase row: Rib 2 (4) (6) (1) (3) (5) (7) (2) (4) (4) (6) (1), *up 1, rib 6; repeat from * to end. – 100 (109) (118) (127) (136) (145) (154) (163) (172) (172) (181) (190) sts.

Change to size 2¾mm. (No. 12) needles and beginning with a k. row s.s. 2 rows.

Now work in FairIsle pattern as follows: This is worked entirely in s.s., so only the colour details are given. Take care not to pull colours not in use tightly across the back of the work, or it will be come puckered.

1st row: *2a., 2m., 3a., 2m.; repeat from * until 1 remains, 1a.

2nd row: All a.

3rd row: All b.

For the first, third, fifth, seventh, ninth, tenth and twelfth sizes: 4th row: 1b., *1c., 2b., 1c., 2b., 1c., 3b., 1c., 3b., 1c., 3b.; repeat from * until 9 remain, 1c., 2b., 1c., 2b., 1c., 2b.

5th row: 4d., *3c., 5d., 2c., 2d., 1c., 5d.; repeat from * until 6 remain, 3c., 3d.

6th row: 3d., 3e., 3d., *2e., 1d., 1e., 1d., 1e., 1d., 2e., 3d., 3e., 3d.; repeat from * until 1 remains, 1e.

For the second, fourth, sixth, eighth and eleventh sizes: 4th row: 1b., *1c., 2b., 1c., 2b., 1c., 3b., 1c., 3b., 1c., 3b.; repeat from * to end.

5th row: 3d., *2c., 2d., 1c., 5d., 3c., 5d.; repeat from * ending last repeat 3d.

6th row: 3d., *3e., 3d., 2e., 1d., 1e., 1d., 1e., 1d., 2e., 3d.; repeat from * ending last repeat 1d.

For all sizes continue as follows: The last 6 rows set the position of the pattern given in the chart; now work the 7th to 46th (58th) (70th) (82nd) (94th) (100th) (100th) (100th) (100th) (100th) (100th) (100th) pattern rows from the chart as set, then work the first nil (nil) (nil) (nil) (nil) (8) (20) (20) (20) (30) (30) (30)rows again.

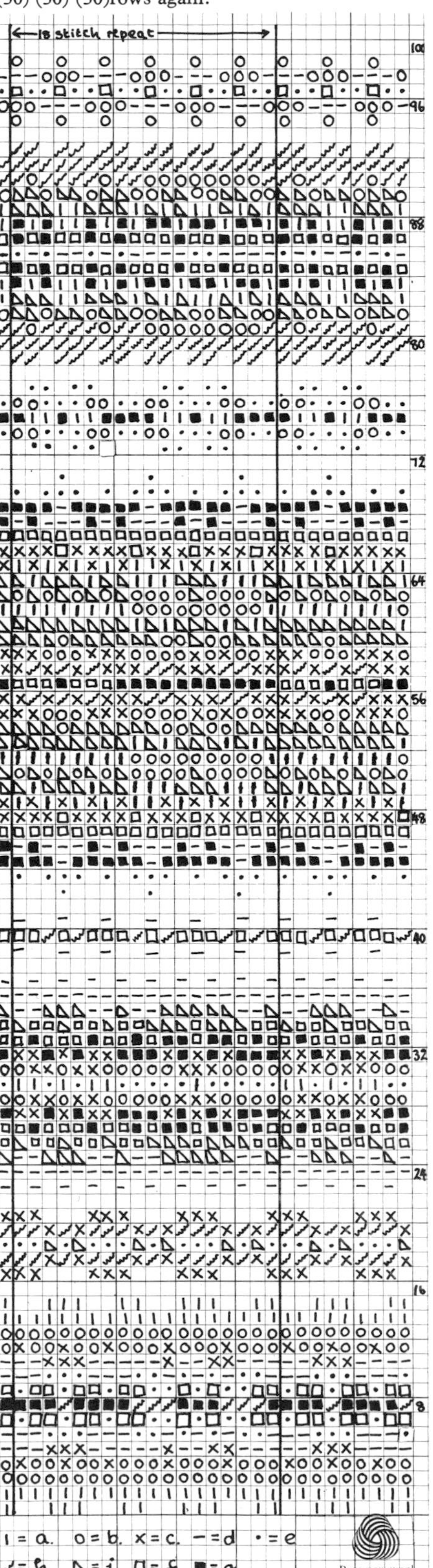

To shape the armholes: Maintaining the continuity of the pattern as set, cast off 4 sts. at the beginning of the next 2 rows, then dec. 1 st. at each end of the next row and the 2 (3) (4) (5) (6) (7) (8) (9) (10) (8) (9) (10) following alternate rows. **

On 86 (93) (100) (107) (114) (121) (128) (135) (142) (146) (153) (160) sts. pattern 37 (39) (43) (45) (49) (51) (53) (53) (53) (61) (61) (61) rows.

To slope the shoulders: Cast off 8 (8) (9) (9) (10) (11) (9) (10) (11) (11) (12) (13) sts. at the beginning of the next 4 (4) (4) (4) (4) (4) (6) (6) (6) (6) (6) (6) rows, then 7 (9) (9) (11) (11) (12) (10) (10) (10) (12) (12) (12) sts. on the 2 following rows. – 40 (43) (46) (49) (52) (53) (54) (55) (56) (56) (57) (58) sts.

Change to size 2¼mm. (No. 13) needles and with m. only, work 6 (6) (6) (8) (8) (8) (10) (10) (10) (12) (12) (12) rows in single rib. Cast off in rib.

THE FRONT
Work as given for the back until ** is reached.

On 86 (93) (100) (107) (114) (121) (128) (135) (142) (146) (153) (160) sts. pattern 22 (22) (22) (22) (22) (22) (22) (22) (22) (30) (30) (30) rows.

Now divide the sts. for the neck: Next row: Pattern 33 (36) (39) (42) (45) (48) (51) (54) (57) (59) (62) (65) and leave these sts. on a spare needle until required for right front shoulder, cast off 20 (21) (22) (23) (24) (25) (26) (27) (28) (28) (29) (30), work to end and continue on these 33 (36) (39) (42) (45) (48) (51) (54) (57) (59) (62) (65) sts. for the left front shoulder.

The left front shoulder: To shape the neck: Dec. 1 st. at the neck edge on each of the next 10 (11) (12) (13) (14) (14) (14) (14) (14) (14) (14) (14) rows.

On 23 (25) (27) (29) (31) (34) (37) (40) (43) (45) (48) (51) sts. work 4 (5) (8) (9) (12) (14) (16) (16) (16) (16) (16) (16) rows.

To slope the shoulder: Cast off 8 (8) (9) (9) (10) (11) (9) (10) (11) (11) (12) (13) sts. at the beginning of the next row and the 1 (1) (1) (1) (1) (1) (2) (2) (2) (2) (2) (2) following alternate rows. On 7 (9) (9) (11) (11) (12) (10) (10) (10) (12) (12) (12) sts. work 1 row, then cast off.

The right front shoulder: With right side of work facing rejoin yarn to inner edge of sts. left on spare needle and work to end of row, then work as given for left front shoulder to end.

THE FRONT NECKBAND
With right side of work facing rejoin m. at left front neck edge and using size 2¼mm. (No. 13) needles pick up and k. 48 (55) (62) (69) (76) (81) (86) (87) (88) (88) (89) (90) sts. from front neck edge. Work 5 (5) (5) (7) (7) (7) (9) (9) (9) (11) (11) (11) rows in single rib, then cast off in rib.

THE SLEEVES (both alike)
With size 2¼mm. (No. 13) needles and m. cast on 52 (54) (57) (60) (63) (66) (69) (72) (75) (79) (81) (84) sts. and work 13 (17) (25) (17) (25) (31) (31) (31) (31) (35) (35) (35) rows in single rib.

Increase row: Rib 4 (4) (8) (8) (3) (3) (4) (2) (5) (7) (1) (7), *up 1, rib 4 (5) (7) (4) (6) (9) (5) (7) (10) (6) (8) (11); repeat from * to end. – 64 (64) (64) (73) (73) (73) (82) (82) (82) (91) (91) (91) sts.

Change to size 2¾mm. (No. 12) needles and beginning with a k. row s.s. 2 rows.

Now work in FairIsle pattern as follows:

For the first size only: Work the first 10 pattern rows as given for first size on back.

For the second and third sizes only: Begin with the 95th pattern row as follows: 95th row: *2m., 1b.; repeat from * until 1 remains, 1m.

96th row: *3b., 3d.; repeat from * ending last repeat 1d.

97th to 100th rows: Work in pattern from chart as set.

1st to 3rd pattern rows: Work in pattern from chart as set.

4th row: 1b., *1c., 2b., 1c., 2b., 1c., 3b., 1c., 3b., 1c., 3b.; repeat from * until 9 remain, 1c., 2b., 1c., 2b., 1c., 2b.

For the fourth, fifth and sixth sizes only: 79th row: 1m., *2h., 1m.; repeat from * to end.

80th row: All h.

81st row: 1h., *8b., 2h., 1b., 4h., 1b., 2h.; repeat from * to end.

82nd row: 1b., *2i., 1b., 2i., 1b., 2i., 2b., 2i., 2b., 2i., 2b.; repeat from * to end.

83rd to 88th rows: Work in pattern from chart as set.

Continued on opposite page.

collette

MATERIALS
Either 8(11)(14)(17)(20)(23)(25)(28)(30) 25 gram balls of "Woollybear Lambswool" by Patricia Roberts or 6(8)(10)(12)(15)(17)(18)(20)(22) 28 gram (ounce) hanks of "Woollybear Real Shetland", or 8(12)(16)(20)(24)(28)(29)(31)(33) 25 gram balls of "Woollybear Fine Cotton", or 6(9)(13)(17)(21)(25)(26)(29)(30) 20 gram balls of "Woollybear Angora"; a pair each of size 2¼mm. (No. 13) and 2¾mm. (No. 12) Aero knitting needles; a fine cable needle.

TENSION
56 stitches – 2 repeats of the pattern to 12½ centimetres (5 inches) in width and 26 rows to 5 centimetres (2 inches) in depth, using size 2¾mm. (No 12) needles. If you cannot obtain the correct tension using the size needles suggested use larger or smaller ones accordingly.

ABBREVIATIONS
K., knit; p., purl; st., stitch; tog., together; dec., decrease (by working 2 sts. tog.); (inc., increase (by working twice into same st.); single rib is k. 1 and p. 1 alternately; up 1, pick up the loop, which lies between the needles, slip it onto left hand needle, then k. into back of it; cable 8f., cable 8 front thus, slip next 4 sts. onto a cable needle and leave at front of work, k.4, then k.4 from cable needle; cable 8b., cable 8 back, as cable 8f., but leaving sts. on cable needle at back of work; sl., slip; p.s.s.o., pass slip st. over.

MEASUREMENTS
The measurements are given in centimetres followed by inches in brackets.

	Children's		
Sizes	1	2	
Underarms	55 (22)	62.5 (25)	
Side seam	15 (6)	19.4 (7¾)	
Length	27.5 (11)	33 (13¼)	
Sleeve seams	15 (6)	21 (8¼)	
	Children's		
Sizes	3	4	5
Underarms	67.5 (27)	75 (30)	80 (32)
Side seam	24.4 (9¾)	28.75 (11½)	33 (13¼)
Length	40 (16)	45.5 (18¼)	51.5 (20¾)
Sleeve seams	26 (10½)	31 (12½)	37 (14¾)
	Women's		
Sizes	6	7	
Underarms	87.5 (35)	92.5 (37)	
Side seam	37.5 (15)	37.5 (15)	
Length	58 (23¼)	59.5 (23¾)	
Sleeve seam	42.5 (17)	42.5 (17)	
	Men's		
Sizes	8	9	
Underarms	100 (40)	105 (42)	
Side seam	40 (16)	40 (16)	
Length	64 (25½)	65 (26)	
Sleeve seam	45 (19)	45 (19)	

NOTE
The instructions are given for the first size. Where they vary, work the figures in the first brackets for the second size and so on. For easier working read through the pattern before commencing work and underline the figures to be worked.

THE BACK
With size 2¼mm. (No. 13) needles cast on 100(112)(122)(134)(144)(158)(168)(180)(190) sts. and work 17(21)(25)(29)(33)(35)(35)(35)(35) rows in single rib.

Increase row: Rib 4(2)(3)(1)(2)(5)(6)(4)(5), *up 1, rib 4; repeat from * ending last repeat rib 4 (2)(3)(1)(2)(5)(6)(4)(5). – 124(140)(152)(168)(180)(196)(208)(224)(236) sts.

Change to size 2¾mm. (No. 12) needles and work in pattern as follows:

For the first, third, fifth, seventh and ninth sizes only: 1st row: K.1, p.1, k.9, p.1, *k.1, p.1, k.13, p.1, k.1, p.1, k.9, p.1; repeat from * to end.

2nd row and every wrong side row: P.1, k.1, p.9, k.1, *p.1, k.1, p.13, k.1, p.1, k.1, p.9, k.1; repeat from * to end.

3rd row: K.1, p.1, cable 8f., k.1, p.1, *k.1, p.1, cable 8f., k.5, p.1, k.1, p.1, cable 8f., k.1, p.1; repeat from * to end.

5th row: As 1st row.

7th row: K.1, p.1, k.9, p.1, *k.1, p.1, k.4, cable 8b., k.1, p.1, k.1, p.1, k.9, p.1; repeat from * to end.

8th row: As 2nd row.

For the second, fourth, sixth and eighth sizes only: 1st row: *K.1, p.1, k.9, p.1, k.1, p.1, k.13, p.1; repeat from * to end.

2nd row and every wrong side row: *P.1, k.1, p.13, k.1, p.1, k.1, p.9, k.1; repeat from * to end.

3rd row: *K.1, p.1, cable 8f., k.1, p.1, k.1, p.1, cable 8f., k.5, p.1; repeat from * to end.

5th row: As 1st row.

7th row: *K.1, p.1, k.9, p.1, k.1, p.1, k.4, cable 8b., k.1, p.1; repeat from * to end.

8th row: As 2nd row.

For all sizes: The last 8 rows form the pattern; repeat them 6(8)(11)(13)(16)(18)(18)(20)(20) times, then work the first 2(6)(2)(6)(2)(4)(4)(2)(2) rows again.

To shape the armholes: Maintaining the continuity of the pattern as set, cast off 5 sts. at the beginning of the next 2 rows, then dec. 1 st. at each end of the next row and the 2(4)(6)(8)(10)(12)(14)(16)(18) following alternate rows.

On 108(120)(128)(140)(148)(160)(168)(180)(188) sts. pattern 53(57)(61)(65)(69)(75)(77)(83)(85) rows as set.

To slope the shoulders: Cast off 7(8)(9)(10)(11)(12)(12)(13)(14) sts. at the beginning of the next 6 rows, then 8(9)(9)(10)(10)(11)(13)(14)(13) sts. on the 2 following rows. – 50(54)(56)(60)(62)(66)(70)(74)(78) sts.

Change to size 2¼mm. (No. 13) needles and work 8(8)(8)(8)(10)(10)(10)(12)(12) rows in single rib, then cast off in rib.

THE FRONT
Work as given for the back until the first armhole shaping row has been worked.

Now divide the sts. for the neck: Next row: Cast off 5 sts. for armhole pattern across next 56(64)(70)(78)(84)(92)(98)(106)(112) sts. and leave these 57(65)(71)(79)(85)(93)(99)(107)(113) sts. on a spare needle until required for right front shoulder, pattern to end and continue on these 57(65)(71)(79)(85)(93)(99)(107)(113) sts. for the left front shoulder.

The left front shoulder: to shape the armhole and to slope the neck: Continuing in pattern as set dec. 1 st. at each end of the next row and the 2(4)(6)(8)(10)(12)(14)(16)(18) following alternate rows. Then dec. 1 st. at the neck edge only on the 22(22)(21)(21)(20)(20)(20)(20)(20) following alternate rows.

On 29(33)(36)(40)(43)(47)(49)(53)(55) sts. pattern 9(13)(19)(23)(29)(35)(37)(43)(45) rows.

To slope the shoulder: Cast off 7(8)(9)(10)(11)(12)(12)(13)(14) sts. at the beginning of the next row and the 2 following alternate rows. On 8(9)(9)(10)(10)(11)(13)(14)(13) sts. work 1 row, then cast off.

The right front shoulder: With right side of work facing rejoin yarn to inner edge of sts. left on spare needle and work to end of row, then work as given for left front shoulder to end.

THE FRONT NECKBAND
With right side of work facing rejoin yarn at left front shoulder and using size 2¼mm. (No. 13) needles pick up and k. 44(48)(52)(56)(60)(64)(68)(74)(78) sts. from left front neck edge, then 44(48)(52)(56)(60)(64)(68)(74)(78) sts. from right front neck edge.

On 88(96)(104)(112)(120)(128)(136)(148)(156) sts. work 1 row in single rib.

Next row: Rib to within 2 sts. of centre front neck, sl.1, k.1, p.s.s.o., k.2 tog., rib to end.

Rib 1 row.

Repeat the last 2 rows 2(2)(2)(2)(3)(3)(3)(4)(4) times.

Cast off loosely in rib.

THE SLEEVES (both alike)
With size 2¼mm. (No. 13) needles cast on 48(52)(56)(60)(64)(68)(72)(76)(78) sts. and work 11(15)(21)(25)(31)(35)(35)(35)(35) rows in single rib.

Increase row: Rib 5(1)(1)(7)(1)(7)(1)(3)(6), *up 1, rib 2(2)(2)(2)(2)(2)(3)(2)(2); repeat from * ending last repeat rib 5(1)(1)(7)(1)(7)(2)(3)(6). – 68(68)(84)(84)(96)(96)(96)(112)(112) sts.

Change to size 2¾mm. (No. 12) needles and work the eight pattern rows as given for the first (first) (second) (second) (first) (first) (first) (second) (second) size given for back.

Continuing in pattern as set and working the extra sts. into the moss stitch pattern at each side of the cables, increase 1 st. at each end of the next row and the 15(19)(15)(19)(17)(21)(24)(19)(22) following 3rd (4th) (6th) (6th) (8th) (8th) (6th) (10th) (8th) rows.

On 100(108)(116)(124)(132)(140)(146)(152)(158) sts. pattern 12(5)(13)(13)(13)(5)(29)(9)(23) rows.

To shape the sleeve top: Continuing in pattern as set, cast off 5 sts. at the beginning of the next 2 rows, then dec. 1st. at each end of the next row and the 2(6)(10)(14)(18)(22)(25)(30)(33) following alternate rows.

Work 1 row straight.

Dec. 1 st. at each end of the next 20(18)(16)(14)(12)(10)(8)(4)(2) rows. – 44(48)(52)(56)(60)(64)(68)(72)(76) sts.

Cast off 3(3)(3)(3)(4)(4)(4)(5)(5) sts. at the beginning of the next 10 rows, then 4(5)(6)(7)(5)(6)(8)(7)(8) sts. on the 2 following rows. Cast off the remaining 6(8)(10)(12)(10)(12)(12)(8)(10) sts.

TO MAKE UP THE SWEATER
Pin out to size and press all parts except the ribbing with a warm iron over a damp cloth. Join shoulder seams. Set in sleeves. Join sleeve and side seams. Press seams.

"**Balmoral**" continued from opposite page.

For the seventh, eighth and ninth sizes only: 79th row: 1m., *2h., 1m.; repeat from * to end.

80th row: All h.

81st row: 2h., *1b., 4h., 1b., 2h., 8b., 2h.; repeat from * until 8 remain, 1b., 4h., 1b., 2h.

82nd row: 1b., 2i., 1b., 2i., 1b., 2i., *2b., 2i., 2b., 2i., 2b., 2i., 1b., 2i., 1b., 2i.; repeat from * until 1 remains, 1b.

83rd to 88th rows: Work in pattern from chart as set.

For the tenth, eleventh and twelfth sizes only: 73rd row: 3m., *2e., 1m., 2e., 4m.; repeat from * ending last repeat 2m.

74th row: 1e., *2b., 3e., 2b., 2e.; repeat from * to end.

75th to 80th rows: Work in pattern from chart as set.

81st row: 1h., *8b., 2h., 1b., 4h., 1b., 2h.; repeat from * to end.

82nd row: 1b., *2i., 1b., 2i., 1b., 2i., 2b., 2i., 2b., 2i., 2b; repeat from * to end.

For all sizes: The last 10 rows set the position of the pattern given in the chart.

Maintaining the continuity of the pattern as set and working the extra sts. into the pattern as they occur, inc. 1 st. at each end of the next row and the 8 (10) (12) (10) (12) (14) (12) (14) (16) (14) (16) (18) following 4th (4th) (4th) (8th) (8th) (8th) (10th) (8th) (8th) (10th) (8th) (8th) rows.

On 82 (86) (90) (95) (99) (103) (108) (112) (116) (121) (125) (129) sts. pattern 3 (13) (17) (13) (9) (15) (11) (19) (3) (7) (19) (3) rows.

To shape the sleevetop: Continuing in pattern as set, cast off 4 sts. at the beginning of the next 2 rows, then dec. 1 st. at each end of the next row and the 1 (3) (5) (8) (11) (14) (15) (16) (17) (16) (17) (18) following alternate rows, then dec. 1 st. at each end of the next 15 (15) (15) (13) (11) (9) (9) (9) (9) (13) (13) (13) rows. – 40 (40) (40) (43) (45) (47) (50) (52) (54) (53) (55) (57) sts.

Cast off 3(3)(3)(3)(3)(3)(4)(4)(4)(4)(4)(4) sts. at the beginning of the next 6 rows, then 4(4)(4)(5)(5)(5)(5)(5)(5)(5)(6)(6) sts. on the 4 following rows.

Cast off the remaining 6 (6) (6) (5) (7) (9) (6) (8) (10) (9) (7) (9) sts.

THE LEFT SHOULDER EDGING (first 3 sizes)
First join left shoulder seam for 1.5 centimetres (½ inch) at armhole edge. With right side of work facing rejoin m. at left back shoulder and using size 2¼mm. (No. 13) needles and m. pick up and k. 23 (25) (27) sts. from left back shoulder, then 23 (25) (27) sts. from left front shoulder.

K.1 row.

Next row: K.25 (27) (29), cast off 3, k. next 12 (14) (16) sts., cast off 3, k. to end.

Next row: K.2, turn, cast on 3, turn, k.13 (15) (17), turn, cast on 3, turn, k. to end.

Cast off loosely.

TO MAKE UP THE SWEATER
Pin out to size and press all parts except the ribbing with a warm iron over a damp cloth. Join shoulder seam(s). Set in sleeves. Join sleeve and side seams. Sew on buttons – on first 3 sizes. Press seams.

dolly blue

gypsy

Rust dress from Brown's, floral skirt from Joseph.

dolly blue

MATERIALS

11 ounce (28 gram) hanks of "Woollybear Real Shetland" by Patricia Roberts in main colour and 3 25 gram balls of "Woollybear 100% Mohair" by Patricia Roberts in each of the 2 contrast colours; a pair each of size 2¼ mm. (No. 13) and size 2¾ mm. (No. 12) Aero knitting needles; 2 fine cable needles.

TENSION

The tension is based on a stocking stitch tension of 16 stitches and 20 rows to 5 centimetres (2 inches) using size 2¾ mm. (No. 12) needles. If you cannot obtain the correct tension using the size needles suggested, use larger or smaller ones accordingly.

ABBREVIATIONS

K., knit; p., purl; st., stitch; tog., together; dec., decrease (by working 2 sts. tog.); inc., increase (by working twice into same st.); single rib is k. 1 and p. 1 alternately; up 1 is pick up the loop which lies between the needles, slip it on to left hand needle, then k. into back of it; cable 4b., cable 4 back thus, slip next 4 sts. onto cable needle and leave at back of work, with a. k.5, then with m. k.4 from cable needle; cable 4f., cable 4 front thus, slip next 4 sts. onto cable needle and leave at front of work, with b. k.5, then with m. k.4 from cable needle; cable 5b., slip next 5 sts. onto cable needle and leave at back of work, with m. k.4, then with a. k.5 from cable needle; cable 5f., slip next 5 sts. onto cable needle and leave at front of work, with m. k.4 then with b. k.5 from cable needle; m., main colour; a., first contrast; b., second contrast.

MEASUREMENTS

The measurements are given in centimetres followed by inches in brackets.

Underarms	85 (34)
Side seam	37.5 (15)
Length	59 (23½)
Sleeve seam	42.5 (17)

THE BACK

With size 2¼ mm. (No. 13) needles and m. cast on 127 sts. and work 33 rows in single rib.

Increase row: Rib 4, *up 1, rib 6, up 1, rib 6, up 1, rib 3, up 1, rib 5, up 1, rib 3, up 1, rib 6, up 1, rib 6, up 1, rib 7; repeat from * ending last repeat rib 4. – 151 sts.

Change to size 2¾ mm. (No. 12) needles and work in pattern as follows. Use separate balls of a. and b. for each cable panel. Take care to purl the up 1s through the back of the sts.

1st row: With m. p.16, *k.4, with a. k.5, with m. p.1, with b. k.5, with m. k.4, p.31; repeat from * ending last repeat p.16.

2nd row: With m. k.16, *p.4, with b. p.5, with m. k.1, with a. p.5, with m. p.4, k.31; repeat from * ending last repeat k.16.

3rd row: With m. p.14, *p.2 tog., k.4, with a. k.5, with m. up 1, p.1, up 1, with b. k.5, with m. k.4, p.2 tog., p.27; repeat from * ending last repeat p.14.

4th row: With m. k.15, *p.4, with b. p.5, with m. k.3, with a. p.5, with m. p.4, k.29; repeat from * ending last repeat k.15.

5th row: With m. p.13, *p.2 tog., cable 4b., with m. up 1, p.3, up 1, cable 5f., with m. p.2 tog., p.25; repeat from * ending last repeat p.13.

6th row: With m. k.14, *with b. p.5, with m. p.4, k.5, p.4, with a. p.5, with m. k.27; repeat from * ending last repeat k.14.

7th row: With m. p.12, *p.2 tog., with a. k.5, with m. k.4, up 1, p.5, up 1, k.4, with b. k.5, with m. p.2 tog., p.23; repeat from * ending last repeat p.12.

8th row: With m. k.13, *with b. p.5, with m. p.4, k.7, p.4, with a. p.5, with m. k.25; repeat from * ending last repeat k.13.

9th row: With m. p.11, *p.2 tog., with a. k.5, with m. k.4, up 1, p.7, up 1, k.4, with b. k.5, with m. p.2 tog., p.21; repeat from * ending last repeat p.11.

10th row: With m. k.12, *with b. p.5, with m. p.4, k.9, p.4, with a. p.5, with m. k.23; repeat from * ending last repeat k.12.

11th row: With m. p.10, *p.2 tog., with a. k.5, with m. k.4, up 1, p.9, up 1, k.4, with b. k.5, with m. p.2 tog., p.19; repeat from * ending last repeat p.10.

12th row: With m. k.11, *with b. p.5, with m. p.4, k.11, p.4, with a. p.5, with m. k.21; repeat from * ending last repeat k.11.

13th row: With m. p.9, *p.2 tog., cable 5b., with m. up 1, p.11, up 1, cable 4f, with m. p.2 tog., p.17; repeat from * ending last repeat k.9.

14th row: With m. k.10, *p.4, with b. p.5, with m. k.13, with a. p.5, with m. p.4, k.19; repeat from * ending last repeat k.10.

15th row: With m. p.8, *p.2 tog., k.4, with a. k.5, with m. up 1, p.13, up 1, with b. k.5, with m. k.4, p.2 tog., p.15; repeat from * ending last repeat p.8.

16th row: With m. k.9, *p.4, with b. p.5, with m. k.15, with a. p.5, with m. p.4, k.17; repeat from * ending last repeat k.9.

17th row: With m. p.7, *p.2 tog., k.4, with a. k.5, with m. up 1, p.15, up 1, with b. k.5, with m. k.4, p.2 tog., p.13; repeat from * ending last repeat p.7.

18th row: With m. k.8, *p.4, with b. p.5, with m. k.17, with a. p.5, with m. p.4, k.15; repeat from * ending last repeat k.8.

19th row: With m. p.6, *p.2 tog., k.4, with a. k.5, with m. up 1, p.17, up 1, with b. k.5, with m. k.4, p.2 tog., p.11; repeat from * ending last repeat p.6.

20th row: With m. k.7, *p.4, with b. p.5, with m. k.19, with a. p.5, with m. p.4, k.13; repeat from * ending last repeat k.7.

21st row: With m. p.5, *p.2 tog., cable 4b., with m. up 1, p.19, up 1, cable 5f., with m. p.2 tog., p.9; repeat from * ending last repeat p.5.

22nd row: With m. k.6, *with b. p.5, with m. p.4, k.21, p.4, with a. p.5, with m. k.11; repeat from * ending last repeat k.6.

23rd row: With m. p.4, *p.2 tog., with a. k.5, with m. k.4, up 1, p.21, up 1, k.4, with b. k.5, with m. p.2 tog., p.7; repeat from * ending last repeat p.4.

24th row: With m. k.5, *with b. p.5, with m. p.4, k.23, p.4, with a. p.5, with m. k.9; repeat from * ending last repeat k.5.

25th row: With m. p.3, *p.2 tog., with a. k.5, with m. k.4, up 1, p.23, up 1, k.4, with b. k.5, with m. p.2 tog., p.5; repeat from * ending last repeat p.3.

26th row: With m. k.4, *with b. p.5, with m. p.4, k.25, p.4, with a. p.5, with m. k.7; repeat from * ending last repeat k.4.

27th row: With m. p.2, *p.2 tog., with a. k.5, with m. k.4, up 1, p.25, up 1, k.4, with b. k.5, with m. p.2 tog., p.3; repeat from * ending last repeat p.2.

28th row: With m. k.3, *with b. p.5, with m. p.4, k.27, p.4, with a. p.5, with m. k.5; repeat from * ending last repeat k.3.

29th row: With m. p.1, *p.2 tog., cable 5b., with m. up 1, p.27, up 1, cable 4f., with m. p.2 tog., p.1; repeat from * to end.

30th row: With m. k.2, *p.4, with b. p.5, with m. k.29, with a. p.5, with m. p.4, k.3; repeat from * ending last repeat k.2.

31st row: With m. p.2 tog., *k.4, with a. k.5, with m. up 1, p.29, up 1, with b. k.5, with m. k.4, p.3 tog.; repeat from * ending last repeat p.2 tog. instead of p.3 tog.

32nd row: With m. k.1, *p.4, with b. p.5, with m. k.31, with a. p.5, with m. p.4, k.1; repeat from * to end.

33rd row: With m. p.1, *k.4, with a. k.5, with m. p.31, with b. k.5, with m. k.4, p.1; repeat from * to end.

34th row: As 32nd row.

35th row: With m. p.1, *up 1, k.4, with a. k.5, with m. p.2 tog., p.27, p.2 tog., with b. k.5, with m. k.4, up 1, p.1; repeat from * to end.

36th to 62nd wrong side rows only: Work as given for 30th back to 4th wrong side rows.

37th row: With m. p.2, *up 1, cable 4b., with m. p.2 tog., p.25, p.2 tog., cable 5f., up 1, p.3; repeat from * ending last repeat p.2.

39th row: With m. p.3, *up 1, with a. k.5, with m. k.4, p.2 tog., p.23, p.2 tog., k.4, with b. k.5, with m. up 1, p.5; repeat from * ending last repeat p.3.

41st row: With m. p.4, *up 1, with a. k.5, with m. k.4, p.2 tog., p.21, p.2 tog., k.4, with b. k.5, with m. up 1, p.7; repeat from * ending last repeat p.4.

43rd row: With m. p.5, *up 1, with a. k.5, with m. k.4, p.2 tog., p.19, p.2 tog., k.4, with b. k.5, with m. up 1, p.9; repeat from * ending last repeat p.5

45th row: With m. p.6, *up 1, cable 5b., with m. p.2 tog., p.17, p.2 tog., cable 4f., with m. up 1, p.11; repeat from * ending last repeat p.6.

47th to 61st rows: Work in cable pattern as set purling 1 extra st. at each end, 2 sts. less between the decreases and 2 sts. more between the up 1 increases on each successive row.

63rd row: With m. p.15, *up 1, k.4, with a. k.5, with m. p.3 tog., with b. k.5, with m. k.4, up 1, p.29; repeat from * ending last repeat p.15.

64th row: As 2nd row.

The last 64 rows form the pattern; now work the first 56 rows again. Work should now measure 37.5 centimetres (15 inches) from beginning.

To shape the armholes: Continuing in pattern as set, cast off 8 sts. at the beginning of the next 2 rows, then dec. 1 st. at each end of the 10 following rows, ending on the 4th pattern row. – 115 sts.

Next row: 5th pattern row: With m. p.1, k.5, p.3, *up 1, cable 5f., with m. p.2 tog., p.25, p.2 tog., cable 4b., with m up 1, p.3; repeat from * once more, k.5, p.1.

6th pattern row: With m. k.10, *p.4, with a. p.5, with m. k.27, with b. p.5, with m. p.4, k.5; repeat from * ending k.10 instead of k.5. * *

Continuing in pattern as set work 44 rows more, then inc. 1 st. at each end of the next row and the following 8th row.

On 119 sts. pattern 9 rows.

To slope the shoulders: Cast off 8 sts. at the beginning of the next 8 rows.

Cast off the remaining 55 sts.

THE FRONT

Work as given for back until * * is reached, then pattern 1 row.

Now divide the sts. for the neck: Next row: Pattern 54 and leave these sts. on a spare needle until required for right front shoulder, cast off 7 sts., pattern to end and continue on these 54 sts. for the left front shoulder.

The left front shoulder: Pattern 27 rows.

To shape the neck: Cast off 10 sts. at the beginning of the next row, then dec. 1 st. at the neck edge on each of the next 14 rows. – 30 sts.

Inc. 1 st. at the beginning – armhole edge on the next row and the following 8th row.

On 32 sts. pattern 9 rows.

To slope the shoulder: Cast off 8 sts. at the beginning of the next row and the 2 following alternate rows. On 8 sts. work 1 row, then cast off.

The right front shoulder: With right side of work facing rejoin yarn to inner edge of sts. left on spare needle and work to end of row, then work as given for left front shoulder to end.

THE SLEEVES (both alike)

With size 2¼ mm. (No. 13) needles and m. cast on 64 sts. and work 29 rows in single rib.

Increase row: Rib 2, *up 1, rib 2; repeat from * to end. – 95 sts.

Change to size 2¾ mm. (No. 12) needles and work in pattern as follows, noting the information given for the back.

41st pattern row: With m. p.1, *up 1, with a. k.5, with m. k.4, p.2 tog., p.21, p.2 tog., k.4, with b. k.5, with m. up 1, p.7; repeat from * ending p.1 instead of p.7.

The last row sets the position of the pattern given for back, work the 42nd to 50th rows as set.

Continuing in pattern as set, inc. 1 st. at each end of the next row and the 6 following 20th rows.

On 109 sts. pattern 13 rows, ending with a 56th pattern row.

To shape the sleevetop: Continuing in pattern as set, cast off 8 sts. at the beginning of the next 2 rows, then dec. 1 st. at each end of the next row and the 15 following alternate rows.

On 61 sts. work 1 row.

Dec. 1 st. at each end of the next 8 rows.

Cast off 5 sts. at the beginning of the next 8 rows. Cast off the remaining 5 sts.

THE COLLAR

With size 2¼ mm. (No. 13) needles and m. cast on 198 sts. and work 10 rows in single rib.

Decrease row: Rib 3, *p.3 tog., rib 6; repeat from * ending least repat rib 3. – 154 sts.

Work 19 rows more in single rib, then cast off.

Continued on opposite page.

gypsy

MATERIALS

For the jacket: 15 (15) (16) 25 gram balls of "Woollybear 100% Mohair" by Patricia Roberts in main colour, 4 balls in each of first and second contrasts and 1 ball in third contrast; a pair each of size 4 mm. (No. 8) and size 3¾ mm. (No. 9) Aero knitting needles; 2 buttons.

For the coat: Add 5 balls in main colour. 2 balls in first and second contrasts and 1 ball in third contrast.

SPECIAL NOTE

These garments may also be knitted in "Woollybear Cotton Bouclé" by Patricia Roberts. The jacket will require 10 (10) (11) 50 gram balls in main colour, 3 balls in each of first and second contrasts and 1 ball in third contrast. For the coat add 3 balls in main colour, and 1 ball in each of first, second and third contrasts. To obtain the correct tension it is necessary to use size 3¾ mm. (No. 9) needles instead of size 4 mm. (No. 8) needles and size 3¼ mm. (No. 10) needles instead of size 3¾ mm. (No. 9) needles throughout.

TENSION

It is essential to work at a tension of 9 stitches and 17 rows to 5 centimetres (2 inches) over the garter stitch using size 4 mm. (No. 8) needles and "Woollybear 100% Mohair" or size 3¾ mm. (No. 9) needles and "Woollybear Cotton Bouclé".

ABBREVIATIONS

K., knit; p., purl; st., stitch; tog., together; dec., decrease (by working 2 sts. tog.); inc., increase (by working twice into same st.); garter st. is k. plain on every row; single rib is k. 1 and p. 1 alternately; sl., slip; p.s.s.o., pass sl. st. over; m., main colour; a., first contrast; b., second contrast; c., third contrast.

NOTE

The instructions are given for the small size. Where they vary, work the figures in the first brackets for the medium size or the figures in the second brackets for the large size.

MEASUREMENTS

The measurements are given in centimetres followed by inches in brackets.

Sizes	small	medium	large
THE JACKET			
Underarms	110 (44)	115 (46)	120 (48)
Side seam	45 (18)	45 (18)	45 (18)
Length	70 (28)	71 (28½)	72.5 (29)
Sleeve seam	40 (16)	40 (16)	40 (16)
THE COAT			
Underarms	110 (44)	115 (46)	120 (48)
Side seam	67.5 (27)	67.5 (27)	67.5 (27)
Length	92.5 (37)	94 (37½)	95 (38)
Sleeve seam	40 (16)	40 (16)	40 (16)

THE JACKET

THE BACK

With size 3¾ mm. (No. 9) needles and m. cast on 100 (106) (110) sts. and work 12 rows in single rib.

Change to size 4 mm. (No. 8) needles and work in pattern as follows. When working the vertical stripes in a. and b. use separate balls of contrast colours for each group of stripes.

1st row: With m. k.2 (5) (7), *with a. k.2, with m. k.2, with a. k.2, with m. k.12, with b. k.2, with m. k.2, with b. k.2, with m. k.12; repeat from * ending last repeat k.2 (5) (7).

2nd row: With m. k.2 (5) (7), *with b. p.2, with m. k.2, with b. p.2, with m. k.12, with a. p.2, with m. k.2, with a. p.2, with m. k.12; repeat from * ending last repeat k.2 (5) (7).

3rd and 4th rows: With m. all k.

5th to 20th rows: Repeat 1st to 4th rows 4 times.

21st and 22nd rows: As 1st and 2nd rows.

23rd and 24th rows: With a. all k.

25th and 26th rows: As 1st and 2nd rows.

27th and 28th rows: With b. all k.

29th and 30th rows: As 1st and 2nd rows.

31st and 32nd rows: With c. all k.

33rd and 34th rows: As 1st and 2nd rows.

35th and 36th rows: With b. all k.

37th and 38th rows: As 1st and 2nd rows.

39th and 40th rows: With a. all k.

The last 40 rows form the pattern; repeat them twice more, then work the first 20 rows again. Work should now measure 45 centimetres (18 inches) from beginning.

To shape the armholes: Maintaining the continuity of the pattern as set, cast off 6 sts. at the beginning of the next 2 rows, then dec. 1 st. at each end of the next row and the 4 (6) (7) following alternate rows.

On 78 (80) (82) sts. pattern 45 (45) (47) rows.

Inc. 1 st. at each end of the next row and the following 12th row.

On 82 (84) (86) sts. pattern 11 rows.

To slope the shoulders: Cast off 9 sts. at the beginning of the next 4 rows, then 8 (9) (10) sts. on the 2 following rows.

Cast off the remaining 30 sts.

THE POCKET BACKS (2 alike)

With size 4 mm. (No. 8) needles and m. cast on 24 sts. and work 44 rows in garter st., then leave these sts. on a stitch-holder until required.

THE LEFT FRONT

With size 3¾ mm. (No. 9) needles and m. cast on 55 (58) (60) sts. and work 12 rows in single rib.

Change to size 4mm. (No. 8) needles and noting the information given for back, work in pattern as follows:

1st row: With m. k.2 (5) (7), with a. k. 2, with m. k.2, with a. k.2, with m. k.12, with b. k.2, with m. k.2, with b. k.2, with m. k.12, with a. k.2, with m. k.2, with a. k.2, with m. k.11.

The last row sets the position of the pattern given for the back. Work the 2nd to 40th rows as set, then work the first 19 rows again.

* * *Now divide the sts. for the pocket: Next row: Pattern 40 and leave these sts. on a spare needle until required, pattern to end.

Next row: Pattern across the remaining 15 (18) (20) sts., then onto the same needle, continue in pattern as set across the 24 sts. of one pocket back.

On 39 (42) (44) sts. pattern 22 rows, then leave these sts. on a spare needle until required.

Returning to the 40 sts. left on a spare needle rejoin yarn to inner edge of sts. and continuing in pattern as set, cast off 2 sts. at the beginning, inner edge, on the next row and the 11 following alternate rows. – 16 sts.

Next row: Pattern across these 16 sts., then onto the same needle pattern across the 39 (42) (44) sts. left on spare needle. – 55 (58) (60) sts. * * *

Pattern 42 rows more as set.

* * * *To slope the front edge: Maintaining the continuity of the pattern as set, dec. 1 st. at the end of the next row and the 3 following 4th rows.

On 51 (54) (56) sts. work 1 row back to side seam edge.

To shape the armhole and to slope the front edge: Continuing to dec. at front edge on every 4th row as before, cast off 6 sts. at the beginning of the next row, work 1 row back to armhole edge, then dec. 1 st. at the beginning – armhole edge – on the next row and the 4 (6) (7) following alternate rows.

Still decreasing at front edge on every 4th row pattern 45 (45) (47) rows. – 26 sts.

Pattern 13 rows, increasing 1 st. at the armhole edge on the 1st and 13th of these rows and, at the same time, decreasing 1 st. at the front edge on the 3rd of these rows on the small and medium sizes and on the 7th row on the small size only. – 26 (27) (28) sts.

On 26 (27) (28) sts. pattern 11 rows.

To slope the shoulder: Cast off 9 sts. at the beginning of the next row and the following alternate row. On 8 (9) (10) sts. work 1 row, then cast off.

THE RIGHT FRONT

With size 3¾ mm. (No. 9) needles and m. cast on 55 (58) (60) sts. and work 12 rows in single rib.

Change to size 4 mm. (No. 8) needles and work in pattern as follows.

1st row: With m. k.11, with b. k.2, with m. k.2, with b. k.2, with m. k.12, with a. k.2, with m. k.2, with a. k.2, with m. k.12, with b. k.2, with m. k.2, with b. k.2, with m. k.2 (5) (7).

The last row sets the position of the pattern given for the back. Work the 2nd to 40th rows as set then work the first 20 rows again.

Now work as given for left front from * * * to * * *.

Pattern 1 row.

1st Buttonhole row: Pattern 3, cast off 4, work to end.

2nd Buttonhole row: Pattern until 3 remain, turn, cast on 4 over those cast off, turn, work to end.

Pattern 36 rows, then work the 2 buttonhole rows again.

Work 1 row straight, then work as given for left front from * * * * to end.

THE SLEEVES (both alike)

With size 3¾ mm. (No. 9) needles and m. cast on 42 (44) (46) sts. and work 8 rows in single rib.

Change to size 4 mm. (No. 8) needles and work as follows:

Increase row: k.21 (22) (23), turn, cast on 20 sts., turn, k. to end. – 62 (64) (66) sts.

K. 1 row.

Now work in pattern as given for back, but beginning with the 13th row as follows: 13th row: With m. k.10 (11) (12), with a. k.2, with m. k.2, with a. k.2, with m. k.12, with b. k.2, with m. k.2, with b. k.2, with m. k.12, with a. k.2, with m. k.2, with a. k.2, with m. k.10 (11) (12).

The last row sets the position of the pattern given for the back, work the 14th to 40th rows as set. Work the 40 pattern rows twice more, then work the first 20 rows again.

To shape the sleevetop: Continuing in pattern as set, cast off 6 sts. at the beginning of the next 2 rows, then dec. 1 st. at each end of the next row and the 9 following 4th rows, then at each end of the 2 (3) (4) following alternate rows.

On 26 sts. work 1 row.

Dec. 1 st. at each end of the next 2 rows, then cast off 3 sts. at the beginning of the next 6 rows, then cast off the remaining 4 sts.

THE HALF COLLARS (both alike)

With size 3¾ mm. (No. 9) needles and m. cast on 24 sts. and work 70 rows in single rib.

Decrease row: Rib 2, sl 1, k.2 tog., p.s.s.o., rib to end.

Rib 3 rows.

Repeat the last 4 rows 8 times, then work the decrease row again.

On 4 sts. work rows in single rib, until the band is long enough to fit down front edge, with last decrease in line with first front edge dec., then cast off.

THE POCKET TOPS (2 alike)

With right side of work facing rejoin m. to the shaped edge of pocket opening and using size 3¾ mm. (No. 9) needles pick up and k. 40 sts. from this edge. Work 5 rows in single rib, then cast off in rib.

TO MAKE UP THE JACKET

Pin out to size and press very lightly on the wrong side with a warm iron over a damp cloth. Join shoulder seams. Set in sleeves, join sleeve and side seams. Neatly sew pocket backs and row ends of pocket tops in place. Join cast on edges of half collar pieces, then sew the shaped row end edges in place all round neck edge and down front edges, so that the first front edge dec. is in line with the last dec. of each half collar. Fold cast on group of sts. at centre of cuffs to wrong side and neatly fold and sew in place. Press seams. Sew buttons in place.

THE COAT

TO WORK

Work as given for the jacket, but working 2 extra repeats of the 40 row pattern on the back, before shaping the armholes and on the left and right fronts before dividing the sts. for the pockets.

"**Dolly Blue**" continued from opposite page.

THE BUTTONBAND

With size 2¼ mm. (No. 13) needles and m. cast on 9 sts. and work 28 rows in single rib, then cast off in rib.

THE BUTTONHOLE BAND

With size 2¼ mm. (No. 13) needles and m. cast on 9 sts. and work 4 rows in single rib.

1st Buttonhole row: Rib 3, cast off 3, rib to end.

2nd Buttonhole row: Rib 3, turn, cast on 3, turn, rib to end.

Rib 18 rows, then work the 2 buttonhole rows again.

Rib 2 rows, then cast off in rib.

TO MAKE UP THE SWEATER

Pin out to size and press all parts except the ribbing with a warm iron over a damp cloth. Join shoulder seams. Set in sleeves. Join sleeve and side seams. Sew cast off edge of collar in place all round neck edge. Sew button and buttonhole bands in place. Press seams. Sew on buttons.

burlington

Trousers, shirts and dress by Kamik

mirage

n Patricia Roberts, Covent Garden.

burlington

MATERIALS
Either 24 25 gram balls of "Woollybear Cashmere" by Patricia Roberts, or 25 25 gram balls of "Woollybear 100% Mohair", or 37 25 gram balls of "Woollybear Cotton Crepe"; a pair each of size 3 mm. (No. 11) and size 3¾ mm. (No. 9) Aero knitting needles; a cable needle; 2 shoulder pads (optional).

TENSION
15 stitches – 1 repeat of the pattern and 16 rows to 5 centimetres (2 inches) using either "Woollybear Cashmere" double or "Cotton Crepe"; or 14 stitches and 16 rows to 5 centimetres (2 inches) using "Woollybear Mohair"; all using size 3¾ mm. (No. 9) knitting needles. If you cannot obtain the correct tension using the size needles suggested, use larger or smaller ones accordingly.

ABBREVIATIONS
K., knit; p., purl; st., stitch; tog., together; dec., decrease (by working 2 sts. tog.); inc., increase (by working twice into same st.); single rib is k. 1 and p. 1 alternately; cable 6 thus, slip next 3 sts. onto cable needle and leave at front of work, k. 3, then k. 3 from cable needle; sl., slip; p.s.s.o., pass sl. st. over.

MEASUREMENTS
The measurements are given in centimetres followed by inches in brackets.

Underarms – in Cashmere or Cotton Crepe	97·5	(39)
Underarms – in Mohair	105	(42)
Side seam	45	(18)
Length	67·5	(27)
Sleeve seam	40	(16)

SPECIAL NOTE
When using "Woollybear Cashmere", the yarn is knitted double – 2 strands together – throughout.

THE BACK AND FRONT (alike)
With size 3 mm. (No. 11) needles cast on 119 sts. and work 23 rows in single rib, beginning right side rows with p. 1 and wrong side rows with k. 1.

Increase row: Rib 4, *inc. p.wise in each of the next 3 sts., rib 9, repeat from * ending last repeat rib 4. – 149 sts.

Change to size 3¾ mm. (No. 9) needles and work in pattern as follows:

1st row: *K. 3, p. 1, k. 6, p. 1, k. 3, p. 1; repeat from * ending last repeat k. 3, instead of k. 3, p. 1.

2nd row: *K. 1, p. 1, k. 1, p. 8, k. 1, p. 1, k. 1, p. 1; repeat from * ending last repeat k. 1, p. 1, k. 1, instead of k. 1, p. 1, k. 1, p. 1.

3rd to 6th rows: Repeat the 1st and 2nd rows twice.

7th row: *K. 3, p. 1, cable 6, p. 1, k. 3, p. 1; repeat from * ending last repeat k. 3.

8th row: As 2nd row.

9th to 12th rows: Repeat 1st and 2nd rows twice.

13th row: As 7th row.

14th row: As 2nd row.

The last 14 rows form the pattern; repeat them 7 times more, then work the first 8 rows again.

To shape the armholes: Maintaining the continuity of the pattern as set, cast off 6 sts. at the beginning of the next 2 rows, then dec. 1 st. at each end of the next row and the 9 following alternate rows. – 117 sts. Pattern 14 rows.

Decrease row: P. 1, *k. 1, p. 3, p. 2tog., p. 3, k. 1, p. 5; repeat from * ending last repeat p. 1 instead of p. 5. – 109 sts.

Leave these sts. on a spare needle until required.

THE SLEEVES (both alike)
With size 3 mm. (No. 11) needles cast on 60 sts. and work 17 rows in single rib.

Increase row: Rib 3, *up 1, rib 5; repeat from * ending last repeat rib 2. – 72 sts.

Change to size 3¾ mm. (No. 9) needles and work in pattern as follows:

1st row: K. 2, *p. 1, k. 6, p. 1, k. 3, p. 1, k. 3; repeat from * until 10 remain, p. 1, k. 6, p. 1, k. 2.

2nd row: P. 1, k. 1, p. 8, k. 1, p. 1, *k. 1, p. 1, k. 1, p. 1, k. 1, p. 8, k. 1, p. 1; repeat from * to end.

The last 2 rows set the position of the pattern given for the back. Work the 3rd to 14th rows as set.

Continuing in cable pattern and working the extra sts. into the pattern as they occur, inc. 1 st. at each end of the next row and the 15 following 6th rows.

On 104 sts. pattern 7 rows.

To shape the sleevetop: Cast off 6 sts. at the beginning of the next 2 rows, then dec. 1 st. at each end of the next row and the 9 following alternate rows. On 72 sts. pattern 14 rows.

Decrease row: K. 2tog., *p. 3, p. 2tog., p. 3, k. 1, p. 5, k. 1; repeat from * once, p. 2, p. 2tog. and leave these 32 sts. on a stitch-holder until required, then work across the remaining sts. as follows: p. 2tog., p. 2, *k. 1, p. 5, k. 1, p. 3, p. 2tog., p. 3; repeat from * once, k. 2tog., leave these 32 sts. on a spare needle until required.

THE BACK YOKE
With right side of work facing rejoin yarn at centre of one sleeve and using size 3 mm. (No. 11) needles, beginning with k. 1, work in single rib across the 32 sts. of one sleeve, then onto the same needle work in single rib across the 109 sts. of the back, then across the first 32 sts. of other sleeve.

On 173 sts. work 3 rows in single rib.

Decrease row: Rib 10, sl. 1, k. 2tog., p.s.s.o., rib until 13 remain, sl. 1, k. 2tog., p.s.s.o., rib to end.

Repeat the last 4 rows twice more.

Work 1 row in single rib.

Next Decrease row: K. 2tog., rib 8, sl. 1, k. 2tog., p.s.s.o., rib until 13 remain, sl. 1, k. 2tog., p.s.s.o., rib until 2 remain, k. 2tog. **

Repeat the last 2 rows 7 times more, working 1 st. less between the first and last decreases on each successive repeat.

On 113 sts. rib 1 row.

To slope the shoulders: Cast off 14 sts. at the beginning of the next 4 rows. – 57 sts.

Work 2 rows in single rib, then cast off in rib.

THE FRONT YOKE
Work as given for the back yoke until ** is reached.

Now divide the sts. for the neck: Next Row: Rib 69 and leave these sts. on a stitch-holder until required for right front shoulder, rib 17 and leave these sts. on a spare double pointed needle until required, rib to end and continue on these 69 sts. for the left front shoulder.

Decrease row: K. 2tog., rib 7, sl. 1, k. 2tog., p.s.s.o., rib until 3 remain, then slip these 3 sts. onto the needle holding the sts. at centre front neck.

Rib 1 row.

Repeat the last 2 rows once more, working 1 st. less between the decreases.

Next Decrease row: K. 2tog., rib 5, sl. 1, k. 2tog., p.s.s.o., rib until 2 remain, slip these 2 sts. onto needle at centre front. Rib 1 row.

Repeat the last 2 rows 4 times more, working 1 st. less between the decreases on each successive repeat.

To slope the shoulder: Next row: Cast off 14 sts., then rib until 2 remain and slip these sts. onto needle at centre front.

Rib 1 row.

Next row: Cast off 14 sts., then leave the 2 remaining sts. on needle at centre front.

The right front shoulder: With right side of work facing rejoin yarn to inner edge of sts. left on stitch-holder and work as follows:

Decrease row: Rib until 12 remain, sl. 1, k. 2tog., p.s.s.o., rib 7, k. 2tog.

Next row: Rib until 3 remain, slip these 3 sts. onto spare needle at centre front.

Repeat the last 2 rows once more, then the decrease row again, but working 1 st. less between the decreases on each successive decrease row.

Next row: Rib until 2 remain, slip these 2 sts. onto needle at centre front.

Repeat the last 2 rows, working 1 st. less between the decreases on each successive repeat, 4 times.

Rib 1 row straight.

To slope the shoulder: Work as given for left front shoulder.

To complete the front: Rejoin yarn to the 57 sts. now on needle at centre front. Work 2 rows in single rib, then cast off very loosely.

THE POCKET BACKS (2 alike)
With size 3¾ mm. (No. 9) needles cast on 40 sts. and work 40 rows in single rib, then cast off.

TO MAKE UP THE SWEATER
Pin out to size and press all parts very lightly on the wrong side with a warm iron over a damp cloth. Join shoulder seams. Neatly sew one row end edge of each pocket at each side of back 5 centimetres (2 inches) above ribbing. Join sleeve seams. Join side seams, neatly sewing pockets backs in place on wrong side of front. Join underarm seams. Catch shoulder pads in place if required.

"**Mirage**" continued from opposite page.

TO MAKE UP THE JACKET
Pin out to size and press all parts very lightly on the wrong side. Join shoulder seams. Set in sleeves. Join sleeve and side seams. Neatly sew pocket backs in place, so that one row end edge of each is sewn to the row end edges of pocket opening nearest the side seams. Sew collar in place, so that the row ends between the marking threads are sewn to the last few sts. cast off at front neck edges. Press seams. Sew on buttons.

mirage

MATERIALS
16 25 gram balls of "Woollybear Lambswool" by Patricia Roberts, plus 10 25 gram balls of "Woollybear 100% Mohair" in main colour, 5 balls in each of the first and second contrast colours and 4 balls in the third contrast; a pair each of size 4 mm. (No. 8) and size 4½ mm. (No. 7) Aero knitting needles; a cable needle; 4 buttons.

TENSION
30 stitches – 2 repeats of the pattern – to 12.5 centimetres (5 inches) in width and 12 rows to 5 centimetres (2 inches) in depth over the cable rib pattern using size 4½ mm. (No. 7) needles and one strand each of mohair and lambswool together.

ABBREVIATIONS
K., knit; p., purl; st., stitch; tog., together; dec., decrease (by working 2 sts. tog.)., inc., increase (by working twice into same st.); single rib is k. 1 and p. 1 alternately; cable 6, slip next 3 sts. onto a cable needle and leave at front of work, k. 3, then k. 3 from cable needle; m., main colour – mohair used with lambswool; a., first contrast colour; b., second contrast colour; c., third contrast; up 1, pick up the loop which lies between the needles, slip it onto left hand needle, then k. into back of it.

MEASUREMENTS
The measurements are given in centimetres followed by inches in brackets.

Underarms	110	(44)
Side seam	40	(16)
Length	65	(26)
Sleeve seam	40	(16)

NOTE
Instructions in brackets are worked the number of times stated after the brackets.

SPECIAL NOTE
The lambswool is used throughout in the same colour – it is knitted together with the mohair in various colours, thus the colour mentioned is always that of the mohair.

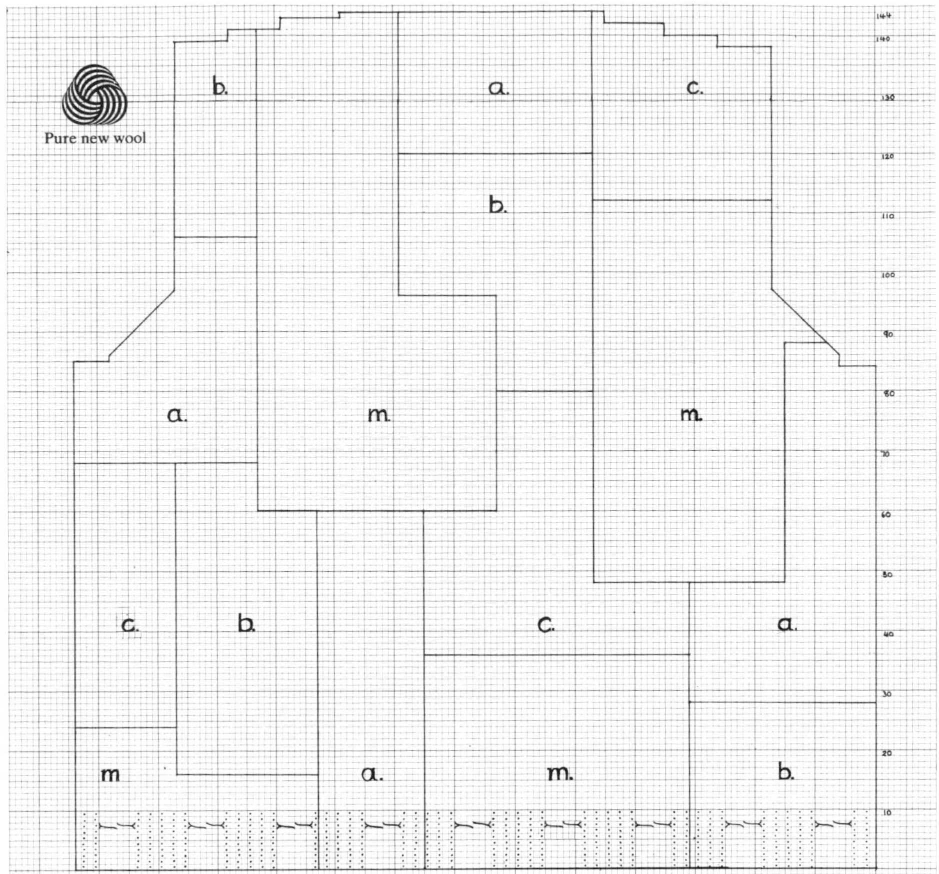

THE BACK
With size 4 mm. (No. 8) needles and m. – one strand of mohair and one strand of lambswool together, cast on 108 sts. and work 11 rows in single rib.

Increase row: Rib 4, *up 1, rib 4; repeat from * to end. – 134 sts.

Change to size 4½ mm. (No. 7) needles and work in pattern as follows; but in blocks of colour as given in the charts, noting that the lambswool is used throughout and that the mohair only changes colour. The stitch pattern only is now given, for the colours see the chart. The garment is worked in cable rib all over.

1st row: (K. 1, p. 1) twice, *k. 6, p. 1, (k. 1, p. 1) 4 times; repeat from * until 10 remain, k. 6, (p. 1, k. 1) twice.

2nd row: (P. 1, k. 1) twice, *p. 6, k. 1, (p. 1, k. 1) 4 times; repeat from * ending last repeat (k. 1, p. 1) twice.

3rd to 6th rows: Repeat 1st and 2nd rows twice.

7th row: (K. 1, p. 1) twice, *cable 6, p. 1, (k. 1, p. 1) 4 times; repeat from * ending last repeat (p. 1, k. 1) twice.

8th row: As 2nd row.

9th and 10th rows: As 1st and 2nd row.

The last 10 rows form the cable rib pattern and the colour details are given in the chart. Thus pattern 74 rows more in cable rib in blocks of colour.

To shape the armholes: Continuing in pattern as set, cast off 6 sts. at the beginning of the next 2 rows, then dec. 1 st. at each end of the next 11 rows.

On 100 sts. pattern 41 rows.

To slope the shoulders: Cast off 9 sts. at the beginning of the next 4 rows and 10 sts. on the 2 following rows.

Cast off the remaining 44 sts.

THE LEFT FRONT
With size 4 mm. (No. 8) needles and m. – one strand each of lambswool and mohair – cast on 70 sts. and work 11 rows in single rib.

Increase row: Rib 3, *up 1, rib 4; repeat from * ending last repeat rib 3. – 87 sts.

Change to size 4½ mm. (No. 7) needles and work in cable rib as given for back in blocks of colour as follows:

1st row: With b. (k. 1, p. 1) twice, k. 6, p. 1, (k. 1, p. 1) 4 times, k. 6, (p. 1, k. 1) 3 times, with m. p. 1, k. 1, p. 1, *k. 6, p. 1, (k. 1, p. 1) 4 times; repeat from * once, k. 6, p. 1, (k. 1, p. 1) twice, with a. (k. 1, p. 1) twice, k. 6, p. 1, k. 1.

The last row sets the position of the cable rib pattern given for back and the blocks of colour given on the right hand side of the chart.

Continuing in pattern work 11 rows straight.

**Now divide the sts. for the pocket. Next row: Work as set across 31 sts. and leave these sts. on a spare needle until required, pattern to end and continue on these 56 sts.

On 56 sts. pattern 27 rows, when working right front, work buttonholes as before on the 25th and 26th of these rows, then leave these sts. on a spare needle.

Return to the 31 sts. left on spare needle, rejoin yarn at inner edge and pattern 27 rows as set.

Next row: Pattern across these 31 sts. then onto the same needle pattern across the 56 sts. left on spare needle before.

On all 87 sts. pattern 43 rows.

To shape the armhole: Continuing in pattern as set and in colours from chart, cast off 6 sts. at the beginning of the next row. Work 1 row back to armhole edge.

Dec. 1 st. at the armhole edge on each of the next 11 rows.

On 70 sts. pattern 22 rows.

To shape the neck: Cast off in pattern 31 sts. at the beginning of the next row, then dec. 1 st. at the neck edge on each of the next 11 rows.

On 28 sts. pattern 7 rows.

To slope the shoulder: Cast off 9 sts. at the beginning of the next row and following alternate row. On 10 sts. work 1 row, then cast off.

THE RIGHT FRONT
With size 4 mm. (No. 8) needles and m. cast on 70 sts. and work 6 rows in single rib.

1st Buttonhole row: Work as set across 5 sts., cast off 3, rib next 12 sts. – work 20 sts. instead of 12 on the next set of buttonhole rows – cast off 3, work to end as set.

2nd Buttonhole row: Work as set, but turning and casting on 3 sts. over those cast off.

Rib 3 rows, then work the increase row given for left front.

Change to size 4½ mm. (No. 7) needles and work in cable rib as given for back in blocks of colour from the chart as follows:

1st row: With m. k. 1, p. 1, k. 6, p. 1, (k. 1, p. 1) 4 times, k. 6, p. 1, k. 1, p. 1, k. 1, p. 1, with a. (k. 1, p. 1) twice, k. 6, (p. 1, k. 1) 4 times, with m. p. 1, *k. 6, p. 1, (k. 1, p. 1) 4 times; repeat from * ending last repeat (p. 1, k. 1) twice.

The last row sets the position of the cable rib pattern given for the back and the blocks of colour given at the left hand side of chart.

Pattern 12 rows as set.

Now work as given for left from ** to end.

THE POCKET BACKS (2 alike)
With size 4 mm. (No. 8) needles and m. – one strand each of lambswool and mohair – cast on 28 sts. and work 28 rows in single rib, then cast off.

THE SLEEVES (both alike)
With size 4 mm. (No. 8) needles and m., cast on 61 sts. and work 11 rows in single rib.

Next row: Rib 6, *up 1, rib 5; repeat from * to end – 72 sts.

Change to size 4½ mm. (No. 7) needles and work in cable rib pattern in blocks of colour as given at the centre of the chart for the back as follows:

1st row: With m. p. 1, k. 1, p. 1, *k. 6, p. 1, (k. 1, p. 1) 4 times; repeat from * once, k. 6, p. 1, k. 1, p. 1, k. 1, p. 1, with a. k. 1, p. 1, k. 1, p. 1, k. 6, (p. 1, k. 1) 4 times, with m. p. 1, k. 6, p. 1, k. 1, p. 1.

The last row sets the position of the pattern and the colour blocks given for the centre of the back. Continuing in pattern as set work 11 rows.

Inc. 1 st. at each end of the next row and the 5 following 12th rows. On 84 sts. work 11 rows.

To shape the sleevetop: Cast off 6 sts. at the beginning of the next 2 rows, then dec. 1 st. at each end of the next row and the 17 following alternate rows. On 36 sts. work 1 row.

Cast off 3 sts. at the beginning of the next 2 rows, 4 sts. on the 2 following rows and 5 sts. on the next 2 rows. Cast off the remaining 12 sts.

THE COLLAR
With size 4 mm. (No. 8) needles and m. cast on 108 sts. and work 10 rows in single rib. Mark each end of the last row with coloured threads. Dec. 1 st. at each end of the next 4 rows, marking each end of the last row with coloured threads.

Cast off 6 sts. at the beginning of the next 4 rows.

Cast off the remaining 76 sts.

Continued on opposite page.

crackers

Skirt and culo

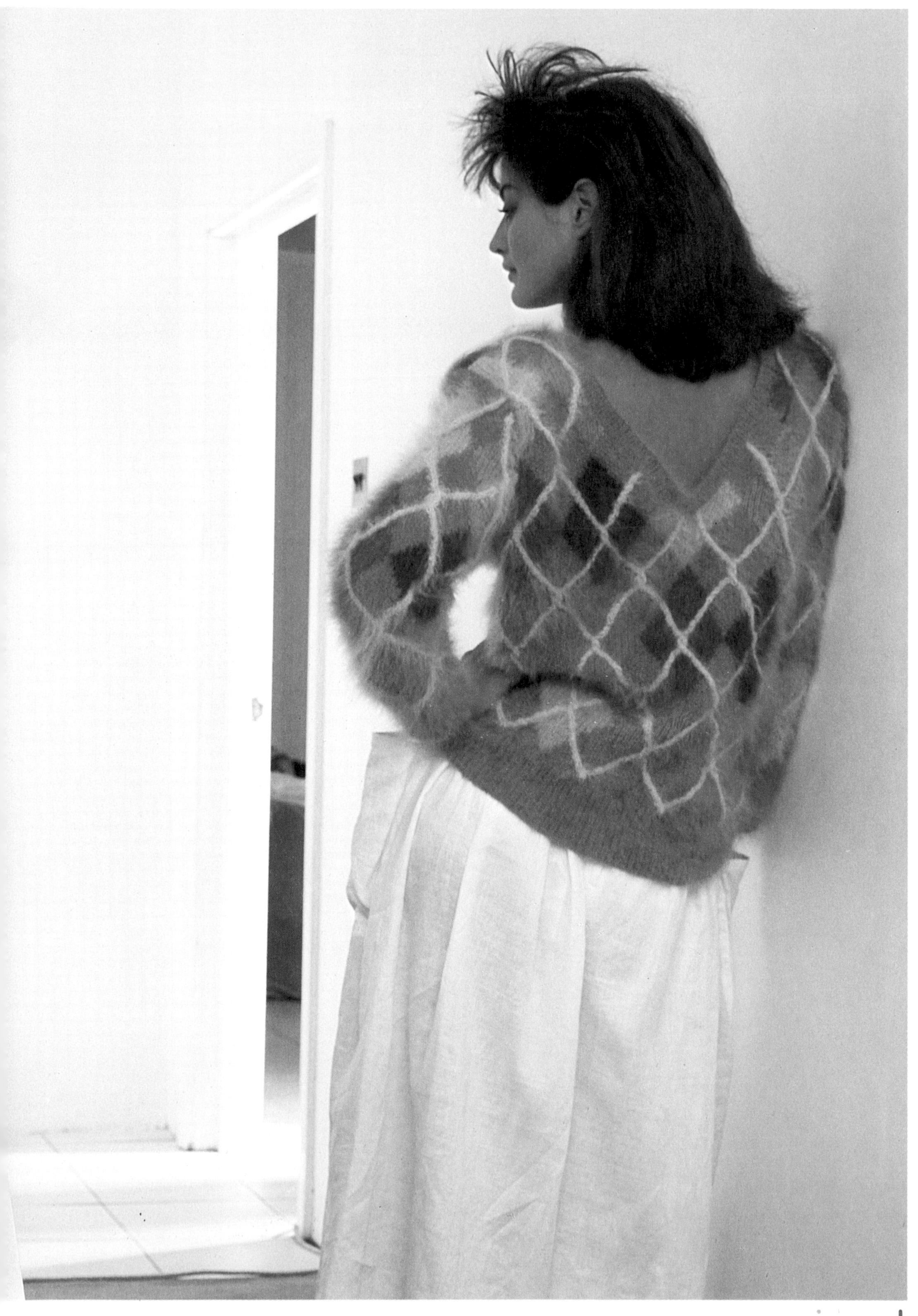

pierrot

ana Lino

pierrot and crackers

The instructions for knitting "Crackers" are on pages 36 & 37 and those for "Pierrot" are on pages 52 & 53. Both patterns may be knitted for winter warmth in "Woollybear Angora" by Patricia Roberts as shown in the pictures on the previous page, this page and on the cover.

MATERIALS
For the "Crackers" cardigan: 12 20 gram balls of "Woollybear Angora" in both main and first contrast colours, plus 2 balls of the same yarn in each of the 4 other contrast colours; 7 buttons.
For the "Crackers" short sweater: 8 20 gram balls "Woollybear Angora" in main colour and 7 balls in first contrast plus 1 ball in each of the 4 other contrast colours.
For the "Pierrot" vee necked sweater or the cardigan: 10 20 gram balls of "Woollybear Angora" in main colour, 3 balls in first contrast and 2 balls in each of the 5 other contrast colours; 5 buttons for the cardigan.
For the "Pierrot" short sweater: 7 20 gram balls of "Woollybear Angora" in main colour, 3 balls in first contrast, 1 ball in second and fourth contrasts and 2 balls in each of the 3 other contrast colours.
For any of these garments a pair each of size 2¼mm (No. 13) and size 2¾mm (No. 12) Aero knitting needles; a fine cable needle.

"**Fudge**" continued from opposite page.
Now divide the sts. for the top of the sleeve: Dec. pattern 25 and leave these 26 sts. on a spare needle until required for second point, cast off 50, pattern until 2 remain, dec., then continue on these 26 sts. for the first point.
The first point: Dec. 1st at each end of the next 12 rows.
Take the 2 remaining sts. tog. and fasten off.
The second point: With right side of work facing, rejoin yarn to inner edge of sts. left on spare needle and work as given for first point.

THE POCKETS (2 alike)
With size 2¾mm. (No. 12) needles cast on 28 sts. and work 114 rows in s.s., then cast off.

THE YOKE
First join raglan seams so that the sts. cast off at underarms are sewn to the straight row ends of sleeves above the marking threads.
Rejoin yarn to top of left back raglan seam and using a circular size 2¼mm (No. 13) knitting needle, pick up and k. 70 sts. from top of left sleeve, 100 sts. from front neck edge, 70 sts. from top of right sleeve and 100 sts. from back neck edge.
Work 7 rounds in single rib.
1st Decrease row: Rib 7, *sl.1, k.2 tog., p.s.s.o., rib 14; repeat from * ending last repeat rib 7.
Rib 7 rows.
2nd Decrease row: Rib 6, *sl.1, k.2 tog., p.s.s.o., rib 12; repeat from * ending last repeat rib 6.
Rib 7 rows.
3rd Decrease row: Rib 5, *sl.1, k.2 tog., p.s.s.o., rib 10; repeat from * ending last repeat rib 5.
Rib 7 rows.
4th Decrease row: Rib 4, *sl.1. k.2 tog., p.s.s.o., rib 8; repeat from * ending last repeat rib 4.
On 180 sts., work 87 rows in single rib, then cast off loosely.

TO MAKE UP THE SWEATER
Pin out to size all parts and press on the wrong side with a warm iron over a damp cloth. Join row ends of back and front ribbing. Fold pockets in half and join the row end edges at each side. Neatly sew pockets in place at side seams above ribbing. Join rest of sleeve and side seams. Press seams.

fudge

MATERIALS
Either 28(29)(30) 25 gram balls of "Woollybear Pure Cashmere" or 36(37)(39) 25 gram balls of "Woollybear Lambswool"; a pair each of size 2¼mm. (No. 13) and 2¾mm. (No. 12) Aero knitting needles, a size 2¼mm. (No. 13) Aero circular knitting needle, a fine cable needle.

STOCKISTS
Woollybear Yarns are available from Patricia Roberts Knitting Shops at 31 James Street, Covent Garden, London W.C.2.; 60 Kinnerton Street, London S.W.1 and 1b Kensington Church Walk, London W.8. Mail order is also available. Please write enclosing a stamped, self-addressed envelope for a price list.

TENSION
83 (85) (87) stitches - 1 repeat of the pattern between the stars * - to 23 (23.5) (24) centimetres [9 (9¼) (9½)] inches in width and 50 rows - 1 repeat of the pattern - to 12 centimetres [4¾] inches in length, using size 2¾mm (No. 12) needles. If you cannot obtain the correct tension, using the size needles suggested, use larger or smaller ones accordingly.

ABBREVIATIONS
K., knit; p., purl; st., stitch; tog., together; dec., decrease (by working 2 sts, tog.); inc., increase (by working twice into same st.); y.f., yarn forward; y.r.n. yarn round needle; m.b., make bobble thus, k.1, y.r.n., k.1, y.r.n., k.1 all into next st., turn., p.5, turn, k.5, turn p.5, turn, pass 2nd, 3rd, 4th and 5th sts. on left hand needle over first st., y.f., p.1 remaining st.; cable 6 thus, slip next 3 sts. onto cable needle and leave at front of work, k.3, then k.3 from cable needle; c.3rt., cross 3 right thus, slip next st. onto cable needle at back of work, k.2, then p.1 from cable needle; c.31t., cross 3 left thus, slip next 2 sts. onto cable needle at front of work, p.1, then k.2 from cable needle; cable 6b., as cable 6, but leaving sts. on cable needle at back of work; cr.5 thus, slip next 2 sts. onto a cable needle at front of work, k.2, p.1, then k.2 from cable needle; double rib is k.2 and p.2 alternately; up 1, pick up the loop which lies between the needles, slip it onto left hand needle, then k. into back of it; single rib is k.1 and p.1 alternately; sl., slip; p.s.s.o., pass sl. st. over; 3 from 1, k.1, y.r.n., k.1 all in next st.

NOTE
The instructions are given for the small size. Where they vary work the figures in the first brackets for the medium size or the figures in the second brackets for the large size.

MEASUREMENTS
The measurements are given in centimetres followed by inches in square brackets.

Underarms	97 [38½]	102[40½]	107[42½]
Side seam	45 [18]	45[18]	45[18]
Length	64.5 [25¾]	65[26]	65.5 [26¼]
Sleeve seam	49 [19½]	49[19½]	49[19½]

THE BACK
With size 2¼mm. (No. 13) needles cast on 128(136)(144) sts. and work 53 rows in double rib.

Increase row: Rib 1(5)(9), *up 1, rib 2, up 1, rib 3, repeat from *until 2(6)(10) remain, up 1, rib 1(5)(9), inc. - 180 (188)(196) sts.

Change to size 2¾mm. (No. 12) needles and work in pattern as follows:

1st row: K.1 (3)(5), *p.4, k.1, p.4, k.1, p.4, m.b., p.4(5)(6), k.6, p.2, k.5, p.7, k.2, m.b., k.2, p.7, k.5, p.2, k.6, p.4 (5)(6), m.b., p.4, k.1, p.4, k.1, p.4*, k.1, p.2, k.6, p.2, k.1; repeat from * to *, k.1(3)(5).

2nd row: P.1(3)(5), *k.4, p.1, k.4, p.1, k.4, p.1, k.4(5)(6), p.6, k.2, p.5, k.7, p.5, k.7, p.5, k.2, p.6, k.4(5)(6), p.1, k.4, p.1, k.4, p.1, k.4, *p.1, k.2, p.6, k.2, p.1; repeat from * to *, p.1(3)(5).

3rd row: K.1(3)(5), *p.4, k.1, p.4, k.1, p.3, m.b., k.1, m.b., p.3(4)(5), cable 6, p.2, k.5, p.6, c.3rt., k.1, c.31t., p.6, k.5, p.2, cable 6, p.3(4)(5), m.b., k.1, m.b., p.3, k.1, p.4, k.1, p.4, *k.1, p.2, cable 6, p.2, k.1; repeat from * to*, then k.1(3)(5).

4th row: P.1(3)(5), *k.4, p.1, k.4, p.1, k.4, p.1, k.4(5)(6), p.6, k.2, p.5, k.6, p.2, k.1, p.1, k.1, p.2, k.6, p.5, k.2, p.6, k.4(5)(6), p.1, k.4, p.1, k.4, p.1, k.4, *p.1, k.2, p.6, k.2, p.1; repeat from * to *, p.1(3)(5).

5th row: K.1(3)(5), *p.4, k.1, p.4, k.1, p.2, m.b., p.1, m.b., p.1, m.b., p.2(3)(4), k.6, p.2, k.5, p.5, c.3rt., p.1, k.1, p.1, c.31t., p.5, k.5, p.2, k.6, p.2(3)(4), m.b., p.1, m.b., p.1, m.b., p.2, k.1, p.4, k.1, p.4*, k.1, p.2, k.6, p.2, k.1; repeat from * to *, then k.1(3)(5).

6th row: P.1(3)(5), *k.4, p.1, k.4, p.1, k.4, p.1, k.4(5)(6), p.6, k.2, p.5, k.5, p.3, k.1, p.1, k.1, p.3, k.5, p.5, k.2, p.6, k.4(5)(6), p.1, k.4, p.1, k.4, p.1, k.4*, p.1, k.2, p.6, k.2, p.1; repeat from * to *, then p.1(3)(5).

7th row: K.1(3)(5), *p.4, m.b., p.4, k.1, p.4, k.1, p.4(5)(6), k.6, p.2, k.2, m.b., k.2, p.4, c.3rt., k.1., p.1, k.1, p.1 k.1, c.31t., p.4, k.2, m.b., k.2, p.2, k.6, p.4(5)(6), k.1, p.4, k.1, p.4, m.b., p.4*, k.1, p.2, k.6, p.2, k.1; repeat from * to *, then k.1(3)(5).

8th row: P.1(3)(5), *k.4, p.1, k.4, p.1, k.4, p.1, k.4(5)(6), p.6, k.2, p.5, k.4, p.2, k.1, p.1, k.1, p.1, k.1, p.1, k.1, p.2, k.4, p.5, k.2, p.6, k.4(5)(6), p.1, k.4, p.1, k.4, p.1, k.4, *p.1, k.2, p.6, k.2, p.1; repeat from * to *, then p.1(3)(5).

9th row: K.1(3)(5), *p.3, m.b., k.1, m.b., p.3, k.1, p.4, k.1, p.4(5)(6), k.6, p.2, k.1, m.b., k.1, m.b., k.1, p.3, c.3rt., p.1, k.1, p.1, k.1, p.1, k.1, p.1, c.31t., p.3, k.1, m.b., k.1, m.b., k.1, p.2, k.6, p.4(5)(6), k.1, p.4, k.1, p.3, m.b., k.1, m.b., p.3,*k.1, p.2, k.6, p.2, k.1; repeat from * to *, then k.1(3)(5).

10th row: P.1(3)(5), *k.4, p.1, k.4, p.1, k.4, p.1, k.4(5)(6), p.6, k.2, p.5, k.3, p.3, k.1, p.1, k.1, p.1, k.1, p.1, k.1, p.3, k.3, p.5, k.2, p.6, k.4(5)(6), p.1, k.4, p.1, k.4, p.1, k.4, *p.1, k.2, p.6, k.2, p.1; repeat from * to *, then p.1(3)(5).

11th row: K.1(3)(5), *p.2, m.b., p.1, m.b., p.1, m.b., p.2, k.1, p.4, k.1, p.4(5)(6), cable 6, p.2, k.5, p.2, c.3rt., k.1, p.1, k.1, p.1, k.1, p.1, k.1, p.1, k.1, c.31t., p.2, k.5, p.2, cable 6, p.4(5)(6), k.1, p.4, k.1, p.2, m.b. p.1, m.b., p.1, m.b., p.2*, k.1, p.2, cable 6, p.2, k.1; repeat from * to *, k.1 (3)(5).

12th row: P.1(3)(5), *k.4, p.1, k.4, p.1, k.4, p.1, k.4(5)(6), p.6, k.2, p.5, k.2, p.2, k.1, p.1, k.1, p.1, k.1, p.1, k.1, p.1, k.1, p.1, k.1, p.2, k.2, p.5, k.2, p.6, k.4(5)(6), p.1, k.4, p.1, k.4, p.1, k.4*, p.1, k.2, p.6, k.2, p.1; repeat from * to *, then p.1(3)(5).

13th to 24th rows: As 1st to 12th rows.

NOTE: There is no continuity between rows 25–50, and rows 1–24, they are two different patterns put together to make one.

25th row: K.1(3)(5), *p.11, cr.5, p.5, k.9, p.2, k.1, p.3(4)(5), m.b., p.2, cr.5, p.2, m.b., p.3(4)(5), k.1, p.2, k.9, p.5, cr.5, p.11*, k.1, p.2, k.6, p.2, k.1; repeat from * to *, k.1(3)(5).

26th row: P.1(3)(5), *k.11, p.2, k.1, p.2, k.5, p.9, k.2, p.1, k.6(7)(8), p.2, k.1, p.2, k.6(7)(8), p.1, k.2, p.9, k.5, p.2, k.1, p.2, k.11*, p.1, k.2, p.6, k.2, p.1; repeat from * to *, p.1(3)(5).

27th row: K.1(3)(5), *p.3, m.b., p.6, c.3rt., p.1, c.31t., p.4, cable 6, k.3, p.2, k.1, p.5(6)(7), c.3rt., p.1, c.31t., p.5 (6)(7), k.1, p.2, cable 6, k.3, p.4, c.3rt., p.1, c.31t., p.6, m.b., p.3*, k.1, p.2, cable 6, p.2, k.1; repeat from * to *, k.1(3)(5).

28th row: P.1(3)(5), *k.10, p.2, k.3, p.2, k.4, p.9, k.2, p.1, k.5(6)(7), p.2, k.3, p.2, k.5(6)(7), p.1, k.2, p.9, k.4, p.2, k.3, p.2, k.10*, p.1, k.2, p.6, k.2, p.1; repeat from * to *, p.1(3)(5).

29th row: K.1(3)(5), *p.9, c.3rt., p.3, c.31t., p.3, k.9, p.2, k.1, p.4(5)(6), c.3rt., p.3, c.31t., p.4(5)(6), k.1, p.2, k.9, p.3, c.3rt., p.3, c.31t., p.9*, k.1, p.2, k.6, p.2, k.1; repeat from * to *, k.1(3)(5).

30th row: P.1(3)(5), *k.9, p.2, k.5, p.2, k.3, p.9, k.2, p.1, k.4(5)(6), p.2, k.5, p.2, k.4(5)(6), p.1, k.2, p.9, k.3, p.2, k.5, p.2, k.9*, p.1, k.2, p.6, k.2, p.1; repeat from * to *, p.1(3)(5).

31st row: K.1(3)(5), *p.1, m.b., p.3, m.b., p.3, k.2, p.5, k.2, p.3, k.3, cable 6b., p.2, k.1, p.3(4)(5), c.3rt., p.2., m.b., p.2, c.31t., p.3(4)(5), k.1, p.2, k.3, cable 6b., p.3, k.2, p.5, k.2, p.3, m.b., p.3, m.b., p.1*, k.1, p.2, k.6, p.2, k.1; repeat from * to *, k.1(3)(5).

32nd row: P.1(3)(5), *k.9, p.2, k.5, p.2, k.3, p.9, k.2, p.1, k.3(4)(5), p.2, k.7, p.2, k.3(4)(5), p.1, k.2, p.9, k.3, p.2, k.5, p.2, k.9*, p.1, k.2, p.6, k.2, p.1; repeat from * to *, p.1(3)(5).

33rd row: K.1(3)(5), *p.9, c.31t., p.3, c.3rt., p.3, k.9, p.2, k.1, p.2(3)(4), c.3rt., p.7, c.31t., p.2(3)(4), k.1, p.2, k.9, p.3, c.31t., p.3, c.3rt., p.9*, k.1, p.2, k.6, p.2, k.1; repeat from * to *, k.1(3)(5).

34th row: P.1(3)(5), *k.10, p.2, k.3, p.2, k.4, p.9, k.2, p.1, k.2(3)(4), p.2, k.9, p.2, k.2(3)(4), p.1, k.2, p.9, k.4, p.2, k.3, p.2, k.10*, p.1, k.2, p.6; k.2, p.1; repeat from * to *, p.1(3)(5).

35th row: K.1(3)(5), *p.3, m.b., p.6, c.31t., p.1, c.3rt., p.4, cable 6, k.3, p.2, k.1, p.1(2)(3), c.3rt., p.2, m.b., p.3, m.b., p.2, c.31t., p.1(2)(3), k.1, p.2, cable 6, k.3, p.4, c.31t., p.1, c.3rt., p.6, m.b., p.3*, k.1, p.2, cable 6, p.2, k.1; repeat from * to *, k.1(3)(5).

36th row: P.1(3)(5), *k.11, p.2, k.1, p.2, k.5, p.9, k.2, p.1, k.1(2)(3), p.2, k.11, p.2, k.1(2)(3), p.1, k.2, p.9, k.5, p.2, k.1, p.2, k.11*, p.1, k.2, p.6, k.2, p.1; repeat from * to *, p.1(3)(5).

37th row: K.1(3)(5), *p.11, cr.5, p.5, k.9, p.2, k.1, p.1 (2)(3), k.2, p.11, k.2, p.1(2)(3), k.1, p.2, k.9, p.5, cr.5, p.11*, k.1, p.2, k.6, p.2, k.1; repeat from * to *, k.1(3)(5).

38th row: As 36th row.

39th row: K.1(3)(5), *p.1, m.b., p.3, m.b., p.4, c.3rt., p.1, c. 31t., p.4, k.3, cable 6b., p.2, k.1, p.1(2)(3), c.31t., p.2, m.b., p.3, m.b., p.2, c.3rt., p.1(2)(3), k.1, p.2, k.3, cable 6b., p.4, c.3rt., p.1, c.31t., p.4, m.b., p.3, m.b., p.1*, k.1, p.2, cable 6, p.2, k.1; repeat from * to *, k.1(3)(5).

40th row: As 34th row.

41st row: Working c.3rt. for c.31t. and c.31t. for c.3rt., work as given for 33rd row.

42nd row: As 32nd row.

43rd row: K.1(3)(5), *p.3, m.b., p.5, k.2, p.5, k.2, p.3, cable 6, k.3, p.2, k.1, p.3(4)(5), c.31t., p.2, m.b., p.2, c.3rt., p.3(4)(5), k.1, p.2, cable 6, k.3, p.3, k.2, p.5, k.2, p.5, m.b., p.3*, k.1, p.2, k.6, p.2, k.1; repeat from * to *, k.1(3)(5).

44th row: As 30th row.

45th row: Working c.3rt. for c.3lt. and c.31t. for c.3rt., work as given for 29th row.

46th row: As 28th row.

47th row: K.1(3)(5), *p.1, m.b., p.3, m.b., p.4, c.31t., p.1, c.3rt., p.4, k.3, cable 6b, p.2, k.1, p.5(6)(7), c.31t., p.1, c.3rt., p.5(6)(7), k.1, p.2, k.3, cable 6b., p.4, c.31t., p.1, c.3rt., p.4, m.b., p.3, m.b., p.1*, k.1, p.2, cable 6, p.2, k.1; repeat from * to *, k.1(3)(5).

48th row: As 26th row.

49th and 50th rows: As 25th and 26th rows.

The last 50 rows form the pattern; repeat them once more, then work the first 36 rows again.

To shape the raglan armholes: Maintaining the continuity of the pattern as set, cast off 4(6)(8) sts. at the beginning of the next 2 rows.

Dec. 1 st. at each end of the next 14 rows.

Dec. 1st. at each end of the next row and the 9(10)(11) following alternate rows. - 124(126)(128) sts.

Now divide the sts. for the neck: Next row: Pattern 42 and leave these sts. on a spare needle until required for the second point, cast off 40(42)(44) sts., pattern to end and continue on these 42 sts. for the first point.

The first point: To shape the neck and continue to slope the raglan.

1st row: Dec. 1 st. at the beginning, pattern to end.

2nd row: Cast off 3 sts., pattern to end.

Repeat the last 2 rows 5 times more.

Pattern 10 rows more decreasing 1 st. at armhole edge as before on every alternate row and decreasing 1 st. at the neck edge on each row. - 3 sts.

S1.1, k.2 tog., p.s.s.o. Fasten off.

The second point: With right side of work facing rejoin yarn to inner edge of sts. left on spare needle and work to end of row, then work as given for first point to end.

THE FRONT
Work as given for back.

THE SLEEVES (both alike)
With size 2¼mm. (No. 13) needles cast on 56(60)(64) sts. and work 35 rows in double rib.

Increase row: K.1(3)(5), *3 from 1; repeat from *until nil(2)(4) remain, k. nil (2)(4). - 166(170)(174) sts.

Change to size 2¾mm. (No. 12) needles and work in pattern as follows:

1st row: Work from * to * on 17th pattern row given for back, then repeat from * to * again.

Thus continuing to work the pattern given between * and * twice on each pattern row given for back, beginning with the 18th pattern row work 169 rows.

Mark each end of the last row with coloured threads.

Pattern 4(6)(8) rows.

To shape the raglan: Dec. 1st. at each end of the next 31(33) (35) rows.

Continued on opposite page.

fudge

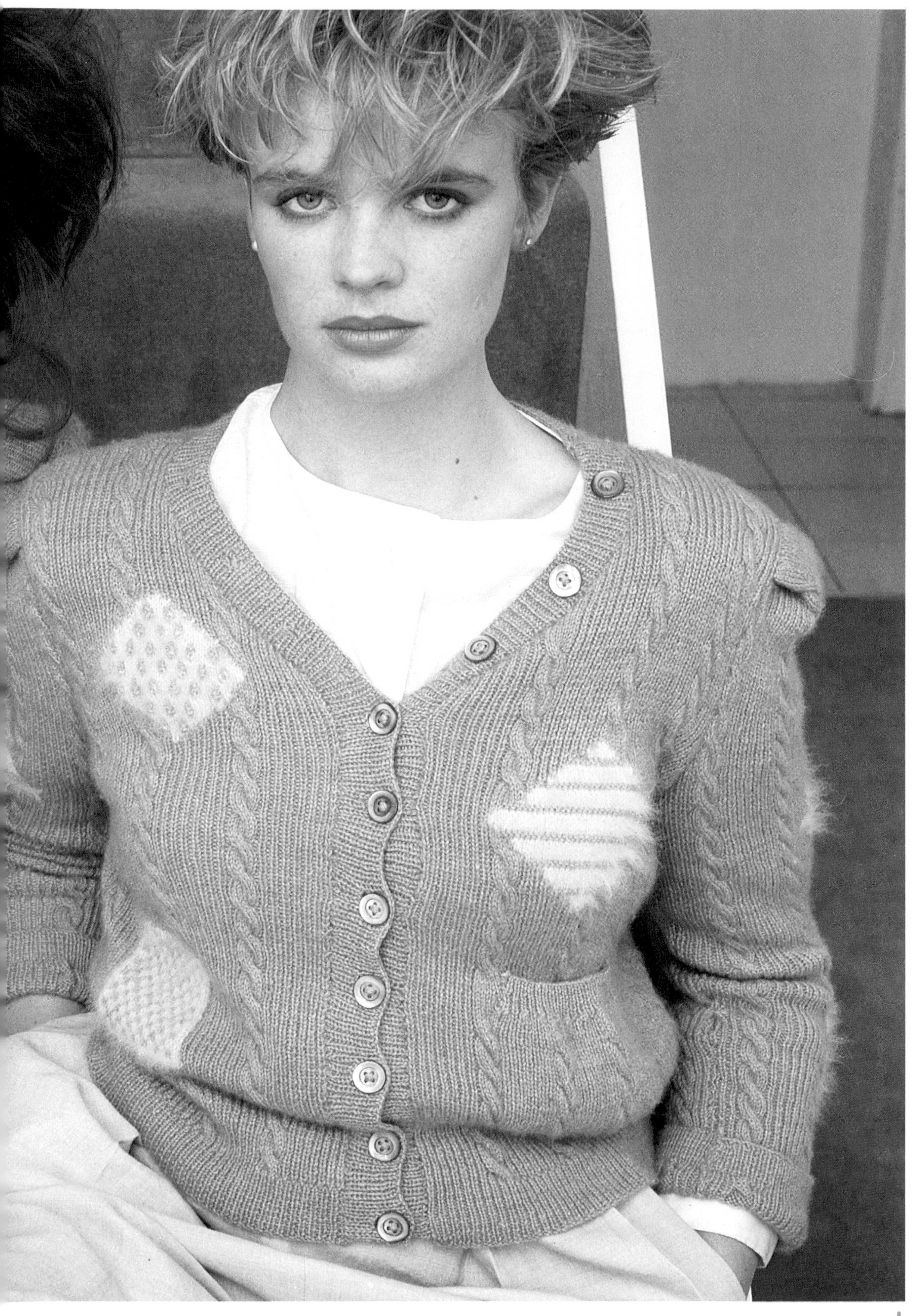

nougat

nougat

MATERIALS
Either: 14 25 gram balls of "Woollybear Pure Cashmere" in main colour and 1 20 gram ball of "Woollybear Angora" in contrast colour, or 16 28 gram (ounce) hanks of "Woollybear Real Shetland" in main colour and 1 hank in contrast colour; a pair each of size 2¾mm (No. 12) Aero knitting needles; 10 buttons.

TENSION
Work at a tension of 21 stitches – 1 repeat of the pattern – and 20 rows to 5 centimetres (2 inches) over the cable and rib pattern using size 2¾mm (No. 12) needles. If you cannot obtain the correct tension using the size needles suggested, use larger or smaller ones accordingly.

ABBREVIATIONS
K., knit; p., purl; st., stitch; tog., together; dec., decrease (by working 2 sts. tog.); inc., increase (by working twice into same st.); single rib is k.1 and p.1 alternately; m., main colour; a., contrast colour; m.b., make bobble thus, k.1, y.r.n., k.1 all into one st., turn, p.3, turn, sl.1, k.2 tog., p.s.s.o.; 3 from 1, k.1, y.r.n., k.1 all into one st.; y.r.n., yarn round needle; cable 6, slip next 3 sts. onto cable needle and leave at front of work, k.3, then k.3 from cable needle; sl., slip; p.s.s.o., pass slip st. over.

MEASUREMENTS
The measurements are given in centimetres followed by inches in brackets.

Underarms	90(36)
Side seam	35(14)
Length	55(22)
Sleeve seam	42.5(17)

THE BACK
With size 2¾mm (No. 12) needles and m. cast on 186 sts. and work 18 rows in single rib.
Now work in cable rib as follows:
1st row: (K.1, p.1) 3 times, k.6, *p.1, (k.1, p.1) 7 times, k.6; repeat from * until 6 remain, (p.1, k.1) 3 times.
2nd row: (P.1, k.1) 3 times, p.6, *k.1, (p.1, k.1) 7 times, p.6; repeat from * until 6 remain, (k.1, p.1) 3 times.
3rd and 4th rows: As 1st and 2nd rows.
5th row: (K.1, p.1) 3 times, cable 6, *p.1, (k.1, p.1) 7 times, cable 6; repeat from * until 6 remain, (p.1, k.1) 3 times.
6th row: As 2nd row.
7th and 8th rows: As 1st and 2nd rows.
The last 8 rows form the cable and rib pattern; repeat them 3 times more, then work the first 2 rows again.
***Now work the checkered patch as follows, using separate balls of m. at each side of patches.
1st row: With m. pattern 132 as set, with a. k.30, with m. pattern to end.
2nd row: With m. pattern 24, with a. p.30, with m. pattern to end as set.
The last 2 rows set the position of the 30 row checkered patch given in the chart, work the 3rd to 30th rows as set.
Next row: With m. pattern 132 as set, then still with m. k.30, pattern to end as set.
Next row: With m. as second cable pattern row.
With m. pattern 22 rows as set.
Now work the striped patch as follows:
1st row: With m. pattern 56, with a. k.1, with m. pattern to end as set.
2nd row: With m. pattern 128 as set, with a. p.3, with m. pattern 55.
The last 2 rows set the position of the striped patch given in the chart, now work the 3rd to 34th rows as set.
To shape the armholes: Continuing in pattern as set, including the striped patch, given in the chart, cast off 8 sts. at the beginning of the next 2 rows.
Dec. 1 st. at each end of the next 2 rows.
Now work the spotted patch as follows:
1st row: With m. k.2 tog., pattern 43, with a. k.3, with m. pattern 70, with a. k.1, with m. pattern 45, k.2 tog.
2nd row: With m. p.2 tog., pattern 43, with a. p.3, with m. pattern 70, with a. p.1, with m. pattern 43, p.2 tog.
The last 2 rows set the position of the spotted patch given in the chart and complete the striped patch. Continuing in pattern as set, dec. 1 st. at each end of the next 9 rows.
On 144 sts. pattern 54 rows, completing the spotted patch on the 22nd of these rows.***
Now divide the sts. for the back neck: Pattern 57 and leave these sts. on a spare needle until required for left back shoulder, cast off 30, pattern to end and continue on these 57 sts. for the right back shoulder.
The right back shoulder: Work 1 row straight. Cast off 4 sts. at the beginning of the next row.
To slope the shoulder and to shape the neck: Cast off 10 sts. at the beginning of the next row and 4 sts. on the following row.
Repeat the last 2 rows twice.
Cast off the remaining 11 sts.
The left back shoulder: With right side of work facing, rejoin m. to inner edge of sts. left on spare needle and work to end of row, then work as given for right back shoulder to end.

THE POCKET BACK
With size 2¾mm (No. 12) needles and m. cast on 43 sts. and work in pattern as follows:
1st row: (K.1, p.1) 4 times, k.6, p.1, (k.1, p.1) 7 times, k.6, (p.1, k.1) 4 times.
2nd row: (P.1, k.1) 4 times, p.6, k.1, (p.1, k.1) 7 times, p.6, (k.1, p.1) 4 times.
The last 2 rows set the position of the 8 row cable pattern given for the back, pattern 47 rows as set, then leave these stitches on a stitch-holder until required.

THE LEFT FRONT
With size 2¾mm (No. 12) needles and m. cast on 90 sts. and work 18 rows in single rib.
Now work in pattern as follows:
1st row: (K.1, p.1) 3 times, *k.6, p.1, (k.1, p.1) 7 times; repeat from * to end.
2nd row: *K.1, (p.1, k.1) 7 times, p.6; repeat from * until 6 remain, (k.1, p.1) 3 times.
The last 2 rows set the 8 row cable pattern given for the back, work the 3rd to 8th rows as set, then work the first 4 rows again.
Next row: Pattern 40 as set, turn, cast on 21, turn, pattern to end. – 111 sts.
Next row: (6th pattern row): *K.1, (p.1, k.1) 7 times, p.6; repeat from * until 6 remain, (k.1, p.1) 3 times.
Thus working in pattern as set work 46 rows.
Next row: Pattern 19 as set, then (k.1, p.3 tog., k.1, p.1) 10 times, k.1, p.2 tog., k.1, then leave these 43 sts. on a stitch-holder until required for pocket top, pattern to end as set.
Next row: Pattern 28 as set, pattern across the 43 sts. of pocket back, work to end of row. – 90sts.
Pattern 26 rows as set.
Now work the striped patch as follows:
1st row: With m. pattern 55, with a. k.1, with m.

pattern 34.
2nd row: With m. pattern 33, with a. p.3, with m. pattern to end.
The last 2 rows set the position of the striped patch given in the chart.
Work the 3rd to 34th rows from the chart as set.
To shape the armhole: Continuing in pattern as set, including the patch, cast off 8 sts. at the beginning of the next row, work 1 row back to armhole edge.
Pattern 13 rows decreasing one st. at the armhole edge on each row and completing the striped patch on the 4th of these rows.
On 69 sts. pattern 7 rows.
**To slope the neck edge: Dec. 1 st. at the end – neck edge of the next row and at the same edge on each of the next 16 rows.
On 52 sts. work 1 row.
Dec. 1 st. at the end – neck edge on the next row and the 10 following alternate rows.
On 41 sts. pattern 11 rows.
To slope the shoulder: Cast off 10 sts. at the beginning of the next row and the 2 following alternate rows.
On 11 sts. work 1 row, then cast off.

THE POCKET TOP
With right side of work facing rejoin m. to the 43 sts. left on stitch-holder. Work 8 rows in single rib, then cast off in rib.

THE RIGHT FRONT
With size 2¾ mm (No. 12) needles and m. cast on 90 sts. and work 18 rows in single rib.
Now work in pattern as follows:
1st row: *P.1, (k.1, p.1) 7 times, k.6; repeat from * until 6 remain, (p.1, k.1) 3 times.
2nd row: (P.1, k.1) 3 times, *p.6, (k.1, p.1) 7 times, k.1; repeat from * to end.
The last 2 rows set the position of the 8 row cable pattern given for the back. Pattern 32 rows more as set.
Now work the checkered patch as follows:
1st row: With m. pattern 37 as set, with a. k.30, with m. pattern 23.
The last row sets the position of the checkered patch given in the chart. Work the 2nd to 30th rows as set.
Next row: With m. pattern 37 as set, then still with m. k.30, pattern to end.
Next row: As 2nd cable pattern row.
With m. pattern 57 rows.
To shape the armhole: Cast off 8 sts. at the beginning of the next row, then dec. 1 st. at the armhole edge on each of the next 2 rows. – 80 sts.

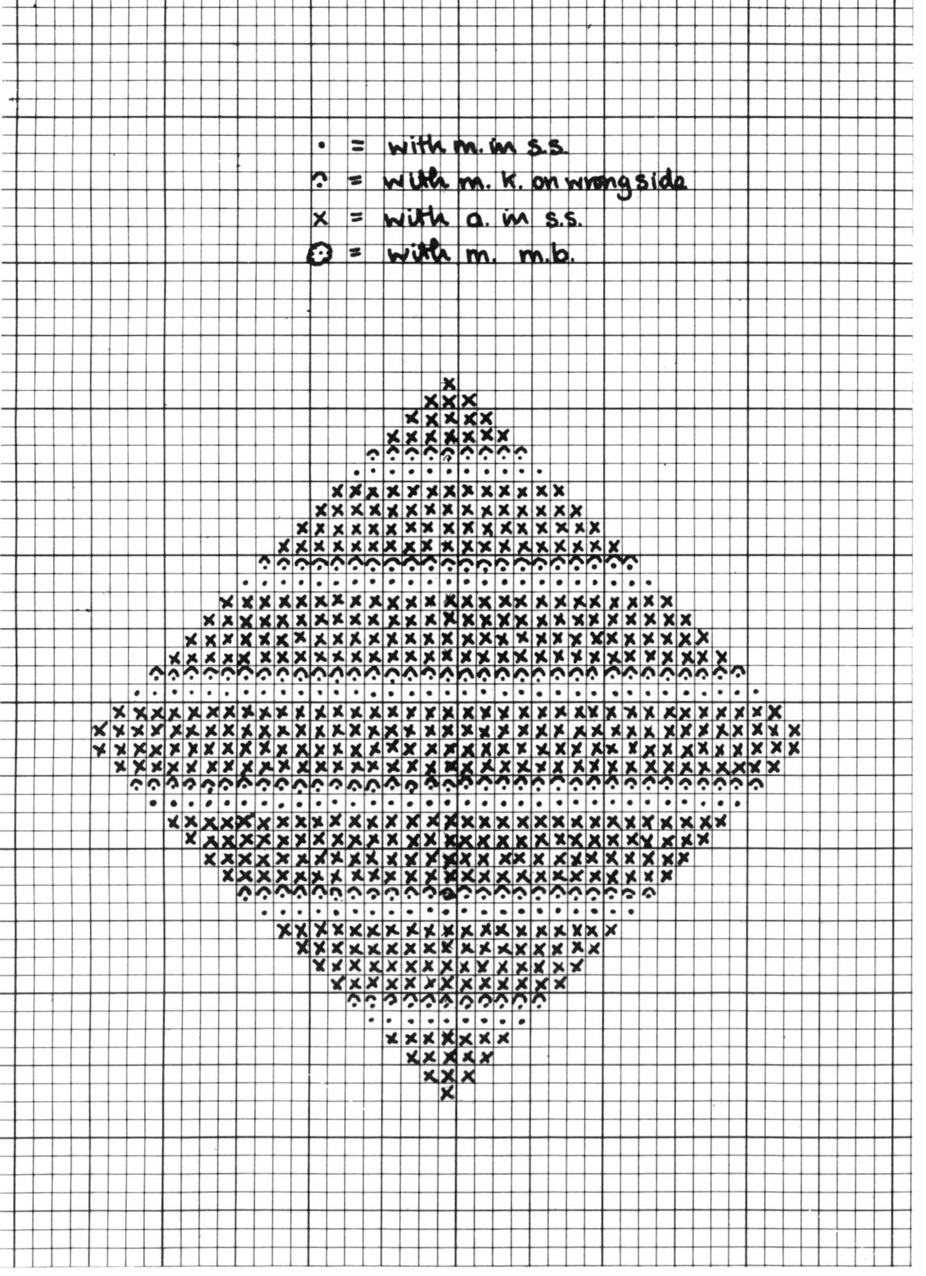

Now work the spotted patch as follows:
1st row: With m. pattern 32, with a. k.1, with m. pattern 45, k.2 tog.
2nd row: With m. p.2 tog., pattern 43, with a. p.3, with m. pattern 31.
The last 2 rows set the position of the spotted patch given in the chart. Continuing in pattern as set dec. 1 st. at the armhole edge on each of the next 9 rows.
On 69 sts. pattern 8 rows.
Work as given for left front from ** to end.

THE SLEEVES (both alike)
With size 2¾ mm (No. 12) needles and m. cast on 102 sts. and work 10 rows in single rib.
Work the 8 cable rib pattern rows given for back 6 times.
Now work the checkered patch as follows:
1st row: With m. pattern 40 as set, with a. k.30, with m. pattern 32 as set.
The last row sets the position of the checkered patch given in the chart, work the 2nd to 30th rows as set, but increasing 1 st. at each end of the 9th and 21st of these rows.
Next row: With m. pattern 42, then still with m. k.30, with m. pattern to end.
Next row: With m. work in cable rib pattern across all 106 sts.
Continuing in pattern as set, inc. 1 st. at each end of the next row and the 4 following 8th rows.
On 116 sts. work 7 rows.
Now work the striped patch as follows:
Next row: With m. pattern 49, with a. k.1, with m. pattern to end.
Next row: With m. pattern 65, with a. p.3, with m. pattern to end.
The last 2 rows set the position of the stripe patch given in the chart, now work the 3rd to 40th rows as set, but increasing 1 st. at each end of the 5th pattern row and the 2 following 12th rows. – 122 sts.
To shape the sleevetop: Continuing in pattern as set, cast off 8 sts. at the beginning of the next 2 rows, then dec. 1 st. at each end of the next row and the 7 following alternate rows.
On 90 sts. pattern 53 rows.
Cast off.

THE BUTTONHOLE BAND
With right side of work facing rejoin m. at lower edge of right front and using size 2¾ mm (No. 12) needles pick up and k. 128 sts. up to first front edge dec., then 60 sts. from shaped row end of right front edge. – 188 sts.
Work 5 rows in single rib.
Note the buttonholes are supposed to go right up the front band.
1st Buttonhole row: Rib 4, *cast off 3, rib next 14 sts.; repeat from * ending last repeat rib 18.
2nd Buttonhole row: Rib 19, *turn, cast on 3 over those cast off, turn, rib 15; repeat from * ending last repeat rib 4.
**Next row: Rib 128, 3 from 1, rib to end.
Next row: Rib as set.
Repeat the last 2 rows once more.
Cast off loosely using a size larger needle.

THE BUTTONBAND
With right side of work facing rejoin m. at left front shoulder and using size 2¾mm (No. 12) needles pick up and k. 60 sts. from left front neck edge down to first front neck dec., then pick up and k. 128 sts. from straight row ends of left front edge.
On 188 sts. work 7 rows in single rib, then work as for button hole band from ** to end.

THE BACK NECKBAND
With right side of work facing rejoin m. and using size 2¾ mm (No. 12) needles pick up and k. 68 sts. from back neck edge. Work 11 rows in single rib, cast off loosely in rib.

TO MAKE UP THE CARDIGAN
Join shoulder seams. Fold the 2 corners at top of sleevetop to centre of sleevetop and catch in place on the wrong side. Neatly sew sleevetops in position. Join sleeve and side seams. Fold cast on group at base of pocket flat on wrong side and catch in place. Sew pocket back and row ends of pocket top in place. Sew on buttons.

brownie

Skirts, belt and girl's trousers from Elle, shirts and his trousers from Margaret Howell.

brownie

MATERIALS
For the woman's sweater: Either 18 ounce (28 gram) hanks of "Woollybear Real Shetland" or 17 25 gram balls of "Woollybear Pure Cashmere" or 27 25 gram balls of "Woollybear Fine Cotton" all by Patricia Roberts; a pair each of size 2¼ mm. (No. 13) and size 2¾ mm. (No. 12) Aero knitting needles, two fine cable needles. For the man's sweater: Add 2 balls or hanks of "Woollybear Real Shetland" or "Woollybear Pure Cashmere" or 3 balls of "Woollybear Fine Cotton".
For the cardigan: Add 3 hanks of "Woollybear Real Shetland", 3 balls of "Woollybear Pure Cashmere" or 5 balls of "Woollybear Fine Cotton" and 8 buttons.

TENSION
Work at such a tension that one repeat of the pattern – 177 sts. measures 47.5 centimetres (19 inches) in width and 22 rows to 5 centimetres (2 inches) in length. If you cannot obtain the correct tension using the size needles suggested, use larger or smaller ones accordingly.

ABBREVIATIONS
K., knit; p., purl; st., stitch; tog., together; dec., decrease (by working 2 sts. tog.); inc., increase (by working twice into same st.); single rib is k. 1 and p. 1 alternately; y.r.n., yarn round needle; m.b., make bobble thus, k. 1, y.r.n., k. 1, y.r.n., k. 1 all into next st., turn, p. 5, turn, k. 5, turn, p. 5, turn, pass 2nd, 3rd, 4th and 5th sts. on left hand needle, over first st., then p. this st.; up 1, pick up the loop which lies between the needles, slip it onto left hand needle, then p. into back of it; c.4f., cable 4 front thus, slip next 2 sts. onto a cable needle and leave at front of work, k. 2, then k. 2 from cable needle; c.4b., cable 4 back as c.4f., but leave sts. on cable needle at back of work; tw.2rt., twist 2 right thus, k. into front of second st. then p. into first st. on left hand needle, allowing both loops to fall from left hand needle together; tw.2lt., twist 2 left thus, p. into back of second st., then k. into front of first st. on left hand needle, allowing both loops to fall from left hand needle together; c.7b., cable 7 back thus, slip next 7 sts. onto cable needle and leave at back of work, p. 5, then p. 1, k. 1, p. 1, k. 1, p. 1, k. 1, p. 1 across the 7 sts. from cable needle; c.7f., cable 7 front, as c.7b., but leaving sts. on cable needle at front of work; c.5b., cable 5 back thus, slip next 5 sts. onto cable needle and leave at back of work, p, 1, k. 1, p. 1, k. 1, p. 1, k. 1, p. 1 across the next 7 sts., then p. 5 from cable needle; c.5f., cable 5 front as c.5b., but leaving sts. on cable needle at front of work; cr.3rt., cross 3 right thus, slip next st. onto cable needle and leave at back of work, k. 2 then p. 1 from cable needle; cr.3rt.k.wise, as cr.3rt. but k. st. from cable needle; cr.3lt., cross 3 left thus, slip next 2 sts. onto cable needle at front of work, p. 1, then k. 2 sts. from cable needle; cr.3lt.k.wise as cr. 3lt., but k. 1 instead of p. 1, s.s.k., slip 1, k. 1, p.s.s.o.; s.s., stocking stitch is k. on the right side and p. on the wrong side; p.s.s.o., pass sl. st. over; c.6b., cable 6 back, slip next 3 sts. onto cable needle and leave at back of work, k. 3 then k. 3 from cable needle; c.6f., cable 6 front, as c.6b. but leave sts. on cable needle at front of work; cable 9 thus, slip next 4 sts. onto cable needle and leave at front of work, slip next st. onto a safety pin and leave at back of work, k. 4, p. 1 from safety pin, then k. 4 from cable needle; cable 12 right thus, slip next 4 sts. onto cable needle and leave at back of work, slip next 4 sts. onto another cable needle at back of work, k. 4, then k. 4 sts. from second cable needle, then k. 4 from first cable needle; cable 12 left thus, slip next 4 sts. onto cable needle and leave at front of work, slip next 4 sts. onto second cable needle at back of work, k. 4, k. 4 from second cable needle, then k. 4 from first cable needle at front of work; sl., slip.

NOTE
The instructions are given in one size only. For the sweater there is a man's version also offered, only the sleeve seam differs from the woman's.
Instructions given in brackets are worked the number of times stated after the last bracket.

MEASUREMENTS
The measurements are given in centimetres followed by inches in brackets.

THE SWEATER	
Underarms	95 (38)
Side seam	40 (16)
Length	60 (24)
Sleeve seam (woman's)	42.5 (17)
Sleeve seam (man's)	47.5 (19)

THE CARDIGAN	
Underarms	97.5 (39)
Side seam	45 (18)
Length	66 (26½)
Sleeve seam	42.5 (17)

THE SWEATER

THE BACK
With size 2¼ mm. (No. 13) needles cast on 134 sts. and work 29 rows in single rib.

Increase row: Rib 2, *up 1, rib 3; repeat from * to end. – 178 sts.

Change to size 2¾ mm. (No. 12) needles and work in pattern as follows:

1st row: (K. 1, p. 3) 3 times, m.b., p. 4, k. 4, p. 2, k. 15, p. 2, k. 4, p. 3, (tw.2rt.) twice, p. 1, (tw.2lt.) twice, **p. 4, k. 1, p. 1, k. 1, p. 1, k. 1, p. 8, m.b., p. 1, m.b., p. 2*, c.4f., work from * back to **, (tw.2rt.) twice, p. 1, (tw.2lt.) twice, p. 3, (k. 4, p. 2) 3 times, k. 4, p. 1, (k. 4, p. 2) 3 times, k. 4, p. 4, m.b., (p. 3, k. 1) 3 times.

2nd row: *** (P. 1, k. 3) 3 times, p. 1, k. 4, (p. 4, k. 2) 3 times, p. 4, k. 1, (p. 4, k. 2) 3 times ***, then **p. 4, k. 3, p. 1, k. 1, p. 1, k. 3, p. 1, k. 1, p. 1, k. 4, p. 1, k. 1, p. 1, k. 1, p. 1, k. 13 **, p. 4, work from last ** back to first **, then *k. 2, p. 15, k. 2, p. 4, k. 4, (p. 1, k. 3) 3 times, p. 1.

3rd row: (K. 1, p. 3) twice, k. 1, p. 2, m.b., k. 1, m.b., p. 3, c.4f., p. 2, c.6b., k. 3, c.6f., p. 2, c.4b., p. 2, (tw.2rt.) twice, p. 3, (tw.2lt.) twice **p. 3, k. 1, p. 1, k. 1, p. 1, k. 1, p. 9, m.b., p. 2*, cr.3rt.k.wise, cr.3lt.k.wise, work from * back to **, (tw.2rt.) twice, p. 3, (tw.2lt.) twice, (p. 2, c.4f., p. 2, k. 4) twice, p. 1, (k. 4, p. 2, c.4b., p. 2) twice, p. 1 more, m.b., k. 1, m.b., p. 2, k. 1, (p. 3, k. 1) twice.

4th row: Work as given for 2nd row from *** to ***, then **p. 4, k. 2, p. 1, k. 1, p. 1, k. 5, p. 1, k. 1, p. 1, k. 3, p. 1, k. 1, p. 1, k. 1, p. 1, k. 12 **, p. 6, work from last ** back to first **, then work as given for 2nd row from * to end.

5th row: (K. 1, p. 3) twice, k. 1, p. 1, m.b., p. 1, m.b., p. 1, m.b., p. 2, k. 4, p. 2, k. 15, p. 2, k. 4, p. 1, (tw.2rt.) twice p. 5, (tw.2lt.) twice, p. 1, c.7b., p. 5, cr.3rt.k.wise, k. 2, cr.3lt.k.wise, p. 5, c.5f., p. 1, (tw.2rt.) twice, p. 5, (tw.2lt.) twice, p. 1, (k. 4, p. 2) 3 times, k. 4, p. 1, (k. 4, p. 2) 3 times, k. 4, p. 2, m.b., p. 1, m.b., p. 1, m.b., p. 1, k. 1, (p. 3, k. 1) twice.

6th row: Work as given for 2nd row from *** to *** then **p. 4, k. 1, p. 1, k. 1, p. 1, k. 7, p. 1, k. 1, p. 1, k. 7, p. 1, k. 1, p. 1, k. 1, p. 1, k. 6**; p. 8, work from last ** back to first **, then work as given for 2nd row from * to end.

7th row: (K. 1, p. 3) 4 times, p. 1 more, c.4f., p. 2, k. 7, m.b., k. 7, p. 2, c.4b., p. 1, m.b., p. 1, tw.2lt., p. 5, tw.2rt., p. 1, m.b., p. 7, k. 1, p. 1, k. 1, p. 1, k. 1, p. 5, cr.3rt, c.4b., cr.3lt., p. 5, k. 1, p. 1, k. 1, p. 1, k. 1, p. 7, m.b., p. 1, tw.2lt., p. 5, tw.2rt., p. 1, m.b., p. 1, c.4f., p. 2, k. 4, p. 2, c.4f., p. 2, cable 9, p. 2, c.4b., p. 2, k. 4, p. 2, c.4b., p. 4, k. 1, (p. 3, k. 1) 3 times.

8th row: Work as given for 2nd row from *** to ***, then **p. 4, k. 4, p. 1, k. 5, p. 1, k. 10, p. 1, k. 1, p. 1, k. 1, p. 1, k. 5, p. 2, k. 1 ****, p. 4, work from **** back to **, then work as for 2nd row from * to end.

9th row: K. 1, p. 3, m.b., (p. 3, k. 1) twice, p. 4, k. 4, p. 2, k. 5, m.b., k. 3, m.b., k. 5, p. 2, k. 4, p. 4, tw.2lt., p. 3, tw.2rt., p. 10, k. 1, p. 1, k. 1, p. 1, k. 1, p. 4, cr.3rt., p. 1, k. 4, p. 1, cr.3lt., p. 4, k. 1, p. 1, k. 1, p. 1, k. 1, p. 10, tw.2lt., p. 3, tw.2rt., p. 4, k. 4, p. 2, up 1, k. 4, (p. 2, k. 4) twice, up 1, p. 1, up 1, (k. 4, p. 2) twice, k. 4, up 1, p. 2, k. 4, p. 4, (k. 1, p. 3) twice, m.b., p. 3, k. 1.

10th row: (P. 1, k. 3) 3 times, p. 1, k. 4, p. 4, k. 3, (p. 4, k. 2) twice, p. 4, k. 3, (p. 4, k. 2) twice, p. 4, k. 3, **p. 4, k. 5, p. 1, k. 3, p. 1, k. 11, p. 1, k. 1, p. 1, k. 1, p. 1, ***, k. 4, p. 2, k. 2 **, p. 4, work from last ** back to first **, then as for 2nd row from * to end.

11th row: K. 1, p. 2, m.b., k. 1, m.b., p. 2, k. 1, p. 3, k. 1, p. 4, c.4f., p. 2, k. 7, m.b., k. 7, p. 2, c.4b., p. 5, k. 1, p. 3, k. 1, p. 5, c.5b., p. 2, cr.3rt., p. 2, c.4b., p. 2, cr.3lt., p. 2, c.7f, p. 5, k. 1, p. 3, k. 1, p. 5, c.4f., p. 3, up 1, k. 4, p. 2 tog., c.4f., p. 2 tog., k. 4, up 1, p. 3, up 1, k. 4, p. 2 tog., c.4b., p. 2 tog., k. 4, up 1, p. 3, c.4b., p. 4, k. 1, p. 3, k. 1, p. 2, m.b., k. 1, m.b., p. 2, k. 1.

12th row: (P. 1, k. 3) 3 times, p. 1, k. 4, p. 4, k. 4, p. 4, k. 1, p. 4, k. 1, p. 4, k. 5, (p. 4, k. 1) twice, p. 4, k. 4, **p. 4, k. 5, p. 1, k. 3, p. 1, k. 6, p. 1, k. 1, p. 1, k. 1, p. 1, k. 8, p. 2, k. 3**, p. 4, work from last ** back to first **, work as for 2nd row from * to end.

13th row: K. 1, p. 1, m.b., p. 1, m.b., p. 1, m.b., p. 1, k. 1, p. 3, k. 1, p. 4, k. 4, p. 2, k. 5, m.b., k. 3, m.b., k. 5, p. 2, **k. 4, p. 5, m.b., p. 3, m.b., p. 6, k. 1, p. 1, k. 1, p. 1, k. 1, p. 7**, cr.3rt., p. 3, k. 4, p. 3, cr.3lt., work from last ** back to first **, p. 4, up 1, k. 3, s.s.k., k. 4, k. 2 tog., k. 3, up 1, p. 5, up 1, k. 3, s.s.k., k. 4, k. 2 tog., k. 3, up 1, p. 4, k. 4, p. 4, k. 1, p. 3, k. 1, p. 1, m.b., p. 1, m.b., p. 1, m.b., p. 1, k. 1.

14th row: (P. 1, k. 3) 3 times, p. 1, k. 4, p. 4, k. 5, p. 12, k. 7, p. 12, k. 5, **p. 4, k. 4, p. 1, (k. 1, p. 1,) 3 times, k. 5, p. 1, k. 1, p. 1, k. 1, p. 1, k. 7, p. 2, k. 4**, p. 4, work from last ** back to first **, then work as for 2nd row from * to end.

15th row: (K. 1, p. 3) 3 times, m.b., p. 4, c.4f., p. 2, k. 7, m.b., k. 7, p. 2, c.4b., p. 3, tw.2rt., tw.2rt., p. 1, tw.2lt., tw.2lt., p. 4, k. 1, p. 1, k. 1, p. 1, k. 1, p. 7, k. 2, p. 4, c.4b., p. 4, k. 2, p. 7, k. 1, p. 1, k. 1, p. 1, k. 1, p. 4, tw.2rt., tw.2rt., p. 1, tw.2lt., tw.2lt., p. 3, c.4f., p. 5, up 1, k. 4, c.4f., k. 4, up 1, p. 7, up 1, k. 4, c.4b., k. 4, up 1, p. 5, c.4b., p. 4, m.b., (p. 3, k. 1) 3 times.

16th row: (P. 1, k. 3) 3 times, p. 1, k. 4, p. 4, k. 6, p. 12, k. 9, p. 12, k. 6, **p. 4, k. 3, p. 1, k. 1, p. 1, k. 3, p. 1, k. 1, p. 1, k. 4, p. 1, k. 1, p. 1, k. 1, p. 1, k. 7, p. 2, k. 4**, p. 4; work from last ** back to first **, then work as for 2nd row from * to end.

17th row: (K. 1, p. 3) twice, k. 1, p. 2, m.b., k. 1, m.b., p. 3, k. 4, p. 2, k. 5, m.b., k. 3, m.b., k. 5, p. 2, k. 4, p. 2, tw.2rt., tw.2rt., p. 3, tw.2lt., tw.2lt., p. 3, k. 1, p. 1, k. 1, p. 1, k. 1, p. 7, cr.3lt., p. 3, k. 4, p. 3, cr.3rt., p. 7, k. 1, p. 1, k. 1, p. 1, k. 1, p. 3, tw.2rt., tw.2rt., p. 3, tw.2lt., tw.2lt., p. 2, k. 4, p. 6, cable 12 right, p. 9, cable 12 left, p. 6, k. 4, p. 3, m.b., k. 1, m.b., p. 2, k. 1, (p. 3, k. 1) twice.

18th row: Work as given for 16th row until first ** is reached, then ***p. 4, k. 2, p. 1, k. 1, p. 1, k. 5, p. 1, k. 1, p. 1, k. 3, p. 1, k. 1, p. 1, k. 1, p. 1, k. 8, p. 2, k. 3*, p. 4, then work from * back to ***, then work as for 2nd row from * to end.

19th row: (K. 1, p. 3) twice, k. 1, p. 1, m.b., p. 1, m.b., p. 1, m.b., p. 2, c.4f., p. 2, k. 7, m.b., k. 7, p. 2, c.4b., p. 1, tw.2rt., tw.2rt., p. 5, tw.2lt., tw.2lt., p. 1, c.7b., p. 2, cr.3lt., p. 2, c.4b., p. 2, cr.3rt., p. 2, c.5f., p. 1, tw.2rt., tw.2rt., p. 5, tw.2lt., tw.2lt., p. 1, c.4f., p. 4, p. 2 tog., k. 4, c.4f., k. 4, p. 2 tog., p. 5, p. 2 tog., k. 4, c.4b., k. 4, p. 2 tog., p. 4, c.4b., p. 2, m.b., p. 1, m.b., p. 1, m.b., p. 1, k. 1, (p. 3, k. 1) twice.

20th row: Work as given for 14th row until first ** is reached, then ***p. 4, k. 1, p. 1, k. 1, p. 1, k. 7, p. 1, k. 1, p. 1, k. 7, p. 1, k. 1, p. 1, k. 1, p. 1, k. 4, p. 2, k. 2*, p. 4, work from * back to ***, then work as for 2nd row from * to end.

21st row: (K. 1, p. 3) 4 times, p. 1 more, k. 4, p. 2, k. 15, p. 2, k. 4, p. 1, m.b., p. 1, tw.2lt., p. 5, tw.2rt., p. 1, m.b., p. 7, k. 1, p. 1, k. 1, p. 1, k. 1, p. 4, cr.3lt., p. 1, k. 4, p. 1, cr.3rt., p. 4, k. 1, p. 1, k. 1, p. 1, k. 1, p. 7, m.b., p. 1, tw.2lt., p. 5, tw.2rt., p. 1, m.b., p. 1, k. 4, p. 3, p. 2 tog., k. 4, up 1, k. 4, up 1, k. 4, p. 2 tog., p. 3, p. 2 tog., k. 4, up 1, k. 4, up 1, k. 4, p. 2 tog., p. 3, k. 4, p. 4, k. 1, (p. 3, k. 1) 3 times.

22nd row: Work as given for 12th row until first ** is reached, then as for 8th row from ** to end.

23rd row: K. 1, p. 3, m.b., (p. 3, k. 1) twice, p. 4, c.4f., p. 2, c.6b., k. 3, c.6f., p. 2, c.4b., p. 4, tw.2lt., p. 3, tw.2rt., p. 10, k. 1, p. 1, k. 1, p. 1, k. 1, p. 5, cr.3lt., c.4b., cr.3rt., p. 5, k. 1, p. 1, k. 1, p. 1, k. 1, p. 10, tw.2lt., p. 3, tw.2rt., p. 4, c.4f., p. 2, p. 2 tog., k. 4, up 1, p. 1, c.4f., p. 1, up 1, k. 4, p. 2 tog., p. 1, p. 2 tog., k. 4, up 1, p. 1, c.4b., p. 1, up 1, k. 4, p. 2 tog., p. 2, c.4b., p. 4, (k. 1, p. 3) twice, m.b., p. 3, k. 1.

24th row: Work as given for 10th row until *** is reached k. 6, p. 8, k. 6, then work from *** back to first ** on 10th row, then work as for 2nd row from * to end.

25th row: K. 1, p. 2, m.b., k. 1, m.b., p. 2, k. 1, p. 3, k. 1, p. 4, k. 4, p. 2, k. 15, p. 2, k. 4, p. 5, k. 1, p. 3, k. 1, p. 5, c.5b., p. 5, cr.3lt., p. 2, cr.3rt., p. 5, c.7f., p. 5, k. 1, p. 3, k. 1, p. 5, k. 4, p. 1, p. 2 tog., k. 4, p. 2, k. 4, p. 2, k. 4, p. 3 tog., k. 4, p. 2, k. 4, p. 2, k. 4, p. 2 tog., p. 1, k. 4, p. 4, k. 1, p. 3, k. 1, p. 2, m.b., k. 1, m.b., p. 2, k. 1.

26th row: Work as given for 2nd row from * * * to * * *, then * * p.4, k.5, p.1, k.3, p.1, k.6, p.1, k.1, p.1, k.1, p.1, k.12 * *, p.6, work from last * * back to first * *, then as for 2nd row from * to end.

27th row: K.1, p.1, m.b., p.1, m.b., p.1, m.b., p.1, k.1, p.3, k.1, p.4, c.4f., p.2, k.15, p.2, c.4b., p.5, m.b., p.3, m.b., p.6, k.1, p.1, k.1, p.1, k.1, p.8, m.b., p.3, cr.3lt., cr.3rt., p.3, m.b., p.8, k.1, p.1, k.1, p.1, k.1, p.6, m.b., p.3, m.b., p.5, c.4f., p.2, k.4, p.2, c.4f., p.2, cable 9, p.2, c.4b., p.2, k.4, p.2, c.4b., p.4, k.1, p.3, k.1, p.1, m.b., p.1, m.b., p.1, m.b., p.1, k.1.

28th row: Work as given for 2nd row from * * * to * * *, then * * p.4, k.4, p.1, k.1, p.1, k.1, p.1, k.1, p.1, k.5, p.1, k.1, p.1, k.1, p.1, k.13 * *, p.4, work from last * * back to first * *, then work as for 2nd row from * to end.

The last 28 rows form the pattern; repeat them 4 times more then work the first 8 rows again.

To shape the armholes: Maintaining the continuity of the pattern as set, cast off 7 sts. at the beginning of the next 2 rows, then dec. 1 st. at each end of the next row and the 7 following alternate rows. – 148 sts.

Pattern 60 rows as set.

Now divide the sts. for the neck: Next row: Pattern 61 and leave these sts. on a spare needle until required for left. back shoulder, pattern 26 and leave these sts. on a stitch-holder until required for neckband, pattern to end and continue on these 61 sts. for the right back shoulder.

The right back shoulder: 1st row: Cast off 9 sts., work to end of row.

2nd row: Pattern 4 sts. then slip these sts. onto stitch-holder at centre back neck, pattern to end.

Repeat the last 2 rows 3 times.

Cast off the remaining 9 sts.

The left back shoulder: With right side of work facing rejoin yarn to inner edge of the 61 sts. left on spare needle and work to end of row, then work as given for right back shoulder to end.

THE FRONT

Work as given for the back until the armhole shaping has been worked.

Pattern 26 rows as set.

Now divide the sts. for the neck: Next row: Pattern 60 and leave these sts. on a spare needle until required for right front shoulder, pattern 28 and leave these sts. on a spare needle until required for neckband, pattern to end and continue on these 60 sts. for the left front shoulder.

The left front shoulder: To shape the neck: Dec. 1 st. at the neck edge on each of the next 15 rows.

On 45 sts. pattern 19 rows.

To slope the shoulder: Cast off 9 sts. at the beginning of the next row and the 3 following alternate rows.

On 9 sts. work 1 row, then cast off.

The right front shoulder: With right side of work facing rejoin yarn to inner edge of sts. left on spare needle and work to end of row, then work as given for left front shoulder to end.

THE SLEEVES (both alike)

With size 2¼ mm. (No. 13) needles cast on 73 sts. and work 37 rows in single rib.

Increase row: Rib 2, *up 1, rib 1, up 1, rib 2; repeat from * ending last repeat rib 1. – 121 sts.

Change to size 2¾ mm. (No. 12) needles and work in pattern as follows:

1st row: (K.1, p.3) 3 times, m.b., p.4, k.4, p.2, k.15, p.2, k.4, p.3, (tw.2rt.) twice, p.1, (tw.2lt.) twice, p.3, (k.4, p.2) 3 times, k.4, p.1, (k.4, p.2) 3 times, k.4, p.4, m.b., (p.3, k.1) 3 times.

2nd row: (P.1, k.3) 3 times, p.1, k.4, (p.4, k.2) 3 times, p.4, k.1, (p.4, k.2) 3 times, p.4*, k.3, p.1, k.1, p.1, k.3, p.1, k.1, p.1, k.3, * * p.4, k.2, p.15, k.2, p.4, k.4, (p.1, k.3) 3 times, p.1.

3rd row: (K.1, p.3) twice, k.1, p.2, m.b., k.1, m.b., p.3, c.4f., p.2, c.6b., k.3, c.6f., p.2, c.4b., p.2, (tw.2rt,) twice, p.3, (tw.21t.) twice, p.2, c.4f., p.2, k.4, p.2, c.4f., p.2, k.4, p.1, (k.4, p.2, c.4b., p.2) twice, p.1 more, m.b., k.1, m.b., p.2, k.1, (p.3, k.1) twice.

4th row: Work as given for 2nd row until * is reached, then k.2, p.1, k.1, p.1, k.5, p.1, k.1, p.1, k.2, then work as given for 2nd row from * * to end.

The last 4 rows set the position of the patterns given at each end of the 28 pattern rows given for back. Now work the 5th to 28th pattern rows as set. Repeat the 28 pattern rows 4 times more, then work the first 8 rows again. – Work an extra 22 rows here when working the man's version.

To shape the sleevetop: Continuing in pattern as set, cast off 7 sts. at the beginning of the next 2 rows, then dec. 1 st. at each end of the next row and the 15 following alternate rows.

On 75 sts. work 1 row.

Dec. 1 st. at each end of the next 12 rows.

Cast off 4 sts. at the beginning of the next 4 rows, and 6 sts. on the 4 following rows.

Cast off the remaining 11 sts.

THE NECKBAND

First join right shoulder seam. With right side of work facing rejoin yarn at left front neck edge and using size 2¼ mm. (No. 13) needles pick up and k. 34 sts. from left front neck edge, k. across the 28 sts. at centre front, then pick up and k. 34 sts. from right front neck edge, then k. across the 58 sts. on stitch-holder at back neck edge.

On 154 sts. work 119 rows in single rib for the polo neck, 53 rows for the roll neck or 27 rows for the crew neck, then cast off.

THE POCKET BACKS (2 alike)

With size 2¾ mm. (No. 12) needles cast on 40 sts. and beginning with a k. row s.s. 50 rows, then cast off.

TO MAKE UP THE SWEATER

Pin out to size and press all parts except the ribbing very lightly with a warm iron over a damp cloth. Join left shoulder seam, continuing seam along neckband. Set in sleeves. Join sleeve and side seams, inserting pockets 5 centimetres (2 inches) above ribbing at side seams. On the crew neck version fold ribbing in half to wrong side and neatly sew in place. Press seams.

THE CARDIGAN

THE BACK

With size 2¼ mm. (No. 13) needles cast on 154 sts. and work 29 rows in single rib.

Increase row: Rib 8, *up 1, rib 6; repeat from * ending last repeat rib 8. – 178 sts.

Change to size 2¾ mm. (No. 12) needles and work the 28 row pattern given for back of sweater 6 times, then work the first 2 rows again.

To shape the armholes: Cast off 7 sts. at the beginning of the next 2 rows, then dec. 1 st. at each end of the next row and the 7 following alternate rows. – 148 sts.

Pattern 67 rows.

To slope the shoulders: Cast off 9 sts. at the beginning of the next 10 rows.

Cast off the remaining 58 sts.

THE POCKET BACKS (2 alike)

With size 2¾ mm. (No. 12) needles cast on 42 sts. and work 54 rows in single rib, then leave these sts. on a stitch-holder until required.

THE LEFT FRONT

With size 2¼ mm. (No. 13) needles cast on 78 sts. and work 29 rows in single rib.

Increase row: Rib 6, *up 1, rib 6; repeat from * ending last repeat rib 6. – 90 sts.

Change to size 2¾ mm. (No. 12) needles and work in pattern as follows:

1st row: (K.1, p.3) 3 times, m.b., p.4, k.4, p.2, k.15, p.2, k.4, p.3, (tw.2rt.) twice, p.1, (tw.2lt.) twice, p.4, k.1, p.1, k.1, p.1, k.1, p.8, m.b., p.1, m.b., p.2, c.4f., p.2, m.b., p.1, m.b., p.3.

2nd row: K.8, p.4, k.13, p.1, k.1, p.1, k.1, p.1, k.4, p.1, k.1, p.1, k.3, p.1, k.1, p.1, k.3, p.4, k.2, p.15, k.2, p.4, k.4, p.1, (k.3, p.1) 3 times.

The last 2 rows set the position of the 28 row pattern given at the beginning of right side rows and the end of wrong side rows for back of sweater. Now work the 3rd to 28th rows as set.

Pattern 28 rows more as set.

Pocket row: Pattern 16, slip next 42 sts. onto a stitch-holder and leave at front of work, in their place pattern across the 42 sts. of one pocket back, pattern to end of row.

Pattern 79 rows more.

* *To slope the front edge: Continuing in pattern as set, dec. 1 st. at the end of the next row and the 8 following 4th rows.

On 81 sts. work 1 row back to side seam edge.

To shape the armhole and continue to slope the front edge: Still decreasing at front edge on every 4th row as set, cast off 7 sts. at the beginning – armhole edge – on the next row, then dec. 1 st. at the same edge on each of the 8 following alternate rows.

On 62 sts. work 1 row.

To slope the front edge only: Dec. 1 st, at the end – front edge on the next row and the 16 following 4th rows.

On 45 sts. work 1 row.

To slope the shoulder: Cast off 9 sts. at the beginning of the next row and the 3 following alternate rows.

On 9 sts. work 1 row, then cast off.

THE RIGHT FRONT

Work as given for left front until the increase row has been worked.

Change to size 2¾ mm. (No. 12) needles and work as follows:

1st row: P.7, k.1, p.1, k.1, p.1, k.1, p.4, (tw.2rt.) twice, p.1, (tw.2lt.) twice, p.3, k.4, (p.2, k.4) 3 times, p.1, (k.4, p.2) 3 times, k.4, p.4, m.b., (p.3, k.1) 3 times.

2nd row: (P.1, k.3) 3 times, p.1, k.4, (p.4, k.2) 3 times, p.4, k.1, p.4, (k.2, p.4) 3 times, k.3, p.1, k.1, p.1, k.3, p.1, k.1, p.1, k.4, p.1, k.1, p.1, k.1, p.1, k.7.

The last 2 rows set the position of the pattern given for the end of right side rows and beginning of wrong side rows for back of sweater. Now work the 3rd to 28th pattern rows, then work these 28 rows once more.

Pocket row: Pattern 32, slip next 42 sts. onto a stitch-holder and leave at front of work, in their place, pattern across the 42 sts. of one pocket back, pattern to end of row.

Pattern 80 rows as set.

Now work as given for left front from * * to end.

THE SLEEVES (both alike)

As given for sleeves on sweater.

THE POCKET TOPS (2 alike)

With right side of work facing rejoin yarn to the 42 sts. left on stitch-holder and using size 2¼ mm. (No. 13) needles work 8 rows in single rib, then cast off in rib.

THE BUTTONBAND AND HALF COLLAR

With size 2¼ mm. (No. 13) needles, cast on 12 sts. and work 166 rows in single rib.

* *Continuing in rib as set, inc. 1 st. at the beginning of the next row and the 17 following 4th rows.

On 30 sts. rib 91 rows.

Cast off in rib.

THE BUTTONHOLE BAND AND HALF COLLAR

With size 2¼ mm. (No. 13) needles cast on 12 sts. and work 10 rows in single rib.

1st Buttonhole row: Rib 4, cast off 4, rib to end.

2nd Buttonhole row: Rib 4, turn, cast on 4, turn, rib to end.

Rib 20 rows.

Repeat the last 22 rows 6 times, then work the 2 buttonhole rows again.

Now work as given for buttonband and half collar from * * to end.

TO MAKE UP THE CARDIGAN

Pin out to size and press all parts except the ribbing lightly on the wrong side with a warm iron over a damp cloth. Join shoulder seams. Set in sleeves. Join sleeve and side seams. Neatly sew pocket backs and row ends of pocket tops in place. Join cast off edges of button and buttonhole bands. Neatly sew shaped row end edges of collar and front bands in place, so that the first front edge decreases are in line with the first increases in the collar. Press seams. Sew buttons in place.

chequered

chequers

Her skirt from Elle, his suit from Paul Smith.

chequered

MATERIALS
For the long sweater: Either 8 (9) (9) 25 gram balls of "Woollybear Pure Silk" by Patricia Roberts in main colour, 7 (8)(8) balls in first contrast colour and 3 balls in each of the other 6 contrast colours or 7 (8) (8) 28 gram (ounce) hanks of "Woollybear Real Shetland" by Patricia Roberts in main colour, 6 (7) (7) hanks in first contrast and 3 hanks in each of the other 6 contrast colours.

For the short sweater: Either 7 25 gram balls of "Woollybear Pure Silk" by Patricia Roberts in main colour, 6 balls in first contrast colour and 2 balls in each of the 6 other contrast colours or 6 28 gram (ounce) hanks of "Woollybear Real Shetland" in main colour, 5 hanks in first contrast and 2 hanks in each of the 6 other contrast colours, 4 25 gram balls of "Woollybear 100% Mohair" in each colour may be substituted for 3 of the contrast colours.

For any of these garments: a pair each of size 2¼mm (No. 13) and size 3mm (No. 11) Aero knitting needles; a fine cable needle.

TENSION
As for "Chequers".

ABBREVIATIONS
As for "Chequers".

NOTES
As for "Chequers"

MEASUREMENTS
The measurements are given in centimetres followed by inches in brackets.

THE LONG SWEATER

Underarms	95(38)	100(40)	105(42)
Side seam	40(16)	40(16)	40(16)
Length	62.5(25)	64(25½)	64(25½)
Sleeve seam	31(12½)	31(12½)	31(12½)

THE SHORT SWEATER

Underarms	100(40)
Side seam	25(10)
Length	50(20)
Sleeve seam	31(12½)

THE LONG SWEATER

THE BACK AND FRONT
As given for "Chequers" man's sweater.

THE SLEEVES (both alike)
As given for the "Chequers" jacket.

THE NECKBAND, SHOULDER EDGING AND POCKETS
As given for the "Chequers" man's sweater.

TO MAKE UP THE SWEATER
Do not press silk. For other yarns pin out to size and press with a warm iron over a damp cloth. Fold the two outer marking threads at top of sleeve to the centre marking thread and pin in place. Neatly sew sleevetops in place, so that the pleat is in line with the shoulder. Sew pocket backs to row ends at each side of back 2.5cms., (1 inch) above the ribbing. Join sleeve and side seams, neatly sewing pocket backs in place on wrong side of fronts. Sew on buttons.

THE SHORT SWEATER

THE BACK
As given for the back of the "Chequers" jacket until the armhole shaping is reached.

To shape the armholes: Work as given for "Chequers" medium sized man's sweater armhole shaping to end.

THE FRONT
Work as given for back until armhole shaping has been worked. Then work as given for front of "Chequers" medium sized man's sweater to end.

THE SLEEVES (both alike)
As given for "Chequers" jacket.

THE NECKBAND
As given for "Chequers" medium sized man's sweater.

TO MAKE UP THE SWEATER
As given for long sweater, omitting pockets.

chequers

MATERIALS

For the sweater: Either 7 (8) (8) 28 gram (ounce) hanks of "Woollybear Real Shetland" by Patricia Roberts in main colour and 6 (7) (7) hanks in first contrast or 8 (9) (9) 25 gram balls of "Woollybear Lambswool" in main colour and 7 (8) (8) balls in first contrast, plus 3 hanks or balls of the same yarn in each of the 6 other contrasts. 4 25 gram balls of "Woollybear 100% Mohair" in each colour may be substituted for 3 of the contrasts; 3 buttons.

For the jacket: 7 (6) 28 gram (ounce) hanks of "Woollybear Real Shetland" in main colour and 6 hanks in first contrast and 2 hanks in each of the 6 other contrasts or 8 25 gram balls of "Woollybear Lambswool" in main colour and 7 balls in first contrast and 3 balls in each of the 6 other contrasts or 4 25 gram balls of "Woollybear 100% Mohair" in each colour substituted for 3 of the contrasts.

For a summer version 8 (7) 25 gram balls of "Woollybear Pure Silk" in main colour and 7 (6) balls in first contrast, plus 2 balls in each of the 6 other contrasts; 4 buttons.

For either garment: a pair each of size 2¼mm. (No. 13), and size 3mm. (No. 11) Aero knitting needles; a fine cable needle.

TENSION

Work at a tension of 24 sts. and 18 rows to 5 centimetres (2 inches) over the pattern using size 3mm. (No. 11) needles. If you cannot obtain the correct tension using the size needles suggested, use larger or smaller ones accordingly.

ABBREVIATIONS

K., knit; p., purl; st., stitch; tog., together; dec., decrease (by working 2 sts. tog.); inc., increase (by working twice into same st.); single rib is k. 1 and p. 1 alternately; s.s., stocking stitch is k. on the right side and p. on the wrong side; 3 from 3, insert needle into next 3 sts. as if to purl, wrap yarn round needle and draw loop through, wrap yarn round needle again, then insert needle back into the 3 sts. on left hand needle, wrap yarn round needle and draw loop through allowing the 3 sts. to fall from left hand needle; cable 6f., slip next 3 sts. onto cable needle and leave at front of work, with m. k.3, then with appropriate contrast colour, k.3 from cable needle; cable 6b., slip next 3 sts. onto cable needle and leave at back of work, with m. k.3, then with appropriate contrast colour, k.3 from cable needle; up 1, pick up the loop, which lies between the needles, slip it onto left hand needle, then k. into back of it; m., main colour; a., first contrast; b., second contrast; c., third contrast; d., fourth contrast; e., fifth contrast; f., sixth contrast; g., seventh contrast.

NOTE

The instructions are given for the small size. Where they vary work the instructions in the first brackets for the medium size or the figures in the second brackets for the large size.

SPECIAL NOTE

Work the instructions in the square brackets [ ] the number of times stated after the brackets.

MEASUREMENTS

The measurements are given in centimetres followed by inches in brackets.

THE SWEATER

Underarms	95	(38)	100	(40)	105	(42)
Side seam	40	(16)	40	(16)	40	(16)
Length	62.5	(25)	64	(25½)	65	(26)
Sleeve seam	47.5	(19)	47.5	(19)	47.5	(19)

THE JACKET

Underarms	100	(40)
Side seam	25	(10)
Length	50	(20)
Sleeve seam	31	(12½)

THE SWEATER

THE BACK

With size 2¼mm. (No. 13) needles and m. cast on 171 (180) (189) sts. and work 33 rows in single rib.

Increase row: Rib 2, * up 1, rib 3; repeat from * ending last repeat rib 1. – 228 (240) (252) sts.

Change to size 3mm. (No. 11) needles and work in pattern as follows. Take care not to pull colours not in use tightly across the back of the work. Use separate balls of m. and a. for each square section. When breaking off colours leave sufficiently long ends to darn in at completion of work, to prevent unravelling.

1st row: [With b. k.3, with m. k.3] 7 (8) (9) times, * [with b. k.4, with a. k.4] 6 times, [with b. k.3, with m. k.3] 8 times; repeat from * ending by working items in last brackets 7 (8) (9) times.

2nd row: [With m. p.3, with b. p.3] 7 (8) (9) times, * [with b. p.1, with a. 3 from 3, with a. p.1, with b. 3 from 3] 6 times, [with m. p.3, with b. p.3] 8 times; repeat from * ending by working items in last brackets 7 (8) (9) times.

3rd row: [With c. and m. cable 6f. – see abbreviations] 7 (8) (9) times, * with c. k.2, [with a. k.4, with c. k.4] 5 times, with a. k.4, with c. k.2, [with c. and m. cable 6f. as before] 8 times; repeat from * ending by working items in last brackets 7 (8) (9) times.

4th row: [With c. p.3, with m. p.3] 7 (8) (9) times, *with c. p.3, [with a. 3 from 3, with a. p.1, with c. 3 from 3, with c. p.1] 5 times, with a. 3 from 3, with a. p.1, with c. p.1 [with c. p.3, with m. p.3] 8 times; repeat from * ending by working items in last brackets 7 (8) (9) times.

5th row: [With m. k.3, with d. k.3] 7 (8) (9) times, * [with a. k.4, with d. k.4] 6 times, [with m. k.3, with d. k.3] 8 times; repeat from *ending by working items in last brackets 7 (8) (9) times.

6th row: [With d. p.3, with m. p.3] 7 (8) (9) times, * [with a. p.1, with d. 3 from 3, with d. p.1, with a. 3 from 3] 6 times. [with d. p.3, with m. p.3] 8 times; repeat from * ending by working items in last brackets 7 (8) (9) times.

7th row: With e. k.3, [with m. and e. cable 6b.] 6 (7) (8) times, with m. k.3, *with a. k.2, [with e. k.4, with a. k.4] 5 times, with e. k.4, with a. k.2, with e. k.3, [with m. and e. cable 6b] 7 times, with m. k.3; repeat from * ending by working items in last brackets 6 (7) (8) times.

8th row: [With m. p.3, with e. p.3] 7 (8) (9) times, *with a. p.3, [with e. 3 from 3, p.1, with a. 3 from 3, p.1] 5 times, with e. 3 from 3, p.1, with a. p.1, [with m. p.3, with e. p.3] 8 times; repeat from * ending by working items in last brackets 7 (8) (9) times.

9th to 16th rows: Using f. instead of b., g. instead of c., b. instead of d. and c. instead of e. work as given for first 8 rows.

17th to 24th rows: Using d. instead of b., e. instead of c., f. instead of d. and g. instead of e., work as given for first 8 rows.

25th to 36th rows: As 1st to 12th rows.

37th row: With b. k.2(nil) (with a.k.2, with b. k.4), [with a. k.4, with b. k.4] 5 (6) (6) times, * [with m. k.3, with b. k.3] 8 times, with a. [k.4, with b. k.4] 6 times; repeat from *, but working instructions in last brackets 5 (6) (6) times, then with a. k.2(nil) (with a. k.4 with b. k.2).

38th row: With a. p.2(nil) (with b. p.3, with a. 3 from 3), [with a. p.1, with b. 3 from 3, with b. p.1, with a. 3 from 3] 5 (6) (6) times, * [with b. p.3, with m. p.3] 8 times, [with a. p.1, with b. 3 from 3, with b. p.1, with a. 3 from 3] 6 times; repeat from * ending by working instructions in last brackets 5 (6) (6) times, then with a. p.2(nil) (with a. p.1, with b. 3 from 3, with b. p.2).

39th row: With a. k.4(2) (nil), [with c. k.4, with a. k.4] 4 (5) (6) times, with c. k.4, with a. k.2, *with c. k.3, [with m. and c. cable 6b.] 7 times, with m. k.3, [with a. k.2, with c. k.4, with a. k.2] 6 times; repeat from *, but working instructions in last brackets 5 (6) (6) times, then with a. k.2(nil) (with a. k.2, with c. k.4).

40th row: With c. p.1 (with a. p.3, with c. 3 from 3, with c. p.1) (with a. p.1, with c. 3 from 3, with c. p.1), [with a. 3 from 3, with a p.1, with c. 3 from 3, with c. p.1] 5 (5) (6) times, with a. p.1, * [with m. p.3, with c. p.3] 8 times, with a. p.3, with c. 3 from 3, [with c. p.1, with a. 3 from 3, with a. p.1, with c. 3 from 3] 5 times with c. p.2; repeat from * ending by working instructions in last brackets 4 (5) (6) times, then with c. p.1, with a. 3 from 3, (with c. p.2) (nil).

41st row: With a. k.2(nil) (with d. k.2, with a. k.4), [with d. k.4, with a. k.4] 6 times, * [with d. k.3, with m. k.3] 8 times, [with d. k.4, with a. k.4] 6 times; repeat from * ending by working instructions in last brackets 5 (6) (6) times, then with d. k.2(nil) (with d. k.4, with a. k.2).

42nd row: With d. p.2(nil) (with a. p.3, with d. 3 from 3), [with d. p.1, with a. 3 from 3, with a. p.1, with d. 3 from 3] 5 (6) (6) times, * [with m. p.3, with d. p.3] 8 times, [with d. p.1, with a. 3 from 3, with a. p.1, with d. 3 from 3] 6 times; repeat from * ending by working instructions in brackets 5 (6) (6) times, then with d. p.2(nil) (with d. p.1, with a. 3 from 3, with a. p.1, with d. p.1).

43rd row: With e. k.2(nil) (with a. k.4, with e. k.2), [with e. k.2, with a. k.4, with e. k.2] 5 (6) (6) times, * [with m. and e. cable 6f.] 8 times, [with e. k.2, with a. k.4, with e. k.2] 6 times; repeat from * ending by working instructions in last brackets 5 (6) (6) times, with e. k.2(nil) (with e. k.2, with a. k.4).

44th row: With a. p.1 (with e. p.3, with a. 3 from 3, p.1) (with e. p.1, with a. 3 from 3, p.1), [with e. 3 from 3, with e. p.1, with a. 3 from 3, with a. p.1] 5 (5) (6) times, with e. p.1, * [with e. p.3, with m. p.3] 8 times, with e. p.3, with a. 3 from 3, p.1, [with e. 3 from 3, p.1, with a. 3 from 3, p.1] 5 times, with e. p.1; repeat from * ending by working instructions in brackets 4 (5) (5) times, then, with e. 3 from 3 (with e. p.1) (with e. 3 from 3, p.1, with a. 3 from 3).

45th to 52nd rows: As 37th to 44th rows, but using f. instead of b., g. instead of c., b. instead of d. and c. instead of e.

53rd to 60th rows: Using d. instead of b., e. instead of c., f. instead of d. and g. instead of e., work as given for 37th to 44th rows.

61st to 72nd rows: As 37th to 48th rows.

The last 72 rows form the pattern; work the first 46 rows again.

To shape the armholes: Continuing in pattern as set cast off 12 sts. at the beginning of the next 2 rows, then dec. 1 st. at each end of the next row and the 11 (13) (15) following alternate rows.

On 180 (188) (196) sts. pattern 51 rows.

To slope the shoulders: Cast off 16 (17) (18) sts. at the beginning of the next 4 rows, then 17 (18) (19) sts. on the 2 following rows. Cast off the remaining 82 (84) (86) sts.

THE FRONT

Work as given for back until the armhole shaping has been worked.

On 180 (188) (196) sts. pattern 14 rows.

Now divide the sts. for the neck: Next row: Pattern 73 (76) (79) and leave these sts. on a spare needle until required for right front shoulder, cast off 34 (36) (38), pattern to end and continue on these 73 (76) (79) sts. for the left front shoulder.

The left front shoulder: To shape the neck: Dec. 1 st. at the neck edge on each of the next 24 rows.

On 49 (52) (55) sts. pattern 12 rows.

To slope the shoulder: Cast off 16 (17) (18) sts. at the beginning of the next row and following alternate row. On 17 (18) (19) sts. work 1 row, then cast off.

The right front shoulder: With right side of work facing rejoin yarn to inner edge of sts. left on spare needle and work to end of row, then work as given for left front shoulder to end.

THE SLEEVES (both alike)

With size 2¼mm. (No. 13) needles and b. or m. – cast on 88 sts. and work 31 rows in single rib.

Increase row: Rib 1, *up 1, rib 2; repeat from * ending last repeat rib 1. – 132 sts.

Change to size 3mm. (No. 11) needles and work in pattern as follows; beginning with a 9th pattern row: 9th pattern row: [with f. k.3, with m. k.3] 7 times, [with f. k.4, with a. k.4] 6 times, [with f. k.3, with m. k.3] 7 times.

The last row sets the position of the pattern given for small size on back. Continuing in pattern as set work 19 (19) (13) rows.

Maintaining the continuity of the pattern and working the extra sts. into the pattern as they occur, inc. 1 st. at each end of the next row and the 17 (19) (21) following 6th rows.

On 168 (172) (176) sts. pattern 23 (11) (5) rows.

To shape the sleevetop: Cast off 12 sts. at the beginning of the next 2 rows, then dec. 1 st. at each end of the next row and the 5 (7) (9) following alternate rows. On 132 sts. work 1 row.

Dec. 1 st. at each end of the next 30 rows. Cast off 5 sts. at the beginning of the next 4 rows, then 7 sts. on the 6 following rows. Cast off.

THE NECKBAND

First join right shoulder seam. With right side of work facing rejoin m. and using size 2¼mm. (No. 13) needles pick up and k. 40 sts. from left front neck edge, 26 (27) (28) sts. from centre front neck, 40 sts. from right front neck edge, then 62 (63) (64) sts. from back neck edge. – 168 (170) (172) sts. Work 9 rows in single rib, then cast off loosely.

Continued on page 116

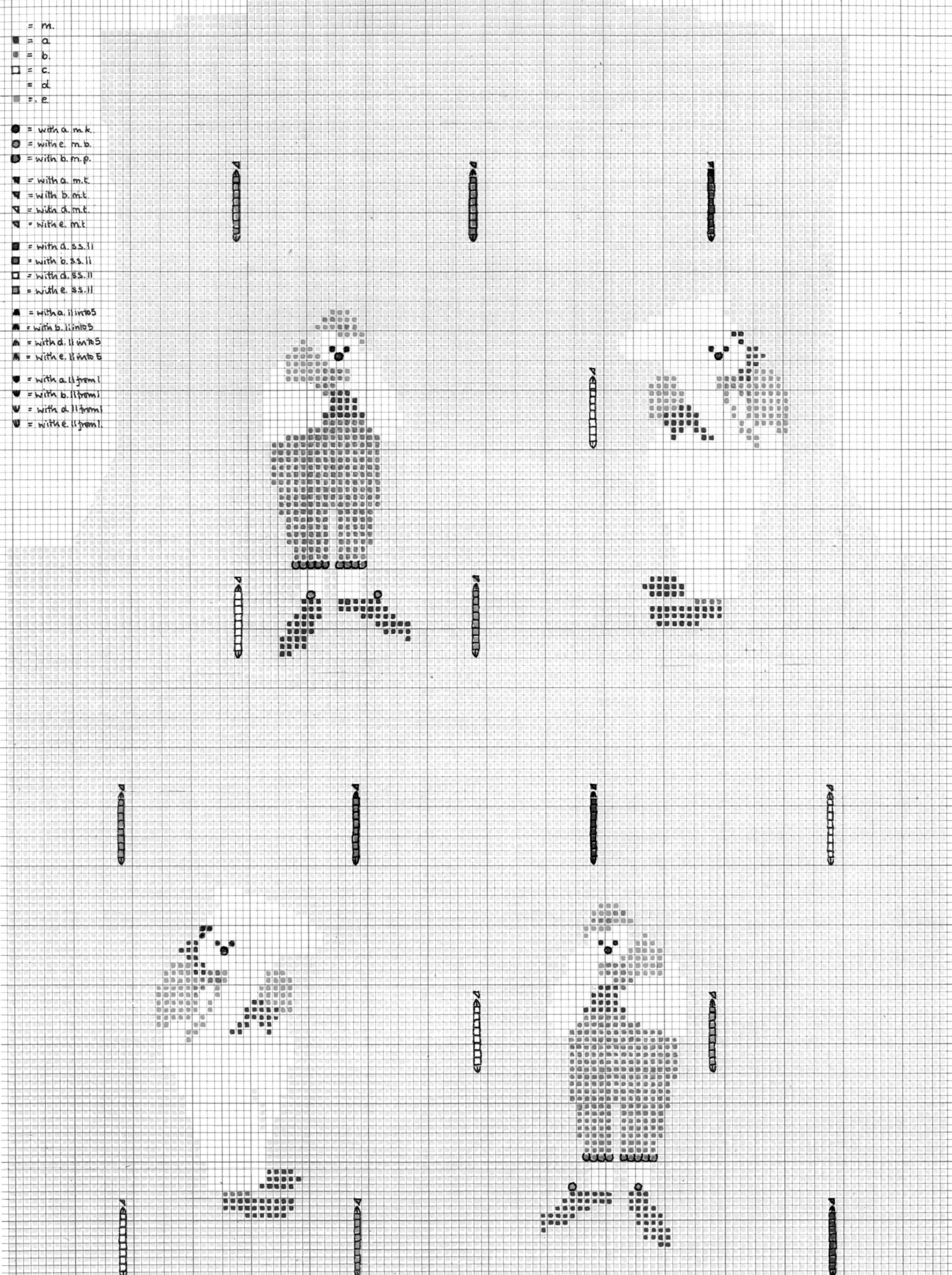
= m.
= a.
= b.
= c.
= d.
= e.
= with a. m.k.
= with e. m.b.
= with b. m.p.
= with a. m.t.
= with b. m.t.
= with d. m.t.
= with e. m.t.
= with a. ss.11
= with b. ss.11
= with d. ss.11
= with e. ss.11
= with a. 11 into 5
= with b. 11 into 5
= with d. 11 into 5
= with e. 11 into 5
= with a. 11 from 1
= with b. 11 from 1
= with d. 11 from 1
= with e. 11 from 1.

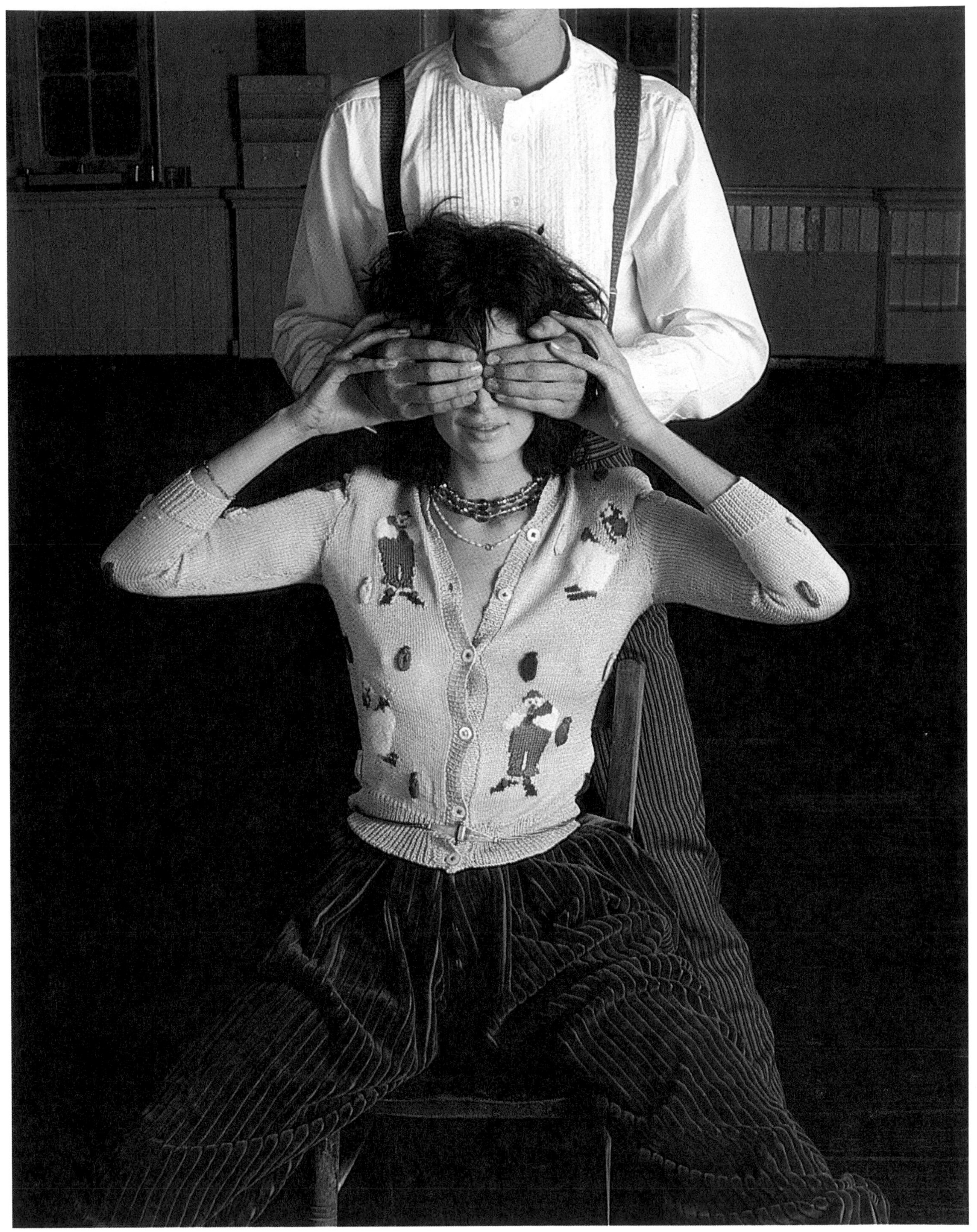

peek-a-boo

Baggy trousers from Brown's.

"Chequers" continued from page 113

THE LEFT SHOULDER EDGING
First join left shoulder at outer edge for 2 centimetres (1 inch), with right side of work facing rejoin m. at left back shoulder, then using size 2¼mm. (No. 13) needles pick up and k. 38 (40) (42) sts. from left back shoulder, then 38 (40) (42) sts. from left front shoulder – including from row ends of neckband.

On 76 (80) (84) sts. work 2 rows in single rib.

1st Buttonhole row: Rib 2, [cast off 2, rib next 12 sts.] twice, cast off 2, rib to end.

2nd Buttonhole row: Rib 42 (46) (50), *turn, cast on 3 over the 2 cast off, turn, rib 13; repeat from * ending rib 2.

Cast off in rib.

THE POCKETS (2 alike optional)
With size 2¼mm. (No. 13) needles and m. cast on 40 sts. and work 50 rows in s.s., then cast off.

TO MAKE UP THE SWEATER
Pin out to size and press all parts except the ribbing lightly on the wrong side with a warm iron over a damp cloth. Set in sleeves. Join sleeve and side seams, inserting pockets in the side seams above the ribbing neatly sewing them in place on wrong side of front. Sew on buttons.

THE CHEQUERS JACKET

THE BACK
With size 2¼mm. (No. 13) needles and m. cast on 160 sts. and work 3 rows in single rib.

Increase row: Rib 1, *up 1, rib 2; repeat from * ending last repeat rib 1. – 240 sts.

Change to size 3mm. (No. 11) needles and noting the information given, work the 72 pattern rows given for the medium – 2nd – size on back of sweater, then work the first 14 rows again. Work should now measure 25 centimetres (10 inches) from beginning.

To shape the armholes: Cast off 12 sts. at the beginning of the next 2 rows, then dec. 1 st. at each end of the next 14 rows.

On 188 sts. pattern 66 rows.

To slope the shoulders: Cast off 15 sts. at the beginning of the next 6 rows and 13 sts. on the 2 following rows. – 72 sts.

Change to size 2¼mm. (No. 13) needles and continue with m. only.

Decrease row: *K.2 tog., k.1, repeat from * to end. – 48 sts. K.3 rows, then cast off loosely.

THE POCKET BACK
With size 2¾mm. (No. 12) needles and m. cast on 36 sts. and beginning with a k. row s.s. 48 rows.

Increase row: K.1, *up 1, k.3; repeat from * ending last repeat k.2. – 48 sts.

P.1 row, then leave these sts. on a stitch-holder until required.

THE LEFT FRONT
With size 2¼mm. (No. 13) needles and m. cast on 89 sts. and work 3 rows in single rib.

Increase row: Rib 3, *up 1, rib 2; repeat from * to end. – 132 sts.

Change to size 3mm. (No. 11) needles and work in pattern as follows: 1st row: [with b. k.3, with m. k.3] 8 times, [with b. k.4, with a. k.4] 6 times, [with b. k.3, with m. k.3] 6 times.

The last row sets the position of the pattern given for the back of the sweater. Work the 2nd to 72nd pattern rows as set. Continuing in pattern work as follows:

Pocket row: Pattern 48, slip next 48 sts. onto a stitch-holder and leave at front of work, in their place pattern across the 48 sts. of pocket back, pattern to end of row.

Work 1 row straight.

**To slope the front edge: Dec. 1 st. at the end – front edge – on the next row, then k.3 sts. tog. at the same edge on the following alternate row. Work 1 row straight.

Repeat the last 4 rows twice more.

To shape the armhole and continue to slope the front edge: Still decreasing at front edge on every alternate row as before, alternating single and double decreases, cast off 12 sts. at the beginning of the next row, then dec. 1 st. at the armhole edge on each of the next 14 rows.

Still decreasing at front edge as before pattern 37 rows. – 58 sts.

On 58 sts. pattern 30 rows.

To slope the shoulder: Cast off 15 sts. at the beginning of the next row and the 2 following alternate rows. On 13 sts. work 1 row, then cast off.

THE RIGHT FRONT
Work as given for left front until the increase row has been worked.

Change to size 3mm. (No. 11) needles and work in pattern as follows, noting the information given for back of sweater: 1st row: [with b. k.3, with m. k.3] 6 times, [with b. k.4, with a. k.4] 6 times, [with b. k.3, with m. k.3] 8 times.

The last row sets the position of the pattern given for the back of the sweater. Work the 2nd to 4th rows as set.

1st Buttonhole row: Pattern 9, cast off 6, pattern to end.

2nd Buttonhole row: Pattern until 9 remain, turn, cast on 6, turn, pattern to end.

Pattern 32 rows.

Repeat the last 34 rows once more, then work the 2 buttonhole rows again.

Pattern 1 row back to side seam edge.

Now work as given for left front from ** to end.

THE HALF COLLAR (1 piece)
With size 2¼mm. (No. 13) needles and a. cast on 2 sts. and k.2 rows.

Increase row: K. into back and front of first st. and k.1, y.r.n., k.1, into last st.

K.5 rows.

Repeat the last 6 rows 13 times, then work the increase row again. On 47 sts. work 1 row.

To shape the neck: Cast off 24 sts. at the beginning of the next row, then dec. 1 st. at the same edge on each of the next 9 rows.

Dec. 1 st. at the beginning of the next row and the 11 following alternate rows.

Take the 2 remaining sts. tog. and fasten off.

THE LEFT FRONT EDGING
With right side of work facing rejoin m. at left front shoulder and using size 2¼mm. (No. 13) needles pick up and k. 96 sts. from row ends of front edge up to first front edge dec., then 80 sts. along front edge to cast on edge.

On 176 sts. k.3 rows, then cast off loosely.

THE RIGHT FRONT EDGING
First sew **long** row end edge of half collar, neatly, in place between first front edge dec. and 2.5 cms. (1 inch) below top of shoulder at neck edge. With right side of work facing rejoin m. at cast on edge of front edge and using size 2¼mm. (No. 13) needles pick up and k. 80 sts. up to first front edge dec., then 56 sts. from row end edge of collar, up to neck shaping.

On 136 sts. k.3 rows, then cast off loosely.

THE RIGHT FRONT NECK EDGING
With size 2¼mm. (No. 13) needles and m. cast on 58 sts. K.3 rows, then cast off loosely.

THE BUTTONHOLE LOOP
With size 2¼mm. (No. 13) needles and m. cast on 16 sts. and k.1 row, then cast off.

THE POCKET TOP
With right side of work facing rejoin m. to the 48 sts. left on stitch-holder and using size 2¼mm. (No. 13) needles work 4 rows in single rib, then cast off.

THE SLEEVES (both alike)
With size 2¼mm. (No. 13) needles and m. cast on 90 sts. and work 7 rows in single rib.

Increase row: Rib 1, *up 1, rib 3; repeat from * ending last repeat rib 2. – 120 sts.

Change to size 3mm (No. 11) needles and work in pattern as follows, noting the information given for back of sweater and starting with a 53rd pattern row.

53rd row: [With d. k.4, with a. k.4] 4 times, with d. k.4, [with m. k.3, with d. k.3] 8 times, [with a. k.4, with d. k.4] 4 times, with a. k.4.

The last row sets the position of the pattern given for back of sweater, work the 54th to 72nd rows.

Continuing in pattern as set and working the extra sts. into the pattern as they occur, inc. 1 st. at each end of the next and the 35 following alternate rows. On 192 sts. pattern 15 rows.

To shape the sleevetop: Cast off 12 sts. at the beginning of the next 2 rows, then dec. 1 st. at each end of the next row and the 25 following alternate rows. On 116 sts. work 1 row.

Dec. 1 st. at each end of the next 18 rows. – 80 sts.

Cast off marking the 20th, 40th and 60th sts. with coloured threads.

TO MAKE UP THE JACKET
Do not press silk. For other yarns pin out and press with a warm iron over a damp cloth. Neatly sew right front neckband in place. Join shoulder seams. Fold the 2 outer marking threads at top of sleeve in to centre marking thread and pin in place. Neatly sew sleevetops in place so that the pleat is in line with shoulder. Join sleeve seams. Sew pocket back and row ends of pocket top in place. Fold buttonhole loop in half, joining first and last 2 sts., then sew loop in place at top of right half collar. Sew on buttons.

peek-a-boo

MATERIALS
10 25 gram balls of either "Woollybear Pure Silk" or 15 25 gram balls of "Woollybear Fine Cotton" or 9 ounce (28 gram) hanks of "Woollybear Real Shetland" all by Patricia Roberts in main colour, one ball of the same yarn in each of 4 contrast colours and one ball of "Woollybear Bunny Fluff Angora" in third contrast colour; a pair each of size 2¾ mm. (No. 12) and size 3 mm. (No. 11) Aero knitting needles; 6 buttons.

TENSION
Work at a tension of 15 stitches and 19 rows to 5 centimetres (2 inches) over the stocking stitch using size 3 mm. (No. 11) needles. If you cannot obtain the correct tension using the size needles suggested, use larger or smaller ones accordingly.

ABBREVIATIONS
K., knit; p., purl; st., stitch; tog., together; dec., decrease (by working 2 sts. tog.); inc., increase (by working twice into same st.); sl., slip; single rib is k.1 and p.1 alternately; p.s.s.o., pass sl. st. over; y.r.n., yarn round needle; 11 from 1., k.1, y.r.n., k.1, y.r.n., k.1., y.r.n., k.1, y.r.n., k.1, y.r.n., k.1 all into next st.; m.k., make knot thus, k.1, y.r.n., k.1 all into next st., turn, p.3, turn, slip 1, k.2 tog., p.s.s.o.; m.b., make bobble thus, k.1, y.r.n., k.1, y.r.n., k.1 all into next st., turn, k.5, turn, p.5, turn, pass 2nd, 3rd, 4th and 5th sts. over first st., k. this st; up 1, pick up the loop, which lies between the needles, slip it onto left hand needle, then k. into back of it; m.p., make picot thus, with b. k.1, turn, cast on 2, then k.1, y.r.n., k.2 tog. across these 3 sts., turn, sl.1, k.2 tog., p.s.s.o.; m., main colour; a. first contrast; b., second contrast; c., third contrast; d., fourth contrast; e., fifth contrast; f., sixth contrast; s.s., stocking stitch, k. on the right side and p. on the wrong side; 11 into 5, with appropriate contrast colour, p.2 tog., p.2 tog., p.3 tog., p.2 tog., p.2 tog.; m.t., make triangle thus, pass 2nd, 3rd, 4th and 5th sts. on left hand needle over first st., then with appropriate contrast colour, k.1, y.r.n., k.1, y.r.n., k.1, all into the remaining st., turn, p.5, turn, cast off 4.

MEASUREMENTS
The measurements are given in centimetres followed by inches in brackets.

All round at underarms	87.5 (35)
Side seam	37.5 (14)
Length	55 (22)
Sleeve seam	43 (17¼)

THE BACK
With size 2¾ mm. (No. 12) needles and m. cast on 115 sts. and work 35 rows in single rib.

Increase row: Rib 7, *up 1, rib 9; repeat from * to end. – 127 sts.

Change to size 3 mm. (No. 11) needles and beginning with a k. row s.s. 8 rows.

Now work in pattern as follows: This is worked entirely in s.s. except where indicated. Use separate small balls of m. at each side of clowns, so that colours not in use will not be taken across the back of the work. When working the balloons pull m. firmly across the back of the contrast colour balloons to emphasise the raised effect.

1st row: 15m., with a. 11 from 1., 63m., with e. 11 from 1, 31 m., with d. 11 from 1, 15m.

2nd row: 15m., 11d., 31m., 11e., 63m., 11a., 15m.

3rd row: 15m., 11a., 63m., 11e., 31m., 11d., 15m.

4th row: As 2nd row.

5th row: 15m., 11a., 21m., 2a., 40m., 11e., 31m., 11d., 15m.

6th row: 15m., 11d., 31m., 11e., 38m., 4a., 21m., 11a., 15m.

7th row: 15m., 11a., 21m., 4a., 13m., 1a., 24m., 11e., 31m., 11d., 15m.

8th row: 15m., 11d., 31m., 11e., 24m., 4a., 9m., 4a., 22m., 11a., 15m.

9th row: 15m., 11a., 22m., 4a., 8m., 5a., 24m., 11e., 9m., 6a., 16m., 11d., 15m.

10th row: 15m, with d., 11 into 5, 13m., 10a., 8m., with e. 11 into 5, 26m., 5a., 5m., 4a., 23m., with a., 11 into 5, 15m.

11th row: 15m., m.t. – see abbreviations. 24m., 3a., 2m., 7a., 27m., m.t., 8m., 10a., 13m., m.t., 15m.

12th row: 29m., 4b., 43m., 6a., 2m., 3a., 40m.

The last 12 rows set the position of the pattern given in the chart.

Now work the 13th to 98th rows from the chart as set.

To shape the armholes: Continuing in pattern as set, cast off 9 sts. at the beginning of the next 2 rows, then dec. 1 st. at each end of the next row and the 5 following alternate rows.

On 97 sts. pattern 37 rows.

Inc. 1 st. at each end of the next row and the following 8th row.

On 101 sts. pattern 11 rows.

To slope the shoulders: Cast off 10 sts. at the beginning of the next 6 rows.

Cast off the remaining 41 sts.

THE LEFT FRONT
With size 2¾ mm. (No. 12) needles and m. cast on 58 sts. and work 35 rows in single rib.

Increase row: Rib 4, *up 1, rib 9; repeat from * to end. – 64 sts.

Change to size 3 mm. (No. 11) needles and beginning with a. k. row s.s. 8 rows.

Now work in pattern as follows, noting the information given for back. * *

1st row: 15m., with a. 11 from 1, 48m.

2nd row: 48m., 11a., 15m.

The last 2 rows set the position of the pattern given at right hand side of the chart given for back.

Now work the 3rd to 98th rows from the chart as set.

* * *To shape the armhole: Cast off 9 sts. at the beginning of the next row.

Work 1 row back to armhole edge, then dec. 1 st. at the armhole edge on the next row and the following 5 alternate rows.

On 49 sts. work 15 rows.

To slope the neck: Continuing in pattern as set, dec. 1 st. at the end – front edge on the next row and the 10 following alternate rows.

On 38 sts. work 1 row.

Continuing to dec. 1 st. at the front edge on every alternate row, inc. 1 st. at the beginning – armhole edge on the next row and following 8th row.

Still decreasing at front edge on every alternate row work 10 rows.

On 30 sts. work 1 row.

To slope the shoulder: Cast off 10 sts. at the beginning of the next row and the following alternate row.

On 10 sts. work 1 row, then cast off.

THE RIGHT FRONT
Work as given for left front until * * is reached.

1st row: 16m., with e. 11 from 1, 31m., with d. 11 from 1, 15m.

2nd row: 15m., 11d., 31m., 11e., 16m.

The last 2 rows set the position of the pattern given at left hand side of chart. Now work the 3rd to 99th rows as set.

To shape the armhole: Work as given for left front from * * * to end.

THE SLEEVES (both alike)
With size 2¾ mm. (No. 12) needles and m. cast on 56 sts. and work 29 rows in single rib.

Increase row: Rib 4, *up 1, rib 4; repeat from * to end. – 69 sts.

Change to size 3mm. (No. 11) needles and work in pattern as follows, noting the information given for back: 1st to 8th rows: With m. beginning with a k. row in s.s.

9th row: 34m., with d. 11 from 1, 34m.

10th to 17th rows: 34m., 11d., 34m.

18th row: 34m., with d. 11 into 5, 34m.

19th row: 34m., m.t. – see abbreviations, 34m.

20th to 36th rows: All m.

37th row: 18m., with b. 11 from 1, 31m., with a. 11 from 1, 18m.

38th row: 18m., 11a., 31m., 11b., 18m.

39th row: 18m., 11b., 31m., 11a., 18m.

40th to 45th rows: Repeat 38th and 39th rows 3 times.

46th row: 18m., with a. 11 into 5, 31m., with b. 11 into 5, 18m.

47th row: 18m., m.t., 31m., m.t., 18m.

48th to 56th rows. All m.

The last 56 rows form the pattern.

Continuing in pattern as set, using e. instead of d., d. instead of b. and b. instead of a. on the first repeat, then a. instead of d., e. instead of b. and d. instead of a. on the second repeat of the pattern. Work as follows: inc. 1 st. at each end of the next row and the 8 following 10th rows.

On 87 sts. pattern 3 rows, ending with the 28th row of the second repeat of the pattern.

To shape the sleevetop: Continuing in pattern as set, cast off 9 sts. at the beginning of the next 2 rows., then dec. 1 st. at each end of the next row and the 17 following alternate rows.

On 33 sts. work 1 row.

Cast off 3 sts. at the beginning of the next 6 rows, then 4 sts. on the 2 following rows.

Cast off the remaining 7 sts.

THE LEFT FRONT BAND AND HALF COLLAR
With size 2¾ mm. (No. 12) needles and m. cast on 240 sts. and work 4 rows in single rib.

1st and 2nd turning rows: Rib 32, turn, slip 1, rib to end, turn.

3rd and 4th turning rows: Rib 36, turn, slip 1, rib to end, turn.

5th and 6th turning rows: Rib 40, turn, slip 1, rib to end, turn.

7th to 20th turning rows: As set, ribbing 4 extra sts. on each successive pair of turning rows.

21st and 22nd turning rows: Rib 72, turn, slip 1, rib to end, turn.

Mark the end of the last row with a coloured thread. * *

Now continuing on all 240 sts. work 6 rows in single rib, then cast off in rib.

THE RIGHT FRONT BAND AND HALF COLLAR
Work as given for left front band and half collar until the 22 turning rows have been worked and * * is reached.

1st Buttonhole row: Rib 73, *cast off 3 sts., rib next 28 sts.; repeat from * 4 times more, cast off 3, rib next 3 sts.

2nd Buttonhole row: Rib 4, *turn, cast on 3 sts. over those cast off, rib 29; repeat from * ending last repeat rib 73.

THE SHOULDER PADS
With size 2¾ mm. (No. 12) needles and m. cast on 40 sts. and work 50 rows in single rib, then cast off in rib. Fold in half diagonally and join outer edges, to form a triangle.

TO MAKE UP THE SWEATER
DO NOT PRESS. Join shoulder seams. Set in sleeves. Join sleeve and side seams. Catch shoulder pads in place. Join long row end edges of half collars, then sew cast off edges of front bands and collar in place, so that the first front edge neck decrease is in line with the coloured marking thread on front bands. Sew on buttons.

goldie

goldie

MATERIALS

6 (7) (8) 25 gram balls of "Woollybear Fine Cotton" by Patricia Roberts in main colour, 3 balls in fifth contrast colour and 2 balls in each of the 4 other contrast colours, plus 7 (7) (8) 25 gram balls of "Woollybear Lurex" by Patricia Roberts or 10 25 gram balls of "Woollybear 100% Mohair" by Patricia Roberts in main colour, 4 balls in fifth contrast colour and 3 balls in each of the 4 other contrast colours; a pair each of size 3¾ mm. (No. 9) and size 4 mm. (No. 8) knitting needles; a medium sized cable needle, 2 buttons.

TENSION

Work at a tension of 10 stitches and 14 rows to 5 centimetres (2 inches) over the moss stitch using one strand of "Woollybear Fine Cotton" together with one strand of "Woollybear Lurex" or "Woollybear 100% Mohair" knitted single, using size 4 mm. (No. 8) needles. If you cannot obtain the correct tension using the size needles suggested, use larger or smaller ones accordingly.

ABBREVIATIONS

K., knit; p., purl; st., stitch; tog., together; dec., decrease (by working 2 sts. tog.); inc., increase (by working twice into same st.); single rib is k. 1 and p. 1 alternately; up1, pick up the loop, which lies between the needles, slip it onto left hand needle, then k. into back of it; cable 8 thus, slip next 4 sts. onto cable needle and leave at front of work, k.4, then k.4 from cable needle; m., main colour, a., first contrast; b., second contrast; c., third contrast; d., fourth contrast; e., fifth contrast.

NOTE

The instructions are given for the small size. Where they vary work the figures in the first brackets for the medium size or the figures in the second brackets for the large size.

MEASUREMENTS

The measurements are given in centimetres followed by inches in brackets.

Sizes	small	medium	large
Underarms	90 (36)	95 (38)	100 (40)
Side seam	42.5 (17)	42.5 (17)	42.5 (17)
Length	62.5 (25)	62.5 (25)	62.5 (25)
Sleeve seam	40 (16)	40 (16)	40 (16)

SPECIAL NOTE

When knitting this garment in "Woollybear Fine Cotton" and "Woollybear Lurex", one strand of each yarn is used together throughout.

THE BACK

With size 3¾ mm. (No. 9) needles and m. cast on 80 (86) (92) sts. and work 15 rows in single rib.

Increase row: Rib 4 (7) (10), *up 1, rib 8; repeat from * ending last repeat rib 4 (7) (10). – 90 (96) (102) sts.

Change to size 4 mm. (No. 8) needles and work pattern as follows:

1st row: With a. p.1, (k.1, p.1) (p.1, k.1, p.1), *k.1, p.1; repeat from * 6 times more, with b. * k.1, p.1; repeat from * 6 times more, then k.1 (k.1, p.1) (k.1, p.1, k.1), with c. p.1 (k.1, p.1) (p.1, k.1, p.1), *k.1, p.1; repeat from * 6 times more, with d. *k.1, p.1; repeat from * 6 times more, k.1 (k.1, p.1) (k.1, p.1, k.1), with m. p.1 (k.1, p.1) (p.1, k.1, p.1), *k.1, p.1; repeat from *6 times more, with e. *k.1, p.1; repeat from * 6 times more, then k.1 (k.1, p.1) (k.1, p.1, k.1).

2nd row: With e. k.1 (p.1, k.1) (k.1, p.1, k.1), *p.1, k.1; repeat from * 6 times more, with m. *p.1, k.1; repeat from * 6 times more, then p.1 (p.1, k.1) (p.1, k.1, p.1), with d. k.1 (p.1, k.1) (k.1, p.1, k.1), *p.1, k.1; repeat from * 6 times more, with c. *p.1, k.1; repeat from * 6 times more, then p.1, (p.1, k.1) (p.1, k.1, p.1), with b. k.1 (p.1, k.1) (k.1, p.1, k.1), *p.1, k.1; repeat from * 6 times more, with a. * p.1, k.1; repeat from * 6 times more, then p.1 (p.1, k.1) (p.1, k.1, p.1).

The last 2 rows form the moss st. When changing colour care should be taken to wrap colours round each other.

3rd to 22nd rows: Repeat 1st and 2nd rows 10 times more.

The last 22 rows form the pattern. Repeat them using c. instead of a., d. instead of b., m. instead of c., e. instead of d., a. instead of m. and b. instead of e.

Now repeat the 22 pattern rows using m. instead of a., e. instead of b., a. instead of c., b. instead of d., c. instead of m. and d. instead of e.

Repeat the 22 pattern rows using b. instead of a., c. instead of b., d. instead of c., m. instead of d., e. instead of m., and a. instead of e.

Using e. instead of a., a. instead of b., b. instead of c., c instead of d., d. instead of m., and m. instead of e., work the first 18 rows of the pattern repeat. Work should now measure 42.5 centimetres (17 inches) from beginning.

To shape the armholes: Continuing in pattern as set, cast of 5 sts. at the beginning of the next 2 rows, dec. 1 st. at each end of the next row, then pattern 1 row.

Using d. instead of a., m. instead of b., e. instead of c., a. instead of d., b. instead of m. and c. instead of e. for the next repeat of pattern, dec. 1 st. at each end of the next row and the 3 (4) (5) following alternate rows, then on 70 (74) (78) sts. pattern 15 (13) (11) rows to complete this pattern repeat.

Work the 22 pattern rows again as set in the original colours.

Change to size 3¾ mm. (No. 9) needles and using m. only k.1 row. * * *

Work 15 rows in single rib, then cast off in rib.

THE FRONT

Work as given for back until * * * is reached.

Work 13 rows in single rib.

1st Buttonhole row: Rib 2 (3) (4), cast off 4, rib next 57 (59) (61) sts., cast off 4 sts., rib to end.

2nd Buttonhole row: Rib 2 (3) (4), turn, cast on 4 over those cast off, turn, rib 58 (60) (62), turn, cast on 4, turn, rib 2 (3) (4).

Cast off in rib.

THE SLEEVES (both alike)

With size 3¾ mm. (No. 9) needles and m. cast on 40 (44) (48) sts. and work 15 rows in single rib.

Increase row: Rib 3 (5) (7), *up 1, rib 2, repeat from * ending last repeat rib 3 (5) (7). – 58 (62) (66) sts.

Change to size 4 mm. (No. 8) needles and work in pattern as follows. Use separate balls of m. and e. for each section of the pattern, so that colours are not taken across the back of the work when not in use.

1st row: With m. *k.1, p.1; repeat from * once (twice) (3 times), with e. k.8, with m. p.1, *k.1, p.1; repeat from last * 5 times more, with e. k.8, with m. p.1, *k.1, p.1; repeat from last * 5 times more, with e. k.8, with m. *p.1, k.1; repeat from last * once (twice) (3 times).

2nd row: With m. *k.1, p.1; repeat from * once (twice) (3 times), with e. p.8, with m. p.1, *k.1, p.1; repeat from last * 5 times more, with e. p.8, with m. p.1, *k.1, p.1; repeat from last * 5 times more, with e. p.8, with m. *p.1, k.1; repeat from last * once (twice) (3 times).

3rd to 6th rows: Repeat 1st and 2nd rows twice.

7th row: With m. moss st. 4 (6) (8) as set, *with e. cable 8, with m. moss st. 13; repeat from * ending last repeat moss st. 4 (6) (8).

8th row: As 2nd row.

9th and 10th rows: As 1st and 2nd rows.

The last 10 rows form the pattern. Repeat them twice more.

Continuing in pattern as set, inc. 1 st. at each end of the next row and the 2 following 20th rows.

On 64 (68) (72) sts. pattern 25 rows.

To shape the sleevetop: Maintaining the continuity of the pattern as set, cast off 5 sts. at the beginning of the next 2 rows, then dec. 1 st. at each end of the next row and the 14 following alternate rows.

On 24 (28) (32) sts. work 1 row.

Cast off 3 sts. at the beginning of the next 2 rows, then 3 (4) (5) sts. on the 4 following rows.

Cast off the remaining 6 sts.

TO MAKE UP THE SWEATER

Pin out to size and press all parts except the ribbing on the wrong side with a warm iron over a damp cloth. Join shoulder seams for 1 centimetre (½ inch) at armhole edges. Set in sleeves. Join sleeve and side seams. Press seams. Sew on buttons.

2

PALM SPRINGS

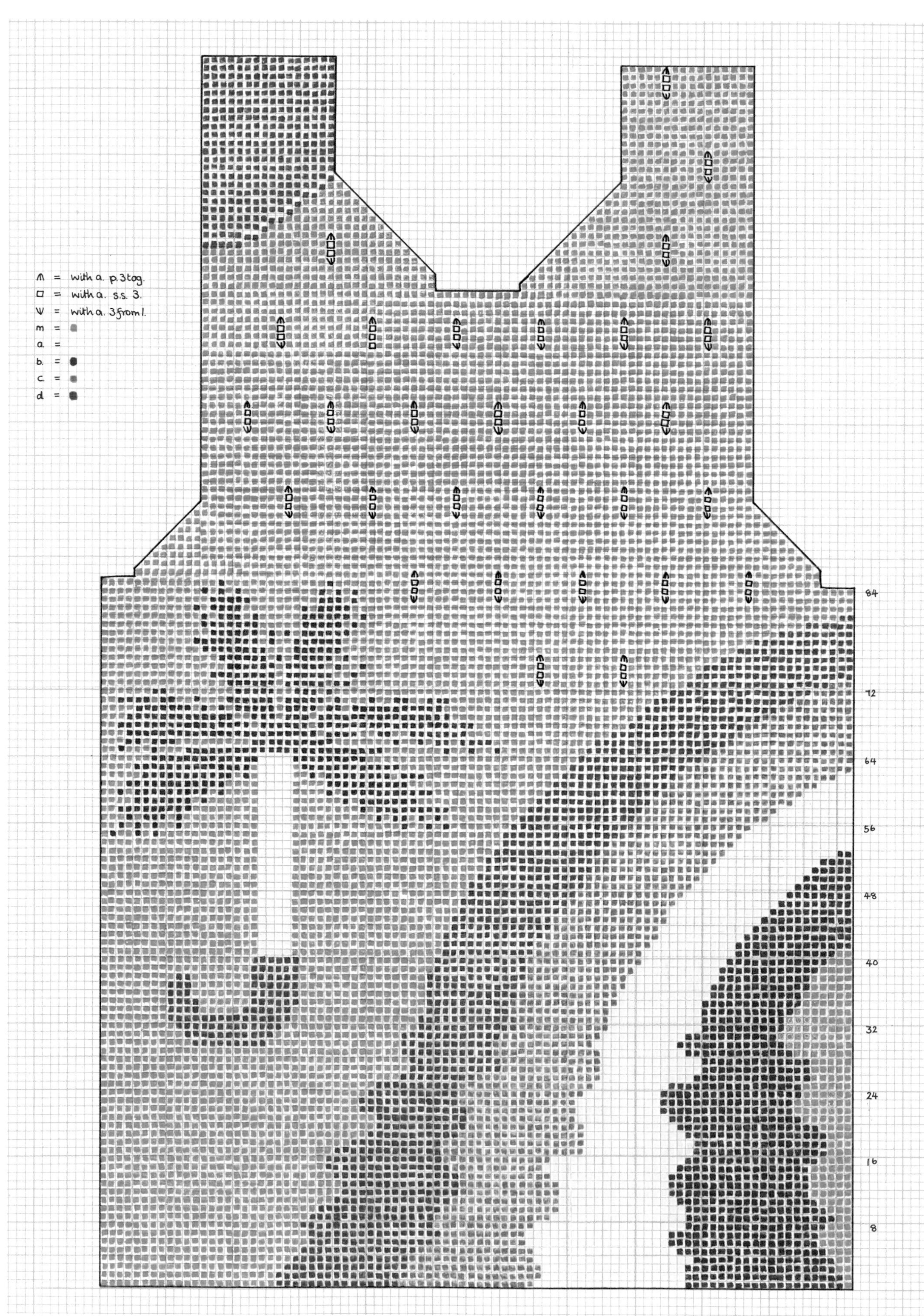

INTERNATIONAL
LONDON
WINNER
BREWEX
1976
EXPORT
BEER

PALM SPRINGS

MATERIALS
11 25 gram balls of 'Woollybear 100% Mohair' by Patricia Roberts in main colour; 2 balls in each of 2 contrast colours – a. and d.; and 1 ball in each of the 2 other contrast colours – b., and c., a pair each of size 3¾ mm. (No. 9) and 4 mm. (No. 8) Aero knitting needles.

SPECIAL NOTE
This garment may also be knitted for summer in 'Woollybear Cotton Bouclé' by Patricia Roberts. The materials required are 8 50 gram balls in main colour, 2 balls in each of 2 contrast colours a. and d., 1 ball in each of the 2 other colours – b. and c.; a pair each of size 3¼ mm. (No. 10) and size 3¾ mm. (No. 9) Aero knitting needles. To obtain the correct tension it will be necessary to use size 3¼ mm. (No. 10) needles instead of size 3¾ mm. (No. 9) needles and size 3¾ mm. (No. 9) instead of size 4 mm. (No. 8) needles throughout the pattern.

TENSION
10 stitches and 14 rows to 5 centimetres (2 inches) over the stocking stitch using size 4 mm. (No. 8) needles and mohair or size 3¾ mm. (No. 9) needles and cotton bouclé. If you cannot obtain the correct tension using the size needles suggested, use larger or smaller ones accordingly.

ABBREVIATIONS
K., knit; p., purl; st., stitch; tog., together; dec., decrease (by working 2 sts. tog.); inc., increase (by working twice into same st.); single rib is k.1 and p.1 alternately; s.s., stocking stitch is k. on the right side and p. on the wrong side; y.r.n., yarn round needle; 3 from 1, k.1, y.r.n., k.1, all into next st.; m., main colour; a., first contrast; b., second contrast; c., third contrast; d., fourth contrast; e., fifth contrast; up 1, pick up the loop which lies between the needles, slip it onto left hand needle, then k. into back of it.

MEASUREMENTS
The measurements are given in centimetres followed by inches in brackets.

Size	Woman's	Man's
Underarms	90 (36)	100 (40)
Side seam	39 (15½)	41 (16½)
Length	61 (24½)	67 (26½)
Sleeve seam	42 (16½)	45 (18)

The instructions are given for the woman's size. To obtain the man's measurements, use a larger size needle throughout and work at a tension of 9 stitches and 13 rows to 5 centimetres (2 inches).

NOTE
When counting the sts. count the 3 sts. of raindrops as one st.

THE BACK
With size 3¾ mm. (No. 9) needles and m. cast on 80 sts. and work 27 rows in single rib.
Increase row: Rib 4, * up 1, rib 8; repeat from * ending last repeat rib 4 – 90 sts.
Change to size 4 mm. (No. 8) needles and work in pattern as follows. This is worked entirely in s.s. except for the raindrops. Use separate balls or lengths of yarn for each colour section of the pattern and for each raindrop, but ensure that sufficiently long ends are left for darning in at completion of work, or the knitting may unravel. **
1st row: 21m., 15d., 16c., 18a., 19b., 1m.
2nd row: 1m., 19b., 17a., 16c., 16d., 21m.
3rd row: 7m., with a. 3 from 1, 9m., with a. 3 from 1, 4m., 15d., 16c., 17a., 18b., 2m.
4th row: 2m., 17b., 19a., 15c., 14d., 5m., 3a., 9m., 3a., 7m.
5th row: 7m., 3a., 9m., 3a., 6m., 14d., 14c., 17a., 18b., 3m.
6th row: 4m., 18b., 17a., 11c., 15d., 7m., with a. p. 3 tog., 9m., with a. p. 3 tog., 7m.
The last 6 rows set the position of the pattern given in the chart for the back. Now work the 7th to 84th rows from the chart as set.
To shape the armholes: Continuing in pattern from chart as set and given in the chart, cast off 4 sts. at the beginning of the next 2 rows, then dec. 1 st. at each end of the next 8 rows.
On 66 sts. pattern 52 rows.
To slope the shoulders: Cast off 16 sts. at the beginning of the next 2 rows – 34 sts.
Change to size 3¾ mm. (No. 9) needles and with m. only work 6 rows in single rib, then cast off in rib.

THE FRONT
Work as given for the back until ** is reached.
1st row: 1m., 19b., 18a., 16c., 15d., 21m.
2nd row: 21m., 16d., 16c., 17a., 19b., 1m.
The last 2 rows set the position of the pattern given in the chart for the front.
Work the 3rd to 84th rows from the chart as set.
To shape the armholes: Continuing in pattern as set and given in the chart, cast off 4 sts. at the beginning of the next 2 rows, then dec. 1 st. at each end of the next 8 rows.
On 66 sts. pattern 25 rows as set.
Now divide the sts. for the neck: Next row: Work as set across 28 sts. and leave these sts. on a spare needle until required for right front shoulder, cast off 10 sts., work to end and continue on these 28 sts. for the left front shoulder.
The left front shoulder: To shape the neck: Dec. 1 st. at the neck edge on each of the next 12 rows.
On 16 sts. work 14 rows, then cast off.
The right front shoulder: With right side of work facing rejoin yarn to inner edge of sts. left on spare needle and work to end of row as set, then work as given for left front shoulder to end.

THE FRONT NECKBAND
With right side of work facing rejoin m. at left front shoulder using size 3¾ mm. (No. 9) needles, pick up and k. 25 sts. from left front neck edge, 10 sts. from those cast off at centre front and 25 sts. from right front neck edge.
On 60 sts. work 5 rows in single rib then cast off loosely in rib.

THE SLEEVES (both alike)
With size 3¾ mm. (No. 9) needles and m. cast on 37 sts. and work 23 rows in single rib.
Increase row: Rib 1, * up 1, rib 2; repeat from * to end – 55 sts.
Change to size 4 mm. (No. 8) needles and beginning with a k. row s.s. 6 rows.
Now work in rain pattern as follows, using separate lengths of a. for each rain drop, and noting the information given for back.
1st row: 7m., * with a. 3 from 1, 9m.; repeat from * ending last repeat 7m.
2nd row: 7m., * 3a., 9m.; repeat from * ending last repeat 7m.
3rd row: 7m., * 3a., 9m.; repeat from * ending last repeat 7m.
4th row: 7m., * with a. p.3 tog., 9m.; repeat from * ending last repeat 7m.
5th to 10th rows: All m.
11th row: 2m., * with a. 3 from 1, 9m.; repeat from * ending last repeat 2m.
12th row: 2m., * 3a., 9m.; repeat from * ending last repeat 2m.
13th row: as 12th row.
14th row: 2m., * with a. p.3 tog., 9m.; repeat from * ending last repeat 2m.
15th to 20th rows: All m.
The last 20 rows form the pattern; work the first 10 rows again.
Continuing in pattern as set and working the extra sts. into the pattern as they occur, inc. 1 st. at each end of the next row and the 2 following 20th rows.
On 61 sts. pattern 19 rows.
To shape the sleevetop: Continuing in pattern as set, cast off 4 sts. at the beginning of the next 2 rows, then dec. 1 st. at each end of the next row and the 10 following alternate rows. On 31 sts. work 1 row.
Dec 1 st. at each end of the next 6 rows – 19 sts. Cast off 3 sts. at the beginning of the next 4 rows, then cast off the remaining 7 sts.

THE SHOULDER PADS (2 alike)
With size 3¾ mm. (No. 9) needles and m. cast on 36 sts. and work 44 rows in single rib, then cast off in rib. Fold in half diagonally and join edges to form a triangle.

TO MAKE UP THE SWEATER
Pin out to size and press all parts except the ribbing with a warm iron over a damp cloth. Join shoulder seams. Set in sleeves. Join sleeve and side seams. Catch shoulder pads in place. Press seams.

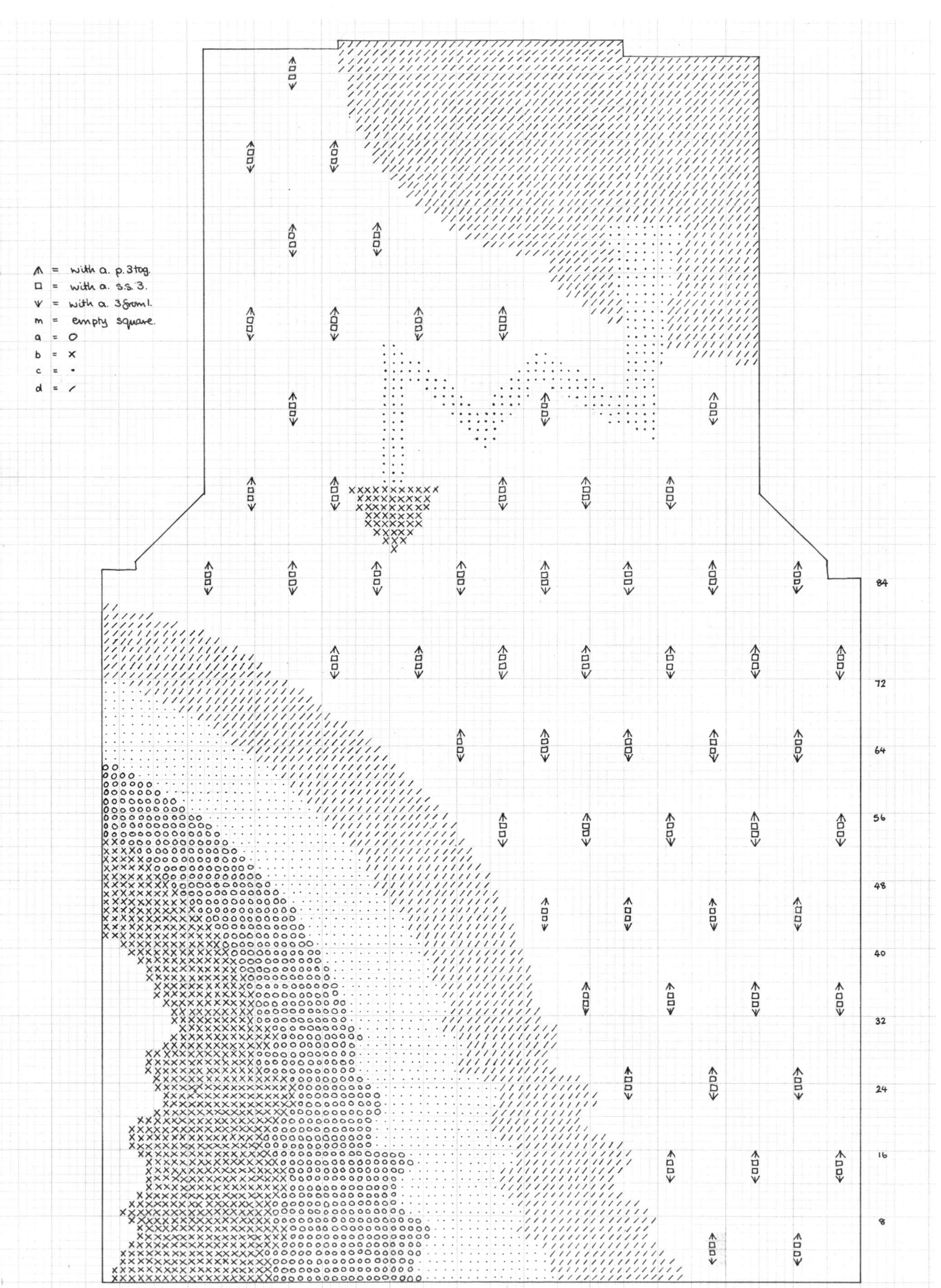

∧ = with a. p.3tog.
□ = with a. s.s.3.
∨ = with a. 3 from 1.
m = empty square.
a = O
b = ×
c = •
d = /
84
72
64
56
48
40
32
24
16
8

FRUIT MACHINE

HAROLD AND MAUD

HAROLD AND MAUD

MATERIALS
12 (13) (14) 25 gram balls of 'Woollybear 100% Mohair' in main colour, 2 balls in first contrast colour, 1 ball in second contrast and 3 (4) (4) balls in third contrast; a pair each of size $3\frac{3}{4}$ mm. (No. 9) and size $4\frac{1}{2}$ mm. (No. 7) Aero knitting needles; 6 buttons.

TENSION
9 stitches and 12 rows to 5 centimetres (2 inches) over the pattern using size $4\frac{1}{2}$ mm. (No. 7) needles. If you cannot obtain the correct tension using the size needles suggested use larger or smaller ones accordingly.

ABBREVIATIONS
K., knit; p., purl; st., stitch; tog., together; dec., decrease (by working 2 sts. tog.); inc., increase (by working twice into same st.); single rib is k.1 and p.1 alternately; y.r.n., yarn round needle; s.s., stocking stitch is k. on the right side and p. on the wrong side; sl., slip; p.s.s.o., pass sl. st. over; up 1, pick up the loop, which lies between the needles, slip it onto left hand needle, then k. into back of it; m., main colour; a., first contrast colour; b., second contrast colour; c., third contrast colour; 5 from 1, k.1, y.r.n., k.1, y.r.n., k.1 all into next st.; m.b., make bobble thus, k.1, y.r.n., k.1, all into next st., turn, p.3, turn, k.3, turn, p.3, turn, sl.1, k.2 tog., p.s.s.o.

NOTE
The instructions are given for the small size. Where they vary work the figures in the first brackets for the medium size, or the figures in the second brackets for the large size.

MEASUREMENTS
The measurements are given in centimetres followed by inches in brackets.

Sizes	Small	Medium	Large
To fit bust	82.5(33)	87.5(35)	92.5(37)
Underarms	87.5(35)	92.5(37)	97.5(39)
Side seam	37.5(15)	37.5(15)	37.5(15)
Length	58(23)	59($23\frac{1}{2}$)	60(24)
Sleeve seam	41($16\frac{1}{2}$)	41($16\frac{1}{2}$)	41($16\frac{1}{2}$)

THE POCKET BACKS (2 alike)
With size $4\frac{1}{2}$ mm. (No. 7) needles and m. cast on 19 sts. and beginning with a k. row s.s. 28 rows. Then leave these sts. on a spare needle until required.

THE MAIN PART
With size $3\frac{3}{4}$ mm. (No. 9) needles and m. cast on 137 (145) (155) sts. and work 29 rows in single rib.

Increase row: Rib 9 (13) (17), * up 1, rib 8; repeat from * ending last repeat rib 8 (12) (18) – 153 (161) (171) sts.

Change to size $4\frac{1}{2}$ mm. (No. 7) needles and work in pattern as follows: Use short lengths or small balls of contrast colours for individual motifs, i.e. each cherry, bunch of grapes or for stems.

1st row: With m. all k.

2nd row: With m. all p.

3rd row: With m. k.2 (6) (2), * with a. 5 from 1, with m. k.17; repeat from * ending last repeat with m. k.6 (10) (6).

4th row: With m. p.6 (10) (6), * with a. p.5, with m. p.17; repeat from * ending last repeat with m. k.2 (6) (2).

5th row: With m. k.2 (6) (2), * with a. k.5, with m. k.17; repeat from * ending last repeat with m. k.6 (10) (6).

6th row: As 4th row.

7th row: With m. k.2 (6) (2), * with a. sl.1, k.1, p.s.s.o., k.1, k.2 tog., with m. k.3, with a. 5 from 1, with m. k.13; repeat from * ending last repeat with m. k.2 (6) (2).

8th row: With m. p.2 (6) (2), * with a. p.5, with m. p.3, with a. p. 3 tog., with m. p.13; repeat from * ending last repeat with m. p.2 (6) (2).

9th row: With m. k.2 (6) (2), * with b. k.1, with m. k.3, with a. k.5, with m. k.13; repeat from * ending last repeat with m. k.2 (6) (2).

10th row: With m. p.2 (6) (2), * with a. p.5, with m. p.3, with b. p.1, with m. p.13; repeat from * ending last repeat with m. p.2 (6) (2).

11th row: With m. k.2 (6) (2), * with m. up 1, with b. k.1, with m. k. 2 tog., k.1, with a. sl.1, k.1, p.s.s.o., k.1, k.2 tog., with m. k.13; repeat from * ending last repeat with m. k.2 (6) (2).

12th row: With m. p.2 (6) (2), * with a. p.3 tog., with m. p.2, with b. p.1, with m. p.14; repeat from * ending last repeat with m. p.3 (7) (3).

13th row: With m. k.3 (7) (3), * with m. up 1, with b. k.1, with m. k. 2 tog., with b. k.1, with m. k.14; repeat from * ending last repeat with m. k.2 (6) (2).

14th row: With m. p.2 (6) (2), * with b. p.1, with m. p.1, with b. p.1, with m. p.15; repeat from * ending last repeat p.4 (8) (4).

15th row: With m. k.4 (8) (4), * with m. up 1, with b. sl.1, k.1, p.s.s.o., k.1, with m. k.15; repeat from * ending last repeat with m. k.2 (6) (2).

16th row: With m. p.2 (6) (2), * with b. p.2, with m. p.16; repeat from * ending last repeat with m. p.5 (9) (5).

17th row: With m. k.5 (9) (5), * with m. up 1, with b. sl.1, k.1, p.s.s.o., with m. k.16; repeat from * ending last repeat with m. k.2 (6) (2).

18th row: With m. all p.

19th row: With m. all k.

20th row: With m. all p.

21st row: With m. k.15 (19) (15), * with c. m.b., with m. k.17; repeat from * ending last repeat with m. k.11 (15) (11).

22nd row: With m. p.10 (14) (10), * with c. p.3, with m. p.15; repeat from * ending last repeat with m. p.14 (18) (14).

23rd row: With m. k.14 (18) (14), * with c. m.b., k.1, m.b., with m. k.15; repeat from * ending last repeat with m. k.10 (14) (10).

24th row: With m. p.9 (13) (9), * with c. p.5, with m. p.13; repeat from * ending last repeat with m. p.13 (17) (13).

25th row: With m. k.13 (17) (13), * with c. m.b., k.1, m.b., k.1, m.b., with m. k.13; repeat from * ending last repeat with m. k.9 (13) (9).

26th row: With m. p.8 (12) (8), * with c. p.7, with m. p.11; repeat from * ending last repeat

FRUIT MACHINE

MATERIALS
For the sleeveless sweater: 6 (6) (7) ounces of 'Woollybear Real Shetland' in main colour and either one ounce of the same wool in each of first 2 contrast colours and 2 ounces in 3rd contrast or 3 25 gram balls of 'Woollybear 100% Mohair' in first contrast colour; 1 ball in second contrast and 6 balls in third contrast; a pair each of size $2\frac{1}{4}$ mm. (No. 13) and size $2\frac{3}{4}$ mm. (No. 12) Aero knitting needles.

For the sweater with sleeves: 10 (11) (12) ounces of 'Woollybear Real Shetland' in main colour and either 2 ounces of the same wool in each of first 2 contrast colours and 3 ounces in 3rd contrast or 4 25 gram balls of 'Woollybear 100% Mohair' in first contrast colour; 2 balls in second contrast and 7 balls in third contrast; a pair each of size $2\frac{1}{4}$ mm. (No. 13) and size $2\frac{3}{4}$ mm. (No. 12) Aero knitting needles.

TENSION
16 stitches and 20 rows to 2 inches (5 centimetres) over the stocking stitch using size $2\frac{3}{4}$ mm. (No. 12) needles. If you cannot obtain the correct tension using the size needles suggested use larger or smaller needles accordingly.

ABBREVIATIONS
K., knit; p., purl; st., stitch; tog., together; dec., decrease (by working 2 sts. tog.); inc., increase (by working twice into same st.); single rib is k.1 and p.1 alternately; s.s., stocking stitch is k. on the right side and p. on the wrong side; sl., slip; p.s.s.o., pass sl. st. over; up 1, pick up the loop which lies between the needles, slip it onto left hand needle, then k. into back of it; y.r.n., yarn round needle; m., main colour; a., first contrast; 5 from 1, k.1, y.r.n., k.1, y.r.n., k.1 all into next st.; m.b., make bobble thus, k.1, y.r.n., k.1 all into next st., turn, p.3, turn, k.3, turn, p.3, turn, sl.1, k. 2 tog., p.s.s.o.; b., second contrast colour; c., third contrast.

NOTE
The instructions are given for the small size. Where they vary work the figures in the first brackets for the medium size or the figures in the second brackets for the large size.

MEASUREMENTS
The measurements are given in centimetres followed by inches in brackets.

Sizes	Small	Medium	Large
To fit bust	80(32)	85(34)	90(36)
Underarms	82.5(33)	87.5(35)	92.5(37)
Side seam	35(14)	35(14)	35(14)
Length	55(22)	56($22\frac{1}{2}$)	57.5(23)
Sleeve seam	42.5(17)	42.5(17)	42.5(17)

THE BACK
With size $2\frac{1}{4}$ mm. (No. 13) needles and m. cast on 120 (128) (136) sts. and work 27 rows in single rib.

Increase row: Rib 6 (10) (14), * up 1, rib 9; repeat from * ending last repeat rib 6 (10) (14) – 133 (141) (149) sts.

Change to size $2\frac{3}{4}$ mm. (No. 12) needles and work in pattern as follows. Use separate lengths or small balls of contrast colours for individual motifs – i.e. each cherry, bunch of grapes or set of stems.

1st row: With m. all k.

2nd row: With m. all p.

3rd row: With m. k.14 (9) (13), * with a. 5 from 1, with m. k.17; repeat from * ending last repeat k.10 (5) (9).

4th row: With m. p.10 (5) (9), * with a. p.5, with m. p.17; repeat from * ending last repeat p.14 (9) (13).

5th row: With m. k.14 (9) (13), * with a. k.5, with m. k.17; repeat from * ending last repeat with m. k.10 (5) (9).

6th row: As 4th row.

7th row: With m. k.14 (9) (13), * with a. sl.1, k.1, p.s.s.o., k.1, k.2 tog., with m. k.3, with a. 5 from 1, with m. k.13; repeat from * ending last repeat with m. k.6 (1) (5).

8th row: With m. p.6 (1) (5), * with a. p.5,

with m. p.12 (16) (12).

27th row: With m. k.12 (16) (12), * with c. m.b., k.1, m.b., k.1 m.b., k.1, m.b., with m. k.11; repeat from * ending last repeat with m. k.8 (12) (8).

28th row: As 24th row.

29th row: As 25th row.

30th row: With m. p.10 (14) (10), * with b. p.3, with m. p.15; repeat from * ending last repeat with m. p.14 (18) (14).

31st row: With m. k.13 (17) (13), * with b. k.5, with m. k.13; repeat from * ending last repeat with m. k.9 (13) (9).

32nd row: With m. p.11 (15) (11), * with b. p.1, with m. p.17; repeat from * ending last repeat with m. p.15 (19) (15).

33rd row: With m. k.15 (19) (15), * with b. k.1, with m. k.17; repeat from * ending last repeat with m. k.11 (15) (11).

34th row: As 32nd row.

The last 34 rows form the pattern. Continuing in pattern as set, work as follows:

Pocket row: K.8, * slip next 19 sts. onto a stitch-holder and leave at front of work until required for pocket top and in their place k. across the 19 sts. of one pocket back *, k.99 (107) (117), repeat from * to *, k.8.

Now beginning with the 2nd pattern row pattern 30 rows more.

Now divide the sts. for the armholes: Next row: Pattern 36 (38) (40) as set and leave these sts. on a spare needle until required for left half front, cast off 4, pattern across next 72 (76) (82) sts. and leave these 73 (77) (83) sts. on a spare needle until required for back, cast off 4, pattern to end and continue on these 36 (38) (40) sts. for right half front.

The right half front: To shape the armhole: Maintaining the continuity of the pattern as set dec. 1 st. at the armhole edge on each of the next 6 (7) (8) rows.

On 30 (31) (32) sts. pattern 18 (19) (20) rows.

To shape the neck: Cast off 4 sts. at the beginning of the next row then dec. 1 st. at the neck edge on each of the next 6 rows.

On 20 (21) (22) sts. pattern 12 rows.

To slope the shoulder: Cast off 10 sts. at the beginning of the next row. On 10 (11) (12) sts. work 1 row, then cast off.

The back: With right side of work facing rejoin yarn to the 73 (77) (83) sts. left on spare needle and continuing in pattern as set, dec. 1 st. at each end of the next 6 (7) (8) rows.

On 61 (63) (67) sts. pattern 38 (39) (40) rows.

To slope the shoulders: Cast off 10 sts. at the beginning of the next 2 rows, then 10 (11) (12) sts. on the 2 following rows – 21 (21) (23) sts.

Change to size 3¾ mm. (No. 9) needles and with m. only work 6 rows in single rib, then cast off.

The left half front: With right side of work facing rejoin yarn to inner edge of sts. left on spare needle and work to end of row, then work as given for right half front to end.

THE SLEEVES (both alike)

With size 3¾ mm. (No. 9) needles and m. cast on 37 (39) (41) sts. and work 20 rows in single rib.

Change to size 4½ mm. (No. 7) needles and beginning with a k. row s.s. 2 rows.

Now work in pattern; beginning with the 21st pattern row as follows: 21st row: With m. k.8 (9) (10), with c. m.b., with m. k.17, with c. m.b., with m. k.10 (11) (12).

The last row sets the position of the pattern given for back. Pattern 7 rows more as set.

Continuing in pattern as set and working the extra sts. into the pattern as they occur inc. 1 st. at each end of the next row and the 8 following 8th rows.

On 55 (57) (59) sts. pattern 7 rows.

To shape the sleevetop: Cast off 2 sts. at the beginning of the next 2 rows, then dec. 1 st. at each end of the next row and the 6 (7) (8) following alternate rows.

On 37 sts. work 1 row.

Dec. 1 st. at each end of the next 10 rows. Cast off 3 sts. at the beginning of the next 4 rows. Cast off the remaining 5 sts.

THE POCKET TOPS (both alike)

With right side of work facing rejoin m. to the 19 sts. left on stitch-holder and using size 3¾ mm. (No. 9) needles work 6 rows in single rib, then cast off.

THE LEFT AND RIGHT FRONT NECKBANDS (both alike)

With right side of work facing rejoin m. and using size 3¾ mm. (No. 9) needles pick up and k.22 sts. from neck edge. Work 5 rows in single rib, then cast off.

THE SHOULDER PADS (2 alike)

With size 3¾ mm. (No. 9) needles and m. cast on 30 sts. and work 2 rows in single rib.

Continuing in rib as set, dec. 1 st. at each end of the next row and the 13 following alternate rows.

Take the 2 remaining sts. tog. and fasten off.

THE BUTTONHOLE BAND

With size 3¾ mm. (No. 9) needles and m. cast on 6 sts. and work 4 (6) (6) rows in single rib.

1st Buttonhole row: Rib 2, cast off 2, rib to end.

2nd Buttonhole row: Rib 2, turn, cast on 2, turn, rib to end.

Rib 22 rows.

Repeat the last 24 rows 4 times more, then work the 2 buttonhole rows again.

Rib 4 (4) (6) rows more.

THE BUTTONBAND

With size 3¾ mm. (No. 9) needles and m. cast on 6 sts. and work 130 (132) (134) rows in single rib, then cast off.

TO MAKE UP THE CARDIGAN

Pin out to size and press all parts except the ribbing on the wrong side with a warm iron over a damp cloth. Join shoulder seams, continuing seams across neckbands. Join sleeve seams. Set in sleeves. Sew button and buttonhole bands in place. Sew pocket backs and row ends of pocket tops in place. Sew shoulder pads in place. Press seams. Sew on buttons.

with m. p.3, with a. p.3 tog., with m. p.13; repeat from * ending last repeat with m. p.14 (9) (13).

9th row: With m. k.14 (9) (13), * with b. k.1, with m. k.3, with a. k.5, with m. k.13; repeat from * ending last repeat with m. k.6 (1) (5).

10th row: With m. p.6 (1) (5), * with a. p.5, with m. p.3, with b. p.1, with m. p.13; repeat from * ending last repeat with m. p.14 (9) (13).

11th row: With m. k.14 (9) (13), * with m. up 1, with b. k.1, with m. k. 2 tog., k.1, with a. sl.1, k.1, p.s.s.o., k.1, k. 2 tog., with m. k.13; repeat from * ending last repeat k.6 (1) (5).

12th row: With m. p.6 (1) (5), * with a. p.3 tog., with m. p.2, with b. p.1, with m. p.14; repeat from * ending last repeat with m. p.15 (10) (14).

13th row: With m. k.15 (10) (14), * with m. up 1, with b. k.1, with m. k.2 tog., with b. k.1, with m. k.14; repeat from * ending last repeat with m. k.6 (1) (5).

14th row: With m. p.6 (1) (5), * with b. p.1, with m. p.1, with b. p.1, with m. p.15; repeat from * ending last repeat p.16 (11) (15).

15th row: With m. k.16 (11) (15), * with m. up 1, with b. sl.1, k.1, p.s.s.o., k.1, with m. k.15; repeat from * ending last repeat with m. k.6 (1) (5).

16th row: With m. p.6 (1) (5),* with b. p.2, with m. p.16; repeat from * ending last repeat with m. p.17 (12) (16).

17th row: With m. k.17 (12) (16), * with m. up 1, with b. sl.1, k.1, p.s.s.o., with m. k.16; repeat from * ending last repeat with m. k.6 (1) (5).

18th row: With m. all p.

19th row: With m. all k.

20th row: With m. all p.

21st row: With m. k.9 (4) (8), * with c. m.b., with m. k.17; repeat from * ending last repeat with m. k.15 (10) (14).

22nd row: With m. p.14 (9) (13), * with c. p.3, with m. p.15; repeat from * ending last repeat with m. p.8 (3) (7).

23rd row: With m. k.8 (3) (7), * with c. m.b., k.1, m.b., with m. k.15; repeat from * ending last repeat with m. k.14 (9) (13).

24th row: With m. p.13 (8) (12), * with c. p.5, with m. p.13; repeat from * ending last repeat with m. p.7 (2) (6).

25th row: With m. k.7 (2) (6), * with c. m.b., k.1, m.b., k.1, m.b., with m. k.13; repeat from * ending last repeat with m. k.13 (8) (12).

26th row: With m. p.12 (7) (11), * with c. p.7; with m. p.11; repeat from * ending last repeat with m. p.6 (1) (5).

27th row: With m. k.6 (1) (5), * with c. m.b., k.1, m.b., k.1, m.b., k.1, m.b., with m. k.11; repeat from * ending last repeat with m. k.12 (7) (11).

28th row: As 24th row.

29th row: As 25th row.

30th row: With m. p.14 (9) (13), * with b. p.3, with m. p.15; repeat from * ending last repeat with m. p.8 (3) (7).

31st row: With m. k.7 (2) (6), * with b. k.5, with m. k.13; repeat from * ending last repeat with m. k.13 (8) (12).

32nd row: With m. p. 15 (10) (14), * with b. p.1, with m. p.17; repeat from * ending last repeat with m. p.9 (4) (8).

33rd row: With m. k.9 (4) (8), * with b. k.1, with m. k.17; repeat from * ending last repeat with m. k.15 (10) (14).

34th row: As 32nd row.

The last 34 rows form the pattern; repeat them twice more, then work the first 14 rows again.

To shape the armholes: Maintaining the continuity of the pattern as set, cast off 4 sts. at the beginning of the next 2 rows, then dec. 1 st. at each end of the next 10 (12) (14) rows.

On 105 (109) (113) sts., pattern 62 (64) (66) rows.

To slope the shoulders: Cast off 11 sts. at the beginning of the next 4 rows, then 10 (11) (12) sts. on the 2 following rows – 41 (43) (45) sts.

Change to size 2¼ mm. (No. 13) needles and with m. only work 6 rows in single rib.

continued on page 130

continued from page 129

THE FRONT
Work as given for back until the 34 pattern rows have been worked twice then work the first 33 rows again.

Now divide the sts. for the neck: Next row: Work as set across 66 (70) (74) sts. then leave these sts. on a spare needle until required for right half front, p. 2 tog., work to end as set and continue on these 66 (70) (74) sts. for the left half front.

The left half front: To slope the neck: Continuing in pattern as set, dec. 1 st. at the neck edge on the next row and the 3 following 4th rows.

On 62 (66) (70) sts. pattern 1 row.

To shape the armhole and continue to slope front edge: While continuing to dec. at neck edge on every 4th row as set, cast off 4 sts. at the beginning – armhole edge on the next row, then dec. 1 st. at the armhole edge on each of the next 10 (12) (14) rows.

Pattern 52 (54) (56) rows decreasing 1 st. at neck edge on every 4th row as set.

On 32 (33) (34) sts., pattern 11 rows.

To shape the shoulder: Cast off 11 sts. at the beginning of the next row and following alternate row. On 10 (11) (12) sts., work 1 row, then cast off.

The right half front: With right side of work facing rejoin yarn to inner edge of sts. left on spare needle and work to end of row, then work as given for left half front to end.

THE FRONT NECKBAND
With right side of work facing rejoin m. and using size 2¼ mm. (No. 13) needles pick up and k. 68 (70) (72) sts. from left front neck edge, then 68 (70) (72) sts. from right front neck edge.

Work 1 row in single rib.

Next row: Rib to within 2 sts. of centre front, sl.1, k.1, p.s.s.o., k.2 tog., rib to end.

Repeat the last 2 rows once more.

Rib 1 row, then cast off in rib.

THE ARMHOLE EDGINGS (both alike)
For the sleeveless version only: First join shoulder seams. With right side of work facing rejoin m. and using size 2¼ mm. (No. 13) needles pick up and k.128 (132) (136) sts. from all round armhole edge.

Work 5 rows in single rib, then cast off in rib.

THE SLEEVES (both alike)
With size 2¼ mm. (No. 13) needles and m. cast on 64 sts. and work 43 rows in single rib.

Increase row: Rib 8, * up 1, rib 12; repeat from * ending last repeat rib 8 – 69 sts.

Change to size 2¾ mm. (No. 12) needles and work 10 rows in pattern as given for second size on back.

Continuing in pattern as set and working the extra sts. into the pattern as they occur, inc. 1 st. at each end of the next row and the 11 (13) (15) following 12th (10th) (8th) rows.

On 93 (97) (101) sts., pattern 7 (9) (19) rows.

To shape the sleevetop: Cast off 4 sts. at the beginning of the next 2 rows, dec. 1 st. at each end of the next row and the 23 (25) (27) following alternate rows.

On 37 sts., work 1 row.

Dec. 1 st. at each end of the next 2 rows.

Next row: * Sl.1, k. 2 tog., p.s.s.o., repeat from * to end.

Cast off the remaining 11 sts.

THE SHOULDER PADS (both alike)
With size 2¼ mm. (No. 13) needles and m. cast on 40 sts. and k. 70 rows, then cast off.

TO MAKE UP THE SWEATER
Pin out to size and press all parts except the ribbing on the wrong side with a warm iron over a damp cloth.

For the sleeveless version: Join side seams.

For the version with sleeves: Join shoulder seams; set in sleeves; join sleeve and side seams; fold shoulder pads in half to form triangles and neatly catch in place.

For both versions: Press seams.

JIGSAW

MATERIALS
6 (6) (7) 25 gram balls of 'Woollybear 100% Mohair' in main colour; 4 balls of the same yarn in first and second contrast colours; 2 balls in white and one ball in each of the 2 other contrast colours; a pair each of size 4½ mm. (No. 7) and size 3¾ mm. (No. 9) Aero knitting needles.

TENSION
9 stitches and 12 rows to 5 centimetres (2 inches) over the stocking stitch using size 4½ mm. (No. 7) needles. If you cannot obtain the correct tension using the size needles suggested use larger or smaller ones accordingly.

ABBREVIATIONS
K., knit; p., purl; st., stitch; tog., together; dec., decrease (by working 2 sts. tog.); inc., increase (by working twice into same st); s.s., stocking stitch (k. on the right side and p. on the wrong side); single rib is k.1 and p.1 alternately; sl., slip; p.s.s.o., pass sl. st. over; m.b., make bobble thus, k.1, y.r.n., k.1 all into next st., turn, p.3, turn, k.3, turn, p.3, turn, sl. 1, k.2 tog., p.s.s.o.; up 1, pick up the loop which lies between the needles, slip it onto left hand needle, then k. into back of it; m., main colour; a., first contrast; b., second contrast; c., third contrast; d., fourth contrast; e., fifth contrast; 3 long from 1, k.1 winding yarn round needle twice, p.1 winding yarn round needle twice, k.1 winding yarn round needle twice, all into next st.; 5 from 1, k.1, p.1, k.1, p.1, k.1. all into next st.; cr. 3 rt., cross 3 right thus, insert right hand needle into front of third st. on left hand needle, then into first st. and k. these 2 sts. tog. allowing first loop to fall from left hand needle, k. into second st. allowing extra loops to fall from left hand needle; cr. 3 lt., cross 3 left thus, slip next long st. off left hand needle to front of work, k. next st., k.1 long st. tog. with next st. on left hand needle.

NOTE
The instructions are given for the small size. Where they vary work the figures in the first brackets for the medium size or the figures in the second brackets for the large size.

MEASUREMENTS
The measurements are given in centimetres followed by inches in brackets.

Size	Small	Medium	Large
To fit bust	82.5 (33)	87.5 (35)	92.5 (37)
Underarms	85 (34)	90 (36)	95 (38)
Side seam	37.5 (15)	37.5 (15)	37.5 (15)
Length	56 (22½)	57.5 (23)	59 (23½)
Sleeve seam	40 (16)	40 (16)	40 (16)

THE BACK
With size 3¾ mm. (No. 9) needles and a. cast on 68 (72) (76) sts. and work 23 rows in single rib.

Increase row: Rib 2 (4) (6), * up 1, rib 8; repeat from * ending last repeat rib 2 (4) (6). – 77 (81) (85) sts.

Change to size 4½ mm. (No. 7) needles. Break off a., join in b. With b. beginning with a k. row s.s. 2 rows.

Join in c. Now work in flower pattern as follows: 1st row: With b. k.5 (4) (3), * with c., 3 long from 1, with b. k.5; repeat from * ending last repeat with b. k.5 (4) (3).

2nd row: With b. p.5 (4) (3), * sl.p. wise the 3 long sts. dropping the extra loops, with b. p.5; repeat from * ending last repeat with b. p.5 (4) (3).

3rd row: With b., k.3 (2) (1), * cr. 3 rt., sl.1, cr. 3 lt., k.1; repeat from * ending last repeat k.3 (2) (1).

4th row: With b. all p.

5th row: With b. all k.

6th row: With b. all p.

7th row: With b. k.2 (7) (6), * with c. 3 long from 1, with b. k.5; repeat from * ending last repeat with b. k.2 (7) (6).

8th row: With b. p.2 (7) (6), * sl. p.wise the 3 long sts., dropping extra loops, with b. p.5; repeat from * ending last repeat with b. p.2 (7) (6).

9th row: With b. k.nil (5) (4), * cr. 3 rt., sl.1, cr. 3 lt., k.1; repeat from * ending last repeat

continued on page 130

JOEY BOY

MATERIALS
27 (29) (30) 50 gram balls of 'Woollybear Wool Bouclé'; a pair each of size 7 mm. (No. 2) and size 4½ mm. (No. 7) Aero knitting needles; 4 buttons.

TENSION
9 stitches and 14 rows to 10 centimetres (4 inches) over the reversed stocking stitch using size 7 mm. (No. 2) needles. If you cannot obtain the correct tension using the size needles suggested use larger or smaller ones accordingly.

ABBREVIATIONS
K., knit; p., purl; st., stitch; tog., together; dec., decrease (by working 2 sts. tog.); inc., increase (by working twice into same st.); single rib is k.1 and p.1 alternately; r.s.s., reversed stocking stitch (p. on the right side and k. on the wrong side); y.r.n., yarn round needle.

NOTE
The instructions are given for the small size. Where they vary work the figures in the first brackets for the medium size or the figures in the second brackets for the large size.

MEASUREMENTS
The measurements are given in centimetres followed by inches in brackets.

Size	Small	Medium	Large
To fit chest	90 (36)	95 (38)	100 (40)
Underarms	97.5 (39)	102.5 (41)	107.5 (43)
Side seam	37.5 (15)	37.5 (15)	37.5 (15)
Length	67.5 (27)	69 (27½)	70 (28)
Sleeve seam	46 (18½)	46 (18½)	46 (18½)

THE BACK
With size 4½ mm. (No. 7) needles cast on 45 (47) (49) sts. and work 14 rows in single rib.
Change to size 7 mm. (No. 2) needles and beginning with a p. row r.s.s. 42 rows.
To slope the raglan armholes: Cast off 2 sts. at the beginning of the next 2 rows, then dec. 1 st. at each end of the next row and the 13 (14) (15) following alternate rows.
On 13 sts., r.s.s. 13 rows.
Cast off.

THE POCKET BACKS (2 alike)
With size 7 mm. (No. 2) needles cast on 12 sts. and beginning with a p. row r.s.s. 13 rows, then leave these sts. on a stitch-holder until required.

THE FRONT
With size 4½ mm. (No. 7) needles cast on 45 (47) (49) sts. and work 14 rows in single rib.
Change to size 7 mm. (No. 2) needles and beginning with a p. row r.s.s. 15 rows.
Now divide the sts. for the pocket: Next row: K.5 (6) (7), then onto same needle k. across the 12 sts. of one pocket back, break off wool, then leave these 17 (18) (19) sts. on a spare needle until required for right side, rejoin wool and k. across the centre 35 sts., break off wool and leave these sts. on a spare needle until required for centre panel, rejoin wool and k. across the 12 sts. of other pocket back, then across the 5 (6) (7) remaining sts. and continue on these 17 (18) (19) sts. for the left side.
The left side: R.s.s. 6 rows, then leave these 17 (18) (19) sts. on a spare needle until required.
The centre panel: With right side of work facing rejoin yarn to the 35 sts. left on spare needle at centre and continuing in r.s.s. cast off 4 sts. at the beginning of the next 6 rows, then leave these remaining 11 sts. on a spare needle until required.
The right side: With right side of work facing rejoin yarn to the 17 (18) (19) sts. left on spare needle and r.s.s. 6 rows, then leave these sts. on a spare needle until required.
Next row: With right side of work facing rejoin yarn to left side p. across these 17 (18) (19) sts., then onto same needle p. across the 11 sts. at centre then across the 17 (18) (19) sts. of right side.
On 45 (47) (49) sts., r.s.s. 4 rows.
Now divide the sts. for the front opening: Next row: K.21 (22) (23) and leave these sts. on a spare needle until required for the right half front, cast off 3 sts. for front opening, k. to end and continue on these 21 (22) (23) sts. for the left half front.
The left half front: R.s.s. 14 rows.
To slope the raglan armhole: Cast off 2 sts. at the beginning of the next row, work 1 row back to armhole edge. Dec. 1 st. at the beginning of the next row and the 1 (2) (3) following alternate row(s).
On 17 sts., work 1 row.
To slope the neck edge and continue to slope the raglan: While continuing to dec. at armhole edge on every alternate row as set, dec. 1 st. at the front edge on the next row and the 3 following 6th rows – 3 sts.
R.s.s. 3 rows, decreasing 1 st. at armhole edge on the 2nd of these rows. Take the 2 remaining sts. tog. and fasten off.
The right half front: With right side of work facing rejoin yarn to inner edge of sts. left on spare needle and work to end of row, then work as given for left half front to end.

THE SLEEVES (both alike)
With size 4½ mm. (No. 7) needles cast on 21 (23) (25) sts. and work 12 rows in single rib.
Change to size 7 mm. (No. 2) needles and beginning with a p. row r.s.s. 8 rows.
Inc. 1 st. at each end of the next row and the 9 following 4th rows.
On 41 (43) (45) sts. r.s.s. 9 rows.
To slope the raglan sleeve top: Cast off 2 sts. at the beginning of the next 2 rows, then dec. 1 st. at each end of the next row and the 13 (14) (15) following alternate rows. On 9 sts. work 1 row, then cast off.

THE POCKET TOPS (both alike)
With right side of work facing rejoin yarn and using size 4½ mm. (No. 7) needles pick up and k.15 sts. from sts. cast off for pocket openings.
Work 3 rows in single rib, then cast off.

continued from page 131

k.nil (5) (4).
10th, 11th and 12th rows: As 4th, 5th and 6th rows.
Repeat the last 12 rows twice more.**
Break off b. and c., join in d.
With d. s.s. 4 rows. Break off d., join in m.
With m. s.s. 28 rows.
*** To shape the armholes: Cast off 3 sts. at the beginning of the next 2 rows. Dec. 1 st. at each end of the next row and the 2(3) (4) following alternate rows.
On 65 (67) (69) sts. s.s. 1 row.
Now work the cloud pattern as follows: Use a separate small ball of c. for each group of clouds.
1st row: With m. k.6 (7) (8), * with c.5 from 1, turn, p.5, turn, k.5, with m. k.1.*; repeat from * to * 3 times more, with m. k.38 more; repeat from * to * 4 times, with m. k.5 (6) (7) more.
2nd row: With m. p.6 (7) (8), * with c. p.5, with m. p.1 *; repeat from * to * 3 times more, with m. p.38 more; repeat from * to * 4 times, with m. p.5 (6) (7) more.
3rd row: With m. k.6 (7) (8), * with c. k.5, turn, p. 2 tog., p.1, p.2 tog., turn, sl.1, k.2 tog., p.s.s.o., with m. k.1 *; repeat from * to * 3 times more, with m. k.38 more; repeat from * to * 4 times, with m. k.5 (6) (7) more.
4th, 5th and 6th rows: With m. in s.s.
7th row: With m. k.16 (17) (18), repeat from * to * on 1st row 4 times, with m. k.18 more; repeat from * to * on 1st row 4 times, with m. k.15 (16) (17) more.
8th row: With m. p.16 (17) (18), repeat from * to * on 2nd row 4 times, with m. p.18 more; repeat from * to * on 2nd row 4 times, with m. p.15 (16) (17) more.
9th row: With m. k.16 (17) (18); repeat from * to * on 3rd row 4 times, with m. k.18 more, repeat from * to * on 3rd row 4 times, with m. k.15 (16) (17) more.
10th, 11th and 12th rows: With m. in s.s.
13th row: With m. k.26 (27) (28); repeat from * to * on 1st row 7 times, with m. k.25 (26) (27) more.
14th row: With m. p.26 (27) (28); repeat from * to * on 2nd row 7 times, with m. p.25 (26) (27) more.
15th row: With m. k.26 (27) (28); repeat from * to * on 3rd row 7 times more, with m. k.25 (26) (27) more.
This completes the cloud pattern.***
With m. only s.s. 19 rows.
To slope the shoulders: Cast off 9 sts. at the beginning of the next 2 rows, then 8 (9) (10) sts. on the 2 following rows – 31 sts.
Leave the remaining sts. on a spare needle until required for neckband.

THE FRONT
Work as given for back until ** is reached.
Break off b. Join in d.
Now work in the trees and houses pattern as follows: This is worked entirely in s.s. except for the bobbles so only the colour details are given. Use separate small balls of contrast colours for each section or motif.
1st row: 3 (5) (7) d., 8c., 14d., 18c., 4d., 12c., 6d., 9c., 3 (5) (7) d.
2nd row: 3 (5) (7) d., 9c., 6d., 12c., 4d., 18c., 14d., 8c., 3 (5) (7) d.
The last 2 rows set the position of the pattern given in the chart, now work the 3rd to 32nd rows from the chart as set. Now work as given for back from *** to ***.
With m. only s.s. 2 rows.
Now divide the sts. for the neck: Next row: P.27 (28) (29) and leave these sts. on a spare needle until required for right front shoulder, p.11 and leave these sts. on a stitch-holder until required for neckband, p. to end and continue on these 27 (28) (29) sts. for the left front shoulder.
The left front shoulder: To shape the neck: Dec. 1 st. at the neck edge on each of the next 10 rows.
On 17 (18) (19) sts., s.s. 6 rows.
To slope the shoulder: Cast off 9 sts. at the beginning of the next row. On 8 (9) (10) sts. work 1 row, then cast off.
The right front shoulder: With right side of work facing rejoin yarn to inner edge of the 27 (28) (29) sts. left on spare needle and work to end of row.
Now work as given for left front shoulder to end.

THE SLEEVES (both alike)
With size 3¾ mm. (No. 9) needles and a. cast on 35 (37) (39) sts. and work 24 rows in single rib.
Change to size 4½ mm. (No. 7) needles.
Break off a., join in b. With b. beginning with a k. row s.s. 2 rows.
Now work the flower pattern as follows: 1st

THE RIGHT HALF COLLAR
With size 4½ mm. (No. 7) needles cast on 50 (52) (54) sts. and work 5 rows in single rib.

**Continuing in rib, cast off 16 sts. at the beginning of the next row.

Rib 1 row, then cast off 4 sts. at the beginning of the next row and 3 following alternate rows.

Cast off the remaining 18 (20) (22) sts.

THE LEFT HALF COLLAR
With size 4½ mm. (No. 7) needles cast on 50 (52) (54) sts. and work 2 rows in single rib.

Buttonhole row: Rib 34 (36) (38), * y.r.n., k. 2 tog., rib 4; repeat from * ending last repeat rib 2.

Rib 2 rows.

Now work as given for right collar from ** to end.

THE RAGLAN RIB BANDS (4 alike)
With size 4½ mm. (No. 7) needles cast on 25 (27) (29) sts. and work 6 rows in single rib, then cast off in rib loosely.

TO MAKE UP THE TOP
Pin out to size and press all parts except the ribbing on the wrong side with a warm iron over a damp cloth. Sew cast on edge of raglan rib bands to the raglan shaping rows on back and front, sew row ends of bands at back to the first 6 straight row end edges of back neck. Join raglan shaping rows of sleeves to cast off edges of raglan rib bands, then join half the sts. cast off at top of sleeves to the remaining 6 row ends at back neck. Join sleeve and side seams. Sew pocket back and row ends of pocket tops in place. Join row end edges of left and right half collars for centre back seam. Sew cast off edges of collar in place all round neck edge. Neatly secure row ends of front bands to the 3 sts. cast off at centre front. Press seams. Sew on buttons. Make a buttonhole loop at outer edge of left half collar.

row: With b. k.5 (3) (4), * with c.3 long from 1, with b. k.5; repeat from * ending last repeat with b. k.5 (3) (4).

The last row sets the position of the 12 row flower pattern given for back. Pattern 1 row more as set.

Maintaining the continuity of the pattern as set and working the extra sts. into the pattern as they occur inc. 1 st. at each end of the next row and the 4 following 8th rows.

On 45 (47) (49) sts. pattern 7 rows more.

Break off b. and c. Join in d. With d. s.s. 4 rows. Break off d., join in m.

With m. continuing in s.s. as set inc. 1 st. at each end of the next row and the 3 following 8th rows.

On 53 (55) (57) sts. s.s. 3 rows.

To shape the sleevetop: Cast off 3 sts. at the beginning of the next 2 rows. Dec. 1 st. at each end of the next row and the 8 (9) (10) following alternate rows.

On 29 sts. work 1 row.

Dec. 1 st. at each end of the next 6 rows. Cast off 3 sts. at the beginning of the next 4 rows. Cast off the remaining 5 sts.

THE NECKBAND
First join right shoulder seam. With right side of work facing rejoin a. and using size 3¾ mm. (No. 9) needles, pick up and k. 18 sts. from left front neck edge, k. across the 11 sts. left on stitch-holder at centre front neck, pick up and k. 18 sts. from right front neck edge, then k. across the 31 sts. on spare needle at back neck edge.

On 78 sts., work 4 rows in single rib.

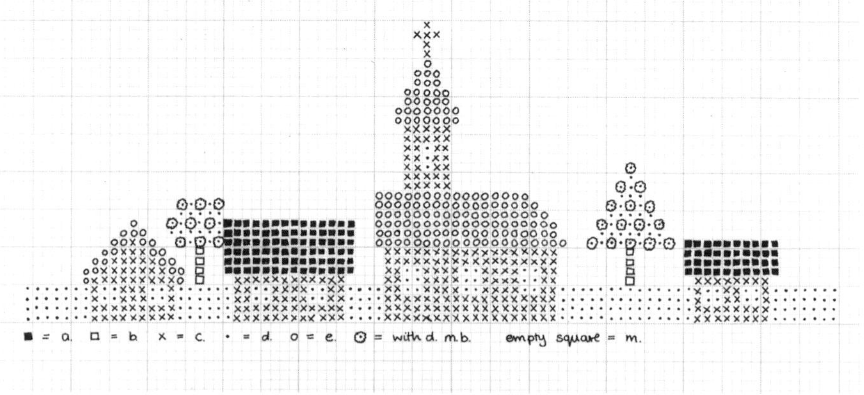

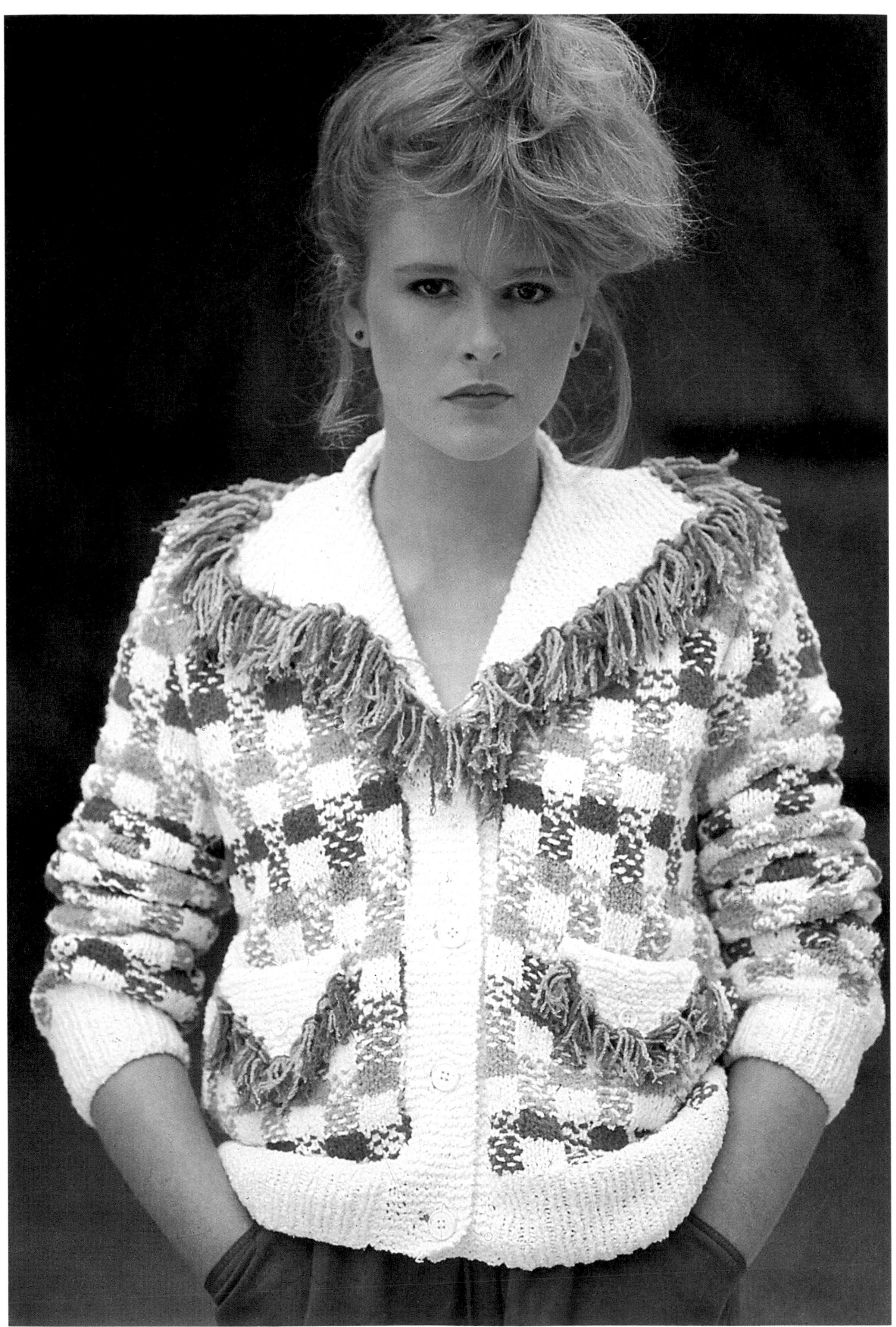

CALAMITY

CALAMITY

MATERIALS
14 25 gram balls of 'Woollybear 100% Mohair' by Patricia Roberts in main colour and 2 balls of the same yarn in each of the 5 contrast colours; a pair each of size 4 mm. (No. 8) and size 3¾ mm. (No. 9) Aero knitting needles, a medium sized crochet hook; 4 medium sized buttons and 2 small ones.

SPECIAL NOTE
This garment may also be knitted in 'Woollybear Cotton Bouclé' by Patricia Roberts. It will require 10 50 gram balls in main colour and 2 balls in each of the 5 contrast colours. However, to obtain the correct tension it is necessary to use size 3¾ mm. (No. 9) needles instead of size 4 mm. (No. 8) needles and size 3¼ mm. (No. 10) needles instead of size 3¾ mm. (No. 9) needles, throughout.

TENSION
10 stitches – 1 repeat of the pattern – to 5 centimetres (2 inches) in width and 23 rows of the pattern to 10 centimetres (4 inches) in depth. If you cannot obtain the correct tension using the size needles suggested use larger or smaller ones accordingly.

ABBREVIATIONS
K., knit; p., purl; st., stitch; tog., together; dec., decrease (by working 2 sts. tog.); inc., increase (by working twice into the same st.); single rib is k.1 and p.1 alternately; s.s., stocking stitch is k. on the right side and p. on the wrong side; sl., slip; f.w., front of work; b.w., back of work; garter st. is k. plain on every row; m., main colour; a., first contrast; b., second contrast; c., third contrast; d., fourth contrast; e., fifth contrast; up 1, pick up the loop which lies between the needles, slip it onto left hand needle then k. into back of it; y.r.n., yarn round needle.

NOTE
The instructions are given for the small/medium size. Where they vary work the figures in the brackets for the large size.

MEASUREMENTS
The measurements are given in centimetres followed by inches in brackets.

Sizes	Small/medium	Large
To fit bust	82.5–85 (33–34)	92.5–95 (37–38)
Underarms	90 (36)	100 (40)
Side seam	39.5 (15)	39.5 (15)
Length	58 (23½)	60 (24)
Sleeve seam	42.5 (17)	42.5 (17)

THE BACK
With size 3¾ mm. (No. 9) needles and m. cast on 80 (90) sts. and work 23 rows in single rib.

Increase row: Rib 7 (12), *up 1, rib 6; repeat from * ending last repeat rib 7 (12). – 92 (102) sts.

Change to size 4 mm. (No. 8) needles and work in pattern as follows. Great care must be taken not to pull colours not in use tightly across the back of the work or the work will become puckered.

1st row: With a. k.1, ** with m. k.5, * with m. to f.w. – right side, with a. k.1, with m. to b.w., with a. k.1; repeat from * once, with m. to f.w., with a. k.1; repeat from ** until 1 remains, with m. k.1.

2nd row: With m. p.1, ** with m. to f.w. – wrong side, with a. p.1, * with m. to b.w., with a. p.1, with m. to f.w., with a. p.1; repeat from * once, with m. p.5; repeat from ** until 1 remains, with a. p.1.

3rd, 4th and 5th rows: As 1st and 2nd rows, then 1st row again.

6th row: With b. p.1, ** with b. to f.w., with m. p.1, * with b. to b.w. with m. p.1, with b. to f.w. with m. p.1; repeat from * once, with b. p.5; repeat from ** until 1 remains, with m. p.1.

7th row: With m. k.1, ** with b. k.5, with b. to f.w. with m. k.1, * with b. to b.w. with m. k.1, with b. to f.w. with m. k.1; repeat from * once; repeat from ** until 1 remains, with b. k.1.

8th, 9th and 10th rows: As 6th and 7th rows, then 6th row again.

11th row: With m. k.1, ** with m. to f.w. with c. k.1, * with m. to b.w. with c. k.1, with m. to f.w. with c. k.1; repeat from * once, with m. k.5; repeat from ** until 1 remains, with c. k.1.

12th row: With c. p.1, ** with m. p.5, * with m. to f.w. with c. p.1, with m. to b.w. with c. p.1; repeat from * once, with m. to f.w. with c. p.1; repeat from ** until 1 remains, with m. p.1.

13th, 14th and 15th rows: As 11th and 12th rows, then 11th row again.

16th row: With m. p.1, ** with d. p.5, with d. to f.w., with m. p.1, * with d. to b.w., with m. p.1, with d. to f.w. with m. p.1; repeat from * once; repeat from ** until 1 remains, with d. p.1.

17th row: With d. k.1, ** with d. to f.w. with m. k.1, * with d. to b.w. with m. k.1, with d. to f.w., with m. k.1; repeat from * once, with d. k.5; repeat from ** until 1 remains, with m. k.1.

18th, 19th and 20th rows: As 16th and 17th rows, then 16th row again.

The last 20 rows form the pattern. Using e. instead of a., a. instead of b., b. instead of c. and c. instead of d. work the 20 pattern rows again.

Thus continuing in the 20 row pattern in the colour sequence of 5 rows in d. and m., 5 rows in e. and m., 5 rows in a. and m., 5 rows in b. and m, and 5 rows in c. and m. pattern 30 rows more.

To shape the armholes: Continuing in pattern in colour sequence as set, cast off 5 (6) sts. at the beginning of the next 2 rows, then dec. 1 st. at each end of the next row and the 4 (6) following alternate rows.

On 72 (76) sts. pattern 11 rows.

Inc. 1 st. at each end of the next row and the following 10th row.

On 76 (80) sts. pattern 9 rows.

To slope the shoulders: Cast off 8 sts. at the beginning of the next 4 rows, then 8 (9) sts. on the 2 following rows.

Cast off the remaining 28 (30) sts.

THE POCKET BACKS (2 alike)
With size 4 mm. (No. 8) needles and m. cast on 20 sts. and beginning with a k. row s.s. 28 rows, then leave these sts. on a stitch-holder until required.

THE LEFT FRONT
With size 3¾ mm. (No. 9) needles and m. cast on 36 (41) sts. and work 23 rows in single rib.

Increase row: Rib 3 (5), *up 1, rib 6; repeat from * ending last repeat rib 3 (6). – 42 (47) sts.

Change to size 4 mm. (No. 8) needles and work in pattern as follows, noting information given for back. ***

1st row: With a. k.1, **with m. k.5, * with m. to f.w. – right side, with a. k.1, with m. to b.w., with a. k.1; repeat from * once, with m. to f.w., with a. k.1; repeat from ** until 1 (6) remain, with m. k.1 (with m. k.5, with a. k.1).

2nd row: With m. p.1 (with a. p.1, with m. p.5), ** with m. to f.w. – wrong side, with a. p.1 *with m. to b.w., with a. p.1, with m. to f.w., with a. p.1; repeat from * once, with m. p.5; repeat from ** until 1 remains, with a. p.1.

The last 2 rows set the position of the pattern given for the back. Now work the 3rd to 20th pattern rows as set. Continuing in pattern as set, and in colour sequence given for back, work 16

ANNIE

MATERIALS
17 (18) (19) 25 gram balls of 'Woollybear 100% Mohair' by Patricia Roberts in main colour and 4 balls in contrast colour; a pair each of size 4 mm. (No. 8) and size 3¾ mm. (No. 9) Aero knitting needles; 4 buttons.

SPECIAL NOTE
This garment may also be knitted in 'Woollybear Cotton Bouclé' by Patricia Roberts. It will require 12 (12) (13) 50 gram balls in main colour and 3 balls in contrast colour. To obtain the correct tension it is necessary to use size 3¼ mm. (No. 10) needles instead of size 4 mm. (No. 8) needles and size 3 mm. (No. 11) needles instead of size 3¾ mm. (No. 9) needles throughout.

TENSION
16 stitches to 7.5 centimetres (3 inches) and 14 rows to 5 centimetres (2 inches) over the rib pattern using either size 4 mm. (No. 8) needles and 'Woollybear 100% Mohair' or size 3 mm. (No. 11) needles and 'Woollybear Cotton Bouclé'. If you cannot obtain the correct tension using the size needles suggested, use larger or smaller ones accordingly.

ABBREVIATIONS
K., knit; p., purl; st., stitch; tog., together; dec., decrease (by working 2 sts. tog.); inc., increase (by working twice into the same st.); single rib is k.1 and p.1 alternately; m., main colour; c., contrast colour; sl., slip; p.s.s.o., pass sl. st. over; up 1, pick up tne loop which lies between the needles, slip it onto left hand needle, then k. into back of it.

NOTE
The instructions are given for the small size. Where they vary work the figures in the first brackets for the medium size or the figures in the second brackets for the large size.

MEASUREMENTS
The measurements are given in centimetres followed by inches in brackets

Sizes	Small	Medium	Large
To fit bust	82.5 (33)	87.5 (35)	92.5 (37)
Underarms	90 (36)	95 (38)	100 (40)
Side seam	44 (17½)	44 (17½)	44 (17½)
Length	64 (25½)	65 (26)	66 (26½)
Sleeve seam	42.5 (17)	42.5 (17)	42.5 (17)

THE BACK
With size 3¾ mm. (No. 9) needles and m. cast on 81 (87) (93) sts. and work 19 rows in single rib.

Increase row: Rib 3 (6) (9), *up 1, rib 5; repeat from * ending last repeat rib 3 (6) (9). – 97 (103) (109) sts.

Change to size 4 mm. (No. 8) needles and work in rib pattern as follows:

1st row: K.2, *p.3, k.3; repeat from * ending last repeat k.2.

2nd row: P.1 *k.1, p.1; repeat from * to end.

The last 2 rows form the pattern; repeat them 51 times more.

To shape the armholes: Continuing in rib as set, cast off 5 sts. at the beginning of the next 2 rows, then dec. 1 st. at each end of the next row and the 5 (6) (7) following alternate rows.

On 75 (79) (83) sts. work 27 (29) (31) rows in rib as set.

Inc. 1 st. at each end of the next row.

On 77 (81) (85) sts. work 9 rows.

To slope the shoulders: Cast off 8 sts. at the beginning of the next 4 rows, then 7 (8) (9) sts. on the 2 following rows.

Cast off the remaining 31 (33) (35) sts.

THE FRONT
Work as given for the back until the 2 rib pattern rows have been worked 8 times.

Now divide the sts. for the pockets: Next row: Pattern 12 (15) (18) and leave these sts. on a s[illegible]older until required, pattern across the next 73 sts. and leave these sts. on a spare needle until required, work to end and continue on these 12 (15) (18) sts.

Continuing in pattern as set work 24 rows increasing 1 st. at the inner edge on each row.

On 36 (39) (42) sts. work 1 row ending at inner edge, then leave these sts. on a spare needle until required.

Return to the 73 sts. left on spare needle at centre and work 24 rows decreasing 1 st. at each end of each row.

On 25 sts. work 1 row, then leave these sts. on a spare needle until required.

Return to the 12 (15) (18) sts. left on stitch-holder and work 24 rows in pattern increasing 1 st. at inner edge on each row.

On 36 (39) (42) sts. work 1 row back to side seam edge.

Next row: Pattern as set across these 36 (39) (42) sts., then across the 25 sts. at centre front and the 36 (39) (42) sts. on spare needle.

rows more.

Pocket row: Pattern 11 (16), slip next 20 sts. onto a stitch-holder until required for pocket top and in their place pattern across the 20 sts. of one pocket back, pattern to end of row.

Pattern 21 rows more.

****To slope the front edge: Continuing in pattern as set dec. 1 st. at the end–front edge on the next row and the following 6th row.

On 40 (45) sts. pattern 5 rows.

To shape the armhole and continue to slope the front edge: Cast off 5 (6) sts. at the beginning and dec. 1 st. at the end – front edge on the next row. Pattern 10 (14) rows decreasing 1 st. at the armhole on every right side row and at the same time decreasing 1 st. at front edge on the 6th (6th and 12th) of these rows.

Still decreasing at front edge on every 6th row as set, work 11 rows straight, then inc. 1 st. at the armhole edge on the next row and the following 10th row.

On 26 (27) sts. pattern 3 (5) rows.

Dec. 1 st. at the front edge on the next row.

On 25 (26) sts. pattern 5 rows.

To slope the shoulder: Cast off 8 sts. at the beginning and dec. 1 st. at the end of the next row. Cast off 8 sts. at the beginning of the following alternate row. On 8 (9) sts. work 1 row, then cast off.

THE RIGHT FRONT

Work as given for the left front until *** is reached.

1st row: With m. k.1 (with a. k.1, with m. k.5), ** with m. to f.w. – right side, with a. k.1, * with m. to b.w., with a. k.1, with m. to f.w., with a. k.1; repeat from * once, with m. k.5; repeat from ** until 1 remains, with a. k.1.

2nd row: With a. p.1, ** with m. p.5, * with m. to f.w. – wrong side, with a. p.1, with m. to b.w., with a. p.1; repeat from * once, with m. to f.w., with a. p.1; repeat from ** until 1 (6) remain, with m. p.1 (with m. p.5, with a. p.1).

The last 2 rows set the position of the pattern given for the back. Work the 3rd to 20th rows as set.

Pattern 16 more rows as set.

Pocket row: Pattern 11, slip next 20 sts. onto a stitch-holder until required for pocket top, and in their place pattern across the 20 sts. of one pocket back, pattern to end of row.

Pattern 22 rows more.

Now work as given for left front from **** to end.

THE SLEEVES (both alike)

With size 3¾ mm. (No. 9) needles and m. cast on 42 sts. and work 23 rows in single rib.

Increase row: Rib 3, *up 1, rib 4; repeat from * ending last repeat rib 3. – 52 sts.

Change to size 4 mm. (No. 8) needles and using d. instead of c. and e. instead of d. work the 11th to 20th rows given for back, then work the 1st to 10th rows with a. and m., then b. and m. as given at beginning of back.

Continuing in pattern as set and working the extra sts. into the pattern as they occur, inc. 1 st. at each end of the next row and the 4 (6) following 12th (8th) rows.

On 62 (66) sts. pattern 11 rows.

To shape the sleevetop: Continuing in pattern as set, cast off 5 (6) sts. at the beginning of the next 2 rows, then dec. 1 st. at each end of the next row and the 8 (9) following alternate rows. On 34 sts. work 1 row.

Dec 1 st. at each end of the next 4 rows – 26 sts.

Cast off 3 sts. at the beginning of the next 2 rows, then 4 sts. on the 4 following rows.

Cast off the 4 remaining sts.

THE BUTTONBAND AND HALF COLLAR

With size 3¾ mm. (No. 9) needles and m. cast on 11 sts. and work 92 rows in garter st.

**Continuing in garter st. as set, inc. 1 st. at the beginning of the next row and the 9 (10) following 4th rows.

On 21 (22) sts. k. 13 rows.

Cast on 14 (15) sts. for back neck at the beginning of the next row.

On 35 (37) sts. k.39 rows, then cast off loosely.

THE BUTTONHOLE BAND AND HALF COLLAR

With size 3¾ mm. (No. 9) needles and m. cast on 11 sts. and work 6 rows in garter st.

1st Buttonhole row: K.4, cast off 3, k. to end.

2nd Buttonhole row: K.4, turn, cast on 3, turn, k. to end.

K.26 rows.

Repeat the last 28 rows twice more, then work the 2 buttonhole rows again.

Now work as given for buttonband and half collar from ** to end.

THE POCKET TOPS (2 alike)

With right side of work facing rejoin m. to the 20 sts. left on stitch-holder at front of work and using size 3¾ mm. (No. 9) needles k.4 rows, then cast off.

THE POCKET FLAPS (2 alike)

With size 3¾ mm. (No. 9) needles and m. cast on 21 sts. and k.4 rows.

Continuing in garter st. dec. 1 st. at each end of the next row and the 4 following alternate rows – 11 sts.

Buttonhole row: K.5, y.r.n., k.2 tog., k. to end.

Dec. 1 st. at each end of the next row and the 3 following alternate rows. – 3 sts.

K.3, then take these 3 sts. tog. and fasten off.

THE SHOULDER PADS (2 alike)

With size 3¾ mm. (No. 9) needles and m. cast on 25 sts. and work 40 rows in garter st. then cast off. Fold in half diagonally and join outer edges to form a triangle.

TO MAKE UP THE JACKET

Pin out to size and press all parts except the garter st. and the ribbing on the wrong side with a warm iron over a damp cloth. Join shoulder seams. Set in sleeves. Join sleeve and side seams. Join short row end edges of half collars for centre back seam. Neatly sew shaped row end and cast on edges of front bands and back collar in place, so that the first inc. of collar is in line with first front edge dec. Sew pocket backs and row ends of pocket tops in place, then sew cast on edges of pocket flaps in place. Press seams. Catch shoulder pads in place. Sew on buttons.

THE FRINGING

To make a tassel, cut a 15 cm. (6 inch) length of yarn in each of the 5 contrast colours. Place all 5 lengths together and fold in half. Insert crochet hook into outer edge of collar 8 rows above last buttonhole and draw looped end of folded yarn through, pass cut ends through looped end and pull firmly, to form one tassel. In the same way make another tassel 4 rows above the previous one. Thus make tassels all round outer edge of collar, then make tassels in the same way along shaped row end edges of pocket flaps. Trim fringing to a finished length of 5 cms. (2 inches) round collar and 3 cms. (1 inch) on pocket flaps. Press lightly.

On all 97 (103) (109) sts. pattern 20 rows.

Now divide the sts. for the front opening: Next row: Pattern 45 (48) (51) sts. and leave these on a spare needle until required for right half front, pattern 7 and leave these sts. on a safety pin until required for buttonhole band, work to end of row and continue on these 45 (48) (51) sts. for the left half front.

The left half front: Pattern 40 rows more ending at armhole edge.

To shape the armhole: Cast off 5 sts. at the beginning of the next row. Work 1 row straight, then dec. 1 st. at the beginning of the next row and the 5 (6) (7) following alternate rows.

On 34 (36) (38) sts. work 14 (16) (18) rows.

To shape the neck: Cast off 5 (6) (7) sts. at the beginning of the next row, then dec. 1 st. at the neck edge on each of the next 2 rows.

To slope the shoulder: Still decreasing 1 st. at the neck edge on each row, cast off 8 sts. at the beginning of the next row and the following alternate row.

Dec. 1 st. at the neck edge on the next row, then cast off the remaining 7 (8) (9) sts.

The right half front: With right side of work facing rejoin m. to inner edge of sts. left on spare needle and work to end of row, then work as given for left half front to end.

THE POCKET BACKS (2 alike)

With size 4 mm. (No. 8) needles and c. cast on 31 sts. and work 30 rows in pattern as given for back, then cast off.

THE SHOULDER INSETS (2 alike)

With size 4 mm. (No. 8) needles and m. cast on 19 sts. and work 30 (32) (34) rows in pattern as given for back, then cast off.

THE SLEEVES (both alike)

With size 3¾ mm. (No. 9) needles and m. cast on 43 sts., and work 20 rows in single rib.

Change to size 4 mm. (No. 8) needles and work 10 (6) (2) rows in rib pattern as given for back.

Continuing in rib as set and working the extra sts. into the pattern as they occur, inc. 1 st. at each end of the next row and the 10 (11) (12) following 8th rows.

On 65 (67) (69) sts. pattern 11 (7) (3) rows.

To shape the sleevetop: Cast off 5 sts. at the beginning of the next 2 rows. Dec. 1 st. at each end of the next row and the 8 (9) (10) following alternate rows.

On 37 sts. work 1 row.

Dec. 1 st. at each end of the next 6 rows.

Cast off 3 sts. at the beginning of the next 6 rows. Cast off the remaining 7 sts.

THE BUTTONBAND

With size 3¾ mm. (No. 9) needles and m. cast on 7 sts. and work 68 (72) (76) rows in single rib, then cast off in rib.

THE BUTTONHOLE BAND

With right side of work facing rejoin m. to the 7 sts. left on safety pin at centre front and work 8 (6) (10) rows in single rib.

1st Buttonhole row: Rib 2, cast off 3, rib to end.

2nd Buttonhole row: Rib 2, turn, cast on 3, turn, rib to end.

Rib 16 (18) (18) rows.

Repeat the last 18 (20) (20) rows twice more, then work the 2 buttonhole rows again.

Rib 4 rows, then cast off in rib.

THE NECKBAND AND COLLAR

With size 4 mm. (No. 8) needles and c. cast on 19 sts. and work 400 rows in rib pattern given for back, marking the end of the 146th (142nd) (138th) and 254th (258th) (262nd) rows with coloured threads. Cast off.

THE SHOULDER PADS (2 alike)

With size 3¾ mm. (No. 9) needles and m. cast on 25 sts. and work 34 rows in single rib, then cast off in rib. Fold in half diagonally, and join outer edges to form triangles.

THE POCKET TOPS (2 alike)

With right side of work facing rejoin m. and using size 3¾ mm. (No. 9) needles pick up and k.31 sts. from shaped edge of pocket opening, turn and cast off.

TO MAKE UP THE SWEATER

Pin out to size and press very lightly on the wrong side with a warm iron over a damp cloth. Sew row end edges of shoulder inserts to back and front shoulders, so that cast off edge forms part of neck edge. Set in sleeves. Join sleeve and side seams. Sew row ends of collar between marking threads in place all round neck edge. Sew button and buttonhole bands in position. Sew pockets in place. Press seams lightly. Sew on buttons. Catch shoulder pads in place.

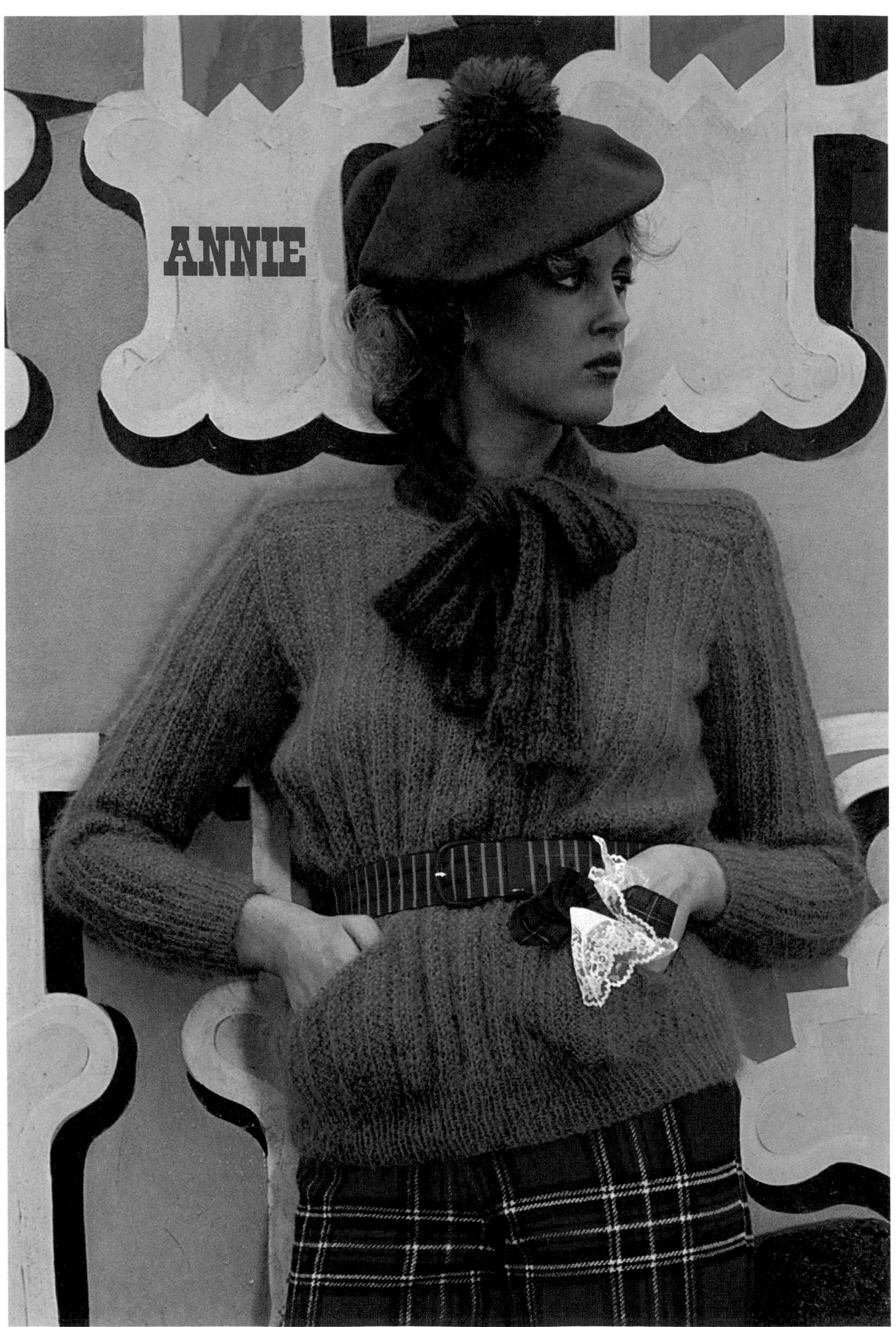
ANNIE

COCO

COCO

MATERIALS
14 50 gram balls of 'Woollybear Wool Bouclé' by Patricia Roberts in main colour, 5 balls of the same yarn in first contrast colour and 4 balls in each of the 3 other contrast colours; 2 ounce (28 gram) hanks of 'Woollybear Real Shetland' by Patricia Roberts in a contrast colour for the ribbings; a pair each of size 2¾ mm. (No. 12) and size 6 mm. (No. 4) and one size 4 mm. (No. 8) Aero knitting needles; 7 buttons.

TENSION
10 stitches and 18 rows to 10 centimetres (4 inches) over the stocking stitch using size 6 mm. (No. 4) needles and 'Woollybear Wool Bouclé'. If you cannot obtain the correct tension using the size needles suggested use larger or smaller ones accordingly.

ABBREVIATIONS
K., knit; p., purl; st., stitch; tog., together; dec., decrease (by working 2 sts. tog.); inc., increase (by working twice into same st.); single rib is k.1 and p.1 alternately; s.s. stocking stitch is k. on the right side and p. on the wrong side; sl., slip; p.s.s.o., pass sl. st. over; m., main colour; a. first contrast; b., second contrast.; c., third contrast; d., fourth contrast.

MEASUREMENTS
The measurements are given in centimetres followed by inches in brackets.

To fit bust	82.5–87.5 (33–35)
Underarms	100 (40)
Side seam	45 (18)
Length	67.5 (27)
Sleeve seam	42.5 (17)

THE BACK
With size 2¾ mm. (No. 12) needles and 'Woollybear Real Shetland' cast on 156 sts. and work 34 rows in single rib.

Using the 4 mm. (No. 8) needle work the Decrease row: *Sl.1, k.2 tog., p.s.s.o.; repeat from * to end.

Change to size 6 mm. (No. 4) needles. Break off Shetland, join in 'Wool Bouclé' in m. and on 52 sts. p.1 row, then work in pattern as follows: This is worked entirely in s.s. beginning with a k. row so only the colour details are given. Use separate small balls of contrast colour for each section of the pattern, so that colours not in use are not taken across the back of the work.

1st row: 4m., 1a., 9m., 18b., 19a., 1m.

2nd row: 2m., 17a., 18b., 8m., 2a., 5m.

The last 2 rows set the position of the pattern given in the chart. Work the 3rd to 68th rows from the chart as set.

To shape the armholes: Continuing in pattern from chart as set, cast off 3 sts. at the beginning of the next 2 rows, then dec. 1st. at each end of the next row and the 4 following alternate rows.

On 36 sts. pattern 15 rows.

Inc. 1 st. at each end of the next row and the following 4th row.

On 40 sts. work 5 rows.

To slope the shoulders: Cast off 6 sts. at the beginning of the next 4 rows. Cast off the remaining 16 sts.

THE POCKET BACKS (2 alike)
With size 6 mm. (No. 4) needles and m. cast on 12 sts. and beginning with a k. row s.s. 22 rows, then leave these sts. on a stitch-holder until required.

THE LEFT FRONT
With size 2¾ mm. (No. 12) needles and 'Woollybear Real Shetland' cast on 84 sts. and work 34 rows in single rib.

Using the size 4 mm. (No. 8) needle work the Decrease row: *sl.1, k.2 tog., p.s.s.o.; repeat from * to end. – 28 sts.

Change to size 6 mm. (No. 4) needles, break off Shetland, join in 'Wool Bouclé' in m. and p.1 row. Then work the pattern as follows noting the information given for back.

1st row: With m. k.1, with a. k.19, with b. k.4, with m. p.4 for front band.

2nd row: With m. p.4, with b. p.5, with a. p.17, with m. p.2.

The last 2 rows set the position of the pattern given at left hand side of chart, working knit rows from left to right and purl rows from right to left to reverse the pattern.

Continuing in pattern from chart as set and purling the 4 sts. at front edge with m. on every row for front band, work the 3rd to 26th rows.

Pocket row: Pattern as set across 8 sts., slip next 12 sts. onto a stitch-holder and leave at front of work, in their place pattern across the 12 sts. of one pocket back, work to end of row as set.

Now work the 28th to 68th rows from chart as set.

To shape the armhole: Cast off 3 sts. at the beginning of the next row, work 1 row back to armhole edge.

Dec. 1 st. at the beginning of the next row and the 4 following alternate rows.

On 20 sts. pattern 10 rows, ending at front edge.

**To shape the neck: Cast off 4 sts. of front band at the beginning of the next row. Pattern 6 rows decreasing 1 st. at the neck edge on each row and at the same time increasing 1 st. at the armhole edge on the 5th of these rows.

On 11 sts. pattern 2 rows.

Inc. 1 st. at the armhole edge on the next row.

On 12 sts. pattern 5 rows.

To slope the shoulder: Cast off 6 sts. at the beginning of the next row. On 6 sts. work 1 row, then cast off.

THE RIGHT FRONT
With size 2¾ mm. (No. 12) needles and 'Woollybear Real Shetland', cast on 84 sts. and work 6 rows in single rib.

1st Buttonhole row: Rib 6, cast off 5, rib to end.

2nd Buttonhole row: Rib until 6 remain, turn, cast on 5, turn, rib to end.

Rib 24 rows, then work the 2 buttonhole rows again.

Using the size 4 mm. (No. 8) needles work the Decrease row: *Sl.1, k.2 tog., p.s.s.o.; repeat from * to end. – 28 sts.

Change to size 6 mm. (No. 4) needles, break off Shetland, join in 'Wool Bouclé' in m. and p.1 row. Then work in pattern as follows:

1st row: With m. p.4 for front band, with b. k.10, with m. k.9, with a. k.1, with m. k.4.

2nd row: With m. p.5, with a. p.2, with m. p.8, with b. p.9, with m. p.4.

The last 2 rows set the position of the pattern given at right hand side of chart, reversing it as for left front and purling the 4 sts. at front edge

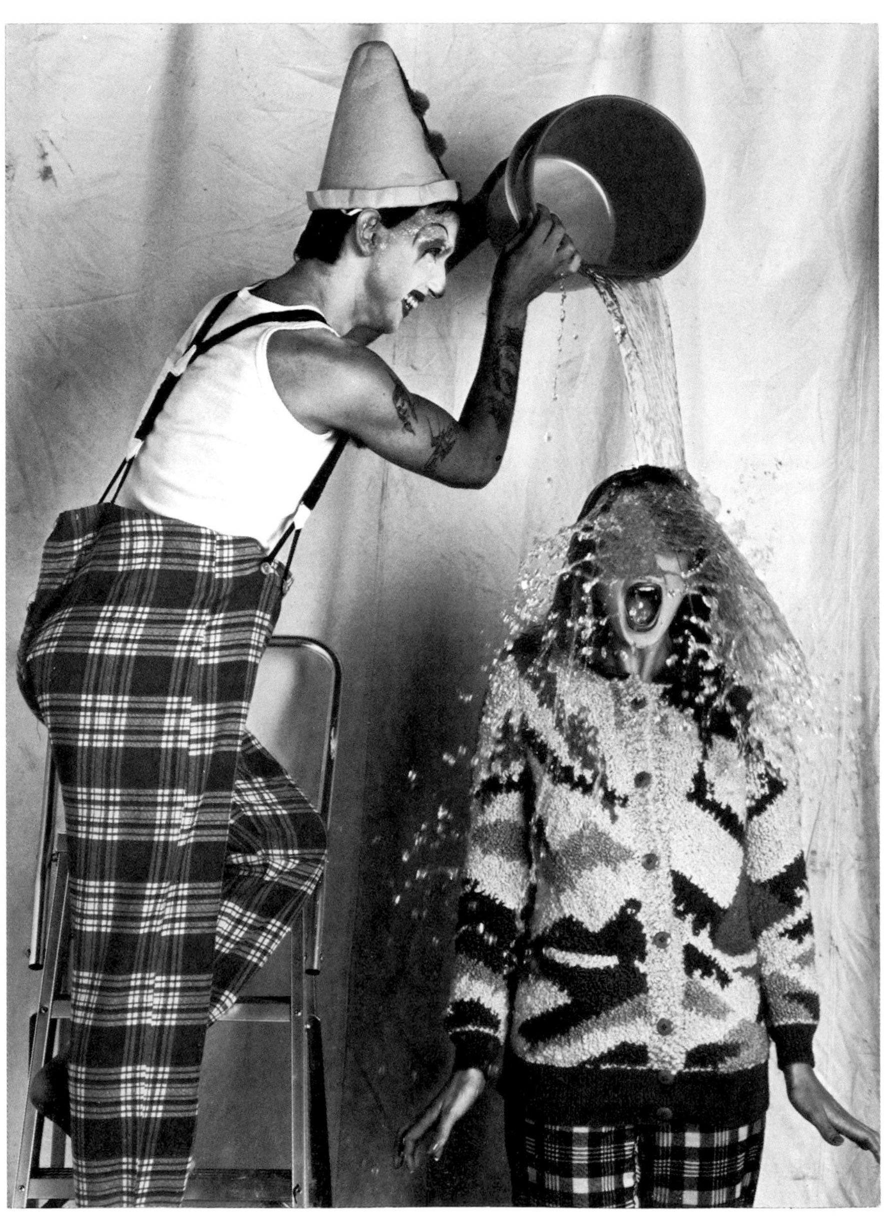

with m. for front band. Work the 3rd to 12th rows as set.

1st Buttonhole row: With m. p.2, cast off 1 p.wise, pattern to end from chart as set.

2nd Buttonhole row: Work as set until 2 remain, turn, cast on 1, turn, p. to end.

Pattern 12 rows as set, then work the pocket row given for left front.

Work the 28th to 69th rows from the chart as set, working buttonholes as before on the 31st and 32nd, 49th and 50th and the 67th and 68th of these rows.

Shape the armhole as given for left front, then on 20 sts. pattern 10 rows, working a buttonhole as before on the 5th and 6th of these rows.

Now work as given for left front from ** to end.

THE SLEEVES (both alike)
With size 2¾ mm. (No. 12) needles and 'Real Shetland' cast on 64 sts. and work 22 rows in single rib.

Using the size 4 mm. (No. 8) needle work this Decrease row: *Sl.1, k.1, p.s.s.o.; repeat from * to end. – 32 sts. Change to size 6 mm. (No. 4) needles.

Break off Shetland, join in 'Wool Bouclé' in m. and p.1 row. Then work in pattern as follows, noting the information given for back.

1st row (K row): 4m., 18b., 10a.

2nd row (P row): 9a., 18b., 5m.

The last 2 rows set the position of the pattern at the centre of the chart given for the back. Now work the 3rd to 68th rows from the chart as set.

To shape the sleevetop: Continuing in pattern from chart as set, cast off 3 sts. at the beginning of the next 2 rows, then dec. 1 st. at each end of the next row and the 6 following 4th rows.

On 12 sts. work 1 row.

Cast off 2 sts. at the beginning of the next 4 rows, then cast off the 4 remaining sts.

THE POCKET TOPS (2 alike)
With right side of work facing rejoin 'Wool Bouclé' in m. to the 12 sts. left on stitch-holder and using size 6 mm. (No. 4) needles k.2 rows, then cast off loosely.

THE COLLAR
With size 2¾ mm. (No. 12) needles and 'Real Shetland' cast on 186 sts. and work 4 rows in single rib.

Decrease row: Rib 4, sl.1, k.2 tog., p.s.s.o., rib until 7 remain, sl.1, k.2 tog., p.s.s.o., rib 4.

Rib 3 rows.

Repeat the last 4 rows 4 times more, then cast off the remaining 166 sts. in rib.

THE SHOULDER PADS (2 alike)
With size 6 mm. (No. 4) needles and 'Wool Bouclé' in m. cast on 13 sts. and work 20 rows in single rib, then cast off. Fold in half diagonally to form a triangle and join outer edges.

TO MAKE UP THE JACKET
Pin out to size and press all parts except the ribbing with a warm iron over a damp cloth. Join shoulder seams. Set in sleeves. Join sleeve and side seams. Neatly sew cast off edge of collar in place all round neck edge, beginning and ending half way across the front band. Sew pocket backs and row ends of pocket tops in place. Press seams. Catch shoulder pads in place. Sew on buttons.

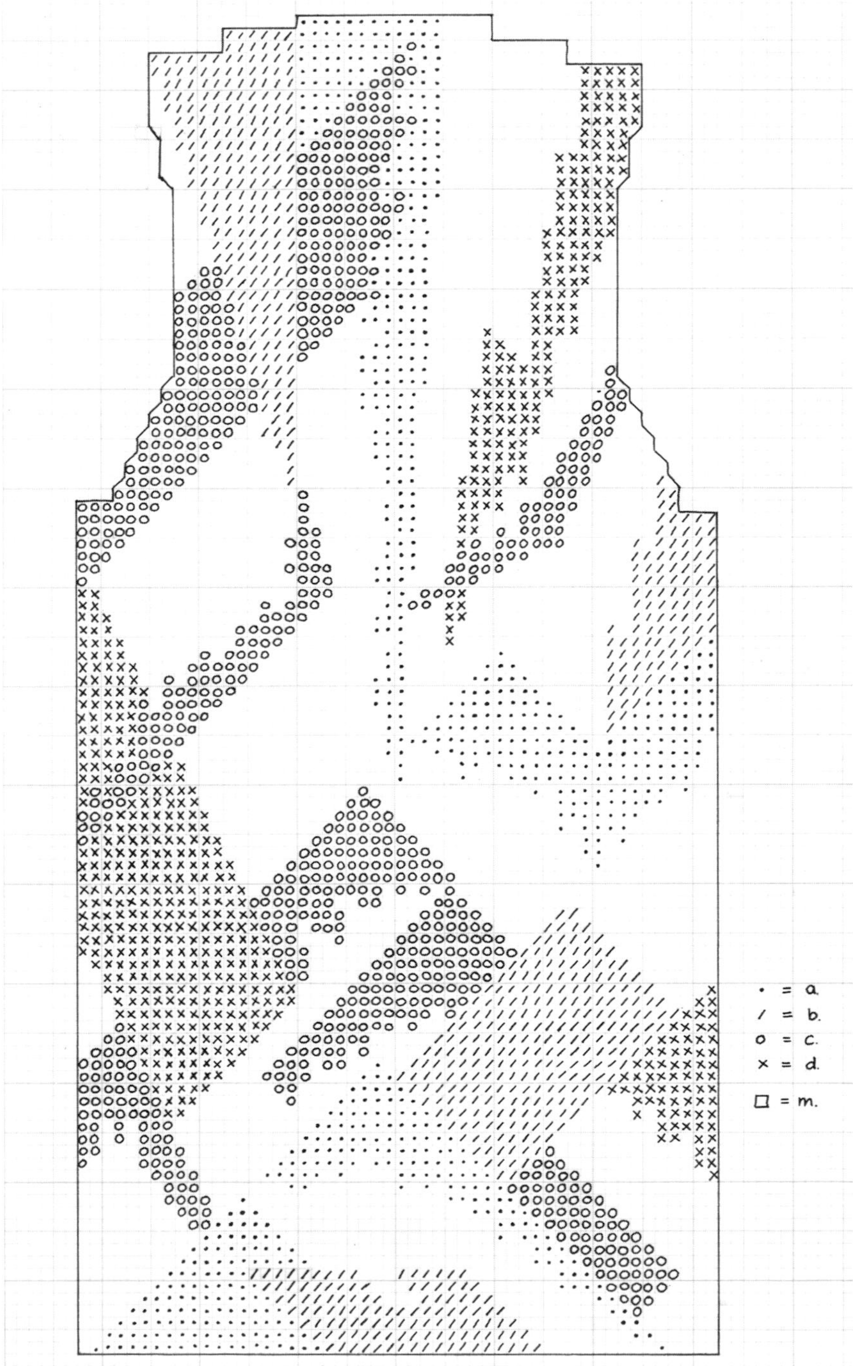

FACADE

MATERIALS
7 (8) ounces of 'Woollybear Real Shetland Wool' by Patricia Roberts in main colour, 2 ounces in each of the first and second contrast colours, and one ounce in each of the 3 other contrast colours.
For the woman's size only: a pair each of size 2¼ mm. (No. 13) and size 2¾ mm. (No. 12) Aero knitting needles.
For the man's size only: a pair each of size 3 mm. (No. 11) and size 3¼ mm. (No. 10) Aero knitting needles.

TENSION
For the woman's sweater work at a tension of 16 stitches and 20 rows to 5 centimetres (2 inches) over stocking stitch using size 2¾ mm. (No. 12) needles.
For the man's sweater work at a tension of 14 stitches and 18 rows to 5 centimetres (2 inches) over stocking stitch using size 3¼ mm. (No. 10) needles.
If you cannot obtain the correct tension using the size needles suggested, use larger or smaller ones accordingly.

ABBREVIATIONS
K., knit; p., purl; st., stitch; tog., together; dec., decrease (by working 2 sts. tog.); inc., increase (by working twice into same st.); single rib is k.1 and p.1 alternately; s.s., stocking stitch is k. on the right side and p. on the wrong side; m., main colour; a., first contrast colour; b., second contrast colour; c., third contrast; d., fourth contrast; e., fifth contrast.

MEASUREMENTS
The measurements are given in centimetres followed by inches in brackets.

Sizes	Women's	Men's
To fit bust/chest	82.5 (33–34)	92.5–95 (37–38)
Underarms	85 (34)	96 (38½)
Side seam	35 (14)	39 (15½)
Length	55 (22)	61 (24½)
Sleeve seam	42.5 (17)	47 (18¾)

SPECIAL NOTE
The different sizes in this sweater are obtained by using different sized needles and working at different tensions. Thus the larger needle sizes for the man's sweater are given in brackets after the smaller needles used for the woman's sweater.

THE BACK
With size 2¼ mm. (No. 13) (size 3 mm. (No. 11)) needles and m. cast on 136 sts. and work 26 rows in single rib.
Change to size 2¾ mm. (No. 12) (size 3¼ mm. (No. 10)) needles and work in pattern as follows. This is worked entirely in s.s., beginning with a k. row, so only the colour details are given. Use separate small balls of contrast colours for each section of the pattern, so that colours not in use will not be taken across the back of the work. **
1st row: 31m., 14b., 91m.
2nd row: 89m., 16b., 31m.
The last 2 rows set the position of the pattern given in the chart. Now work the 3rd to 116th rows from the chart as set.
To shape the armholes: Continuing in pattern as set, cast off 6 sts. at the beginning of the next 2 rows, then dec. 1 st. at each end of the next row and the 9 following alternate rows.
On 104 sts. pattern 29 rows.
Inc. 1 st. at each end of the next row and the 2 following 8th rows.
On 110 sts. pattern 7 rows.
To slope the shoulders: Cast off 10 sts. at the beginning of the next 4 rows, then 11 sts. on the 2 following rows.
Leave the remaining 48 sts. on a spare needle until required for neckband.

THE FRONT
Work as given for the back until ** is reached.
1st row: 91m., 14b., 31m.
2nd row: 31m., 16b., 89m.
The last 2 rows set the position of the pattern given in the chart, but reversing it so that the knit rows are worked from left to right and the purl rows from right to left. Now work the 3rd to 116th rows from the chart as set.
To shape the armholes: Continuing in pattern as set, cast off 6 sts. at the beginning of the next 2 rows, then dec. 1 st. at each end of the next row and the 9 following alternate rows.
On 104 sts. pattern 20 rows.
Now divide the sts. for the neck: Next row: Pattern 41 and leave these sts. on a spare needle until required for right front shoulder, cast off 22, pattern to end and continue on these 41 sts. for the left front shoulder.
The left front shoulder: To shape the neck: Dec. 1 st. at the neck edge on each of the next 8 rows – 33 sts.
Inc. 1 st. at the beginning and dec. 1 st. at the end of the next row.
Dec. 1 st. at the neck edge on each of the next 4 rows.
This completes the neck shaping. On 29 sts. work 3 rows.
Inc. 1 st. at the beginning of the next row and the following 8th row.
On 31 sts. pattern 7 rows.
To slope the shoulder: Cast off 10 sts. at the beginning of the next row and the following alternate row. On 11 sts. work 1 row, then cast off.
The right front shoulder: With right side of work facing rejoin yarn to inner edge of sts. left on spare needle and work to end of row, then work as given for left front shoulder to end.

THE SLEEVES (both alike)
With size 2¼ mm. (No. 13) (size 3 mm. (No. 11)) needles and m. cast on 64 sts. and work 28 rows in single rib.
Change to size 2¾ mm. (No. 12) (size 3¼ mm. (No. 10)) needles and work in pattern as follows. This is worked entirely in s.s. so only the colour details are given. Use a separate ball of m. at each side of the half circles, for neater and easier work.
1st row: 27m., 5a., 32m.
2nd row: 32m., 8a., 24m.
The last 2 rows set the position of the pattern given in the chart. Now work the 3rd to 12th rows from the chart as set.
Continuing in pattern as set, inc. 1 st. at each end of the next row and the 15 following 8th rows.
On 96 sts. pattern 11 rows.
To shape the sleeve top: Cast off 6 sts. at the beginning of the next 2 rows, then dec. 1 st. at each end of the next row and the 21 following alternate rows.
On 40 sts. work 1 row.
Cast off 3 sts. at the beginning of the next 10 rows. Cast off the remaining 10 sts.

THE NECKBAND
First join right shoulder seam. With right side of work facing rejoin m. at left front neck edge and using size 2¼ mm. (No. 13) (size 3 mm. (No. 11)) needles pick up and k.36 sts. from left front neck edge, 22 sts. from centre front neck edge and 36 sts. from right front neck edge, then k. across the 48 sts. at back neck edge.
On 142 sts. work 9 rows in single rib, then cast off in rib.

THE SHOULDER PADS (2 alike – optional)
With size 2¼ mm. (No. 13) needles and m. cast on 48 sts. and work 60 rows in single rib, then cast off in rib. Fold in half diagonally to form a triangle and join outer edges.

TO MAKE UP THE SWEATER
Pin out to size and press all parts except the ribbing on the wrong side with a warm iron over a damp cloth. Join left shoulder seam. Set in sleeves. Join sleeve and side seams. Neatly catch shoulder pads in place on wrong side if required. Press seams.

X = a
O = b
· = c
/ = d
■ = e
□ = m
116
108
100
92
84
76
68
60
52
44
36
28
20
12

GENTLEMEN PREFER BLONDES

MIDNIGHT LACE

GENTLEMEN PREFER BLONDES

MATERIALS
For the jacket: 25 (27) (28) 50 gram balls of 'Woollybear Wool Bouclé'; a pair each of size 6½ mm. (No. 3) and size 4½ mm. (No. 7) Aero knitting needles.

For the scarf: 2 50 gram balls of 'Woollybear Wool Bouclé' in each of 2 colours; a pair of size 6½ mm. (No. 3) Aero knitting needles.

TENSION
4 stitches and 7 rows to 5 centimetres (2 inches) over the moss stitch using size 6½ mm. (No. 3) needles. If you cannot obtain the correct tension using the size needles suggested use larger or smaller ones accordingly.

ABBREVIATIONS
K., knit; p., purl; st., stitch; tog., together; dec., decrease (by working 2 sts. tog.); inc., increase (by working twice into same st.); single rib is k.1 and p.1 alternately; sl., slip; p.s.s.o., pass sl. st. over; m., main colour; c., contrast colour.

NOTE
The instructions are given for the small size. Where they vary work the figures in the first brackets for the medium size or the figures in the second brackets for the large size.

MEASUREMENTS
The measurements are given in centimetres followed by inches in brackets.

THE JACKET

Size	Small	Medium	Large
To fit bust	85 (34)	90 (36)	95 (38)
Underarms	120 (48)	127.5 (51)	135 (54)
Side seam	36 (14½)	36 (14½)	36 (14½)
Length	61 (24½)	62.5 (25)	64 (25½)
Sleeve seam	40 (16)	40 (16)	40 (16)

THE SCARF
12.5 centimetres (5 inches) in width and 110 centimetres (44 inches) in length.

THE JACKET

THE BACK
With size 6½ mm. (No. 3) needles cast on 50 (52) (54) sts. and work in moss st. as follows:

1st row: * K.1, p.1; repeat from * to end.

2nd row: * P.1, k.1; repeat from * to end.

The last 2 rows form the moss st. pattern; repeat them 24 times more.

To shape the armholes: Continuing in moss st. as set, cast off 2 sts. at the beginning of the next 2 rows, then dec. 1 st. at each end of the next row and the 2 following alternate rows.

On 40 (42) (44) sts. moss st. 11 (13) (15) rows

Change to size 4½ mm. (No.7) needles and work 20 rows in single rib.

To slope the shoulders: Cast off 12 (13) (14) sts. at the beginning of the next 2 rows.

Cast off the remaining 16 sts.

THE POCKET BACKS (2 alike)
With size 6½ mm. (No. 3) needles cast on 10 sts. and work 19 rows in moss st. as given for back, then leave these sts. on a stitch-holder until required.

THE LEFT FRONT
With size 6½ mm. (No. 3) needles cast on 32 (34) (36) sts. and work 28 rows in moss st. as given for back.

1st Pocket row: Moss st. 8 (10) (12), cast off 10, moss st. to end.

2nd Pocket row: Moss st. 14, moss st. across the 10 sts. of one pocket back left on stitch-holder in place of those sts. cast off, moss st. to end.

Moss st. 20 rows.

MIDNIGHT LACE

MATERIALS
For the sweater: 10 (10) (11) 25 gram balls of either 'Woollybear 100% Mohair' or 'Woollybear Brushed Alpaca' in main colour and one ball of the same yarn in contrast colour; a pair each of size 6 mm. (No. 4), size 5½ mm. (No. 5), size 5 mm. (No, 6) and size 4 mm. (No. 8) Aero knitting needles; sequins.

For the bolero: 7 (8) (8) 25 gram balls of either 'Woollybear 100% Mohair' or 'Woollybear Brushed Alpaca' in main colour and one ball in contrast colour; a pair each of size 4 mm. (No. 8) and size 3¾ mm. (No. 9) Aero knitting needles; sequins.

TENSION
12 stitches – 2 repeats of the lace pattern to 9 centimetres (3½ inches) in width and 16 rows – 2 repeats of the pattern to 7.5 centimetres (3 inches) in depth over the lace pattern using size 6 mm. (No. 4) needles. 10 stitches and 13 rows to 5 centimetres (2 inches) over the stocking stitch using size 4 mm. (No. 8) needles.

ABBREVIATIONS
K., knit; p., purl; st., stitch; tog., together; dec., decrease (by working 2 sts. tog.); inc., increase (by working twice into same st.); s.s., stocking stitch (k. on the right side and p. on the wrong side); single rib is k.1 and p.1 alternately; y.r.n., yarn round needle; sl., slip; p.s.s.o., pass sl. st. over; s.s.k., sl.1, k.1, p.s.s.o.; m., main colour; c., contrast colour; garter st. is k. plain on every row.

NOTE
The instructions are given for the small size. Where they vary work the figures in the first brackets for the medium size or the figures in the second brackets for the large size.

MEASUREMENTS
The measurements are given in centimetres followed by inches in brackets.

THE SWEATER

Size	Small	Medium	Large
To fit bust	80 (32)	87.5 (35)	95 (38)
Underarms	80 (32)	87.5 (35)	95 (38)
Side seam	37.5 (15)	37.5 (15)	37.5 (15)
Length	56 (22½)	57.5 (23)	59 (23½)
Sleeve seam	41 (16½)	41 (16½)	41 (16½)

THE BOLERO

Size	Small	Medium	Large
Underarms excluding edging	80 (32)	87.5 (35)	95 (38)
Side seam excluding edging	10 (4)	10 (4)	10 (4)
Length excluding edging	30 (12)	31 (12½)	32 (13)
Sleeve seam excluding edging	10 (4)	10 (4)	10 (4)

THE SWEATER

THE BACK
With size 5 mm. (No. 6) needles and m. cast on 55 (61) (67) sts. and work 10 rows in single rib.

Change to size 6 mm. (No. 4) needles and work in pattern as follows: 1st row: K.1,* y.r.n., s.s.k., k.1, k. 2 tog., y.r.n., k.1 repeat from * to end.

2nd row and every wrong side row: All p.

3rd row: K.1, * y.r.n., k.1, sl.1, k. 2 tog., p.s.s.o., k.1, y.r.n., k.1 repeat from * to end.

5th row: K.1, * k. 2 tog., y.r.n., k.1, y.r.n., s.s.k., k.1 repeat from * to end.

7th row: K.2 tog., * k.1, y.r.n., k.1, y.r.n., k.1, sl.1, k. 2 tog., p.s.s.o. repeat from * ending last repeat s.s.k. instead of sl.1, k. 2 tog., p.s.s.o.

8th row: As 2nd row.

The last 8 rows form the pattern; repeat them twice more.

Change to size 5½ mm. (No. 5) needles and repeat the pattern twice more.

Change to size 6 mm. (No. 4) needles and repeat the 8 pattern rows 4 times more.

To shape the armholes: Maintaining the continuity of the pattern as set cast off 2 sts. at the beginning of the next 2 rows, then dec. 1 st. at each end of the next row and the 2 (3) (4) following alternate rows.**

On 45 (49) (53) sts., pattern 28 rows.

Now divide the sts. for the neck: Next row: P.15 (17) (19) and leave these sts. on a spare needle until required for the left back shoulder, p.15 and leave these sts. on a stitch-holder until required for the back neckband, p. to end and continue on these 15 (17) (19) sts. for the right back shoulder.

The right back shoulder: To slope the shoulder and to shape the neck: Cast off 4 (5) (6) sts. at the beginning of the next row for the shoulder, then 6 (7) (8) sts. at the beginning of the next row for the neck. Cast off the remaining 5 sts. for the shoulder.

The left back shoulder: With right side of work facing rejoin yarn to inner edge of the 15 (17) (19) sts. left on spare needle and work to end of row, then work as given for right back shoulder to end.

THE FRONT
Work as given for back until ** is reached.

On 45 (49) (53) sts. pattern 6 rows.

Now divide the sts. for the neck: Next row: P.15 (17) (19) and leave these sts. on a spare needle until required for right front shoulder, p.15 and leave these sts. on a stitch-holder until required for neck, p. to end and continue on these 15 (17) (19) sts. for the left front shoulder.

The left front shoulder: To shape the neck: Dec. 1 st. at the neck edge on the next row and the 5 (6) (7) following alternate rows.

On 9 (10) (11) sts., pattern 11 (9) (7) rows.

To slope the shoulder: Cast off 4 (5) (6) sts. at the beginning of the next row. On 5 sts., work 1 row, then cast off.

The right front shoulder: With right side of work facing rejoin yarn to inner edge of sts. left on spare needle and work to end of row, then work as given for left front shoulder to end.

THE SLEEVES (both alike)
With size 5 mm. (No. 6) needles and m. cast on 25 sts. and work 10 rows in single rib.

Change to size 6 mm. (No. 4) needles and work 8 rows in pattern as given for back.

Continuing in pattern as set and working the extra sts. into the pattern as they occur inc. 1 st. at each end of the next row and the 5 (6) (7) following 12th (10th) (8th) rows.

On 37 (39) (41) sts., pattern 11 (11) (15) rows.

To shape the sleevetop: Cast off 2 sts. at the beginning of the next 2 rows, then dec. 1 st. at each end of the next row and the 3 (4) (5) following 4th rows.

On 25 sts., work 3 (1) (1) row(s).

Dec. 1 st. at each end of the next 2 rows.

Cast off 4 sts. at the beginning of the next 4 rows. Cast off the remaining 5 sts.

To shape the armhole: Cast off 2 sts. at the beginning of the next row, work 1 row back to armhole edge. Dec. 1 st. at the beginning of the next row and the 2 (3) (4) following alternate rows.

Moss st. 2 rows.

To slope the front edge: Decrease row: Moss st. 9, sl.1, k. 2 tog., p.s.s.o., moss st. to end.

Moss st. 7 rows.

Now divide the sts. for the shoulder and the collar: Next row: Moss st. 9 and leave these sts. on a stitch-holder until required for collar, sl.1, k. 2 tog., p.s.s.o. for front slope, moss st. to end – 14 (15) (16) sts.

Change to size 4½ mm. (No. 7) needles and work 20 rows in single rib, decreasing 1 st. at front edge on the 7th and 13th of these rows.

Cast off these 12 (13) (14) sts.

To complete the collar: Rejoin yarn to inner edge of the 9 sts. left on stitch-holder and using size 6½ mm. (No. 3) needles work 25 rows in moss st., then cast off.

THE RIGHT FRONT
Work as given for left front as the fabric is reversible.

THE SLEEVES (both alike)
The first part: With size 6½ mm. (No. 3) needles cast on 12 (14) (16) sts. and work 10 rows in moss st. as given for back, then leave these sts. on a stitch-holder until required.

The second part: With size 6½ mm. (No. 3) needles cast on 8 sts. and work 10 rows in moss st.

Now join the 2 parts together as follows: Next row: Moss st. across 8 sts. of second part, then onto same needle moss st. across the 12 (14) (16) sts. of first part.

On 20 (22) (24) sts., moss st. 5 rows.

Continuing in moss st. as set and working the extra sts. into the pattern as they occur, inc. 1 st. at each end of the next row and the 3 following 10th rows.

On 28 (30) (32) sts., moss st. 9 rows.

To shape the sleevetop: Cast off 2 sts. at the beginning of the next 2 rows.

On 24 (26) (28) sts. pattern 26 (28) (30) rows, then cast off.

TO MAKE UP THE JACKET
Pin out to size and press all parts except the ribbing on the wrong side with a warm iron over a damp cloth. Join shoulder seams. Join cast off edges of left and right half collar. Then sew collar in place all round neck edge. Neatly sew pocket backs in place. Join side seams. Join sleeve seams. Fold the corners at top of sleevetop to centre of cast off edge of sleeve and catch in position. Set in sleeves. Press seams. Make one buttonhole loop on each cuff opening. Sew on buttons.

THE SCARF
With size 6½ mm. (No. 3) needles and m. cast on 10 sts. and working in moss st. as given for back work in stripes of 8 rows m., 8 rows c.

The last 16 rows form the stripe pattern; repeat them 8 times more, then work the first 8 rows again. Cast off.

THE FRINGING
To make one tassel: Cut 3 lengths of m. each 6 inches long. Fold these in half together. Using a crochet hook draw the 3 looped ends through one corner of cast on edge. Pass cut ends through looped ends. Pull firmly to form tassel. Now make another 5 tassels in the same way evenly spaced along cast on edge. Then make 6 tassels in the same way along cast off edge. Press scarf as for jacket.

THE SHOULDER PADS (both alike)
With size 4 mm. (No. 8) needles and m. cast on 33 sts. and k. 2 rows, continuing in garter st. dec. 1 st at each end of the next row and the 14 following alternate rows – 3 sts.

K.3, then take these 3 sts. tog. and fasten off.

THE NECKBAND
First join right shoulder seam, with right side of work facing rejoin m. and using size 5 mm. (No. 6) needles pick up and k.19 (20) (21) sts. from left front neck edge, k. across the 15 sts. at centre front neck edge, pick up and k. 19 (20) (21) sts. from right front neck edge and 7 (8) (9) sts. from right back neck edge, k. across the 15 sts. at centre back neck, then pick up and k. 7 (8) (9) sts. from left back neck edge.

On 82 (86) (90) sts., work 5 rows in single rib. Cast off in rib.

THE BELT
With size 4 mm. (No. 8) needles and c. cast on 12 sts. and work in s.s. until the belt measures 140 centimetres (56 inches) from beginning, then cast off.

TO MAKE UP THE SWEATER
Pin out to size and press all parts except the ribbing on the wrong side with a warm iron over a damp cloth. Join left shoulder seam, continuing seam across neckband. Set in sleeves. Join sleeve and side seam. Neatly catch shoulder pads in position. Sew sequins all over right side of belt. Press seams.

THE BOLERO
THE POCKET BACK
With size 4 mm. (No. 8) needles and m. cast on 15 sts. and beginning with a k. row s.s. 20 rows, then leave these sts. on a stitch-holder until required.

THE MAIN PART
With size 4 mm. (No. 8) needles and m. cast on 160 (175) (190) sts. and beginning with a k. row s.s. 25 rows.

Now divide the sts. for the armholes. Next row: P.32 (36) (40) and leave these sts. on a spare needle until required for left half front, cast off 6 sts. for armhole, p. next 83 (90) (97) sts. and leave these 84 (91) (98) sts. on a spare needle until required for half back, cast off 6 sts. for armhole, p. to end and continue on these 32 (36) (40) sts. for the right half front.

The right half front: To shape the armhole: Dec. 1 st. at the end – armhole edge – on the next row and the 6 (8) (10) following alternate rows.

On 25 (27) (29) sts., s.s. 7 rows.

** To slope the front edge: Dec. 1 st. at the beginning – front edge on the next row and the 2 (3) (4) following 8th (8th) (6th) rows.

On 22 (23) (24) sts., s.s. 9 (1) (1) row(s).

To slope the shoulder: Cast off 7 sts. at the beginning of the next row and the following alternate row. On 8 (9) (10) sts., work 1 row, then cast off.

The half back: With right side of work facing rejoin m. to the 84 (91) (98) sts. left on spare needle for half back and work as follows: To shape the armholes: Dec. 1 st. at each end of the next row and the 6 (8) (10) following alternate rows.

On 70 (73) (76) sts. s.s. 33 rows.

To slope the shoulders: Cast off 7 sts. at the beginning of the next 4 rows, then 8 (9) (10) sts. on the 2 following rows.

Cast off the remaining 26 (27) (28) sts.

The left half front: With right side of work facing rejoin m. to inner edge of sts. left on spare needle for left half front and work as follows: To shape the armhole: Dec. 1 st. at the beginning – armhole edge – on the next row and the 6 (8) (10) following alternate rows.

On 25 (27) (29) sts. work 1 row.

Pocket row: K.5 (6) (7), slip next 15 sts. onto a stitch-holder and leave at front of work, in their place k. across the 15 sts. of pocket back, k. to end of row.

On 25 (27) (29) sts., s.s. 6 rows.

Now work as given for right half front from ** to end.

THE POCKET TOP
With right side of work facing rejoin m. to the 15 sts. left on stitch-holder and using size 3¾ mm. (No. 9) needles work 4 rows in single rib, then cast off in rib.

THE SLEEVES (both alike)
With size 4 mm. (No. 8) needles and m. cast on 52 (55) (58) sts. and beginning with a k. row s.s. 4 rows.

Inc. 1 st. at each end of the next row and the 4 following 4th rows.

On 62 (65) (68) sts. s.s. 5 rows.

To shape the sleevetop: Cast off 3 sts. at the beginning of the next 2 rows, then dec. 1 st. at each end of the next row and the 8 (9) (10) following 4th rows.

On 38 (39) (40) sts. s.s. 3 (1) (1) row(s).

Next row: K.2 (nil) (1), * sl.1, k. 2 tog., p.s.s.o.; repeat from * to end.

Cast off the remaining 14 (13) (14) sts.

THE SLEEVE EDGINGS (both alike)
With size 3¾ mm. (No. 9) needles and m. cast on 5 sts. and work in single rib until the edging is long enough to fit along cast on edge of sleeve; cast off.

THE MAIN EDGING
First join shoulder seams. With size 3¾ mm. (No. 9) needles and m. cast on 5 sts. and work in single rib until the edging is long enough to fit from right shoulder across back neck edge, down left front, along cast on edge, up right front edge. Neatly sew in place, casting off when correct length is assured. Join cast on and cast off edges of edging.

THE HANKIE (2 pieces both alike)
With size 4 mm. (No. 8) needles and c. cast on 15 sts. and beginning with a k. row s.s. 4 rows.

Continuing in s.s. dec. 1 st. at each end of the next row and the 5 following alternate rows – 3 sts., p.3, then take these 3 sts. tog. and fasten off.

TO MAKE UP THE BOLERO
Pin out to size and press all parts except the ribbing on the wrong side with a warm iron over a damp cloth. Sew sleeve edging along cast on edge of sleeves. Join sleeve seams. Set in sleeves. Sew sequins all over right side of the hankie pieces. Sew pocket back in place. Sew row ends of pocket top in place. Neatly sew hankie pieces in place as in picture. Press seams.

CHERRY LIPS

= a
= b.
= c
= d
= e
= m
= with f. p.3tog.
= withf. s.s. 3.
= with f. 3from1.
= with d. m.b.
= with a. m.b.

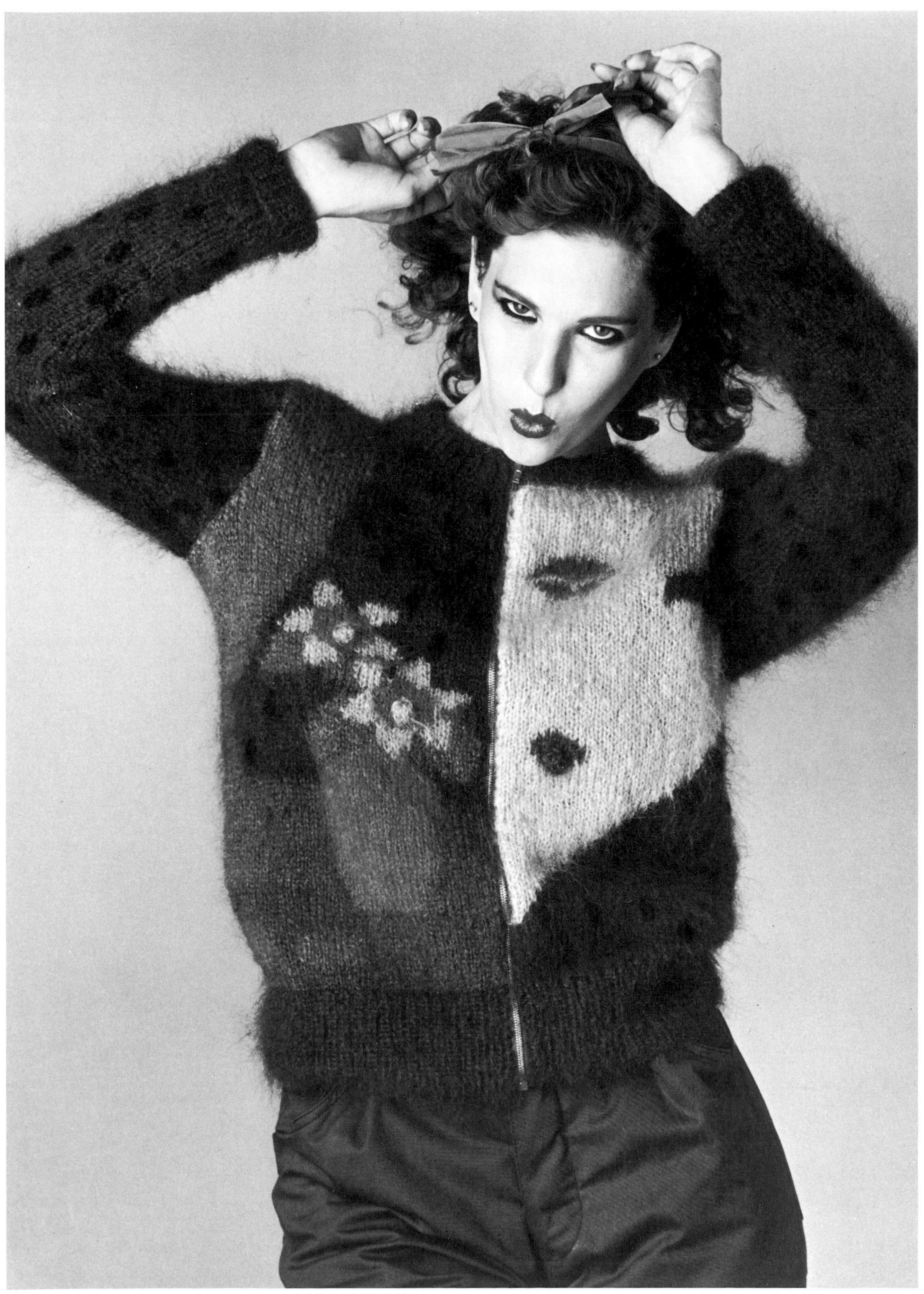

CHERRY LIPS and APRIL

MATERIALS
For the cardigan: 10 25 gram balls of 'Woollybear 100% Mohair' by Patricia Roberts in main colour – m., 3 balls of the same yarn in f., 2 balls in each of b., and e.; and 1 ball in each of a., c. and d.; a 50 centimetre (20 inch) open ended zip fastener.

For the sweater; 8 balls of the same yarn in main colour – m., 3 balls in f., 2 balls in each of a. and b. and 1 ball in each of c., d. and e.

For both the cardigan and the sweater: a pair each of size 4 mm. (No. 8) and size 3¾ mm. (No. 9) Aero knitting needles.

SPECIAL NOTE
These garments may also be knitted in 'Woollybear Cotton Bouclé' by Patricia Roberts. Using this yarn the amounts required are as follows: for the cardigan 8 50 gram balls in main colour – m., 2 balls in b., e. and f. and 1 ball in each of a., c. and d.; for the sweater 7 balls in m., 2 balls in a., b. and f. and 1 ball in c., d. and e.

TENSION
10 stitches and 14 rows to 5 centimetres (2 inches) over the stocking stitch using size 4 mm. (No. 8) needles. If you cannot obtain the correct tension using the size needles suggested, use larger or smaller ones accordingly.

ABBREVIATIONS
K., knit; p., purl; st., stitch; tog., together; dec., decrease (by working 2 sts. tog.); inc., increase (by working twice into same st.); single rib is k.1 and p.1 alternately; s.s., stocking stitch is k. on the right side and p. on the wrong side; 3 from 1, k.1, p.1, k.1 all into next st; m., main colour; a., first contrast; b., second contrast; c., third contrast; d., fourth contrast; e., fifth contrast; f., sixth contrast; m.b., make bobble thus, k.1, p.1, k.1, p.1, k.1, all into next st., turn, p.5, turn, k.5, turn, p.2 tog., p.1, p.2 tog., turn, sl.1, k.2 tog., p.s.s.o.; sl., slip; p.s.s.o., pass sl. st. over; up 1, pick up the loop which lies between the needles, slip it onto left hand needle, then k. into back of it.

NOTE
The instructions are given in one size only.

MEASUREMENTS
The measurements are given in centimetres followed by inches in brackets.

To fit bust	85 (34)
Underarms	87.5 (35)
Side seams	37.5 (15)
Length	58 (23¼)
Sleeve seam	42.5 (17)

THE CARDIGAN
THE BACK
With size 3¾ mm. (No. 9) needles and m. cast on 88 sts. and work 24 rows in single rib.

Change to size 4 mm. (No. 8) needles and work in pattern as follows. This is worked entirely in s.s. except for the raindrops and the bobbles, so only the colour details are given. Use separate small balls of colour for each section of the pattern for both ease and neatness of work.

1st row (right side): With a. k.44 with m. k.44.

2nd row: With m. p.44, with a. p.44.

3rd to 4th rows: As 1st and 2nd rows.

5th row: 4a., 5c., 7a., 5b., 23a., 8m., * with f. 3 from 1, 7m.; repeat from * ending last repeat 3m.

6th row: 3m., * 3f., 7m.; repeat from * 3 times more, 3f., 8m., 22a., 7b., 5a., 7c., 3a.

7th row: 2a., 9c., 3a., 9b., 21a., 8m., * 3f., 7m.; repeat from * ending last repeat 3m.

8th row: 3m., * with f. p.3 tog., 7m.; repeat from * 3 times more, with f. p.3 tog., 8m., 21a., 9b., 3a., 9c., 2a.

The last 8 rows set the position of the pattern; now work the 9th to 84th rows from the chart as set.

To shape the armholes: Continuing in pattern from chart as set, cast off 4 sts. at the beginning of the next 2 rows, then dec. 1 st. at each end of the next row and the 3 following alternate rows.

On 72 sts. pattern 29 rows from chart.

Inc. 1 st. at each end of the next row and the following 8th row.

On 76 sts. pattern 7 rows.

To slope the shoulders: Cast off 11 sts. at the beginning of the next 2 rows then 12 sts. on the 2 following rows. – 30 sts.

Change to size 3¾ mm. (No. 9) needles and with m. only work 8 rows in single rib, then cast off loosely in rib.

THE LEFT FRONT
With size 3¾ mm. (No. 9) needles and m. cast on 44 sts. and work 24 rows in single rib.

Change to size 4 mm. (No. 8) needles and work in pattern as follows, noting the information for the back. **

1st to 4th rows: All m.

5th row: 3m., * with f. 3 from 1, 7m.; repeat from * ending last repeat 8m.

6th row: 8m., * 3f., 7m.; repeat from * ending last repeat 3m.

The last 6 rows set the position of the pattern given on the left hand side of the chart, but reversing it, so that the knit rows are worked from left to right and the purl rows from right to left. Now work the 7th to 84th rows from the chart as set.

To shape the armhole: Continuing in pattern from chart as set, cast off 4 sts. at the beginning of the next row. Work 1 row back to armhole edge, then dec. 1 st. at the armhole on the next row and the 3 following alternate rows.

On 36 sts. pattern 20 rows.

*** To shape the neck: Cast off 9 sts. at the beginning of the next row, then dec. 1 st. at the neck edge on each of the next 6 rows.

On 21 sts. work 2 rows.

To shape the armhole: Inc. at the beginning of the next row and the following 8th row.

On 23 sts. pattern 7 rows.

To slope the shoulder: Cast off 11 sts. at the beginning of the next row. On 12 sts. work 1 row, then cast off.

THE RIGHT FRONT
Work as given for left front until ** is reached.

1st to 4th rows: All a.

5th row: 23a., 5b., 7a., 5c., 4a.

6th row: 3a., 7c., 5a., 7b., 22a.

The last 6 rows set the position of the pattern given on the right hand side of the chart, but reversing it so that the knit rows are worked from left to right and the purl rows are worked from right to left. Now work the 7th to 85th rows from the chart as set.

To shape the armhole: Cast off 4 sts. at the beginning of the next row, then dec. 1 st. at the armhole edge on the next row and the 3 following alternate rows.

On 36 sts. pattern 21 rows.

Now work as given for left front from *** to end.

THE LEFT AND RIGHT FRONT NECKBANDS (both alike)
With right side of work facing rejoin m. and using size 3¾ mm. (No. 9) needles pick up and k.30 sts. from all round neck edge. Work 7 rows in single rib, then cast off in rib.

THE SLEEVES (both alike)
With size 3¾ mm. (No. 9) needles and m. cast on 41 sts. and work 22 rows in single rib.

Change to size 4 mm. (No. 8) needles and beginning with a k. row s.s. 4 rows.

Now work in pattern as follows. Use a separate short length of f. for each raindrop. This pattern is worked entirely in s.s. except for the raindrops so only the colour details are given.

1st row: 4m., * with f. 3 from 1, 7m.; repeat from * ending last repeat 4m.

2nd row: 4m., * 3f., 7m.; repeat from * ending last repeat 4m.

3rd row: As 2nd row.

4th row: 4m., * with f. p.3 tog., 7m.; repeat from * ending last repeat 4m.

5th to 8th rows: All m.

9th row: 8m., * with f. 3 from 1, 7m.; repeat from * ending last repeat 8m.

10th row: 8m., * 3f., 7m.; repeat from *

ending last repeat 8m.
11th row: As 10th row.
12th row: 8m., * with f. p.3 tog., 7m.; repeat from * ending last repeat 8m.
13th to 16th rows: All m.
The last 16 rows form the pattern. Continuing in pattern as set and working the extra sts. into the pattern as they occur, inc. 1 st. at each end of the next row and the 9 following 8th rows.
On 61 sts. pattern 7 rows.
** To shape the sleevetop: Maintaining the continuity of the pattern as set, cast off 4 sts. at the beginning of the next 2 rows. Dec. 1 st. at each end of the next row and the 13 following alternate rows.
On 25 sts. work 1 row.
Cast off 3 sts. at the beginning of the next 4 rows and 4 sts. on the 2 following rows.
Cast off the remaining 5 sts.

THE SHOULDER PADS (2 alike)
With size 3¾ mm. (No. 9) needles and m. cast on 36 sts. and work 44 rows in single rib, then cast off in rib. Fold in half diagonally, and join edges to form a triangle.

TO MAKE UP THE JACKET
Pin out to size and press all parts except the ribbing on the wrong side with a warm iron over a damp cloth. Join shoulder seams. Set in sleeves. Join sleeve and side seams. Catch shoulder pads in place, on wrong side. Neatly sew zip fastener in position. Press seams.

THE SWEATER
THE BACK
With size 3¾ mm. (No. 9) needles and m. cast on 81 sts. and work 23 rows in single rib.
Increase row: Rib 6, * up 1, rib 10; repeat from * ending last repeat rib 5 – 89 sts.
Change to size 4 mm. (No. 8) needles. Join in a. and beginning with a k. row s.s. 4 rows. Now work in pattern as follows. This is worked entirely in s.s. except for the bobbles and raindrops so only the colour details are given. Use separate small balls of colour for each section of the pattern for both ease and neatness of work. **
5th row: 4a., 5c., 7a., 5b., with a. work to end.
6th row: 67a., 7b., 5a., 7c., 3a.
The last 2 rows set the position of the pattern given in the chart. Now work the 7th to 84th rows from the chart as set.
To shape the armholes: Continuing in pattern from the chart as set, cast off 4 sts. at the beginning of the next 2 rows, then dec. 1 st. at each end of the next row and the 3 following alternate rows.
On 73 sts. pattern 29 rows from the chart.
Inc. 1 st. at each end of the next row and the following 8th rows.
On 77 sts. work 7 rows.
To slope the shoulders: Cast off 11 sts. at the beginning of the next 2 rows, then 12 sts. on the 2 following rows.
Leave the remaining 31 sts. on a spare needle until required for neckband.

THE FRONT
Work as given for the back until ** is reached.
5th row: 68a., 5b., 7a., 5c., 4a.
6th row: 3a., 7c., 5a., 7b., 67a.
The last 6 rows set the position of the pattern given in the chart, but reversing it so that the knit rows are worked from left to right and the purl rows from right to left. Now work the 7th to 84th rows from the chart as set.
To shape the armholes: Continuing in pattern from chart as set, cast off 4 sts. at the beginning of the next 2 rows, then dec. 1 st. at each end of the next row and the 3 following alternate rows.
On 73 sts. pattern 20 rows.
Now divide the sts. for the neck. Next row: Pattern 29 and leave these sts. on a spare needle until required for right front shoulder, cast off 15, work to end and continue on these 29 sts. for the left front shoulder.
The left front shoulder: To shape the neck. Dec. 1 st. at the neck edge on each of the next 8 rows.
Inc. 1 st. at the beginning – armhole edge on the next row and the following 8th row.
On 23 sts. pattern 7 rows.
To slope the shoulder: Cast off 11 sts. at the beginning of the next row. On 12 sts. work 1 row, then cast off.
The right front shoulder: With right side of work facing rejoin yarn to inner edge of sts. left on spare needle and work to end of row, then work as given for left front shoulder to end.

THE NECKBAND
First join right shoulder seam. With right side of work facing rejoin m. at left front neck edge and using size 3¾ mm. (No. 9) needles pick up and k.24 sts. from left front neck edge, 15 sts. from centre front neck; and 24 sts. from right front neck edge, then k. across the 31 sts. left on spare needle at back.
On 94 sts. work 5 rows in single rib, then cast off loosely in rib.

THE LEFT SLEEVE
Work as given for sleeves of cardigan until ** is reached.
To shape the sleevetop: Maintaining the continuity of the pattern as set, cast off 4 sts. at the beginning of the next 2 rows.
Dec. 1 st. at each end of the next row; work 1 row straight.
Continuing in pattern as set, but using e. instead of m. work 8 rows, decreasing 1 st. at each end of the 3rd and 7th rows.
Now using b. instead of m. and continuing in pattern as set, work 10 rows decreasing 1 st. at each end of the 3rd, 7th and 9th rows.
Continuing in pattern as set, with m. as before, dec. 1 st. at each end of the next row and the 2 following alternate rows, then at each end of the next 7 rows.
Cast off 3 sts. at the beginning of the next 2 rows, then 4 sts. on the 2 following rows.
Cast off the remaining 7 sts.

THE RIGHT SLEEVE
Work as given for left sleeve, but using m. and f. only throughout.

THE SHOULDER PADS (2 alike)
With size 3¾ mm. (No. 9) needles and m. cast on 36 sts. and work 44 rows in single rib, then cast off in rib. Fold in half diagonally and join edges to form a triangle.

TO MAKE UP THE SWEATER
Pin out to size and press all parts on the wrong side with a warm iron over a damp cloth. Join left shoulder seam. Set in sleeves. Join sleeve and side seams. Press seams. Catch shoulder pads in place.

APRIL SHOWER

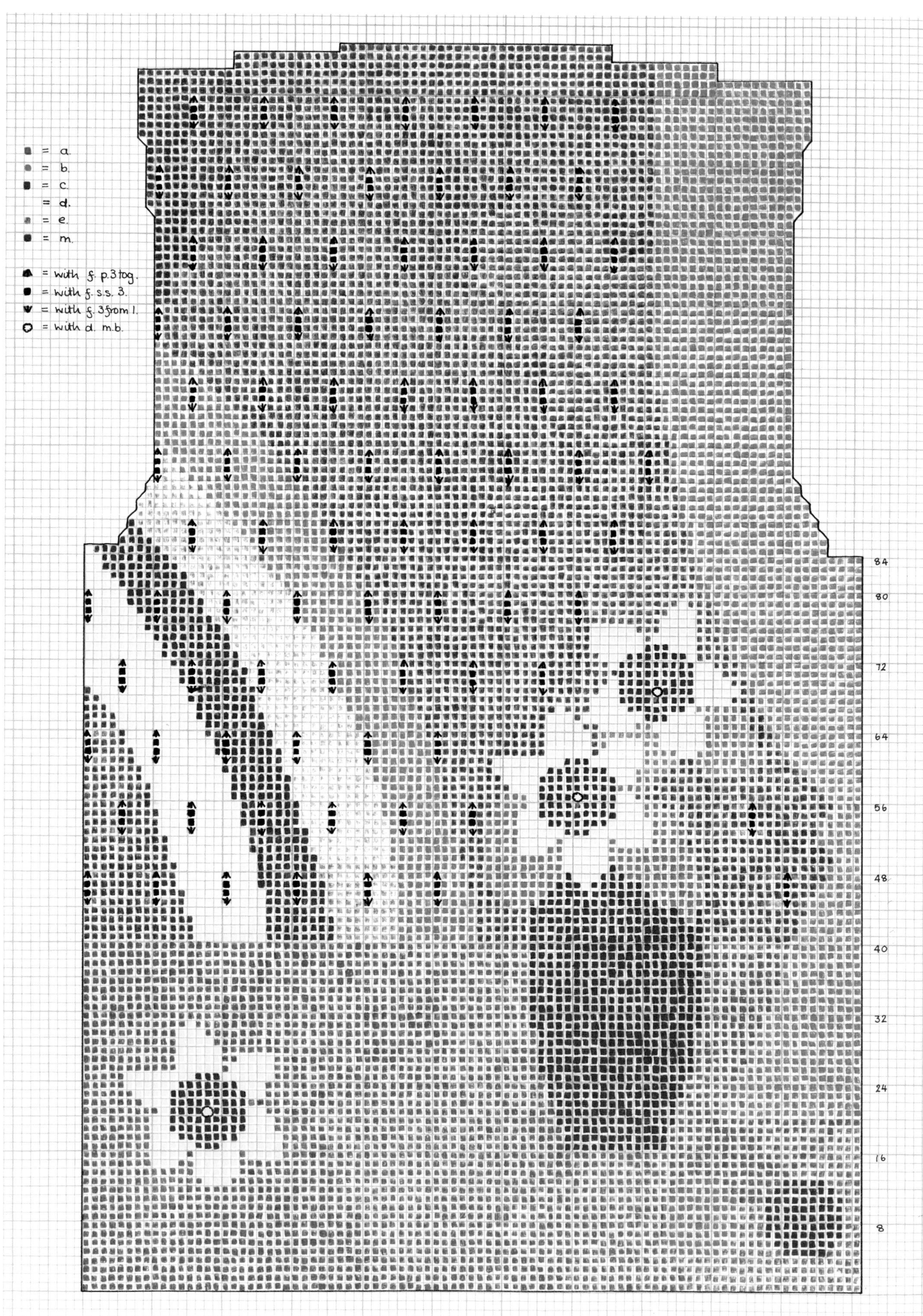

KALEIDOSCOPE

MATERIALS

For the waistcoat: 5 (6) (7) ounces of 'Woollybear Real Shetland' in main colour and 1 (2) (2) ounces of the same wool in each of 4 contrast colours.

For the cardigan: 8 (9) (10) ounces of 'Woollybear Real Shetland' in main colour and 2 ounces of the same wool in each of 4 contrast colours.

For both garments: A pair each of size 2¼ mm. (No. 13) and size 2¾ mm. (No. 12) Aero knitting needles; 6 buttons.

TENSION

16 stitches and 19 rows to 5 centimetres (2 inches) over the pattern using size 2¾ mm. (No. 12) needles. If you cannot obtain the correct tension using the size needles suggested use larger or smaller ones accordingly.

ABBREVIATIONS

K., knit; p., purl; st., stitch; tog., together; dec., decrease (by working 2 sts. tog.); inc., increase (by working twice into same st.); single rib is k.1 and p.1 alternately; s.s., stocking stitch is k. on the right side and p. on the wrong side; m.b. make bobble thus, p. into back and front of next st., turn, k.2, turn, p. 2 tog.; m., main colour; a., first contrast; b., second contrast colour; c., third contrast colour; d., fourth contrast colour; up 1, pick up the loop which lies between the needles, slip it onto left hand needle, then k. into back of it; sl., slip; p.s.s.o., pass sl. st. over.

NOTE

The instructions are given for the small size. Where they vary work the figures in the first brackets for the medium size or the figures in the second brackets for the large size.

MEASUREMENTS

The measurements are given in centimetres followed by inches in brackets.

Size	Small	Medium	Large
To fit bust	80–83 (32–33)	88–90 (35–36)	92–95 (37–38)
Underarms	81 (32½)	89 (35½)	94 (37½)
Side seam	32.5 (13)	32.5 (13)	32.5 (13)
Length	51 (20½)	52.5 (21)	54 (21¾)
Sleeve seam	41 (16½)	41 (16½)	41 (16½)

THE BACK

With size 2¼ mm. (No. 13) needles and m. cast on 116 (128) (134) sts. and work 33 rows in single rib.

Increase row: Rib 10 (16) (19), * up 1, rib 12; repeat from * ending last repeat rib 10 (16) (19). – 125 (137) (143) sts.

Change to size 2¾ mm. (No. 12) needles and beginning with a k. row s.s. 2 rows.

Now work in colour pattern as follows: This is worked entirely in s.s. except for the bobbles. Take care not to pull colours not in use tightly across the back of the work or it will become puckered.

1st row: 2m., * 1a., 2m.; repeat from * to end.

2nd row: 1a., * 3m., 1a., with a. m.b., 1a.; repeat from * until 4 remain, 3m., 1a.

3rd row: As 1st row.

4th row: All m.

5th row: 2m., * 1b., 2m.; repeat from * to end.

6th row: 1m., * 1b., with b., m.b., 1b., 3m.; repeat from * ending last repeat 1m.

7th row: As 5th row.

8th row: All m.

9th to 16th rows: As 1st to 8th rows, but using c. instead of a. and d. instead of b.

The last 16 rows form the pattern. Repeat them 4 times more, then work the first 12 rows again.

To shape the armholes: Cast off 6 sts. at the beginning of the next 2 rows, then dec. 1 st. at each end of the next row and the 9 (11) (13) following alternate rows.

On 93 (101) (103) sts., pattern 45 (47) (49) rows.

To slope the shoulders: Cast off 9 sts. at the beginning of the next 4 rows and 8 (10) (11) sts. at the beginning of the next 2 rows.

Cast off the remaining 41 (45) (45) sts.

THE POCKET BACKS (2 alike)

With size 2¼ mm. (No. 13) needles and m. cast on 31 sts. and beginning with a k. row s.s. 38 rows, then leave these sts. on a stitch-holder until required.

THE LEFT FRONT

With size 2¼ mm. (No. 13) needles and m. cast on 60 (66) (72) sts. and work 33 rows in single rib.

Increase row: Rib 6 (9) (12), * up 1, rib 12; repeat from * ending last repeat rib 6 (9) (12) – 65 (71) (77) sts.

Change to size 2¾ mm. (No. 12) needles and beginning with a k. row s.s. 2 rows.

Now work 36 rows in pattern as given for back.

Pocket row: Pattern across 17 (20) (23) sts., slip next 31 sts. onto a stitch-holder and leave at front of work, in their place pattern across the 31 sts. of one pocket back, pattern to end.

Pattern 43 rows – work 1 extra row here when working right front.

To slope the front edge: Maintaining the continuity of the pattern as set, dec. 1 st. at the end – front edge on the next row and at the same edge on the 3 following 3rd rows. On 61 (67) (73) sts., pattern 2 rows.

To shape the armhole and continue to slope the front edge: Continuing to dec. at front edge on every 3rd row as before, cast off 6 sts. for armhole at the beginning of the next row, then dec. 1 st. at the armhole edge on the 10 (12) (14) following alternate rows.

Pattern 34 (36) (41) rows decreasing at front edge on every 3rd row as set.

On 26 (28) (29) sts. pattern 11 (11) (8) rows.

To slope the shoulder: Cast off 9 sts. at the beginning of the next row and following alternate row.

On 8 (10) (11) sts., work 1 row, then cast off.

THE RIGHT FRONT

Work as given for left front noting the variation in the number of rows before sloping front edge.

THE POCKET TOPS (both alike)

With right side of work facing rejoin m. to the 31 sts. left on stitch-holder and using size 2¼ mm. (No. 13) needles work 5 rows in single rib, then cast off.

THE FRONTBAND

First join shoulder seams. With size 2¼ mm. (No. 13) needles and m. cast on 10 sts. and work 6 rows in single rib.

1st Buttonhole row: Rib 3, cast off 4, rib to end.

2nd Buttonhole row: Rib 3, turn, cast on 4, turn, rib to end.

Rib 20 rows.

Repeat the last 22 rows 4 times more, then work the 2 buttonhole rows again.

Continue in rib until the band is long enough to fit up right front edge across back neck edge and down left front edge.

Neatly sew band in place, casting off when correct length is assured.

THE ARMBANDS FOR THE WAISTCOAT (both alike)

With right side of work facing rejoin m. and using size 2¼ mm. (No. 13) needles pick up and k.122 (130) (140) sts. from all round armhole edge.

Work 5 rows in single rib, then cast off in rib.

THE SLEEVES FOR THE CARDIGAN (both alike)

With size 2¼ mm. (No. 13) needles and m. cast on 65 (65) (71) sts. and work 32 rows in single rib.

Change to size 2¾ mm. (No. 12) needles and beginning with a k. row s.s. 2 rows.

Now work 12 (4) (8) rows in pattern as given for back.

Continuing in pattern as set and working the extra sts. into the pattern as they occur inc. 1 st. at each end of the next row and the 13 (15) (14) following 8th rows.

On 93 (97) (101) sts., pattern 11 (3) (7) rows.

To shape the sleevetop: Cast off 6 sts. at the beginning of the next 2 rows, then dec. 1 st. at each end of the next row and the 16 (17) (18) following 4th rows.

On 47 (49) (51) sts., work 1 (3) (1) row(s).

Next row: With m. only, * sl.1, k. 2 tog., p.s.s.o.; repeat from * ending last repeat k.2 (1) (nil).

Cast off the remaining 17 sts.

THE SHOULDER PADS

With size 2¼ mm. (No. 13) needles and m. cast on 49 sts. and work 4 rows in single rib.

Continuing in rib dec. 1 st. at each end of the next row and the 22 following alternate rows.

Take the 3 remaining sts. tog. and fasten off.

TO MAKE UP THE GARMENT

Pin out to size and press all parts except the ribbing on the wrong side with a warm iron over a damp cloth. Neatly sew pocket backs and row ends of pocket tops in place.

For the waistcoat: Join side seams.

For the cardigan: Set in sleeves, join sleeve and side seams. Sew in shoulder pads.

For both garments: Press seams, sew on buttons.

COLUMBINE

COLUMBINE

MATERIALS
For the sweater with bows in main colour: 14 25 gram balls of 'Woollybear Bunny Fluff' by Patricia Roberts in main colour and one ball in contrast colour; or 11 ounce (28 gram) hanks of 'Woollybear Real Shetland' by Patricia Roberts in main colour and one hank in contrast colour.
For the sweater with bows in contrast colour: allow one less ball or hank of main colour and one extra in contrast colour.
For the cardigan with bows in contrast colour: 13 ounce (28 gram) hanks of 'Woollybear Real Shetland' by Patricia Roberts in main colour and 3 hanks in contrast colour or 17 25 gram balls of 'Woollybear Bunny Fluff' by Patricia Roberts in main colour and 4 balls in contrast colour; 9 buttons.
For the cardigan with bows in main colour; allow 2 fewer balls or hanks in contrast colour and 2 extra ones in main colour.
For both the sweater and the cardigan: A pair each of size 2¼ mm. (No. 13) and size 3 mm. (No. 11) Aero knitting needles.
For the gloves: One ball or hank of either 'Woollybear Bunny Fluff' or 'Woollybear Real Shetland' in main colour and one in contrast colour; a pair each of size 2¾ mm. (No. 12) and size 2¼ mm. (No. 13) Aero knitting needles.

TENSION
Work at a tension of 24 stitches – 4 repeats of the 6 stitch all over pattern to 9 centimetres (3½ inches) in width and 17 rows to 5 centimetres (2 inches) in length over the pattern. If you cannot obtain the correct tension using the size needles suggested, use larger or smaller ones accordingly.

ABBREVIATIONS
K., knit; p., purl; st., stitch; tog., together; dec., decrease (by working 2 sts. tog.); inc., increase (by working twice into same st.); single rib is k.1 and p.1 alternately; k.1 down thus, insert right hand needle into the stitch below next st. on left hand needle and k. into this st., allowing st. to slip from left hand needle in the usual way; y.r.n., yarn round needle; 9 from 1, k.1, y.r.n., k.1, y.r.n., k.1, y.r.n. k.1, y.r.n. k.1 all into next st.; m., main colour; c., contrast colour; sl., slip; p.s.s.o., pass sl. st. over; s.s., stocking st. is k. on the right side and p. on the wrong side.

NOTE
The instructions are given for the small size. Where they vary work the figures in the brackets for the medium size.

MEASUREMENTS
The measurements are given in centimetres followed by inches in brackets.

SWEATER		
Sizes	Small	Medium
Underarms	85 (34)	94 (37½)
Side seam	44 (17½)	44 (17½)
Length	64 (25½)	65 (26)
Sleeve seam	42.5 (17)	42.5 (17)
CARDIGAN		
Underarms	94 (37½)	102.5 (41)
Side seam	60 (24)	60 (24)
Length	81 (32½)	82.5 (33)
Sleeve seam	42.5 (17)	42.5 (17)

THE SWEATER

THE BACK
With size 2¼ mm. (No. 13) needles and m. cast on 117 (129) sts. and work 22 rows in single rib.
Change to size 3 mm. (No. 11) needles and work in pattern as follows. The instructions are given for the bows in main colour with contrast colour dots. The pattern may also be knitted with the bows in contrast colour with the spots in main colour, by using c. instead of m. and m. instead of c. when working the bows – between ** and ** on 9th to 15th and 33rd to 39th rows.
1st row: With m. all k.
2nd row: With m. p.3, *k.3, p.3; repeat from * to end.
3rd row: With m. k.3, *p.1, k.1 down, p.1, ..3; repeat from * to end.
4th row: With m. all p.
5th row: With m. all k.
6th row: With m. k.3, *p.3, k.3; repeat from * to end.
7th row: With m. p.1, k.1 down, p.1, *k.3, p.1, k.1 down, p.1; repeat from * to end.
8th row: With m. all p.
9th row: With m. k.15 (21), **then for a bow with m. turn, cast on 12, turn, k.1, 9 from 1, k.1, turn, cast on 12, turn**, with m. k.39; repeat from ** to ** with m., k.39; repeat from ** to **, with m. k.15 (21).
10th row: With m. p.3, *k.3, p.3; repeat from * once (twice), ** for the bow with m. p.35 **, with m. p.3, *k.3, p.3; repeat from last * 5 times more; repeat from first ** ending last repeat, repeat from last * once (twice).
11th row: With m. k.3, *p.1, k.1 down, p.1, k.3; repeat from * once (twice), ** for the bow with m. k.2, with c. k.1, with m. k.3, with c. k.1, with m. k.3, with c. k.1, with m. k.1, turn, with m. p. these 12 sts., turn, and k. these 12 sts., with m. k.1, with c. k.1, with m. k.3, with c. k.1, with m. k.3, with c. k.1, with m. k.2, with c. k.1, with m. k.3, with c. k.1, with m. k.3, with c. k.1, with m. k.2, turn, with m. p.12, turn, k.12 **, now with m. pattern 39 as set and given for 3rd row; repeat from first ** ending last repeat pattern 15 (21) as for 3rd row.
12th row: With m. p.15 (21), **for the bow with m. p.4, with c. p.1, with m. p.3, with c. p.1, with m. p.17, with c. p.1, with m. p.3, with c. p.1, with m. p.4 **, with m. p.39; repeat from first ** ending last repeat p. 15 (21).
13th row: With m. k.15 (21), **for the bow with m. k.12, turn, p.12, turn, k.2, with c. k.1, with m. k.3, with c. k.1, with m. k.3, with c. k.1, with m. k.4, with c. k.1, with m. k.3, with c. k.1, with m. k.15, turn, p.12, turn, k.1, with c. k.1, with m. k.3, with c. k.1, with m. k.3, with c. k.1, with m. k.2 **, with m. k.39; repeat from first ** ending last repeat k.15 (21).
14th row: With m. work as given for 6th row across 15 (21) sts., then ** for the bow, with m. p. 35 **, pattern 39 as set; repeat from first ** ending last repeat pattern 15 (21) sts.
15th row: With m. pattern 15 (21) as for 7th row, ** for the bow with m. cast off 12, pass 2nd, 3rd, 4th, 5th, 6th, 7th, 8th and 9th sts. on left hand needle one at a time over first st., k. this st., then k.1, cast off 12, this completes the bow**, pattern next 38 sts.; repeat from first ** ending last repeat pattern next 14 (20).
16th row: With m. all p.
17th to 32nd rows: Repeat 1st to 8th rows twice.
33rd row: With m. k. 36 (42), ** for a bow with m. turn, cast on 12, turn, k.1, 9 from 1, k.1, turn, cast on 12, turn **, with m. k.39; repeat from ** to **, with m. k. 36 (42).
34th row: Pattern 36 (42) as for 2nd row, for bow with m. p.35, with m. pattern 39, for bow with m. p.35, with m. pattern to end.
35th row: With m. pattern 36 (42) as for 3rd row, work as given for bow from ** to ** on 11th row, with m. pattern 39, work as for bow from ** to ** on 11th row, with m. pattern to end.
36th row: With m. p.36 (42), work as given for bow from ** to ** on 12th row, with m. p.39, work as for bow from ** to ** on 12th row, with m. p.36 (42).
37th row: With m. k. 36 (42), work as for bow from ** to ** on 13th row, with m. k.39, work as for bow from ** to ** on 13th row, with m. k. 36 (42).
38th row: With m. pattern 36 (42), ** for bow with m. p.35**, with m. pattern 39, **for bow with m. p.35**, with m. pattern to end.
39th row: With m. pattern 36 (42), work as for bow from ** to ** on 15th pattern row, with m. pattern 39, work as for bow from ** to ** on 15th pattern row, with m. pattern to end.
40th row: With m. all p.
41st to 48th rows: As 1st to 8th rows.
The last 48 rows form the pattern; repeat them once more, then work the first 36 rows again.
To shape the armholes: Continuing in pattern as set, cast off 6 (7) sts. at the beginning of the next 2 rows, then dec. 1 st. at each end of the next row and the 5 (7) following alternate rows.
On 93 (99) sts. pattern 31 rows.
Inc. 1 st. at each end of the next row and the two following 6th rows.
On 99 (105) sts. pattern 5 rows.
To slope the shoulders: Cast off 10 (11) sts. at the beginning of the next 4 rows and 10 sts. on the 2 following rows.
Leave the remaining 39 (41) sts. on a spare needle until required for neckband.

THE FRONT
With size 2¼ mm. (No. 13) needles and m. cast on 117 (129) sts. and work 22 rows in single rib.
Change to size 3 mm. (No. 11) needles and beginning with the 25th pattern row given for back pattern 132 rows – ending with a 12th pattern row.
To shape the armholes: Continuing in pattern as set, cast off 6 (7) sts. at the beginning of the next 2 rows, then dec. 1 st. at each end of the next row and 1 (2) following alternate rows – 101 (109) sts.
Now divide the sts. for the neck: Next row: Pattern 50 (54) and leave these sts. on a spare needle until required for right front shoulder, p.1 and leave this st. on a safety pin until required for neckband, work to end and continue on these 50 (54) sts. for the left front shoulder.
The left front shoulder: To slope the neck and continue to shape the armhole: Dec. 1 st. at each end of the next row and the 3 (4) following alternate rows.
On 42 (44) sts. work 1 row.
Dec. 1 st. at the end – neck edge on the next row and the 14 following alternate rows. – 27 (29) sts. This completes the neck shaping. Work 1 row straight.
Inc. 1 st. at the beginning of the next row and the 2 following 6th rows.
On 30 (32) sts. work 5 rows.
To slope the shoulder: Cast off 10 (11) sts. at the beginning of the next row and the following alternate row. On 10 sts. work 1 row, then cast off.
The right front shoulder: With right side of work facing rejoin yarn to inner edge of sts. left on spare needle and work to end of row, then work as given for left front shoulder to end.

THE SLEEVES (both alike)
With size 2¼ mm. (No. 13) needles and m. cast on 63 sts. and work 22 rows in single rib.
Change to size 3 mm. (No. 11) needles and work the 5th to 8th pattern rows as given for back.
9th row: With m. k.9, **for the bow with m. turn, cast on 12, turn, k.1, 9 from 1, k.1, turn, cast on 12, turn ** with m. k.39; repeat from ** to ** with m., k.9.
The last row sets the position of the bow pattern given for the back. Continuing in pattern as set, work 3 rows more.***
Maintaining the continuity of the pattern and working the extra sts. into the pattern as they occur, inc. 1 st. at each end of the next row and the 9 (11) following 12th (10th) rows.
On 83 (87) sts. pattern 11 (9) rows.
To shape the sleevetop: Continuing in pattern as set, cast off 6 (7) sts. at the beginning of the next 2 rows, then dec. 1 st. at each end of the next row and the 17 (18) following alternate rows.
On 35 sts. work 1 row.
Cast off 3 sts. at the beginning of the next 2 rows and 5 sts. on the 4 following rows.
Cast off the remaining 9 sts.

THE NECKBAND
First join right shoulder seam. With right side of work facing rejoin m. at left front shoulder and using size 2¼ mm. (No. 13) needles pick up and k. 63 (65) sts. from left front neck edge, k.1 st. from centre front, pick up and k. 63 (65) sts. from right front neck edge, then k. across the 39 (41) sts. left on spare needle at back neck edge – 166 (172) sts.
1st row: *P.1, k.1; repeat from * to end.
2nd row: Rib as set to within 4 sts. of centre st., sl.1, k.2 tog., p.s.s.o., p.1, k. centre st., then p.1, sl.1, k.2 tog., p.s.s.o., rib to end.
Repeat the last 2 rows 4 times more, then cast off the remaining 146 (152) sts. in rib.

THE SHOULDER PADS (2 alike)
With size 2¼ mm. (No. 13) needles and m. cast on 44 sts. and work 54 rows in single rib, then cast off in rib. Fold in half diagonally to form a triangle and join outer edges.

TO MAKE UP THE SWEATER
Pin out to size and press all parts except the ribbing with a warm iron over a damp cloth. Join left shoulder seam. Set in sleeves. Join sleeve and side seams. Press seams. Catch the shoulder pads in place.

THE CARDIGAN
THE BACK
With size 2¼ mm. (No. 13) needles and m. cast on 129 (141) sts. and work 32 rows in single rib.
Change to size 3 mm. (No. 11) needles and work the first 8 pattern rows given for the back of the sweater and noting the information on colour permutations.
9th row: With m. k.21 (27), **for a bow with m. turn, cast on 12, turn, k.1, 9 from 1, k.1, turn, cast on 12, turn**, with m. k.39; repeat from ** to ** with m. k.39; repeat from ** to **, with m. k.21 (27).
The last row sets the position of the pattern given for the sweater, now work the 10th to 48th pattern rows as set.
Repeat the 48 pattern rows twice more, then work the first 36 rows again.
To shape the armholes: Cast off 7 (8) sts. at the beginning of the next 2 rows, then dec. 1 st. at each end of the next row and the 7 (9) following alternate rows.
On 99 (105) sts. pattern 31 rows.
Increase 1 st. at each end of the next row and the 2 following 6th rows.
On 105 (111) sts. pattern 5 rows.
To slope the shoulders: Cast off 11 sts. at the beginning of the next 4 rows and 10 (12) sts. on the 2 following rows – 41 (43) sts.
Change to size 2¼ mm. (No. 13) needles and work 4 rows in single rib. Continuing in rib, dec. 1 st. at each end of the next row and the 2 following 4th rows.
On 35 (37) sts. work 3 rows, then cast off in rib.

THE POCKET BACKS (2 alike)
With size 3 mm. (No. 11) needles and m. cast on 33 sts. and work the first 8 pattern rows given for back of sweater 5 times, then work the first 4 rows again. Leave these sts. on a spare needle until required.

THE LEFT FRONT
With size 2¼ mm. (No. 13) needles and m. cast on 63 (69) sts. and work 32 rows in single rib.
Change to size 3 mm. (No. 11) needles and work the first 8 pattern rows given for back of sweater, noting the information on colour permutations.
9th row: With m. k.21 (27), work as given for bow between ** and ** on 9th row given for back of sweater, with m. k.39.
Now work the 10th to 48th pattern rows as set. Repeat these 48 rows once more.
Pocket row: K.15 (21), slip the next 33 sts. onto a stitch-holder and leave at front of work, in their place pattern across the 33 sts. of one pocket back, work to end of row.
On 63 (69) sts. pattern 73 rows.
****To slope the front edge: Continuing in pattern as set, dec. 1 st. at the end – front edge on the next row and the 2 following 4th rows.
Work 1 row straight – ending at side seam edge.
To shape the armhole: Continuing to dec. 1 st. at the front edge on every 4th row as before, cast off 7 (8) sts. at the beginning of the next row. Work 1 row back to armhole edge, then dec. 1 st. at the armhole edge on the next row and the 7 (9) following alternate rows.
Still decreasing at the front edge on every 4th row pattern 31 rows straight, then inc. 1 st. at the armhole edge on the next row and the 2 following 6th rows.
On 33 (35) sts. work 1 row.
Dec. 1 st. at the front edge on the next row.
On 32 (34) sts. work 3 rows.

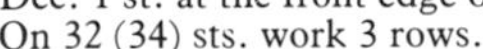

continued on page 164

CONFETTI

CONFETTI

MATERIALS
For the bobble patterned coat: 34 50 gram balls of 'Woollybear Wool Bouclé' by Patricia Roberts in main colour and 4 balls in each of the 5 contrast colours; 4 buttons.

For the one colour version allow 13 balls extra in main colour.

For the striped jacket: 20 balls of the same yarn in main colour and 12 balls in contrast colour; 3 buttons.

For either version: a pair of size 6 mm. (No. 4) Aero knitting needles.

TENSION
5 stitches and 10 rows to 5 centimetres (2 inches) over the garter stitch using size 6 mm. (No. 4) needles. If you cannot obtain the correct tension using the size needles suggested, use larger or smaller ones accordingly.

ABBREVIATIONS
K., knit; p., purl; st., stitch; tog., together; dec., decrease (by working 2 sts. tog.); inc. increase (by working twice into same st.); garter st. is k. plain on every row; y.r.n., yarn round needle; sl., slip; p.s.s.o., pass sl. st. over; m.b., make bobble thus, k.1, y.r.n., k.1, y.r.n., k.1 all into next st., turn, p.5, turn, k.5, turn, p.5, turn, k.5, turn, p.2 tog., p.1, p.2 tog., turn, sl.1, k.2 tog., p.s.s.o.; m., main colour; a., first contrast colour; b., second contrast; c., third contrast; d., fourth contrast; e., fifth contrast; up 1., pick up the loop which lies between the needles, slip it onto left hand needle, then k. into back of it.

MEASUREMENTS
The measurements are given in centimetres followed by inches in brackets.

	JACKET	COAT
To fit bust	80–90 (32–36)	80–90 (32–36)
Underarms	112 (44¾)	112 (44¾)
Side seam	40 (16)	65 (26)
Length	65 (26)	90 (36)
Sleeve seam	42.5 (17)	42.5 (17)

THE COAT

THE BACK
With size 6 mm. (No. 4) needles and m. cast on 57 sts. and work in pattern as follows. The instructions are given for the coat with multicoloured bobbles. For the one colour version work the bobbles in main colour.

1st to 6th rows: With m. all k.

7th row: With m. k.4, join in a., with a. m.b., break off a., and knot ends, leaving sufficiently long ends to darn in at completion of work, with m. k.7, *with b. m.b. as before, with m. k.7, with a. m.b., with m. k.7; repeat from * ending last repeat with m. k.4.

8th to 14th rows: With m. all k.

15th row: With m. k.8, *with c. m.b., with m. k.7, with d. m.b., with m. k.7; repeat from * ending last repeat with m. k.8.

16th row: With m. all k.

17th to 32nd rows: As 1st to 16th rows, but using e. instead of a., a. instead of b., b. instead of c., and c. instead of d. for the bobbles.

33rd to 48th rows: As 1st to 16th rows, but using d. instead of a., e. instead of b., a. instead of c., and b. instead of d. for the bobbles.

49th to 64th rows: As 1st to 16th rows, but using c. instead of a., d. instead of b., e. instead of c., and a. instead of d. for the bobbles.

65th to 80th rows: As 1st to 16th rows, but using b. instead of a., c. instead of b., d. instead of c., and e. instead of d. for the bobbles.

The last 80 rows form the pattern. Work the first 50 rows again.

To shape the armholes: Maintaining the continuity of the pattern as set cast off 3 sts. at the beginning of the next 2 rows, then dec. 1 st. at each end of the next row and the 4 following alternate rows.

On 41 sts. pattern 23 rows.

Inc. 1 st. at each end of the next row and the following 6th row.

On 45 sts. pattern 5 rows.

To slope the shoulder: Cast off 8 sts. at the beginning of the next 2 rows, then 7 sts. on the 2 following rows.

Cast off the remaining 15 sts.

THE POCKET BACKS (2 alike)
With size 6 mm. (No. 4) needles and m. cast on 13 sts. and work 24 rows in garter st., then leave these sts. on a stitch-holder until required.

THE LEFT FRONT
With size 6 mm. (No. 4) needles and m. cast on 31 sts. and work in pattern as follows.

1st to 6th rows: With m. all k.

7th row: With m. k.4, with a. m.b., with m. k.7, with b. m.b., with m. k.7, with a. m.b., with m. k.10.

8th to 14th rows: With m. all k.

15th row: With m. k.8, with c. m.b., with m. k.7, with d. m.b., with m. k.7, with c. m.b., with m. k.6.

16th row: With m. all k.

The last 16 rows set the position of the 80 row colour sequence given for back. Now work the 17th to 80th rows as set.

**Pocket row: Pattern 6, slip next 13 sts. onto a stitch-holder and leave at front of work in their place; pattern across the 13 sts. of one pocket back, work to end of row.

Pattern 48 rows more as set.

***Now divide the sts. for the collar: Next row: K.5 and leave these sts. on a safety pin until required for collar, work to end and continue on these 26 sts.

To shape the armhole and to slope the front edge: Cast off 3 sts. at the beginning for armhole and dec. 1 st. at the end for front edge on the next row. Pattern 10 rows decreasing 1 st. at the armhole edge on each right side row and at the same time decreasing 1 st. at the front edge on the 8th of these rows.

On 16 sts. work 5 rows.

Dec. 1 st. at the front edge on the next row and the 2 following 8th rows.

On 13 sts. work 1 row.

Work 7 rows, increasing 1 st. at the armhole edge on the 1st and 7th of these rows, and at the same time marking the 3rd of these rows with a coloured thread at front edge.

On 15 sts. work 5 rows.

To slope the shoulder: Cast off 8 sts. at the beginning of the next row. On 7 sts. work 1 row, then cast off.

THE RIGHT FRONT
With size 6 mm. (No. 4) needles and m. cast on 31 sts. and work as follows:

1st to 6th rows: With m. all k.

7th row: With m. k.10, with a. m.b., with m. k.7, with b. m.b., with m. k.7, with a. m.b., with m. k.4.

8th to 14th rows: With m. all k.

15th row: With m. k.6, with d. m.b., with m. k.7, with c. m.b., with m. k.7, with d. m.b., with m. k.8.

16th row: With m. all k.

continued from page 161

To slope the shoulder: Cast off 11 sts. at the beginning of the next row and the following alternate row. On 10 (12) sts. work 1 row, then cast off.

THE RIGHT FRONT
Work as given for the left front until 8 pattern rows have been worked.

9th row: With m. k.39, work as for bow between ** and ** on the 9th row given for back of sweater, with m. k.21 (27).

The last row sets the position of the pattern given for the back of the sweater. Work the 10th to 48th rows as set, then work these 48 rows again.

Pocket row: K.15, slip the next 33 sts. onto a stitch-holder and leave at front of work, in their place pattern across the 33 sts. of pocket back, work to end of row.

On 63 (69) sts. pattern 74 rows.

Now work as given for left front from **** to end.

THE POCKET TOPS (2 alike)
With right side of work facing rejoin m. to the 33 sts. left on stitch-holder and using size 2¼ mm. (No. 13) needles work 8 rows in single rib, then cast off in rib.

THE SLEEVES (both alike)
Work as given for sleeves of sweater until *** is reached.

Maintaining the continuity of the pattern as set and working the extra sts. into the pattern as they occur, inc. 1 st. at each end of the next row and the 11 (13) following 10th (8th) rows.

On 87 (91) sts. pattern 9 (15) rows.

To shape the sleevetop: Cast off 7 (8) sts. at the beginning of the next 2 rows, then dec. 1 st. at each end of the next row and the 18 (19) following alternate rows.

On 35 sts. work 1 row.

Cast off 3 sts. at the beginning of the next 2 rows and 5 sts. on the 4 following rows. Cast off the remaining 9 sts.

THE SHOULDER PADS
Work as given for shoulder pads of sweater.

THE BUTTONBAND AND HALF COLLAR
With size 2¼ mm. (No. 13) needles and m. cast on 12 sts. and work 202 rows in single rib.

***Continuing in rib as set, inc. 1 st. at the beginning of the next row and the 29 (31) following alternate rows.

On 42 (44) sts. rib 1 row.

Cast on 12 sts. at the beginning of the next row.

On 54 (56) sts. rib 15 rows, then cast off in rib.

THE BUTTONHOLE BAND AND HALF COLLAR
With size 2¼ mm. (No. 13) needles and m. cast on 12 sts. and work 8 rows in single rib.

1st Buttonhole row: Rib 4, cast off 4, rib to end.

2nd Buttonhole row: Rib 4, turn, cast on 4, turn, rib to end.

Rib 22 rows.

Repeat the last 24 rows 7 times, then work the 2 buttonhole rows again.

Now work as given for buttonband from *** to end.

TO MAKE UP THE CARDIGAN
Pin out to size and press all parts on the wrong side with a warm iron over a damp cloth. Join shoulder seams. Set in sleeves. Join sleeve and side seams. Sew shaped row end and cast on edges of front bands and half collars in place. Sew pocket backs and row ends of pocket tops in place. Press seams. Catch shoulder pads in place. Sew on buttons.

THE GLOVES

THE LEFT GLOVE
With size 2¼ mm. (No. 13) needles and c. cast on 51 sts. and work 20 rows in single rib.

The last 16 rows set the position of the pattern given for back. Continuing in pattern as set, work as follows:

1st Buttonhole row: K.2, cast off 1, work to end as set.

2nd Buttonhole row: K. until 2 remain, turn, cast on 1, turn, k. to end.

Pattern 34 rows, then work the 2 buttonhole rows again.

Pattern 26 rows.

Pocket row: Work as set across 12 sts., slip next 13 sts. onto a stitch-holder and leave at front of work, in their place pattern across the 13 sts. of other pocket back, work to end of row.

Pattern 49 rows, working buttonholes on the 8th/9th and 44th/45th of these rows.

Now work as given for left front from *** to end.

THE POCKET TOPS (2 alike)
With right side of work facing rejoin m. to the 13 sts. left on stitch-holder at front of work and using size 6 mm. (No. 4) needles k.2 rows, then cast off loosely.

THE LEFT AND RIGHT FRONT COLLARS (alike)
Rejoin m. to the inner edge of the 5 sts. left on safety pin at front edge and using size 6 mm. (No. 4) needles, continuing in garter st., inc. 1 st. at the beginning – inner edge – on the next row and the 8 following 4th rows.

On 14 sts. k.3 rows.

Cast off loosely.

THE SLEEVES (both alike)
With size 6 mm. (No. 4) needles and m. cast on 23 sts. and k. 11 rows.

Increase row: With m. k.3, *up 1, k.2; repeat from * to end. – 33 sts.

Beginning with the 17th pattern row given for back work 74 rows in pattern, increasing 1 st. at each end of the 31st of these rows. – 35 sts.

To shape the sleevetop: Cast off 3 sts. at the beginning of the next 2 rows, then dec. 1 st. at each end of the next row and the 7 following alternate rows.

On 13 sts. work 1 row.

Dec. 1 st. at each end of the next 5 rows.

Cast off the remaining 3 sts.

THE BACK COLLAR
With size 6 mm. (No. 4) needles and m. cast on 29 sts. and k.6 rows. Inc. 1 st. at each end of the next row. K.13 rows. Then cast off loosely.

THE SHOULDER PADS (2 alike)
With size 6 mm. (No. 4) needles and m. cast on 13 sts. and k. 25 rows, then cast off. Fold in half diagonally and join outer edges to form a triangle.

TO MAKE UP THE COAT
Pin out to size and press lightly on the wrong side with a warm iron over a damp cloth. Join shoulder seams. Set in sleeves. Join sleeve and side seams. Neatly sew pocket backs and row ends of pocket tops in place. Sew cast on edge of back collar in place between the marking threads. Sew row ends of left and right front collars in place. Then join row end edges of back collar to cast off edges of front collars for 5 cms (2 inches) at inner edge. Press seams. Catch shoulder pads in place. Sew on buttons.

THE JACKET

THE BACK
With size 6 mm. (No. 4) needles and m. cast on 57 sts. and working in garter st. in the sequence of 6 rows m., 6 rows a., k.80 rows.

To shape the armholes: Continuing in stripe pattern as set, work as given for armhole shaping on back of coat to end.

THE POCKET BACKS (2 alike)
Work as given for coat.

THE LEFT FRONT
With size 6 mm. (No. 4) needles and m. cast on 31 sts. and work in stripe pattern with front band in m. as follows:

1st to 6th rows: With m. all k.

7th row: With a. k.26, with m. k.5 for front band.

8th row: With m. k.5, with a. k.26.

9th to 12th rows: Repeat 7th and 8th rows twice.

Repeat the last 12 rows once, then work the first 6 rows again.

Continuing in stripe pattern as set, work as given for left front of coat from ** to end.

THE RIGHT FRONT
With size 6 mm. (No. 4) needles and m. cast on 31 sts. and work as follows:

1st to 6th row: With m. all k.

7th row: With m. k.5 for front band, with a. k. to end.

8th row: With a. k.26, with m. k.5.

9th to 12th rows: Repeat 7th and 8th rows twice.

Continuing in the 12 row stripe pattern as set work 2 rows straight. Work the 2 buttonhole rows given for right front of coat. Pattern 14 rows, then work the pocket row given for the right front of coat.

Pattern 49 rows working buttonholes on the 16th/17th and 48th/49th of these rows.

Now work as given for left front of the coat from *** to end.

THE POCKET TOPS (2 alike)
As given for coat.

THE LEFT AND RIGHT FRONT COLLARS (alike)
As given for coat.

THE SLEEVES (both alike)
With size 6 mm. (No. 4) needles and m. cast on 23 sts. and k.11 rows.

Increase row: With m. k.3, *up 1, k.2; repeat from * to end. – 33 sts.

Now working in stripe pattern of 6 rows a., 6 rows m., work 74 rows, increasing 1 st. at each end of the 31st of these rows. – 35 sts.

To shape the sleevetop: Cast off 3 sts. at the beginning of the next 2 rows, then dec. 1 st. at each end of the next row.

On 27 sts. work 1 row.

Now working in stripe sequence of 4 rows m. and 4 rows a. dec. 1 st. at each end of the next row and the 3 following 4th rows, then on the 4 following alternate rows.

Dec. 1 st. at each end of the next 4 rows.

Cast off the remaining 3 sts.

THE BACK COLLAR
As given for coat.

THE SHOULDER PADS (2 alike)
As given for coat.

TO MAKE UP THE JACKET
As given for coat.

Change to size 2¾ mm. (No. 12) needles and work the first 8 pattern rows given for back of sweater 3 times.

Now work the bow as follows: ***

1st row: With c. k.36, join in m., turn and with m. cast on 12, turn, k.1, 9 from 1, k.1, turn, cast on 12, turn, with c. k.12.

2nd row: With c. pattern 12 as set, with m. p.35, with c. pattern to end as set.

3rd row: With c. pattern 36, then work as given for bow between ** and ** on 11th row of back of sweater, with c. pattern to end as set.

4th to 7th rows: With c. pattern as set up to bow, then work as given between ** and ** on 12th to 15th rows of back of sweater, with c. work to end of row.

This completes the bow. Continuing with c. only, work 1 row.

Now divide the sts. for the thumb: Next row: K.15, slip next 9 sts. onto a safety pin until required for thumb, turn, cast on 9 sts., turn, k. to end.

****On 51 sts. pattern 15 rows as before.

Now divide the sts. for the fingers: Next row: k.4, inc. in next st., then leave these 6 sts. on a piece of yarn until required for little finger, inc., k.4, inc., and leave these 8 sts. on a piece of yarn until required for third finger, inc., k.5, inc. and leave these 9 sts. on a piece of yarn until required for second finger, inc., pattern 12, inc. and leave these 16 sts. on a piece of yarn until required for first finger, inc., k.5, inc. and leave these 9 sts. on a piece of yarn until required for second finger, inc., k.4, inc. and leave these 8 sts. on a piece of yarn until required for third finger, k.6 for little finger, then onto same needle, k. across the 6 sts. left for little finger, and continue on these 12 sts.

The little finger: Beginning with a p. row s.s. 19 rows.

**Next row: *K.2 tog.; repeat from * to end. Break off yarn, leaving a long end, thread through remaining sts. and draw up firmly. Later the long end may be used to join row ends.

The third finger: With wrong side of work facing rejoin c. to one set of 8 sts. left for 3rd finger, p. across these 8 sts., then across the other set of 8 sts. – 16 sts.

Beginning with a k. row s.s. 24 rows.

Work as given for little finger from ** to end.

The second finger: With wrong side of work facing rejoin c. to one set of 9 sts. left for second finger, p. across these sts., then across the other set of 9 sts. – 18 sts.

Beginning with a k. row s.s. 28 rows then work as given for little finger from ** to end.

The first finger: With wrong side of work facing, rejoin c. to the 16 sts. left for first finger and beginning with a p. row s.s. 25 rows, then work as given for little finger from ** to end.

The thumb: With right side of work facing rejoin c. to the 9 sts. left for thumb, cast on 10 sts., then on 19 sts. beginning with a k. row s.s. 22 rows. Work as given for little finger from ** to end.

THE RIGHT GLOVE
Using m. instead of c. and c. instead of m. work as given for left glove until *** is reached.

1st row: With m. k.12, join in c., turn, cast on 12, turn, k.1, 9 from 1, k.1, turn, cast on 12, turn, with m. k. to end.

The last row sets the position of the bow, now work the 2nd to 7th rows of bows as set. Work 1 row straight.

Next row: K. 27, slip next 9 sts. onto a safety pin until required for thumb, turn, cast on 9 sts., turn, k. to end.

Now work as given for left glove from **** to end.

TO MAKE UP THE GLOVES
Press lightly on the wrong side. Join row end edges of side seams and individual fingers and thumbs. Join cast on edges of thumbs.

TUTTI-FRUTTI

MATERIALS
4 (4) (5) 50 gram balls of 'Woollybear Cotton Bouclé' by Patricia Roberts in main colour and 2 (2) (3) balls in each of the 4 contrast colours; a 10 centimetre (4 inch) zip fastener, a pair each of size 3¼ mm. (No. 10) and size 3¾ mm. (No. 9) Aero knitting needles.

SPECIAL NOTE
This garment may also be knitted in 'Woollybear 100% Mohair' by Patricia Roberts. The yarn required is 6 (6) (7) 25 gram balls in main colour and 3 balls in each of the 4 other contrast colours. To obtain the correct tension it will be necessary to use size 3¾ mm. (No. 9) instead of size 3¼ mm. (No. 10) needles and the size 4 mm. (No. 8) instead of size 3¾ mm. (No. 9) needles throughout.

TENSION
10 stitches and 15 rows to 5 centimetres (2 inches) over the pattern using size 3¾ mm. (No. 9) needles and cotton bouclé. If you cannot obtain the correct tension using the size needles suggested, use larger or smaller ones accordingly.

ABBREVIATIONS
K., knit; p., purl; st., stitch; tog., together; dec., decrease (by working 2 sts. tog.); inc., increase (by working twice into same st.); s.s., stocking st. is k. on the right side and p. on the wrong side; single rib is k.1. and p.1. alternately; m., main colour; a., first contrast; b., second contrast; c., third contrast; d., fourth contrast; up 1, pick up the loop which lies between the needles, slip it onto left hand needle, then k. or p. into back of it.

NOTE
The instructions are given for the small size. Where they vary work the figures in the first brackets for the medium size or the figures in the second brackets for the large size.

MEASUREMENTS
The measurements are given in centimetres followed by inches in brackets.

Sizes	Small	Medium	Large
To fit bust	82.5 (33)	87.5 (35)	92.5 (37)
Underarms	85 (34)	90 (36)	95 (38)
Side seam	30 (12)	30 (12)	30 (12)
Length	48.5 (19¼)	49 (19½)	49.5 (19¾)
Sleeve seam	23 (9¼)	23 (9¼)	23 (9¼)

THE BACK
With size 3¼ mm. (No. 10) needles and m. cast on 75 (80) (85) sts. and work 23 rows in single rib.

Increase row: Rib 1 (4) (7), * up 1, rib 8; repeat from * ending last repeat rib 2 (4) (6) – 85 (90) (95) sts.

Change to size 3¾ mm. (No. 9) needles and work in pattern as follows.

1st and 2nd row: With a. all k.

3rd to 12th row: With b. beginning with a k. row s.s. 10 rows.

13th to 24th rows: Using c. instead of b. as 1st to 12th rows.

25th to 36th rows: Using m. instead of b. as 1st to 12th rows.

37th to 48th rows: Using d. instead of b. as 1st to 12th rows.

The last 48 rows form the pattern.

Work the 1st to 18th rows again.

To shape the armholes: Continuing in stripe pattern as set, cast off 4 sts. at the beginning of the next 2 rows. Then dec. 1 st. at each end of the next row and the 5 (6) (7) following alternate rows.

On 65 (68) (71) sts. pattern 19 rows.

Inc. 1 st. at each end of the next row and the 2 following 6th rows.

On 71 (74) (77) sts. work 5 rows.

To slope the shoulders: Cast off 10 sts. at the beginning of the next 2 rows and 10 (11) (12) sts. on the 2 following rows.

Leave the remaining 31 (32) (33) sts. on a spare needle until required for neckband.

SMARTY-PANTS

MATERIALS
14 (15) ounces of 'Woollybear Real Shetland' by Patricia Roberts in main colour and 2 balls of 'Woollybear 100% Mohair' by Patricia Roberts in each of 5 Contrast colours: a pair each of size 2¼ mm. (No. 13) and size 2¾ mm. (No. 12) Aero knitting needles; a size 2¼ mm. (No. 13) and a size 2¾ mm. (No. 12) Aero circular knitting needles.

TENSION
16 stitches and 20 rows to 5 centimetres (2 inches) over the bobble pattern, using size 2¾ mm. (No. 12) needles. If you cannot obtain the correct tension using the size needles suggested, use larger or smaller ones accordingly.

ABBREVIATIONS
K., knit; p., purl; st., stitch; tog., together; dec., decrease (by working 2 sts. tog.); inc., increase (by working twice into same st.); single rib is k.1 and p.1 alternately; s.s., stocking stitch is k. on the right side and p. on the wrong side; m., main colour – shetland; a., first contrast – mohair; b., second contrast; c., third contrast; d., fourth contrast; e., fifth contrast; sl., slip; p.s.s.o., pass sl. st. over; y.r.n., yarn round needle; m.b., make bobble thus, with appropriate colour contrast, k.1, y.r.n., k.1, y.r.n., k.1, all into next st., turn, p. these 5 sts., turn, k.5, turn, p.5, turn, k.5, turn, p.2 tog., p.1, p.2 tog., turn, sl.1, k.2 tog., p.s.s.o., break off contrast colour and knot loose ends together.

NOTE
The instructions are given for the small size. Where they vary work the figures in the brackets for the medium size.

MEASUREMENTS
The measurements are given in centimetres followed by inches in brackets.

Sizes	Small	Medium
Underarms	87.5 (35)	94 (37½)
Side seam	36 (14½)	36 (14½)
Length	55.5 (22¼)	57.5 (23)
Sleeve seam	42.5 (17)	42.5 (17)

THE BACK AND FRONT (both alike)
With size 2¼ mm. (No. 13) needles and m. cast on 142 (152) sts. and work 30 rows in single rib.

Change to size 2¾ mm. (No. 12) needles and beginning with a k. row s.s. 4 rows.

Now work in pattern as follows. This is worked entirely in s.s. except for the bobbles, so only the colour details are given. Use a separate length of mohair for each bobble, knotting each one off after working it and threading in the ends at the completion of knitting.

1st row: 3 (8)m., * with a. m.b., 9m., with b. m.b., 9m.; repeat from * ending last repeat 8m. (with a. m.b., 3m.).

2nd to 8th rows: All m.

9th row: 8 (3)m., * with c. m.b., 9m., with d. m.b., 9m.; repeat from * ending last repeat 3m. (with c. m.b., 8m.).

10th to 16th rows: All m.

17th row: Using e. instead of a. and a. instead of b., work as for 1st row.

18th to 24th rows: All m.

25th row: Using b. instead of c. and c. instead of d., work as given for 9th row.

26th to 32nd rows: All m.

33rd row: Using d. instead of a. and e. instead of b., work as given for 1st row.

34th to 40th rows: All m.

THE FRONT

Work as given for back until the 48 pattern rows have been worked once, then work the first 17 rows again.

Now divide the sts. for the neck. Next row: P.43 (45) (48) and leave these sts. on a spare needle until required for right front shoulder, on the small and large sizes only, up 1, then on all sizes p. to end and continue on these 43 (45) (48) sts. for the left front shoulder.

The left front shoulder: To shape the armhole: Continuing in pattern as set, cast off 4 sts. at the beginning of the next row. Work 1 row back to armhole edge, then dec. 1 st. at the armhole edge on the next row and the 5 (6) (7) following alternate rows.

On 33 (34) (36) sts. pattern 12 rows.

To shape the neck: Cast off 6 (6) (7) sts. at the beginning of the next row, then dec. 1 st. at the neck edge on each of the next 6 rows.

Inc. 1 st. at the armhole edge and dec. 1 st. at the neck edge on the next row.

Dec. 1 st. at the neck edge on each of the next 3 rows.

On 18 (19) (20) sts. work 2 rows.

Inc. 1 st. at the armhole edge on the next row and the following 6th row.

On 20 (21) (22) sts. work 5 rows.

To slope the shoulder: Cast off 10 sts. at the beginning of the next row. On 10 (11) (12) sts. work 1 row, then cast off.

The right front shoulder: With right side of work facing rejoin yarn to inner edge of sts. left on spare needle and work to end of row, then work as given for left front shoulder to end.

THE NECKBAND

First join shoulder seams. With right side of work facing rejoin m. at right front neck edge and using size 3¼ mm. (No. 10) needles, pick up and k.31 (32) (33) sts. from right front neck edge, k. across the 31 (32) (33) sts. at back neck edge then pick up and k.31 (32) (33) sts. from left front.

On 93 (96) (99) sts. work 5 rows single rib, then cast off in rib.

THE SLEEVES (both alike)

With size 3¼ mm. (No. 10) needles and m. cast on 50 (53) (56) sts. and work 15 rows in single rib.

Increase row: Rib 2 (4) (6), * up 1, rib 5; repeat from * ending last repeat rib 3 (4) (5) – 60 (63) (66) sts.

Change to size 3¾ mm. (No. 9) needles and beginning with the 13th pattern row given for back; pattern 54 rows.

To shape the sleevetop: Continuing in pattern as set, cast off 4 sts. at the beginning of the next 2 rows, then dec. 1 st. at each end of the next row and the 13 (14) (15) following alternate rows.

On 24 (25) (26) sts. work 1 row.

Dec. 1 st. at each end of the next 4 rows.

Cast off 3 sts. at the beginning of the next 4 rows.

Cast off the remaining 4 (5) (6) sts.

THE SHOULDER PADS (2 alike)

With size 3¼ mm. (No. 10) needles and m. cast on 36 sts. and work 44 rows in single rib, then cast off. Fold in half diagonally to form a triangle and join outer edges.

THE NECK INSET

With size 3¾ mm. (No. 9) needles and b. cast on 30 sts. and k. 4 rows.

Beginning with a k. row s.s. 20 rows.

K. 4 rows, then cast off.

TO MAKE UP THE SWEATER

Pin out to size and press all parts except the ribbing on the wrong side with a warm iron over a damp cloth. Set in sleeves. Join sleeve and side seams. Neatly sew zip fastener in place at neck opening. Neatly sew neck inset in position. Press seams. Catch shoulder pads in place on wrong side.

41st row: Using a. instead of c. and b. instead of d., work as given for 9th row.

42nd to 48th rows: All m.

49th row: Using c. instead of a. and d. instead of b., work as given for 1st row.

50th to 56th rows: All m.

57th row: Using e. instead of c. and a. instead of d., work as given for 9th row.

58th to 64th rows: All m.

65th row: Using b. instead of a. and c. instead of b., work as given for 1st row.

66th to 72nd rows: All m.

73rd row: Using d. instead of c. and e. instead of d., work as given for 9th row.

74th to 80th rows: All m.

The last 80 rows form the pattern; work the first 36 rows again.

To shape the armholes: Continuing in pattern as set, cast off 2 (3) sts. at the beginning of the next 2 rows, then dec. 1 st. at each end of the next row and the 8 (12) following alternate rows.

On 120 sts. p.1 row, then leave these sts. on a spare needle until required for yoke.

THE SLEEVES (both alike)

With size 2¼ mm. (No. 13) needles and m. cast on 62 (72) sts. and work 30 rows in single rib.

Change to size 2¾ mm. (No. 12) needles and beginning with a k. row s.s. 4 rows.

Now beginning with the 57th row, work 4 rows in pattern as given for back and front.

Maintaining the continuity of the pattern as set and working the extra sts. into the pattern as they occur, inc. 1 st. at each end of the next row and the 16 following 8th rows.

On 96 (106) sts. pattern 7 rows.

To shape the sleevetop: Cast off 2 (3) sts. at the beginning of the next 2 rows, then dec. 1 st. at each end of the next row and the 2 (6) following alternate rows, then on the 3 following 4th rows.

On 80 sts. p.1 row, then leave these sts. on a spare needle until required for the yoke.

THE YOKE

With right side of work facing rejoin yarn to the 80 sts. of one sleeve and using the size 2¾ mm. (No. 12) circular needle, pattern as set across the 80 sts. of one sleeve, then onto same needle pattern across the 120 sts. of front, the 80 sts. of other sleeve, then across the 120 sts. of back – 400 sts.

Noting that stocking stitch is k. plain on every round, when knitting circular, pattern 31 rounds.

1st Decrease round: With m. k.1, * sl.1, k.2 tog., p.s.s.o., k.3, with appropriate colour m.b., with m. k.3; repeat from * ending last repeat k.2 – 320 sts.

Pattern 15 rounds as set, but working 2 sts. less between the bobbles on the bobble round.

2nd Decrease round: * with m. sl.1, k.2 tog., p.s.s.o., k.2, with appropriate colour m.b., with m. k.2; repeat from * to end.

On 240 sts. s.s. 7 rounds.

3rd Decrease round: * With appropriate contrast colour m.b., with m. k.1, sl.1, k.2 tog., p.s.s.o.; k.1; repeat from * to end.

On 160 sts. work 1 round.

Change to the 2¼ mm. (No. 13) circular knitting needle and work 10 rows in single rib, then cast off loosely in rib.

TO MAKE UP THE SWEATER

Darn in the ends. Pin out to size and press all parts except the ribbing on the wrong side with a warm iron over a damp cloth. Join sleeve and side seams. Press seams.

Petro

TARZAN

MATERIALS
9 25 gram balls of 'Woollybear 100% Mohair' by Patricia Roberts in main colour, 3 balls in each of first and sixth contrast colours and one ball in each of the 4 other contrast colours; a pair each of size 4 mm. (No. 8) and size 3¾ mm. (No. 9) Aero knitting needles; a cable needle.

SPECIAL NOTE
This garment may also be knitted in 'Woollybear Cotton Bouclé' by Patricia Roberts. It will require 7 50 gram balls in main colour, 2 balls in each of the first and sixth contrast colours, and one ball in each of the 4 other contrast colours. To obtain the correct tension it is necessary to use size 3¾ mm. (No. 9) needles instead of size 4 mm. (No. 8) needles and size 3¼ mm. (No. 10) needles instead of size 3¾ mm. (No. 9) needles throughout.

TENSION
10 stitches and 14 rows to 5 centimetres (2 inches) over the stocking stitch using size 4 mm. (No. 8) needles and 'Woollybear 100% Mohair'. Using 'Woollybear Cotton Bouclé' the same tension should be obtained by using size 3¾ mm. (No. 9) needles. If you cannot obtain the correct tension using the size needles suggested, use larger or smaller ones accordingly.

ABBREVIATIONS
K., knit; p., purl; st., stitch; tog., together; dec., decrease (by working 2 sts. tog.); inc., increase (by working twice into same st.); single rib is k.1 and p.1 alternately; s.s., stocking stitch (k. on the right side and p. on the wrong side); up 1, pick up the loop which lies between the needles, slip it onto left hand needle, then k. into back of it; sl., slip; p.s.s.o., pass slip st. over; y.r.n., yarn round needle; 5 from 1, k.1, y.r.n., k.1, y.r.n., k.1 all into next st.; 4 over 1, pass 2nd, 3rd, 4th and 5th sts. on left hand needle over first st. one at a time, then with f. k. this st.; cr. 8 lt., cross 8 left thus, slip next 7 sts. onto a cable needle and leave at front of work, with m. k.1, then with c. k.7 from cable needle; cr. 7 rt., cross 7 right thus, slip next st. onto a cable needle and leave at back of work, with d. k.6, then with m. k.1 from cable needle; p.1 s.p. is purl 1, then slip this st. onto a safety pin at front of work until required; 2 over 1, pass 2nd and 3rd sts. on left hand needle over first st., then with m. k. this st.; m., main colour; a., first contrast; b., second contrast; c., third contrast; d., fourth contrast; e., fifth contrast; f., sixth contrast.

MEASUREMENTS
The measurements are given in centimetres followed by inches in brackets.

To fit bust	85 (34)
Underarms	87.5 (35)
Side seam	37.5 (15)
Length	58 (23¼)
Sleeve seam	42.5 (17)

THE BACK
With size 3¾ mm. (No. 9) needles and m. cast on 80 sts. and work 23 rows in single rib.

Increase row: Rib 8, *up 1, rib 9; repeat from * to end. – 88 sts.

Change to size 4 mm. (No. 8) needles and work in pattern as follows: this is worked entirely in s.s. beginning with a k. row, so only the colour details are given. Use separate small balls of colour for each section of the pattern, so that colours not in use are not taken across the back of the work, but leave sufficiently long ends to darn in at the completion of a colour section.

1st row (k. row): 15m., 34a., 39m.

2nd row: 37m., 12a., 2b., 23a., 14m.

The last 2 rows set the position of the pattern given in the chart, now work the 3rd to 62nd rows from the chart as set.

63rd row: 3m., 11a., 2m., 1b., 15a., 2b., 18a., 1b., 19m., with d. k.1, * up 1, k.1; repeat from * 5 times, 9m.

64th row: 9m., * slip next st. onto a safety pin at right side of work, with d. p.1.; repeat from * 5 times more, slip next st. onto a safety pin and leave these 7 sts. until required for banana leaves, work to end of row as set and given in chart.

Now work the 65th to 84th rows as set.

To shape the armholes: Continuing in pattern from chart as set, cast off 4 sts. at the beginning of his next 2 rows, then dec. 1 st. at each end of the next row and the 3 following alternate rows. **

On 72 sts. pattern 29 rows.

Inc. 1 st. at each end of the next row and the following 8th row.

On 76 sts. pattern 7 rows.

To slope the shoulders: cast off 10 sts. at the beginning of the next 4 rows. Leave the remaining 36 sts. on a spare needle until required for neckband.

THE FRONT
Work as given for back until ** is reached. On 72 sts. pattern 26 rows. Now divide the sts. for the neck. Next row: pattern as set across 30 sts., noting that each group of 5 sts. in c. are counted as one st., and leave these sts. on a spare needle until required for right front shoulder, cast off 12, work to end and continue on these 30 sts. for the left front shoulder.

The left front shoulder: To shape the neck: Continuing in pattern from chart as set, dec. 1 st. at the neck edge on each of the next 12 rows, and at the same time inc. 1 st. at armhole edge on the 3rd and 11th of these rows. – 20 sts.

Pattern 6 rows straight.

To slope the shoulder: Cast off 10 sts. at the beginning of the next row. On 10 sts. work 1 row, then cast off.

The right front shoulder: With right side of work facing rejoin yarn to inner edge of sts. left on spare needle and work to end of row, then work as given for left front shoulder to end.

THE SLEEVES (both alike)
With size 3¾ mm. (No. 9) needles and m. cast on 41 sts. and work 22 rows in single rib.

Change to size 4 mm. (No. 8) needles and beginning with a k. row s.s. 7 rows. Now work the banana motifs as follows. This is worked in s.s. except where indicated. Pull m. firmly across the back of each motif to accentuate the raised effect.

8th row (wrong side): 20m., lc., 20m.

9th row: 20m., with c. 5 from 1, 20m.

10th row: 20m., 5c., 20m.

11th row: 20m. with c. k.1, up 1, k.3, up 1, k.1, 20m.

12th row: 20m., 7c., 20m.

13th row: 20m., cr. 8 lt., 19m.

14th row: 19m., 7c., 21m.

15th row: 21m., cr. 8 lt., 18m.

16th row: 18m., 7c., 22m.

17th row: 22m., 7c., 18m.

18th row: 18m., 7d., 22m.

19th row: 22m., with d. k.1, * up 1, k.1; repeat from * 5 times, 18m.

20th row: 18m., * with d. p.1 and slip this st. onto a safety pin at right side of work, with d. p.1 as usual; repeat from * 5 times more, then with d. p.1 more and slip this st. onto the safety pin, then leave these 7 sts. until required for leaves, with m. work to end of row.

21st row: With m. inc., k.21, with d. k.6, with m. k. to end increasing in last st.

22nd row: 19m., 6d., 23m.

23rd row: 22m., cr. 7 rt., 19m.

24th row: 20m., 6d., 22m.

25th row: 21m., cr. 7 rt., 20m.

26th row: 21m., with d. p.2 tog., p.2 tog., p.2 tog., 21m.

27th row: 21m., 2 over 1, 21m.

The last 27 rows set the position of the banana motif pattern given in the chart. Continuing in pattern from chart as set, work 1 row straight, then inc. 1 st. at each end of the next row and the 8 following 8th rows.

On 61 sts. pattern 7 rows.

To shape the sleevetop: Cast off 4 sts. at the beginning of the next 2 rows, then dec. 1 st. at each end of the next row and the 13 following alternate rows.

On 25 sts. work 1 row.

Cast off 3 sts. at the beginning of the next 4 rows, then 4 sts. on the 2 following rows. Cast off the 5 remaining sts.

THE BANANA LEAVES (all alike)
With right side of work facing slip 3 sts. of the 7 from safety pin onto a size 4 mm. (No. 8) needle, rejoin d. and k.10 rows, then sl.1., k.2 tog., p.s.s.o., and fasten off leaving a long end. Now slip remaining 4 sts. onto needles and k.10 rows, then, k.2 tog., k.2 tog., turn, k.2 tog. and fasten off leaving a long end.

THE NECKBAND
First join right shoulder seam. With right side of work facing, rejoin m. at left front shoulder, and using size 3¾ mm. (No. 9) needles pick up and k. 23 sts. from left front neck edge, 12 sts. from centre front neck edge, and 23 sts. from right front neck edge, then k. across the 36 sts. at back neck edge.

On 94 sts. work 7 rows in single rib, then cast off in rib.

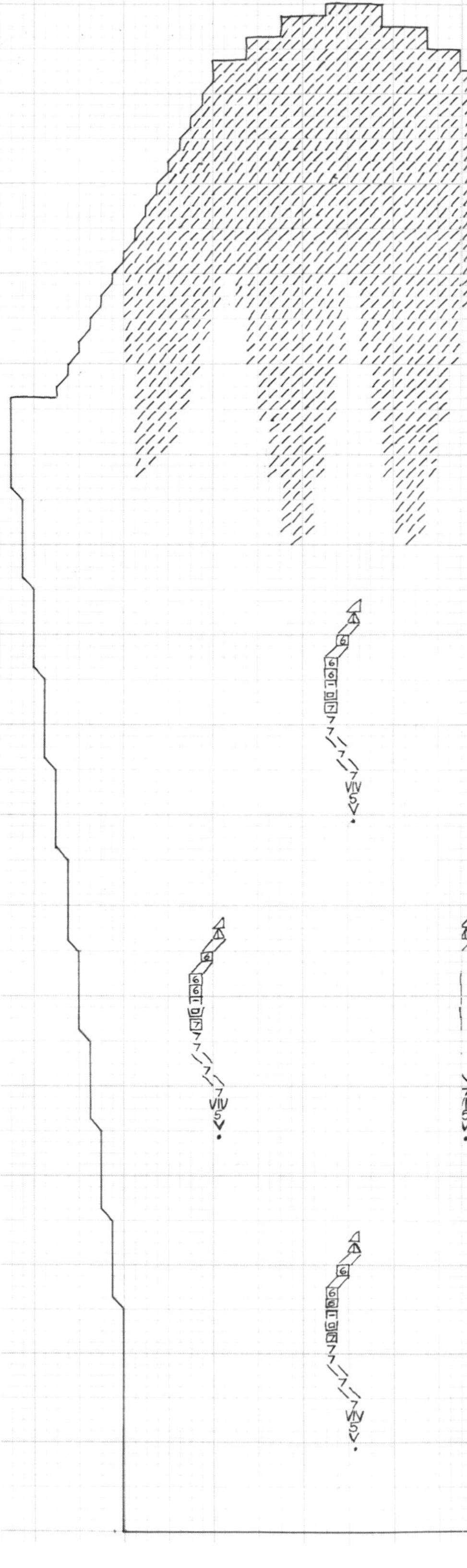

TO MAKE UP THE SWEATER

Pin out to size and press all parts except the ribbing with a warm iron over a damp cloth. Join right shoulder seam. Set in sleeves. Join sleeve and side seams. Press seams. Secure tips of banana leaves.

TWO FOR THE ROAD

JOHN AND MARY

TWO FOR THE ROAD

MATERIALS
13 (13) (14) (14) four ounce hanks of 'Woollybear Teddy Fleece'; a pair of size 6 mm. (No. 4) Aero knitting needles; 2 large buttons and 4 small ones.

TENSION
9 stitches and 8 rows to 5 centimetres (2 inches) over the single rib. If you cannot obtain the correct tension using the size needles suggested use larger or smaller ones accordingly.

ABBREVIATIONS
K., knit; p., purl; st., stitch; tog., together; dec., decrease (by working 2 sts. tog.); inc., increase (by working twice into the same st.); single rib is k.1 and p.1 alternately; sl., slip; p.s.s.o., pass sl. st. over; garter stitch is k. plain on every row.

NOTE
The instructions are given for the small woman's size. Where they vary work the figures in the first brackets for the medium woman's size; the figures in the second brackets for the small man's size; or the figures in the third brackets for the medium man's size.

MEASUREMENTS
The measurements are given in centimetres followed by inches in brackets.

	Women's	
Size	Small	Medium
To fit bust	82.5 (33)	87.5 (35)
Underarms	95 (38)	100 (40)
Side seam	47.5 (19)	47.5 (19)
Length	71 (28½)	72.5 (29)
Sleeve seam	42.5 (17)	42.5 (17)

	Men's	
Size	Small	Medium
To fit chest	92.5 (37)	97.5 (39)
Underarms	100 (40)	105 (42)
Side seam	47.5 (19)	47.5 (19)
Length	72.5 (29)	74 (29½)
Sleeve seam	45 (18)	45 (18)

THE BACK
With size 6 mm. (No. 4) needles cast on 86 (90) (90) (94) sts. and work 76 rows in single rib – work should now measure 47.5 centimetres (19 inches) from beginning.

To shape the armholes: Cast off 2 sts. at the beginning of the next 2 rows, then dec. 1 st. at each end of the next 10 (11) (8) (9) rows.

On 62 (64) (70) (72) sts. work 22 (23) (26) (27) rows in single rib.

To slope the shoulders: Cast off 11 sts. at the beginning of the next 2 rows and 8 (8) (11) (11) sts. on the 2 following rows.

Cast off the remaining 24 (26) (26) (28) sts.

THE LEFT FRONT
With size 6 mm. (No. 4) needles cast on 52 (54) (54) (56) sts. and work 76 rows in single rib.

**To shape the armhole: Cast off 2 sts. at the beginning of the next row. Work 1 row back to armhole edge. Dec. 1 st. at armhole edge on each of the next 10 (11) (8) (9) rows.

On 40 (41) (44) (45) sts. rib 9 (10) (13) (14) rows.

To shape for the rever collar and the neck: Cast off 17 (18) (18) (19) sts. at the beginning of the next row, then dec. 1 st. at the neck edge on each of the next 4 rows.

On 19 (19) (22) (22) sts. work 8 rows in single rib.

To slope the shoulder: Cast off 11 sts. at the beginning of the next row. Work 1 row. Then cast off the remaining 8 (8) (11) (11) sts.

JOHN AND MARY

MATERIALS
For the sleeveless sweater: 4 (4) (5) (5) (6) ounces of 'Woollybear Real Shetland' in main colour and one ounce of the same wool in each of the 7 contrast colours; a pair each of size 2¼ mm. (No. 13) and size 2¾ mm. (No. 12) Aero knitting needles.

For the sweater with sleeves: 7 (7) (8) (8) (9) ounces of 'Woollybear Real Shetland' in main colour and 2 ounces of the same wool in each of 7 contrast colours; a pair each of size 2¼ mm. (No. 13) and size 2¾ mm. (No. 12) Aero knitting needles.

TENSION
19 stitches and 20 rows to 5 centimetres (2 inches) over the FairIsle pattern using size 2¾ mm. (No. 12) needles. If you cannot obtain the correct tension using the size needle suggested, use larger or smaller ones accordingly.

ABBREVIATIONS
K., knit; p., purl; st., stitch; tog., together; dec., decrease (by working 2 sts. tog.); inc., increase (by working twice into same st.); single rib is k.1 and p.1 alternately; s.s., stocking stitch is k. on the right side and p. on the wrong side; m., main colour; a., first contrast colour; b., seventh contrast colour; up 1, pick up the loop, which lies between the needles, slip it onto left hand needle, then k. into back of it.

NOTE
The instructions are given for the small woman's size. Where they vary work the figures in the first brackets for the medium woman's size, the figures in the second brackets for the small man's size; the figures in the third brackets for the medium man's size; or the figures in the fourth brackets for the large man's size.

MEASUREMENTS
The measurements are given in centimetres followed by inches in brackets.

	Women's	
Size	Small	Medium
To fit bust	80 (32)	85 (34)
Underarms	80 (32)	85 (34)
Side seam	32.5 (13)	32.5 (13)
Length	51 (20½)	52.5 (21)
Sleeve seam	42.5 (17)	42.5 (17)

	Men's		
Size	Small	Medium	Large
To fit chest	90 (36)	95 (38)	100 (40)
Underarms	90 (36)	95 (38)	100 (40)
Side seam	37.5 (15)	37.5 (15)	37.5 (15)
Length	59 (23½)	60 (24)	61 (24½)
Sleeve seam	45 (18)	45 (18)	45 (18)

THE BACK
With size 2¼ mm. (No. 13) needles and m. cast on 131 (141) (151) (161) (171) sts. and work 33 rows in single rib.

Increase row: Rib 8 (4) (9) (5) (10), * up 1, rib 6 (7) (7) (8) (8); repeat from * ending last repeat rib 9 (4) (9) (4) (9).

Change to size 2¾ mm. (No. 12) needles and on 151 (161) (171) (181) (191) sts. beginning with a k. row s.s. 2 rows.

Now work in FairIsle pattern as follows: This is worked entirely in s.s. so only the colour details are given. It is not necessary to weave in the wools, but care should be taken not to pull colours not in use tightly across the back of the work or it will become puckered.

For the small woman's and medium man's sizes: 1st row: 1m., * 2a., 2m., 1a., 1m., 1a., 4m., 1a., 1m., 1a., 1m., 1a., 1m., 1a., 4m., 1a., 1m., 1a., 2m., 2a., 1m., *; repeat from * to * to end.

2nd row: 2a., * 2m., 1a., 1m., 1a., 6m., 1a., 1m., 1a., 1m., 1a., 6m., 1a., 1m., 1a., 2m., 3a. *; repeat from * to * ending last repeat 2a. instead of 3a.

For the medium woman's and large man's sizes: 1st row: 1a., 2m., 2a., 1m.; repeat from * to * as for 1st row of first size until 5 remain, 2a., 2m., 1a.

2nd row: 1m., 1a., 2m., 3a.; repeat from * to * given for 2nd row of first size until 4 remain, 2m., 1a., 1m.

For the small man's size: 1st row: 3m., 1a., 1m., 1a., 2m., 2a., 1m., now repeat from * to * given for 1st row of first size until 10 remain, 2a., 2m., 1a., 1m., 1a., 3m.

2nd row: 4m., 1a., 1m., 1a., 2m., 3a.; now repeat from * to * as given for 2nd row of first size until 9 remain, 2m., 1a., 1m., 1a., 4m.

For all sizes the last 2 rows set the position of the pattern given in the chart.

Now work the 3rd to 98th rows from the chart as set, then work the first 2 (2) (22) (22)((22) rows again.

To shape the armholes: Maintaining the continuity of the pattern as set, cast off 4 sts. at the beginning of the next 2 rows, then dec. 1 st. at each end of the next 10 (12) (14) (16) (18) rows.

On 123 (129) (135) (141) (147) sts., pattern 60 (62) (66) (68) (70) rows.

To slope the shoulders: Cast off 19 (20) (21) (22) (23) sts. at the beginning of the next 4 rows – 47 (49) (51) (53) (55) sts.

Change to size 2¼ mm. (No. 13) needles and with m. only work 10 rows in single rib, then cast off in rib.

THE FRONT
Work as given for back until 89 (89) (109) (109) (109) rows have been worked in FairIsle pattern.

Now divide the sts. for the neck: Next row: Work as set across 75 (80) (85) (90) (95) sts., and leave these sts. on a spare needle until required for right half front, p. 2 tog., work to end as set and continue on these 75 (80) (85) (90) (95) sts. for the left half front.

The left half front: To slope the neck: Maintaining the continuity of the pattern as set dec. 1 st. at the neck edge on the next row and the 3 following 3rd rows.

To shape the armhole and continue to slope the neck edge: Continuing to dec. at neck edge on every 3rd row as before, cast off 4 sts. at the beginning of the next row, then dec. 1 st. at the armhole edge on each of the next 10 (12) (14) (16) (18) rows.

Pattern 46 (47) (48) (49) (50) rows decreasing 1 st. at neck edge on every 3rd row as before.

On 38 (40) (42) (44) (46) sts. pattern 15 (16) (19) (20) (21) rows.

To slope the shoulder: Cast off 19 (20) (21) (22) (23) sts. at the beginning of the next row. On 19 (20) (21) (22) (23) sts. work 1 row, then cast off.

The right half front: With right side of work facing rejoin wool to inner edge of sts. left on spare needle and work to end of row, then work as given for left half front to end.

THE RIGHT FRONT
With size 6 mm. (No. 4) needles cast on 52 (54) (54) (56) sts. and work 36 rows in single rib.

1st Buttonhole row: Rib 4, cast off 3, rib to end.

2nd Buttonhole row: Rib until 4 remain, turn, cast on 3 over those cast off, turn, rib to end.

Rib 18 rows.

Work the 2 buttonhole rows again.

Rib 19 rows more.

Now work as given for left front from ** to end.

THE SLEEVES (both alike)
With size 6 mm. (No. 4) needles cast on 45 (47) (51) (53) sts. and work 12 rows in single rib.

Continuing in rib as set, inc. 1 st. at each end of the next row and the 8 following 6th rows.

On 63 (65) (69) (71) sts. rib 7 (7) (11) (11) rows.

To shape the sleevetop: Cast off 2 sts. at the beginning of the next 2 rows. Dec. 1 st. at each end of the next row and the 1 (2) (2) (3) following alternate rows.

On 55 (55) (59) (59) sts. rib 1 row.

Dec. 1 st. at each end of the next 16 (16) (18) (18) rows. Cast off 4 sts. at the beginning of the next 4 rows. Cast off the remaining 7 sts.

THE LARGE POCKETS (2 alike)
With size 6 mm. (No. 4) needles cast on 25 sts. and work 24 rows in single rib, then cast off.

THE SMALL POCKET
With size 6 mm. (No. 4) needles cast on 21 sts. and work 20 rows in single rib, then cast off.

THE EPAULETTES (2 alike)
With size 6 mm. (No. 4) needles cast on 5 sts. and work 14 rows in single rib.

Dec. 1 st. at each end of the next row. Rib 1 row. Next row: Sl.1, k.2 tog., p.s.s.o. Fasten off.

THE CUFF BANDS
With size 6 mm. (No. 4) needles cast on 5 sts. and work 30 (30) (32) (32) rows in single rib.

Dec. 1 st. at each end of the next row. On 3 sts. rib 1 row.

Next row: Sl.1, k.2 tog., p.s.s.o. Fasten off.

THE BACK COLLAR
With size 6 mm. (No. 4) needles cast on 65 (67) (67) (69) sts. and work 9 rows in single rib.

Dec. 1 st. at each end of the next 3 rows. Cast off the remaining 59 (61) (61) (63) sts.

THE SHOULDER PADS
With size 6 mm. (No. 4) needles cast on 22 sts. and k. 1 row. Continuing in garter st. dec. 1 st. at each end of the next row and the 9 following alternate rows. Take the 2 remaining sts. tog. and fasten off.

TO MAKE UP THE JACKET
Pin out to size and press all parts on the wrong side with a warm iron over a damp cloth. Join shoulder seams. Set in sleeves. Join sleeve and side seams. Pin cast off edge of back collar in place all round neck edge, beginning and ending at front neck shaping rows, then pin shaped row ends of back collar to the last few sts. cast off for reverse. Sew collar in position. Sew cast on edges of cuff bands to the sleeve seam 6 centimetres (2½ inches) above cast on edge. Sew cast on edge of epaulettes in place at armhole edge of each shoulder. Sew pockets in place. Sew on buttons, securing epaulettes and cuff bands with buttons. Sew shoulder pads in place. Press seams.

THE FRONT NECKBAND
With right side of work facing rejoin m. and using size 2¼ mm. (No. 13) needles pick up and k.68 (72) (78) (82) (86) sts. from left front neck edge and 68 (72) (78) (82) (86) sts. from right front neck edge.

Work 1 row in single rib.

Next row: Work in single rib as set to within 2 sts. of centre front, slip 1, k.1, pass slip st. over, k. 2 tog., rib to end.

Repeat the last 2 rows 3 times more.

Rib 1 row, then cast off.

THE ARMBANDS (both alike)
(For the sleeveless version)
First join shoulder seams, then with right side of work facing rejoin m. and using size 2¼ mm. (No. 13) needles pick up and k.128 (136) (144) (152) (160) sts. from all round armhole edge.

Work 7 rows in single rib, then cast off in rib.

THE SLEEVES (both alike)
With size 2¼ mm. (No. 13) needles and m. cast on 81 (81) (91) (91) (91) sts. and work 34 (34) (28) (28) (28) rows in single rib.

Change to size 2¾ mm. (No. 12) needles and beginning with a k. row s.s. 3 rows.

Now work in FairIsle pattern as follows; noting the information given for back and beginning with the 66th pattern row.

For the small and medium woman's sizes: 66th row: 4m., * 2b., 3m., 1b., 1m., 1b., 3m., 2b., 6m., 5b., 6m.; repeat from * once more, 2b., 3m., 1b., 1m., 1b., 3m., 2b., 4m.

For the small, medium and large man's sizes: 66th row: 3b., * 6m., 2b., 3m., 1b., 1m., 1b., 3m., 2b., 6m., 5b.; repeat from * ending last repeat 3b. instead of 5b.

For all sizes: Pattern 8 rows more as set.

Maintaining the continuity of the pattern as set, inc. 1 st. at each end of the next row and the 14 (16) (14) (16) (19) following 8th (6th) (10th) (8th) (6th) rows.

On 111 (115) (121) (125) (131) sts. pattern 11 (27) (3) (15) (29) rows.

To shape the sleevetop: Cast off 4 sts. at the beginning of the next 2 rows. Dec. 1 st. at each end of the next row and the 4 following alternate rows.

Work 1 row straight.

Dec. 1 st. at each end of the next 24 (26) (28) (30) (32) rows. Cast off 4 sts. at the beginning of the next 10 rows. Cast off the remaining 5 (5) (7) (7) (9) sts.

THE SHOULDER PADS (2 alike optional)
With size 2¼ mm. (No. 13) needles and m. cast on 51 sts. and work 2 rows in single rib. Dec. 1 st. at each end of the next row and the 23 following alternate rows.

Take the 3 remaining sts. tog. and fasten off.

TO MAKE UP THE SWEATER
Pin out to size and press all parts except the ribbing on the wrong side with a warm iron over a damp cloth. For the sweater with sleeves. Join shoulder seams continuing seams across neckband. Set in sleeves. Join sleeve and side seams. Press seams. Sew shoulder pads in place if required. For the sleeveless version, join side seams. Press seams.

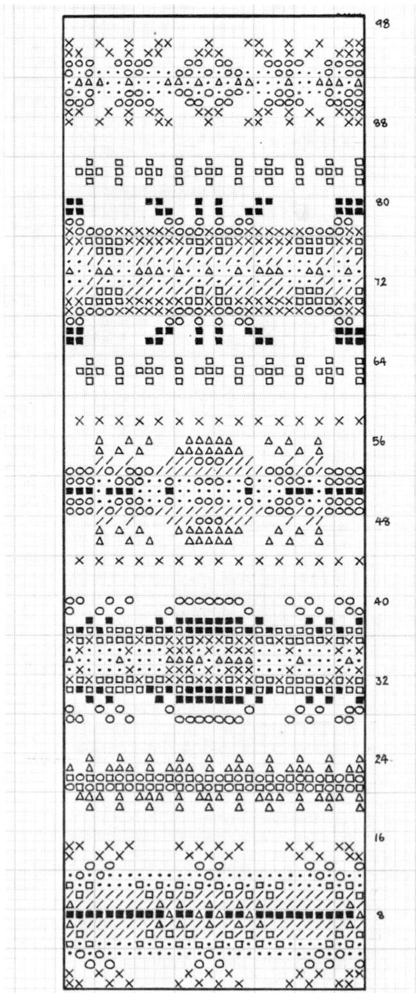

ROSE PETAL

NUT-CASE

ROSE PETAL

MATERIALS
26 (28) 50 gram balls of 'Woollybear Wool Bouclé' by Patricia Roberts, a pair of size 5 mm. (No. 6) Aero knitting needles; 5 large buttons; 4 small buttons.

TENSION
6 stitches and 10 rows to 5 centimetres (2 inches) over the single rib using size 5 mm. (No. 6) needles. If you cannot obtain the correct tension using the size needles suggested, use larger or smaller ones accordingly.

ABBREVIATIONS
K., knit; p., purl; st., stitch; tog., together; dec., decrease (by working 2 sts. tog.); inc., increase (by working twice into same st.); single rib is k.1 and p.1 alternately; sl., slip; p.s.s.o., pass sl. st. over; up 1, pick up the loop which lies between the needles, slip it onto left hand needle, then k. into back of it, thus making 1 st.

NOTE
The instructions are given for the small size. Where they vary work the figures in the brackets for the medium size.

MEASUREMENTS
The measurements are given in centimetres followed by inches in brackets.

Sizes	Small	Medium
To fit bust	85 (34)	90 (36)
Underarms	85 (34)	90 (36)
Side seam	32.5 (13)	32.5 (13)
Length	55 (22)	56 ($22\frac{1}{2}$)
Sleeve seam	42.5 (17)	42.5 (17)

THE BACK
With size 5 mm. (No. 6) needles cast on 59 (63) sts. and work 8 rows in single rib, beginning right side rows with k.1 and wrong side rows with p.1.

1st Decrease row: K.2 tog., rib 13, sl.1, k.2 tog., p.s.s.o., rib 23 (27), sl. 1, k.2 tog., p.s.s.o., rib 13, k.2 tog. – 53 (57) sts.

Rib 7 rows.

2nd Decrease row: K.2 tog., rib 11, sl.1, k.2 tog., p.s.s.o., rib 21 (25), sl. 1, k.2 tog., p.s.s.o., rib 11, k.2 tog. – 47 (51) sts.

Rib 7 rows.

3rd Decrease row: K.2 tog., rib 9, sl.1, k.2 tog., p.s.s.o., rib 19 (23), sl.1, k.2 tog., p.s.s.o., rib 9, k.2 tog.

On 41 (45) sts. rib 3 rows.

Increase row: Rib 4 (6), * up 1, inc. in next st., rib 7; repeat from * ending last repeat rib 4 (6).

On 51 (55) sts. work 37 rows in single rib.

To shape the armholes: Cast off 2 sts. at the beginning of the next 2 rows, then dec. 1 st. at each end of the next row and the 2 (3) following alternate rows.

On 41 (43) sts. rib 21 rows.

Inc. 1 st. at each end of the next row and the following 6th row,

On 45 (47) sts. rib 5 rows.

To slope the shoulders: Cast off 7 sts. at the beginning of the next 4 rows.

Leave the remaining 17 (19) sts. on a stitch-holder until required for collar.

THE LARGE POCKET BACKS (2 alike)
With size 5 mm. (No. 6) needles cast on 12 sts. and work 20 rows in single rib, then leave these sts. on a stitch-holder until required.

THE SMALL POCKET BACK
With size 5 mm. (No. 6) needles cast on 9 sts. and beginning right side rows with k.1 and wrong side rows with p.1, work 16 rows in single rib, then leave these sts. on a stitch-holder until required.

THE LEFT FRONT
With size 5 mm. (No. 6) needles cast on 33 (35) sts. and beginning with right side rows with k.1 and wrong side rows with p.1, work 8 rows in single rib.

1st Decrease row: K.2 tog., rib 13, sl.1, k.2 tog., p.s.s.o., rib to end. – 30 (32) sts.

Rib 7 rows.

2nd Decrease row: K.2 tog., rib 11, sl.1, k.2 tog., p.s.s.o., rib to end. – 27 (29) sts.

Rib 5 rows.

Pocket row: Rib 8 (10), slip next 12 sts. onto a stitch-holder and leave at front of work, in their place rib across the 12 sts. of one large pocket back, rib to end of row.

Rib 1 row.

3rd Decrease row: K.2 tog., rib 9, sl.1, k.2 tog., p.s.s.o., rib to end.

On 24 (26) sts. rib 3 rows.

Increase row: Inc. in first st., rib 7, up 1, inc. in next st., rib 7, up 1, inc. in next st., rib 7 (9).

On 29 (31) sts. rib 37 rows.

To shape the armhole: Cast off 2 sts. at the beginning of the next row. Work 1 row back to armhole edge. Dec. 1 st. at the beginning of the next row and the 2 (3) following alternate rows.

On 24 (25) sts. rib 3 (1) row(s).

Pocket row: Rib 3, slip next 9 sts. onto a stitch-holder and leave at front of work, in their place, rib across the 9 sts. of small pocket back, rib to end of row.

On 24 (25) sts. rib 12 rows.

** Now divide the sts. for the collar: Next row: Rib 6 and leave these sts. on a stitch-holder until required for collar, work to end of row.

NUT-CASE

MATERIALS
For the sleeveless sweater: 2 ounces of 'Woollybear Real Shetland Wool' by Patricia Roberts in main colour.

For the sweater with sleeves 3 (3) (4) (4) ounces of the same wool in main colour.

For either version 1 ounce of the same wool in each of the 8 other colours; a pair each of size $2\frac{1}{4}$ mm. (No. 13) and $2\frac{3}{4}$ mm. (No. 12) Aero knitting needles.

TENSION
18 stitches and 18 rows to 5 centimetres (2 inches) over the pattern using size $2\frac{3}{4}$ mm. (No. 12) needles. If you cannot obtain the correct tension using the size needles suggested, use larger or smaller ones accordingly.

ABBREVIATIONS
K., knit; p., purl; st., stitch; tog., together; dec., decrease (by working 2 sts. tog.); inc., increase (by working twice into same st.); single rib is k.1 and p.1 alternately; s.s., stocking stitch is k. on the right side and p. on the wrong side; up 1., pick up the loop which lies between the needles, slip it onto left hand needle, then k. into back of it; m., main colour; a., first background colour; b., second background colour; c., third background colour; d., first pattern colour; e., second pattern colour; f., third pattern colour; g., fourth pattern colour; h., fifth pattern colour.

NOTE
The instructions are given for the small woman's size. Where they vary, work the figures in the first brackets for the large woman's size, the figures in the second brackets for the small man's size or the figures in the third brackets for the large man's size.

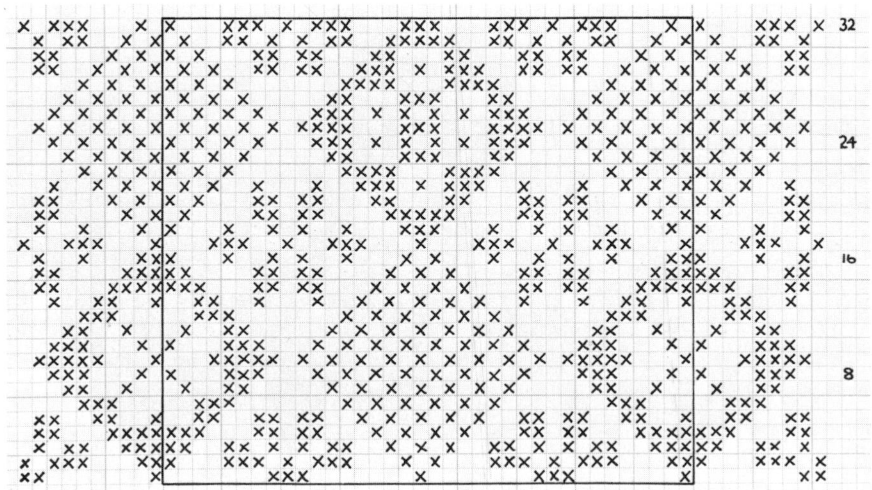

MEASUREMENTS
The measurements are given in centimetres followed by inches in brackets.

Women's	Small	Large
To fit bust	80 (32)	90 (36)
Underarms	80 (32)	90 (36)
Side seam	35 (14)	35 (14)
Length	55 (22)	56 ($22\frac{1}{2}$)
Sleeve seam	42.5 (17)	42.5 (17)
Men's	**Small**	**Large**
To fit chest	90 (36)	100 (40)
Underarms	90 (36)	100 (40)
Side seam	40 (16)	40 (16)
Length	63 ($25\frac{1}{4}$)	64 ($25\frac{3}{4}$)
Sleeve seam	47.5 (19)	47.5 (19)

THE BACK
With size $2\frac{1}{4}$ mm. (No. 13) needles and m. cast on 121 (139) (139) (157) sts. and work 31 rows in single rib.

Increase row: Rib 3 (12) (12) (21), * up 1, rib 5; repeat from * ending last repeat rib 3 (12) (12) (21). – 145 (163) (163) (181) sts.

Change to size $2\frac{3}{4}$ mm. (No. 12) needles and work in shetland colour pattern as follows. The pattern is worked entirely in s.s. beginning with a k. row. Take great care not to pull colours not in use tightly across the back of the work.

For the small woman's and large man's sizes: 1st row: 1d., * 7m., 3d., 7m., 1d.; repeat from * to end.

2nd row: 2d., * 3m., 3d., 1m., 1d., 1m., 3d., 3m., 1d., 1m., 1d., 3m., 3d., 1m., 1d., 1m., 3d., 3m., 3d. *; repeat from * to * ending last repeat 2d.

3rd row: 3e., ** 2m., 2e., 1m., 1e., 1m., 1e., 1m., 2e., 2m., * 1e., 1m., 1e., 1m., 1e., repeat from ** to *, 5e. **; repeat from ** to ** ending last repeat 3e.

4th row: 4e., * 3a., 2e., 1a., 2e., 3a., 1e., 1a., 1e., 1a., 1e., 1a., 1e., 3a., 2e., 1a., 2e., 3a., 7e.,* repeat from * to * ending last repeat 4e.

5th row: 1e., * 2a., 2e., 2a., 2e., 1a., 2e., 2a., 1e., 1a., 1e., 1a., 1e., 1a., 1e., 1a., 1e., 2a., 2e., 1a., 2e., 2a., 2e., 2a., 1e. *; repeat from * to * to end.

To shape the neck: Dec. 1 st. at the neck edge on each of the next 4 (6) rows.

Inc. 1 st. at the beginning – armhole edge and dec. 1 st. at the end – neck edge on the next row.

On the small size only: Dec. 1 st. at the neck edge on the next row.

For both sizes: On 13 sts. work 4 (5) rows.

Inc. 1 st. at the armhole edge on the next row.

On 14 sts. rib 5 rows.

To slope the shoulder: Cast off 7 sts. at the beginning of the next row. On 7 sts. work 1 row, then cast off.

THE RIGHT FRONT

With size 5 mm. (No. 6) needles cast on 33 (35) sts. and work 8 rows in single rib.

1st Decrease row: Rib 15 (17), sl.1, k.2 tog., p.s.s.o., rib 13, k.2 tog.

Rib 7 rows.

2nd Decrease row: Rib 14 (16), sl.1, k.2 tog., p.s.s.o., rib 11, k.2 tog.

Rib 3 rows.

1st Buttonhole row: Rib 2, cast off 2, rib to end.

2nd Buttonhole row: Rib until 2 remain, turn, cast on 2, turn, rib to end.

Pocket row: Rib 7, slip next 12 sts. onto a stitch-holder and leave at front of work, in their place rib across the 12 sts. of one large pocket back, rib to end.

On 27 (29) sts. rib 1 row.

3rd Decrease row: Rib 13 (15), sl.1, k.2 tog., p.s.s.o., rib 9, k.2 tog.

On 24 (26) sts. rib 3 rows.

Increase row: Rib 7 (9), up 1, inc. in next st., rib 7, up 1, inc. in next st., rib 7, inc. in next st.

On 29 (31) sts. rib 9 rows.

Work the 2 buttonhole rows again.

Rib 16 rows, then work the 2 buttonhole rows again.

Rib 9 rows.

To shape the armhole: Cast off 2 sts. at the beginning of the next row. Work 1 row back to armhole edge, then dec. 1 st. at the beginning of the next row and the 2 following alternate rows.

Work the 2 buttonhole rows again, but decreasing 1 st. at the armhole edge on the second size only, on the 2nd of these rows.

On 24 (25) sts. rib 14 rows.

Now work as given for left front from ** to end.

THE POCKET TOPS (all alike)

With right side of work facing rejoin yarn to the sts. left on stitch-holder and using size 5 mm. (No. 6) needles work 1 row in single rib, then cast off in rib.

THE COLLAR

First join shoulder seams. With right side of work facing rejoin yarn to the 6 sts. left on stitch-holder at right front edge and using size 5 mm. (No. 6) needles rib across these sts. then pick up and k.15 (16) sts. from right front neck edge, rib across the 17 (19) sts. at back neck edge, pick up and k.15 (16) sts. from left front neck edge, then rib across the 6 sts. left on stitch-holder.

On 59 (63) sts. rib 1 row.

Work the 2 buttonhole rows given for right front.

Rib 2 rows.

Continuing in rib, dec. 1 st. at each end of the next 2 rows.

Cast off loosely in rib.

THE SLEEVES (both alike as the fabric is reversible)

The first part: With size 5 mm. (No. 6) needles cast on 8 sts. and work 14 rows in single rib, then leave these sts. on a spare needle until required.

The second part: With size 5 mm. (No. 6) needles cast on 18 (20) sts. and work 14 rows in single rib.

The main part: Rib across the 18 (20) sts. of second part, then rib across the 8 sts. of first part.

On 26 (28) sts. rib 3 rows.

Continuing in rib inc. 1 st. at each end of the next row and the 5 following 10th rows.

On 38 (40) sts. rib 15 rows.

To shape the sleevetop: Cast off 2 sts. at the beginning of the next 2 rows, then dec. 1 st. at each end of the next row and the 8 (9) following alternate rows.

On 16 sts. work 1 row.

Cast off 3 sts. at the beginning of the next 4 rows. Cast off the remaining 4 sts.

THE SHOULDER PADS (2 alike)

With size 5 mm. (No. 6) needles cast on 15 sts. and work 25 rows in single rib, then cast off.

TO MAKE UP THE JACKET

Pin out to size and press lightly on the wrong side with a warm iron over a damp cloth. Set in sleeves, so that the slits at the lower edges are towards the back of the garment. Join sleeve and side seams. Sew in pocket backs and row ends of pocket tops in place.

Fold shoulder pads in half diagonally to form triangles and neatly join outer edges. Catch shoulder pads in place on wrong side. Press seams. Sew large buttons in place at front edge. Overlap cuffs towards back of garment and secure with 2 small buttons on each sleeve.

6th row: 3a., * 3f., 7a., 1f., 1a., 1f., 1a., 1f., 1a., 1f., 1a., 1f., 1a., 1f., 7a., 3f., 5a., *; repeat from * to * ending last repeat 3a.

For the large woman's and small man's sizes; 1st row: 2d., * 7m., 1d., 7m., 3d.; repeat from * ending last repeat 2d.

2nd row: 1d., 1m., 3d., 3m., 3d., repeat from * to * on 2nd row of small woman's size until 8 remain, 3m., 3d., 1m., 1d.

3rd row: 1m., 1e., 1m., 2e., 2m., 5e., repeat from ** to ** on 3rd row given for small woman's size until 7 remain, 2m., 2e., 1m., 1e., 1m.

4th row: 1a., 2e., 3a., 7e., repeat from * to * on 4th row given for small woman's size, until 6 remain, 3a., 2e., 1a.

5th row: 1a., 2e., 2a., 2e., 2a., 1e.; repeat from * to * on 5th row given for small woman's size until 9 remain, 2a., 2e., 2a., 2e., 1a.

6th row: 4a., 3f., 5a., repeat from * to * on 6th row given for small woman's size until 7 remain, 3f., 4a.

For all sizes: The last 6 rows set the position of the 32 row stitch repeat pattern given in the chart and the colour sequence which is as follows: the background colours are worked in a sequence of 3 rows m., 3 rows a., 3 rows b., 3 rows c., and the pattern colours are worked in the sequence of 2 rows d., 3 rows e., 3 rows f., 3 rows g., 3 rows h., 1 row d.

Thus working in pattern as set, work the 7th to 32nd rows, then work a further 68 (68) (86) (86) rows in pattern in colour sequence as given.

To shape the armholes: Maintaining the continuity of the pattern as set, cast off 6 (8) (6) (8) sts. at the beginning of the next 2 rows, then dec. 1 st. at each end of the next row and the 9 (11) (13) (15) following alternate rows.

On 113 (123) (123) (133) sts. pattern 13 (13) (17) (17) rows.***

Maintaining the continuity of the pattern as set and working the extra sts. into the pattern as they occur, inc. 1 st. at each end of the next row and the 3 following 8th rows.

On 121 (131) (131) (141) sts. pattern 7 rows.

To slope the shoulders: Cast off 12 (13) (13) (14) sts. at the beginning of the next 4 rows, and 11 (13) (12) (14) sts. on the 2 following rows.

Leave the remaining 51 (53) (55) (57) sts. on a spare needle until required for neckband.

THE FRONT

Work as given for the back until *** is reached.

Inc. 1 st. at each end of the next row – 115 (125) (125) (135) sts.

Now divide the sts. for the neck:

Next row: Pattern 48 (52) (51) (55) and leave these sts. on a spare needle until required for right front shoulder, cast off 19 (21) (23) (25) sts. for neck, pattern to end and continue on these 48 (52) (51) (55) sts. for the left front shoulder.

The left front shoulder: To shape the neck and continue to shape for the armhole: Pattern 16 rows decreasing 1 st. at the neck edge on each row and at the same time increasing 1 st. at the armhole edge on the 7th and 15th of these rows.

On 34 (38) (37) (41) sts. pattern 6 rows, then inc. 1 st. at the armhole edge on the next row.

On 35 (39) (38) (42) sts. pattern 7 rows.

To slope the shoulder: Cast off 12 (13) (13) (14) sts. at the beginning of the next row and the following alternate row. On 11 (13) (12) (14) sts. work 1 row, then cast off.

The right front shoulder: With right side of work facing rejoin yarn to inner edge of sts. left on spare needle and work to end of row, then work as given for left front shoulder to end.

THE NECKBAND

First join right shoulder seam: With right side of work facing rejoin m. at left front neck edge and using size 2¼ mm. (No. 13) needles pick up and k. 47 sts. from left front neck edge, 19 (21) (23) (25) sts. from centre front neck and 47 sts. from right front neck edge, then k. across the 51 (53) (55) (57) sts. left on spare needle at back neck edge.

On 164 (168) (172) (176) sts. work 8 rows in single rib, then cast off loosely in rib.

THE SLEEVES (both alike)

With size 2¼ mm. (No. 13) needles and m. cast on 63 (65) (67) (69) sts. and work 27 rows in single rib.

Increase row: Rib 4 (4) (8) (10), * up 1, rib 6 (8) (10) (16); repeat from * ending last repeat rib 5 (5) (9) (11).

Change to size 2¾ mm. (No. 12) needles and on 73 sts. work 6 rows in pattern as given for small woman's size on back but beginning the colour sequence given for back as follows.

1st row: Background in a., pattern in h.
2nd row: Background in a., pattern in d.
3rd row: Background in b., pattern in d.
4th row: Background in b., pattern in d.
5th row: Background in b., pattern in e.
6th row: Background in c., pattern in e.

The last 6 rows set the position of the pattern given for the back. Continuing in pattern as set and working the extra sts. into the pattern as they occur, inc. 1 st. at each end of the next row and the 17 (19) (21) (23) following 6th rows.

On 109 (113) (117) (121) sts. pattern 23 (11) (17) (5) rows.

To shape the sleevetop: Maintaining the continuity of the pattern as set, cast off 6 (8) (6) (8) sts. at the beginning of the next 2 rows.

Dec. 1 st. at each end of the next row and the 14 (18) (22) (26) following alternate rows. Work 1 row straight.

Dec. 1 st. at each end of the next 10 (6) (6) (2) rows. Then cast off 5 sts. at the beginning of the next 8 rows.

Cast off the remaining 7 sts.

THE ARMBANDS (both alike)
(for the sleeveless version)

First join left shoulder seam. With right side of work facing rejoin m. and using size 2¼ mm. (No. 13) needles pick up and k. 124 (136) (148) (160) sts. and work 10 rows in single rib, then cast off in rib.

THE SHOULDER PADS (optional)

With size 2¼ mm. (No. 13) needles and m. cast on 54 sts. and work 66 rows in single rib, then cast off. Fold in half diagonally and join outer edges to form triangles.

TO MAKE UP THE SWEATER

Pin out to size and press all parts except the ribbing on the wrong side with a warm iron over a damp cloth. Join left shoulder seam. Set in sleeves. Join sleeve and side seams. Press seams.

BLITHE SPIRIT

THE WHISPERERS

BLITHE SPIRIT

MATERIALS

For the sweater: 12 (13) (14) ounces of 'Woollybear Real Shetland' in main colour and 2 ounces in contrast colour; a pair each of size 2¼ mm. (No. 13) and size 3 mm. (No. 11) Aero knitting needles; 5 small buttons.

TENSION

30 stitches – 2 repeats of the lace pattern to 9.5 centimetres (3¾ inches) in width and 20 rows – 2 repeats of the pattern to 5 centimetres (2 inches) in depth, using size 3 mm. (No. 11) needles. If you cannot obtain the correct tension using the size needles suggested use larger or smaller ones accordingly.

ABBREVIATIONS

K., knit; p., purl; st., stitch; tog., together; dec., decrease (by working 2 sts. tog.); inc., increase (by working twice into same st.); single rib is k.1 and p.1 alternately; sl., slip; p.s.s.o., pass sl. st. over; s.s.k., sl.1, k.1, p.s.s.o.; y.r.n., yarn round needle; up 1, pick up the loop which lies between the needles, slip it onto left hand needle, then k. into back of it; m., main colour; c., contrast colour.

NOTE

The instructions are given for the small size. Where they vary work the figures in the first brackets for the medium size or the figures in the second brackets for the large size.

MEASUREMENTS

The measurements are given in centimetres followed by inches in brackets.

THE SWEATER

Size	Small	Medium	Large
To fit bust	82.5 (33)	90 (36)	97.5 (39)
Underarms	84 (33¾)	94 (37½)	102.5 (41)
Side seam	32.5 (13)	32.5 (13)	32.5 (13)
Length	51 (20½)	52.5 (21)	54 (21½)
Sleeve seam	40 (16)	40 (16)	40 (16)

THE SWEATER

THE BACK

With size 2¼ mm. (No. 13) needles and m. cast on 128 (142) (156) sts. and work 33 rows in single rib.

Increase row: Rib 8 (7) (6), * up 1, rib 16; repeat from * ending last repeat rib 8 (7) (6) – 136 (151) (166) sts.

Change to size 3 mm. (No. 11) needles and work in pattern as follows: 1st row: K.1, * y.r.n., k.1, s.s.k., p.1, k. 2 tog., k.1, y.r.n., p.1, s.s.k., p.1, k. 2 tog., y.r.n., k.1, y.r.n., k.1; repeat from * to end.

2nd row; P.5, * k.1, p.1, k.1, p.3, k.1, p.8; repeat from * ending last repeat p.4.

3rd row: K.1, * y.r.n., k.1, s.s.k., p.1, k. 2 tog., k.1, p.1, sl.1, k. 2 tog., p.s.s.o., y.r.n., k.3, y.r.n., k.1; repeat from * to end.

4th row: P.7, * k.1, p.2, k.1, p.10; repeat from * ending last repeat p.4.

5th row: K.1, * y.r.n., k.1, y.r.n., s.s.k., p.1, k. 2 tog., k. 2 tog., y.r.n., k.5, y.r.n., k.1, repeat from * to end.

6th row: P.8, * k.1, p.1, k.1, p.12; repeat from * ending last repeat p.5.

7th row: K.1, * y.r.n., k.3, y.r.n., sl.1, k. 2 tog., p.s.s.o., p.1, y.r.n., k.1, s.s.k., p.1, k. 2 tog., k.1, y.r.n., k.1; repeat from * to end.

8th row; P.4, * k.1, p.3, k.1, p.10; repeat from * ending last repeat p.7.

9th row: K.1, * y.r.n., k.5, y.r.n., s.s.k., k.1, s.s.k., p.1, k. 2 tog., k.1, y.r.n., k.1; repeat from * to end.

10th row: P.4, * k.1, p.2, k.1, p.11; repeat from * ending last repeat p.8.

The last 10 rows form the pattern, repeat them 9 times more. Work should now measure 32.5 centimetres (13 inches) from beginning.

To shape the armholes: Maintaining the continuity of the pattern as set cast off 7 sts. at the beginning of the next 2 rows, then dec. 1 st. at each end of the next 8 (11) (14) rows.

On 106 (115) (124) sts., pattern 29 (32) (31) rows. **

Now divide the sts. for the back neck opening: Next row: Work as set across 53 (57) (62) sts. and leave these sts. on a spare needle until required for left back shoulder, on the second size only p. 2 tog., then on all sizes work

THE WHISPERERS

MATERIALS

For the waistcoat: 12 (13) (14) (15) 25 gram balls of either 'Woollybear Brushed Alpaca' or 'Woollybear 100% Mohair'; a pair each of size 3¾ mm. (No. 9) and size 4 mm. (No. 8) Aero knitting needles; 5 (5) (6) (6) buttons; a medium sized cable needle.

For the scarf: 5 25 gram balls of either 'Woollybear Brushed Alpaca' or 'Woollybear 100% Mohair'; a pair of size 3¾ mm. (No. 9) Aero knitting needles.

TENSION

18 stitches and 20 rows to 7.5 centimetres (3 inches) over the pattern using size 4 mm. (No. 8) needles. If you cannot obtain the correct tension using the size needles suggested use larger or smaller ones accordingly.

ABBREVIATIONS

K., knit; p., purl; st., stitch; tog., together; dec., decrease (by working 2 sts. tog.); inc., increase (by working twice into same st.); single rib is k.1 and p.1 alternately; cable 4, thus, slip next 2 sts. onto a cable needle and leave at front of work, k.2, then k.2 from cable needle; up 1, pick up the loop which lies between the needles, slip it onto left hand needle, then k. into back of it.

NOTE

The instructions are given for the small woman's size. Where they vary work the figures in the first brackets for the medium woman's size; the figures in the second brackets for the small man's size or the figures in the third brackets for the medium man's size.

MEASUREMENTS

The measurements are given in centimetres followed by inches in brackets.

THE WAISTCOAT

	Women's Small	Medium
To fit bust	82.5 (33)	90 (36)
Underarms	82.5 (33)	90 (36)
Side seam	32.5 (13)	32.5 (13)
Length	51 (20½)	52.5 (21)

	Men's Small	Medium
To fit chest	90 (36)	97.5 (39)
Underarms	90 (36)	97.5 (39)
Side seam	37.5 (15)	37.5 (15)
Length	59 (23½)	60 (24)

THE SCARF

19 centimetres (7½ inches) in width and 120 centimetres (48 inches) in length.

THE WAISTCOAT

THE BACK

With size 3¾ mm. (No. 9) needles cast on 85 (93) (93) (101) sts. and work 19 rows in single rib.

Increase row: Rib 6, * up 1, rib 8; repeat from * ending last repeat rib 7.

Change to size 4 mm. (No. 8) needles and on 95 (104) (104) (113) sts., work in pattern as follows: 1st row: P.1, k.1, p.1, k.1, p.1, * k.4, p.1, k.1, p.1, k.1, p.1; repeat from * to end.

2nd row: K.1, p.1, k.1, p.1, k.1, * p.4, k.1, p.1, k.1, p.1, k.1; repeat from * to end.

3rd and 4th rows: As 1st and 2nd rows.

5th row: P.1, k.1, p.1, k.1, p.1, * cable 4, p.1, k.1, p.1, k.1, p.1; repeat from * to end.

6th row: As 2nd row.

The last 6 rows form the pattern; repeat them 10 (10) (12) (12) times more then on the men's sizes only work 2 rows more.

To shape the armholes: Continuing in pattern as set cast off 3 (4) (4) (5) sts. at the beginning of the next 2 rows, then dec. 1 st. at each end of the next row and the 5 (6) (6) (7) following alternate rows.

On 77 (82) (82) (87) sts. pattern 33 (33) (37) (39) rows.

To slope the shoulders: Cast off 12 sts. at the beginning of the next 2 rows, then 11 (13) (13) (15) sts. on the 2 following rows.

Cast off the remaining 31 (32) (32) (33) sts.

THE LEFT FRONT

With size 3¾ mm. (No. 9) needles cast on 44 (48) (48) (52) sts. and work 19 rows in single rib.

Increase row: Rib 5 (3) (3) (5), * up 1, rib 7; repeat from * ending last repeat rib 4 (3) (3) (5) – 50 (55) (55) (59) sts.

Change to size 4 mm. (No. 8) needles and work in pattern as follows: 1st row: * P.1, k.1, p.1, k.1, p.1, k.4; repeat from * until 5 (1) (1) (5) remain, rib to end as set.

The last row sets the position of the 6 row cable pattern given for back. Pattern 29 rows more as set and given for back.

Pocket row: Pattern 12 (14) (14) (16), slip next 25 (25) (27) (27) sts. onto a stitch-holder to end as set and continue on these 53 (57) (62) sts. for the right back shoulder. The right back shoulder: Pattern 30 (28) (30) rows.

To slope the shoulder: Cast off 11 (12) (13) sts. at the beginning of the next row and the 2 following alternate rows. On 20 (21) (23) sts., work 1 row, then cast off.

The left back shoulder: With right side of work facing rejoin m. to inner edge of sts. left on spare needle and work to end of row, then work as given for right back shoulder to end.

THE FRONT

Work as given for back until ** is reached.

Now divide the sts. for the neck: Next row: Pattern as set across 45 (49) (53) sts. and leave these sts. on a spare needle until required for right front shoulder, cast off 16 (17) (18) sts. for neck, pattern to end of row and continue on these 45 (49) (53) sts. for the left front shoulder.

The left front shoulder: To shape the neck: Dec. 1 st. at the neck edge on each of the next 12 (13) (14) rows. On 33 (36) (39) sts. pattern 18 (15) (16) rows.

To slope the shoulder: Cast off 11 (12) (13) sts. at the beginning of the next row and following alternate row. On 11 (12) (13) sts. work 1 row, then cast off.

The right front shoulder: With right side of work facing rejoin m. to inner edge of sts. left on spare needle and work to end of row, then work as given for left front shoulder to end.

THE SLEEVES (both alike)

With size 3 mm. (No. 11) needles and m. cast on 61 sts. and work 10 rows in pattern as given for back.

Maintaining the continuity of the pattern and working the extra sts. into the pattern as they occur, inc. 1 st. at each end of the next row and the 14 (16) (18) following 10th (8th) (8th) rows.

On 91 (95) (99) sts. pattern 9 (21) (5) rows.

To shape the sleevetop: Cast off 7 sts. at the beginning of the next 2 rows. Dec. 1 st. at each end of the next row and the 19 (20) (21) following alternate rows.

On 37 (39) (41) sts. work 1 row.

Cast off 5 sts. at the beginning of the next 6 rows. Cast off the remaining 7 (9) (11) sts.

THE COLLAR (2 halves both alike)

With size 2¼ mm. (No. 13) needles and c. cast on 73 (75) (79) sts. and work in moss st. as follows:

Moss st. row: K.1, * p.1, k.1; repeat from * to end. Repeat the moss st. row 3 times more.

Continuing in moss st. as set, dec. 1 st. at each end of the next row and the 4 following 4th rows.

On 63 (65) (69) sts. moss st. 3 rows, then cast off.

THE CUFFS (both alike)

With size 2¼ mm. (No. 13) needles and c. cast on 71 sts. and work 4 rows in moss st. as given for collar. Continuing in moss st. dec. 1 st. at each end of the next row and the 4 following 4th rows.

On 61 sts. moss st. 3 rows, then cast off.

THE SHOULDER PADS (2 alike)

With size 2¼ mm. (No. 13) needles and m. cast on 40 sts. and work 70 rows in moss st., then cast off.

THE NECKTIES (2 alike)

With size 2¼ mm. (No. 13) needles and c. cast on 99 sts. and work 2 rows in moss st. as given for collar, then cast off loosely.

TO MAKE UP THE SWEATER

Pin out to size and press all parts except the ribbing on the wrong side with a warm iron over a damp cloth. Join shoulder seams. Set in sleeves, join sleeve and side seams. Neatly sew cast off edges of half collars in place. Sew cast off edges of cuffs in position at cast on edge of sleeves. Fold cuffs back and secure with 2 buttons on each. Make a buttonhole loop at left back neck edge. Sew button in place at right back neck edge. Sew ends of ties at back neck edges. Fold shoulder pads in half to form triangles, then neatly catch shoulder pads in place. Press seams.

THE HEADBAND

With size 2¼ mm. (No. 13) needles cast on 19 sts. and work in moss st. as given for collar until the band measures 100 centimetres (40 inches). Cast off.

and leave at front of work, in their place pattern across the 25 (25) (27) (27) sts. of one pocket back, pattern to end.

Pattern 29 rows then work the pocket row again.

Pattern 1 (1) (15) (15) row(s).

**To slope the front edge: Dec. 1 st. at the end front edge on the next row and the following alternate row.

Work 1 row back to armhole edge.

To shape the armhole and continue to slope the front edge: While continuing to dec. at front edge on every alternate row as before, cast off 3 (4) (4) (5) sts. at the beginning of the next row, for armhole, then decrease 1 st. at the armhole edge on the 6 (7) (7) (8) following alternate rows.

Pattern 18 (18) (18) (16) rows decreasing at front edge on every alternate row as before.

On 23 (25) (25) (27) sts., pattern 15 (15) (19) (23) rows.

To slope the shoulder: Cast off 12 sts. at the beginning of the next row. On 11 (13) (13) (15) sts. work 1 row, then cast off.

THE RIGHT FRONT

Work as given for left front until the increase row has been worked.

Change to size 4 mm. (No. 8) needles and work in pattern as follows: 1st row: Beginning with p.1, rib 5 (1) (1) (5), * k.4, p.1, k.1, p.1, k.1, p.1,; repeat from * to end.

The last row sets the position of the 6 row cable pattern given for back. Pattern 29 rows more as set.

Pocket row: Pattern 13 (16) (14) (16), slip next 25 (25) (27) (27) sts. onto a stitch-holder and leave at front of work, in their place pattern across the sts. of one pocket back, pattern to end.

Pattern 29 rows, then work the pocket row again.

Pattern 2 (2) (16) (16) rows.

Now work as given for left front from ** to end.

THE POCKET BACKS (4 alike)

With size 4 mm. (No. 8) needles cast on 25 (25) (27) (27) sts. and work 30 rows in single rib, then leave these sts. on a stitch-holder until required.

THE POCKET TOPS (4 alike)

With right side of work facing rejoin yarn to the 25 (25) (27) (27) sts. left on stitch-holder and using size 3¾ mm. (No. 9) needles work 6 rows in single rib. Cast off in rib.

THE ARMBANDS (both alike)

First join shoulder seam. With right side of work facing rejoin yarn and using size 3¾ mm. (No. 9) needles pick up and k.96 (102) (108) (114) sts. from all round armhole edge.

Work 5 rows in single rib.

Cast off in rib.

THE FRONTBAND

With size 3¾ mm. (No. 9) needles cast on 7 sts. and work 6 (6) (4) (4) rows in single rib.

1st Buttonhole row: Rib 2, cast off 3, rib to end.

2nd Buttonhole row: Rib 2, turn, cast on 3, turn, rib to end.

Rib 16 rows.

Repeat the last 18 rows 3 (3) (4) (4) times more, then work the 2 buttonhole rows again.

Continue in rib until the band is long enough to fit up one front edge across back neck edge and down other front edge.

Sew front band in position, casting off when correct length is assured.

TO MAKE UP THE WAISTCOAT

Pin out to size and press very lightly on the wrong side with a warm iron over a damp cloth. Join side seams. Neatly sew pocket backs and row ends of pocket tops in place. Press seams. Sew on buttons.

THE SCARF

With size 3¾ mm. (No. 9) needles cast on 45 sts. and work in single rib until the scarf measures 120 centimetres (48 inches), then cast off in rib.

THE TASSELS

For each tassel cut 6 lengths of yarn each 15 centimetres (6 inches) long, fold all 6 lengths of yarn in half together. Using crochet hook pull looped ends through one corner of cast on edge. Pass cut ends through looped ends and draw up firmly.

In the same way make 7 more tassels evenly along cast on edge, then a further 8 tassels along cast off edge.

Press scarf lightly.

POPCORN

POPCORN

MATERIALS
For the sweater or the cardigan: 9 ounce (28 gram) hanks of 'Woollybear Real Shetland' by Patricia Roberts in main colour; 3 hanks in first contrast colour and one hank in each of the 5 other contrast colours, or 14 25 gram balls of 'Woollybear Bunny Fluff' in main colour; 3 balls in first contrast colour; one ball in 2nd, 3rd, 4th and 5th contrast colours and one hank of 'Real Shetland' in 6th contrast – black; a pair each of size 2¾ mm. (No. 12) and size 3 mm. (No. 11) Aero knitting needles; for the cardigan only, 8 buttons.

TENSION
Work at a tension of 14 stitches and 18 rows to 5 centimetres (2 inches) over the stocking stitch using size 3 mm. (No. 11) needles. If you cannot obtain the correct tension using the size needles suggested, use larger or smaller ones accordingly.

ABBREVIATIONS
K., knit; p., purl; st., stitch; tog., together; dec., decrease (by working 2 sts. tog.); inc., increase (by working twice into same st.); single rib is k.1 and p.1 alternately; s.s., stocking stitch is k. on the right side and p. on the wrong side; sl., slip; p.s.s.o., pass sl. st. over; up 1, pick up the loop which lies between the needles, slip it onto left hand needle, then k. into back of it; m.k., make knot thus, with a. k.1, p.1, k.1 all into next st., turn, p.3, turn, sl.1, k.2 tog., p.s.s.o.; make ties thus, working into next st., cast on 24 sts., cast off these 24 sts., thus one st. from left hand needle has been transferred to right hand needle; m., main colour; a., first contrast colour; b., second contrast; c., third contrast; d., fourth contrast; e., fifth contrast; f., sixth contrast; y.r.n., yarn round needle.

MEASUREMENTS
The measurements are given in centimetres followed by inches in brackets.

To fit bust	85 (34)
Underarms (sweater)	86 (34½)
Underarms (cardigan)	88.5 (35½)
Side seam	37.5 (15)
Length	57.5 (23)
Sleeve seam	42.5 (17)

THE SWEATER

THE BACK
With size 2¾ mm. (No. 12) needles and m. cast on 111 sts. and work 29 rows in single rib.

Increase row: Rib 11, *up 1, rib 10; repeat from * to end. – 121 sts.

**Change to size 3 mm. (No. 11) needles and beginning with a k. row s.s. 4 rows.

Now work in pattern as follows. This is worked in s.s. except where indicated, so only the colour details are given. Use separate small balls of contrast colours for each section of the pattern. When working the snow knots take care not to pull a. tightly across the back of the work.

1st row: 6m., *with a. m.k., 5 m.; repeat from * ending last repeat 6m.

2nd, 3rd and 4th rows with m. in s.s.

5th row: 3m., *with a. m.k., 5m; repeat from * ending last repeat 3m.

6th row: All m. **

7th row: 26m., 8e., 87m.

8th row: 86m., 11e., 24m.

The last 8 rows set the position of the pattern given in the chart. Now working in pattern from chart as set, work the 9th to 106th rows.

To shape the armholes: Continuing in pattern from chart as set, cast off 7 sts. at the beginning of the next 2 rows, then dec. 1 st. at each end of the next row and the 5 following alternate rows.

On 95 sts. pattern 37 rows.

Inc. 1 st. at each end of the next row and the following 8th row.

On 99 sts. work 7 rows.

To slope the shoulders: Cast off 11 sts. at the beginning of the next 2 rows, 10 sts. on the 2 following rows and 9 sts. on the 2 following rows.

Cast off the remaining 39 sts.

THE FRONT
Work as given for the back until the armhole shaping has been worked.

On 95 sts. pattern 30 rows as set.

Now divide the sts. for the neck: Next row: Pattern 43 and leave these sts. on a spare needle until required for right front shoulder, cast off 9, work to end and continue on these 43 sts. for the left front shoulder.

The left front shoulder: Continuing in pattern as set, dec. 1 st. at the neck edge on each of the next 6 rows. Still decreasing at the neck edge on each row, inc. 1 st. at the armhole edge on the next row and the following 8th row.

On 30 sts. pattern 7 rows.

To slope the shoulder: Cast off 11 sts. at the beginning of the next row and 10 sts. on the following alternate row. On 9 sts. work 1 row, then cast off.

The right front shoulder: With right side of work facing rejoin yarn to inner edge of sts. left on spare needle and work to end of row. Work as given for left front shoulder to end.

THE SLEEVES (both alike)
With size 2¾ mm. (No. 12) needles and m. cast on 57 sts. and work 23 rows in single rib.

Increase row: Rib 2, *up 1, rib 4; repeat from * ending last repeat rib 3. – 71 sts.

Change to size 3 mm. (No. 11) needles and beginning with a k. row s.s. 2 rows.

Now work in the snow and parcel pattern as follows, noting the information given on back:

1st row: 2m., *with a. m.k., 5m.; repeat from * ending last repeat 2m.

2nd, 3rd and 4th rows: All m.

5th row: 5m., *with a. m.k., 5m; repeat from * to end.

6th, 7th and 8th rows: All m.

9th to 16th rows: Repeat 1st to 8th rows.

17th to 20th rows: As 1st to 4th rows.

21st row: Work in snow pattern as set across 8 sts., then for the parcel 6d., with m. make tie – see abbreviations, – 6d., pattern 29 as set, 6d., with m. make tie, 6d., pattern as set across 8 sts.

22nd row: Pattern 8 as set, 6d., 1m., 6d., work 29 as set, 6d., 1m., 6d., pattern 8 as set.

23rd to 26th rows: As given for 22nd row.

27th and 28th rows. All m.

29th to 34th rows: As 22nd row.

35th row: 14m., with m. make tie, 41m., with m. make tie, 14m.

36th row: All m.

37th to 52nd rows: As 5th to 20th rows.

53rd to 56th rows: As 5th to 8th rows.

57th row: Pattern 29 as set, then for parcel 6c., with m. make tie, 6c., pattern 29 as set.

58th row: Pattern 29 as set, 6c., 1m., 6c., pattern to end as set.

59th to 62nd rows: As 58th row.

63rd and 64th rows: All m.

65th to 70th rows: As 58th row.

71st row: 35m., with m. make tie, 35m.

72nd row: All m.

The last 72 rows form the parcel pattern; continuing in pattern as set, but using b. instead of d. and d. instead of c. and working the extra sts. into the pattern as they occur inc. 1 st. at each end of the next row and the 6 following 8th rows, then on 85 sts. pattern 7 rows.

To shape the sleevetop: Continuing in pattern as set, cast off 7 sts. at the beginning of the next 2 rows, then dec. 1 st. at each end of the next row and the 16 following alternate rows.

On 37 sts. work 1 row.

Cast off 4 sts. at the beginning of the next 8 rows, then cast off the remaining 5 sts.

THE COLLAR
With size 2¾ mm. (No. 12) needles and m. cast on 154 sts. and work 80 rows in single rib, then cast off loosely in rib.

THE SHOULDER PADS (2 alike)
With size 2¾ mm. (No. 12) needles and m. cast on 50 sts. and work 60 rows in single rib, then cast off in rib. Fold in half diagonally to form a triangle and join outer edges.

TO MAKE UP THE SWEATER
Pin out to size and press all parts except the ribbing with a warm iron over a damp cloth. Join shoulder seams. Set in sleeves. Join sleeve and side seams. Join row end edges of collar, then sew cast off edge of collar in place all round neck edge. Press seams. Catch shoulder pads in place.

THE CARDIGAN

THE BACK
Work as given for sweater.

THE LEFT FRONT
With size 2¾ mm. (No. 12) needles and m. cast on 56 sts. and work 29 rows in single rib.

Increase row: Rib 6, *up 1, rib 10; repeat from * to end. – 61 sts.

Now work as given for back from ** to **

7th row: 26m., 8e., 27m.

8th row: 26m., 11e., 24m.

The last 8 rows set the position of the pattern given at the right hand side of the chart. Now work the 9th to 106th rows from the chart as set

To shape the armhole: Continuing in pattern from chart as set, cast off 7 sts. at the beginning of the next row; work 1 row back to armhole edge, then dec. 1 st. at the beginning of the next row and the 5 following alternate rows.

On 48 sts. pattern 30 rows, ending at front edge.

To shape the neck: Cast off 5 sts. at the beginning of the next row.

Now work as given for the left front shoulder of the sweater front to end.

THE RIGHT FRONT
Work as given for the left front until the 6th pattern row has been worked.

7th and 8th rows: All m.

9th to 12th rows: As 1st to 4th rows.

13th row: Work in snow pattern as for 5th row across 36 sts., then for parcel 6b., with m. make tie, 6b., pattern to end as set.

14th row: 12m., 6b., 1m., 6b., 36m.

The last 14 rows set the position of the pattern given at the left hand side of the chart. Now work the 15th to 107th rows from the chart as set.

To shape the armhole: Work as given for left front armhole shaping to end.

THE SLEEVES (both alike)
Work as given for sweater.

THE BUTTONBAND
With size 2¾ mm. (No. 12) needles and m. cast on 10 sts. and work 192 rows in single rib, then cast off in rib.

THE BUTTONHOLE BAND
With size 2¾ mm. (No. 12) needles and m. cast on 10 sts. and work 4 rows in single rib.

1st Buttonhole row: Rib 4, cast off 2, rib to end.

2nd Buttonhole row: Rib 4, turn, cast on 2, turn, rib to end.

Rib 24 rows.

Repeat the last 26 rows 6 times more, then work the 2 buttonhole rows again.

Rib 4 rows, then cast off in rib.

THE SHOULDER PADS (2 alike)
As given for sweater.

THE NECKBAND
First join shoulder seams. With right side of work facing rejoin m. at right front neck edge and using size 2¾ mm. (No. 12) needles pick up and k. 29 sts. from right front neck edge, 40 sts. from back neck edge and 29 sts. from left front neck edge.

On 98 sts. work 1 row in single rib.

Eyelet hole row: Rib 2, *y.r.n., k.2 tog., rib 2, y.r.n., k.2 tog., rib 5; repeat from * ending last repeat rib 2.

On 98 sts. rib 5 rows more, then cast off in rib.

THE DOGS' SCARVES (4 pieces)
With size 2¾ mm. (No. 12) needles and b. cast on 6 sts. and k. 26 rows, then cast off. Neatly sew one piece at each side of dogs' necks. Tie and secure.

THE CORD
Cut 4 lengths of m. each 225 centimetres (90 inches) long. Knot these together at one end. Twist firmly in a clockwise direction. Fold in half allowing the 2 halves to twist together in opposite directions. Knot ends and trim.

TO MAKE UP THE CARDIGAN
Press as for sweater. Set in sleeves. Join sleeve and side seams. Sew front-bands in place. Press seams. Catch shoulder pads in place. Sew on buttons. Thread cord through eyelet holes in neckband. With b. make 2 pompoms 5 centimetres (2 inches) in diameter. Sew one pompom to each end of cord.

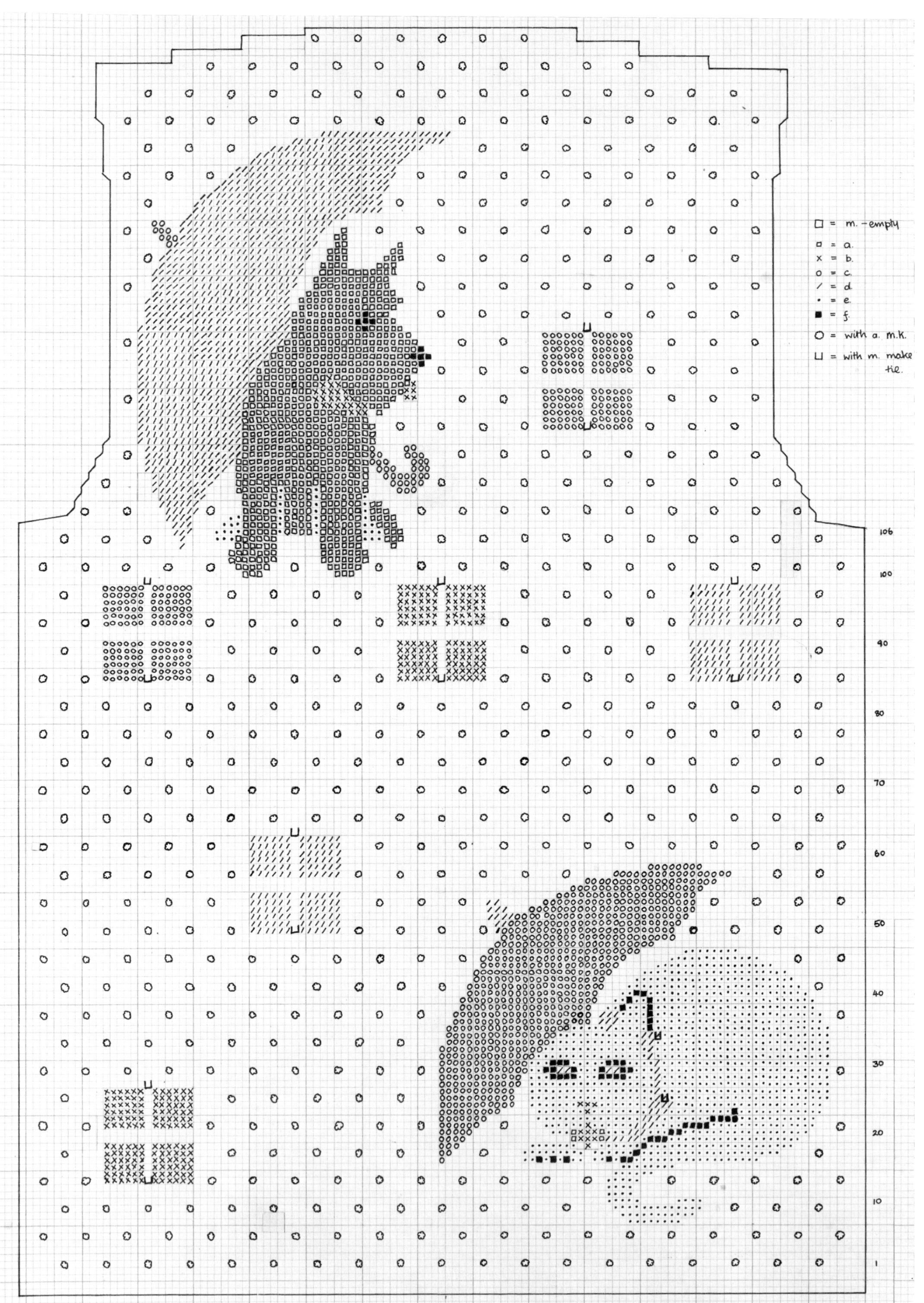

□ = m. - empty
▫ = a.
× = b.
o = c.
/ = d.
• = e.
■ = f.
O = with a. m.K.
⊔ = with m. make tie.
106
100
90
80
70
60
50
40
30
20
10
1

BULLSEYE

MATERIALS
For the sweater: 6 (7) (7) 25 gram balls of 'Woollybear 100% Mohair' by Patricia Roberts in main colour and 5 (5) (6) balls in contrast colour.
For the hat: 1 ball of the same yarn in each of the 2 colours.
For both items: a pair each of size 3¾ mm. (No. 9) and size 4 mm. (No. 8) Aero knitting needles.

TENSION
10 stitches and 14 rows to 5 centimetres (2 inches) over the stocking stitch using size 4 mm. (No. 8) needles. If you cannot obtain the correct tension using the size needles suggested, use larger or smaller ones accordingly.

ABBREVIATIONS
K., knit; p., purl; st., stitch; tog., together; dec., decrease (by working 2 sts. tog.); inc., increase (by working twice into same st.); single rib is k.1 and p.1 alternately; s.s., stocking st. is k. on the right side and p. on the wrong side; up 1, pick up the loop which lies between the needles, slip it onto left hand needle, then k. into back of it; sl., slip; p.s.s.o., pass sl. st. over; m., main colour; c., contrast colour.

NOTE
The instructions are given for the small size. Where they vary, work the figures in the first brackets for the medium size or the figures in the second brackets for the large size.

MEASUREMENTS
The measurements are given in centimetres followed by inches in brackets.

Sizes	Small	Medium	Large
To fit bust	80 (32)	85 (34)	90 (36)
Underarms	82.5 (33)	87.5 (35)	92.5 (37)
Side seam	30 (12)	30 (12)	30 (12)
Length	50 (20)	50.5 (20¼)	51 (20½)
Sleeve seam	20 (8)	20 (8)	20 (8)

THE SWEATER

THE BACK
With size 3¾ mm. (No. 9) needles and m. cast on 70 (74) (80) sts. and work 23 rows in single rib.
Increase row: Rib 2 (4) (7), * up 1, rib 5; repeat from * ending last repeat rib 3 (5) (8).
Change to size 4 mm. (No. 8) needles and on 84 (88) (94) sts. join in c. and work in s.s. in 2 colours as follows.
1st row: With c. k.42 (44) (47) with m. k. to end.
2nd row: With m. p.42 (44) (47) with c. p. to end.
Repeat the last 2 rows 29 times more.
Next row: With m. k.42 (44) (47), with c. k. to end.
Next row: With c. p.42 (44) (47), with m. p. to end.
Repeat the last 2 rows once.
To shape the armholes: Continuing to work one side of the garment in c. and the other half in m. as set, cast off 4 sts. at the beginning of the next 2 rows, then dec. 1 st. at each end of the next row and the 5 (6) (7) following alternate rows. **
On 64 (66) (70) sts. work 27 rows.
Inc. 1 st. at each end of the next row and the following 6th row.
On 68 (70) (74) sts. work 5 rows.
To slope the shoulders: Cast off 10 sts. at the beginning of the next 2 rows and 10 (11) (12) sts. on the 2 following rows.
Leave the remaining 28 (28) (30) sts. on a spare needle until required for neck band.

THE FRONT
Work as given for the back until ** is reached.
On 64 (66) (70) sts. work 14 rows.
Now divide the sts. for the neck: Next row: p.27 (28) (29) and leave these sts. on a spare needle until required for right front shoulder,

HUMBUG

MATERIALS
20 50 gram balls of 'Woollybear Wool Bouclé' by Patricia Roberts in main colour and 17 balls in contrast colour; a pair each of size 5½ mm. (No. 5) and size 6 mm. (No. 4) Aero knitting needles.

TENSION
11 stitches and 16 rows to 10 centimetres (4 inches) over the stocking stitch using size 6 mm. (No. 4) needles. If you cannot obtain the correct tension using the size needles suggested, use larger or smaller ones accordingly.

ABBREVIATIONS
K., knit; p., purl; st., stitch; tog., together; dec., decrease (by working 2 sts. tog.); inc., increase (by working twice into same st.); s.s. stocking stitch is k. on the right side and p. on the wrong side; single rib is k.1 and p.1 alternately; m., main colour; c., contrast colour.

NOTE
The instructions are given for one size only.

MEASUREMENTS
The measurements are given in centimetres followed by inches in brackets.

To fit bust	80–90 (32–36)
Underarms excluding edging	107.5 (43)
Side seam	62.5 (25)
Length	87.5 (35)
Sleeve seam	42.5 (17)

THE BACK
With size 5½ mm. (No. 5) needles and m. cast on 60 sts. and work 4 rows in single rib.
Change to size 6 mm. (No. 4) needles and work in pattern as follows. This is worked entirely in s.s. so only the colour details are given. Use separate balls of colour for each square.
1st row: * 10m., 10c.; repeat from * to end.
2nd row: * 10c., 10m.; repeat from * to end.
3rd to 16th rows: Repeat the 1st and 2nd rows 7 times.
17th row: * 10c., 10m.; repeat from * to end.
18th row: * 10m., 10c.; repeat from * to end.
19th to 32nd rows: Repeat the 17th and 18th rows 7 times.
The last 32 rows form the pattern; repeat them twice more.
To shape the armholes: Continuing in pattern as set, cast off 3 sts. at the beginning of the next 2 rows, then dec. 1 st. at each end on the next row and the 2 following alternate rows.
On 48 sts. work 21 rows.
Inc. 1 st. at each end of the next row and the following 4th row.
On 52 sts. work 3 rows.
To slope the shoulders: Cast off 9 sts. at the beginning of the next 4 rows.
Cast off the remaining 16 sts.

THE POCKET BACKS (2 alike)
With size 6 mm. (No. 4) needles and c. cast on 14 sts. and beginning with a k. row s.s. 20 rows, then leave these sts. on a spare needle until required.

THE LEFT FRONT
With size 5½ mm. (No. 5) needles and m. cast on 30 sts. and work 4 rows in single rib.
Change to size 6 mm. (No. 4) needles and work in pattern as follows, noting the information given for the back. **
1st row: 10m., 10c., 10m.
2nd row: 10m., 10c., 10m.
The last 2 rows set the position of the 32 row pattern given for the back.
*** Pattern 46 rows more as set.
Pocket row: Work as set across 8 sts., slip next 14 sts. onto spare needle and leave at front of work, in their place k. across the 14 sts. of one pocket back, k. to end.
Pattern 47 rows. Work 1 extra row here, when working right front.
To shape the armhole and to slope the front edge: Cast off 3 sts. at the beginning for armhole and dec. 1 st. at the end for front edge on the next row.

cast off 10 (10) (12), p. to end and continue on these 27 (28) (29) sts. for the left front shoulder.

The left front shoulder: To shape the neck, continuing with m. as before, dec. 1 st. at the neck edge on each of the next 9 rows – 18 (19) (20) sts.

S.s. 3 rows.

Inc. 1 st. at the beginning of the next row and the following 6th row.

On 20 (21) (22) sts. work 5 rows.

To slope the shoulder: Cast off 10 sts. at the beginning of the next row. On 10 (11) (12) sts. work 1 row, then cast off.

The right front shoulder: With right side of work facing rejoin c. and work to end of row. Now continuing with c. as set, work as given for left front shoulder to end.

THE NECKBAND

First join right shoulder seam. With right side of work facing, rejoin m. at left front neck edge and using size 3¾ mm. (No. 9) needles, pick up and k.24 sts. from left front neck edge, 10 (10) (12) sts. from centre front neck edge and 24 sts. from right front neck edge, then k. across the 28 (28) (30) sts. left on spare needle at back neck edge.

On 86 (86) (90) sts. work 7 rows in single rib, then cast off in rib.

THE LEFT SLEEVE

With size 3¾ mm. (No. 9) needles and m. cast on 50 (52) (54) sts. and work 15 rows in single rib.

Increase row: Rib 2 (3) (4), * up 1, rib 5; repeat from * ending last repeat rib 3 (4) (5).

Change to size 4 mm. (No. 8) needles, break off m. and join in c. and with c. only on 60 (62) (64) sts., beginning with a k. row s.s. 42 rows.

To shape the sleevetop: Cast off 4 sts. at the beginning of the next 2 rows, then dec. 1 st. at each end of the next row and the 12 (13) (14) following alternate rows.

On 26 sts. work 1 row.

Cast off 3 sts. at the beginning of the next 4 rows and 4 sts. on the 2 following rows.

Cast off the remaining 6 sts.

THE RIGHT SLEEVE

Work as given for left sleeve, but using c. instead of m. and m. instead of c.

THE LEFT SHOULDER PAD

With size 3¾ mm. (No. 9) needles and m. cast on 36 sts. and work 48 rows in single rib then cast off.

THE RIGHT SHOULDER PAD

Using c. instead of m. work as given for left shoulder pad.

TO MAKE UP THE SWEATER

Pin out to size and press all parts except the ribbing with a warm iron over a damp cloth. Join left shoulder seam. Set in sleeves. Join sleeve and side seams. Press seams. Fold shoulder pads in half diagonally and join outer edges to form triangles. Then catch in place on wrong side.

THE HAT

QUARTER SECTION (Work 2 with m. and 2 with c.)

With size 3¾ mm. (No. 9) needles cast on 24 sts. and work 16 rows in single rib.

Change to size 4 mm. (No. 8) needles and beginning with a k. row s.s. 24 rows.

1st Decrease row: * Sl.1, k.2 tog., p.s.s.o., k.5; repeat from * to end.

S.s. 7 rows.

2nd Decrease row: * Sl.1, k.2 tog., p.s.s.o., k.3; repeat from * to end.

On 12 sts. s.s. 5 rows.

3rd Decrease row: * Sl.1, k.2 tog., p.s.s.o., k.1; repeat from * to end.

On 6 sts. s.s. 3 rows.

4th Decrease row: * Sl.1, k.2 tog., p.s.s.o.; repeat from * to end. Take the 2 remaining sts. tog. and fasten off.

TO MAKE UP THE HAT

Press as for sweater. Join row end edges.

Pattern 6 rows as set, decreasing 1 st. at the armhole edge on the 2nd, 4th and 6th rows and at the same time, decreasing 1 st. at front edge on the 4th of these rows.

On 22 sts. pattern 1 row.

Dec. 1 st. at the front edge on the next row and the 4 following 4th rows.

On 17 sts. work 3 rows.

Inc. 1 st. at the beginning and dec. 1 st. at the end of the next row.

On 17 sts. work 3 rows.

Inc. 1 st. at the beginning of the next row.

On 18 sts. work 3 rows.

To slope the shoulder: Cast off 9 sts. at the beginning of the next row.

On 9 sts. work 1 row, then cast off.

THE RIGHT FRONT

Work as given for left front until ** is reached.

1st row: 10c., 10m., 10c.

2nd row: 10c., 10m., 10c.

The last 2 rows set the position of the 32 row pattern given for the back.

Now working in pattern as set, work as given for left front from *** to end, noting the variation in the number of rows before shaping the armhole.

THE LEFT POCKET TOP

With right side of work facing, rejoin m. to the 14 sts. left on stitch-holder and using size 5½ mm. (No. 5) needles work 2 rows in single rib, then cast off.

THE RIGHT POCKET TOP

Using c. instead of m. work as given for left pocket top.

THE LEFT AND RIGHT FRONT BANDS AND HALF COLLARS (both alike)

With size 5½ mm. (No. 5) needles and m. cast on 104 sts. and work 4 rows in single rib.

Cast off 68 sts. loosely at the beginning of the next row.

Dec. 1 st. at the end of the next row and at the same edge on each of the next 12 rows.

Cast off the remaining 23 sts.

THE SLEEVES (both alike)

With size 5½ mm. (No. 5) needles and m. cast on 28 sts. and work 4 rows in single rib.

Change to size 6 mm. (No. 4) needles and work in pattern as follows:

1st row: 9m., 10c., 9m.

2nd row: 9m., 10c., 9m.

The last 2 rows set the position of the 32 row pattern given for back.

Pattern 6 rows more as set.

Continuing in pattern as set and working the extra sts. into the pattern as they occur, inc. 1 st. at each end of the next row and the 3 following 14th rows.

On 36 sts. pattern 13 rows as set.

To shape the sleevetop: Break off c. and continue in s.s. with m. only. Cast off 3 sts. at the beginning of the next 2 rows, then dec. 1 st. at each end of the next row and the 5 following alternate rows.

On 18 sts. work 1 row.

Cast off 2 sts. at the beginning of the next 2 rows, and 4 sts. on the 2 following rows.

Cast off the remaining 6 sts.

THE SHOULDER PADS (2 alike)

With size 5½ mm. (No. 5) needles and c. cast on 18 sts. and work 24 rows in single rib, then cast off in rib. Fold in half diagonally and join outer edges to form triangles.

TO MAKE UP THE COAT

Pin out to size and press all parts except the ribbing on the wrong side with a warm iron over a damp cloth. Join shoulder seams. Set in sleeves. Join sleeve and side seams. Sew pocket backs and row ends of pocket tops in place. Join long row end edges of half collars for centre back neck seam. Sew shaped row end and cast off edges of collar and front bands in position. Neatly catch shoulder pads in place on wrong side. Press seams.

ALLSORTS

MATERIALS
For the jacket or the sweater: 10 (11) 50 gram balls of 'Woollybear Cotton Bouclé' by Patricia Roberts in main colour and one ball in each of the 5 contrast colours; a pair each of size 3¾ mm. (No. 9) and 3¼ mm. (No. 10) Aero knitting needles; For the jacket 7 medium sized buttons.

SPECIAL NOTE
These garments may also be knitted in 'Woollybear 100% Mohair'. You will require 15 (16) 25 gram balls of 'Woollybear 100% Mohair' by Patricia Roberts in main colour and 2 balls of the same yarn in each of the 5 contrast colours. To obtain the correct tension it will be necessary to use size 4 mm. (No. 8) needles instead of 3¾ mm. (No. 9) needles and size 3¾ mm. (No. 9) needles instead of 3¼ mm. (No. 10) needles throughout.

TENSION
10 stitches and 14 rows to 5 centimetres (2 inches) over the stocking stitch using size 3¾ mm. (No. 9) needles and 'Woollybear Cotton Bouclé'. Using 'Woollybear 100% Mohair' you should obtain the same tension using size 4 mm. (No. 8) needles. If you cannot obtain the correct tension using the size needles suggested, use larger or smaller ones accordingly.

ABBREVIATIONS
K., knit; p., purl; st., stitch; tog., together; dec., decrease (by working 2 sts. tog.); inc., increase (by working twice into same st.); sl., slip; p.s.s.o., pass sl. st. over; y.r.n., yarn round needle; single rib is k.1 and p.1 alternately; s.s. stocking stitch is k. on the right side and p. on the wrong side; m.b., make bobble thus: k.1, y.r.n., k.1, all into next st., turn, p.3, turn, k.3, turn, p.3, turn, sl.1, k.2 tog., p.s.s.o.; m., main colour; a., first contrast; b., second contrast; c. third contrast; d., fourth contrast; e., fifth contrast; m.l.b., make large bobble thus, k.1, y.r.n., k.1, y.r.n., k.1, all into next st., turn, p.5, turn, k.5, turn, p.5, turn, k.5, turn, p.2 tog., p.1, p.2 tog., turn, sl.1, k.2 tog., p.s.s.o.

NOTE
The instructions are given for the small size. Where they vary work the figures in the brackets for the medium size.

MEASUREMENTS
The measurements are given in centimetres followed by inches in brackets.

THE JACKET

Sizes	Small	Medium
To fit bust	85 (34)	90 (36)
Underarms	90 (36)	95 (38)
Side seam	40 (16)	40 (16)
Length	60 (24)	60.5 (24¼)
Sleeve seam	42.5 (17)	42.5 (17)

THE SWEATER

Sizes	Small	Medium
To fit bust	85 (34)	90 (36)
Underarms	87.5 (35)	92.5 (37)
Side seam	40 (16)	40 (16)
Length	60 (24)	60.5 (24¼)
Sleeve seam	42.5 (17)	42.5 (17)

THE JACKET

THE BACK
With size 3¼ mm. (No. 10) needles and m. cast on 88 (94) sts. and work 16 rows in single rib.

Change to size 3¾ mm. (No. 9) needles and beginning with a k. row s.s. 4 rows.

Now work in pattern as follows. This is worked entirely in s.s. except for the bobbles, so only the colour details are given. Use separate small balls of contrast colours for each motif and take great care not to pull colours not in use tightly across the back of the work or it will become puckered.

1st row: 4 (7)m., * with a. m.b., 1a., with a. m.b., 1a., with a. m.b. *, 25m., 5b., 25m.; repeat from * to *, 19 (22)m.

2nd row: 18 (21)m., 7a., 23m., 7b., 23m., 7a., 3 (6)m.

The last 2 rows set the position of the pattern given in the chart. Work the 3rd to 42nd rows from the chart as set. Using e. instead of a., a. instead of d., and d. instead of e., work the 42 pattern rows again.

Using d. instead of a., e. instead of d., and a. instead of e., for the next repeat of the pattern, work the first 10 pattern rows.

To shape the armholes: Continuing in pattern as set, cast off 4 sts. at the beginning of the next 2 rows, then dec. 1 st. at each end of the next row and the 5 (6) following alternate rows.

On 68 (72) sts. pattern 21 rows, noting that the last repeat of the pattern will be in the original colours.

Inc. 1 st. at each end of the next row and the 2 following 6th rows.

On 74 (78) sts. pattern 5 rows.

To slope the shoulders: Cast off 11 sts. at the beginning of the next 2 rows and 11 (12) sts. on the 2 following rows.

Cast off the remaining 30 (32) sts.

THE POCKET BACKS (2 alike)
With size 3¾ mm. (No. 9) needles and m., cast on 24 sts. and beginning with a k. row s.s. 34 rows, then leave these sts. on a spare needle until required.

THE LEFT FRONT
With size 3¼ mm. (No. 10) needles and m. cast on 44 (47) sts. and work 16 rows in single rib.

Change to size 3¾ mm. (No. 9) needles and beginning with a k. row, s.s. 4 rows. Now work in pattern as follows, noting the information given for the back.**

1st row: 4 (7)m., * with a. m.b., 1a., with a. m.b., 1a., with a. m.b.,* 25m., 5b., 5m.

2nd row: 4m., 7b., 23m., 7a., 3 (6)m.

The last 2 rows set the position of the pattern given in the chart. Now work the 3rd to 34th rows from the chart as set.

Pocket row: K.10 (13), slip next 24 sts. onto a stitch-holder and leave at front of work, then in their place k. across the 24 sts. of one pocket back, k. to end.

***Now work the 36th to 42nd rows.

Using e. instead of a., a. instead of d., and d. instead of e., work the 42 pattern rows again.

Using d. instead of a., e. instead of d., and a. instead of e., for the next repeat pattern, work the first 10 pattern rows. Work 1 extra row here when working the right front.

****To shape the armhole and to slope the front edge: Continuing in pattern as set, cast off 4 sts. at the beginning for armhole and dec. 1 st. at the end for front slope on the next row.

Pattern 12 (14) rows decreasing 1 st. at armhole edge on every right side row and at the same time dec. 1 st. at the front edge on the 3rd, 6th, 9th and 12th of these rows.

Pattern 21 rows, decreasing 1 st. at front edge on every 3rd row as before – 22 (24) sts.

Still decreasing at front edge on every 3rd row, inc. 1 st. at the armhole edge on the next row and the following 6th row.

Work 5 rows decreasing 1 st. at the front edge on the 2nd (3rd) of these rows. This completes the front slope shaping.

Inc. 1 st. at the armhole edge on the next row.

On 22 (23) sts. pattern 5 rows.

To slope the shoulder: Cast off 11 sts. at the beginning of the next row. On 11 (12) sts. work 1 row, then cast off.

THE RIGHT FRONT
Work as given for left front until ** is reached.

1st row: 20m., with a. m.b., 1a., with a. m.b., 1a., with a. m.b., 19 (22)m.

2nd row: 18 (21)m., 7a., 19m.

The last 2 rows set the position of the pattern given in the chart. Now work the 3rd to 34th rows from the chart as set.

Pocket row: K.10, slip next 24 sts. onto a stitch-holder and leave at front of work, in their place, k. across the 24sts. of other pocket back, k. to end.

Now work as given for left front from *** to end, noting that 1 extra row is worked before shaping the armhole.

THE POCKET TOPS (2 alike)
With right side of work facing rejoin m. and using size 3¼ mm. (No. 10) needles work 6 rows in single rib, then cast off in rib.

THE FRONT BANDS AND HALF COLLARS (both alike the fabric is reversible)
With size 3¼ mm. (No. 10) needles and m. cast on 6 sts. and work 114 rows in single rib.

Continuing in single rib, inc. 1 st. at the beginning of the next row and at the same edge on the 21 (22) following alternate rows.

On 28 (29) sts. work 1 row back to shaped edge.

Cast on 25 (26) sts. at the beginning of the next row.

On 53 (55) sts. work 11 rows in single rib, then cast off loosely in rib.

THE SLEEVES (both alike)
With size 3¼ mm. (No. 10) needles and m. cast on 43 (45) sts. and work 22 rows in single rib.

Change to size 3¾ mm. (No. 9) needles and beginning with a k. row s.s. 4 rows. Now work in pattern as follows, noting the information given for back.

1st row: 4 (5)m., with a. m.b., 1a., with a. m.b., 1a., with a. m.b., 25m., 5b., 4 (5)m.

2nd row: 3 (4)m., 7b., 23m., 7a., 3 (4)m.

The last 2 rows set the position of the pattern given in the chart.

Now work the 3rd and 4th rows from the chart as set.

Maintaining the continuity of the pattern as set and changing the order of the colours on each repeat of the pattern as given for back, inc. 1 st. at each end of the next row and the 8 following 10th rows.

On 61 (63) sts. pattern 9 rows.

To shape the sleevetop: Continuing in pattern as set, cast off 4 sts. at the beginning of the next 2 rows, then dec. 1 st. at each end of the next row and the 11 (12) following alternate rows.

On 29 sts. work 1 row.

Dec. 1 st. at each end of the next 2 rows – 25 sts.

Cast off 3 sts. at the beginning of the next 6 rows. Cast off the remaining 7 sts.

THE SHOULDER PADS (2 alike)
With size 3¼ mm. (No. 10) needles and m. cast on 36 sts. and work 40 rows in single rib, then cast off in rib. Fold in half diagonally to form a triangle and join outer edges.

TO MAKE UP THE JACKET
Pin out to size and press all parts except the ribbing on the wrong side with a warm iron over a damp cloth. Join shoulder seams. Set in sleeves. Join sleeve and side seams. Join short row end edges of collar for centre back neck seam. Sew shaped row end and cast on edges of front bands in position. Neatly sew pocket backs and row ends of pocket tops in place. Make 7 buttonhole loops evenly spaced along right front edge. Sew on buttons. Press seams. Neatly catch shoulder pads in place on wrong side.

THE SWEATER

THE BACK
Work as given for the back of the jacket.

THE FRONT
Work as given for the back until the 42 pattern rows have been worked twice, then work the first 9 pattern rows again, changing the order of the colours on each repeat as for back.

Now divide the sts. for the neck. Next row: P.44 (47) and leave these sts. on a spare needle until required for the right front shoulder, p. to end and continue on these 44 (47) sts. for the left front shoulder.

The left front shoulder: Work as given for the left front of jacket from **** to end.

The right front shoulder: With right side of work facing rejoin yarn to inner edge of sts. left on spare needle and work to end of row.

Now work as given for the left front of jacket from **** to end.

THE SLEEVES (both alike)
Work as given for the jacket sleeves.

THE SHOULDER PADS (2 alike)
Work as given for the shoulder pads on jacket.

THE NECKBAND
First join right shoulder seam. With right side of work facing rejoin m. at left front neck edge. Using size 3¼ mm. (No. 10) needles pick up and k.46 (48) sts. from left front neck edge, 46 (48) sts. from right front neck edge and 30 (32) sts. from back neck edge – 122 (128) sts.

Work 1 row in single rib.

Next row: Rib to within 2 sts. of centre front, sl.1, k.1, p.s.s.o., k.2 tog., rib to end.

Repeat the last 2 rows 3 times more.

Cast off loosely in rib.

TO MAKE UP THE SWEATER
Pin out to size and press all parts except the ribbing on the wrong side with a warm iron over a damp cloth. Join left shoulder seam, continuing seam across neckband. Set in sleeves. Join sleeve and side seams. Press seams. Neatly catch shoulder pads in place on wrong side.

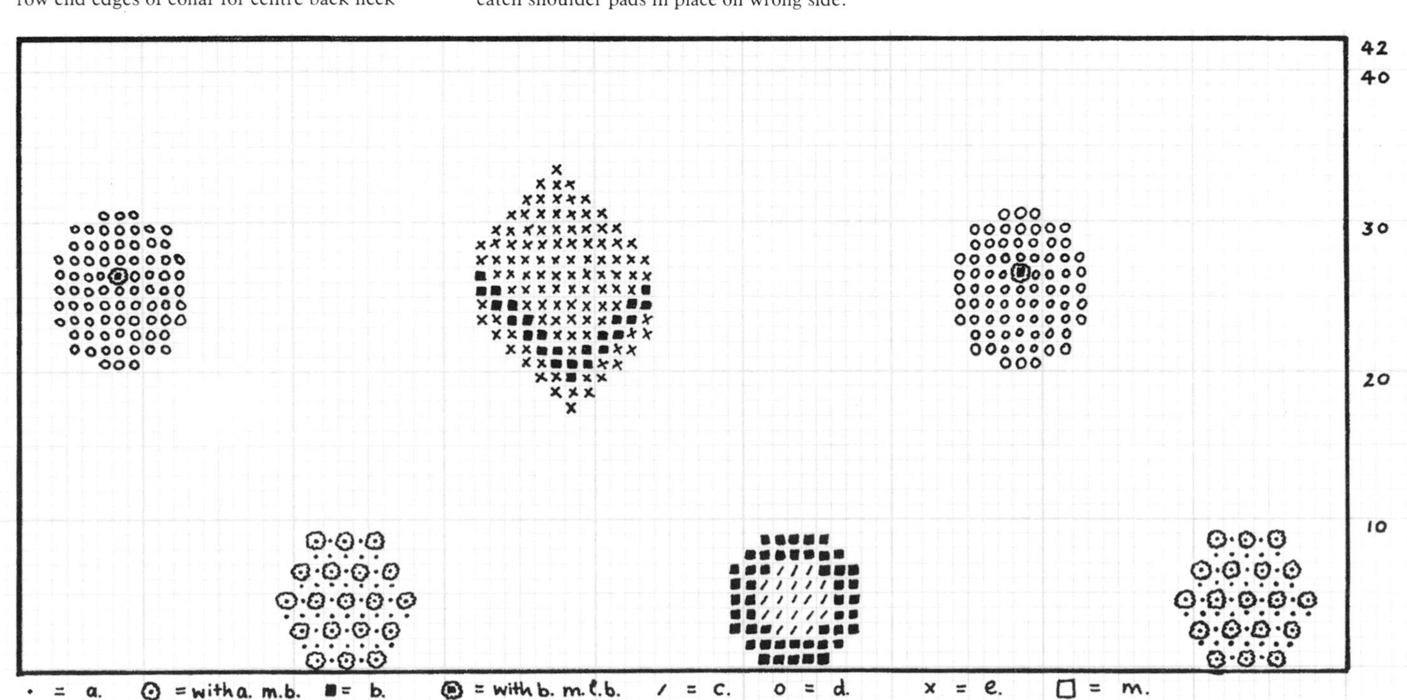

NEAPOLITAN

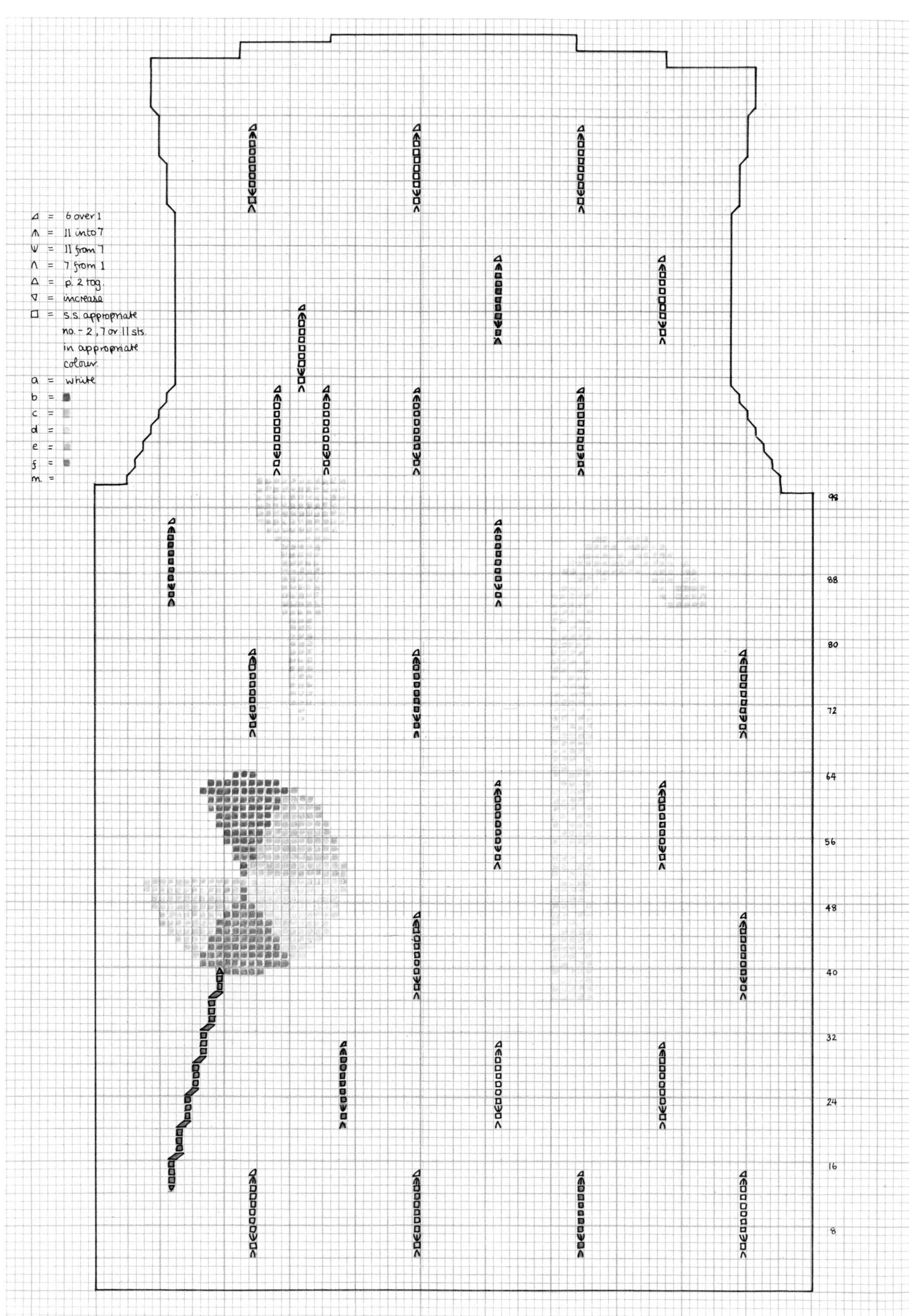

⊿ = 6 over 1
⩚ = 11 into 7
⩛ = 11 from 7
∧ = 7 from 1
Δ = p. 2 tog.
∇ = increase
□ = s.s. appropriate no. – 2, 7 or 11 sts. in appropriate colour.
a = white
b =
c =
d =
e =
f =
m. =
96
88
80
72
64
56
48
40
32
24
16
8

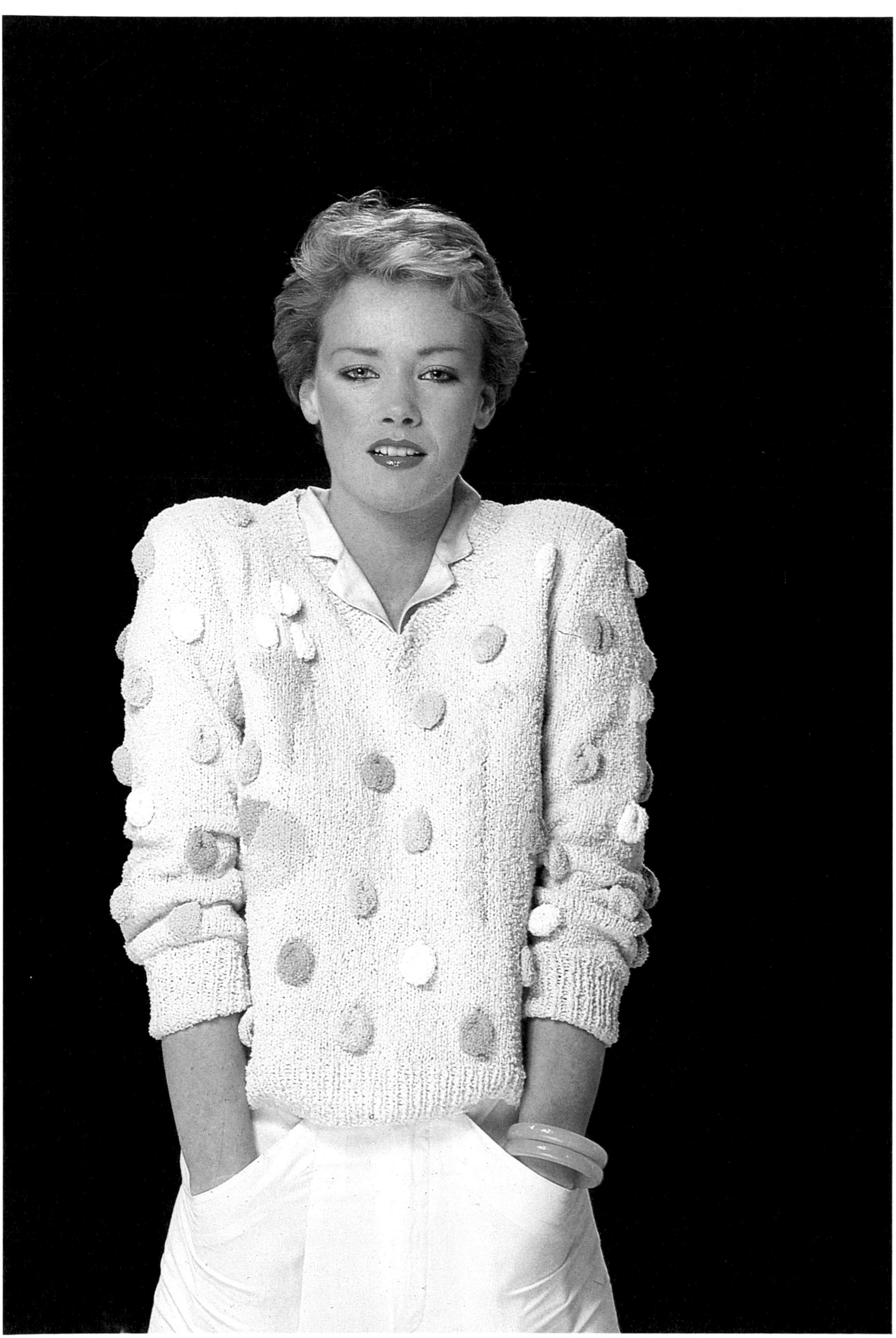

NEAPOLITAN

MATERIALS
For the long sleeved version: 10 50 gram balls of 'Woollybear Cotton Boucle' in main colour and 1 ball in each of the 6 contrast colours; a pair each of size 3¼ mm. (No. 10) and size 3¾ mm. (No. 9) Aero knitting needles, a cable needle.
For the short sleeved version: allow 2 balls less in the main colour.

SPECIAL NOTE
This garment may also be knitted in 'Woollybear 100% Mohair' by Patricia Roberts. It will require 15 25 gram balls in main colour and 2 balls in each contrast colour. To obtain the correct tension it is necessary to use size 4 mm. (No. 8) needles instead of size 3¾ mm. (No. 9) needles, and size 3¾ mm. (No. 9) needles instead of size 3¼ mm. (No. 10) needles.

TENSION
10 stitches and 14 rows to 5 centimetres (2 inches) over the stocking stitch using size 3¾ mm. (No. 9) needles and 'Woollybear Cotton Boucle'. Using 'Woollybear 100% Mohair' the same tension should be obtained by using the size 4 mm. (No. 8) needles. If you cannot obtain the correct tension using the size needles suggested, use larger or smaller ones accordingly.

ABBREVIATIONS
K., knit; p., purl; st., stitch; tog., together; dec., decrease (by working 2 sts. tog.); inc., increase (by working twice into same stitch); s.s., stocking stitch is k. on the right side and p. on the wrong side; single rib is k.1 and p.1 alternately; m., main colour; a., first contrast; b., second contrast; c., third contrast; d., fourth contrast; e., fifth contrast; f., sixth contrast; sl., slip; p.s.s.o., pass sl. st. over; up 1, pick up the loop which lies between the needles, slip it onto left hand needle, then k. into back of it; y.r.n., yarn round needle; 7 from 1, k.1, y.r.n., k.1, y.r.n., k.1, y.r.n., k.1, all into next st.; twist 2 right, slip next st. onto cable needle and leave at back of work, with b. k.2, then with m. k.1 from cable needle; 6 over 1, pass 2nd, 3rd, 4th, 5th, 6th and 7th sts. on left hand needle over 1st st., then with m. k. this st.; 11 into 7, with appropriate contrast colour, p.2 tog., p.2 tog., p.3, p.2 tog., p.2 tog.; 11 from 7, with appropriate contrast colour, k.1, up 1, k.1, up 1, k.3, up 1, k.1, up 1, k.1.

MEASUREMENTS
The measurements are given in centimetres followed by inches in brackets.

To fit bust	85 (34)
Underarms	88 (35)
Side seam	40 (16)
Length	60 (24)
Long sleeve seam	42.5 (17)
Short sleeve seam	10 (4)

THE BACK
With size 3¼ mm. (No. 10) needles and m. cast on 88 sts. and work 16 rows in single rib.
Change to size 3¾ mm. (No. 9) needles and beginning with a k. row s.s. 4 rows.
Now work in colour pattern as follows. This is worked entirely in s.s. except where indicated, so only the colour details are given. When working the ice cream cone and the top of the lollipop use separate balls of m. at each size of motifs. When working the ice cream bobbles do not worry about pulling m. firmly across the back of the work as a raised effect is desired.
5th row: 8m., with a. 7 from 1, 19m., with b. 7 from 1, 19m., with c. 7 from 1, 19m., with d. 7 from 1, 19m.
6th row: 19m., 7d., 19m., 7c., 19m., 7b., 19m., 7a., 8m.
7th row: 8m., with a. 11 from 7 – see abbreviations, 19m., with b. 11 from 7., 19m., with c. 11 from 7., 19m., with d. 11 from 7; 19m.
8th row: 19m., 11d., 19m., 11c., 19m., 11b., 19m., 11a., 8m.
9th row: 8m., 11a., 19m., 11b., 19m., 11c., 19m., 11d., ** 19m.
10th and 11th rows: As 8th and 9th rows.
12th row: As 8th row.
13th row: Work as given for 9th row until ** is reached, 9m., with b. k.1 and p.1 into next st., 9m.
14th row: 9m., 2b., 9m., with d. 11 into 7., 19m., with c. 11 into 7., 19m., with b. 11 into 7., 19m., with a. 11 into 7., 8m.
15th row: 8m., * 6 over 1, 19m.; repeat from * ending last repeat 9m., 2b., 9m.
16th row: 9m., 2b., 78m.
17th row: 77m., twist 2 right, 9m.
18th row: 10m., 2b., 77m.
The last 18 rows set the position of the pattern given in the chart. Now work the 19th to 98th rows from the chart as set.
To shape the armholes: Maintaining the continuity of the pattern as set and given in the chart work as follows, noting that the extra sts. of each ice cream bobble will be counted as 1 st. when counting sts.: Cast off 4 sts. at the beginning of the next 2 rows, then dec. 1 st. at each end of the next row and the 5 following alternate rows. – 68 sts.
Pattern 21 rows more.
Inc. 1 st. at each end of the next row and the 2 following 6th rows.
On 74 sts. work 5 rows.
To slope the shoulders: Cast off 11 sts. at the beginning of the next 4 rows.
Leave the remaining 30 sts. on a spare needle until required for neckband.

THE FRONT
Work as given for the back until 97 pattern rows have been worked.
Now divide the sts. for the neck. Next row: Work as set across 44 sts. and leave these sts. on a spare needle until required for right front shoulder, p. to end and continue on these 44 sts. for the left front shoulder.
**The left front shoulder: To shape the neck

HOME SWEET HOME

MATERIALS
For the short sleeved version: 8 50 gram balls of 'Woollybear Cotton Bouclé' by Patricia Roberts in main colour and 1 ball in each of the 7 contrast colours, a pair each of size 3¼ mm. (No. 10) and size 3¾ mm. (No. 9) Aero knitting needles; 7 buttons.
For the long sleeved version: add one ball in main colour.

SPECIAL NOTE
This garment may also be knitted in 'Woollybear 100% Mohair' by Patricia Roberts. It will require 12 25 gram balls in main colour and 2 balls in each of 1st, 4th, 5th and 6th contrast colours and 1 ball in each of 2nd, 3rd and 7th contrast colours. To obtain the correct tension it is necessary to use size 4 mm. (No. 8) needles instead of size 3¾ mm. (No. 9) needles and size 3¾ mm. (No. 9) needles instead of size 3¼ mm. (No. 10) needles.

TENSION
10 stitches and 14 rows to 5 centimetres (2 inches) over the stocking stitch using size 3¾ mm. (No. 9) needles and 'Woollybear Cotton Boucle'. Using 'Woollybear 100% Mohair' the same tension should be obtained by using size 4 mm. (No. 8) needles. If you cannot obtain the correct tension using the size needles suggested, use larger or smaller ones accordingly.

ABBREVIATIONS
K., knit; p., purl; st., stitch; tog., together; inc., increase (by working twice into same st.); dec., decrease (by working 2 sts. tog.); single rib is k.1 and p.1 alternately; s.s. stocking stitch is k. on the right side and p. on the wrong side; 7 from 1, k.1, y.r.n., k.1, y.r.n., k.1, y.r.n., k.1 all into next st.; y.r.n., yarn round needle; m.b., make bobble thus: k.1, y.r.n., k.1 all into next st., turn, k.3, turn, sl.1, k.2 tog., p.s.s.o.; sl., slip; p.s.s.o., pass sl. st. over; up 1, pick up the loop which lies between the needles, slip it onto left hand needle, then k. into back of it; m., main colour; a., first contrast; b., second contrast; c., third contrast; d., fourth contrast; e., fifth contrast; f., sixth contrast, g., seventh contrast.

MEASUREMENTS
The measurements are given in centimetres followed by inches in brackets.

To fit bust	85 (34)
Underarms	90 (36)
Side seam	35 (14)
Length	55 (22)
Long sleeve seam	42.5 (17)
Short sleeve seam	12.5 (5)

THE BACK
With size 3¼ mm. (No. 10) needles and m. cast on 81 sts. and work 23 rows in single rib.
Increase row: Rib 6, *up 1, rib 10; repeat from * ending last repeat rib 5. – 89 sts. Break off m., join in a.
Change to size 3¾ mm. (No. 9) needles and beginning with a k. row s.s. 3 rows. Now work in pattern as follows: – Use separate small balls of colour for each section of the pattern for both ease and neatness of work.
4th row: 56a., 7d., 26a.
5th row: 22a., 13d., 54a.
The last 5 rows set the position of the pattern given in the chart. Now work the 6th to 76th rows from the chart as set.
To shape the armholes: Continuing in pattern as set and given in chart, cast off 4 sts. at the beginning of the next 2 rows, then dec. 1 st. at each end of the next row and the 3 following alternate rows.
On 73 sts. pattern 29 rows.
Inc. 1 st. at each end of the next row and the following 8th row.
On 77 sts. work 7 rows.
To slope the shoulders: Cast off 12 sts. at the beginning of the next 4 rows.
Leave the remaining 29 sts. on a spare needle until required for collar.

THE LEFT FRONT
With size 3¼ mm. (No. 10) needles and m. cast on 40 sts. and work 23 rows in single rib.
Increase row: Rib 4, *up 1, rib 8; repeat from * ending last repeat rib 4. – 45 sts. Break off m. and join in a.
Change to size 3¾ mm. (No. 9) needles and beginning with a k. row with a. s.s. 21 rows.
22nd row: 14a., 19b., 12a.
23rd row: 13a., 17b., 15a.
The last 2 rows set the position of the pattern given in the chart – at left hand side but reversing it so that the knit rows are worked from left to right and the purl rows from right to left. Now work the 24th to 76th rows from the chart as set.
**To shape the armhole: Continuing in pattern from chart as set, cast off 4 sts. at the beginning of the next row. Work 1 row back to armhole edge.

and to shape the armhole: Maintaining the continuity of the pattern as set and given in the chart, cast off 4 sts. for armhole at the beginning and dec. 1 st. at the end for neck on the next row.

Pattern 12 rows, decreasing 1 st. at armhole edge on each right side row and at the same time decreasing 1 st. at the neck edge on the 3rd, 6th, 9th, and 12th rows.

Continuing to dec. 1 st. at neck edge on every 3rd row as set, pattern 21 rows.

Still decreasing 1 st. at neck edge on every 3rd row as before, inc. 1 st. at the armhole edge – at the beginning of the next row and the following 6th row.

Work 1 row straight.

Dec. 1 st. at the neck edge on the next row. This completes the neck shaping.

Pattern 3 rows straight.

Inc. 1 st. at the beginning – armhole edge on the next row.

On 22 sts. work 5 rows.

To slope the shoulder: Cast off 11 sts. at the beginning of the next row. On 11 sts. work 1 row, then cast off.

The right front shoulder: With right side of work facing rejoin yarn to inner edge of sts. left on spare needle and work to end of row, then work as given for left front shoulder from ** to end.

THE NECKBAND
First join right shoulder seam. With right side of work facing rejoin m. at left front neck edge and using size $3\frac{1}{4}$ mm. (No. 10) needles pick up and k. 46 sts. from left front neck edge and 46 sts. from right front neck edge, then k. across the 30 sts. at back neck edge. – 122 sts.

Work 1 row in single rib.

Next row: Rib to within 2 sts. of centre front, sl.1, k.1, p.s.s.o., k.2 tog., rib to end.

Repeat the last 2 rows twice more.

Cast off loosely in rib.

THE SHORT SLEEVES (both alike)
With size $3\frac{1}{4}$ mm. (No. 10) needles and m. cast on 51 sts. and work 9 rows in single rib.

Increase row: Rib 3, *up 1, rib 5; repeat from * ending last repeat rib 3. – 61 sts.

Change to size $3\frac{3}{4}$ mm. (No. 9) needles and beginning with a k. row s.s. 4 rows.

Now work in pattern as follows, noting the information given for the back. ***1st row: 10m., with b. 7 from 1, 19m., with c. 7 from 1, 19m., with d. 7 from 1, 10m.

2nd row: 10m., 7d., 19m., 7c., 19m., 7b., 10m.

The last 2 rows set the position of the ice cream bobbles given in the chart for the back, now work 12 rows more in pattern as set.

To shape the sleevetop: Cast off 4 sts. at the beginning of the next 2 rows.

Next row: K.2 tog., 14m., with a. 7 from 1, 19m., with b. 7 from 1, 14m., k.2 tog.

The last row sets the position and colour of the next 2 ice cream bobbles. Pattern 1 row as set.

Now continuing in pattern as set, dec. 1 st. at each end of the next row and the 6 following alternate rows.

On 37 sts. work 1 row.

Next row: K.2 tog., 16m., with e. 7 from 1, 16m., k.2 tog.

The last row sets the position of the last bobble.

Work 1 row straight.

Continuing in pattern as set, dec. 1 st. at each end of the next row and the 4 following alternate rows.

Work 1 row straight.

Cast off 3 sts. at the beginning of the next 4 rows and 4 sts. on the 2 following rows.

Cast off the remaining 5 sts.

THE LONG SLEEVES (both alike)
With size $3\frac{1}{4}$ mm. (No. 10) needles and m. cast on 41 sts. and work 21 rows in single rib.

Increase row: Rib 3, *up 1, rib 4; repeat from * ending last repeat rib 2. – 51 sts.

Change to size $3\frac{3}{4}$ mm. (No. 9) needles and beginning with a k. row s.s. 4 rows.

Now work in pattern as follows noting the information given for the back.

1st row: 15m., with e. 7 from 1, 19m., with a. 7 from 1, 15m.

2nd row: 15m., 7a., 19m., 7e., 15m.

The last 2 rows set the position and colour of the ice cream bobbles given in the chart, now work the 3rd to 14th rows as set. Inc. 1 st. at each end of the next row then work 1 row straight. – 53 sts.

Next row: 6m., with c. 7 from 1, 19m., with d. 7 from 1, 19m., with e. 7 from 1, 6m.

The last row sets the position and colour of the next row of bobbles, pattern 15 rows more, increasing 1 st. at each end of the 14th of these rows. – 55 sts.

Next row: 17m., with b. 7 from 1, 19m., with c. 7 from 1, 17m.

The last row sets the position of the bobbles. Pattern 15 rows more increasing 1 st. at each end of the 14th of these rows. – 57 sts.

Next row: 8m., with e. 7 from 1, 19m., with a. 7 from 1, 19m., with b. 7 from 1, 8m.

Pattern 15 rows as set, increasing 1 st. at each end of the 14th of these rows. – 59 sts.

Next row: 19m., with d. 7 from 1, 19m., with e. 7 from 1, 19m.

Pattern 15 rows as set, increasing 1 st. at each end of the 14th of these rows. – 61 sts.

Now work as given for the short sleeves from *** to end.

THE SHOULDER PADS (both alike)
With size $3\frac{1}{4}$ mm. (No. 10) needles and m. cast on 30 sts. and work 42 rows in single rib, then cast off. Fold in half diagonally and join outer edges to form a triangle.

TO MAKE UP THE SWEATER
Darn in ends, always make sure that sufficiently long ends are left or the work will unravel. Pin out to size and press all parts except the ribbing with a warm iron over a damp cloth. Join left shoulder seam. Set in sleeves. Join sleeve and side seams. Press seams. Catch shoulder pads in position.

Dec. 1 st. at the beginning of the next row and the 3 following alternate rows.

On 37 sts. pattern 20 rows.

To shape the neck: Cast off 7 sts. at the beginning of the next row, then dec. 1 st. at the neck edge on each of the next 8 rows. – 22 sts.

Inc. 1 st. at the beginning of the next row and the following 8th row.

On 24 sts. work 7 rows.

To slope the shoulder: Cast off 12 sts. at the beginning of the next row. On 12 sts. work 1 row, then cast off.

THE RIGHT FRONT
Work as given for left front until the increase row has been worked.

Break off m., join in a. Change to size $3\frac{3}{4}$ mm. (No. 9) needles and beginning with a k. row, with a. s.s. 3 rows.

4th row: 26a., 7c., 12a.

5th row: 10a., 13c., 22a.

The last 2 rows set the position of the pattern given on the right hand side of the chart, but reversing it so that the purl rows are worked from right to left, and the knit rows from left to right.

Work the 6th to 77th rows from the chart as set.

Continuing in pattern from chart as set, work as given for left front from ** to end.

THE LONG SLEEVES (both alike)
With size $3\frac{1}{4}$ mm. (No. 10) needles and m. cast on 41 sts. and work 22 rows in single rib.

Change to size $3\frac{3}{4}$ mm. (No. 9) needles and beginning with a k. row s.s. 4 rows.

Now work in wallpaper pattern as follows, but using short lengths of contrast colours for each motif:

1st row: 4m., 1f., 31m., 1f., 4m.

2nd row: 3m., 3f., 29m., 3f., 3m.

The last 2 rows set the position of the pattern given in the chart.

Work the 3rd to 16th rows from the chart as set.

Continuing in pattern as set and working the extra sts. into the pattern as they occur, inc. 1 st. at each end of the next row and the 9 following 8th rows.

On 61 sts. pattern 7 rows.

To shape the sleevetop: Maintaining the continuing of the pattern as set, cast off 4 sts. at the beginning of the next 2 rows. Dec. 1 st. at each end of the next row and the 13 following alternate rows.

On 25 sts. work 1 row.

Cast off 3 sts. at the beginning of the next 4 rows and 4 sts. on the 2 following rows.

Cast off the remaining 5 sts.

THE SHORT SLEEVES (both alike)
With size $3\frac{1}{4}$ mm. (No. 10) needles and m. cast on 57 sts. and work 12 rows in single rib.

Change to size $3\frac{3}{4}$ mm. (No. 9) needles and beginning with a k. row s.s. 4 rows.

1st row: 12m., 1f., 31m., 1f., 12m.

2nd row: 11m., 3f., 29m., 3f., 11m.

The last 2 rows set the position of the 32 row repeat wallpaper pattern outlined on the chart. Work the 3rd and 4th rows as set.

Continuing in pattern as set, inc. 1 st. at each end of the next row and the following 8th row.

On 61 sts. pattern 7 rows.

To shape the sleevetop: Work as given for the sleevetop on long sleeves.

THE SHOULDER PADS (2 alike)
With size $3\frac{1}{4}$ mm. (No. 10) needles and m. cast on 30 sts. and work 42 rows in single rib, then cast off. Fold in half diagonally and join outer edges to form a triangle.

THE BUTTON BAND
With size $3\frac{1}{4}$ mm. (No. 10) needles and m. cast on 6 sts. and work 130 rows in single rib, then cast off.

THE BUTTONHOLE BAND
With size $3\frac{1}{4}$ mm. (No. 10) needles and m. cast on 6 sts. and work 6 rows in single rib.

1st Buttonhole row: Rib 2, cast off 2, rib to end.

2nd Buttonhole row: Rib 2, turn, cast off 2, turn, rib to end.

Rib 18 rows.

Repeat the last 20 rows 5 times, then work the 2 buttonhole rows again.

Rib 2 rows, then cast off.

THE COLLAR
First join shoulder seams, with right side of work facing rejoin m. at the right front neck edge using size $3\frac{1}{4}$ mm. (No. 10) needles, pick up and k. 31 sts. from right front neck edge, k. across the 29 sts. at back neck edge, then pick up and k. 31 sts. from left front neck edge. – 91 sts.

Work 13 rows in single rib, then cast off loosely in rib.

TO MAKE UP THE CARDIGAN
Pin out to size and press all parts except the ribbing with a warm iron over a damp cloth. Set in sleeves. Join sleeve and side seams. Neatly sew front bands in place. Press seams. Sew on buttons. Catch shoulder pads in place.

HOME SWEET HOME

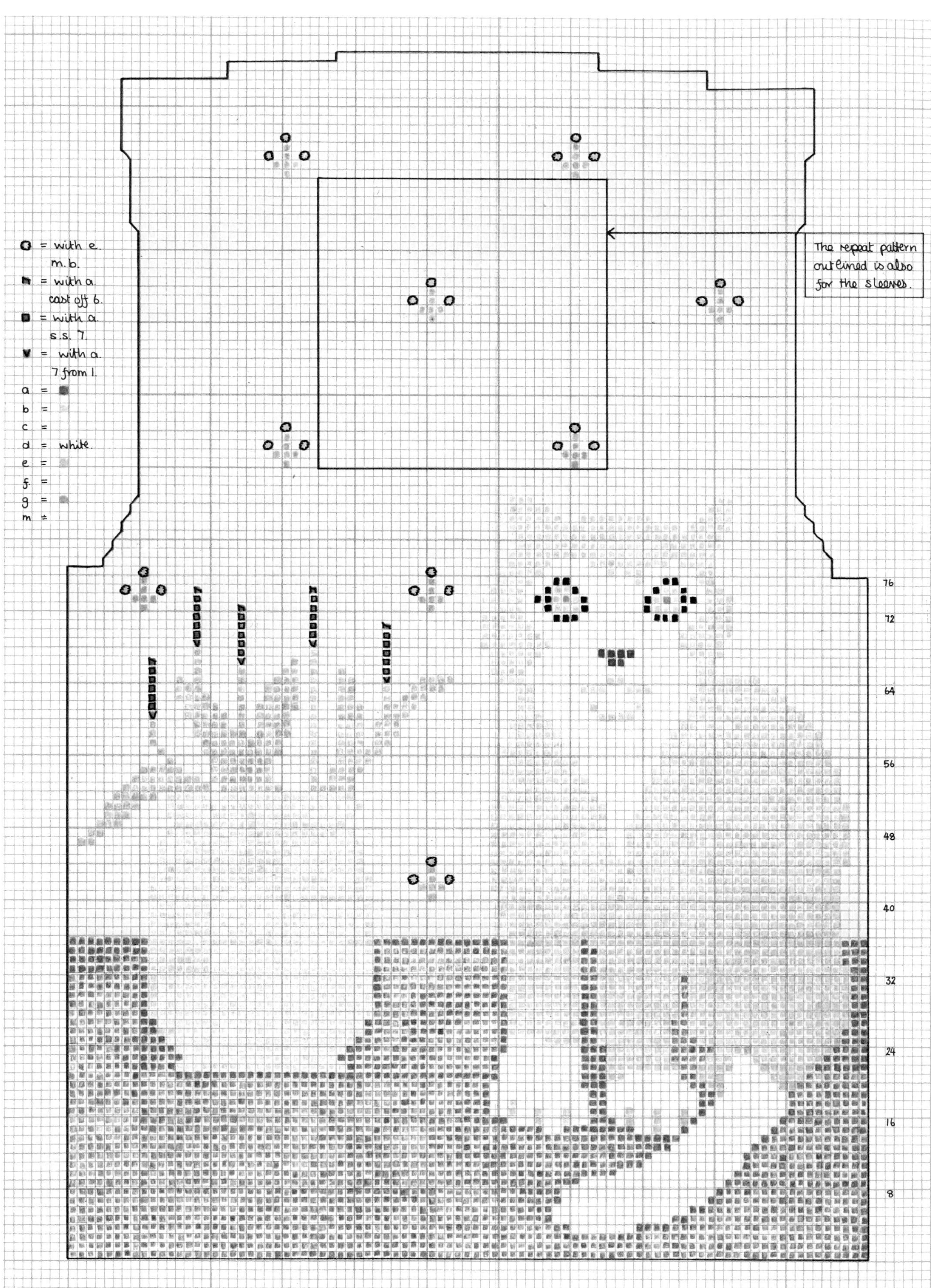

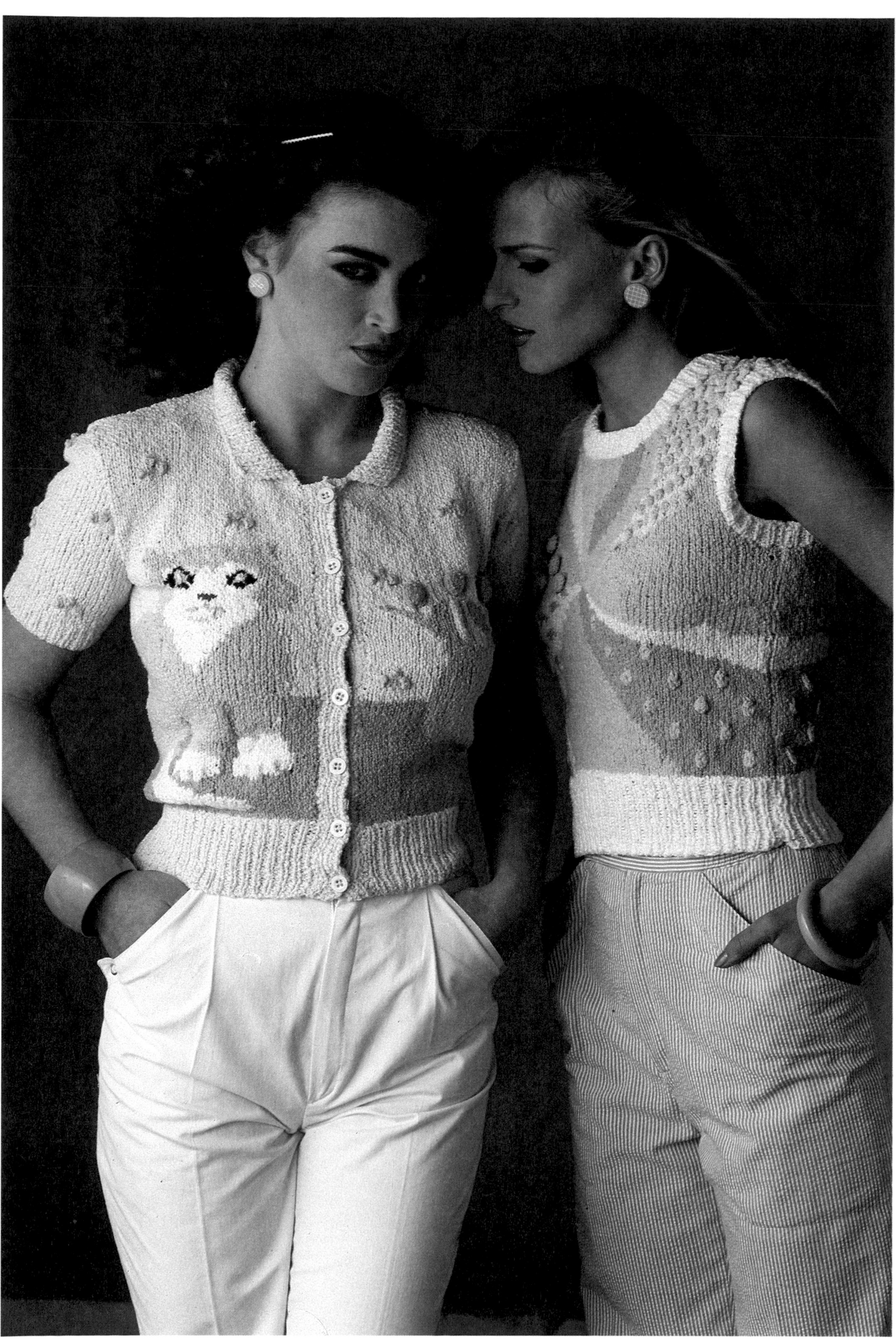

CASSATA

MATERIALS
One 50 gram ball of 'Woollybear Cotton Bouclé' in main colour, second, third, and fourth contrast colours, and 2 balls in each of the first and fifth contrast colours; a pair each of size 3¼ mm. (No. 10) and size 3¾ mm. (No. 9) Aero knitting needles.

TENSION
10 stitches and 14 rows to 5 centimetres (2 inches) over the stocking stitch using size 3¾ mm. (No. 9) needles. If you cannot obtain the correct tension using the size needle suggested, use larger or smaller ones accordingly.

ABBREVIATIONS
K., knit; p., purl; st., stitch; tog., together; dec., decrease (by working 2 sts. tog.); inc., increase (by working twice into same st.); single rib is k.1 and p.1 alternately; s.s., stocking stitch is k. on the right side and p. on the wrong side; up 1, pick up the loop which lies between the needles, slip it onto left hand needle and k. into the back of it; m., main colour; a., first contrast; b., second contrast; c., third contrast; d., fourth contrast; e., fifth contrast; sl., slip; p.s.s.o., pass sl. st. over; y.r.n., yarn round needle; m.b., make bobble thus, k.1, y.r.n., k.1., y.r.n., k.1, all into next st., turn, p.5, turn, k.5, turn, p.5, turn, k.5, turn, p.2 tog., p.1, p.2 tog., turn, sl.1, k.2 tog., p.s.s.o; m.k., make knot thus, k.1, y.r.n., k.1, turn, k.3, turn, sl.1, k.2 tog., p.s.s.o.; 3 from 1, k.1, p.1, k.1, all into next st.

MEASUREMENTS
The measurements are given in centimetres followed by inches in brackets.

Underarms	80 (32)
Side seam	34 (13½)
Length	52.5 (21)

THE BACK
With size 3¼ mm. (No. 10) needles and e. cast on 72 sts. and work 23 rows in single rib.

Increase row: Rib 8, *up 1, rib 8; repeat from * to end. – 80 sts.

Change to size 3¾ mm. (No. 9) needles and work in pattern as follows: This is worked entirely in s.s. except for the bobbles and knots. Use separate balls of colour for each section for both ease and neatness of work. Always ensure that sufficiently long ends have been left for darning in.

1st row: *3b., 3a.; repeat from * 4 times more, 2b., 1a., 31c., 16b.

2nd row: 16b., 31c., 1a., 1b., * 5a., 1b.; repeat from * 4 times, 1a.

The last 2 rows set the position of the pattern given in the chart. Now work the 3rd to 70th rows from the chart as set.

To shape the armholes: Continuing in pattern from chart as set, cast off 3 sts. at the beginning of the next 2 rows, then dec. 1 st. at each end of the next row and the 3 following alternate rows.

On 66 sts. pattern 25 rows.

Inc. 1 st. at each end of the next row and the following 8th row.

On 70 sts. pattern 7 rows.

To slope the shoulders: Cast off 10 sts. at the beginning of the next 4 rows. Leave the remaining 30 sts. on a spare needle until required for neckband.

THE FRONT
Work as given for back until the increase row has been worked.

Change to size 3¾ mm. (No. 9) needles and work in pattern as follows, noting the information given for the back.

1st row: 16b., 31c., 1a., 2b., *3a., 3b.; repeat from * to end.

2nd row: 1a., 1b., *5a., 1b.; repeat from * 4 times, 1a., 31c., 16b.

The last 2 rows set the position of the pattern given in the chart, but working k. rows from left to right and p. rows from right to left, thus reversing the pattern.

Now work the 3rd to 70th rows from the chart as set.

To shape the armholes: Continuing in pattern as set, cast off 3 sts. at the beginning of the next 2 rows, then dec. 1 st. at each end of the next row and the 3 following alternate rows.

On 66 sts. pattern 16 rows.

Now divide the sts. for the neck: Next row: Work as set across 26 sts. and leave these sts. on a spare needle until required for right front shoulder, cast off 14 sts. for neck, work to end and continue on these 26 sts. for left front shoulder.

To shape the neck: Continuing in pattern as set, dec. 1 st. at the neck edge on each of the next 8 rows.

Inc. 1 st. at the beginning – armhole edge on the next row and the following 8th row.

On 20 sts. pattern 7 rows.

To slope the shoulder: Cast off 10 sts. at the beginning of the next row. On 10 sts. work 1 row, then cast off.

The right front shoulder: With right side of work facing, rejoin yarn to inner edge of sts. left on spare needle and work to end of row.

Then work as given for left front shoulder to end.

THE NECKBAND
First join right shoulder seam. With right side of work facing rejoin e. and using size 3¼ mm. (No. 10) needles pick up and k. 23 sts. from left front neck edge, 14 sts. from centre front neck, 23 sts. from right front neck edge and k.30 sts. from back neck edge. On 90 sts. work 7 rows in single rib, then cast off in rib.

THE ARMBANDS (both alike)
First join left shoulder seam. With right side of work facing rejoin e. and using size 3¼ mm. (No. 10) needles pick up and k. 72 sts. from all round armhole edge. Work 7 rows in single rib, then cast off loosely in rib.

TO MAKE UP THE SWEATER
Pin out to size and press all parts on the wrong side with a warm iron over a damp cloth. Join side seams. Press seams.

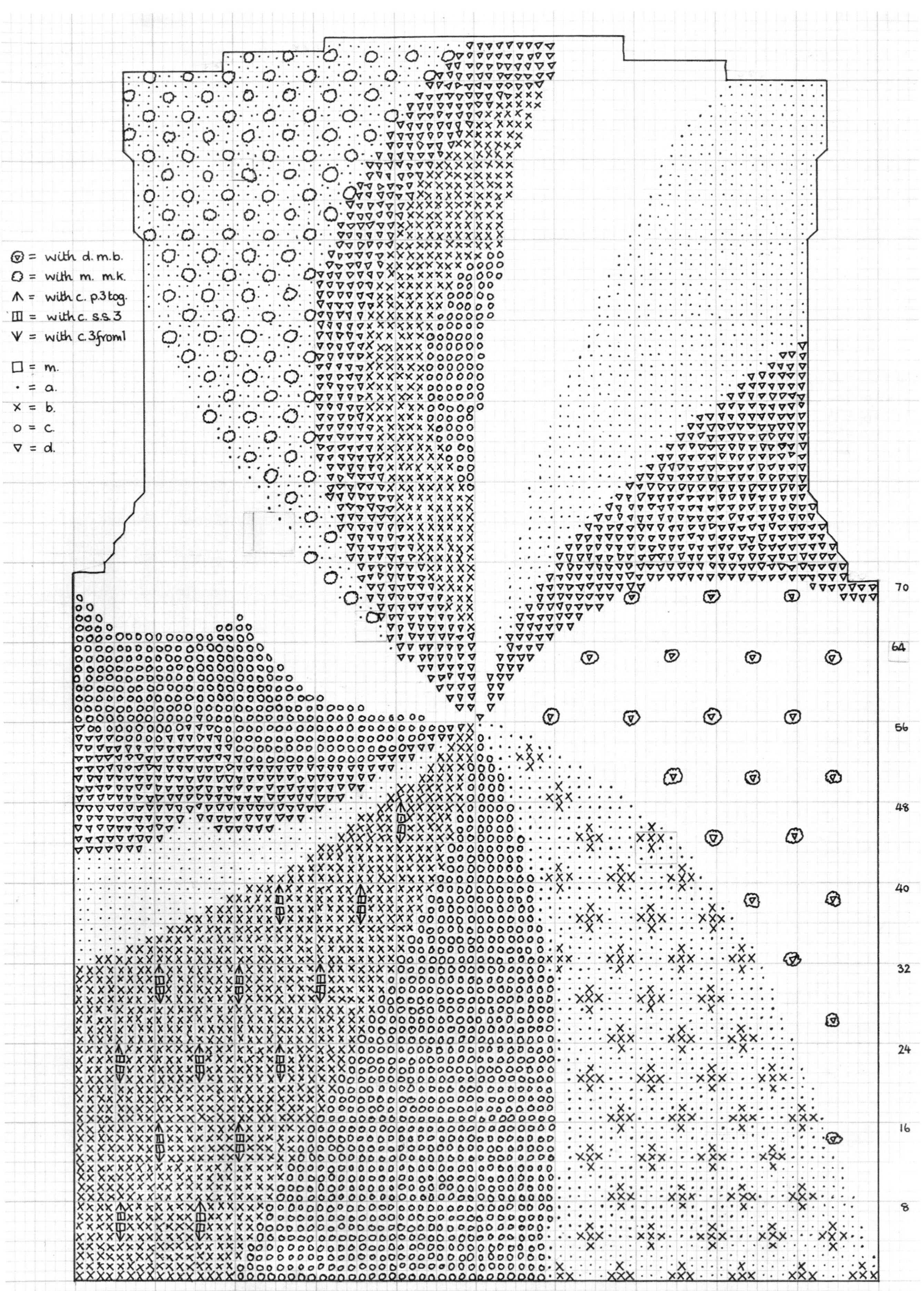

⊚ = with d. m.b.
O = with m. m.k.
Λ = with c. p.3 tog.
▥ = with c. s.s.3
V = with c. 3 from 1
□ = m.
· = a.
× = b.
o = c.
▽ = d.
70
64
56
48
40
32
24
16
8

PIERROT

PIERROT

MATERIALS
For the sweater: 13 (14) (15) ounce (28 gram) hanks of 'Woollybear Real Shetland' by Patricia Roberts or 17 (18) (19) 25 gram balls of 'Woollybear Bunny Fluff' by Patricia Roberts; 3 buttons.

For the dress: 20 ounce (28 gram) hanks of 'Woollybear Real Shetland' by Patricia Roberts or 26 25 gram balls of 'Woollybear Bunny Fluff' by Patricia Roberts.

For the sweater or the dress: a pair each of size $2\frac{1}{4}$ mm. (No. 13) and size $2\frac{3}{4}$ mm. (No. 12) Aero knitting needles; a fine cable needle.

TENSION
Work at a tension of 16 stitches and 20 rows to 5 centimetres (2 inches) over the stocking stitch using size $2\frac{3}{4}$ mm. (No. 12) needles. If you cannot obtain the correct tension using the size needles suggested, use larger or smaller ones accordingly.

ABBREVIATIONS
K., knit; p., purl; st., stitch; tog., together; dec., decrease (by working 2 sts. tog.); inc., increase (by working twice into same st.); s.s., stocking stitch is k. on the right side and p. on the wrong side; double rib is k.2 and p.2 alternately; c.8f., cable 8 front thus, slip next 4 sts. onto a cable needle and leave at front of work, k.4, then k.4 from cable needle; c.8b., cable 8 back as cable 8f. but leave sts. on cable needle at back of work; c.12, cable 12 thus, slip next 6 sts. onto a cable needle and leave at back of work, k.6, then k.6 from cable needle; c.6, cable 6 thus, slip next 3 sts. onto a cable needle and leave at back of work, k.3, then k.3 from cable needle; up 1, pick up the loop which lies between the needles, slip it onto left hand needle, then k. into back of it.

NOTE
The instructions are given for the small size. Where they vary work the figures in the first brackets for the medium size or the figures in the second brackets for the large size.

MEASUREMENTS
The measurements are given in centimetres followed by inches in brackets.

THE SWEATER

Sizes	Small	Medium	Large
To fit chest	92.5 (37)	97.5 (39)	102.5 (41)
Underarms	92.5 (37)	97.5 (39)	102.5 (41)
Side seam	40 (16)	40 (16)	40 (16)
Length	62.5 (25)	64 ($25\frac{1}{2}$)	65 (26)
Sleeve seam	47.5 (19)	47.5 (19)	47.5 (19)

THE DRESS

To fit bust	80–90 (32–36)
Underarms	102.5 (41)
Side seam	70 (28)
Length	95 (38)
Sleeve seam	42.5 (17)

THE SWEATER

THE BACK
With size $2\frac{1}{4}$ mm. (No. 13) needles cast on 136 (144) (152) sts. and work 35 rows in double rib.

Increase row: Rib 7 (11) (15), *up 1, rib 11; repeat from * ending last repeat rib 8 (12) (16). – 148 (156) (164) sts.

Change to size $2\frac{3}{4}$ mm. (No. 12) needles and beginning with a k. row s.s. 35 rows.

Foundation row: P.5 (9) (13), *up 1, p.8; repeat from * 4 times more, up 1, p.16, up 1, p.6, up 1, p.14, up 1, p.6, up 1, p.16, *up 1, p.8; repeat from last * ending last repeat p.5 (9) (13). – 164 (172) (180) sts.

Now work in pattern as follows:

1st row: K. 58 (62) (66), p.2, k.44, p.2, k.58 (62) (66).

2nd row: P.5 (9) (13), k.1, p.8, k.1, p.8, k.1, p.8, k.1, p.8, k.1, p.8, k.1, p.6, k.1, p.2, k.1, p.6, k.1, p.6, k.1, p.6, **, k.2; work from ** back to beginning of row.

3rd row: K.56 (60) (64), p.1, k.1, p.2, k.1, p.1, k.40, p.1, k.1, p.2, k.1, p.1, k.56 (60) (64).

4th row: P.5 (9) (13), k.1, p.8, k.1, p.8, k.1, p.8, k.1, p.8, k.1, p.8, k.1, * p.4, k.1, p.1., k.1, p.2, k.1, p.1, k.1, p.4, k.1, p.6, k.1, p.6 **, k.2; work from ** back to beginning of row.

5th row: P.5 (9) (13), k.1, c.8b., k.1, p.8, k.1, c.8b., k.1, p.8, k.1, c.8b., *, k.4, p.1, k.1, p.1, k.1, p.2, k.1, p.1, k.1, p.1, k.4, c.6, k.1, c.6**, k.2; work from ** back to beginning of row.

6th row: Work as given for 4th row until * is reached, p.2, k.1, p.1, k.1, p.1, k.1, p.2, k.1, p.1, k.1, p.1, k.1, p.2, k.1, p.6, k.1, p.6**, k.2; work from ** back to beginning of row.

7th row: K.52 (56) (60), p.1, k.1, p.1, k.1, p.1, k.1, p.2, k.1, p.1, k.1, p.1, k.1, p.1 **, k.32; work from ** back to beginning of row.

8th row: Work as for 4th row until * is reached, k.1 more, p.1, k.1, p.1, k.1, p.1, k.1, p.2, k.1, p.1, k.1, p.1, k.1, p.1, k.2, p.6, k.1, p.6 **, k.2; work from ** back to beginning of row.

9th row: K.51 (55) (59), p.1, k.1, p.1, k.1, p.1, k.1, p.1, k.2, p.1, k.1, p.1, k.1, p.1, k.1, p.1, ** k.30; work from ** back to beginning.

10th row: Work as for 4th row until * is reached, p.1, k.1, p.1, k.1, p.1, k.1, p.1, k.2, p.1, k.1, p.1, k.1, p.1, k.1, p.1, k.1, p.6, k.1, p.6 **, k.2; work from ** back to beginning of row.

11th row: K.53 (57) (61), p.1, k.1, p.1, k.1, p.1, k.2, p.1, k.1, p.1, k.1, p.1 **, m. k.34; work from ** back to beginning.

12th row: Work as for 4th row until * is reached, p.3, k.1, p.1, k.1, p.1, k.2, p.1, k.1, p.1, k.1, p.3, k.1, p.6, k.1, p.6 **, k.2; work from ** back to beginning.

13th row: P.5 (9) (13), k.1, c.8f., k.1, p.8, k.1, c.8f., k.1, p.8, k.1, c.8f., k.5, p.1, k.1, p.1, k.2, p.1, k.1, p.1, k.5, c.6, k.1, c.6 **, k.2; work from ** back to beginning.

14th row: Work as for 4th row until * is reached, p.5, k.1, p.1, k.2, p.1, k.1, p.5, k.1, p.6, k.1, p.6 **, k.2; work from ** back to beginning.

15th row: K.57 (61) (65), p.1, k.2, p.1, k.42, p.1, k.2, p.1, k. to end.

16th row: Work as for 4th row until * is reached, p.7, k.2, p.7, k.1, p.6, k.1, p.6 **, k.2; work from ** back to beginning.

17th row: K.52 (56) (60), *p.2, k.2, p.2, k.2, p.2, k.2, p.2, k.32, p.2, k.2, p.2, k.2, p.2, k.2, p.2*, k.52 (56) (60).

18th row: Work as for 4th row until * is reached, p.1, k.2, p.2, k.2, p.2, k.2, p.2, k.2, p.1, k.1, p.6, k.1, p.6 **, k.2; work from ** back to beginning of row.

19th row: K.51 (55) (59), p.1, k.2, p.2, k.2, p.2, k.2, p.2, k.2, p.1 **, k.30, work from ** back to beginning.

20th row: Work as for 4th row until * is reached, k.1 more, p.2, k.2, p.2, k.2, p.2, k.2, p.2, k.2, p.6, k.1, p.6**, k.2; work from ** back to beginning.

21st row: Work as given for 5th row until * is reached, k.2, work from * to * on 17th row, k.2; work from * on 5th row back to beginning of row.

22nd, 23rd and 24th rows: As 18th, 19th and 20th rows.

25th to 48th rows: As 1st to 24th rows, but working c.8f. instead of c.8b. and c.8b. instead of c.8f.

Now work the first 39 rows again.

***Next row: Work as given for 4th row until * is reached, p.7, k.2, p.7, k.1, p.6, p.2 tog., p.5. **, k.2; work from ** back to beginning – 162 (170) (178) sts.

Now work in pattern as follows.

1st row: k.1, then p.2 (p.2, k.2, p.2) (p.2, k.2, p.2, k.2, p.2), k.12, p.2, k.2, p.2, k.12, p.2, k.2, p.2, k.13, p.2, k.2, p.2, k.2, p.2, k.2, p.2 **, k.30; work from ** back to beginning of row.

2nd row and every wrong side row: P.5 (9) (13), k.1, p.8, k.1, p.8, k.1, p.8, k.1, p.8, k.1, p.8, k.2, p.2, k.2, p.2, k.2, p.2, k.2, p.2, k.2, p.12 ** k.2; work from ** back to beginning.

3rd row: K.3, then p.2 (p.2, k.2, p.2) (p.2, k.2, p.2, k.2, p.2), k.12, p.2, k.2, p.2 k.12, p.2, k.2, p.2, k.11, p.2, k.2, p.2, k.2, p.2, k.2, p.2 ** k.30; work from ** back to beginning.

5th row: K.1, then p.2 (p.2, k.2, p.2) (p.2, k.2, p.2, k.2, p.2), k.3, c.8b., k.1, p.2, k.2, p.2, k.3, c.8b., k.1, p.2, k.2, p.2, k.3, c.8b., k.2, p.2, k.2, p.2, k.2, p.2, k.2, p.2, ** k.30; work from ** back to beginning.

7th row: As 3rd row.

9th row: Work as for 1st row until ** is reached, k.2, c.12, k.2, c.12, k.2; work from ** on 1st row back to beginning to row.

11th to 20th rows: As 3rd to 8th rows, then 1st to 4th rows.

21st row: Work as for 5th row until ** is reached, k.2, c.12, k.2, c.12, k.2; work from ** on 5th row back to beginning.

22nd to 24th rows: As 2nd, 3rd and 4th rows.

The last 24 rows form the cable pattern.

To shape the armholes: Continuing in the 24 row cable pattern as set, cast off 8 sts. at the beginning of the next 2 rows, then dec. 1 st. at each end of the next row and the 9 (11) (13) following alternate rows.

On 126 (130) (134) sts. pattern 45 (47) (49) rows.

Inc. 1 st. at each end of the next row and the 3 following 8th rows.

On 134 (138) (142) sts. pattern 9 rows.

To slope the shoulders: Cast off 11 sts. at the beginning of the next 6 rows and 10 (11) (12) sts. on the 2 following rows.

Cast off the remaining 48 (50) (52) sts.

THE FRONT
Work as given for back until the armhole shaping has been worked.

On 126 (130) (134) sts. pattern 38 (40) (42) rows.

Now divide the sts. for the neck: Next row: Pattern 50 (51) (52) and leave these sts. on a spare needle until required for right front shoulder, cast off 26 (28) (30) for neck, pattern to end and continue on these 50 (51) (52) sts. for the left front shoulder.

The left front shoulder: To shape the neck: Pattern 11 rows decreasing 1 st. at the neck edge on each row and at the same time increasing 1 st. at the armhole edge on the 7th of these rows.

On 40 (41) (42) sts. pattern 3 rows.

Inc. 1 st. at the armhole edge on the next row and the 2 following 8th rows.

On 43 (44) (45) sts. pattern 9 rows.

To slope the shoulder: Cast off 11 sts. at the beginning of the next row and the 2 following alternate rows. On 10 (11) (12) sts. work 1 row, then cast off.

The right front shoulder: With right side of work facing rejoin yarn to inner edge of sts. left on spare needle and work to end of row, then work as given for left front shoulder to end.

THE SLEEVES (both alike)
With size $2\frac{1}{4}$ mm. (No. 13) needles cast on 76 (80) (84) sts. and work 36 rows in double rib.

Change to size $2\frac{3}{4}$ mm. (No. 12) needles and beginning with a k. row s.s. 6 rows.

Continuing in s.s. inc. 1 st. at each end of the next row and the 13 following 10th rows. On 104 (108) (112) sts. s.s. 3 rows.

Now work in cable pattern as follows:

1st row: P.2 (k.2, p.2) (p.2, k.2, p.2), *k.2, p.2; repeat from * 3 times more, k.13, p.2, k.2, p.2, ** k.30, ** p.2, k.2, p.2, k.13, *p.2, k.2; repeat from last * ending last repeat p.2 (k.2) (p.2).

2nd row and every wrong side row: P.20 (22) (24), k.1, p.8, k.2, p.2, k.2, p.2, k.2, p.12 **, k.2; work from ** back to beginning.

3rd row: K.2 (p.2, k.2) (k.2, p.2, k.2), p.2, *k.2, p.2; repeat from * 3 times more, k.11, p.2, k.2, p.2, k.30, p.2, k.2, p.2, k.11, *p.2, k.2; repeat from last * ending last repeat k.2 (p.2) (k.2).

5th row: P.2 (k.2, p.2) (p.2, k.2, p.2), *k.2, p.2; repeat from * 3 times more, k.3, c.8b., k.2, p.2, k.2, p.2, ** k.30, ** p.2, k.2, p.2, k.2, c.8b., k.3, * p.2, k.2; repeat from * ending last repeat p.2 (k.2) (p.2).

7th row: As 3rd row.

9th row: As 1st row until first ** is reached, k.2, c.12, k.2, c.12, k.2, then work from second ** on first row to end.

10th to 16th rows: As 2nd to 8th rows.

17th to 20th rows: As 1st to 4th rows.

21st row: As 5th row until ** is reached, k.2, c.12, k.2, c.12, k.2, then as for 5th row from second ** to end.

22nd to 24th rows: As 2nd, 3rd and 4th rows.

The last 24 rows form the cable pattern.

To shape the sleevetop: Continuing in cable pattern as set, cast off 8 sts. at the beginning of the next 2 rows, then dec. 1 st. at each end of the next row and the 23 following alternate rows.

On 40 (44) (48) sts. work 1 row.

Dec. 1 st. at each end of the next 4 (6) (8) rows.

Cast off 3 sts. at the beginning of the next 4 rows and 4 sts. on the 4 following rows. Cast off the remaining 4 sts.

THE NECKBAND

First join right shoulder seam. With right side of work facing rejoin yarn at left front neck edge and using size 2¼ mm. (No. 13) needles pick up and k.34 sts. from left front neck edge, 26 (28) (30) sts. from centre front neck, 34 sts. from right front neck edge, then 48 (50) (52) sts. from back neck edge.

On 142 (146) (150) sts. work 11 rows in double rib, then cast off loosely in rib.

THE LEFT SHOULDER EDGING

First join first 9 (10) (11) sts. of left shoulder at armhole edge. Rejoin yarn to neckband at left back shoulder, then using size 2¼ mm. (No. 13) needles pick up and k.40 sts. from left back shoulder, then 40 sts. from left front shoulder. On 80 sts. k.1 row.

1st Buttonhole row: K.43, *cast off 3, k. next 12 sts.; repeat from * ending last repeat k.1.

2nd Buttonhole row: K.2, *turn, cast on 3 over those cast off, turn, k.13, repeat from * once, turn, cast on 3, turn, k. to end.

Cast off.

TO MAKE UP THE SWEATER

Pin out to size and press all parts except the ribbing on the wrong side with a warm iron over a damp cloth. Set in sleeves. Join sleeve and side seams. Press seams. Sew on buttons.

THE DRESS

THE BACK

With size 2¼ mm. (No. 13) needles cast on 180 sts. and work in rib as follows:

1st row: *K.3, p.3; repeat from * to end.

2nd row: *K.1, p.1; repeat from * to end.

Repeat the last 2 rows 15 times more.

Change to size 2¾ mm. (No. 12) needles and work the 48 pattern rows given for large size of back of sweater 5 times, then work the first 39 rows again.

Now work as given for large size of back of sweater from *** to end.

THE FRONT

Work as given for the back until the armhole shaping has been worked, then work as given for large size of front of sweater to end.

THE SLEEVES (both alike)

With size 2¼ mm. (No. 13) needles cast on 68 sts. and work 35 rows in rib pattern as given for back.

Increase row: Rib 5, *up 1, rib 1, up 1, rib 2; repeat from * ending last repeat rib 5. – 108 sts.

Change to size 2¾ mm. (No. 12) needles and work the 24 row cable pattern given for middle size on sleeves of sweater 7 times.

To shape the sleeve top: Continue in pattern as set, work as given for sleeve top on middle size of sweater.

THE COLLAR

With size 2¼ mm. (No. 13) needles cast on 168 sts. and work 120 rows in rib as given for back, then cast off in rib.

THE SHOULDER PADS (both alike)

With size 2¼ mm. (No. 13) needles cast on 48 sts. and work 60 rows in rib as given for back. Fold in half diagonally and join outer edges to form triangles.

TO MAKE UP THE DRESS

Pin out to size and press lightly on the wrong side with a warm iron over a damp cloth. Join shoulder seams. Set in sleeves. Join sleeve and side seams. Press seams. Catch shoulder pads in place. Join row end edges of collar. Sew collar in place all round neck edge.

GRENADINE

MATERIALS
13 (14) (17) (18) 25 gram balls of either 'Woollybear 100% Mohair' by Patricia Roberts or 'Woollybear Brushed Alpaca' by Patricia Roberts; a pair each of size 4 mm. (No. 8) and size $3\frac{3}{4}$ mm. (No. 9) Aero knitting needles.

TENSION
10 stitches and 14 rows to 5 centimetres (2 inches) over the stocking stitch using size 4 mm. (No. 8) needles. If you cannot obtain the correct tension using the size needles suggested, use larger or smaller ones accordingly.

ABBREVIATIONS
K., knit; p., purl; st., stitch; tog., together; dec., decrease (by working 2 sts. tog.); single rib is k.1 and p.1 alternately; s.s., stocking stitch is k. on the right side and p. on the wrong side; sl., slip.; p.s.s.o., pass sl. st. over; inc., increase (by working twice into same st.).

NOTE
The instructions are given for the small woman's size. Where they vary work the figures in the first brackets for the medium woman's size, the figures in the second brackets for the small man's size or the figures in the third brackets for the medium man's size.

MEASUREMENTS
The measurements are given in centimetres followed by inches in brackets.

Sizes	Women's Small	Medium
To fit bust	85 (34)	90 (36)
Underarms	85 (34)	90 (36)
Side seam	34 ($13\frac{1}{2}$)	34 ($13\frac{1}{2}$)
Length	56 ($22\frac{1}{2}$)	57 ($22\frac{3}{4}$)
Sleeve seam	42.5 (17)	42.5 (17)

Sizes	Men's Small	Medium
To fit chest	95 (38)	100 (40)
Underarms	95 (38)	100 (40)
Side seam	39 ($15\frac{1}{2}$)	39 ($15\frac{1}{2}$)
Length	63 (25)	64 ($25\frac{1}{2}$)
Sleeve seam	47.5 (19)	47.5 (19)

THE BACK
With size $3\frac{3}{4}$ mm. (No. 9) needles and m. cast on 86 (90) (96) (100) sts. and work 20 rows in single rib.

Change to size 4 mm. (No. 8) needles and beginning with a k. row s.s. 78 (78) (92) (92) rows.

To shape the armholes: Cast off 4 sts. at the beginning of the next 2 rows, then dec. 1 st. at each end of the next row and the 5 (6) (6) (7) following alternate rows.

On 66 (68) (74) (76) sts. s.s. 35 (35) (37) (37) rows.

Inc. 1 st. at each end of the next row and the following 6th row.

On 70 (72) (78) (80) sts. s.s. 5 rows.

To slope the shoulders: Cast off 10 (11) (12) (13) sts. at the beginning of the next 2 rows, then 11 (11) (12) (12) sts. on the 2 following rows.

Leave the remaining 28 (28) (30) (30) sts. on a spare needle until required for neckband.

THE FRONT
Work as given for the back until 77 (77) (91) (91) rows have been worked in s.s.

Now divide the sts. for the neck: Next row: P.43 (45) (48) (50) and leave these sts. on a spare needle until required for right front shoulder, p.

BUTTERSCOTCH

MATERIALS
For the one colour version: 8 (8) (9) (10) 100 gram hanks of 'Woollybear Teddy Fleece' and 11 (11) (13) (14) 25 gram balls of 'Woollybear 100% Mohair' both by Patricia Roberts.

For the 3 colour version: 3 (3) (4) (4) 100 gram hanks of 'Woollybear Teddy Fleece' in each of 3 different colours and 4 (4) (5) (5) 25 gram balls of 'Woollybear 100% Mohair' in each of 3 different colours.

For either version: A pair of size 7 mm. (No. 2) Aero knitting needles; 4 medium sized buttons and 4 small buttons.

TENSION
6 stitches and 11 rows to 5 centimetres (2 inches) over the check stitch using size 7 mm. (No. 2) needles. If you cannot obtain the correct tension using the size needles suggested use larger or smaller ones accordingly.

ABBREVIATIONS
K., knit; p., purl; st., stitch; tog., together; dec., decrease (by working 2 sts. tog.); inc., increase (by working twice into same st.); sl., slip; a., first colour; b., second colour; c., third colour; y.f., yarn forward; y.b., yarn back; single rib is k.1 and p.1 alternately; p.s.s.o., pass slip stitch over.

NOTE
The instructions are given for the small woman's size. Where they vary work the figures in the first brackets for the medium woman's size; the figures in the second brackets for the small man's size or the figures in the third brackets for the medium man's size.

MEASUREMENTS
The measurements are given in centimetres followed by inches in brackets.

Sizes	Women's Small	Medium
To fit bust	85 (34)	90 (36)
Underarms	87.5 (35)	92.5 (37)
Side seam	35 (14)	35 (14)
Length	55 (22)	55.5 ($22\frac{1}{4}$)
Sleeve seam	40 (16)	40 (16)

Sizes	Men's Small	Medium
To fit chest	95 (38)	100 (40)
Underarms	95 (38)	100 (40)
Side seam	40 (16)	40 (16)
Length	62 ($24\frac{3}{4}$)	62.5 (25)
Sleeve seam	45 (18)	45 (18)

THE BACK
With size 7 mm. (No. 2) needles and one strand each of 'Mohair' and 'Teddy Fleece' in first colour – a., cast on 53 (55) (59) (61) sts. and work in pattern as follows:

For the one colour version: 1st row: sl.1, * y.f., sl.1 p. wise., y.b., k.1; repeat from * to end.

2nd row: Sl.1, p.1, * y.b., sl.1 p. wise, y.f., p.1; repeat from * until 1 remains, k.1.

The last 2 rows form the pattern; repeat them 37 (37) (42) (42) times more.

For the three colour version: 1st row: With a. work as given for 1st row of one colour version; leave a. hanging.

2nd row: With b. – one strand of 'Mohair' and one strand of 'Teddy Fleece' in second colour – work as given for 2nd row of one colour version; leave b. hanging.

3rd row: With c. – one strand of 'Mohair' and one strand of 'Teddy Fleece' in third contrast – work as given for 1st row, leave c. hanging.

4th row: With a. as second row.

5th row: With b. as first row.

6th row: With c. as second row.

The last 6 rows form the 3 colour pattern; repeat them 11 (11) (13) (13) times more, then work the first 4 (4) (2) (2) rows again.

For either version: To shape the armholes: Continuing in pattern as set, cast off 2 sts. at the beginning of the next 2 rows, then dec. 1 st. at each end of the next row and the 2 (3) (3) (4) following alternate rows.

On 43 (43) (47) (47) sts. work 29 (29) (31) (31) rows in pattern as set.

Inc. 1 st. at each end of the next row.

On 45 (45) (49) (49) sts. pattern 4 rows.

Now divide the sts. for the neck: Next row: Pattern 14 (14) (15) (15) and leave these sts. on a spare needle until required for second back shoulder, cast off 17 (17) (19) (19) for neck, pattern to end and continue on these 14 (14) (15) (15) sts. for the first back shoulder.

The first back shoulder: Cast off 6 sts. at the beginning and dec. 1 st. at the end of the next row. Dec. 1 st. at the beginning – neck edge on the next row. Cast off the remaining 6 (6) (7) (7) sts.

The second back shoulder: Rejoin yarn to inner edge of sts. left on spare needle and work to end of row, then work as given for first back shoulder to end.

THE LARGE POCKET BACKS (2 alike)
With size 7 mm. (No. 2) needles and a. cast on 15 sts. and work 18 (24) rows in pattern as given for back, then leave these sts. on a spare needle until required.

THE SMALL POCKET BACK
With size 7 mm. (No. 2) needles and a. cast on 11 sts. and work 16 rows in pattern as given for back, then leave these sts. on a spare needle until required.

THE FIRST FRONT
With size 7 mm. (No. 2) needles and a. cast on 29 (31) (33) (35) sts. and work 14 (14) (18) (18) rows in pattern as given for back.

1st Buttonhole row: Pattern 24 (26) (28) (30) sts. cast off 2, work to end.

2nd Buttonhole row: Pattern 3, turn, cast on 2, turn, pattern to end.

Pattern 12 (12) (14) (14) rows.

Pocket row: Pattern 6 (7) (8) (9) sts. slip next 15 sts. onto a stitch-holder and leave at front of work, in their place pattern across the 15 sts. of one large pocket back, pattern to end of row.

Pattern 5 rows.

Work the 2 buttonhole rows again.

Pattern 18 (18) (20) (20) rows, then work the 2 buttonhole rows again.

Repeat the last 20 (20) (22) (22) rows again.

Work 1 extra row here when working

to end and continue on these 43 (45) (48) (50) sts. for the left front shoulder.

The left front shoulder: To shape the armhole and to slope the neck: Cast off 4 sts. at the beginning and dec. 1 st. at the end of the next row. Work 1 row back to armhole edge.

Pattern 11 (13) (13) (15) rows, decreasing 1 st. at the armhole edge on every right side row and at the same time decreasing 1 st. at the neck edge on the 3rd of these rows and the 2 (2) (2) (3) following 4th rows.

Pattern 35 (35) (37) (37) rows decreasing 1 st. at neck edge on every 4th row as before.

Still decreasing 1 st. at the neck edge on every 4th row, inc. 1 st. at the armhole edge on the next row, then s.s. 5 rows – 20 (21) (23) (24) sts.

Inc. 1 st. at the beginning of the next row.

On 21 (22) (24) (25) sts. s.s. 5 rows.

To slope the shoulder: Cast off 10 (11) (12) (13) sts. at the beginning of the next row. On 11 (11) (12) (12) sts. work 1 row, then cast off.

The right front shoulder: With right side of work facing rejoin yarn to inner edge of sts. left on spare needle and work to end of row, then work as given for left front shoulder to end.

THE NECKBAND

First join right shoulder seam. With right side of work facing rejoin yarn at left front neck edge and using size 3¾ mm. (No. 9) needles pick up and k.48 (50) (52) (54) sts. from left front neck edge, and 48 (50) (52) (54) sts. from right front neck edge, then k. across the 28 (28) (30) (30) sts. left on spare needle at back neck edge – 124 (128) (134) (138) sts.

Work 1 row in single rib.

Next row: Rib to within 2 sts. of centre front neck, sl.1, k.1, p.s.s.o., k.2 tog., rib to end.

Repeat the last 2 rows 3 times more.

Cast off loosely in rib.

THE SLEEVES (both alike)

With size 3¾ mm. (No. 9) needles cast on 40 (42) (48) (50) sts. and work 20 rows in single rib.

Change to size 4 mm. (No. 8) needles and beginning with a k. row, s.s. 4 rows.

Continuing in s.s. inc. 1 st. at each end of the next row and the 9 following 10th rows.

On 60 (62) (68) (70) sts. s.s. 7 (7) (21) (21) rows.

To shape the sleevetop: Cast off 4 sts. at the beginning of the next 2 rows. Dec. 1 st. at each end of the next row and the 13 (14) (15) (16) following alternate rows.

On 24 (24) (28) (28) sts. work 1 row.

Dec. 1 st. at each end of the next 4 rows. Cast off 3 sts. at the beginning of the next 4 rows, then cast off the remaining 4 (4) (8) (8) sts.

THE SHOULDER PADS (2 alike – optional)

With size 3¾ mm. (No. 9) needles, cast on 36 sts. and work 48 rows in single rib, then cast off.

Fold in half diagonally and join outer edges to form a triangle.

TO MAKE UP THE SWEATER

Pin out to size and press all parts except the ribbing on the wrong side with a warm iron over a damp cloth. Join left shoulder seam, continuing seam across neckband. Set in sleeves. Join sleeve and side seams. Press seams.

women's three colour version or men's one colour version.

To shape the armhole: Continuing in pattern as set, cast off 2 sts. at the beginning of the next row, work 1 row back to armhole edge, then dec. 1 st. at the beginning of the next row and the 2 (3) (3) (4) following alternate rows. – 24 (25) (27) (28) sts.

**Work 1 row back to armhole edge.

To slope the front edge: Decrease row: Pattern until 7 remain, sl.1, k.2 tog. on a k. row or p.2 tog. on a p. row, then p.s.s.o., pattern to end.

Pattern 7 (5) (5) (3) rows.

Repeat the last 8 (6) (6) (4) rows 2 (3) (3) (4) times, then work the decrease row again.

On 16 (15) (17) (16) sts. pattern 3 (3) (5) (9) rows.

Inc. 1 st. at the beginning of the next row.

On 17 (16) (18) (17) sts. pattern 5 rows.

To slope the shoulder: Cast off 6 sts. at the beginning of the next row. Work 1 row straight.

Next row: Cast off 6 (6) (7) (7) sts. for the shoulder, then on the second and fourth sizes only inc. in next st., then for all sizes work to end. – 5 sts.

On 5 sts. pattern 16 rows, then cast off.

THE SECOND FRONT

With size 7 mm. (No. 2) needles and a. cast on 29 (31) (33) (35) sts. and work 28 (28) (34) (34) rows in pattern as given for back.

Pocket row: Pattern 8 (9) (10) (11), slip next 15 sts. onto a stitch-holder and leave at front of work, in their place pattern across the 15 sts. of one pocket back, pattern to end of row.

Pattern 48 (48) (52) (52) rows. – work 1 row less here when working the women's three colour version or men's one colour version.

To shape the armhole: Continuing in pattern as set, cast off 2 sts. at the beginning of the next row, work 1 row back to armhole edge, then dec. 1 st. at the beginning of the next row and the 1 (2) (2) (3) following alternate rows. Work 1 row back to armhole edge.

Pocket row: K.2 tog. then pattern as set across 4 (5) (6) (7) sts., slip next 11 sts. onto a stitch-holder and leave at front of work until required for pocket top and in their place pattern across the 11 sts. of small pocket back, pattern to end of row.

Now work as given for first front from ** to end.

THE SLEEVES

The first part: With size 7 mm. (No. 2) needles and one strand each of 'Mohair' and 'Teddy Fleece' in first colour a. cast on 21 (23) (23) (25) sts. and work 14 rows in pattern as given for back, then leave these sts. on a spare needle until required.

The second part: With size 7 mm. (No. 2) needles and one strand each of 'Mohair' and 'Teddy Fleece' in first colour – a. cast on 13 sts. and work 13 rows in pattern as given for back.**

Cast off 3 sts. at the beginning of the next row.

Now join the two parts together: Next row: Pattern across the 10 sts. of second part, then onto same needle pattern across the 21 (23) (23) (25) sts. of first part.

***On 31 (33) (33) (35) sts. pattern 5 rows.

Maintaining the continuity of the pattern as set, and working the extra sts. into the pattern as they occur, inc. 1 st. at each end of the next row and the 2 (2) (3) (3) following 20th rows.

On 37 (39) (41) (43) sts. pattern 27 (27) (17) (17) rows.

To shape the sleevetop: Cast off 2 sts. at the beginning of the next 2 rows.

Dec. 1 st. at each end of the next row and the 4 following 4th rows.

On 23 (25) (27) (29) sts. pattern 1 row.

Dec. 1 st. at each end of the next row and the 1 (2) (3) (4) following alternate rows. On 19 sts. work 1 row.

Dec. 1 st. at each end of the next 6 rows.

Cast off the remaining 7 sts.

THE SECOND SLEEVE

Work as given for first sleeve until ** is reached.

Next row: Pattern until 3 remain, cast off the 3 remaining sts. Leave the remaining 10 sts. on a spare needle.

Now join the two parts together: Next row: Pattern as set across the 21 (23) (23) (25) sts. of first part, then across the 10 sts. of second part.

Now work as given for first sleeve from *** to end.

THE POCKET TOPS (3 alike)

Rejoin one strand of 'Mohair' and one strand of 'Teddy Fleece' in a. to the sts. left on stitch-holder and using size 7 mm. (No. 2) needles work 2 rows in single rib, then cast off.

THE SHOULDER PADS (2 alike)

With size 7 mm. (No. 2) needles and one strand of 'Mohair' and one strand of 'Teddy Fleece' in a. cast on 19 sts. and work 30 rows in pattern. Cast off. Fold the shoulder pads in half diagonally to form a triangle. Neatly join open edges.

TO MAKE UP THE JACKET

Pin out to size and press all parts on the wrong side with a warm iron over a damp cloth. For the one coloured jacket the purl side of the fabric will be right side and for the 3 colour jacket the knit side of the fabric will be the right side.

Join shoulder seams. Set in sleeves. Join sleeve and side seams. Join cast off edges of collar pieces. Neatly sew row end edge of collar to back neck edge. Neatly sew pocket backs in place, then sew row ends of pocket tops in position. Neatly sew 3 sts. cast off on second part of sleeve behind first part. Sew 4 medium sized buttons in place at front. Catch cuff slits together with 2 small buttons on each cuff. Neatly catch shoulder pads in position. Press seams.

BANDANA

MATERIALS
For the sweater with sleeves: 17 (18) (20) (21) ounces of 'Woollybear Real Shetland' by Patricia Roberts.

For the sleeveless version: 11 (12) (14) (15) ounces of 'Woollybear Real Shetland' by Patricia Roberts.

For either version: A pair each of size 4 mm. (No. 8) and 3¾ mm. (No. 9) Aero knitting needles; a medium sized cable needle.

TENSION
Work at a tension of 15 stitches and 15 rows to 5 centimetres (2 inches) over the pattern using size 4 mm. (No. 8) needles using Shetland double. If you cannot obtain the correct tension using the size needles suggested use larger or smaller needles accordingly.

ABBREVIATIONS
K., knit; p., purl; st., stitch; tog., together; inc., increase (by working twice into same st.); dec., decrease (by working 2 sts. tog.); 3 from 1, k.1, p.1, k.1, all into next st.; cable 8f, slip next 4 sts. onto a cable needle and leave at front of work, k.4, then k.4 from cable needle; cable 8b., as cable 8f., but leaving 4 sts. on cable needle at back of work; cable 12, slip next 6 sts. onto a cable needle and leave at front of work, k.6, then k.6 from cable needle; single rib is k.1 and p.1, alternately; sl., slip; p.s.s.o., pass sl. st. over; up 1, pick up the loop which lies between the needles, slip it onto left hand needle, then k. into back of it.

NOTE
The instructions are given for the small woman's size. Where they vary work the figures in the first brackets for the medium woman's size; the figures in the second brackets for the small man's size or the figures in the third brackets for the medium man's size.

SPECIAL NOTE
When using 'Real Shetland Wool' use two strands of yarn together throughout this garment.

MEASUREMENTS
The measurements are given in centimetres followed by inches in brackets.

	Women's	
Sizes	Small	Medium
To fit bust	82.5 (33)	87.5 (35)
Underarms	85 (34)	90 (36)
Side seam	35 (14)	35 (14)
Length	55.5 (22¼)	57 (22¾)
Sleeve seam	40 (16)	40 (16)
	Men's	
To fit chest	95 (38)	100 (40)
Underarms	95 (38)	100 (40)
Side seam	40 (16)	40 (16)
Length	64 (25½)	65 (26)
Sleeve seam	45 (18)	45 (18)

THE SWEATER WITH SLEEVES

THE BACK
With size 3¾ mm. (No. 9) needles cast on 104 (112) (116) (124) sts. and work 21 rows in single rib.

Increase row: Rib 6 (10) (4) (8), * up 1, rib 4; repeat from * ending last repeat rib 6 (10) (4) (8) – 128 (136) (144) (152) sts.

Change to size 4 mm. (No. 8) needles and work in pattern as follows: 1 st row: K.2, p.8 (12) (16) (20), k.1, p.2, k.8, p.1, k.8, p.2, k.1, p.2, k.3, p.2, k.2, p.2, k.9, p.2, k.1, p.2, k.12, p.2, k.1, p.2, k.9, p.2, k.2, p.2, k.3, p.2, k.1, p.2, k.8, p.1, k.8, p.2, k.1, p.8 (12) (16) (20), k.2.

2nd row: K.2, * 3 from 1, p.3 tog; repeat from * 1 (2) (3) (4) time(s), ** p.1, k.2, p.8, k.1, p.8, k.2, p.1, k.2, p.1, k.2, p.2, k.2, p.11, k.2, p.1, k.2, p.12, k.2, p.1, k.2, p.11, k.2, p.2, k.2, p.1, k.2, p.1, k.2, p.8, k.1, p.8, k.2, p.1. **, then *p.3 tog., 3 from 1; repeat from last * until 2 remain, k.2.

3rd row: As 1st row.

4th row: K.2, * p.3 tog., 3 from 1; repeat from * 1 (2) (3) (4) times, now work as given for 2nd row from ** to ** then * 3 from 1, p.3 tog; repeat from last * 1 (2) (3) (4) times, k.2.

5th row: K.2, p.8 (12) (16) (20), k.1, p.2, cable 8f., p.1, cable 8b., p.2, k.1, p.2, k.3, p.2, k.2, p.2, cable 8f., k.1, p.2, k.1, p.2, cable 12, p.2, k.1, p.2, k.1, cable 8b., p.2, k.2, p.2, k.3, p.2, k.1, p.2, cable 8f., p.1, cable 8b., p.2, k.1, p.8 (12) (16) (20), k.2.

6th, 7th and 8th rows: As 2nd, 3rd and 4th rows.

9th and 10th rows: As 1st and 2nd rows.

11th row: *K.2, p.8 (12) (16) (20), k.1, p.2, k.8, p.1, k.8, p.2, k.1, p.2, k.9, p.2, k.2, p.2, k.3, p.2, k.1, p.2 **, k.12; work from ** back to *.

12th row: K.2, * p.3 tog., 3 from 1; repeat from * 1 (2) (3) (4) time(s), ** p.1, k.2, p.8, k.1, p.8, k.2, p.1, k.2, p.11, k.2, p.2, k.2, p.1, k.2, p.1, k.2, p.12, k.2, p.1, k.2, p.1, k.2, p.2, k.2, p.11, k.2, p.1, k.2, p.8, k.1, p.8, k.2, p.1 **, then * 3 from 1, p.3 tog.; repeat from last * 1 (2) (3) (4) time(s), k.2.

13th row: As 11th row.

14th row: K.2, * 3 from 1, p.3 tog.; repeat from * 1 (2) (3) (4) time(s), work as given for 12th row from ** to **, then * p.3 tog., 3 from 1, repeat from last * 1 (2) (3) (4) time(s), k.2.

15th row: K.2, p.8 (12) (16) (20), k.1, p.2, cable 8f., p.1, cable 8b., p.2, k.1, p.2, k.1, cable 8f., p.2, k.2, p.2, k.3, p.2, k.1, p.2, cable 12, p.2, k.1, p.2, k.3, p.2, k.2, p.2, cable 8b., k.1, p.2, k.1, p.2, cable 8f., p.1, cable 8b., p.2, k.1, p.8 (12) (16) (20), k.2.

16th, 17th and 18th rows: As 12th, 13th and 14th rows.

19th and 20th rows: As 11th and 12th rows.

The last 20 rows form the pattern. Repeat them 3 times more then work the first 2 (2) (18) (18) rows again. **

To shape the raglan armholes: Maintaining the continuity of the pattern as set, cast off 2 sts. at the beginning of the next 2 rows, then work as follows:

1st row: K.2, sl.1, k.2 tog., p.s.s.o., pattern until 5 remain, k.3 tog., k.2.

2nd row: P.3, pattern as set until 3 remain, p.3.

3rd row: K.3, pattern as set until 3 remain, k.3.

4th row: As 2nd row.

Repeat the last 4 rows 9 (9) (10) (10) times.

Next row: K.2, sl.1, k.2 tog., p.s.s.o., pattern until 5 remain, k.3 tog., k.2.

Next row: P.3, pattern as set until 3 remain, p.3.

Repeat the last 2 rows 9 (11) (11) (13) times ***.

Change to size 3¾ mm. (No. 9) needles and work 8 rows in single rib, then cast off the remaining 44 (44) (48) (48) sts.

THE FRONT
Work as given for the back until the 20 pattern rows have been worked 4 times, then work the first 1 (1) (17) (17) rows again.

Now divide the sts. for the neck: Next row: Pattern as set across 64 (68) (72) (76) sts. and leave these sts. on a spare needle until required for right front shoulder, pattern to end and continue on these sts. for the left front shoulder. **.

The left front shoulder: To shape the raglan armhole and to slope the neck: Maintaining the continuity of the pattern as set, cast off 2 sts. at the beginning – armhole edge and dec. 1 st. at the end – neck edge on the next row.

Work 1 row back to armhole edge then work as follows: 1st row: K.2, sl.1, k.2 tog., p.s.s.o., pattern until 2 remain, k.2 tog.

2nd row: Pattern until 3 remain, p.3.

3rd row: K.3, pattern until 2 remain, k.2 tog.

4th row: As 2nd row.

Repeat the last 4 rows 9 (9) (10) (10) times.

This completes the neck shaping.

Next row: K.2, sl.1, k.2 tog., p.s.s.o., pattern to end.

Next row: Pattern until 3 remain, p.3.

Repeat the last 2 rows 8 (10) (10) (12) times – 3 sts.

Take the 3 remaining sts. tog. and fasten off.

The right front shoulder: With right side of work facing rejoin yarn to inner edge of sts. left on spare needle and work to end of row. Cast off 2 sts. at the beginning and dec. 1 st. at the end of the next row, then work as follows.

1st row: K.2 tog., – for neck, then pattern until 5 remain, k.3 tog., k.2.

2nd row: P.3, pattern to end.

3rd row: K.2 tog., pattern until 3 remain, k.3.

4th row: As 2nd row.

Repeat the last 4 rows 9 (9) (10) (10) times.

Next row: Pattern until 5 remain, k.3 tog., k.2.

Next row: P.3, pattern to end.

Repeat the last 2 rows 8 (10) (10) (12) times.

Take the 3 remaining sts. tog. and fasten off.

THE SLEEVES (both alike)

With size 3¾ mm. (No. 9) needles cast on 42 (46) (50) (54) sts. and work 17 rows in single rib.

Increase row: Rib 2, * up 1, rib 1; repeat from * to end – 82 (90) (98) (106) sts.

Change to size 4 mm. (No. 8) needles and work in pattern as follows: 1st row: K.2, p.4 (8) (12) (16), k.1, p.2, k.8, p.1, k.8, p.2, k.1, p.1, k.1, p.1, k.1, p.2, k.12, p.2, k.1, p.1, k.1, p.1, k.1, p.2, k.8, p.1, k.8, p.2, k.1, p.4 (8) (12) (16), k.2.

2nd row: K.2, * 3 from 1, p.3 tog.; repeat from * nil (1) (2) (3) time(s),** p.1, k.2, p.8, k.1, p.8, k.2, p.1, k.1, p.1, k.1, p.1, k.2, p.12, k.2, p.1, k.1, p.1, k.1, p.1, k.2, p.8, k.1, p.8, k.2, p.1 **, then * p.3 tog., 3 from 1; repeat from last * until 2 remain, k.2.

3rd row: As 1st row.

4th row: K.2, * p.3 tog., 3 from 1; repeat from * nil (1) (2) (3) time(s), work as given for 2nd row from ** to **, then * 3 from 1, p.3 tog.; repeat from last * until 2 remain, k.2.

5th row: K.2, p.4 (8) (12) (16), k.1, p.2, cable 8f., p.1, cable 8b., p.2, k.1, p.1, k.1, p.1, k.1, p.2, cable 12, p.2, k.1, p.1, k.1, p.1, k.1, p.2, cable 8f., p.1, cable 8b., p.2, k.1, p.4 (8) (12) (16), k.2.

6th, 7th and 8th rows: As 2nd, 3rd and 4th rows.

9th to 12th rows: As 1st to 4th rows.

13th and 14th rows: As 1st and 2nd rows.

15th row: As 5th row.

16th row: As 4th row.

17th to 20th rows: As 1st to 4th rows.

The last 20 rows form the pattern: Continuing in pattern as set and working the extra sts. into the trinity st. edging as they occur, inc. 1 st. at each end of the next row and the 3 following 20th rows.

On 90 (98) (106) (114) sts. pattern 21 (21) (37) (37) rows.

To shape the raglan sleevetop: Work as given for raglan armhole shaping on back until *** is reached.

Cast off the remaining 6 (6) (10) (10) sts.

THE FRONT NECKBAND

First join the front raglan seams. With right side of work facing rejoin yarn at left front neck edge and using size 3¾ mm. (No. 9) needles pick up and k.62 (66) (70) (74) sts. from left front neck edge and 62 (66) (70) (74) sts. from right front neck edge.

** Work 1 row in single rib.

Next row: Rib to within 2 sts. of centre front, sl.1, k.1, p.s.s.o., k.2 tog., rib to end.

Rib 1 row.

Repeat the last 2 rows twice.

Cast off in rib.

TO MAKE UP THE SWEATER

Pin out to size and press lightly on the wrong side with a warm iron over a damp cloth. Join back raglan seams. Join sleeve and side seams. Press seams.

THE SLEEVELESS SWEATER

THE BACK

Work as given for the back of the raglan sleeved sweater until ** is reached.

To shape armholes: Maintaining the continuity of the pattern as set, cast off 3 sts. at the beginning of the next 2 rows, then dec. 1 st. at each end of the next row and the 6 (6) (10) (10) following alternate rows.

On 108 (116) (116) (124) sts. pattern 43 (47) (43) (47) rows.

To slope the shoulders: Cast off 16 (17) (17) (19) sts. at the beginning of the next 2 rows and 16 (18) (18) (19) sts. on the 2 following rows – 44 (46) (46) (48) sts.

Change to size 3¾ mm. (No. 9) needles and work 8 rows in single rib, then cast off in rib.

THE FRONT

Work as given for the version with sleeves until ** is reached.

The left front shoulder: To shape the armhole and to slope the neck: Maintaining the continuity of the pattern as set, cast off 3 sts. at the beginning and dec. 1 st. at the end of the next row. Work 1 row back to armhole edge.

Dec. 1 st. at each end of the next row and the 6 (6) (10) (10) following alternate rows.

On 46 (50) (46) (50) sts. work 1 row.

To slope the neck edge only: Dec. 1 st. at the end of the next row and the 13 (14) (10) (11) following alternate rows.

On 32 (35) (35) (38) sts. pattern 15 (17) (21) (23) rows.

To slope the shoulder: Cast off 16 (17) (17) (19) sts. at the beginning of the next row. On 16 (18) (18) (19) sts. work 1 row, then cast off.

The right front shoulder: With right side of work facing rejoin yarn to inner edge of sts. left on spare needle and work to end of row. Now work as given for left front shoulder to end.

THE FRONT NECKBAND

With right side of work facing rejoin yarn at left front neck edge and using size 3¾ mm. (No. 9) needles pick up and k.62 (66) (70) (74) sts. from left front neck edge, then 62 (66) (70) (74) sts. from right front neck edge.

Now work as given for neckband of sweater from ** to end.

THE ARMBANDS (both alike)

First join shoulder seams. With right side of work facing rejoin yarn and using size 3¾ mm. (No. 9) needles pick up and k.100 (108) (116) (124) sts. from all round armhole edge.

Work 5 rows in single rib.

Cast off in rib.

TO MAKE UP THE SWEATER

Pin out to size. Press on the wrong side with a warm iron over a damp cloth. Join side seams. Press seams.

HARLEQUIN

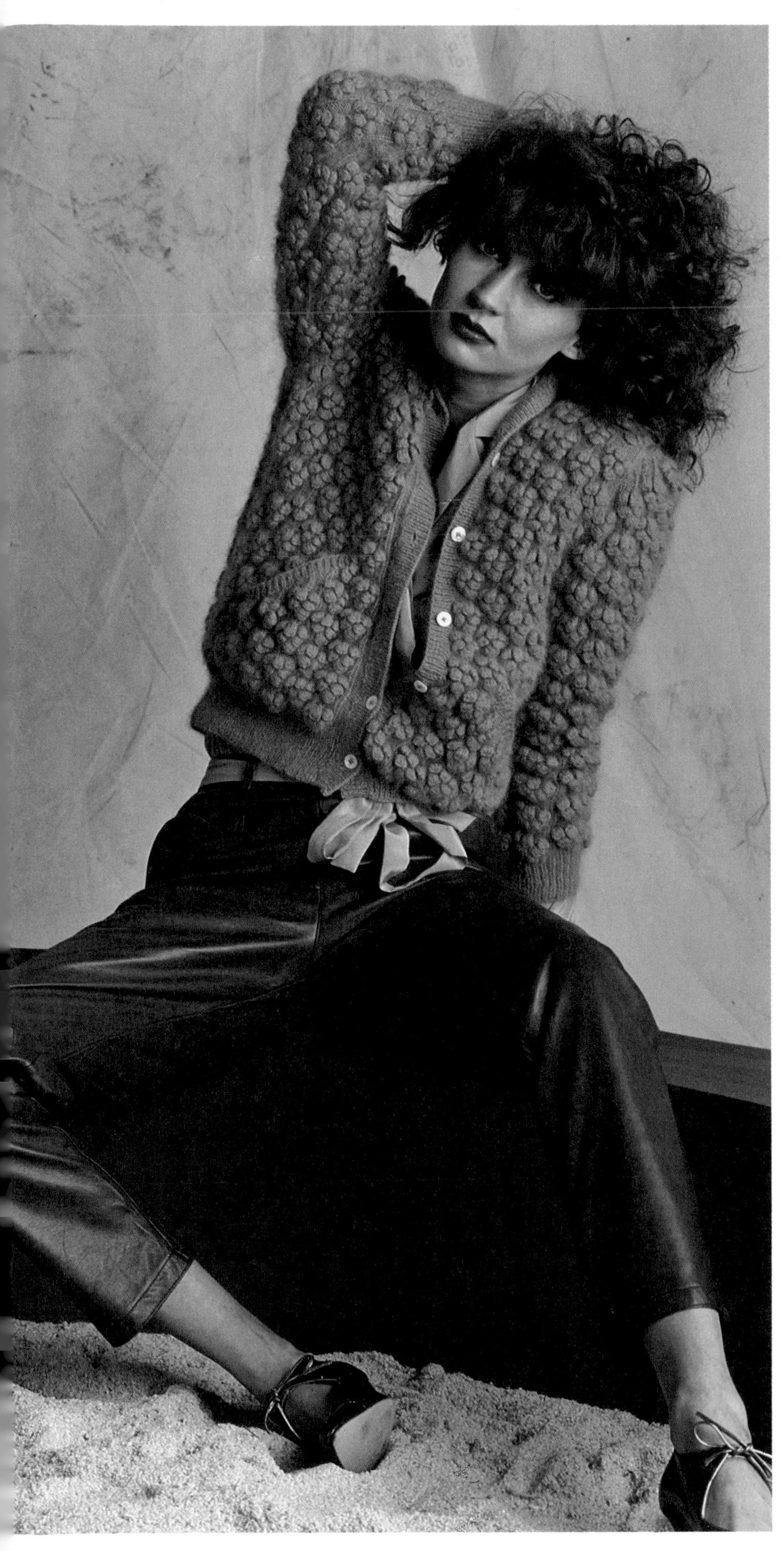

HARLEQUIN

MATERIALS
For the cardigan: 22 (23) 25 gram balls of 'Woollybear Bunny Fluff' by Patricia Roberts or 17 (18) ounces (28 gram) hanks of 'Woollybear Real Shetland' by Patricia Roberts; a pair each of size 2¼ mm. (No. 13) and size 3 mm. (No. 11) Aero knitting needles; 6 buttons.
For the sweater: 12 (13) 25 gram balls of 'Woollybear Bunny Fluff' by Patricia Roberts in main colour and 2 balls in each of the 5 contrast colours, or 9 (10) ounces (28 gram) hanks of 'Woollybear Real Shetland' by Patricia Roberts in main colour and 2 balls of each of the 5 contrast colours; a pair each of size 2¼ mm. (No. 13) and size 3 mm. (No. 11) knitting needles.

TENSION
32 stitches – 2 repeats of the pattern – to 11 centimetres (4½ inches) in width and 24 rows – 2 repeats of the pattern – to 7.5 centimetres (3 inches) in depth, using size 3 mm. (No. 11) needles. If you cannot obtain the correct tension using the size needles suggested, use larger or smaller ones accordingly.

ABBREVIATIONS
K., knit; p., purl; st., stitch; tog., together; dec., decrease (by working 2 sts. tog.); inc., increase (by working twice into same st.); single rib is k.1 and p.1 alternately; sl., slip; p.s.s.o., pass sl. st. over; y.r.n., yarn round needle; m.b., make bobble thus, k.1, y.r.n., k.1, y.r.n., k.1 all into next st., turn, p.5 turn, k.5, turn, p.2 tog., p.1, p.2, tog., turn, sl.1, k.2 tog., p.s.s.o.; m., main colour; a., first contrast; b., second contrast; c., third contrast; d., fourth contrast; e., fifth contrast.

NOTE
The instructions are given for the small size, where they vary work the instructions in the brackets for the medium size.

MEASUREMENTS
The measurements are given in centimetres followed by inches in brackets.

Sizes	Small	Medium
To fit bust	82.5–85 (33–34)	87.5–90 (35–36)
Underarms (cardigan)	87.5 (35)	92.5 (37)
Underarms (sweater)	85 (34)	90 (36)
Side seam	37.5 (15)	37.5 (15)
Length	57.5 (23)	59 (23½)
Sleeve seam	42.5 (17)	42.5 (17)

THE CARDIGAN
THE BACK
With size 2¼ mm. (No. 13) needles cast on 121 (129) sts. and work 32 rows in single rib.
Change to size 3 mm. (No. 11) needles and work in pattern as follows:
1st row: K.1, *p.3, m.b., p.3, k.1, p.3, k.1, p.3, k.1; repeat from * until 8 remain, p.3, m.b., p.3, k.1 (repeat from * to end).
2nd row and every wrong side row: P.1, *k.3, p.1; repeat from * to end.
3rd row: K.1, *p.2, m.b., k.1, m.b., p.2, k.1, p.3., k.1, p.3, k.1; repeat from * until 8 remain, p.2, m.b., k.1, m.b., p.2, k.1 (repeat from * to end).
5th row: K.1, *p.1, m.b., p.1, m.b., p.1, m.b., p.1, k.1, p.3, k.1, p.3, k.1; repeat from * until 8 remain, p.1, m.b., p.1, m.b., p.1, m.b., p.1, k.1 (repeat from * to end).
7th row: K.1, *p.3, k.1, p.3, k.1, p.3, m.b., p.3, k.1; repeat from * until 8 remain, p.3, k.1, p.3, k.1 (repeat from * to end).
9th row: K.1, *p.3, k.1, p.3, k.1, p.2, m.b., k.1, m.b., p.2, k.1; repeat from * until 8 remain, p.3, k.1, p.3, k.1 (repeat from * to end).
11th row: K.1, *p.3, k.1, p.3, k.1, p.1, m.b., p.1, m.b., p.1, m.b., p.1, k.1; repeat from * until 8 remain, p.3, k.1, p.3, k.1 (repeat from * to end).
12th row: As 2nd row.
The last 12 rows form the pattern; repeat them 7 times more.
To shape the armholes: Maintaining the continuity of the pattern as set, cast off 7 sts. at the beginning of the next 2 rows, then dec. 1 st. at each end of the next row and the 6 (7) following alternate rows. – 93 (99) sts.
Pattern 25 (27) rows as set.
Inc. 1 st. at each end of the next row and the 2 following 6th rows.
On 99 (105) sts. pattern 5 rows.
To slope the shoulders: Cast off 10 (11) sts. at the beginning of the next 4 rows and 9 sts. at the beginning of the next 2 following rows.
Cast off the remaining 41 (43) sts.

THE POCKET BACKS (2 alike)
With size 3 mm. (No. 11) needles cast on 33 sts. and work in rib as follows:
1st row: K.1, *p.3, k.1; repeat from * to end.
2nd row: P.1, *k.3, p.1; repeat from * to end.
Repeat the last 2 rows 11 times more, then work the first row again, then leave these sts. on a stitch-holder until required.

THE LEFT FRONT
With size 2¼ mm. (No. 13) needles cast on 61 (65) sts. and work 32 rows in single rib.
Change to size 3 mm. (No. 11) needles and work in pattern as follows:
1st row: K.1, *p.3, m.b., p.3, k.1, p.3, k.1 **, p.3, k.1; repeat from * 3 times, but ending at ** on the last repeat on the small size only.
2nd row and every wrong side row: P.1, *k.3, p.1; repeat from * to end.
The last 2 rows set the position of the pattern given for the back. Now work the 3rd to 12th rows as set, then continuing in pattern work a further 12 rows.
Now divide the sts. for the pocket: Next row: Pattern as set across 16 sts. then leave these sts. on a spare needle until required, pattern to end and continue on these 45 (49) sts.
Continuing in pattern as set, dec. 1 st. at the end – inner edge on the next row and at the same edge on each of the next 32 rows – ending at inner edge, leave the remaining 12 (16) sts. on a spare needle until required.
Rejoin yarn to the 33 sts. of one pocket back and pattern as set across these sts., then onto the same needle pattern across the 16 sts. left on spare needle.
On 49 sts. work 32 rows in bobble pattern as set by the group of 16 sts.
Next row: Pattern as set across these 49 sts. then onto the same needle pattern across the 12 (16) sts. left on spare needle. This completes the pocket.
On 61 (65) sts. pattern 37 rows.
***To shape the armhole: Cast off 7 sts at the beginning of the next row, work 1 row back to armhole edge, then dec. 1 st. at the armhole edge on the next row and the 6 (7) following alternate rows. – 47 (50) sts. This completes the armhole shaping.
Work 1 row back to armhole edge.
To slope the front edge: Dec. 1 st. at the end of the next row and the 11 (12) following alternate rows. Work 1 row straight.
Pattern 18 rows, decreasing 1 st. at the front edge on every alternate row as before and at the same time increasing 1 st. at armhole edge on the 1st, 7th and 13th of these rows. – 29 (31) sts.
To slope the shoulders: Cast off 10 (11) sts. at the beginning of the next row and the following alternate row. On 9 sts. work 1 row, then cast off.

THE RIGHT FRONT
With size 2¼ mm. (No. 13) needles cast on 61 (65) sts. and work 32 rows in single rib.
Change to size 3 mm. (No.11) needles and work in pattern as follows:
For small size only: 1st row: K.1, *p.3, k.1, p.3, m.b., p.3, k.1**, p.3, k.1; repeat from * ending last repeat at **.
For medium size only: 1st row: K.1, *p.3, m.b., p.3, k.1, p.3, k.1, p.3, k.1; repeat from * to end.
For both sizes: 2nd row: P.1, *k.3, p.1; repeat from * to end.
The last 2 rows set the position of the pattern given for back. Now work the 3rd to 12th rows as set, then continuing in pattern work 12 rows more.
Now divide the sts. for the pocket:
Next row: Pattern as set across 45 (49) sts. and leave these sts. on a spare needle until required, pattern to end and continue on these 16 sts.
Next row: Work as set across these 16 sts., then onto the same needle work in bobble st. across the 33 sts. of pocket back.
On 49 sts. pattern 32 rows, then leave these sts. on a spare needle until required.
Rejoin yarn to inner edge of 45 (49) sts. left on spare needle and work 33 rows decreasing 1 st. at inner edge on each row.
Next row: Pattern across the remaining 12 (16) sts. then onto the same needle pattern across the 49 sts. left on spare needle.
On 61 (65) sts. pattern 38 rows. Now work as given for left front from *** to end.

THE SLEEVES (both alike)
With size 2¼ mm. (No. 13) needles cast on 57 sts. and work 28 rows in single rib.

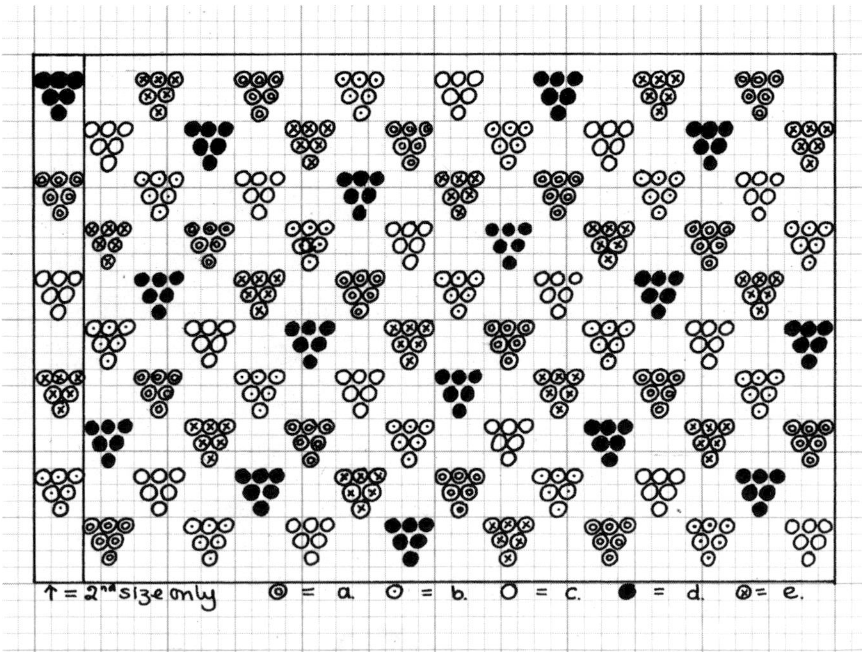

Change to size 3 mm. (No. 11) needles and work 8 rows in pattern as given for small size on back.

***Continuing in pattern as set, and working the extra sts. into the pattern as they occur, inc. 1 st. at each end of the next row and the 13 (15) following 8th (6th) rows.

On 85 (89) sts. pattern 3 (17) rows.

To shape the sleevetop: Continuing in pattern as set, cast off 7 sts. at the beginning of the next 2 rows, then dec. 1 st. at each end of the next row and the 13 following alternate rows.

On 43 (47) sts. work 1 row.

Dec. 1 st. at each end of the next 4 (6) rows, then cast off 3 sts. at the beginning of the next 4 rows and 4 sts. on the 4 following rows.

Cast off the remaining 7 sts.

THE BUTTONBAND AND HALF COLLAR

With size 2¼ mm. (No. 13) needles cast on 216 (220) sts. and work 4 rows in single rib.

1st and 2nd turning rows: Rib 44 (48), turn, slip 1, rib to end, turn.

3rd and 4th turning rows: Rib 48 (52), turn, slip 1, rib to end, turn.

5th and 6th turning rows: Rib 52 (56), turn, slip 1, rib to end, turn.

7th and 8th turning rows: Rib 56 (60), turn, slip 1, rib to end, turn.

9th and 10th turning rows: Rib 60 (64), turn, slip 1, rib to end, turn.

11th and 12th turning rows: Rib 64 (68), turn, slip 1, rib to end, turn.

13th and 14th turning rows: Rib 68 (72), turn, slip 1, rib to end, turn.

15th and 16th turning rows: Rib 72 (76), turn, slip 1, rib to end, turn.

17th and 18th turning rows: Rib 76 (80), turn, slip 1, rib to end, turn.

19th and 20th turning rows: Rib 80 (84), turn, slip 1, marking this st. with a coloured thread, rib to end, turn.**

Now continuing on all 216 (220) sts. work 6 rows in single rib, then cast off loosely in rib.

THE BUTTONHOLE BAND AND HALF COLLAR

Work as given for buttonband and half collar until ** is reached. Then continue on all 216 (220) sts. as follows:

1st Buttonhole row: Rib 82 (86), *cast off 3, rib next 21 sts.; repeat from * 4 times more, cast off 3, rib next 5 sts.

2nd Buttonhole row: Rib 6, *turn, cast on 3 sts. over those cast off, rib 22; repeat from * ending last repeat rib 82 (86).

Work 4 rows in single rib, then cast off loosely in rib.

THE POCKET TOPS (2 alike)

With right side of work facing rejoin yarn to the shaped edge of pocket and using size 2¼ mm. (No. 13) needles pick up and k. 40 sts. from this edge.

Work 5 rows in single rib, then cast off in rib.

THE SHOULDER PADS (2 alike)

With size 2¼ mm. (No. 13) needles cast on 40 sts. and work 50 rows in single rib, then cast off in rib. Fold in half diagonally and join outer edges, to form a triangle.

TO MAKE UP THE CARDIGAN

Pin out to size and press all parts except the ribbing with a warm iron over a damp cloth. Join shoulder seams. Set in sleeves. Join sleeve and side seams. Neatly sew pocket backs and row ends of pocket tops in place. Join long row end edges of half collars and sew cast off edge of front bands and collar in place so that the first front edge decreases are in line with marking threads. Catch shoulder pads in place. Sew on buttons. Press seams.

THE SWEATER

THE BACK

Work as given for the back of the cardigan with m. but working the bobbles in contrast colours in the sequence given in the chart. This is a 60 row repeat colour pattern. Use separate small balls of colour for each set of coloured bobbles, leaving sufficiently long ends to darn in at completion of work.

THE FRONT

Work as given for back until the armhole shaping has been worked. – 93 (99) sts.

Pattern 16 (18) rows as set.

Now divide the sts. for the neck: Next row: Pattern 40 (42) and leave these sts. on a spare needle until required for right front shoulder, cast off 13 (15) sts. for neck, pattern to end and continue on these 40 (42) sts. for the left front shoulder.

The left front shoulder: To shape the neck: Continuing in pattern as set dec. 1 st. at the neck edge on each of the next 8 rows.

Pattern 13 rows, decreasing 1 st. at the neck edge on each of the first 6 rows and at the same time increasing 1 st. at the armhole edge on the 1st, 7th and 13th of these rows.

On 29 (31) sts. pattern 5 rows.

To slope the shoulder: Cast off 10 (11) sts. at the beginning of the next row and the following alternate row. On 9 sts. work 1 row, then cast off.

The right front shoulder: With right side of work facing rejoin yarn to the inner edge of sts. left on spare needle and work to end of row, then work as given for left front shoulder to end.

THE SLEEVES (both alike)

With size 2¼ mm. (No. 13) needles cast on 57 sts. and work 28 rows in single rib.

Change to size 3 mm. (No. 11) needles and work in pattern as follows:

1st row: Working in pattern as given for first size on back of cardigan, work the first bobble with a., the second bobble with e., the third with d., and the fourth with c.

2nd row: In m. as given for back of cardigan.

The last 2 rows set the position of the 60 row colour sequence. Continuing in pattern as given for small size of back in the colour sequence given at the centre of the chart, work 6 rows straight, then still in colour pattern work as given for the cardigan sleeves from *** to end.

THE COLLAR

With size 2¼ mm. (No. 13) needles and m. cast on 154 (158) sts. and work 4 rows in single rib.

Decrease row: Rib 4, sl.1, k.2 tog., p.s.s.o., rib until 7 remain, sl.1, k.2 tog., p.s.s.o., rib 4.

Rib 3 rows.

Repeat the last 4 rows 5 times more, then cast off in rib the remaining 130 (134) sts.

THE SHOULDER PADS (2 alike)

Work as given for shoulder pads on cardigan.

TO MAKE UP THE SWEATER

Pin out to size and press all parts except the ribbing with a warm iron over a damp cloth. Join shoulder seams. Set in sleeves. Join sleeve and side seams. Sew cast off edge of collar in place. Press seams.

A TOUCH OF CLASS

SOME LIKE IT HOT

A TOUCH OF CLASS

MATERIALS
For the jacket: 19 (20) (21) 25 gram balls of either 'Woollybear Brushed Alpaca' or 'Woollybear 100% Mohair'; a pair of size 4½ mm. (No. 7) Aero knitting needles; 2 medium sized buttons; 4 small buttons.
For the hat: 2 balls of the same yarn; a pair of size 4½ mm. (No. 7) Aero knitting needles.

TENSION
11 stitches and 13 rows to 5 centimetres (2 inches) over the single rib using size 4½ mm. (No. 7) needles. If you cannot obtain the correct tension using the size needles suggested use larger or smaller ones accordingly.

ABBREVIATIONS
K., knit; p., purl; st., stitch; tog., together; dec., decrease (by working 2 sts. tog.); inc., increase (by working twice into same st.); single rib is k.1 and p.1 alternately; sl. slip; p.s.s.o., pass slip st. over; 3 from 1, p.1, k.1, p.1 all into next st.

NOTE
The instructions are given for the small size. Where they vary work the figures in the first brackets for the medium size or the figures in the second brackets for the large size.

MEASUREMENTS
The measurements are given in centimetres followed by inches in brackets.

THE JACKET

Size	Small	Medium	Large
To fit bust	85 (34)	90 (36)	95 (38)
Underarms	91 (36½)	96 (38½)	101 (40½)
Side seam	31 (12½)	31 (12½)	31 (12½)
Length	55 (22¼)	56 (22½)	57 (22¾)
Sleeve seam	40 (16)	40 (16)	40 (16)

THE JACKET

THE BACK
With size 4½ mm. (No. 7) needles cast on 105 (111) (117) sts. and work 22 rows in single rib beginning right side rows with k.1 and wrong side rows with p.1.
1st Decrease row: Rib 25 (27) (29), sl.1 p.wise, p. 2 tog., p.s.s.o., rib 49 (51) (53), sl.1 p.wise, p. 2 tog., p.s.s.o., rib 25 (27) (29).
Rib 11 rows.
2nd Decrease row: Rib 24 (26) (28), sl.1 p.wise, p. 2 tog., p.s.s.o., rib 47 (49) (51), sl.1 p.wise, p. 2 tog., p.s.s.o., rib 24 (26) (28).
Rib 11 rows.
3rd Decrease row: Rib 23 (25) (27), sl.1 p.wise, p. 2 tog., p.s.s.o., rib 45 (47) (49), sl.1 p.wise, p. 2 tog., p.s.s.o., rib 23 (25) (27).
On 93 (99) (105) sts., rib 11 rows.
1st Increase row: Rib 23 (25) (27), 3 from 1, rib 45 (47) (49), 3 from 1, rib 23 (25) (27).
Rib 11 rows.
2nd Increase row: Rib 24 (26) (28), 3 from 1, rib 47 (49) (51), 3 from 1, rib 24 (26) (28).
On 101 (107) (113) sts., rib 11 rows.
To shape the armholes: Cast off 5 sts. at the beginning of the next 2 rows, then dec. 1 st. at each end of the next row and the 5 (6) (7) following alternate rows.
On 79 (83) (87) sts., rib 21 rows.
Inc. 1 st. at each end of the next row and the 2 following 8th rows.
On 85 (89) (93) sts., rib 7 rows.
To slope the shoulders: Cast off 9 sts. at the beginning of the next 4 rows, then 8 (9) (10) sts. on the 2 following rows.
Cast off the remaining 33 (35) (37) sts.

THE LARGE POCKET BACKS (2 alike)
With size 4½ mm. (No. 7) needles cast on 27 sts. and work 32 rows in single rib, then leave these sts. on a spare needle until required.

THE SMALL POCKET BACKS (2 alike)
With size 4½ mm. (No. 7) needles cast on 17 sts. and work 20 rows in single rib, then leave these sts. on a spare needle until required.

THE LEFT FRONT
With size 4½ mm. (No. 7) needles cast on 43 (45) (49) sts. and work 2 rows in single rib, beginning right side rows with k.1 and wrong side rows with p.1. Now increase for front edge as follows:
Increase row: Rib until 5 remain, 3 from 1, rib 4.
Rib 1 row.
Repeat the last 2 rows 4 times more, then work the increase row again.
Rib 3 rows, work the increase row, rib 3 rows more, then work the increase row again.
On 59 (61) (65) sts., rib 1 row.
1st Decrease row: Rib 25 (27) (29), sl.1 p.wise, p. 2 tog., p.s.s.o., rib 31 (31) (33).
Rib 11 rows.
2nd Decrease row: Rib 24 (26) (28), sl.1 p.wise, p. 2 tog., p.s.s.o., rib 30 (30) (32).
On 55 (57) (61) sts., rib 1 row.
Pocket row: Rib 6 (8) (10), slip next 27 sts. onto a stitch-holder until required for pocket top and in their place rib across the 27 sts. of one large pocket back, rib 22 (22) (24). **
Rib 9 rows.
3rd Decrease row: Rib 23 (25) (27), sl.1 p.wise, p. 2 tog., p.s.s.o., rib 29 (29) (31).
On 53 (55) (59) sts., rib 11 rows.
1st Increase row: Rib 23 (25) (27), 3 from 1, rib 29 (29) (31).
Rib 11 rows.
*** 2nd Increase row: Rib 24 (26) (28), 3 from 1, rib 30 (30) (32).
On 57 (59) (63) sts., rib 11 rows.
To shape the armhole: Cast off 5 sts. at the beginning of the next row, work 1 row back to armhole edge. Then dec. 1 st. at the beginning of the next row and the 5 (6) (7) following alternate rows.
On 46 (47) (50) sts., rib 1 row.
Next pocket row: Rib 7 (8) (9), slip next 17 sts. onto a stitch-holder until required for pocket top and in their place rib across the 17 sts. of one small pocket back, rib 22 (22) (24).

SOME LIKE IT HOT

MATERIALS
For the sleeveless version; 5 (6) (6) (7) 25 gram balls of 'Woollybear Brushed Alpaca' or 'Woollybear 100% Mohair' in main colour; 3 (4) (4) (4) ounces of 'Woollybear Real Shetland' in first contrast colour and 2 (3) (3) (3) ounces in second contrast; a pair each of size 2¼ mm. (No. 13) and size 3¼ mm. (No. 10) Aero knitting needles.
For the sweater with sleeves: 7 (7) (8) (9) 25 gram balls of 'Woollybear Brushed Alpaca' or 'Woollybear 100% Mohair' in main colour; 4 (4) (5) (5) ounces of 'Woollybear Real Shetland' in first contrast colour and 3 (3) (4) (4) ounces in second contrast colour; a pair each of size 2¼ mm. (No. 13) and size 3¼ mm. (No. 10) Aero knitting needles.

TENSION
12 stitches and 24 rows to 5 centimetres (2 inches) over the garter stitch stripe pattern, using size 3¼ mm. (No. 10) needles. If you cannot obtain the correct tension using the size needles suggested use larger or smaller ones accordingly.

ABBREVIATIONS
K., knit; p., purl; st., stitch; tog., together; dec., decrease (by working 2 sts. tog.); inc., increase (by working twice into same st.); garter st. is k. plain on every row; single rib is k.1 and p.1 alternately; m., main colour – Brushed Alpaca or Mohair; a., first contrast – Shetland; b., second contrast – Shetland.

NOTE
The instructions are given for the small woman's size. Where they vary work the figures in the first brackets for the medium woman's size or the figures in the second brackets for the small man's size or the figures in the third brackets for the medium man's size.

MEASUREMENTS
The measurements are given in centimetres followed by inches in brackets.

	Women's	
Size	Small	Medium
To fit bust	80 (32)	85 (34)
Underarms	82.5 (33)	87.5 (35)
Side seam	31 (12½)	31 (12½)
Length	51 (20½)	52.5 (21)
Sleeve seam with cuffs folded in half	42.5 (17)	42.5 (17)

	Men's	
Size	Small	Medium
To fit chest	90 (36)	95 (38)
Underarms	92.5 (37)	97.5 (39)
Side seam	36 (14½)	36 (14½)
Length	59 (23½)	60 (24)
Sleeve seam with cuffs folded in half	45 (18)	45 (18)

THE BACK
With size 2¼ mm. (No. 13) needles and a. cast on 100 (106) (112) (118) sts. and work 38 rows in single rib.
Change to size 3¼ mm. (No. 10) needles. Join in m. and b. and work in garter stitch in stripe sequence of 2 rows m., 4 rows b., 2 rows m., 4 rows a.
The last 12 rows form the stripe sequence; repeat them 8 (8) (10) (10) times more.
To shape the armholes: Continuing in stripe pattern as set, cast off 4 sts. at the beginning of the next 2 rows, then dec. 1 st. at each end of the next row and the 4 (5) (6) (7) following alternate rows.
On 82 (86) (90) (94) sts. work 79 (83) (87) (91) rows.
To slope the shoulders: Cast off 8 sts. at the beginning of next 4 rows and 7 (8) (9) (10) sts. on the 2 following rows – 36 (38) (40) (42) sts.
Break off m. and b.
Change to size 2¼ mm. (No. 13) needles and with a. work 10 rows in single rib, then cast off loosely in rib.

Rib 1 row.

To shape the front edge: Next row: Rib until 7 remain, sl.1, k. 2 tog., p.s.s.o., rib 4.

Rib 7 rows.

Repeat the last 8 rows once more then work the decrease row again.

Rib 1 row.

To shape the armhole: Inc. 1 st. at the beginning of the next row.

Rib 5 rows.

Next row: Rib until 7 remain, sl.1, k. 2 tog., p.s.s.o., rib 4.

Repeat the last 8 rows once (once) (twice) more.

Rib 1 row.

For the small and medium sizes only: Inc. 1 st. at the beginning of the next row, then rib 7 rows.

For all sizes: To slope the shoulder: Cast off 9 sts. at the beginning of the next row and following alternate row, then 8 (9) (10) sts. on the next alternate row.

On 13 sts., rib 21 (21) (23) rows, then cast off.

THE RIGHT FRONT

Work as given for left front noting that the fabric is reversible until ** is reached. Rib 1 row.

1st Buttonhole row: Rib 47 (49) (53), cast off 4, rib to end.

2nd Buttonhole row: Rib 4, turn, cast on 4, turn, rib to end.

Rib 6 rows.

3rd Decrease row: Rib 23 (25) (27), sl.1 p.wise, p. 2 tog., p.s.s.o., rib 29 (29) (31).

On 53 (55) (59) sts., rib 11 rows.

Increase row: Rib 23 (25) (27), 3 from 1, rib 29 (29) (31).

Rib 7 rows.

Work the 2 buttonhole rows again.

Rib 2 rows.

Now work as given for left front from *** to end.

THE SLEEVES (both alike as the fabric is reversible)

The first part: With size 4½ mm. (No. 7) needles cast on 35 (37) (39) sts. and work 19 rows in single rib, then leave these sts. on a spare needle until required.

The second part: With size 4½ mm. (No. 7) needles cast on 21 sts. and work 18 rows in single rib. Cast off 3 sts. at the beginning of the next row.

Next row: Rib across the 18 sts. of second part then onto same needle rib across the 35 (37) (39) sts. of first part.

On 53 (55) (57) sts., rib 4 rows.

Continuing in rib, inc. 1 st. at each end of the next row and the 7 following 10th rows.

On 69 (71) (73) sts., rib 9 rows.

To shape the sleevetop: Cast off 5 sts. at the beginning of the next 2 rows, then dec. 1 st. at each end of the next row and the 12 (13) (14) following alternate rows.

On 33 sts. rib 1 row.

Dec. 1 st. at each end of the next 4 rows. Cast off 3 sts. at the beginning of the next 6 rows.

Cast off the remaining 7 sts.

THE POCKET TOPS (all 4 alike)

With right side of work facing rejoin yarn to the sts. left on stitch-holder and using size 4½ mm. (No. 7) needles work 2 rows in single rib, then cast off.

THE SHOULDER PADS (both alike)

With size 4½ mm. (No. 7) needles cast on 27 sts. and work 32 rows in single rib, then cast off.

TO MAKE UP THE JACKET

Pin out to size and press all parts on the wrong side with a warm iron over a damp cloth. Join shoulder seams. Set in sleeves. Join sleeve and side seams. Neatly sew pocket backs and row ends of pocket tops in place. Join cast off edges of back collar. Join back collar to back neck edge. Neatly sew 3 sts. cast off at top of 2nd part of sleeves behind those of the 1st part. Press seams. Sew 2 medium sized buttons at left front edge. Secure sleeve openings with small buttons. Fold shoulder pads in half to form triangles and neatly sew in place.

THE HAT

THE MAIN PART

With size 4½ mm. (No. 7) needles cast on 99 sts. and work 16 rows in single rib.

1st Decrease row: Rib 3, * sl.1, k. 2 tog., p.s.s.o., rib 13; repeat from * to end – 87 sts.

Rib 3 rows.

2nd Decrease row: Rib 3, * sl.1, k. 2 tog., p.s.s.o., rib 11; repeat from * to end – 75 sts.

Rib 3 rows.

3rd Decrease row: Rib 3, * sl.1, k. 2 tog., p.s.s.o., rib 9; repeat from * to end – 63 sts.

Rib 1 row.

4th Decrease row: Rib 3, * sl.1, k. 2 tog., p.s.s.o., rib 7; repeat from * to end – 51 sts.

Rib 1 row.

5th Decrease row: Rib 3, * sl.1, k. 2 tog., p.s.s.o., rib 5; repeat from * to end – 39 sts.

Rib 1 row.

6th Decrease row: Rib 3, * sl.1, k. 2 tog., p.s.s.o., rib 3; repeat from * to end – 27 sts.

7th Decrease row: Rib 3, * sl. 1, k. 2 tog., p.s.s.o., rib 1; repeat from * to end – 15 sts.

8th Decrease row: * Sl.1, k. 2 tog., p.s.s.o.; repeat from * to end – 5 sts.

Break off yarn leaving a long end, thread this end through the 5 remaining sts. draw up firmly and secure. Using the same end, join row end edges for centre back seam.

THE HATBAND

With size 4½ mm. (No. 7) needles cast on 13 sts. and work in single rib until the band measures 100 centimetres (40 inches) in length. Neatly sew bands in place around cast on edge of hat, leaving the two ends free to tie in a bow at left side of head. Press seams.

THE FRONT

Work as given for back until the armhole shaping has been worked.

On 82 (86) (90) (94) sts. work 42 (44) (46) (48) rows in stripe pattern as set.

Now divide the sts. for the neck as follows: Next row: K. 35 (36) (37) (38) and leave these sts. on a spare needle until required for right front shoulder, k. 12 (14) (16) (18) and leave these sts. on a stitch-holder until required for front neckband, k. to end and continue on these 35 (36) (37) (38) sts. for the left front shoulder.

The left front shoulder: To shape the neck: Dec. 1 st. at the neck edge on each of the next 12 rows.

On 23 (24) (25) (26) sts., work 24 (26) (28) (30) rows.

To slope the shoulder: Cast off 8 sts. at the beginning of the next row and the following alternate row.

On 7 (8) (9) (10) sts., work 1 row, then cast off.

The right front shoulder: With right side of work facing rejoin yarn to inner edge of the 35 (36) (37) (38) sts. left on spare needle and work to end of row, then work as given for left front shoulder to end.

THE FRONT NECKBAND

With right side of work facing rejoin a. and using size 2¾ mm. (No. 13) needles pick up and k. 36 (37) (38) (39) sts. from left front neck edge, k. across the 12 (14) (16) (18) sts. left on stitch-holder at centre front neck edge, then pick up and k. 36 (37) (38) (39) sts. from right front neck edge.

On 84 (88) (92) (96) sts. work 9 rows in single rib, then cast off loosely in rib.

THE ARMBANDS (2 alike for the sleeveless version)

First join shoulder seams, then with right side of work facing rejoin a. and using size 2¾ mm. (No. 13) needles pick up and k. 136 (144) (152) (160) sts. from all round armhole edge.

Work 7 rows in single rib, then cast off loosely in rib.

THE SLEEVES (both alike)

With size 2¾ mm. (No. 13) needles and a. cast on 48 (50) (54) (56) sts. and work 44 rows in single rib.

Change to size 3¼ mm. (No. 10) needles. Join in m. and b. and work 12 rows in garter st. stripe pattern as given for back.

Continuing in stripe pattern as set, inc. 1 st. at each end of the next row and the 11 following 14th rows.

On 72 (74) (78) (80) sts., work 13 (13) (25) (25) rows in stripe pattern as set.

To shape the sleevetop: Cast off 4 sts. at the beginning of the next 2 rows, then dec. 1 st. at each end of the next row and the 20 (21) (23) (24) following alternate rows. On 22 sts. work 1 row.

Cast off 3 sts. at the beginning of the next 6 rows, then cast off the remaining 4 sts.

THE SHOULDER PADS (2 alike optional)

With size 3¼ mm. (No. 10) needles and m. cast on 32 sts. and work 36 rows in garter st., then cast off.

TO MAKE UP THE SWEATER

Pin out to size and press all parts on the wrong side with a warm iron over a damp cloth. For the sleeveless version: Join side seams, continuing seams across armbands. Press seams. For the sweater with sleeves: Join shoulder seams continuing seam across neckband. Set in sleeves. Join sleeve and side seams. Press seams. Fold shoulder pads in half to form triangles and neatly sew in place.

HIGH FLYER

HIGH FLYER

MATERIALS
15 (16) 25 gram balls of 'Woollybear 100% Mohair' by Patricia Roberts in main colour: 2 balls in each of the five contrast colours; a pair each of size 4 mm. (No. 8) and size $3\frac{3}{4}$ mm. (No. 9) Aero knitting needles; a cable needle; 2 buttons for the open necked version.

SPECIAL NOTE
This garment may also be knitted in 'Woollybear Cotton Bouclé' by Patricia Roberts. It will require 10 (11) 50 gram balls in main colour and 1 ball in each of the five contrast colours. To obtain the correct tension it is necessary to use size $3\frac{3}{4}$ mm. (No. 9) needles instead of size 4 mm. (No. 8) needles and size $3\frac{1}{4}$ mm. (No. 10) needles instead of size $3\frac{3}{4}$ mm. (No. 9) needles throughout.

TENSION
10 stitches and 14 rows to 5 centimetres (2 inches) over the stocking stitch using size 4 mm. (No. 8) needles and 'Woollybear 100% Mohair'. Using 'Woollybear Cotton Bouclé' the same tension should be obtained using size $3\frac{3}{4}$ mm. (No. 9) needles. If you cannot obtain the correct tension using the size needles suggested, use larger or smaller ones accordingly.

ABBREVIATIONS
K., knit; p., purl; st., stitch; tog., together; dec., decrease (by working 2 sts. tog.); inc., increase (by working twice into same st.); single rib is k.1 and p.1 alternately; up 1, pick up the loop which lies between the needles, slip it onto left hand needle then k. into back of it; y.r.n., yarn round needle; 3 from 1, k.1, y.r.n., k.1 all into next st.; cr. 5 rt., cross 5 right thus, slip next st. onto a cable needle and leave at back of work, with appropriate contrast colour k.5 then with m. k.1 from cable needle; m., main colour; a., first contrast colour; b., second contrast; c., third contrast; d., fourth contrast; e., fifth contrast; s.s., stocking st. is k. on the right side and p. on the wrong side; sl., slip; p.s.s.o., pass sl. st. over.

SPECIAL NOTE
When counting stitches, count the extra sts. of crayons as one st.

MEASUREMENTS
The measurements are given in centimetres followed by inches in brackets.

	Women's	Men's
To fit bust or chest	85 (34)	92.5 (37)
Underarms	87.5 (35)	92 ($36\frac{3}{4}$)
Side seam	40 (16)	40 (16)
Length	60 (24)	64 ($25\frac{1}{2}$)
Sleeve seam	42.5 (17)	47.5 (19)

THE BACK
With size $3\frac{3}{4}$ mm. (No. 9) needles and m. cast on 80 (84) sts. and work 19 rows in single rib.
Increase row: Rib 8 (10), *up 1, rib 9; repeat from * ending last repeat rib 9 (11). – 88 (92) sts.
Change to size 4 mm. (No. 8) needles and beginning with a k. row s.s. 4 rows.
Now work in pattern as follows. This is worked entirely in s.s. except where indicated, so only the colour details are given. Use separate small balls of contrast colour for each section of the pattern. When working the pencils, pull m. firmly across the back of the work, as a raised effect is required. At completion of each section leave sufficiently long ends to darn in at completion of work.
1st row: 3m., 3a., 19 (20) m., 3b., 19 (20)m., 3a., 19 (20)m., 3b., 16 (17)m.
2nd row: 15 (16)m., 1b., 3m., 1b., 17 (18)m., 1a., 3m., 1a., 17 (18)m., 1b., 3m., 1b., 17 (18)m., 1a., 3m., 1a., 2m.
3rd row: 1m., 1a., 5m., 1a., 15 (16)m., 1b., 5m., 1b., 15 (16)m., 1a., 5m., 1a., 15 (16)m., 1b., 5m., 1b., 14 (15)m.
4th row: 13 (14)m., 1b., 6m., 1b., 14 (15)m., 1a., 6m., 1a., 14 (15)m., 1b., 6m., 1b., 14 (15)m., 1a., 6m., 1a., 1m.
5th row: 1m., * 1a., 7m., 1b., 13 (14)m., 1b., 7m., 1a., 13 (14)m; repeat from * ending 12 (13)m. instead of 13 (14)m.
6th row: 2m., *2a., 8 (9)m., 1a., 7m., 1b., 3m., 2b., 8 (9)m., 1b., 7m., 1a., 3m.; repeat from * ending 1m.
7th row: 1a., *8m., with e. 3 from 1, 7 (8)m., 1b., 2m., 3b., 8m., with e. 3 from 1, 7 (8)m., 1a., 2m., 3a.; repeat from * ending 2a.
8th row: 4m., * 1a., 7 (8)m., 3e., 13m., 1b., 7 (8)m., 3e., 13m.; repeat from * ending 9m.
9th row: 9m., *1e., with e. up 1, 1e., with e. up 1, 1e., 7 (8)m., 1b., 13m.,1e., with e. up 1, 1e., with e. up 1, 1e., 7 (8)m., 1a., 13m.; repeat from * ending 4m.
10th row: 3m., *1a., 8 (9)m., 5a., 12m., 1b., 8 (9)m., 5b., 12m., repeat from * ending 9m.
11th row: 8m., *with b. cr.5 rt., 9 (10)m., 1b., 10m., with a. cr. 5 rt., 9 (10)m., 1a., 10m.; repeat from * ending 2m.
12th row: 2m., *1a., 10 (11)m., 5a., 10m., 1b., 10 (11)m., 5b., 10m.; repeat from * ending 8m.
13th row: 7m., *with b. cr. 5 rt., 10 (11)m., 1b., 9m., with a. cr. 5 rt., 10 (11)m., 1a., 9m.; repeat from * ending 2m.
14th row: 3m., *5a., 6(7)m., 5a., 10m., 5b., 6 (7)m., 5b., 10m.; repeat from * ending 7m.
15th row: 6m., *with b. cr. 5 rt., 5 (6)m., 1b., 14m., with a. cr. 5 rt., 5 (6)m., 1a., 14m.; repeat from * ending 8m.
16th row: 9m., *1a., 5 (6)m., 5a., 15m., 1b., 5 (6)m., 5b., 15m.; repeat from * ending 6m.
17th row: 5m., *with b. cr. 5 rt., 5 (6)m., 1b., 14m., with a. cr. 5 rt., 5 (6)m., 1a., 14m.; repeat from * ending 9m.
18th row: 9m., *1a., 6 (7)m., 5a., 14m., 1b., 6 (7)m., 5b., 14m.; repeat from * ending 5m.
19th row: 4m. * with b. cr. 5 rt., 6 (7)m., 1b., 13m., with a. cr. 5 rt., 6 (7)m., 1a., 13m.; repeat from * ending 9m.
20th row: 9 m., *1a., 7 (8)m., 5a., 13m., 1b., 7 (8)m., 5b., 13m.; repeat from * ending 4m.
21st row: 3m., * with b. cr. 5 rt., 20 (21)m., with a. cr. 5 rt., 20 (21)m.; repeat from * ending 17 (18)m.
22nd row: 18 (19)m., 5a., 21 (22)m., 5b., 21 (22)m., 5a., 21 (22)m., 5b., 3m.
23rd row: 2m., * with b. cr. 5 rt., 20 (21)m., with a. cr. 5 rt., 20 (21)m.; repeat from * ending 18 (19)m.
24th row: 19 (20)m., * 5b.– note colour change – 21 (22)m., 5a., 21 (22)m.; repeat from * ending 2m.
25th row: 2m., * with a. cast off 4, 21 (22)m., with b. cast off 4, 21 (22)m.; repeat from * ending 19 (20)m.
26th to 30th rows: All m.
31st row: 14m., *3c., 19 (20)m., 3d., 19 (20)m.; repeat from * ending 5 (6)m.
32nd row: 4 (5)m., *1d., 3m., 1d., 17 (18)m., 1c., 3m., 1c., 17 (18)m.; repeat from * ending 13m.
33rd row: 12m., *1c., 5m., 1c., 15 (16)m., 1d., 5m., 1d., 15 (16)m.; repeat from * ending 3 (4)m.
34th row: 2 (3)m., *1d., 6m., 1d., 14 (15)m., 1c., 6m., 1c., 14 (15)m.; repeat from * ending 12m.
35th row: 12m, * 1c., 7m., 1d., 13 (14)m., 1d., 7m., 1c., 13 (14)m.; repeat from * ending 1 (2)m.
36th row: 1 (2)m., *1c., 7m., 1d., 3m., 2d., 8 (9)m., 1d., 7m., 1c., 3m., 2c., 8 (9)m.; repeat from * ending 7m.
37th row: 6m., *1c., 2m., 3c., 8m., with e. 3 from 1, 7 (8)m., 1d., 2m., 3d., 8m., with e. 3 from 1, 7 (8)m.; repeat from * ending 1 (2)m.
38th row: 1 (2)m., *3e., 13m., 1d., 7 (8)m., 3e., 13m., 1c., 7 (8)m.; repeat from * ending 6m.
39th row: 6m., *1c., 13m., 1e., with e. up 1, 1e., with e. up 1, 1e., 7 (8)m., 1d., 13m., 1e., with e. up 1, 1e., with e. up 1, 1e., 7 (8)m.; repeat from * ending 1 (2)m.
40th row: 1 (2)m., *5c., 12m., 1d., 8 (9)m.,

5d., 12m., 1c., 8 (9)m.; repeat from * ending 7m.

41st row: 8m., *1c., 10m., with d. cr. 5 rt., 9 (10)m., 1d., 10m., with c. cr. 5 rt., 9 (10)m.; repeat from * ending 1 (2)m.

42nd row: 2 (3)m., *5c., 10m., 1d., 10 (11)m., 5d., 10m., 1c., 10 (11)m.; repeat from * ending 8m.

43rd row: 8m., *1c., 9m., with d. cr. 5 rt., 10 (11)m., 1d., 9m., with c. cr. 5 rt., 10 (11)m.; repeat from * ending 2 (3)m.

44th row: 3 (4)m., *5c., 10m., 5d., 6 (7)m., 5d., 10m., 5c., 6 (7)m.; repeat from * ending 3m.

45th row: 2m., *1c., 14m., with d. cr. 5 rt., 5 (6)m., 1d., 14m., with c. cr. 5 rt., 5 (6)m.; repeat from * ending 3 (4)m.

46th row: 4 (5)m., *5c., 15m., 1d., 5 (6)m., 5d., 15m., 1c., 5 (6)m.; repeat from * ending 1m.

47th row: 1m., *1c., 14m., with d. cr. 5 rt., 5 (6)m., 1d., 14m., with c. cr. 5 rt., 5 (6)m.; repeat from * ending 4 (5)m.

48th row: 5 (6)m., *5c., 14m., 1d., 6 (7)m., 5d., 14m., 1c., 6 (7)m.; repeat from * ending 1m.

49th row: 1m., *1c., 13m., with d. cr. 5 rt., 6 (7)m., 1d., 13m., with c. cr. 5 rt., 6 (7)m.; repeat from * ending 5 (6)m.

50th row: 6 (7)m., *5c., 13m., 1d., 7 (8)m., 5d., 13m., 1c., 7 (8)m.; repeat from * ending 1m.

51st row: 14m., *with d. cr. 5 rt., 20 (21)m., with c. cr. 5 rt., 20 (21)m.; repeat from * ending 6 (7)m.

52nd row: 7 (8)m., 5c., 21 (22)m., 5d., 21 (22)m., 5c., 21 (22)m., 5d., 14m.

53rd row: 13m., *with d. cr. 5 rt., 20 (21)m., with c. cr. 5 rt., 20 (21)m.; repeat from * ending 7 (8)m.

54th row: 8 (9)m., 5d. – note colour change – 21 (22)m., 5c., 21 (22)m., 5d., 21 (22)m., 5c., 13m.

55th row: 13m., *with c. cast off 4, 21 (22)m., with d. cast off 4, 21 (22)m.; repeat from * ending 8m.

56th to 60th rows: All m.

The last 60 rows form the pattern; work the first 30 rows again.

To shape the armholes: Maintaining the continuity of the pattern as set, cast off 5 sts. at the beginning of the next 2 rows, then dec. 1 st. at each end of the next row and the 5 following alternate rows.

On 66 (70) sts. pattern 25 (31) rows.

Inc. 1 st. at each end of the next row and the following 6th (8th) row.

On 70 (74) sts. work 7 (9) rows.

To slope the shoulders: Cast off 10 (11) sts. at the beginning of the next 2 rows and 10 sts. on the 2 following rows.

Cast off the remaining 30 (32) sts.

THE FRONT (crew neck)

Work as given for the back until the armhole shaping has been worked.

On 66 (70) sts. pattern 14 (20) rows.

Now divide the sts. for the neck: Next row: Pattern 28 (29) and leave these sts. on a spare needle until required for right front shoulder, cast off 10 (12), work to end and continue on these 28 (29) sts. for the left front shoulder.

The left front shoulder: To shape the neck: Dec. 1 st. at the neck edge on each of the next 10 rows. Inc. 1 st. at the beginning – armhole edge, on the next row and the following 6th (8th) row.

On 20 (21) sts. work 7 (9) rows.

To slope the shoulder: Cast off 10 (11) sts. at the beginning of the next row. On 10 sts. work 1 row, then cast off.

The right front shoulder: With right side of work facing rejoin yarn to inner edge of the 28 (29) sts. left on spare needle and work to end of row, then work as given for left front shoulder to end.

THE FRONT (open necked)

Work as given for the back until the first 2 armhole shaping rows have been worked, then dec. 1 st. at each end of the next row and the following alternate row. – 74 (78) sts.

Now divide the sts. for the neck opening: Next row: Pattern 34 (36) and leave these sts. on a spare needle until required for right front shoulder, pattern 6 and leave these sts. on a stitch-holder until required for buttonhole band, work to end and continue on these 34 (36) sts. for the left front shoulder.

The left front shoulder: Dec. 1 st. at the armhole edge on the next row and the 3 following alternate rows.

On 30 (32) sts. pattern 14 (20) rows – work 1 extra row here when working right front shoulder – ending at neck.

To shape the neck: Cast off 2 (3) sts. at the beginning of the next row.

Now work as given for left front shoulder of crew necked version to end.

The right front shoulder: With right side of work facing rejoin yarn to inner edge of sts. left on spare needle and work as given for left front shoulder, noting the variation in number of rows.

THE SLEEVES (both alike)

With size 3¾ mm. (No. 9) needles and m. cast on 40 (42) sts. and work 27 rows in single rib.

Increase row: Rib 5 (6), *up 1, rib 10; repeat from * ending rib 5 (6). – 44 (46) sts.

Change to size 4 mm. (No. 8) needles and beginning with a k. row s.s. 4 rows.

Now work in pattern as follows: 1st row: 3m., 3a., 19 (20)m., 3b., 16 (17)m.

The last row sets the position of the pattern given for back.

Pattern 9 rows more as set.

Continuing in pattern as set and working the extra sts., into the pattern as they occur, inc. 1 st. at each end of the next row and the 7 (8) following 10th rows.

On 60 (64) sts. work 9 (13) rows.

To shape the sleevetop: Continuing in pattern as set, cast off 5 sts. at the beginning of the next 2 rows, then dec. 1 st. at each end of the next row and the 12 (14) following alternate rows.

On 24 sts. work 1 row.

Cast off 3 sts. at the beginning of the next 6 rows.

Cast off the remaining 6 sts.

THE NECKBAND (for crew neck)

First join right shoulder seam. With right side of work facing rejoin m. and using size 3¾ mm. (No. 9) needles pick up and k. 25 (27) sts. from left front neck edge, 10 (12) sts. from centre front neck, 25 (27) sts. from right front neck edge, and 30 (32) sts. from back neck edge.

On 90 (98) sts. work 7 rows in single rib, then cast off in rib.

THE BUTTONBAND (for open neck)

With size 3¾ mm. (No. 9) needles and m. cast on 6 sts. and work 22 (28) rows in single rib, then cast off.

THE BUTTONHOLE BAND (for open neck)

With right side of work facing rejoin m. to the 6 sts. left on stitch-holder at centre front, and using size 3¾ mm. (No. 9) needles work 4 (6) rows in single rib.

1st Buttonhole row: Rib 2, cast off 2, rib to end.

2nd Buttonhole row: Rib 2, turn, cast on 2, turn, rib to end.

Rib 12 (16) rows then work the 2 buttonhole rows again.

Rib 2 rows, then cast off.

THE COLLAR (for open neck)

With size 3¾ mm. (No. 9) needles and m. cast on 102 (110) sts. and work 4 rows in single rib.

THE SHOULDER PADS (2 alike optional)

With size 3¾ mm. (No. 9) needles and m. cast on 25 sts. and work 34 rows in single rib, then cast off. Fold in half diagonally and join outer edges to form a triangle.

Decrease row: Rib 2, sl.1, k.2 tog., p.s.s.o., rib until 5 remain, sl.1, k.2 tog., p.s.s.o., rib 2.

Rib 3 rows.

Repeat the last 4 rows twice more, then cast off in rib.

TO MAKE UP THE SWEATER

Pin out to size and press all parts except the ribbing lightly on the wrong side with a warm iron over a damp cloth. Join shoulder seam(s). Set in sleeves. Join sleeve and side seams. Catch shoulder pads in place.

For the open necked version: Sew cast off edge of collar in place all round neck edge. Sew button and buttonhole band in place. Press seams. Sew on buttons.

DOLLY MIXTURE

MATERIALS
Either 18 25 gram balls of 'Woollybear Bunny Fluff Angora' by Patricia Roberts, or 15 ounce (28 gram) hanks of 'Woollybear Real Shetland' by Patricia Roberts, in main colour and 3 balls or hanks of either yarn in each of the second and third contrast colours, and 4 balls or hanks in first contrast; 4 25 gram balls of 'Woollybear 100% Mohair' by Patricia Roberts in 4th contrast colour and 3 balls in 5th contrast colour; a pair each of size 2¼ mm. (No. 13) and size 2¾ mm. (No. 12) Aero knitting needles, plus one spare size 2¾ mm. (No. 12) needle; a set of 4 double pointed size 2¾ mm. (No. 12) Aero knitting needles; 4 buttons.

TENSION
Work at a tension of 16 stitches and 20 rows to 5 centimetres (2 inches) over the stocking stitch using size 2¾ mm. (No. 12) needles. If you cannot obtain the correct tension using the size needles suggested, use larger or smaller ones accordingly.

ABBREVIATIONS
K., knit; p., purl; st., stitch; tog., together; dec., decrease (by working 2 sts. tog.); inc., increase (by working twice into same st.); single rib is k.1 and p.1 alternately; s.s., stocking stitch is k. on the right side and p. on the wrong side; y.r.n., yarn round needle; m.h.b., make half bobble thus, with c. k.1, y.r.n., k.1, y.r.n., k.1 all into next st., then k.1, y.r.n., k.1, y.r.n., k.1 all into the following st., turn, p.10, turn, k.10, turn, p.10, turn, k.10, turn, p.10, turn, k.10; f.h.b., finish half bobble thus, with c. p.10, turn, k.10, turn, p.10, turn, k.2 tog., k.2 tog., k.2, k.2 tog., k.2 tog., turn, p.3 tog., p.3 tog.; m.s., make streamer thus, using the spare size 2¾ mm. (No. 12) needle and working into next st. on left hand needle, with d. cast on 30 sts., then cast off these 30 sts., transfer the one st. on spare needle to right hand needle; m., main colour; a., first contrast colour; b., second contrast; c., third contrast; d., fourth contrast; e., fifth contrast; m.d., make dot thus, with appropriate contrast colour k.1, y.r.n., k.1 all into next st., turn, p.3, turn, slip 1, k.2 tog., pass slip st. over; sl., slip; p.s.s.o., pass sl. st. over; garter st. is k. plain on every row; up 1, pick up the loop which lies between the needles, slip it onto left hand needle, then k. into back of it.

MEASUREMENTS
The measurements are given in centimetres followed by inches in brackets.

Underarms	99 (39½)
Side seam	52.5 (21)
Length	77.5 (31)
Sleeve seam	42.5 (17)

THE BACK
With size 2¼ mm. (No. 13) needles and m. cast on 159 sts. and work 32 rows in single rib.
Change to size 2¾ mm. (No. 12) needles and beginning with a k. row s.s. 4 rows.
Now work in colour pattern as follows. This is worked entirely in s.s. except where indicated. Use separate small balls of contrast colour for each motif, thus ensuring that contrast colours are not taken across the back of the work when not in use. Do not weave in main colour at the back of contrast colour motifs.
1st row: 2m., *7a., 14m.; repeat from * ending last repeat 3m.
2nd row: 3m., *6a., 15m.; repeat from * ending last repeat 3m.
The last 2 rows set the position of the pattern given in the chart; now work the 3rd to 12th rows as set.
13th row: 3m., with c. m.h.b., – see abbreviations, 7m., *7b., 5m., with c. m.h.b., 7m.; repeat from * to end.
14th row: 7m., with c. f.h.b., – see abbreviations, 6m., *5b., 8m., with c. f.h.b., 6m.; repeat from * ending last repeat 3m.
15th row: 14m., *3b., 18m.; repeat from * ending last repeat 16m.
16th row: 17m., *1b., 20m.; repeat from * ending last repeat 15m.
17th and 18th rows: All m.
19th row: 7m., *with d. m.s. – see abbreviations, 20m.; repeat from * ending last repeat 4m.
20th to 22nd rows: All m.
The last 22 rows form the streamer pattern.
Now work in dot pattern as follows. This is worked entirely in s.s. except for the dots.
1st row: 4m., *with a. m.d. – see abbreviations, 5m.; repeat from * ending last repeat 4m.
2nd, 3rd and 4th rows: All m.
5th row: 1m., *with b. m.d. – see abbreviations, 5m.; repeat from * ending last repeat 1m.
6th to 8th rows: All m.
9th to 16th rows: As 1st to 8th rows, but using c. instead of a. and d. instead of b.
17th to 24th rows: As 1st to 8th rows, but using e. instead of a. and a. instead of b.
25th to 32nd rows: As 1st to 8th rows, but using b. instead of a. and c. instead of b.
33rd to 40th rows: As 1st to 8th rows, but using d. instead of a. and e. instead of b.
The last 40 rows form the dot pattern; repeat them twice more, then work the first 36 rows again. – Work should now measure 52.5 centimetres (21 inches).
To shape the armholes: Continuing in pattern as set, cast off 2 sts. at the beginning of the next 2 rows, then dec. 1 st. at each end of the next row and the 13 following alternate rows. – 127 sts.
Now divide the sts. for the yoke: Next row: Work as set across 35 sts. and leave these sts. on a stitch-holder until required for left half back, work across next 31 sts. and leave these sts. on a double pointed size 2¾ mm. (No. 12) needle until required for left back yoke, working into next st. cast on 5 sts., then p. across these 5 sts., then across the next 26 sts. and leave these 31 sts. on a double pointed size 2¾ mm. (No. 12) needle until required for right back yoke, p. to end of row and continue on these 35 sts. for right half back.
The right half back: 1st row: Dec. 1 st., pattern as set to end.
2nd row: Work across 6 sts., then slip these sts. onto double pointed needle holding sts. of right back yoke**, work to end of row.
Repeat the last 2 rows 4 times more ending at ** on the last repeat as no sts. will remain, but there will be 61 sts. on needle for right back yoke.
The left half back: Rejoin m. to inner edge of 35 sts. left on stitch-holder and p. to end of row, then work as given for right half back to end, but transferring sts. to needle holding sts. of left half back yoke. On completion there will be 61 sts. on needle for left back yoke.

THE FRONT
Work as given for back until the 40 dot pattern rows have been worked 3 times, then work the first 35 rows again.
Now divide the sts. for the yoke: Next row: P.61 and leave these sts. on a stitch-holder until required for right half front, p.37 and leave these sts. on a double pointed size 2¾ mm. (No. 12) needle until required for front yoke, p. to end and continue on these 61 sts. for the left half front.
The left half front: Cast off 2 sts. at the beginning – for armhole, on the next row, then work as follows:
1st row: Pattern 3, then slip these 3 sts. onto double pointed needle, holding the sts. of front yoke **, work to end.
2nd row: Dec., work to end.
3rd row: Pattern 3, up 1, then slip these 4 sts. onto the double pointed needle holding the sts. of front yoke, work to end.
4th row: Dec., work to end.
Repeat the last 4 rows 6 times more then work as given for 1st row until ** is reached. No sts. will remain.
The right half front: With right side of work facing rejoin m. to inner edge of 61 sts. left on stitch-holder and work to end of row, then work as given for left half front to end.
There will now be 141 sts. on double pointed needle for front yoke.

THE LEFT SLEEVE
With size 2¼ mm. (No. 13) needles and m. cast on 64 sts. and work 29 rows in single rib.
Increase row: Rib 1, *up 1. rib 2; repeat from * ending last repeat rib 1. – 96 sts.
Change to size 2¾ mm. (No. 12) needles and beginning with a k. row s.s. 4 rows.
Now work the 22 row streamer pattern given for back, then work the 40 row dot pattern.
Continuing in dot pattern as set, inc. 1 st. at each end of the next row and the 6 following 10th rows.
On 110 sts. pattern 15 rows.
To shape the sleevetop: Continuing in dot pattern cast off 2 sts. at the beginning of the next 2 rows, then dec. 1 st. at each end of the next row and the 13 following alternate rows.
On 78 sts. work 1 row; work 1 extra row here when working right sleeve.
1st and 2nd turning rows: Dec., work as set until 12 remain, turn, work to end, turn.
3rd and 4th turning rows: Dec., work as set until 24 remain, turn, work to end, turn.
5th and 6th turning rows: Dec., work as set until 36 remain, turn, work to end, turn.

17 stitch repeat

21 stitch repeat

O = a. X = b.

Ш = with c. m.h.b.

⊓ = with d. m.s.

ᗰ = with c. f.h.b.

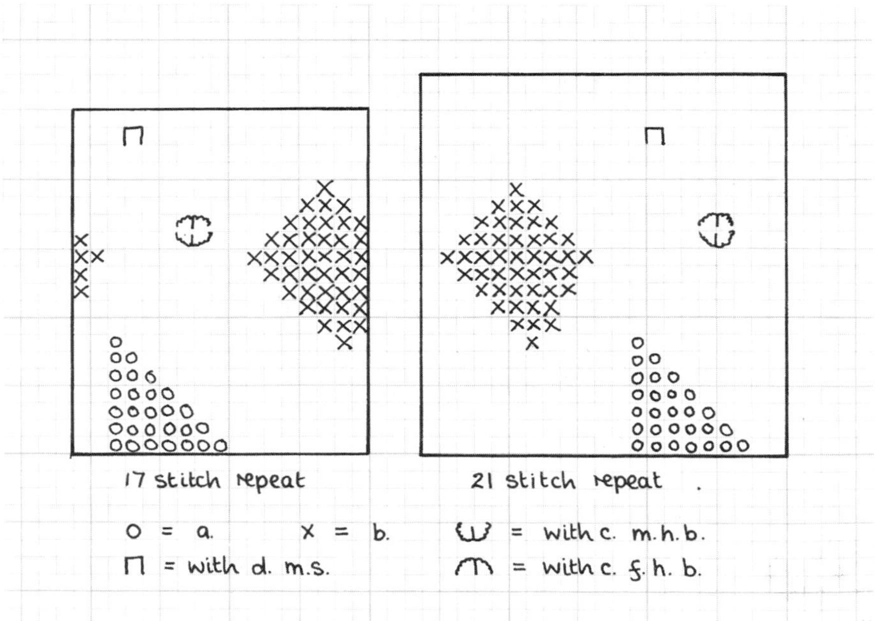

continued on page 232

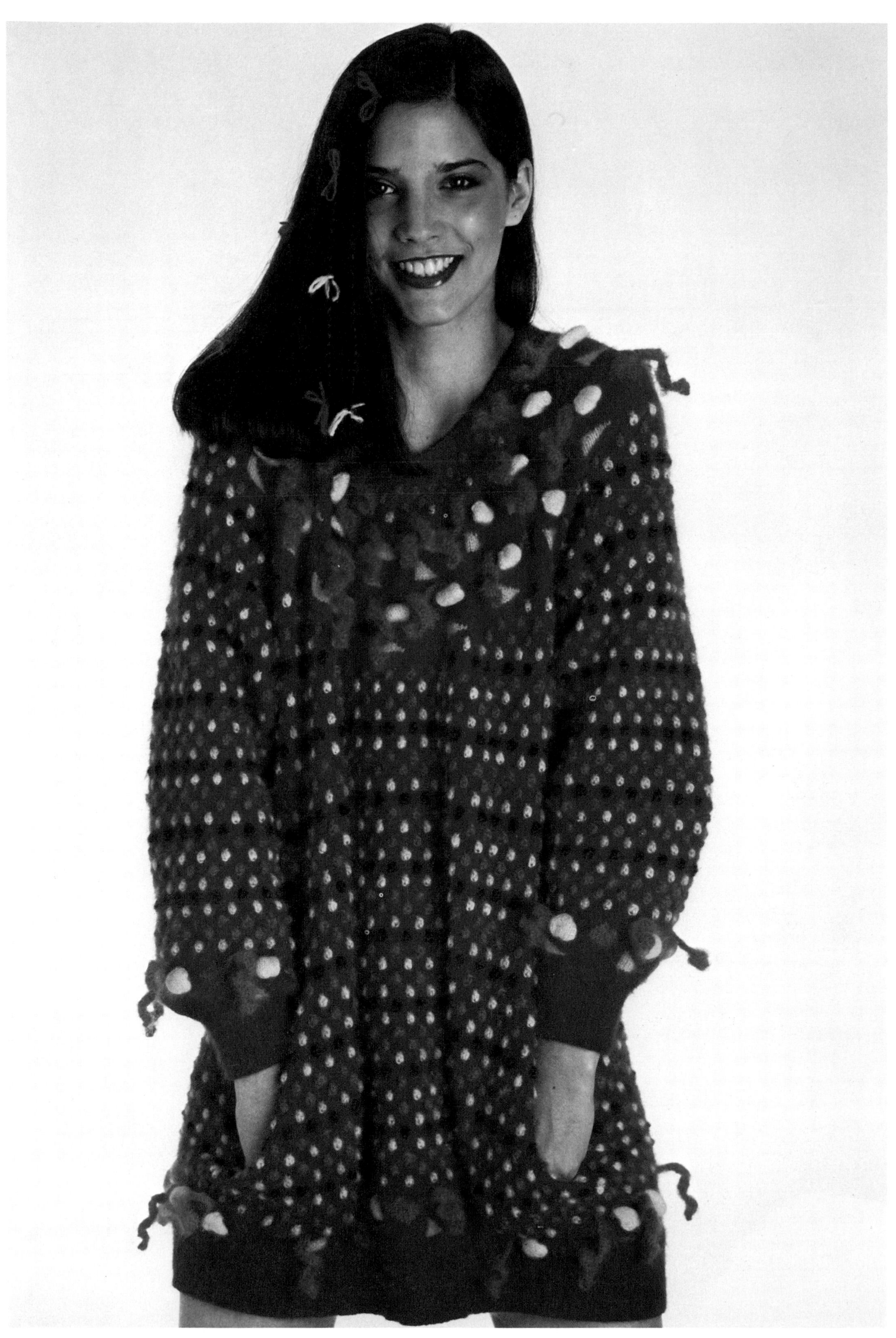

continued from page 231

7th and 8th turning rows: Dec., work as set until 48 remain, turn, work to end, turn.

9th and 10th turning rows: Dec., work as set until 60 remain, turn, work to end. – 73 sts.

Now slip these onto the double pointed needle holding the sts. for the left half back yoke at side edge.

THE RIGHT SLEEVE

Work as given for left sleeve, noting the variation in the number of rows, before working the turning rows.

At completion, position the remaining 73 sts. at right hand side of sts. of right half back yoke on double pointed needle.

THE YOKE

With right side of work facing rejoin m. at centre back to the 61 sts. of left half back yoke, and using 4th double pointed size 2¾ mm. (No. 12) needle k. across these sts., then across the 73 sts. of left sleeve, continuing with next needle k. across the 141 sts. of front yoke, then using next needle k. across the 73 sts. of right sleeve and the 61 sts. of back yoke, turn. – 409 sts.

Next row: With m. k.5, p. until 5 remain, k.5.

Now working backwards and forwards in rows, using the 4 double pointed needles as set work in colour pattern in s.s. as given for back, but with 5 sts. at beginnings and ends of rows – centre back opening – in garter st., as follows.

1st row: With m. garter st. 5, then in s.s. 1m., *7a., 14m.; repeat from * ending last repeat 13m., with m. garter st. 5.

2nd row: With m. garter st. 5, then in s.s. 13m., *6a., 15m.; repeat from * ending last repeat 2m., with m. garter st. 5.

The last 2 rows set the position of the 21 st. repeat pattern given in the chart, now work the 3rd to 20th rows from chart as set.

1st Decrease row: With m. k.12, *sl. 2, k.1, pass 2 sl. sts. over, k.1, k.3 tog., k.14; repeat from * ending last repeat k.12. – 333 sts.

Next row: With m. garter st. 5, p. until 5 remain, garter st. 5.

Now work the 17 st. repeat colour pattern with garter st. edging as follows.

1st row: With m. garter st. 5, then in s.s. 8m., *7a., 10m.; repeat from * ending last repeat 2m., with m. garter st. 5.

2nd row: With m. garter st. 5, then in pattern 2m., *6a., 11m.; repeat from * ending last repeat 9m., with m. garter st. 5.

The last 2 rows set the position of the 17 st. repeat pattern given in the chart. Now work the 3rd to 20th rows from the chart as set.

Next decrease row: With m. k.10, *sl. 2, k.1, pass 2 sl. sts. over, k.2 tog., k.3 tog., k.9; repeat from * to end. – 238 sts.

Work 1 row with m. as set.

Now work in dot pattern with garter st. edging as follows: 1st row: with m. garter st. 5, then in s.s., 1m., *with a. m.d., 5m.; repeat from * ending last repeat 4m., with m. garter st. 5.

2nd, 3rd and 4th rows: With m. in s.s. with garter st. edging.

5th row: With m. garter st. 5, 4m., *with b. m.d., 5m.; repeat from * ending last repeat 1m., with m. garter st. 5.

6th row: As 2nd row.

Next dec. row: With m. k.8, *sl.2, k.1, pass 2 sl. sts. over, k.1, k.3 tog., k.5; repeat from * ending last repeat k.7. – 162 sts.

Next row: With m. as set.

Next row: With m. k.6, *with d. m.d., 3m., repeat from * ending last repeat 7m.

Work 3 rows with m. in s.s. with garter st. edging as set.

Change to size 2¼ mm. (No. 13) needles and work 8 rows in single rib, but with 5 st. garter st. edging as set at each end of each row. Cast off loosely in rib.

THE POCKET BACKS (2 alike)

With size 2¾ mm. (No. 12) needles and m. cast on 40 sts. and work 46 rows in s.s., then cast off.

TO MAKE UP THE SWEATER

Pin out to size and press lightly on the wrong side with a warm iron over a damp cloth. Join armhole shaping rows on back and front to those on sleevetops. Join sleeve seams. Join side seams, inserting pocket backs neatly, 12.5 cms. (5 inches) from lower edges of sweater. Press seams.

THE BUTTONHOLES

Insert a large knitting needle into the centre of the garter st. band 4 rows from top at left back; and oversew the hole. Make 3 more buttonholes evenly spaced along this edge. Sew buttons in place.